T0319475

CONTROLLING CONTAGION

The Princeton Economic History of the Western World

Joel Mokyr, Series Editor

A list of titles in this series appears in the back of the book.

Controlling Contagion

Epidemics and Institutions from the Black Death to Covid

Sheilagh Ogilvie

PRINCETON UNIVERSITY PRESS
PRINCETON AND OXFORD

Published by Princeton University Press
41 William Street, Princeton, New Jersey 08540
99 Banbury Road, Oxford OX2 6JX

press.princeton.edu

All Rights Reserved

Library of Congress Cataloging-in-Publication Data

Names: Ogilvie, Sheilagh C., author.
Title: Controlling contagion : epidemics and institutions from the black death
    to Covid / Sheilagh Ogilvie.
Other titles: Princeton economic history of the Western world.
Description: Princeton : Princeton University Press, [2025] | Series: Princeton economic
    history of the Western world | Includes bibliographical references and index.
Identifiers: LCCN 2024018421 (print) | LCCN 2024018422 (ebook) | ISBN 9780691255569
    (hardback) | ISBN 9780691267418 (ebook)
Subjects: MESH: Epidemics—history | Communicable Disease Control—history | Social
    Structure | Sociological Factors | History of Medicine | BISAC: HISTORY / World |
    BUSINESS & ECONOMICS / Development / Economic Development
Classification: LCC RA649 (print) | LCC RA649 (ebook) | NLM WA 11.1 |
    DDC 614.4/9—dc23/eng/20240827
LC record available at https://lccn.loc.gov/2024018421
LC ebook record available at https://lccn.loc.gov/2024018422

British Library Cataloging-in-Publication Data is available

Editorial: Hannah Paul and Josh Drake
Production Editorial: Kathleen Cioffi
Jacket Design: Benjamin Higgins
Production: Erin Suydam
Publicity: William Pagdatoon and Charlotte Coyne
Copyeditor: Maia Vaswani

Jacket images: Details of a nineteenth-century engraving by Enrico Pratesi, based on a painting attributed to Luigi Baccio del Bianco (d. 1657), showing the 1630 plague in Florence, located in the Sala di Compagnia in the headquarters of the Venerabile Arciconfraternita della Misericordia di Firenze. Virus illustration by vidimages / Shutterstock

This book has been composed in Adobe Text and Gotham

10 9 8 7 6 5 4 3 2 1

In memory of Ticca Margaret Alison Ogilvie, 1962–2023

Bon voyage, little sister

CONTENTS

Figures and Maps

Tables

ACKNOWLEDGEMENTS

At all times, but especially during a pandemic, I feel very fortunate to be a member of an international community of scholars who generate exhilarating encouragement and tough criticism.

In writing this book, I would like to express my great thanks to those who provided generous and inspiring comments on earlier versions of the manuscript. Guido Alfani shared his wisdom about pandemics down the ages, posing far-reaching questions on inequality, state capacity, and modern policies; I especially enjoyed the news item on how eating mice caused Covid. Robin Briggs shed light on broad vistas of early modern Europe, including esoteric publications on the Habsburg–Ottoman sanitary cordon. Tracy Dennison inspired me to consider the wider implications of state overreach, community vigilantism, and murky markets. Jeremy Edwards, as always, adjured me to look at the whole forest, while nonetheless spurring me to analyse every tree. Mattia Fochesato shared a rich literature on state capacity and Italian plague, making me think again about pesthouse internment. Tim Guinnane provided trenchant comments on economics and demography, nailing them down during vital fieldwork in country pubs. John Henderson shared his encyclopaedic knowledge of plague, hospitals, and Italian art, while charting the shoals of medical history. John Landers provided comprehensive feedback and shared his fascination (if that's the right word) with morbidity and mortality. Richard Saller alerted me to lively debates among historians of antiquity on plagues and marriage patterns. Felix Schaff thoughtfully commented not just on inequality but on everything else. Paul Seabright was exceptionally generous with written comments and café conversations for two years while visiting All Souls, and even partially resolved my bafflement about religion and economics. Chris Wickham made lively comments on the whole manuscript and made me rethink early medieval history and anthropology.

I am also grateful to friends and colleagues who shared their thoughts on epidemics during a time when many might have preferred to address more cheerful subjects: André Carus for his philosophical insistence on explication; Adolf Češka for inviting me in March 2020 to write a short essay for botanists on history and pandemics; Romola Davenport for delivering on her remark that "surprisingly few people seem to enjoy a good chat about smallpox, alas!";

Friederike Fisher and Alexander Johnston for teatime conversations about policy implications; Ajit Karnik for literature on Indian epidemics; Bjørn Poulsen for explaining the Odense journeymen's guild in the "great pestilence" of 1405; Emily Sellars for her analyses of communities and forced labour during the Columbian Exchange; and Peter Wilson for advice on nineteenth-century German constitutions.

My thanks go to audience members at the NIESR Prais Lecture on Productivity in 2021, the Souq Economics Keynote Lecture in 2022, and the Swedish Economic History Society Keynote Lecture in 2023, who listened to some of the ideas in this book and posed stimulating questions about state capacity in economic and epidemiological crises down the centuries.

Finally, I thank Joel Mokyr and two anonymous readers for Princeton University Press for lightning-fast, knowledgeable, and rigorous reports, inspiring me to look at epidemics from other perspectives.

1

Epidemics and Institutions

In many cases the houses of the dead had to be shut up, for no one dared enter them or touch the belongings of the dead. No one knew what to do. Everyone, one by one, fell in turn to death's dart.

—ACCOUNT OF THE BLACK DEATH IN PIACENZA BY THE NOTARY GABRIELE DE MUSSIS, 1348-56[1]

In the early 1340s, the Black Sea port of Caffa was a city of about 17,000 households from many cultures—Italian, Mongolian, Jewish, Greek, Armenian, Vlach, Trapezuntine, Circassian, Mingrelian, Sutar, Polish, Georgian, Russian, Tartar, Turkic, Arab, Iranian. Genoa, an Italian city-state, had bought the place 80 years earlier from the Golden Horde, after which Caffa flourished as a trade hub.[2] But in 1343 the khan of the Golden Horde resolved to strengthen his own authority and that of Islam. He sent an army to harry European trading posts in the Black Sea region, confiscating wares and ships, ejecting Italians from the Venetian entrepôt of Tana on the Sea of Azov and pursuing them to the

---

1. Quoted in Horrox 1994, 23. De Mussis, a notary (lawyer) who lived from *c.*1280 to *c.*1356 in the Italian city of Piacenza, did not personally witness the rise of plague in Caffa. His *Istoria de Morbo sive Mortalitate quae fuit anno dni MCCCXLVIII* (History of the Disease, or the Great Dying, which took place in the year of our Lord 1348) dates from between 1348 and 1356.

2. The "Golden Horde" is the most commonly used term for the Mongol (later Turkicized) khanate that was established in the thirteenth century in the north-western sector of the Mongol Empire. The name this khanate used to refer to itself was "Ulug Ulus", Turkic for Great State. The expression "Golden Horde" emerged in the sixteenth century, when Russian chroniclers began to refer to this khanate as the "Zolotaia Orda", the Golden Camp or Palace. Modern specialists sometimes refer to it as the "Kipchak Realm" or the "Jochid Realm". For reasons of intelligibility, this book uses "Golden Horde" as the mostly widely understood term for this complex medieval polity.

Genoese fortress at Caffa, which he besieged. In 1346 bubonic plague—probably originating in Mongolia, where marmots kept it smouldering—blazed up in the khan's army. In the vivid account of Gabriele de Mussis, a Piacenza notary, the epidemic broke up the besieging army but also the city of Caffa, whose inhabitants fled in all directions.[3] Other accounts describe how plague arose in the Mongolian army after the siege, diffused around Crimea to Venetian Tana, and voyaged across the Black Sea with grain shipments when trade embargoes were relaxed in 1347 after the hostilities.[4]

Over the next seven years, plague travelled by sea to Constantinople, Alexandria, Sicily, Genoa, and Venice, and thence throughout the Mediterranean, Asia Minor, and Europe. It journeyed with merchants, sailors, soldiers, refugees, pilgrims, migrants, and the rats and fleas that accompanied them.[5] It moved at a pace of 40 kilometres daily by ship, 2 by land in the warm and populous south, and 0.5 by land in the cold and desolate north, reaching nearly every society in Asia Minor, the Middle East, North Africa, and Europe by 1353.[6] This disease became the most lethal epidemic in recorded history, the Black Death, killing 33–58 per cent of the entire population in the societies it struck.

Each of the institutions analysed in this book—market, state, community, religion, guild, and family—played a role in this spectacular act of contagion. The market brought immunologically naive Italians to a region where they met carriers of plague from the Mongolian steppe and bore the infection onwards to societies where plague had been rare or absent for centuries. The state established the privileged Italian entrepôts in Crimea and brought the Golden Horde army to Caffa, setting up sieges and encampments where humans, rats, and fleas crowded together, along with their waste.[7] Local communities in Italy repulsed returning ships, sending them onwards to other communities, which in turn ejected marginal inhabitants such as paupers, beggars, Jews, and

3. Wheelis 2002; Slater 2006, 271–2, 274–7; Benedictow 2004, 44, 49–54, 60–1, 64, 69, 130, 181, 183, 212, 227; M. Harrison 2012, 3; Benedictow 2021, 164, 178–9, 187, 248, 431, 451; Favereau 2021, 248–9, 256.

4. H. Barker 2021; Favereau 2021, 249–51.

5. Plague was probably transmitted from the Black Sea region to Europe through a multiplicity of routes and mechanisms in 1347. But most scholars think that the Black Death emerged from encounters between Mongol armies and European merchants in the Black Sea region, in which military, political, commercial, and religious forces combined to create a perfect epidemiological storm.

6. On the pace of transmission, see Benedictow (2004, 229–31). Biraben (1975, 90) estimates a faster diffusion of plague, at a rate of 0.66–5 km/day on land, averaging 4 km daily.

7. As discussed earlier, this medieval polity referred to itself as "Ulug Ulus", Turkic for "Great State". On the reasons for regarding it as a "state" in the fourteenth century, see Trepavlov (2018) and Favereau (2021, esp. ch. 7).

migrants, who then carried disease into nearby villages and on to new towns. Religion created pressures in the Golden Horde, which brought a Muslim army to Caffa, and soon impelled penitent Christianity to organize superspreader gatherings in plague-struck Europe. Guilds of physicians, surgeons, and apothecaries claimed exclusive privileges over their professions, defending ancient knowledge against disruptive innovations, and limiting the supply of medical services to patients and communities. Families insisted on deathbed and funeral gatherings in the teeth of official prohibitions, as in Piacenza in 1348, where, "when one person had contracted the illness, he poisoned his whole family even as he fell and died, so that those preparing to bury his body were seized by death in the same way".[8]

But each of our six institutions also helped to mitigate this epidemic, and many others before and since. The market responded by shutting down even without being ordered to do so, as in Alexandria and Bilbais, where the caravanserais closed in 1350 not by public order but when merchants and customers refused to attend.[9] Market exchange created gains from trade and rising incomes, helping people accumulate savings so they could stay away from the market temporarily and pay taxes to finance public health measures. The state responded by providing public goods such as information, sanitation, and isolation measures, with Italian city-states appointing health boards to control contagion as early as 1348. The community deployed norms, information, and peer pressure to enforce sanitation and social distancing. Religions exhorted the faithful to obey public health regulations and donate alms to help the poor comply without starving. Doctors' guilds supplied medical advice and recruited volunteers to serve in pesthouses. The family provided a basic safety net, enabling members to stay away from the labour market for longer than if kin-based risk-pooling had been unavailable, and supporting contagion controls to safeguard vulnerable family members.

All six institutions thus played central roles in both transmitting contagion and controlling it. But, as this book will show, institutions do not behave the same way in all societies. Every human society has markets, states, communities, religions, occupational associations, and families. But these take different forms and act differently in different times and places. Even when they take similar forms themselves, they are embedded in a different overall institutional framework, where they cooperate and compete in different ways. Societies vary in how they deal with epidemics.

This book uses the past seven centuries of history to investigate how human societies dealt with epidemic disease. It focuses on contagion. How do social institutions enable us to contract, coerce, and coordinate so that we take

8. De Mussis 1348–56, quoted in Horrox 1994, 19.
9. Dols 1977, 160, 278

account of the effects our infectious behaviour has on others? What weaknesses make an institution fail to control epidemic contagion—or even exacerbate it? How is each institution constrained by others? Do some societies have better institutions than others? Can societies learn? What does history tell us about institutional solutions to the problems posed by epidemic disease?

1. How to Think about Contagion

If you went to church in London near the end of the 1563 plague, Bishop Edward Grindal would have exhorted you to practise social distancing. This was not to save you—at least, not from plague. It was to redeem your soul. But it was also to protect others, since "all men are bound in conscience not to do any thing that by common judgment and experience may bring a manifest peril and danger to their brethren or neighbours". Bishop Grindal's exhortation was based on the idea of the "negative externality"—where some action of mine imposes costs on others on top of the costs I incur. If my getting a disease imposes costs on others, society would like me to do less of it than I would if I were acting altogether selfishly. As Bishop Grindal added, I should avoid being infected not just out of "the rule of charity" but out of collective "profit". Shunning needless interaction during plague was, he urged, "very like to be profitable for this afflicted city".[10]

Epidemics are one of the most extreme examples of negative externalities that human societies know. The classic example is pollution: my factory profits only me, yet poisons everyone. But pollution pales to insignificance beside contagion. In terms of conspicuous costs that one person imposes on others, it is hard to think of a more dramatic example than infection. Epidemics thus create one of the best laboratories for understanding how societies deal with negative externalities—situations where a choice I make inflicts costs on others on top of any I myself incur.

A major way societies deal with externalities is through institutions. Institutions are systems of rules, customs, and practices that structure the way we interact as human beings. By giving us systematic ways to cooperate, institutions reduce transaction costs—costs of search, information, bargaining, decision, policing, and enforcement. These are the costs we incur in trying to reach agreements to act together. Economists mostly focus on how institutions reduce our transaction costs in producing, consuming, and trading. But institutions also lower the costs of ensuring that I take account of the spillover costs my choices inflict on others. That means they not only help us allocate resources efficiently, achieve technological progress, increase overall output, and redistribute resources to the needy. They also help us deal with infectious

10. Grindal 1843, 271.

diseases. This book will argue that assessing institutions in terms of how well they help society cope with epidemics is no less relevant than assessing how they help us improve economic performance—and indeed that the two activities are deeply interconnected.

Different institutions help us deal with infectious disease in different ways. The market offers mechanisms for people to bargain to compensate one another for contagion or pollution. The state offers ways to compel people to stop infecting or polluting others to begin with. The local community, the guild, and the family offer low-cost ways for a group to coordinate individual decisions to benefit all its members—and perhaps even the wider society. Religion teaches ethical norms of altruism, inspiring—or even, as with Bishop Grindal, admonishing—us to care about other people. The family provides emotional motivation for individuals to protect their members by avoiding and controlling contagion. The best institutional solution to a particular instance of contagion will differ according to the attributes of the disease, the technology available to deal with it, and the social context in which it occurs. But in principle, social institutions help us deal with the problem that my infection has spillover effects that I do not take into account, giving rise to contagion that inflicts unintended costs on everyone.

In practice, institutional solutions to epidemic contagion do not always work out well. For one thing, institutions do not just reduce the costs of dealing with infectious disease. They reduce the costs of many human interactions that have nothing to do with contagion. These can take precedence, interfering with how well any institution deals with epidemics. States wage war, religions organize pilgrimages, communities eject migrants, guilds profit their members, families feed their children. These activities benefit states, religions, communities, guilds, and families in other ways. But they also worsen contagion, as we shall see.

Second, most institutions serve some groups more than others—the state favours rulers over ruled, the community privileges citizens over outsiders, religion benefits priests over parishioners and heretics, the guild profits members over interlopers, the family nurtures kin over non-kin. Even if preventing an epidemic is in the interest of society, powerful groups have interests they prioritize more. Rulers and bureaucrats prefer higher tax revenues. Communities and their citizens prefer to favour locals and eject outsiders. Priests prefer to hold religious assemblies and preach against science. Guild masters prefer to control their occupations and monopolize their customers. Families prefer to help relatives instead of complying with lockdown. Swayed by such interests, even an institution capable in principle of mitigating an epidemic can fail to do so. It can even make contagion worse.

Does this mean we should just give up on understanding or improving our institutions? On the contrary, this book will argue. The same infectious disease works out differently in different times and places. This is not so much because of biological characteristics of microbe or human host. It comes from how biological features interact with social ones. The same institution acts differently in different societies. This book analyses how key social institutions deal with epidemics in different places and times, and explores the reasons they succeed, fail, or make things worse.

2. A Brief History of Epidemics

History seethes with epidemics. This is not surprising. For most of history, infectious disease has killed many more people than war or hunger. Counting victims is hard because identifying cause of death is complicated and records are imperfect. Minimum estimates show infectious disease causing 45 per cent of all deaths in England and Wales in 1850, 36 per cent in Britain in 1900, and 40 per cent in low-income countries in 2018.[11] In 2019, the year before Covid-19 struck, communicable diseases caused over 26 per cent of the disease burden across the world, rising to 33 per cent in South Asia and 66 per cent in Sub-Saharan Africa.[12]

Not all these diseases were epidemics. A disease is "endemic" ("within a certain people") when it is permanently prevalent in a place at a predictable level—like smallpox in seventeenth-century China or cholera in eighteenth-century Bengal. It turns into an "epidemic" ("on a certain people") when it starts to infect exceptional numbers in a particular place and time—as with plague around the Black Sea region in 1346–47 or cholera when it broke out of India after 1816. A disease becomes a "pandemic" ("pertaining to all the people") when it spreads across an entire country, continent, or planet—like the Black Death in 1347 or Covid-19 in 2020.[13] In this sense, the difference between endemic, epidemic, and pandemic disease is mainly a matter of scale.

Increasing the spatial scale of disease triggers new social challenges. Endemic disease often varies across regions of the same country. When that disease turns into an epidemic it affects places that are normally spared. These may lack biological immunity as well as social mechanisms to cope with the new disease. In turn, when a disease becomes a pandemic, it spills across

---

11. Alfani and Ó Gráda 2018, 137.

12. "Share of Disease Burdon from Communicable Diseases vs. GDP per Capita, 2019", Our World in Data, accessed 19 May 2024, https://ourworldindata.org/grapher/share-of-disease-burden-from-communicable-diseases-vs-gdp?tab=table&time=2019. Disease burden is measured in disability-adjusted life years (DALYs), defined as years of life lost to due to premature mortality plus years of healthy life lost due to disability. According to current estimates, infectious diseases cause around one-quarter of deaths in the world today: see "Infectious Disease", Wellcome, accessed 1 June 2024, https://wellcome.org/what-we-do/infectious-disease.

13. Pelling 2020; Alfani 2022, 6; Alfani 2023a, 3–4.

political, commercial, communal, religious, and cultural frontiers. So a pandemic often disables institutions such as state, market, community, and religion which normally help people coordinate responses to contagion. It also creates the cross-border externalities we examine in later chapters.

Differences in scale also create differences in kind. When a disease is endemic it is often limited to particular demographic and social groups—children, the elderly, the poor and homeless. When it becomes an epidemic, it penetrates deeply into new social groups. Ultimately, an epidemic or pandemic threatens everyone, though as we shall see in chapter 2 the poorest almost always suffer most.

Endemic, epidemic, and pandemic disease challenge human societies in many of the same ways. So many of the analytical points this book makes about how institutions affect epidemics apply to all infectious diseases. But the negative externalities of contagion and the positive externalities of sanitation, social distancing, and immunization become much more salient when a disease is, or threatens to become, an epidemic or a pandemic. Consequently, the actions of the institutions analysed in this book have much more acute repercussions—for good or ill—in an epidemic situation. Moreover, institutional failures make it more likely that an endemic disease will flare up into an epidemic or pandemic. This book focuses on how institutions affect epidemics and pandemics, while bearing in mind that many of the analytical points apply to all infectious diseases.

Table 1.1 shows the historical epidemics that spread most widely—that is, approached pandemic scale—over the past two millennia. In the 1,855 years between the Antonine plague (possibly smallpox) and the Covid-19 pandemic (a coronavirus), there were 15 severe pandemics, one every five generations on average. Of these, 6 (40 per cent) were bubonic plague, 2 were influenza, 1 was mixed (smallpox, typhus, measles, and influenza), and there was 1 each of ancestral smallpox, haemorrhagic fever, syphilis, cholera, HIV/AIDS, and coronavirus. Pandemics thus struck every 125 years or so over the past two millennia. These 15 pandemics were merely the most notable episodes of a constant and lethal struggle between microbes and humans in Europe, the Mediterranean basin, the Middle East, China, India, other parts of Asia, the Americas, and Africa. This was bad for people in all these times and places. But it was good for science, because it created a huge variety of contexts in which to analyse epidemic disease and human responses to it.

We do not have evidence on all epidemics. This book extends geographically and chronologically as far as reasonably reliable evidence survives. Geographically, the historical record gets fragile once we move outside Europe and the Middle East. The book therefore analyses as much as is known about China, India, and the Americas, but perforce discusses Europe and the Middle East more intensively because of the availability of archival sources, data collection,

TABLE 1.1. Major Lethal Pandemics of the Past Two Millennia

Era	Dates	Epidemic name	Infection	Regions affected	Victims (millions)	Mortality (% of population)	Source
Epidemics of late antiquity	165	Antonine "plague"	Ancestral smallpox (possibly)	Roman Empire	7–8	10–30	1, 3
Epidemics of late antiquity	249–70	Cyprianic "plague"	Haemorrhagic fever (speculative)	Roman Empire		15–25	1
Plagues (main), first pandemic	541, possibly up to 550 in N. Europe	Justinianic plague[a]	Yersinia pestis	Europe, Mediterranean	Up to 25–50 overall	25–50 overall (50 in Egypt and other densely populated areas)	1, 4
Post-Justinianic plagues, first pandemic	565, 627–717, 740s	Five Great Islamic plagues,[b] other post-Justinianic plagues	Yersinia pestis	Italy (565); Middle East, esp. Iraq, Syria, Palestine (627–717); Mediterranean (740s)			4
Plagues (main), second pandemic	1347–52	Black Death	Yersinia pestis	Europe, Mediterranean, Middle East, C. Asia, possibly parts of China	Up to 50 in Europe and the Mediterranean; unknown elsewhere	35–60 in Europe and the Mediterranean; unknown elsewhere	1
Plagues (main), second pandemic	1356–66	Pestis secunda	Yersinia pestis	Europe, Mediterranean, Middle East	Up to 5–10 in Europe and the Mediterranean; unknown elsewhere	15–20 in Europe and the Mediterranean; unknown elsewhere	6
Plagues (main), second pandemic	1625–32	Second plague pandemic	Yersinia pestis	Most of C. and W. Europe (excluding most of Spain and C.-S. Italy)	Up to 2 in northern Italy; up to 1.15 in France; up to 0.25 in Switzerland; up to 0.16 in the Dutch Republic; unknown elsewhere	30–35 in N. Italy; 20–25 in Switzerland; 20–25 in S. Germany, Rhineland, and Alsace (up to 40 incl. victims of famine and Thirty Years' War); 8–11 in the Dutch Republic; unknown elsewhere	6

Plagues (main), second pandemic	1647–57	Second plague pandemic	*Yersinia pestis*	Andalusia, Spanish Mediterranean, and C.-S. Italy	Up to 1.25 in the Kingdom of Naples; up to 0.5 in Spain; up to 0.33 in France; unknown elsewhere	30–43 in Kingdom of Naples; at least 25 in Andalusia; 15–20 in Catalonia; unknown elsewhere [1]
Other extreme early modern epidemics	1492–1550	Columbian Exchange (New to Old World)[c]	Syphilis[d]	Europe, Asia	Up to 2–5 in Europe; unknown elsewhere	Up to 4–5 in Europe; unknown elsewhere [1]
Other extreme early modern epidemics	1492–1650	Columbian Exchange (Old to New World)[e]	Smallpox, typhus, measles, influenza, etc.	American continent		Up to 80–90 in the first century (confounded with direct impact of colonization) [1, 5]
Cholera pandemic	1817–1923	Cholera pandemics 1–6	Cholera	Worldwide	At least 1 (probably many more)	[1]
Third plague pandemic	1894–1920	Third plague pandemic	*Yersinia pestis*	China, India, Europe, USA	12	[1]
Russian flu	1889–90	Russian flu	Influenza	Russia, Asia, Europe	1	[1]
Influenza pandemic	1918–19	Spanish flu	Influenza	Worldwide	50–100	Globally 2.5–5; Italy 1.1–1.3; USA 0.65; Germany 0.37; China up to 2; British India 5–6; South Africa 6 [1, 2, 6]
HIV/AIDS global pandemic	1983–2025 (ongoing)	HIV/AIDS global pandemic	HIV/AIDS	Worldwide, worst in sub-Saharan Africa	75 infections, 30 deaths[f]	[2]

(continued)

TABLE 1.1. (*continued*)

Era	Dates	Epidemic name	Infection	Regions affected	Victims (millions)	Mortality (% of population)	Source
Covid-19 pandemic	2020–25 (ongoing)	Covid-19 pandemic	Covid-19	Worldwide	771 infections, 6.9 deaths (officially reported); 12–18 excess deaths (estimated)[g]		[7]

Sources: [1] Alfani and Murphy 2017, esp. table 1 (pp. 316–17), sources cited in main text of that article. [2] Heinrich 2021, 4. [3] Harper 2017, 18, 115; Haldon et al. 2018, 2; Duncan-Jones 2018, 44; Shabana 2021, 6. [4] Dols 1977, 17, 20–6. [5] Newson 1985, 41–2, 48. [6] Alfani 2023a, 6–7 (table 1), 26. [7] "WHO COVID-19 Dashboard", World Health Organization, accessed 3 October 2023, https://covid19.who.int/; "Estimated Excess Mortality from the World Health Organization", Our World in Data, accessed 3 October 2023, https://ourworldindata.org/excess-mortality-covid#estimated-excess-mortality-from-the-world-health-organization.

Notes: Table does not include pandemics whose characteristics and dimensions are still under-researched, e.g. some large waves of the second plague pandemic; the undiagnosed non-bubonic-plague pestilences of the 1480s–90s and 1550s; and a number of possible pandemics of influenza, yellow fever, typhus, and smallpox.

[a] Figures for Justinianic plague refer to the initial outbreak only, not to the outbreaks which make up the "first pandemic" ending in 750.

[b] The concept of "five Islamic plagues" is based on contemporary sources and has been questioned by some modern scholars.

[c] After the mid-sixteenth century, syphilis mutated into a less aggressive disease.

[d] Given data scarcity, the number of victims of syphilis provides a very uncertain upper boundary only; it is debatable whether all (or any) post-1490s pox outbreaks were caused by syphilis.

[e] Following colonization, epidemics recurred frequently for centuries where the population was not entirely eradicated, yet the greatest demographic toll took place roughly in the first 150 years.

[f] Figures as of 30 April 2021.

[g] Official figures include only confirmed cases and deaths reported to WHO; excess mortality = gap between actual deaths and expected deaths without Covid-19.

quantitative analyses, and historiographical works on epidemics. Similarly, the historical record gets very fragile for the centuries before the Black Death, so this book inevitably concentrates on the seven centuries or so since the 1340s. This book takes the view that it is counterproductive to report guess-work or unreliable research just because they extend into less well recorded eras and regions. But it also seeks to illuminate the questions, methods, and theoretical approaches that can be used once better data are collected on times and places that have yet to be analysed.

Even though this book is about human societies, microbial biology mat-ters. Table 1.2 shows some of the diversity in how different epidemic diseases behave. Some differences are epidemiological—the share of the population that catches the disease (infection rate), the share of the infected who die (case fatality), the share of the whole population that the disease kills (population mortality). The infection rate varies from under 2 per cent for nineteenth-century cholera to nearly 100 per cent for pre-vaccination smallpox. The case fatality rate ranges from 2–3 per cent for Spanish flu and Covid-19 to 80–90 per cent for bubonic plague and Ebola. The population mortality rate ranges from under 1 per cent for cholera to 50–60 per cent for the Black Death plague variant.

Death is not the only problem. Infection matters by itself, since it reduces people's ability to work and—more important—enjoy life. Surviving infec-tion does not lead to living in health. Most epidemic diseases leave some patients with serious sequelae—after-effects of infection—such as blindness, neurocognitive decline, or fatigue. These have repercussions not just for the individual survivor but for the rest of society.

The social distribution of infection and death also differs across diseases, as table 1.2 shows. Some epidemics infect and kill the young and those in the prime of life (like the Spanish flu), others kill the old (like Covid-19), and still others find victims across the entire age spectrum (like plague). Some epidemics show little gap between rich and poor, as with natural smallpox, Ebola, or SARS. Others are diseases of poverty—plague, typhus, cholera. Women have a slight advantage over men in fighting off most diseases, because they have stronger natural immune systems, but pregnancy greatly increases case fatality rates for many diseases, including bubonic plague, smallpox, measles, influenza, SARS, and Covid-19.

Epidemics are not a matter of simple biology. Epidemiological differences evoke differing social responses. A high infection rate alone does not necessar-ily attract concern if case fatality is low, since few people die. Conversely, high case fatality does not necessarily attract attention, since population mortality is low if infection rates are low. It is the combination of non-trivial infections with non-trivial case fatality that results in high population mortality and attracts social attention. A disease that attacks the rich typically attracts more resources

TABLE 1.2. Morbidity, Mortality, and Social Selectivity of Major Pandemics in History

Disease	When	Infection rate (%)	Case fatality rate (%)	Population mortality rate (%)	Sequelae	Poverty	Age	Gender
Plague	1347–52	51–67	80	50–60	Gangrene, clots, meningitis	Weak		No conclusive evidence
Plague	16th–17th century	24–53	80	20–40	Gangrene, clots, meningitis	Medium		No conclusive evidence
Plague	Pre-antibiotic		50–80		Gangrene, clots, meningitis	Strong		Pregnant women
Plague	1890s	c.100	c.80		Gangrene, clots, meningitis	Strong		No conclusive evidence
Smallpox	Pre-vaccination		30–40	10–20	Blindness, scarring	Weak		Pregnant women
Typhus	Pre-antibiotic		>50		Sepsis, seizures, neurocognition, fatigue	Strong		No conclusive evidence
Measles	Pre-vaccination		10		Blindness, neurocognition	Medium		Pregnant women
Cholera	19th century	0.7–2	50	0.5–1	Chronic enteropathy, malnutrition	Strong		No conclusive evidence
Spanish flu	1918–19	c.33	2.5	0.3–6.0	Heart risk	Medium	25–40	Pregnant women
Ebola	1990s–present		60–90		Fatigue, pain, blindness, neurocognition	Weak		No conclusive evidence
SARS	2003		10		Fatigue, osteoporosis, breathing	Weak		Pregnant women
Covid-19	Pre-vaccination		2.3–3.6		Fatigue, neurocognition, breathing, dizziness	Medium	>65	Pregnant women

Sources: Alfani 2023a; Alfani 2023b; Atmar, Englund, and Hammill 1992; Dixon 1962, 2, 6–7; Fleck-Derderian et al. 2020; Haider et al. 2022, 1, 93; Hassett 2003, 14–15; S.-T. Liang et al. 2021, 273–4; Livi-Bacci 2006, 206, 210; Matsuo et al. 2023; E. Smith et al. 2023; Snowden 2019, 29, 84, 95, 163, 241, 334, 471, 475–6.

Notes: Infection rate = % of population that contracts the disease; case fatality rate = % of cases that end in death; population mortality rate = % of population that dies of the disease; sequelae = post-infection conditions resulting from previous infection with the disease; poverty = strength of association between poverty and susceptibility to the disease; age = age-group(s) most strongly affected by the disease; gender = whether women or men are more strongly affected by the disease.

than one that hits just the poor. A disease that afflicts the very young or very old attracts less concern than one that strikes down householders and tax-payers in the prime of life. Historically, a disease that killed pregnant women attracted less attention than one that killed men of military age—hence state smallpox immunization for nineteenth-century soldiers, which long predated universal vaccination mandates. The biological features of different epidemic diseases thus already create differing institutional incentives to contain them. These biological features interact with the capacities of each institution and the interests of those who dominate its use, shaping responses to contagion.

Epidemics have afflicted large zones of the globe repeatedly across many centuries of recorded history, as tables 1.1 and 1.2 show. Indeed, they remain an active and present threat into the present day, as shown by recent and emerging diseases such as HIV/AIDS, SARS, and Covid-19. Yet we must recognize one big fact. The risks of epidemics across the globe as a whole declined enormously over the past seven centuries, and did so at an accelerating rate. Acute episodes of infectious disease weakened, they occurred less frequently, and they infected and killed fewer people when they did take place.[14] By the later seventeenth century, epidemic infection and mortality were lower than in the mid-fourteenth century. Between the late seventeenth and the late nineteenth century, they declined faster. By the early twenty-first century they had fallen even more spectacularly.

"Epidemiological transition" is the term demographers give this development, during which societies are supposed to make a happy exodus from pandemics of infectious disease into the sunlit uplands of non-communicable ailments and longer life expectancy. The epidemiological transition model holds that human populations pass through three stages of mortality and morbidity. In the first stage, "the age of pestilence and famine", societies suffer high and fluctuating mortality, in which infections cause most deaths and epidemics are common. In the second stage, "the age of receding pandemics", mortality declines, pandemics are fewer and smaller, medical knowledge advances, and infections gradually recede. The third and happy stage, "the age of degenerative and man-made diseases", is one in which mortality is low and still decreasing, infectious disease is rare, and most deaths are caused by cardio- and cerebrovascular ailments, metabolic diseases, cancers, injuries, stress-related disorders, and dementia. Epidemiological transition theory sees key changes occurring between 1670 and 1850, when colossal pandemics largely disappeared from western Europe, followed by accelerating improvement around 1900, as many lethal epidemic diseases declined simultaneously and were supplanted by non-communicable ailments.[15]

14. Omran 1971; Santosa et al. 2014; Mackenbach 2020; Mackenbach 2021; Alfani 2022, 33–4.
15. Omran 1971.

The idea of epidemiological transition is a stimulating point of departure, but we now know it does not tell the full story of the war between man and microbe. The concept was invented in 1971 and postulated a universal development based on the experience of a small number of modern, rich countries, whose history was assumed to prefigure the future of poor ones. The past 50 years have shown that this view was too hopeful. Even in Europe, infectious diseases did not all follow the same transition, but rather rose and fell, as shown in table 1.3. Infectious diseases, including epidemics, continue to display this typical rise-and-fall pattern to this day.[16]

Even more seriously, not all societies followed the same epidemiological pattern. The onset, speed, direction, and pattern of mortality developments display huge gaps across societies.[17] The elimination of infectious disease is still far from complete. Some old diseases came back because controls lapsed, as with tuberculosis and whooping cough. Others became much harder to fight because of antibiotic resistance, as with staphylococcal infections. Serious new infections emerged, such as Legionnaires' disease, AIDS, SARS, Ebola, and Covid-19.[18]

Sadly, no uniform epidemiological transition model applies to all societies. It might be argued that at least we can all accept that infectious diseases declined on average between around 1670 and 1900, and that this was mainly caused by advances in scientific and medical knowledge. Only up to a point. Knowledge about microbes and scientific approaches to medicine did ultimately play a key role in reducing epidemic mortality to the level we enjoy today. But their influence was much slower, later, and more partial than optimistic analyses would have it—for reasons this book will discuss. Scientific approaches to medicine gained force only in the final decades of the nineteenth and the early decades of the twentieth century, largely failed to control the 1918 flu pandemic, were still imperfect as late as HIV/AIDS, and are not universally accepted in most societies to this day—as became evident during Covid-19. Scientific knowledge about contagion, sanitation, social distancing, immunization, microbes, and antibiotics certainly gave us better technology for limiting epidemics. But knowledge was not enough. In many societies, new ideas and techniques for tackling epidemics were widely rejected. Why?

Social institutions, this book will argue, played a decisive role. New ideas and practices always create winners and losers. Institutions often enable the losers to block new knowledge, even though accepting it would benefit society at large. Market, state, community, religion, medical associations, and familial

---

16. Mackenbach 2020; Mackenbach 2021.
17. See the survey in Santosa et al. (2014).
18. Mackenbach 2020; Mackenbach 2021.

TABLE 1.3. Rise and Fall of Infectious Diseases in Europe, Ordered by Timing of Decline

Disease	Rise and fall?	Start of rise[a]	Start of fall[b]
Plague[c]	Rise and fall	1347	17th century
Typhus	Rise and fall	Late 15th century	17th century?
Smallpox	Rise and fall	6th century	18th century
Malaria	Rise and fall	16th century	18th century
Cholera	Rise and fall	1829–37	1846–60
Three intestinal infections (dysentery, typhoid fever, paratyphoid)	Rise and fall	6500 BCE[d]	Mid-19th century
Tuberculosis	Rise and fall	18th century	Mid-19th century
Puerperal fever	Rise and fall	18th century	Mid-19th century
Four childhood infections (scarlet fever, measles, whooping cough, diphtheria)	Rise and fall	18th century	Late 19th century
Syphilis	Rise and fall	Late 15th century	Early 20th century
Pneumoconiosis	Rise and fall	19th century	Early 20th century
Pneumonia	Fall only	N/A	Early 20th century
Influenza	Rise and fall	16th century	1918–19
AIDS	Rise and fall	Early 1980s	Mid-1990s
Covid-19	Rise and fall	2020	2021–23

Sources: Mackenbach 2020, 46–7; Mackenbach 2021, 1201.

[a] Approximate start of rise in Europe

[b] Approximate start of fall (or peak year) for north-western Europe only

[c] Second pandemic only

[d] In Europe, the Neolithic or first agricultural revolution started in the Aegean around 6500 BCE

institutions all have the capacity to accept and disseminate scientific approaches to epidemic disease, as we shall see. But they also have the capacity—and often create the incentive—to hinder these approaches. As this book will show, science seldom had a direct effect on epidemic outcomes. Rather, its acceptance and adoption were mediated by the institutional framework. Science, medicine, and technology greatly improve our capacity to limit infectious diseases. But how we use this capacity depends on social institutions.[19]

19. Santosa et al. 2014; Mackenbach 2020, 6–7, 76, 288–91; Mackenbach 2021.

3. What Do We Mean by Institutions?

"Institution" means different things in different contexts. In ordinary language, we use it to refer to specific organizations—the London Stock Exchange, the US government, the United Nations, the Derbyshire village of Eyam, the Catholic Church, the American Medical Association, the British royal family. But social scientists use "institution" to refer to a system of rules, customs, and practices governing how we interact in society—in North's famous formulation, "the rules of the game in a society or, more formally . . . the humanly devised constraints that shape human interaction".[20] The London Stock Exchange is a specific example of an abstract institution: the market. The US government is a specific example of the state, as is the United Nations—a supranational state institution. The Derbyshire village of Eyam, with its legendary communal action against the 1665 plague, which we analyse in chapter 4, is a specific example of a local community. Likewise, the Catholic Church is a specific manifestation of the institution of religion, the American Medical Association a modern instance of a corporative occupational group or guild, and the British royal family a famous example of the institution of the family. This book uses "institution" in this second, abstract sense, to refer to a system of rules and practices governing how we interact in society.

Some scholars argue that institutions encompass both external rules and internal preferences. This book draws a distinction between the two: internal preferences are part of culture, while external rules make up institutions. Human action, as this book thinks about it, involves both culture and institutions: people try to satisfy their preferences subject to a set of constraints. This book sees culture as contributing to the preferences, while institutions are part of the constraints. Of course, on the informal end of the spectrum, institutional rules shade into customs, norms, expectations, and preferences—that is, into culture. Almost certainly, there are two-way causal links between the systems of rules a society ends up with and the preferences held by its members.[21] But this book focuses on the constraints social institutions create for human choices via external rules, customs, and practices which do not take place primarily inside people's minds.

Why do institutions matter for epidemics? Surely disease is just a game between humans and nature—albeit a violent and lethal one? Microbes try to kill us, our immune systems try to kill them, and one side survives to play again. Institutions, by contrast, are games purely among humans. Human beings try to cooperate or compete, institutions channel how we do so, and the rules of that game decide who survives to play again. What do the two games—natural

---

20. North 1990, 3.
21. See the discussion in Ogilvie (2007, 660–1) and Vollrath (2019, pt. 4).

and institutional—have to do with each other? This book shows that the rules of the institutional game among humans change the outcome of the natural game between us and microbes.

Which institutions matter? Probably they all do, but which matter more? Human societies are multifarious, and we do not have evidence on them all. Even for one society, we do not know everything about all its rules, customs, and practices. So this book focuses on half a dozen key institutions: the market, the state, the community, religion, the occupational association, and the family. All six were central to most societies over the past two millennia, though in widely differing forms. All six set the rules for how humans interacted with microbes down the centuries, and still do in most societies to this day.

Our first institution is the market, the name we give to the set of rules, customs, practices, and procedures that people use to buy and sell. According to William Laud in 1637, plague epidemics were caused by people's "greediness to receive into their houses infected goods".[22] This point of view was echoed in 2021 by Dani Rodrik, who claimed that the Covid-19 pandemic would have been milder "if we had spent a little bit less time opening up our borders to trade and investment and doing the bidding of multinational corporations and banks".[23]

As these views illustrate, and as chapter 2 explores in detail, the market is often blamed for making epidemics worse. The market causes contagion, the argument goes, both when it fails and when it succeeds. The market fails when market prices do not take account of the costs individual decisions inflict on others, creating negative externalities such as contagion. Market prices also fail adequately to reward individuals and firms for creating public goods such as health information, sanitary infrastructure, vaccinations, and other medical innovations, which produce positive externalities by controlling infection. But even when the market does exactly what it is good at, facilitating voluntary exchange, it exacerbates contagion because it encourages trade and migration, along with the movement of microbes carried by goods and people.

Yet vigorous market institutions, as chapter 2 shows, also help mitigate epidemics. Measures to control contagion are costly. Border guards, street patrols, corpse inspectors, and other public servants must be paid. Sewerage and water systems must be built and maintained. Quarantined citizens have to be provisioned, or they will break out to find work or food. Medical innovations must be diffused and implemented. The Pfizer vaccine against Covid in 2021 involved assembling 280 components made by 86 suppliers in 19 countries, which would have been impossible without the market transactions and

22. Quoted in Slack 1985, 22.
23. Rodrik 2021, 69.

global production chains denounced by Laud and Rodrik.[24] To pay for public anti-contagion measures requires strong fiscal capacity, which is historically much higher in societies experiencing market-driven economic growth.[25] Communities, religions, occupational associations, and families, too, have more resources to tackle contagion in market societies, where economic growth and per capita incomes are higher.

Chapter 2 investigates how the market has interacted with epidemics down the centuries, and analyses those aspects of market activities that exacerbated or ameliorated the damage epidemic disease inflicts on human well-being.

A second key institution in tackling contagion is the state, a set of practices imposing compulsory rules over people in a territory, claiming priority over the rules of other organizations, and backed by legitimate coercion.[26] In March 1348, very soon after the Black Death reached Europe, the Large Council of the Republic of Venice set up a subcommittee of three, whose task was "to consider diligently all possible ways to preserve public health and avoid the corruption of the environment".[27] In 2020 during Covid-19, Francis Fukuyama declared that the key to dealing with a great pandemic is "whether citizens trust their leaders, and whether those leaders preside over a competent and effective state".[28]

The state has many features that deal with epidemics, as we see in chapter 3. A high-capacity state possesses policy levers enabling it to collect and diffuse information, provide sanitary infrastructure, and subsidize medical innovations—all helping to internalize contagion externalities. States also offer welfare support to motivate and enable poor citizens to comply with anti-contagion measures, instead of being compelled to leave home to buy food or earn a living.

On the other hand, there is such a thing as state failure—and not just in failed states. In 1353 Giovanni Boccaccio described how the Florentine state, one of richest and most sophisticated in the world, failed during the Black Death, when "no learning nor measure was of any use, such as the clearing of the city of much refuse by officials, who were appointed for that purpose, and the prohibition of any sick person from entering and many counsels given for the preservation of health".[29] In 2020, the editor-in-chief of the *Journal of the Royal Society of Medicine* declared uncompromisingly that in England, a rich modern democracy, "the government has indulged in a level of state negligence that may be unprecedented".[30]

---

24. Jecker and Atuire 2021, 597.

25. Besley and Persson 2009.

26. For overlapping definitions to this effect, see Weber ([1922] 1978, 54–5) and Tilly (1990, 1–2).

27. Cipolla 1976, 11.

28. Fukuyama 2020.

29. Quoted in Henderson 2019, 2.

30. Abbasi 2020, 419.

The state fails to deal with contagion, as chapter 3 shows, because of inaccurate information, low fiscal capacity, flawed bureaucratic capacity, *Realpolitik*, and poor incentives. It also exacerbates epidemics as it pursues its other interests. European states historically allocated 50–90 per cent of fiscal capacity to military purposes.[31] The resulting wars, as at Caffa in 1346, exacerbated epidemics through sieges, campaigns, camps, colonies, persecution, prisons, and refugee flows. State expenditure on civilian purposes such as sanitation, social distancing, quarantines, public information, vaccination programmes, or welfare support accounted for a vanishingly small share of public spending well into the twentieth century, and continues to be inadequate in many poor economies to this day.

Chapter 3 explores state capacity, state failure, and state motivation in dealing with contagious diseases. It identifies and analyses those features of the state that have historically helped or hindered societies in managing contagion during epidemics.

A third institution that influences epidemic contagion is the local community—the set of rules, customs, and practices connecting people living in spatial proximity within a town, village, or neighbourhood. During the 1631 plague epidemic, the Florentine village of Pinzidimonte imposed an autonomous community lockdown, incarcerating a number of families in their dwellings and intimidating everyone else out of "frequenting the churches, the streets, work, and everywhere they were threatened".[32] During the Covid-19 pandemic, some scholars lauded similar communal autonomy in China, where "civil society organizations took responsibility of isolating residents in every community".[33]

Community "social capital", as we see in chapter 4, fostered collective action to monitor and penalize individual choices that might transmit infection, ranging from waste disposal to breaking quarantine to neglecting immunization. Communities also provided much charitable relief and informal assistance among neighbours, enabling poor local residents to comply with anti-contagion measures during epidemics.

But communities can also fail. In 1353 Boccaccio described how in Florence during the Black Death "one citizen fled after another, and one neighbour had not any care of another".[34] Even in communities where solidarity survives, it is not always deployed in a good way. In 1630 the community of Prato excluded non-locals from the communal pesthouse, even when the grand-ducal government in Florence pointed out that "by eradicating the disease outside the walls, its eradication within is made easier".[35] In Indian villages during

31. Hoffman 2015, 315.
32. Quoted in Henderson 2019, 144.
33. S. Zhang et al. 2020, 216.
34. Quoted in Alfani and Murphy 2017, 333.
35. Quoted in Cipolla 1973, 123.

the Covid-19 epidemic, Hindu mobs violently attacked Muslims whom they accused of "corona jihad", and Muslim families concealed Covid-19 infections and neighbours' attacks for fear the village would throw them out.[36] Community trust supports exclusion of outsiders and ejection of marginal groups, whose banishment spreads contagion. Communities ration welfare relief, denying it to local minorities, attenuating their incentive and capacity to comply with anti-contagion measures. Communal social capital organizes collective resistance to public health measures, as in the popular anti-vaccination riots that erupted in many villages and towns across the globe between 1796 and the present day.

Chapter 4 analyses the strengths and weaknesses of community institutions. It seeks to identify those features that enable communities to internalize contagion externalities, but also those that make local communities collapse in the face of an epidemic or even organize activities that exacerbate the calamity.

Religion is a central institution of every human society, comprising not just a system of beliefs about spiritual beings but also a set of rules, customs, and practices governing human relationships with the spiritual world.[37] In Boston in 1721, the Puritan minister Cotton Mather proselytized for smallpox immunization in the name of religion, claiming that "Almighty GOD in His great Mercy to Mankind, has taught us a Remedy, to be used when the dangers of the Small Pox distress us."[38] During the 2020 Covid-19 pandemic, the *Scientific American* blog argued that "religion and science can complement one another, as indeed they are already doing by reinforcing public health messages during the current pandemic".[39]

Religious institutions played an important role in dealing with epidemics, as we see in chapter 5. Religions used moral suasion to motivate the faithful to comply with public health measures, adopt medical innovations, and coordinate social distancing or immunization. They exhorted their adherents to make charitable donations in the name of sacred beings and directly organize hospitals and medical care, increasing people's capacity and motivation to comply with anti-contagion measures.

But religions, as we shall see in chapter 5, also interact with epidemics in malignant ways. They facilitate contagion by mandating religious assemblies, pilgrimages, and religious wars. They preach opposition to public health measures such as quarantine or vaccination. Religions deny care to some of the neediest victims by discriminating against those it categorizes as sinners or unbelievers, reducing their ability to comply with anti-contagion measures.

36. Ellis-Petersen and Rahman 2020.
37. See the discussion in Seabright (2024).
38. Mather and Boylston 1721, 18–19.
39. Barmania and Reiss 2020.

Chapter 5 explores how religions use their moral authority and worldly power when epidemics strike. It analyses which features of a religion make it more able and willing to control contagion, but also those characteristics that lead religions to resist public health measures and persecute victims, hobbling epidemic control.

The occupational association or "guild" lays down norms, rules, and practices governing a specified branch of production activities in a particular locality. This type of institution has existed for centuries across the globe, and is especially widespread in medicine. Guilds, "colleges", and "faculties" of physicians, surgeons, and apothecaries governed their professions from before the Black Death into the nineteenth century, and were succeeded by the medical associations that regulate health-care activities to this day. Unsurprisingly, medical associations played a major role in dealing with epidemics. In the Dresden plague epidemic of 1680, the authorities canvassed the local surgeons' guild to provide expert personnel for the plague isolation hospital.[40] In the summer of 2021, the Royal College of Physicians of Edinburgh emphasized its role during the Covid-19 pandemic as "an advocate for our Fellows and Members and, ultimately for the patients that we serve".[41]

Guilds and associations of medical practitioners, as we shall see in chapter 6, contributed to managing epidemics. They advised governments on public health measures and provided skilled volunteers. They donated guild funds to charitable and medical projects, improving the capacity and incentive of poor people to comply with anti-contagion measures. They regulated medical training, quality, and knowledge, addressing information asymmetries between experts and ordinary people.

But medical associations also dealt with epidemics in less beneficent ways. They exacerbated contagion by erecting non-merit-based entry barriers, creating shortages of medical expertise and making contagion advice unaffordable for the poor. They used their authority to oppose knowledge and practices that threatened their professional privileges, blocking innovations that promised to limit epidemic contagion.

Chapter 6 examines the benefits of medical associations during epidemics, along with the costs they imposed. It seeks to identify the features of a medical association that facilitated contagion control, and those that made it more likely that it would seek its members' advantage at the expense of everyone else.

The family, as an institution, coordinates how a group of relatives resides, reproduces, nurtures, consumes, and produces. In Leiden in 1484 during the plague, Govert die Ketelboeter's daughter hastened to cleanse her own family

40. Schlenkrich 2002, 39–40.
41. A. Thomas et al. 2021, S10.

of infection by hanging bedclothes over a town bridge, exposing the neighbourhood to contagion.[42] In England in 1808 thousands of women scrambled to get their children vaccinated, while anti-vaxx activists scoffed at how "mothers fly to [vaccination] as they have done to Ching's Lozenges for the cure of worms".[43] In 2020 during the Covid-19 pandemic, the Pew Research Center ascribed high infection rates in some areas to family patterns "where many people live together, [so] the risk of contagion is heightened if anyone in the household falls ill or becomes an asymptomatic carrier of the coronavirus".[44]

The family influences epidemic contagion in many ways—through residential arrangements, death-related obligations, female autonomy, migration flows, and the balance between familial and societal responsibilities. All these activities, as we see in chapter 7, interact with epidemic disease. Social scientists and demographers stress the distinction between nuclear-family systems with weak kinship links and extended-family systems with strong kin obligations. Contagion, it is argued, is better controlled in nuclear-family systems where households are small, contain fewer generations, involve weaker kin relationships, relax death-related obligations, empower females to make household health choices, direct migration flows in epidemiologically safe channels, and foster prosociality beyond the family.

By contrast, extended-family or clan systems are thought to exacerbate epidemics. In kin-intensive systems, contagion is worse because households are large, interact with wider networks of relatives, mandate kin attendance at deathbeds and funerals, deprive women of health autonomy, unleash migration flows by solitary males in epidemiologically primitive conditions, and foster "amoral familism".

These effects of families on contagion make sense in theory. Chapter 7 examines whether they prevailed in practice—either universally or at all. The family is always embedded in a wider institutional system that influences whether any particular family form acts beneficially or harmfully in response to the external shock of an epidemic. The same, it turns out, applies to every other social institution.

4. The Road Behind and the Way Ahead

Epidemics are so shocking that many see them as natural or supernatural retribution. Historically, people saw plagues as divine punishment for man's sins against God. In the modern era, we think of epidemics as a reckoning for sins against nature: reproducing too fast, ceasing to hunt and gather, inventing

---

42. Coomans 2021, 223.
43. M. Bennett 2008, 506.
44. Kramer 2020.

agriculture, moving into towns, eating animals, globalizing trade. Our unnatural choices are blamed for creating environments where microbes to evolve to attack us.[45] These concerns alert us to natural constraints on human life.

But they neglect other constraints. People do not just submit to nature passively. We also respond actively. We act not just as individuals but in groups, societies, and even sometimes globally. We develop social rules, customs, and practices that constrain and facilitate how we coordinate and compete over how we respond to nature, including to microbial attacks.

This book analyses these societal responses. It asks how different institutions channel our behaviour in times of mass disease, enabling us to respond collectively to natural challenges—for good or ill.

One thing it finds is that history yields no universal laws of resilience. But it does reveal systematic ways of understanding variegated outcomes. In recorded history, epidemics affect different societies differently. Why such divergence?

Institutions, this book argues, play a major role. To foster resilience to epidemic disease, we must understand how rules and practices inside societies respond to natural shocks. But the present is often too close for understanding. History, precisely because it is more variegated and further away, can help.

What, then, is the best institution for dealing with epidemic contagion? The answer is a combination of institutions, chapter 8 argues, interlinked in an interdependent institutional framework, each playing to its strengths and checking the others' weaknesses. Why is this diverse and interdependent institutional framework so important?

First, we need multiple lines of approach. Fighting epidemics requires resources, coercion, monitoring, exhortation, expertise, nurturing. Each human institution is good at mobilizing some of these, but no institution is good at them all. A social framework in which multiple institutions coexist has a better chance of tackling the multiplicity of challenges posed by contagion.

Indeed, as later chapters show, each institution has special strengths. The market can allocate resources efficiently and foster economic growth, generating resources that individuals, families, governments, communities, guilds, and religions need to control contagion. The state and the community can provide coordination, monitoring, and regulation to internalize the negative externalities of contagion and the positive externalities of disease control. Religion can provide moral suasion and exhortation, motivating people to care about each other. Medical associations can monitor training, quality, and information, solving information asymmetries between producers and consumers of epidemiological expertise. The family can reduce risks of coresidence, death

45. McNeill 1976; Diamond 1997; Harper 2017; Arenas 2021.

practices, and migration, empower women, and protect vulnerable relatives by supporting prosocial behaviour.

But every institution has weaknesses. The market can convey price signals motivating people to work, trade, or socialize without taking account of how they affect others. The state can reject or falsify information and wage wars that consume resources and spread contagion. The community can make collective health decisions that favour powerful locals and harm society beyond its borders. Religion can mandate superspreader events and preach against science. Medical associations can impose entry barriers, limit competition, and block epidemiological innovations. The family can unleash risky residential, funerary, and migration choices, suppress female autonomy, and mandate kinship obligations that ignore societal effects.

As history shows, each institution takes different forms in different societies. The state, for instance, may have features in one society which give it greater capacity than the state in another society in the same historical period facing the same epidemic disease. Alternatively, the state may have the same capacity in two different societies, but different incentives, leading one state to devote all its capacity to war, while another allocates more to public health. Sometimes the difference arises not only out of features of that specific institution but also out of how it is embedded in the surrounding institutional framework. Do communities, religious institutions, or medical associations limit the tendency of the state to allocate resources to war or, alternatively, encourage it to allocate resources to public health? This is another reason controlling epidemics needs a combination of institutions—to make up for failures by other institutions and curb their most harmful actions.

The history of epidemics illuminates institutional combinations that work well to address contagion, as chapter 8 argues. It does not usually explain, though, how to achieve such happy institutional equilibria. But even revealing the features of an institutional framework that managed to control an epidemic is worthwhile, and creates the basis for future research on how a society might bring such a framework into being.

This book does not show that certain institutions—or even certain institutional frameworks—are bad or good. It does identify the strengths that enable a particular institution to help people devise and adopt effective ways of tackling epidemics. It also detects the weaknesses in each institution that make things work out badly. It demonstrates how diverse and interdependent institutions in a framework can work together to affect epidemic contagion—for good or ill. It identifies the features which have made institutional frameworks better at coordinating responses to epidemics and better at devising innovations to improve societal learning.

2

The Market

And it is now as clear as the sun, that the last increase [of plague] came by the carelessness of the people, and the greediness to receive into their houses infected goods.

—WILLIAM LAUD TO THOMAS WENTWORTH, 1637[1]

Now shops are shut in, people rare and very few that walk about, in so much that the grass begins to spring up in some places, and a deep silence almost in every place . . . no prancing horses, no rattling coaches, no calling in customers nor offering wares.

—THOMAS VINCENT, *GOD'S TERRIBLE VOICE IN THE CITY*, 1637[2]

We think of the market as a place where people buy and sell—a town square, trade fair, stock exchange, supermarket, or shopping arcade. But the market is also an institution—a set of practices, customs, and procedures by which people do that buying and selling. It is an institution that facilitates exchange by means of prices that convey information to producers and consumers about the scarcity and value of goods and services.

The market is often blamed for making epidemics worse. For one thing, it facilitates exchange of pathogens as well as goods. The first section of this chapter looks at this idea. Does history show that trade caused epidemics? If it did, were places better off if they were free of market exchange and, consequently, free of epidemics?

---

1. Quoted in Slack 1985, 22.
2. Quoted in Slack 1985, 173.

A second way the market is thought to aggravate epidemics is by facilitating trade in specific, disease-bearing goods. Trade in animals and animal products—cattle, sheep, fish, game, wool, furs—is seen as particularly harmful. This is because of zoonoses: pathogens that jump from animals to humans and underlie many emerging diseases. Section 2 of this chapter examines whether the market historically caused zoonoses. Would human societies have been better off without the market in certain goods if that reduced risks of catching diseases from animals?

The third and most important way the market exacerbates epidemics is by failing to convey full information to individuals about some of the costs of their actions. Market failures arise because of externalities and information problems. The market entices me to benefit myself by selling and buying, even though that might harm others by transmitting contagion. The market conveys some information to me via prices, but much information is a public good—the term economists give a good that is non-rival and non-excludable. Non-rival means I can consume information even if others have already consumed it. Non-excludable means I can consume much information without paying for it. Because producers find it hard to get anyone to pay them to produce information, markets will induce them to produce too little of it. Lacking information, people may fail to stay away from the market when they or others are spreading contagion.

As section 3 discusses, people did withdraw from market participation—as from many interpersonal contacts—during epidemics. But did they withdraw as much as if they were fully informed of the risks and incurred a personal cost when they infected others? How big was the gap between voluntary market withdrawal and compulsory market closure?

The market also helps societies cope with epidemics. As section 4 discusses, across the centuries the market has played a major role in improving economic performance. The level and growth rate of per capita gross domestic product (GDP) were historically higher in societies where the market performed well. Where markets allocated resources efficiently, reduced prices, and increased real incomes, people were better able to get health inputs that enabled them to avoid and resist infection themselves, limiting the contagion externalities they inflicted on others.

The market is widely known to fail when it comes to knowledge and technology because, as discussed earlier, information is non-rival and non-excludable. But as section 5 shows, the market played a role in medical innovation. The hope of market profits motivated people to devise and improve preventive measures such as immunization—variolation in the eighteenth century, vaccination in the centuries after 1796. More importantly, the market provided an efficient mechanism to diffuse anti-contagion techniques once they had been devised, making useful medical knowledge available to society as a whole.

1. Does the Market Cause Epidemics?

The market enables exchange of pathogens as well as goods. This plain fact is sometimes held to imply that market exchange causes epidemics. Pandemics in particular, where infections spread across multiple countries, are often thought to arise from the globalization of trade. "The significance of trade in the spread of bubonic plague was clear," according to one recent account: "The plague was carried to Europe via major trading centres. Disease spread through the networks of colonialism."[3] Cholera and smallpox epidemics are also ascribed to the market, with contagion exacerbated by laissez-faire policies in the growing cities of the Industrial Revolution.[4] Some go so far as to argue that Covid-19 is only the latest in a long history of pandemics caused by "mechanisms of unlimited profit, unlimited growth, and unlimited commodification".[5]

Does history show that the market causes epidemics? The market, we now know, existed in virtually every society in history.[6] It was always circumscribed by state, community, religion, guild, and family—all the institutions this book investigates. But in the interstices of other institutions, voluntary exchange between sellers and buyers sprang up in every society historians have studied. When market exchange involved movement of human beings—whether traders or workers—it inevitably also involved transmission of human infections. Trade in animals and animal products transmitted zoonoses, as we shall see. But other trade goods also transmitted pathogens, as with grain and textiles where fleas carrying bubonic plague survived independently of their animal hosts for up to 50 days.[7]

So it is not surprising that epidemics often spread via market exchange, as traders carried pathogens to new places. As early as 160 CE, the Antonine plague (possibly smallpox) spread particularly fast in Egypt, the commercial crossroads between the Mediterranean, the Red Sea, and tropical Africa.[8] In 541, the Justinianic plague is thought to have travelled in grain shipments across the Mediterranean.[9] The great plagues that struck the Mediterranean and the Middle East between 627 and 717 followed trade routes from city to city.[10] In 1346–47, the Black Death travelled with shipments of grain from

---

3. Mauelshagen 2020, 128.
4. Szreter 1997, 710, 715; M. Harrison 2012.
5. Arenas 2021, 371.
6. Ogilvie 2001; Hatekar 2003; Temin 2004a; Temin 2004b; McCloskey 2010; Dennison 2011; Ogilvie 2014a.
7. Dols 1977, 71; Benedictow 2004, 200–1.
8. Duncan-Jones 1996, 120; Scheidel 2002, 98.
9. H. Barker 2021, 106; McCormick 2003.
10. Dols 1977, 28, 43.

Tana across the Black Sea,[11] and voyaged into Europe and the Middle East on merchant ships.[12] Sixteenth-century plagues spread via networks of Dutch merchants throughout north-west Europe,[13] and with the caravan trade from East Africa through Sudan to Egypt and North Africa.[14] In Japan, measles epidemics escalated in the sixteenth century as commerce expanded, and died down after 1616 when the Tokugawa rulers closed down foreign trade.[15] In the seventeenth century, plague repeatedly struck great European trading cities such as Venice, Amsterdam, and London.[16] In 1720 one of the last plague epidemics in western Europe broke out in Marseille when wares off a ship from Lebanon evaded quarantine.[17] Smallpox came to northern Australia in the 1780s via Indonesian fishermen seeking sea slugs to trade in Sulawesi.[18] African epidemics increased sharply with the growth of long-distance trade, spreading in Madagascar in the later eighteenth century,[19] and along Tanzanian caravan routes in the nineteenth.[20] Cholera waves were borne across the world in the nineteenth century partly through the globalization of trade, which accelerated after 1865 via steamships and railways.[21] Scarlet fever epidemics were propagated and synchronized in nineteenth-century Europe and North America through international trading links.[22] After 1894 the third plague pandemic spread quickly across the world partly because trains and steamships increased the speed of trade.[23] The grain trade brought plague to San Francisco in 1900, Ipswich in 1910, and Vietnam in the 1960s.[24]

Inside particular countries, too, epidemics followed trade. During the Black Death, Essex suffered stratospheric mortality because rats and fleas entered on merchant ships through its many ports.[25] In 1545, plague broke out in Devon because harvest failure attracted grain deliveries from other regions and displaced hordes of migrant labourers seeking work.[26] In early modern Japan, measles epidemics moved from south-west to north-east because

11. H. Barker 2021.
12. Benedictow 2004, 68–73.
13. Curtis 2021b, 131; Noordegraaf and Valk 1988, 46–7.
14. Dols 1977, 15.
15. Jannetta 1987, 116, 126, 134.
16. Alfani and Murphy 2017, 327; Biraben 1975; Alfani 2013b, 418.
17. Mauelshagen 2005, 244.
18. M. Bennett 2009, 45, 329.
19. G. Campbell 1991, 427.
20. Koponen 1988, 665–6.
21. M. Harrison 2012, 140–1.
22. Davenport 2020b, 479–80.
23. Echenberg 2007.
24. Barnes 2014, 167; H. Barker 2021, 106; Glatter and Finkelman 2021, 177.
25. Gottfried 1983, 62; Aberth 1995, 275–6.
26. Slack 1985, 84.

the south-west port of Nagasaki was the only one officially open to trade.[27] Seventeenth-century London and Kent saw repeated plague and smallpox epidemics because their ports and docklands teemed with merchant shipping.[28] In nineteenth-century India, trade amplified local plague outbreaks in the north by carrying them across the whole country.[29]

Trade thus often carried epidemic disease. But does this mean epidemics were mainly caused by trade? One reason for caution is that international trade made up a tiny share of economic activity until the twentieth century. Around 1800, trade that crossed national borders made up less than 5 per cent of GDP in Europe and China, trade between continents less than 2 per cent.[30] Long after 1900, most of the market activity in the world was local and regional. International, long-distance trade was just not big enough to be the main cause of epidemics.

Nonetheless, trade did gradually increase across the centuries. It grew between late antiquity and the late Middle Ages, and expanded even more between 1500 and 1800.[31] Over the same period, the speed with which epidemics spread probably increased. Two historians recently calculated that the Black Death of 1347–51 spread faster than the Justinianic plague of 541–47, as illustrated in figures 2.1 and 2.2. Transmission speed more than doubled in 800 years.

Was this caused by trade? This particular study lacks direct evidence on trade intensity. But it tries to rule out other influences by testing whether political borders affected transmission speed. It finds no effect of borders on transmission speed in 541–47 but a significant effect in 1347–51.[32] From this it concludes that plague spread faster mainly because trade grew: "Both diseases were spread by human interaction, particularly through trade activities."[33]

But do these findings establish that plague was transmitted mainly by trade? Probably not. For one thing, the insignificant effect of political borders on the Justinianic plague in the 540s may simply reflect lack of evidence, with only 22 observations for which both transmission date and political borders are known. Moreover, political borders involve two potentially offsetting effects: less market exchange but more military activity. A net zero effect does not tell us whether both trade and war had small effects on plague or both had big ones. Third, many other factors that affect epidemics also changed between

27. Jannetta 1987, 116, 126, 134.
28. Dobson 1992, 85–6.
29. Barnes 2014, 167–8.
30. Ogilvie 2011, 197–8; Wickham 2023.
31. Ogilvie 2011, 197–8.
32. Boerner and Severgnini 2021.
33. Boerner and Severgnini 2021, 351.

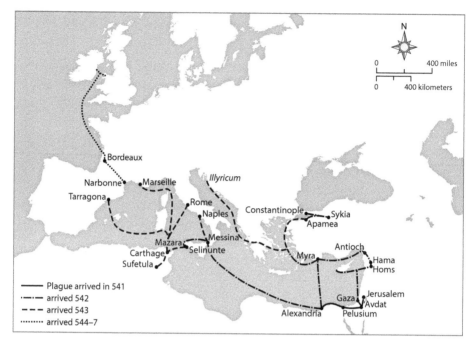

FIGURE 2.1. The spread of the Justinianic plague, 541–47 (first outbreak). The map covers all towns for which information on first infection is known. *Source*: Based on Boerner and Severgnini 2021, 339.

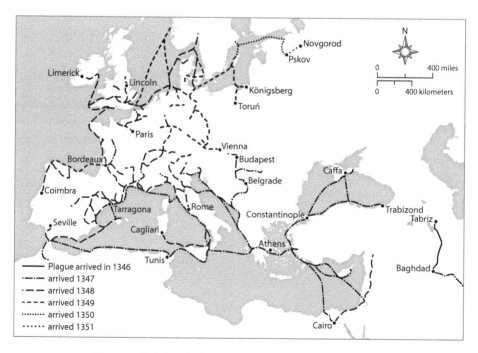

FIGURE 2.2. The spread of the Black Death, 1347–51. The map covers all towns for which information on first infection is known. *Source*: Based on Boerner and Severgnini 2021, 333.

the 540s and the 1340s—transport technology, religious conflict, population density, urbanization, human migration, agriculture, climate, rat ecology, bacteria genetics.

Other studies emphasize these other factors. One looks at how fast plague spread across London, comparing 1348 (the Black Death) to 1665 (the Great Plague). It finds a big acceleration across these 317 years, with plague moving across the city more than four times as fast in the 1660s as in the 1340s. It explains this acceleration not by market trade but by climate change, rat ecology, and human population density.[34]

In sober fact, neither study provides an explanation. Each finds that plague moved faster across the centuries. Each speculates what might have made this happen. But neither study measures the possible causal variables, so they cannot confirm or refute any causal link.

Plague locations suggest that transportation mattered—and this might (or might not) show a link to the market. Analysis of 5,559 plague outbreaks in Europe and its near abroad between 1347 and 1760 finds that over 95 per cent were located within 10 kilometres of navigable rivers. The number of outbreaks declined with distance from city to river, there were more outbreaks near wider rivers, and the link between plague outbreaks and water transport declined over time as land transport technology improved.[35] Good transport links made epidemics spread faster.

City-based analyses claiming that trade caused plague should be taken with more than a grain of internationally traded salt. They rely on data sets of plague locations which vastly over-represent large cities.[36] Yet plague was not exclusively or even predominantly urban, since plague rats favoured grain-rich, rural environments.[37] When we see plague being associated with commerce, trade routes, and navigable rivers, we may just be observing factors that favoured big cities and selection into plague data sets, not a causal chain linking epidemics to trade.

Transportation routes and transport technology reduce the cost of moving people and pathogens. But many institutions used transport links, as we see in later chapters. The state used them for warfare, transmitting epidemics through troop marches, refugee flows, and military supplies, as we see in chapter 3. The community used transport routes to provision itself and sell its surplus, even though this risked infection, as chapter 4 discusses. Religions used transport routes for pilgrimages, crusades, and missions, all of

34. Earn et al. 2020.
35. Yue, Lee, and Wu 2016.
36. Roosen and Curtis 2018, 5.
37. Alfani 2013b, 413, 416–17, 419–21; Dimitrov 2020, 108–10; Curtis 2016, 140, 162–70; Benedictow 2021, 23, 32–3, 276, 298–301, 307, 327, 341.

which spread epidemics, as we see in chapter 5. Occupational guilds used roads and rivers for their "wandering" or "tramping" requirements, which moved journeyman workers across long distances, as discussed in chapter 6. Families used transport links when they sought new places to find jobs, get training, find marriage partners, and make other life decisions, as we see in chapter 7. Thus all the institutions analysed in this book facilitated, encouraged, or mandated movement of people and goods. All these movements took place along the same transportation routes as market-driven trade. And they all carried contagion.

It might be argued that transportation routes were mainly developed for market trade, and non-market forms of travel were less important. But this would need to be established empirically, not just assumed a priori. Available evidence warns against dismissing non-market forms of travel as unimportant in transmitting epidemics. A quantitative study of European plague epidemics from 1347 to 1840 finds that they were strongly associated with military conflicts. Plague followed not just major transportation routes but secondary ones and affected peripheral as well as central towns, suggesting that contagion was often detached from trade nodes. This suggests that epidemics also followed troop movements and refugee flows.[38]

Market-driven trade moved people and goods, which often carried pathogens. In that sense, the market facilitated epidemics. But there are many other movements of people, goods, animals, and pathogens that have little to do with the market. What facilitated contagion was the movement of people and pathogens, by whatever institutional mechanisms.[39]

2. What about the Market in Infectious Goods?

The market is also blamed for exacerbating contagion by enabling trade in specific, disease-bearing goods. Many diseases are zoonoses—infections naturally transmitted to humans from other vertebrate animals, particularly wild ones. In the twenty-first century, 61 per cent of pathogen species causing human disease are zoonotic, rising to 75 per cent among "emerging" pathogens.[40] This has led some to argue that commodification of the natural world is "a major culprit behind the rise and spread of pandemics in general".[41]

Some emerging zoonoses cause just sporadic infections. But others indeed give rise to epidemics. The 1323 European influenza epidemic, it is thought, spread via thousands of pigs imported every year into great cities such as

---

38. Kaniewski and Marriner 2020, 5.
39. Slack 1985, 94.
40. Taylor, Latham, and Woolhouse 2001, 985–6.
41. Arenas 2021, 374.

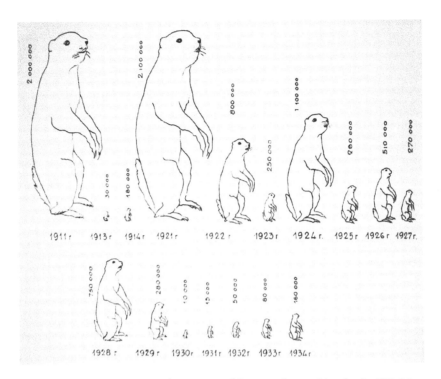

FIGURE 2.3. Tarbagan marmot skins exported from north-west Manchuria, 1911–34. Tarbagan marmots were the main hosts of the plague bacillus in the Manchurian plague epidemic of 1910–11. Traditionally, tarbagans had been a low-quality subsistence food source for locals. But shortly after 1900, international demand for their fur attracted local and incoming trappers, hugely increasing zoonotic transmission of plague to humans. By 1911, over two million tarbagan skins were being exported from north-west Manchuria, along with the plague bacilli they carried. Oversupply, the First World War, and the Russian Revolution choked off the tarbagan fur trade until 1921, when exports again exceeded two million, but only briefly. After that date, exports and tarbagans themselves gradually declined because of overhunting and habitat damage. *Source*: Shen 2019, 314.

Florence.[42] The Black Death, some surmise, jumped from tarbagan marmots to humans in Mongolia, before being carried by humans and rats in the Golden Horde army to the Black Sea basin.[43] The 1910–11 Manchurian plague spread to humans from tarbagans, with blame typically attached to market-oriented immigrant trappers seeking to profit from exporting marmot fur, as shown in figure 2.3.[44] The 2002–4 SARS epidemic emerged from the trade in palm civets

42. Bauch 2020, 59–60.
43. Schmid et al. 2015; Ditrich 2017, 28; Favereau 2021, 251–2.
44. Lynteris 2016, ix–x, 27, 125–6 and passim; Shen 2019.

as a culinary delicacy in East Asian countries.[45] Against this background, it is unsurprising that one hypothesis about the origins of Covid-19 ascribes it to the wild meat trade at the Huanan Seafood Wholesale Market in Wuhan in 2019–20, leading to widespread condemnation of Chinese "wet markets".[46]

Grain, raw cotton, and textiles are not animal products, but their trade is nonetheless blamed for pandemics because they provide a welcoming environment for disease vectors to travel independently of humans.[47] The sixth-century Justinianic plague is blamed partly on the grain trade needed to feed swollen Mediterranean cities.[48] The Black Death is likewise thought to have travelled in grain shipments containing rat fleas.[49] Later medieval European plagues are blamed on the Hanseatic stockfish trade, which hosted colonies of infected black rats.[50] Fifteenth-century Middle Eastern plagues are ascribed partly to the trade in woollen cloth and furs linking the Ottoman lands, the Black Sea basin, Russia, the Mediterranean, and the Silk Road.[51] Nineteenth-century East Asian plagues are thought to have moved into China through raw cotton imported from northern Burma.[52]

Should we blame epidemics on market trade in animal products, grain, or textiles? Probably not. Even when these goods were not traded in the market, they transmitted disease. Grain hosted plague-infected rat fleas whether it was traded in Sicilian merchant ships, hauled in army victualling wagons, or transported to provision pilgrims and crusaders. Norwegian stockfish attracted rats no matter what: any plague they carried can be blamed neither on the market in which stockfish were traded, nor on the Catholic and Orthodox Churches whose dietary rules fuelled demand for Friday and Lenten fare.[53] Tarbagan marmots were infected with *Yersinia pestis* whether their fur was traded by Han merchants on the international market or consumed by indigenous Manchurians for subsistence.[54] The Covid-19 virus is carried by live animals and dead meat, whether consumed by Chinese game hunters on the spot, sold in the Wuhan wet market, or wrapped in Vancouver meat-packing plants.

The market for all these goods also creates benefits. Market trade in pigs, cattle, fish, and grain supported urbanization in central and northern Italy, the

45. Song et al. 2005.
46. Beech 2020.
47. Dols 1977, 71; Benedictow 2004, 200–1; Andreozzi 2015, 128.
48. H. Barker 2021, 106; McCormick 2003.
49. Benedictow 2004, 200–1.
50. Benedictow 2004, 200–1.
51. Varlik 2015, 154.
52. Benedict 1988, 123–5.
53. Benedictow 2004, 200–1.
54. Lynteris 2016, ix–x, 26–7.

European zone with the highest per capita GDP in the fourteenth century. In early modern Holland and England, the grain market created incentives for peasants to produce surpluses, traders to move food from areas of plenty to areas of dearth, and all regions to specialize in producing the crops in which they were most productive. These activities helped increase living standards, urbanization, and economic growth.[55] Banning the pre-modern grain and animal market would have choked off the livelihoods of millions of peasants and increased food prices for millions of urban families. Modern Chinese wet markets, though less central to society than pre-modern European grain markets, nonetheless supply essential foodstuffs to millions of consumers, sustain critical food supply chains, employ hundreds of thousands of workers, generate gains from trade, and are central to culture and sociability. Breeding and selling wild animals in wet markets contributes to rural development and poverty alleviation, provides a living to tens of thousands of Chinese farm families, and was valued in 2017 at 520 billion yuan (US$74 billion).[56]

Even if the benefits generated by trade in particular goods are outweighed by the costs of zoonoses, the solution is not to ban the market outright, but to target those of its activities that endanger public health. For twenty-first-century Chinese wet markets, a recent study established that health risks arose almost entirely from sales of living wild animals.[57] In January 2020, the Chinese government closed the Huanan Seafood Wholesale Market in Wuhan and temporarily banned sales of wild animals for consumption.[58] Even that policy was not ideal, since it pushed exchange into the black market, making it hard to control.[59] A better solution is not to suppress a harmful market but to legalize, monitor, and regulate it.[60]

The long history of trade in particular goods casts clearer light on the link between the market and epidemics. Some goods derive directly from animals and thus easily increase the risk of zoonoses. Others such as grain and textiles are easily contaminated with pathogens. Mass movements of such goods undoubtedly helped spread epidemics, and the market certainly facilitated such trade (though so did state, religion, and other institutions). But the market in particular wares exists because it increases welfare for producers and consumers—as we shall see in later sections of this chapter. Abolishing the market means abolishing the human benefits it brings and the resources it generates, which can be used for, among other things, controlling contagion.

55. De Vries 1976; Ogilvie 2000.
56. Beech 2020; Huber 2021; Lin et al. 2021.
57. Lin et al. 2021.
58. Beech 2020; S. Zhang et al. 2020, 215.
59. Beech 2020; Lin et al. 2021.
60. Huber 2021; Lin et al. 2021.

If trade in a particular good creates contagion costs beyond those the individual market participant incurs then the solution is to target the source of contagion, not close down the whole market. Historically, state and community targeted infected wares through inspections and quarantines, regarding market closures as the suicide option, since it led to starvation. Nowadays, scientific knowledge enables better targeting. Only where monitoring and regulation are impossible—say, with a new pathogen such as Covid-19—may market closure be the best policy. Even then, history suggests it should be temporary, pending better targeting of the risks.

3. Market Withdrawal

Market and non-market institutions are often portrayed as substitutes—indeed rivals—when it comes to epidemic contagion. Either the market is left open, sustaining the economy but fuelling contagion, or other institutions shut it down, extinguishing contagion but ravaging the economy.

Historical epidemics show that this dichotomy is false. Market and non-market institutions are not substitutes but complements. People reduce market participation during epidemics even without state or community compulsion. Social scientists call this response "market withdrawal". A simpler term might be "natural caution". Information about epidemic disease and fear of contagion leads consumers, producers, and traders to withdraw from in-person market activity, as from any face-to-face interaction. Businesses and investors respond to market withdrawal—or even anticipate it—by reducing their own market activity. People thus avoid the market voluntarily during epidemics to protect themselves. They do not avoid it as much as if they were also protecting others. That usually needs coordination from the state and other institutions, as we shall see. But voluntary market withdrawal takes place, and can be substantial.

3.1. WHO WITHDREW?

Non-local merchants left early and often—not surprisingly, given their outside options. During the Black Death in Alexandria, the caravanserais closed, not by public order but because customers were unwilling to frequent them.[61] During the fourteenth-century plagues, markets were deserted in Bilbais on the caravan route between Cairo and Palestine, not because the ruler closed them but because foreign traders stayed away.[62] In the plagues of 1497–98 and 1513–14 in Damascus, foreign merchants immediately left for Cyprus.[63] In the

---

61. Dols 1977, 279.
62. Dols 1977, 160, 278.
63. Dols 1977, 279.

1512 Istanbul plague, with 300 deaths a day, Venetian merchants decamped to the countryside.[64] In the 1625 plague in England, an exodus of merchant shipping left Exeter desolate, and "no-one wanted to buy anything in London".[65] In seventeenth-century plague years, Marseille was hit by recurrent downticks in trade because "merchants preferred to use the smaller, nearby coastal ports, believing them to be healthier".[66] In eighteenth-century England, smallpox outbreaks made merchants avoid towns and shun trade fairs.[67] In the 1864 smallpox epidemic in Angola, commerce in the east ceased altogether as the Imbangala stopped trading, and Cokwe, Ginga and Songo traders refused to enter cities like Kasanje.[68] In the 1896 Mumbai plague epidemic, a local newspaper described how "the exodus and the plague scare have had a serious effect in curtailing trade".[69]

Even local traders avoided the market, though they had fewer outside options. During the Black Death in Bilbais, local sellers moved their stalls out into suburbs and orchards where they could practise social distancing.[70] In sixteenth-century French plagues, shops closed one after another as the epidemic advanced.[71] In Bristol during the 1603 plague, town markets were so idle that they dragged down the rural economy of Herefordshire.[72] In Exeter during the 1625–26 plague, local traders moved their shops to the countryside and refused to return.[73] In the Great Plague of London in 1665–66, "the Exchange was not kcpt shut indeed, but it was no more frequented".[74] In the 1831 plague in Baghdad, shops were left deserted and commerce ceased.[75] In the 1832 cholera epidemic in Alexandria, business came to a standstill without official market closures.[76] In the 1835 Cairo plague, a visiting French observer exclaimed, "What quiet everywhere! No more lines of camels in the streets, no more merchants in all the bazaars, the little shops formerly so busy were closed, now clients and merchants were closed up with their families."[77] In the 1918 flu epidemic in Ghana, within 10 days of the first case being reported,

64. Varlik 2015, 150.
65. Slack 1985, 115, 189.
66. Kettering 2001, 55.
67. Davenport, Satchell, and Shaw-Taylor 2018, 84; Davenport 2020a, 65–6.
68. Dias 1981, 365–6, 369.
69. M. Harrison 1992, 139 (quotation); M. Harrison 2012, 183.
70. Dols 1977, 160, 278.
71. Lucenet 1985, 133.
72. Slack 1985, 188–9.
73. Slack 1985, 115.
74. Defoe 1722, 197–8.
75. Bolaños 2019, 606–7.
76. Kuhnke 1990, 53–4.
77. Quoted in Rue 2016, 38.

town markets were deserted, places of business closed, and trade was at a standstill.[78] In December 1918 when flu arrived in the northern provinces of Nigeria, merchants and petty traders withdrew from the market so that "food became more scarce and dearer".[79]

The labour market also stalled, as employers withdrew to avoid contagion. In 1630, just four months after plague arrived in Florence, a contemporary reported that "in Via Camaldoli all the [inhabitants of the] houses are without work, because the workshop owners no longer provide work, from the suspicion that they would thus infect the cloth".[80] In early modern English plagues, urban employers fled to the countryside, leaving workers without jobs.[81] In the 1720 Marseille plague, an English observer described how rich townsmen fled, and "by this means Trade stops, Employment ceases, and the Poor wanting Work, must of consequence have their Subsistance [*sic*] cut off".[82] In the 1832 cholera epidemic in New York City, richer citizens left town, business dried up, streets fell silent, and the only jobs were those of "Doctors, Undertakers, Coffinmakers".[83]

Even workers tried to avoid the market if they could afford it. During the 1577 Lyon plague, the local lawyer Claude de Rubys recounted how:

These humble people, frightened by the dread of death, still remembering the great plague of 1564, began to pack up, to withdraw with their wives and children to villages here and there, so as to get a change of air and avoid contagion from their infected neighbours. It was a very pitiable thing to see these poor people withdrawing, some with their little children in their arms, others with donkeys, horses and carts, each according to his means, laden with their wives and children, their furniture and clothes, bidding farewell through the town to their relatives and friends.[84]

In Japan during the 1857 Ainu smallpox epidemic, fishermen and porters refused to work, disrupting fisheries and state visits.[85] In Tanzania during the 1859 cholera epidemic, porters withdrew from the market, bringing the caravan trade to a halt.[86] In the 1890–91 Angola smallpox epidemic, the Ovimbundu porters who dominated the transport of wares between Luanda, Dondo, and Cazengo refused to work, stalling 4 million kg of coffee with no means of

78. Scott 1965, 191.
79. Ohadike 1981, 384.
80. Henderson 2019, 132.
81. Slack 1985, 189.
82. Quoted in Ermus 2020.
83. Quoted in Tumbe 2020, 47.
84. Quoted in Lucenet 1985, 132.
85. Walker 1999, 142.
86. Koponen 1988, 662.

transport and throwing the European plantation economy into crisis.[87] In the 1918 flu epidemic in Raleigh, North Carolina, 50–75 per cent of workers stayed away from the textile mills.[88] In Philadelphia in 1918, according to one survivor, "We did not go to work. Could not go to work. Nobody came into work. . . . [T]hey were all afraid."[89] In Japanese textile factories in January 1920,

> Female workers were seized with a panic to see the death of their colleagues. Many female workers politely asked their employers to let them go back to their hometowns. The employer was very upset and refused to allow their parents, who wanted to pick them up, to meet them. Some female workers solicited aid from the police to go home.[90]

Peasants, too, withdrew from the market for fear of contagion. When the Justinianic plague broke out in 542, peasants refused to bring goods into the city of Myra, declaring that "if we give the city [a] wide berth then we will not die of this disease".[91] During the Black Death in Egypt and Andalusia, peasants left towns unsupplied with foodstuffs.[92] In 1457, the peasantry around the Peloponnesian town of Modon (Methoni) fled plague, depriving urban markets of wheat.[93] In 1575 when the first signs of plague appeared in Verona, the surrounding peasantry stopped bringing food to sell in the city.[94] In Salisbury during the 1627 plague epidemic, farmers refused to attend the grain market, triggering hunger riots.[95] In the 1680 plague in České Budějovice (Budweis), municipal officials ordered people to stock up on food and other necessities, since "the neighboring villages were ceasing to communicate with the town and soon nothing will be imported into Budějovice".[96] In the 1818 cholera epidemic in Tamil Nadu, peasants in the countryside around Tanjore (Thanjavur) refused to leave their villages or admit outsiders, damaging the grain trade.[97] In Baghdad during the 1831 plague, peasants in the surrounding countryside left the city unsupplied and triggered famine.[98]

Consumers also withdrew as much as they could. In the Justinianic plague of the 540s, people in Constantinople locked themselves in their houses for

87. Dias 1981, 365–6, 369.
88. Bodenhorn 2020, 34.
89. Quoted in Barry 2018, 332.
90. Quoted in Noy, Okubo, and Strobl 2020, 8.
91. Quoted in Stathakopoulos 2007, 213; see also Eisenberg and Mordechai 2022, 296.
92. Dols 1977, 162.
93. Dimitrov 2020, 111.
94. Alfani 2013a, 108.
95. Slack 1985, 258–9.
96. Quoted in Holasová 2005, 15.
97. Brimnes 2013, 101.
98. Bolaños 2019, 606–7.

fear of infection.[99] In the Great Plague of London in 1665–66, according to Daniel Defoe, "The Markets were but very thinly furnished with provisions, or frequented with Buyers, compair'd to what they were before."[100] Across England that year, the excise collectors reported a huge fall in revenues because fear of plague kept people away from alehouses and inns.[101] In Marseille during the 1720 plague, markets were deserted by rich and poor alike, long before the corrupt city government finally closed them.[102] In eighteenth-century England, adults who had never had smallpox stayed away from town during epidemics, leading markets to be closed.[103] In St Albans in 1794, when 18-year-old William Hart caught smallpox, his landlady threw him out because she was "an old maiden woman who kept a shop and was afraid of losing her customers".[104] In Minnesota in the autumn of 1918, before public gatherings were forbidden by the local government, locals reported that "fear of influenza contagion in crowded places has reduced the patronage of St. Paul motion picture theaters by nearly half".[105]

Market withdrawal struck contemporary observers. In the 1467 plague in Constantinople, according to Critobulus of Imbros (who arrived in the city in 1466 and probably died there shortly after 1468),

> The City was emptied of its inhabitants, both citizens and foreigners. It had the appearance of a town devoid of all human beings, some of them dead or dying of the disease, others, as I have said, leaving their homes and fleeing, while still others shut themselves into their homes as if condemned to die.[106]

In London during the Great Plague of 1665–66, according to Daniel Defoe, "A vast Number of People lock'd themselves up, so as not to come abroad into any Company at all, nor suffer any, that had been abroad in promiscuous Company, to come into their Houses, or near them."[107] In the Romanian town of Craiova in 1795, an exiled Bulgarian wrote to a relative in Turkey that plague had brought all economic activity to a standstill.[108] In London during the 1854 cholera epidemic, the pioneering epidemiologist John Snow observed that "in less than six days . . . the most afflicted streets were deserted by more than three-quarters of

99. Eisenberg and Mordechai 2022, 296.
100. Defoe 1722, 94.
101. Slack 1985, 189.
102. Biraben 1968; Ermus 2020.
103. Davenport, Satchell, and Shaw-Taylor 2018, 84; Davenport 2020a, 65–6.
104. Quoted in Davenport 2020a, 61.
105. Quoted in Ott et al. 2007, 805.
106. Quoted in Dimitrov 2020, 111.
107. Defoe 1722, 241.
108. Robarts 2017, 224–5.

their inhabitants".[109] In rural Kentucky during the 1918–19 influenza epidemic, market withdrawal was so acute that the Red Cross reported "people starving to death not from lack of food but because the well were panic stricken and would not go near the sick".[110]

3.2. HOW BIG WAS MARKET WITHDRAWAL?

Qualitative anecdotes such as these can be multiplied indefinitely. They illuminate people's reasoning when they withdrew from the market. But how much difference did individual withdrawal make to market activity?

Table 2.1 reports quantitative measures of voluntary market withdrawal, independent of public market closures. The first six rows show surviving estimates from the second plague pandemic in the Ottoman Empire, England, and Italy between 1491 and 1666. It finds non-trivial effects on measures as varied as beer purchases, urban retailing, use of the postal system, wool and silk exports, and textile output. The bottom 12 rows of table 2.1 show estimates for modern pandemics between 1918 and 2022—influenza, Ebola, and Covid-19—in the USA, England, Japan, and globally. It again finds non-trivial effects on measures as varied as coal output, income per worker, GDP, retail sales, average daily contacts, plans to leave the home, nightclub attendance, and rail travel.

At the high end, we see a 96–97 per cent decline in textile exports and merchant postal activity in seventeenth-century Italian plagues. On the low end, we find just a 4–5 per cent decline in aggregate income per worker or the economic activity index in the 1918 US flu pandemic and the 2021 UK Covid-19 pandemic (although it must be remembered that the UK Covid pandemic had been brought largely under control by July 2021).

Across all 18 quantitative observations, the average decline in market activity is over 42 per cent. But this masks a large gap between the medieval and early modern plagues, with an average of 69 per cent, and the twentieth- and twenty-first-century epidemics with an average of 29 per cent.[111] This does not necessarily mean that market withdrawal was higher in the past than it is now. But it does show that voluntary market withdrawal during epidemics was non-trivial.

This raises a second question. How big was individual market withdrawal relative to mandatory market closures by states or communities? In most epidemics, individual withdrawal and mandatory closures coexist, and all we

---

109. Quoted in Tulchinsky 2018, 81.

110. Quoted in Barry 2005, 66.

111. The same goes for the median decline, which is 32.5% across all 18 observations, but 78.5% for the 6 early modern plagues and only 20% for the 12 modern influenza, Ebola, and Covid epidemics.

TABLE 2.1. Decline in Market Activity Due to Private Responses to Epidemics, 1491/2022

Place	Date	Epidemic	Indicator	% decline	Source
Bursa	1491	Plague	Sales by shops selling millet beer	32	a
London	1603	Plague	Shortcloth exports	33	b
Chester	1604	Plague	Cloth exports	90	c
Florence	1628–32	Plague	Merchant payments to postal service	97	d
Genoa	1657	Plague	Silk cloth exports	96	d
Colchester	1666	Plague	Textile output	67	e
Kentucky and West Virginia	1918	Influenza	Coal output	15	f
St Paul, Minnesota	1918	Influenza	Theatre attendance	50	g
Southern US cities	1918–19	Influenza	Aggregate income per worker	4	h
Guinea, Liberia, Sierra Leone	2015	Ebola	GDP	12	i
England	Jun.–Jul. 2021	Covid-19	Adults' average daily contacts	60	j
England	Jun.–Jul. 2021	Covid-19	People willing to visit nightclubs	75	k
England	20 Jul. 2021	Covid-19	Economic activity index	5	k
Japan	Spring 2020	Covid-19	Rail passenger numbers	25	l
Japan	Autumn 2021	Covid-19	Rail passenger numbers	25	l
World excluding China	10 Sept. 2022	Covid-19	Global normalcy index	13	m
China	Nov. 2022	Covid-19	Retail sales compared to 1 year earlier	7	n
China	20 Dec. 2022	Covid-19	Intend to stay at home or go out less	61	n
Mean 1491/1666				69.2	
Mean 1918/2022				29.3	
Mean 1491/2022				42.6	

Sources: [a] Varlik 2015, 146 (weighted average across all shops); [b] Slack 1985, 188–9; [c] Victoria County History 2003, 90–7; [d] Cipolla 1976, 40; [e] Slack 1985, 190; [f] Bodenhorn 2020, 4; [g] Ott et al. 2007, 805; [h] Bodenhorn 2020, 45–6; [i] M. Thomas et al. 2015; [j] Cuffe 2021; [k] *Economist* 2021b; [l] Shizume 2022, 10; [m] *Economist* 2022a, 89; [n] *Economist* 2022b, 50.

Notes: Decline in market activity is described in study as resulting primarily from private choices rather than from public regulation.

observe is the outcome. This makes it hard to identify their relative effects. But some studies try.

The earliest epidemic with good enough data is the 1918–19 flu pandemic. Correia, Luck, and Verner analysed monthly data from 43 major US cities and concluded that voluntary market withdrawal was more important than public initiatives in reducing economic activities in 1918–19.[112] But this study turned out to be flawed. Lilley, Lilley, and Rinaldi argued that the finding was driven by pre-existing growth trends in the cities in question.[113] Qualitative evidence shows that voluntary market withdrawal and public anti-contagion initiatives operated simultaneously, with no way to disentangle the two effects.[114]

Studies of the 2020–21 Covid-19 pandemic likewise yield contradictory findings. Some early studies argued that reduction in economic activity was mainly caused by lockdowns rather than market withdrawal.[115] Others claimed that voluntary market withdrawal played a much greater role, and even that public health measures were unnecessary.[116] Studies of countries without strict lockdowns, such as South Korea and Sweden, found that voluntary market withdrawal caused significant economic contraction, but not as much as mandatory market closures did in countries that had them.[117]

High-frequency data on mobility in 128 countries and job postings in 22 countries during the first seven months of the 2020 Covid-19 pandemic, shown in figure 2.4, reveal that government lockdowns and voluntary market withdrawal played comparable roles in reducing economic activity across the whole sample.[118] But societies differed greatly. In high-income economies and "emerging markets" (i.e. middle-income economies), voluntary social distancing played a greater role than government lockdowns, accounting for more than half the economic contraction. These were economies where people could more easily work from home and sustain temporary unemployment by using savings and welfare benefits. But in low-income countries, voluntary social distancing accounted for only about one-fifth of the decline. It is not surprising that voluntary social distancing plays a smaller role in poor economies, since it results from individual calculations of costs of withdrawing from the market. These costs are higher where savings are lower, welfare benefits smaller,

112. Correia, Luck, and Verner 2020.

113. Lilley, Lilley, and Rinaldi 2020.

114. Gelman 2020.

115. J. Baker et al. 2020; Beland et al. 2020; Carvalho et al. 2020; Chronopoulos, Lukas, and Wilson 2020; Gupta et al. 2020.

116. Baek et al. 2020; Bartik et al. 2020; Chen et al. 2020; Chetty et al. 2020; Forsythe et al. 2020; Goolsbee and Syverson 2020; Maloney and Taskin 2020; Rojas et al. 2020.

117. Andersen et al. 2020; Aum, Lee, and Shin 2020; Born, Dietrich, and Müller 2020.

118. Caselli, Grigoli, and Sandri 2022, 251.

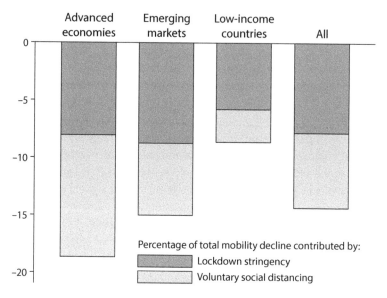

FIGURE 2.4. The relative contributions of government lockdown and voluntary social distancing to mobility decline (per cent) in 122 countries during the 2020 Covid-19 pandemic. Bars denote cross-country averages, computed using coefficients on lockdowns and log of daily Covid-19 cases multiplied by average of corresponding variables for each country group during the first three months of each country's epidemic. *Source*: Based on Caselli, Grigoli, and Sandri 2022, 251.

and remote-working infrastructure less adequate. Low-income people cannot afford to withdraw from the market during pandemics, even when they see the risks of staying.

It might be argued that the magnitude of voluntary market withdrawal was efficient, since it reflected individuals' rational balancing of the risks of infection against the risks of poverty and starvation. But there are reasons to doubt this. First, as we have seen, contagion has negative externalities—costs beyond those incurred by the individual. And second, information is a public good, with the result that individuals and organizations produce less of it than is efficient for society at large because it is non-rival and non-excludable. So people probably did not practise enough voluntary market withdrawal.

The Florentine plague of 1630–31 shows these forces at work. A vivid instance of individuals not taking account of contagion externalities arose in the autumn of 1630, when the nearby village of Tavola had an excellent grape harvest. The only snag was that Tavola was infected with plague. Yet individual Florentine labourers flooded into Tavola to work as grape pickers. Many caught plague and carried it back to Florence, where the infection spread rapidly in the winter of

1630–31.[119] The grape pickers thought their earnings worth the costs to themselves, including the risk of catching plague, but did not take into account the costs of the contagion they spread. We know the grape pickers did spread plague, since contemporaries traced subsequent infections to the Tavola harvest.

Information problems also played a role. Cristofano Ceffini, the public health officer in nearby Prato, described them clearly:

> The epidemic started in the month of August 1630, slowly at first so that people took no notice of its gathering momentum, thinking that any day it would end. In truth people went about their business and took little account of what was beginning to happen because they had no experience of such a catastrophe.[120]

Individuals lack information about epidemics—then as now. Florentine citizens in August 1630 realized that there was some plague around but did not know how much, just as citizens in most countries of the world in February 2020 realized there was some Covid-19 around but did not know how much. Florentine citizens in 1630, like most of us in 2020, also lacked information on how fast the epidemic might spread. Because information is under-provided in markets, non-market institutions such as the state or the community may collect the quantity of information that is more efficient for society as a whole, and use it to close the market before individuals themselves assemble sufficient information to calculate the risks to themselves and others.

The Florentine epidemic of 1630–31 killed 12–14 per cent of the population.[121] This suggests that even in a poor seventeenth-century economy, the degree of market withdrawal achieved by individual decisions alone was not efficient for the wider society. There was a role to be played by the state or the community in imposing mandatory market closures to compensate for how the externalities of contagion and the public-good features of information can make the market fail. Unfortunately, states also fail, as we shall see. The Florentine state did collect information about local infections in the summer of 1630 and placed the village of Tavola under quarantine before the harvest. Unfortunately, the Florentine state failed to enforce the quarantine—for reasons analysed in chapter 3.

Individuals always withdrew from the market during epidemics. But that does not imply that it was unnecessary for communities or states to coordinate on closing markets. On the contrary, individuals, communities, and states can support one another. Individuals can do part of the heavy lifting by calculating their own costs and benefits and assembling the information relevant to

119. Cipolla 1973, 60.
120. Quoted in Cipolla 1973, 59–60.
121. Alfani (2013b, 417) gives the mortality rate of 137 per 1,000; Ammannati (2020, 3) gives 12%.

themselves. Community and state can fill the gaps created by the fact that individuals pay only some of the costs of their own contagion decisions and reap only some of the benefits of collecting epidemic information. The market and other institutions are thus interdependent. In the best case they can make up for one another's weaknesses, though in the worst case they can exacerbate them—as we shall see.

4. Do Markets Matter for Health?

The market facilitated exchange of bad things like pathogens as well as good things like the necessities of life. The market also failed to cope with contagion and information. Did this mean that society was better off without the market? The answer is a clear "no"—even if the sole measure of well-being is epidemic control.

4.1. MARKETS AND ECONOMIC GROWTH

The market made both individuals and societies richer, on average. This was important, since poverty kills. Every recorded epidemic over the past seven centuries hit the poor harder than the rich. When the market generated higher incomes, they were available for individuals, families, communities, religions, guilds, and governments to fight epidemics.

True, low-trade areas sometimes avoided epidemics. In antiquity, areas of the Roman Empire lying outside the main trade routes largely escaped epidemics—Africa, for instance, is sometimes thought to have escaped contagion because its coast was so unwelcoming to shipping that it lacked trade with Asia.[122] This may not be strictly accurate, since ports as far south as Ethiopia were used for trade in the ancient world, and the coasts of Kenya and Tanzania had several major trading ports in the Middle Ages. Furthermore, although Africa was long believed to have escaped the Black Death,[123] recent research shows mid-fourteenth-century abandonment of longstanding settlements, mass burials, and aborted construction projects, suggesting that the pandemic may have reached the continent after all.[124] Russia is another society whose weak market links were originally believed to have spared it the Black Death. But now we know that plague merely arrived there five years late, repeatedly afflicting even this low-trade society from 1352 on.[125]

---

122. Duncan-Jones 1996, 128, 135.
123. Scott 1965, 1–2.
124. Chouin 2018; Gallagher and Dueppen 2018; M. Green 2018.
125. Savinetsky and Krylovich 2011, 203–7; J. T. Alexander 1980; Kollmann 2000; Benedictow 2021, 211–15.

In fact, isolation cut both ways. Being isolated spared places from epidemics if they could avoid contact altogether. But an isolated area was more vulnerable once it got exposed to a disease that was endemic elsewhere—most spectacularly during the Columbian Exchange, when infectious diseases from highly urbanized Europe decimated sparsely populated regions of the Americas. Moreover, even if societies with less market exchange had less epidemic disease, they also had less economic growth. Without exception, they had little non-agricultural activity, few gains from trade, little productivity improvement, low per capita GDP, and glacial economic growth.[126]

The same was true inside societies. Regions with less market exchange had less epidemic disease, but also less prosperity. In sixteenth- and seventeenth-century Devon, for instance, the pastoral highlands lacked market links. This kept them plague-free but it also kept them poor. The fruitful lowland region was densely penetrated with market communications, creating the conditions for both epidemics and wealth.[127] Sixteenth-century Plymouth suffered constant epidemics because of its vigorous maritime trade, but enjoyed almost complete freedom from famine or dearth because that very trade kept it well supplied with cheap food from the Baltic.[128] After 1600, Essex repeatedly suffered lethal epidemics as its growing textile trade and market links with London imported disease; but the county was one of the richest in England because its vigorous markets also fostered prosperity.[129] Across early modern England, the remote inland and upland regions lacked market connections and were therefore largely free of epidemics; but they were also largely free of economic growth, with low productivity, high poverty, and perpetual out-migration. Labourers and young people moved away to seek their fortune in places like London, where they got diseases but also got jobs.[130]

The market indeed facilitated movements of pathogens. But thousands of migrants continued to move every year from healthy villages into lethal towns. Once smallpox immunization appeared, villagers planning to migrate to towns for work got themselves inoculated before they moved, as we shall see. But even before that was possible, thousands of people moved from villages to towns year after year. This suggests that the people with most at stake believed that the economic benefits of urban markets outweighed their epidemiological risks.

The difference in welfare between rich market centres and poor places without market links was smaller than the disparities in income would

126. Crafts 1997a; Crafts 1997b; Prados de la Escosura 2022a; Prados de la Escosura 2022b; Broadberry and Fouquet 2015; Broadberry and Wallis 2017.
127. Slack 1985, 92.
128. Slack 1985, 96–7.
129. Slack 1985, 105.
130. Dobson 1992, 88–9.

suggest—people traded off higher incomes against higher risks of dying of epidemic disease. But places where the market was inactive were not necessarily better off overall. Poverty kills—not just directly through deprivation, but indirectly because poverty exacerbates contagion, as we shall see.

What was it about the market that increased average real incomes? International trade played a minor—though sometimes crucial—role. As we saw earlier, trade that crossed international frontiers made up a trivial share of GDP until well into the nineteenth century. Little output was traded over long distances with foreigners. But a non-trivial and growing share was exchanged over shorter distances in everyday market transactions. Economic growth depended much more on exchange between nearby regions, settlements, and households. This kind of market exchange was widespread even in antiquity, and expanded further during the Middle Ages.[131] By the late medieval period, pure subsistence production—living entirely from what one produced oneself—was the exception rather than the rule, even in the least developed regions of Europe, the Middle East, and northern Africa.[132]

When harvests failed, both interregional and international trade could be the key to survival, especially for towns and the proto-industrial countryside. Long before 1300, grain was being regularly exported from eastern Germany, Poland, Prussia, and the Baltic countries to England and the Netherlands—not replacing western European wheat cultivation but supplementing it, especially in years of harvest failure, high prices, or famine.[133] Grain was also traded across longer distances, as in the Great Famine of 1315–17, when both England and the Baltic were afflicted with harvest failure, but shortages were mitigated by massive wheat imports via Mediterranean merchants.[134] Conversely, England exported grain to the continent when European harvests failed or merchant cartels threatened famine by blockading trade, as the German Hanse did to Norway in 1284, Flanders in 1358 and 1388, Bruges in 1436, and Holland in 1438–41.[135] From the thirteenth century onwards, the international European grain trade helped reduce prices, alleviate famine, and mitigate both harvest failures and merchant blockades, even though shorter-distance interregional or local trade did most of the heavy lifting in normal times.

It was not just the market for goods that mattered. Labour markets played a major role in generating economic growth and improving living standards. Where there was a market for labour, people—including serfs, women, youths, minorities, immigrants, and others at the bottom of society—could find jobs

131. Wickham 2023.
132. De Vries 1976; Ogilvie 2000; Dennison 2011; Ogilvie 2014a; Wickham 2023.
133. Hybel 2002, 221, 225–8; Sharp 2016, 36.
134. Hybel 2002, 237–8; Sharp 2016, 47–8.
135. Hybel 2002, 221, 226, 229; Sarnowsky 2015, 67–8, 79–80, 91–2; Sharp 2016, 45–6.

in which they were more productive than toiling for subsistence inside the family, community, or feudal demesne. The market for labour made it possible for workers to bargain with employers and get better pay than if they had to work for husbands, fathers, rich relatives, exploitive landlords, or local bigwigs. Conversely, the labour market enabled employers—including modest farmers, craftsmen, shopkeepers, and other tradespeople—to find workers to supply scarce skills and cover demand peaks (e.g. during harvests) far more easily than using only household or village members. The market for labour also made it possible for knowledge to travel, embodied in migrating workers who laboured in other households, communities, and regions, where they introduced—and themselves learned—new products, processes, and techniques. As we shall see in later chapters, the knowledge embodied in migrating workers included awareness of better institutional mechanisms for controlling contagion. Societal learning owed much to migrants, who responded to market signals by seeking jobs in places where their labour and knowledge were more productive and better paid.

Land markets also improved economic performance. Where there was a market for land, the key agricultural input could pass into the hands of those who valued it most and were able to use it most productively.[136] If a peasant knew she could sell, lease out, or mortgage her land, she would have the incentive and capacity to maintain it, improve it, and experiment with innovations. Being able to sell one's land, mortgage it, or use it for collateral also made it possible to obtain agricultural micro-credit, increasing a peasant's capacity to improve or maintain her holding. A more productive peasant was then able to accumulate savings, enabling her family to survive an epidemic or pay taxes to fund community or government health measures. More efficient agriculture also reduced food prices, making it easier for the poor to feed themselves, which, as we shall see, increased their ability to withstand epidemic diseases.

Markets for credit also played a surprisingly important role, as far back as the medieval period.[137] Where there was a market for credit, peasants could borrow to improve their land and animals, craftsmen to finance new tools or workshops, traders to fund the gap between purchase and sale, and individuals and households to hold their savings in financial form and survive periods of unemployment, dearth, and plague. The credit market made it possible for small-scale producers to obtain micro-loans enabling them to expand their farms and workshops beyond the scale possible if they had to rely solely on their own savings. The resulting increase in prosperity helped individuals support themselves during epidemics, withdrawing from the market to avoid contagion and complying with public quarantines and lockdowns. It also gave

136. Ogilvie 2000, 102–4; Ogilvie and Carus 2014, 437–41.
137. Ogilvie 2000, 105–6; Briggs 2009; Ogilvie and Carus 2014, 441–3.

them more resources to make charitable donations and welfare payments to support their poorer neighbours, helping them not just survive but also withdraw from markets. Finally, it helped people pay taxes to support public health measures.

The market also played a key role in specialization, which itself enhanced productivity even without technological innovation. Where there was a market for agricultural products and craft wares, individuals, households, communities, and regions could specialize in producing those goods and services in which they were most efficient, because of local skills, soil, climate, location, or resource endowments. This increased productivity, since each producer no longer had to produce everything inefficiently at home. The market was needed for this to happen. For farmers to find the risks of agricultural expansion worthwhile, they needed to know they could sell their surplus at a profit, and that meant being able to reach consumers easily in the market. For craftsmen or proto-industrial workers to risk investing in new skills and specializing in producing things they could not eat, they needed to know they could sell their wares and be sure of buying food. Market exchange made it possible for individuals and regions to specialize in the crops and goods their natural and social endowments made them best at producing. The market gave innovators a better prospect of getting the inputs of labour, capital, and land they needed to implement their new ideas in concrete business situations, and to sell their output at a profit. Market exchange brought competitive pressures to bear on individual monopolists, cartelistic guilds, privileged towns, and powerful landlords, forcing them to lower their prices and control their costs. The day-to-day business of interregional exchange and local shopkeeping benefited both consumers and producers. Greater efficiency in agriculture, crafts, and commerce lowered the price of goods, making subsistence more affordable even for people whose incomes remained low.

For all these reasons, societies with active markets for labour, land, credit, food, raw materials, craft wares, and services generated faster economic growth and higher real incomes than those without. In the Middle Ages, central and northern Italy had the best-functioning market institutions in Europe and the highest per capita GDP. By the fifteenth century Flanders was developing them too. Between 1560 and around 1650 these precocious zones were joined and surpassed by the Northern Netherlands during the Dutch Golden Age. And from 1650 onwards England started growing fast and ultimately took the lead after the Industrial Revolution of the 1760s.[138] In each case, vigorous and well-functioning factor and product markets were associated with, and played a major role in causing, rapid economic growth and rising per capita GDP.

138. Ogilvie 2000, 2019; Broadberry 2021.

It is not that the market is absent in poor economies—whether in the historical past or in the modern day. Voluntary exchange sprang up in every society, in the interstices left by other social institutions. But the market functioned less well where institutional privileges entitled special-interest groups—autocratic rulers, predatory churchmen, coercive landlords, monopolistic merchants, cartelistic craft guilds, closed village and town oligarchies—to manipulate the market to extract resources for themselves at the expense of less powerful groups and the economy at large.[139] The same pattern can be observed in all continents down the centuries—Europe, China, Japan, Mughal India, the medieval Middle East—where episodes of vigorous market growth alternated with episodes of elite extraction and decline.[140] What differed across societies was not so much whether the market existed but how well it functioned. Was it open to all without regard to gender, religion, race, citizenship, parentage, or identity? Did it allocate resources efficiently or was it manipulated by special-interest groups that enjoyed coercive privileges and imposed deadweight costs on the rest of the economy? Did political, communal, religious, occupational, or clan elites make the market work better or worse? Where the market functioned better, economic growth was faster, per capita incomes were higher, health inputs were more affordable, and—as we shall see in chapter 3—fiscal capacity rose, enabling (though not guaranteeing) public action to control epidemic disease.

It might be objected that market exchange also led to urbanization, which fostered epidemics through contagion, congestion, and pollution. Market specialization lay at the root of town growth, since it enabled urban inhabitants to specialize in crafts and services, which they exchanged for rural food and raw materials.[141] Urban markets also performed particularly well because of what economists call "agglomeration economies", spillover benefits from access to clusters of suppliers, customers, workers, skills, specialized inputs, finance, business information, and innovative ideas.[142] But cities also produce agglomeration *diseconomies*, including congestion, pollution, and contagion. Urbanization typically made people much richer, but it also made them much more diseased.

This urban trade-off between wealth and health varied across pathogens, it weakened across the centuries, and it has now almost disappeared. It did not apply to plague, whose prevalence and mortality was higher in the countryside

139. Ogilvie 2000, 102–30; Ogilvie and Carus 2014, 428–36.

140. Jones 1981.

141. Towns could also expand based on non-market institutions, particularly the state, which could establish its seat of government there and use taxation or coercion to force rural producers to supply the urban population. But urbanization typically depended more on market exchange.

142. Ogilvie 2019, 457–61, 473, 508, 540, 544, 552, 558.

than in cities because plague rats and their fleas favoured grain-rich habitats.[143] Smallpox, typhus, cholera, and influenza, by contrast, were much worse in cities because they were conveyed by air, water, or personal contact. Nonetheless, millions of people continued to migrate from healthy villages into insalubrious cities. Rural life kept them in poverty, which poor people will do almost anything to escape—then as now. Urban wealth also gradually began to fund local fiscal capacity. During the nineteenth century, as we shall see in chapter 3, cities gradually built sewerage and water infrastructure, which reduced gastrointestinal epidemics below the levels observed in surrounding rural areas.[144] Cities became even more attractive to migrants, now offering not only much better economic opportunities but somewhat lower epidemic risks. By the twenty-first century, epidemic outcomes were measurably better in cities than the countryside. Across 81 countries in 2020, controlling for other country characteristics, Covid-19 infection rates and excess mortality were lower where urbanization was higher. Infection spread faster in cities, but urbanized countries were richer, generating more resources for individuals, communities, and governments to fight contagion.[145]

Of course, what matters is not just the level of per capita GDP but how it is distributed. Inequality in pre-modern societies was high, and it increased from the Black Death into the twentieth century. But there is no evidence that inequality was worse in market-oriented societies such as those of northwest Europe, with high and rising per capita incomes, than in central or southern Europe, where the level and growth of per capita GDP were lower. On the contrary. The early modern Low Countries (roughly the area of modern Belgium and the Netherlands) had extraordinarily well-functioning markets, the highest per capita GDP in Europe, and—as we shall see—the highest fiscal capacity. This region of Europe also enjoyed levels of inequality which, compared to other parts of Europe, were unusually low and slow growing in the period 1500–1800.[146] Growth in per capita GDP often disproportionately benefited the rich and powerful, especially in most societies before the twentieth century where fiscal systems were highly regressive.[147] But some of the benefits of better economic performance went to ordinary people, who used them to protect themselves from the epidemic diseases that raged around them—as we shall now explore.

143. Alfani 2013b; Curtis 2016, 140, 162–70; Dimitrov 2020, 108–10; Benedictow 2021, 23, 32–3, 276, 298–301, 307, 327, 341.

144. John Brown 1988; Baldwin 1999, 128–9; Alfani and Melegaro 2010; Alfani 2022, 27, 32–3; Aidt, Davenport, and Gray 2023.

145. Naudé and Nagler 2022, 10.

146. Alfani and Ryckbosch 2016, 146 (fig. 2); Alfani, Gierok, and Schaff 2022, esp. 115 (fig. 6).

147. Alfani and Di Tullio 2019, 147–79.

4.2. DO EPIDEMICS DISCRIMINATE?

Popular views often repeat the trope that severe epidemics are universal killers, striking rich and poor alike.[148] Not so. In nearly every major epidemic, being poor was bad. The link between poverty and epidemic disease varied by pathogen, as we saw in table 1.2. Susceptibility to epidemics also varied with age, gender, exposure, density, and biological frailty. But when an epidemic arrived, the poor typically got infected earlier, more frequently, and more intensely than the better-off, and when they did fall ill they were more likely to die. This was bad for them. But it was also bad for everyone else.

People living at the time thought epidemics hit the poor hardest. Bubonic plague was called "the beggars' disease", "the plague of the poor", and "miseriae morbus" (misery disease).[149] During the 744 Syrian plague epidemic, according to the 775 *Zūqnīn Chronicle*, "When the poor vanished, the plague passed on to the wealthy—as long as those whom death could seize were still around—from the small to the great."[150] In Florence during the Black Death, according to the chronicler Matteo Villani, "The lower and middle orders suffered more than the upper classes, because they were weaker to begin with, because they were hit first and hardest, and because they had less aid and lived in poorer conditions."[151] Describing the 1574–75 Milan plague epidemic, the historian Bugati wrote in 1587 that "only the plebs and the populace caught and spread it among their friends and kin and occasionally to those they served".[152] In the 1630 plague epidemic, a Milan priest described how "the poor are most harmed",[153] and the Prato podesta wrote that "those who die here are all poor people".[154] In Florence in February 1631, a contemporary recorded that "the number of deaths from the beginning of the evil up to now, including the Contado, has reached about 10,000, all poor and mendicant people. . . . [T]here have not been twenty deaths among nobles and the well-off".[155] In Yorkshire in 1631, when plague infected a female member of a noble household it was not at first even recognized, because "no man could suspect a lady to die of the plague".[156] In 1844, the British consul of Cape Verde reported that the yellow fever epidemic "prevailed mostly amongst the lower orders, and consequently

---

148. Margerison and Knüsel 2002; Naphy and Spicer 2000.
149. Cipolla 1973, 108.
150. Quoted in Preiser-Kapeller 2023, slide 36.
151. Quoted in Park 1985, 4.
152. Quoted in Cohn 2010b, 49.
153. Quoted in Cipolla 1976, 35.
154. Quoted in Cipolla 1973, 107–8.
155. Quoted in Litchfield 2008, para. 322.
156. Quoted in Slack 1985, 195.

there was much misery, even for the want of common food".[157] At a meeting on cholera in 1892, a Russian doctor declared that "the epidemic might in truth be called 'cholera of the poor' because without a doubt the educated people fulfilled all preventive measures, unlike the simple folk".[158] In the 1918 Punjab influenza epidemic, the sanitary commissioner wrote that "the people who suffer most are the poor and the rural classes, whose housing conditions, medical attendance, food and clothing are in defect".[159] In April 2021, Christina Pagel, director of the Clinical Operational Research Unit at University College London, wrote in the *British Medical Journal* that "there is a real danger that Covid-19 will become entrenched as a disease of poverty".[160]

Epidemic contagion typically struck poor places first and hardest. Medieval and early modern plague epidemics, for instance, usually started in the poorer urban neighbourhoods. In Muslim Almeria in June 1348, plague first appeared in the city's poorest quarter.[161] In Turin in 1599–1600, a doctor described the plague epidemic as being concentrated in "the city's vilest neighbourhoods", inhabited by "leather-workers, grooms, stable boys, working girls ('mulierculularum'), the lowest of the whores ('meretricum sintina'), and the meanest of the plebs".[162] In early modern London, Exeter, Bristol, and Norwich, plague typically struck poor suburbs and slums where individual deprivation and low-quality housing combined to favour contagion; better-off neighbourhoods sometimes escaped altogether.[163] In London between 1560 and 1665, plague almost always broke out first in the poorer parishes, while richer ones were spared.[164] In Augsburg in 1627, the plague epidemic broke out in the Kappenzipfel district, where the average property tax was less than 1 per cent of the average tax paid in the rich upper city.[165] In Rome, the 1656 plague arrived first in the bitterly poor neighbourhood of Trastevere.[166] In Hamburg in 1712–14, plague was first detected in the Neustadt quarter, inhabited mainly by the poor.[167] In Stockholm during the severe smallpox epidemic of 1873–74, infections and mortality were highest in the poorest parishes.[168] Across the 23 districts of Hamburg in the 1896 cholera epidemic, infections

---

157. Quoted in M. Harrison 2012, 94.
158. Quoted in Frieden 1977, 546.
159. Quoted in Arnold 2019, 192.
160. Pagel 2021.
161. Dols 1977, 66.
162. Cohn 2010c, 214.
163. Slack 1985, 112–13, 116–19, 121–4, 137, 153, 164–5.
164. Cummins, Kelly, and Ó Gráda 2016.
165. Mauelshagen 2005, 252.
166. Risse 1999, 190–2.
167. Benedictow 1987, 403.
168. Sköld 1996b, 474.

were strongly and positively correlated with the share of wage workers in the district.[169]

Mortality, too, was typically higher in poor neighbourhoods. In the 1523 Milan epidemic, 42 per cent of plague victims came from just 4 of the 60 parishes—the poorest, most densely inhabited, and most filled with recent immigrants.[170] In sixteenth- and seventeenth-century Amsterdam during plague periods, relative mortality in the poor Jordaan quarter was 50 per cent higher than in richer neighbourhoods.[171] In Bristol from 1575 to 1603, even within the same neighbourhood, plague mortality was higher in the poor backstreets than the rich main thoroughfares.[172] In London between 1560 and 1665, poorer parishes had higher plague mortality.[173] In Florence in 1630–31, plague mortality was higher in streets inhabited by poor people, non-patricians, textile workers, small households, widows, and people lacking surnames (a sign of poverty).[174] In the 1635 Reims epidemic, the 335 plague-stricken houses were mainly in the poor quarters.[175] In the 1647 Chester plague epidemic, overall mortality was 35 per cent, but in the rich parish of St Peter's it was just 9–11 per cent.[176] In Rome in 1656, plague mortality in the slum neighbourhood of Trastevere was over 50 per cent, six times higher than in the rest of the city.[177] In the Great Plague of London in 1665, the crisis mortality rate was higher in poor suburbs than wealthy parishes inside the walls.[178] In Naples during the 1837 cholera epidemic, mortality was 8 per 1,000 for the city as a whole but over 30 in the notoriously poor borough of Porto.[179] In Braunschweig in 1850, cholera mortality was 5.3 per 1,000 in streets where incomes averaged less than 75 marks, 3.0 in streets where it was 75–100 marks, and 1.4 where it was 100–200 marks.[180] In the 1870–72 smallpox epidemic, poor neighbourhoods of Amsterdam had much higher mortality than richer ones.[181] In the 1918 Spanish flu epidemic in Kristiania (Oslo), mortality was 49 per cent higher in impoverished Grønland-Wesels than in wealthy Frogner.[182]

169. R. Evans 1992, 156.
170. Cohn and Alfani 2007, 193–4.
171. Francke and Korevaar 2021, 4.
172. Slack 1985, 124–6.
173. Cummins, Kelly, and Ó Grada 2016.
174. Litchfield 2008, para. 328.
175. Lucenet 1985, 152.
176. Victoria County History 2003, 90–7.
177. Risse 1999, 213.
178. Champion 1993, 42.
179. Snowden 2019, 243
180. R. Evans 1992, 155.
181. Muurling, Riswick, and Buzasi 2021.
182. Mamelund 2006, 935.

In the Covid-19 pandemic, 86 out of 95 peer-reviewed studies found that Covid mortality was significantly and often substantially higher in poorer neighbourhoods, towns, and regions.[183]

Poorer social groups also had higher epidemic mortality. In the Black Death in England, mortality was 40–50 per cent in the general population but only 15–25 per cent for bishops and higher nobles.[184] On 17 Glastonbury Abbey manors, Black Death mortality was about 5 percentage points higher for the landless strata of cottars, day labourers, and sub-tenants than for customary tenants who owned at least enough land to subsist on.[185] Analysis of Black Death plague skeletons finds that "people who experienced physiological stressors, and who developed stress markers in response to those stressors, at some point (perhaps even long) before the arrival of the epidemic were subsequently more likely to die during the Black Death compared to their peers who lacked the stress markers".[186] In the fourteenth-century Florentine parish of Santo Spirito, plague mortality was higher for the poor than the better off.[187] In the 1523 Milan plague epidemic, "characteristically, plague victims came from the poorest families".[188] In the 1631 Clermont epidemic, over half the lowest-taxed people disappeared from tax registers in the course of the plague, compared with one-third of the moderately taxed and just one-fifth of the most highly taxed.[189] In the Königsberg plague of 1709–10, the better-off died much less than the poor.[190] The 1713 Cape Town smallpox epidemic killed a quarter of Europeans but a third of enslaved people.[191] In Moscow in 1770–71, a contemporary reported how the plague,

> as is generally the case, raged chiefly among the common people; the nobles and better sort of inhabitants escaped the contagion, a few only excepted, who fell victims to their rashness and negligence. . . . Amid so great a number of deaths, . . . there were only three persons of family, few of the principal citizens, and not more than 300 foreigners of the common class, who fell victims to the plague; the rest consisted of the lowest order of the Russian inhabitants.[192]

183. McGowan and Bambra 2022.
184. Benedictow 2004, 264, 343.
185. Benedictow 2004, 265.
186. DeWitte 2014, 114.
187. Carmichael 1986, 74–5.
188. Cohn and Alfani 2007, 194.
189. Lucenet 1985, 152.
190. Frandsen 2010, 37.
191. A. White 2018, 139.
192. Mertens 1799, 34–5.

In nineteenth-century London, smallpox mortality was nearly nine times higher among the poor than the better-off.[193] In Aix-en-Provence in 1835, cholera disproportionately struck poor occupations such as workers, day labourers, beggars, paupers, artisans, small traders, and minor peasant farmers.[194] In the 1855–56 Brazilian cholera epidemic, 4 per cent of Belem inhabitants perished, but deaths were "chiefly confined to the negro, the mixed races, and the Indians".[195] In Mumbai in 1897–1900, plague mortality was over 20 per 1,000 for "ordinary" and "low-caste" Hindus; 15 for Brahmins; 10 for Parsis, Jews, and Eurasians; and just 2 for Europeans.[196] In the 1896–1900 Hong Kong plague, case fatality was 92 per cent for the Chinese population but only 59 per cent for the non-Chinese.[197] In Spain during the influenza pandemic of 1918–19, excess mortality averaged 69 per cent for low-income, 62 per cent for middle-income, and 29 per cent for high-income groups.[198] In Mumbai in 1918, influenza mortality was 61.6 per 1,000 among low-caste Hindus, 18.9 among other Hindus, 9.0 among Parsees, and 8.3 among Europeans; these gaps were much wider than for non-flu mortality, suggesting that poverty was particularly lethal during epidemics.[199]

Mortality rates reflect both incidence (rate of infection) and case fatality (death rate once infected). But for the 1918 influenza epidemic we can measure incidence and case fatality separately. Poor people caught influenza more than rich ones, as the left-hand graph in figure 2.5 shows. Across nine American towns covering around 100,000 individuals in 1918, incidence of influenza (the rate of contracting the disease) was significantly higher among the poor, controlling for race and sex. The data underlying this graph show that over all nine localities, age-adjusted influenza incidence was 326–64 per 1,000 for the poor and very poor, compared to only 252–72 for the rich and middling groups.[200] The incidence gap persisted across all age groups, from newborns to the very old. The poor thus suffered from higher contagion. The case fatality gap was much

193. Hardy 1993, 133–4: it was 1.76 per 1,000 among the poor but just 0.2 per 1,000 among the better-off.

194. R. Evans 1992, 155.

195. Quoted in Tumbe 2020, 48.

196. Tumbe 2020, 84.

197. Ó Gráda 2020, 12.

198. Basco, Domènech, and Rosés 2021, 3, 12–13.

199. Phipson 1923, 517; Mills 1986, 33.

200. Sydenstricker 1931, 158–60, 164. The economic classification was made by each study enumerator, who "was instructed to record at the time of her visit to the household her impression of its economic condition in one of four categories—'well-to-do', 'moderate', 'poor', and 'very poor'. The enumerators . . . were purposely given no standards for comparison or more detailed instructions on this point, the intention being to have them record their own impressions naturally and according to their own standards" (156).

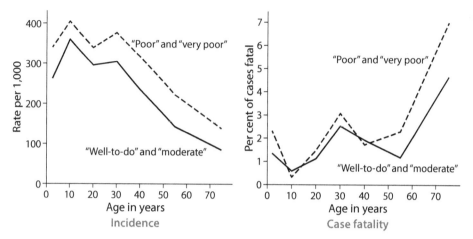

FIGURE 2.5. Incidence and case fatality of influenza by income and age in nine American towns, 1918. Incidence = number of persons contracting the disease per 1,000 population. Case fatality = number of persons dying of the disease per 100 persons infected. *Source*: Based on Sydenstricker 1931, 158.

narrower, as the right-hand graph in figure 2.5 shows. Up to age 40, different economic groups had similar case fatality; but after that age, it was higher for the poor and very poor than the rich and middling groups. Poverty, therefore, increased contagion at all ages; but after age 40 it heightened case fatality, too.

Covid-19 shows a similar strong association between poverty and epidemic contagion. In South Korea in the first six months of 2020, analysis of 126,687 individual health records showed that poorer people had a significantly higher probability of becoming infected with Covid-19, though not of dying of it.[201] In a number of American populations, too, low income significantly and substantially increased the incidence of Covid-19 in 2020 and 2021.[202] Across 81 communities in Los Angeles between July 2020 and September 2021, for instance, Covid incidence was much higher among low-income groups before the introduction of vaccination.[203] The significant association between poverty and the probability of infection with epidemic disease even in modern rich economies with social safety nets is poignant testimony to the importance of individual consumption of health inputs in helping to limit epidemic contagion.

201. S. Kim et al. 2021.
202. See the brief overview in Masterson et al. (2023, 728).
203. Masterson et al. 2023.

4.3. CAN YOU BUY HEALTH?

It is not surprising that poverty increases epidemic contagion. As people's incomes rise, they allocate part of them to protection against disease. Better-off people spend money on health inputs: food, which helps their immune systems resist infection; housing, which keeps out disease vectors; hygiene, which cleans bodies and implements; and care, which prevents intrahousehold infection. They set aside savings to cushion market withdrawal. They rent or buy country residences to avoid urban epidemics, they travel away from infected places, and they pay for immunization. The market increases availability of these inputs by raising incomes, lowering prices, and increasing supplies. Both a well-functioning market and the higher incomes it generates enable people to invest in anti-contagion inputs for themselves and their families.

This is good for better-off individuals. But it also creates social benefits. It not only increases individual well-being by reducing infection, suffering, and death. It also reduces the number of infected individuals inflicting contagion externalities on everyone else. This does not mean that non-market institutions are unnecessary—they are, as we see in later chapters. But even before state, community, or religion step in, individuals do some of the heavy lifting themselves by consuming things which help them stave off infectious disease. Conversely, when real incomes are low, people cannot invest in health inputs, increasing infection for themselves and contagion for everyone else.

First, poor people often cannot afford food. Poor nutrition affects immune response for many infectious diseases. Even for diseases where it does not sap immunity, malnutrition impairs labour productivity, preventing people from earning or saving enough to procure housing, hygiene, sanitation, and other inputs into avoiding contagion.[204] In Italy in 79 CE, the eruption of Vesuvius was followed first by famine as the ash cloud damaged the harvest, then by epidemics as the starving failed to fight off disease.[205] In London during the Black Death, skeletal analysis shows that short stature increased adults' risk of dying of plague, whether from poor nutrition in childhood or poor nutritional status when the plague struck.[206] In the medieval Middle East, famine often led to plague, as undernourished people failed to fight off infection.[207] In 1628–29, severe famine struck northern Italy, reducing resistance to the plague epidemic which arrived in 1630.[208] In the Madras Presidency in 1877,

204. Ravallion 1997, 1210–11, 1231.
205. Duncan-Jones 2018, 60–1.
206. DeWitte and Wood 2008; DeWitte and Hughes-Morey 2012.
207. Dols 1977, 22.
208. Cipolla 1973, 17.

the 10 districts worst hit by preceding famine suffered cholera mortality of 18 per 1,000, compared to just 4.6 in the 6 districts least hit by famine.[209]

Contemporaries were vividly aware of the association between nutrition and susceptibility to epidemic infection. In 1549, the Englishman John Cheke referred to "that vehemence of plague, which naturally followeth the dint of hunger".[210] In Sicily after the 1558 influenza epidemic, the physician Giovan Filipo Ingrassia advised the ruler to provide his subjects with good bread and bullock meat ("carne di gienco"), "which will be of the greatest protection for the afflicted poor as well as the healthy during an epidemic".[211] In Turin in 1599–1600, the concentration of plague among the poor was ascribed partly to the fact that their food was "fatty, corrupt and spoilt".[212] William Boghurst's 1665 book ascribed the Great Plague of London to the fact that the poor lacked "good dyett".[213] The young Englishwoman Julia Charlotte Maitland, who travelled through southern India in the late 1830s, described how during a cholera epidemic near Rajahmundry, "there is little fear of cholera among Europeans, except in travelling. It is caused among the poor natives by bad feeding, dirt, and exposure to the climate."[214] In 1917, a correspondent of the *North China Herald* described how in rural Shanxi, "every spring sees a great deal of sickness and epidemic ailments and this year is no exception . . . The indescribable poverty of the food used by the poorer classes when their wheat flour is exhausted, or its cost prohibitive, must be responsible for many maladies."[215] In the 1918–19 flu epidemic in Delhi, according to the sanitary commissioner of India, "Given nourishing food in a readily assimilable form . . . it was surprising what apparently desperate cases ultimately recovered".[216]

Another material input affecting epidemic contagion was housing. In the 1575–78 Venice epidemic, the astronomer and physician Annibale Raimondo wrote in his plague treatise that women died in greater numbers than men "because of poverty . . . and lack of good housing [*di buone stanze*]".[217] In Turin in 1599–1600, a doctor ascribed the early and lethal plague mortality in poor neighbourhoods to squalid little dwellings called "habitacula", with their overflowing latrines.[218] In July 1665, as the Great Plague gathered force in London, Roger L'Estrange observed that the plague was worst among the

---

209. Arnold 1986, 125.
210. Quoted in Slack 1985, 76.
211. Quoted in Cohn 2010c, 242.
212. Cohn 2010c, 214.
213. Quoted in Champion 1993, 35.
214. Quoted in Tumbe 2020, 51.
215. "Want Threatening in Shansi", *North China Herald*, 2 June 1917, p. 488.
216. Quoted in Tumbe 2020, 157.
217. Quoted in Cohn 2010b, 51.
218. Cohn 2010c, 214.

poor because they were "crowded up into corners, and smothered for want of air".[219] Seventeenth-century Marseille, according to a colleague of Jean-Baptiste Colbert, suffered frequent plagues because "its houses are without water, badly built, crammed full of people from the cellars to the attics and filthy".[220] In the 1834–35 Egyptian epidemic, the French doctor Clot-Bey described how plague particularly struck "the unfortunate who live in filthy and poorly ventilated quarters, just as those who suffer from all sorts of privations"; enslaved Africans, who slept on mats on the floor at street level, were more accessible to infected rats and fleas.[221] In the 1871 Amsterdam smallpox epidemic, the overcrowded, unventilated, and unsanitary "cellar dwellings" recorded mortality of 1 per 28.3 inhabitants, compared with 1 per 37 in the city as a whole.[222] In the 1873–74 Stockholm smallpox epidemic, contemporaries ascribed the higher infection and mortality rates in the poorest parishes to the wretched housing, in which 9 or 10 persons shared the same cellar room.[223] In Kristiania (modern Oslo) in 1918, influenza mortality was 50 per cent lower on average for those living in dwellings with four to six rooms than for those living in one-room apartments.[224] In Baltimore during the plague outbreak of 1947–49, cleaning, repairing, and "rehabilitation of substandard dwellings" reduced the rat population by nearly 85 per cent (from 400,000 to 65,000), dramatically reducing the number of plague cases.[225] In the Indian city of Surat in the 1990s, the poor caught plague more than the better-off partly because they could not afford residential arrangements that limited contagion.[226] Housing mattered because of overcrowding, inadequate ventilation, contaminated water, poor waste disposal, lack of sewerage, and failure to control rats and other disease vectors. Improving all these aspects of housing costs resources. Lacking those resources, poor people caught epidemics and passed them on.

Hygiene was a further input into avoiding epidemic disease, as contemporaries increasingly recognized. But sanitation was costly. Poverty meant people could not afford to be clean. In his 1576 plague treatise, Gratiolo di Salò pointed out that the poor were more likely to die of plague because, "as continued experience clearly shows us, the more dirty and foul the individual, the more likely he is to be afflicted, certainly more so than the clean and noble".[227] In Turin in 1599–1600, according to a contemporary commentator, plague struck the poor

219. Quoted in Champion 1993, 35.
220. Quoted in Kettering 2001, 48.
221. Quoted in Rue 2016, 33–4.
222. Muurling, Riswick, and Buzasi 2021, 15–16.
223. Sköld 1996b, 474.
224. Mamelund 2006, 933, 937.
225. Borsch and Sabraa 2017, 65–6.
226. Barnes 2014, 167.
227. Quoted in Cohn 2010b, 50.

much more severely because they were "without means for washing away the fetid odours that brought the disease seeping through their nostrils".[228] In 1665, William Boghurst ascribed the Great Plague of London to lack of "washing, want of good conveyances of filth; standing and stinking waters; dunghills, excrements, dead bodies lying unburied and putrefying".[229]

Travelling away from infected places was another way of avoiding epidemics, but poor people could seldom afford to leave. Since antiquity, doctors had advised that the only sure way of preventing plague was "pills made of three ingredients called *cito*, *longe*, and *tarde* (swiftly, far, and tardy), namely, run swiftly, go far and return tardily".[230] The sentiment had long circulated in vernacular form, as in the poem by the English poet-monk John Lydgate of Bury (*c*.1370–*c*.1451), whose rules for healthy living included exhortations to "resist the stroke of pestilence . . . flee wicked airs, eschew the presence of infected places".[231] But fleeing epidemics was too costly for the poor. In the 1467 Amiens plague, for instance, many of the "better persons of this place" fled the city, including several members of the town council, but the poor had to stay.[232] In 1553, Bishop Hooper pointed out that when plague struck a place, "there be certain persons that cannot flee although they would: as the poorer sort of people that have no friends nor place to flee unto, more than the poor house they dwell in".[233] The Basel plague epidemic of 1609–11 saw the flight of one-third of the population, mainly the better-off, because the poor had nowhere to go and had to keep on working to survive; one-third of those who stayed died.[234] In the Adrianople (Edirne) plague epidemic of the 1670s, an English observer described how "the best sort of people fled to other places, as the Turkes likewise themselves did from Adrianople to their houses here . . . all fled, but such as were poor, or had offices about Court, and could not get away".[235] In the 1713 Prague plague, 2,000 of the 11,000-strong Jewish community fled to the countryside, mostly the wealthy: "All day long they were seen carrying cases, and what are they to do, the poor who remember seeing the rich people leaving to save their own skin?"[236] In the 1720 Marseille plague, according to one observer, "The Weight of the Judgment generally falls

228. Cohn 2010c, 214.
229. Quoted in Champion 1993, 35.
230. Quoted in Cipolla (1973, 23), as uttered by the sixteenth-century Sicilian physician Giovanni Ingrassia, though the admonition is thought to go back to Hippocrates and Galen.
231. Quoted in Jeremy Brown 2022, 47; spelling modernized ("And resiste the strok of pestilence . . . Flee wikkyd heires, eschew the presence Off infect placys").
232. Quoted in N. Murphy 2013, 157.
233. Quoted in Slack 1985, 43.
234. Benedictow 1987, 416–17.
235. Quoted in Boyar 2018, 221.
236. Quoted in Jeremy Brown 2022, 93.

heaviest upon the poor; . . . their unhappy Circumstances . . . expose them to it . . . The Rich, allarm'd by the Danger of the Infection, fly the infected Ground."[237] In Japan during the 1858 cholera epidemic, an official notice stated explicitly: "People of low rank (*genin*) are more prone to fall ill to the disease than nobles (*shōnin*)".[238] After plague struck the Chinese province of Yunnan in 1883, the British explorer William Gill was told that it appeared so deserted because "there was no one left except a few poverty-stricken wretches who could not afford to move".[239]

Even local market withdrawal was a luxury reserved to people with reasonable incomes, steady jobs, or at least some savings. The poor had to go on working, or die of other causes. In Florence in 1630–31, for instance, poor wool workers, plumbers, lantern makers, coopers, and shoemakers risked plague and prosecution by sneaking out of lockdown so that they could go on earning.[240] The 2020 Covid-19 pandemic showed the same pattern across 729 regions of Africa, Latin America, Asia, and the Middle East, where poorer regions showed 42–62 per cent lower reduction in work-related mobility than rich ones. The poor were less able to withdraw from the market voluntarily and could not afford to obey stay-at-home orders.[241] Market withdrawal is always less affordable for the less well-off. This harms both them and all their contacts.

Poor people also struggled to pay for immunization, once it became available. Sometimes, as we shall see, variolation or vaccination were offered free of charge by state, community, church, or welfare system. Otherwise, the inoculator had to be paid. After around 1720, Western societies learned from the Ottomans, Africans, and Chinese about variolation, which offered lifelong immunity against smallpox using weakened smallpox lymph or powder. But even in England, where the practice spread fastest, variolation was hard for many to afford. In the 1760s, the average charge to variolate one person was 5 shillings (five days' earnings for an agricultural labourer). By the 1780s it had fallen to just 1 shilling (a day's earnings), not because labourers' wages had risen but because market competition among commercial variolators had reduced the cost by 500 per cent.[242] In eighteenth-century Sweden, according to contemporaries, cost was the main reason peasants failed to get their children immunized. In 1767, the official variolation fee charged by a Swedish physician was 12 coppers, equivalent to five to six days' earnings for a worker or peasant.

237. Quoted in Ermus 2020.
238. Quoted in Gramlich-Oka 2009, 46–7.
239. Quoted in Benedict 1988, 126.
240. Litchfield 2008, para. 335.
241. Aminjonov, Bargain, and Bernard 2021a; Aminjonov, Bargain, and Bernard 2021b.
242. Brunton 1990, 144–5. According to Bob Allen's (n.d.) London database, in the 1760s and 1780s, an English agricultural labourer's day wage was 12 pence (1 shilling).

Commercial variolators charged much lower fees, but were thin on the ground because the Swedish government banned them to protect the monopoly of the physicians, as we shall see in chapter 6.[243]

Vaccination with cowpox was invented in 1796, but was often too costly for the poor to afford. In 1809 in rural Slovakia, a smallpox epidemic was spreading and the feudal overlords ordered priests to preach to peasants about the need to get vaccinated. But even though vaccination was in the public interest, the fee was 15 denars—the price of six loaves of bread, and thus an expensive matter for a peasant of the time.[244] In 1815, getting a child vaccinated in the south-west German territories of Baden and Württemberg cost 12–18 *Kreuzer*, the price of 5 to 7 pounds of bread; well-off people could easily afford this price, and those formally classified as "poor" were entitled to free vaccination, but families just above the poverty line had to decide between nutrition and vaccination. This is consistent with historical evidence that most of the people who failed to get vaccinated in early-nineteenth-century Baden and Württemberg were "low-income households, which typically belonged to traditional or rural milieus".[245]

A final reason low incomes made it hard to avoid epidemic disease was that poverty impelled the poor to make risky consumption choices. In Milan in 1576, plague entered the city because several poor peasants robbed the corpse of a plague-infected noble and passed his infected goods on to urban relatives.[246] In Kent in 1610, a poor man privately came into ownership of a plague victim's clothing, and "by that coat was infected and died of the pestilence".[247] In Milan in 1630, a poor soldier contracted plague by wearing garments looted from German plague victims, spreading pestilence across the city before he died.[248] In Florence in 1630–31, a builder's daughter caught plague because she wore a shirt bequeathed by her diseased aunt.[249] In Dalmatia during the 1731 plague, the Morlachs (Black Vlachs) were so poor that they used pieces of waste cloth to insulate their dwellings, even though they knew that such rags harboured plague fleas.[250] In the Russian town of Vetlyanka in 1878–79, the plague epidemic was traced back to second-hand garments of poor migrant workers: "These clothes, purchased by workers, who go to Mongolia, have been used as a vehicle for germs of epidemic disease."[251] Infected goods were transferred not just in the second-hand market but through private transfers,

243. Sköld 1996b, 295.
244. Vavrinec Žeňuch, personal communication, 21 October 2023.
245. Mühlhoff 2022, 5.
246. Cohn 2010c, 101.
247. Quoted in Slack 1985, 11.
248. Cipolla 1973, 19–20.
249. Henderson 2019, 90.
250. Andreozzi 2015, 132.
251. Quoted in Lynteris 2016, 94.

thefts, bequests, and gifts. Poverty motivated people to make life-threatening consumption choices. The market, by increasing real incomes, could free more people from such lethal incentives.

4.4. WHAT ABOUT MEDICAL INPUTS?

The market, and the rising incomes created by market-driven growth, also enabled people to buy medical inputs. As we shall see in chapter 6, medical knowledge was largely useless until the later nineteenth century. Most medical inputs consisted of lifestyle advice, straightforward nursing, and placebo effects. Medical practitioners did not know that microbes caused infection, so they could not provide useful preventive advice, no matter how much they were paid. But there were other medical inputs that made a difference, and rising incomes enabled more people to afford them.

Nursing care mattered, even in pandemics. During the Black Death, better-off families and individuals (even parish priests, who were supposed to attend plague victims' deathbeds) enjoyed higher survival rates because they could afford to employ servants and nurses to provide basic nursing, hygiene, and feeding.[252] In the 1575–78 Venice epidemic, the astronomer and physician Annibale Raimondo wrote in his plague treatise that women died of plague more than men because they were too poor to afford medical care.[253] In the great Chinese plague epidemics of the mid-1890s, case fatality rates for Europeans were just 40–50 per cent, compared with 80 per cent for locals. This was partly because Europeans had better housing, food, and clothing, but even more because they could pay people to care for them.[254] In Punjab in 1918, the influenza case fatality rate was over 50 per cent for Indians of the poorer classes but just 6 per cent for "better class" Indians and those provided with medical care.[255]

Care mainly mattered for recovery once someone had contracted an infectious disease. But it also affected contagion. First, nursing and tending by trained or immune carers could protect other household members. This helped limit intrahousehold transmission, which, as we see in chapter 7, is a major source of contagion in most epidemics. Second, nursing curtailed the duration of illness, limiting the period during which contagion externalities could be transmitted from an infected individual to society more widely.

What about prophylactic remedies? These certainly existed, although medical ignorance meant that most of them were useless before the development

252. Benedictow 2004, 347–53.
253. Cohn 2010b, 51.
254. Benedictow 2004, 351 incl. n35.
255. Tumbe 2020, 151.

of antibiotics in 1928. Nonetheless, anxious consumers demanded them, producers offered them, and the market was one of the institutions that mediated their provision.

The existence of a market for prophylactic remedies, even ones that do not actually work, arises from two features of infectious disease: it is an existential threat, and people do not know what causes it. Individuals are so afraid of contagion that they are willing to pay high prices for even a small chance of avoiding it. This toxic combination of fear and ignorance can worsen a common problem—the asymmetry of information between producers and consumers. Producers often know that their remedy does not actually prevent infection, but consumers do not have that information, so they buy it anyway.

This might seem to be merely a market failure resulting from asymmetric information about product quality which enables producers to fleece gullible consumers. But it can have even worse effects, by creating "moral hazard"— an incentive to take more risks because one believes one is insured against an adverse outcome. A consumer who buys a fake remedy will falsely believe himself to be protected from infection, and will therefore take fewer precautions than otherwise. This increases not only his own risk of infection, but also the external risks he inflicts on others. The moral hazard fostered by false preventive remedies thus exacerbates contagion.

Every epidemic in history gave rise to nostrums that were falsely claimed to prevent infection. In the Antonine plague, an epidemic afflicting many Mediterranean societies in 160–180 CE, the Greek mystic Alexander of Abonouteichos sold a fake remedy consisting of a line of oracular verse, which he advertised as protecting against the pestilence.[256] In Christian Europe after the Black Death, people eagerly purchased theriac, or "plague treacle", a wonder drug brewed from opium, vipers' flesh, and up to 400 other ingredients, which was widely held not just to cure plague but to prevent it.[257] In the Islamic world, too, the Black Death aroused a desperate demand for preventive treatments, as described by the Muslim author Abu Hafs Umar ibn al-Wardi in 1348:

> Oh, if you could see the nobles of Aleppo studying their inscrutable books of medicine! They multiply its remedies by eating dried and sour foods. The buboes which disturb men's healthy lives are smeared with Armenian clay. Each man treated his humors and made life more comfortable. They perfumed their homes with ambergris and camphor, cypress, and sandal. They wore ruby rings and put onions, vinegar, and sardines together with

256. Duncan-Jones 1996, 119.
257. Brévart 2008, 50n165. For a sceptical view of theriac, see Slack (1985, 31); for a more optimistic view, see Fabbri (2007).

the daily meal. They ate less broth and fruit but ate the citron and similar things.[258]

Throughout the centuries after the Black Death, people eagerly bought nostrums that were claimed to prevent plague. These included aromatic globes (composed of different ingredients for rich and poor); precious stones; cordials containing gold, pearls, and gems; rose- or barleywater into which gold coins had been dipped; and alchemical elixirs of gold and distilled wine.[259] In the 1575–76 Venetian plague, 22 citizens petitioned the Health Office and the Council of Ten for patents relating to "secrets, remedies, preservatives, antidotes, precents and electuaries for plague".[260] In the 1657 Rome plague, the Tuscan grand-duke's representative described how:

> A few days ago a certain Neapolitan alchemist, formerly in the pay of his lordship the duke of Bracciano, entered into the pesthouse to treat the sick with a certain powder of his. On the day he arrived in Rome he caught the plague and, taking his medicament, was cured; and then they presented him with four plague sufferers, to whom he gave his powder, and they are all better, the medicament causing copious sweating. They are now negotiating his contract (*condotta*): he was requesting 500 *scudi* a month, whilst the Congregation [government health board] was prepared to pay a set amount for each plague sufferer cured.[261]

Not just the market but also the state provided institutional mechanisms to facilitate the supply of remedies that were claimed to prevent epidemics.

Modern epidemics of cholera, smallpox, influenza, and Covid-19 likewise kindled eager demand for preventive remedies. In the Netherlands in the first cholera epidemics of 1832, pharmacists took advantage of patients by selling a costly "cholera powder", which they claimed would stave off the disease.[262] In nineteenth-century Britain, concoctions containing opium were widely prescribed as preventive remedies against cholera.[263] In nineteenth-century Japan, red ribbons, red oiled paper, boiled eels, straw hats, and sacred pebbles were prescribed and purchased as preventives during smallpox epidemics.[264] In the 1918–19 flu epidemic in the USA, quacks prescribed raw onions, creosote baths, and brown sugar to stave off infection, while reputable doctors peddled bloodletting and bacteria-based vaccines (completely useless against the flu

---

258. Quoted in Vanneste 2010, 37.
259. Crisciani and Pereira 1998; Brévart 2008, 26–8.
260. Gentilcore 2012, 166.
261. Quoted in Gentilcore 2012, 162.
262. Jensen 2023, 125.
263. Lomax 1973, 168.
264. Rotermund and Tyler 2001.

virus).[265] In the Covid-19 pandemic, so many quack preventives against the novel coronavirus were on sale that by 2023 the Wikipedia page "List of Unproven Methods against COVID-19" ran to 9,764 words.[266]

The long history of the production, sale, and consumption of fake preventive measures against epidemic diseases raises the question of whether it would have been better if this market had not existed. The market for fake preventive remedies undoubtedly had the potential to harm consumers, and, to the extent that it provided patients with a false sense of security, made them more likely to engage in risky behaviour that spread contagion to others. On the other hand, the market was not necessary for purveying medicines and practices that claimed to prevent infectious disease. Governments also commissioned and licensed preventive remedies that we now know to have been ineffectual or harmful—as when the Rome Congregation of Health negotiated with a Neapolitan alchemist for doses of his plague powder in 1657.[267] Communities, as chapter 4 discusses, used their social capital to transmit information about disease preventives which were popularly desired and consumed but did not actually work. Religions, too, as we see in chapter 5, touted preventive measures against epidemics, both supernatural practices and medications blessed by religious personnel, which extracted money and effort from the faithful but did not actually prevent infection. Cardinal Gregorio Barbarigo, health overseer for the ward of Trastevere during the Rome plague of 1656–57, resorted to a variety of plague antidotes, including vinegar, quicksilver, viper's powder, and toad pills, and was constantly "on the look-out for preservatives, recipes, electuaries".[268] Medical associations, as we see in chapter 6, threw their authority behind medicines and practices that were falsely purported to prevent infectious diseases—including formal prescriptions for compounds containing opium, arsenic, prussic acid, strychnine, vegetable alkaloids, aconite, belladonna, and cantharides, as well as completely ineffectual vaccinations such as the bacteria-based inoculations used in the 1918–19 influenza pandemic.[269] The market thus facilitated the supply of fake preventives, but so too did other institutions, including those such as governments and medical associations that are widely believed to address the market failure arising from information asymmetries between producers and consumers of medical and pharmaceutical services.

Preventive remedies against epidemic disease are supplied because consumers demand them. During epidemics, that demand unsurprisingly increases—

265. Navarro 2010, 12; S. Liang et al. 2021, 273.

266. Wikipedia contributors, "List of Unproven Methods against COVID-19," *Wikipedia, The Free Encyclopedia*, accessed 7 June 2023, https://en.wikipedia.org/wiki/List_of_unproven_methods_against_COVID-19.

267. Gentilcore 2012, 162.

268. Gentilcore 2012, 165.

269. Leeson, King, and Fegley 2020, 275.

early modern European plague epidemics saw a big upsurge in the activities of "charlatans" and "mountebanks",[270] a phenomenon also widely observed during the Covid-19 pandemic in 2020.[271] It is understandable that states, communities, religions, medical associations, and market providers should seek to benefit by addressing this demand, even if the imperfect state of medical knowledge often means that the remedies they endorse are ineffectual.

Some "quack" remedies actually did prevent epidemic disease. A notable example is variolation against smallpox, which, as we shall see shortly, was sold on the market in China, India, Africa, and the Ottoman Empire long before 1700. Variolation was introduced into England around 1720 and was commercially available on the market there for the rest of the eighteenth century. But in many parts of Europe and America smallpox variolation was vilified as a fraudulent practice, legally and religiously prohibited, or at best rendered costly and inaccessible for ordinary people. Markets helped people circumvent these obstacles to this remedy, which was in practice the only way to prevent smallpox contagion. In many societies in central, eastern, and southern Europe, aristocrats, rich burghers, and other members of the elite circumvented legal and religious prohibitions by paying the high prices charged by freelance, quasi-illicit commercial variolators from England, Ireland, and Scotland. Other members of the European elite sent their children to London, or travelled there themselves, to purchase variolation on the market because medical, religious, and governmental institutions in their own societies defined it as a quack practice, banned it, and prohibited any market provision of variolation.[272]

Other prophylactics that were offered in the market contained the seeds of understanding microbial infection. The popular English quack doctor Joseph Browne earned profits in 1720 through market sales of a book in which he wrote that:

> The Power and Efficacy of Worms and Insects, to procure Diseases . . . Is very extensive and the Vulgar have not only err'd in this, if it be an Error, but many learned Physicians and Naturalists have been, and are still of Opinion, that the *Plague* arises from an animated or living Putrefaction. *Kircher*, in his Treatise of the *Plague*, brings this upon the Stage; from whence the Learned at that time asserted, that the Air might be demonstrated to be Verminous by the Microscope; which seems to stand confirmed by *Malhighius, Leuwenhoock, Morgagni, Redi* and *Mangetus*.[273]

270. Gentilcore 2012, 164–5.
271. Freckleton 2020.
272. Penschow 2022, 42–6, 56–8, 64.
273. Browne 1720, 16.

Browne's own preventive remedies did not actually work, but the ideas in the book he sold to readers were more accurate than those of most medical writers in 1720, when contagionism was still widely rejected by the medical establishment. Diseases really were caused by vermin invisible to the naked eye, and Browne told his readers how Leuwenhoock had seen them using his microscope.[274]

Some prophylactics did not prevent infection but helped with the symptoms, as with "plague treacle" and a number of nineteenth-century nostrums. These contained enough opium to alleviate plague and cholera symptoms such as pain, cough, fever, and diarrhoea. Some putative prophylactics did not prevent infection but had placebo benefits that helped the marginal patient recover. Some, such as nostrums containing arsenic, mercury, or ivermectin, not only failed to prevent infection but actually harmed consumers. The majority—except for the ones like variolation that actually worked—created moral hazard, encouraging contagion externalities by giving consumers a false sense of protection.

Does this mean that the market for unlicensed preventive remedies was on balance harmful? Historically, suppressing such markets would have helped limit the spread of false remedies. But it would also have choked off the supply of true preventives such as smallpox variolation, nostrums containing opium that alleviated plague and cholera symptoms, and self-help books warning against microscopic vermin. Moreover, as we shall see in chapter 5, the most knowledgeable and skilled medical practitioners in the world were still operating on the basis of non-scientific approaches and supernatural beliefs until the emergence of scientific medicine. They still disagreed about basic questions such as microorganisms well into the later nineteenth century. Medical knowledge was thus characterized by lack of consensus and lack of confidence—what Joel Mokyr has termed the absence of "tightness".[275]

This lack of confidence and consensus about medical knowledge, even by experts, meant that until the second half of the nineteenth century, non-market institutions such as states, communities, religions, and medical associations lacked any reliable arbiter to define what was medical fraud and what was not. In such a context, if a medical remedy was demonstrably harmful, then the solution was to target that specific remedy, not close down the entire market for preventive remedies against infectious diseases. Likewise, if questionable remedies created moral hazard, then the solution was to require individuals to comply with sanitation, social distancing, and immunization measures, whether or not they had treated themselves with unlicensed prophylactics.

274. Robertson 2022.
275. Mokyr 2002, 6; Mokyr 2005, 213. On the absence of "tightness" in medical knowledge even in western Europe into the later nineteenth century, see Petroff (2023, 6, 9–10, 21, 30–1).

In rich countries during the twentieth century, markets for medical reme-dies began to be monitored and certified by governments. Around 1935, Norway and Sweden established regulation of drugs before they reached market. The United States followed in the 1938–50 period, establishing the Food and Drug Administration (FDA), now widely viewed as "the world's most powerful regu-latory agency".[276] Yet vigorous debate still rages about whether such agencies carry out appropriate cost–benefit calculations. Do they reach the right balance between safety, access, market incentives, and contagion externalities in the best interests of patients and society? From the 1970s onwards, for instance, a number of studies have argued that the FDA significantly increased the cost of developing pharmaceuticals, needlessly prolonged approval times relative to other advanced economies, and deterred innovation.[277] During the Covid-19 pandemic, the FDA was censured for delaying approval of Covid-19 tests, rem-desivir treatments, and vaccines, increasing infections and leading to unneces-sary deaths. The fact that Covid-19 tests, remedies, and vaccines were rapidly and safely approved and adopted when the FDA issued Emergency Use Autho-rizations (EUAs) was held to demonstrate that prevailing FDA regulations were needlessly strict and had exacerbated the pandemic.[278] Yet other publications vigorously criticized the FDA for granting EUAs which allowed tests, remedies, and vaccines to be developed with less than its customary regulatory stringency during the Covid-19 pandemic, regardless of the benefits.[279]

Regulatory agencies in different rich countries certainly displayed signifi-cantly different behaviour in regulating markets for Covid-19 prophylactics such as testing kits, face masks, and vaccines. The South Korean regulatory agency, for instance, was much faster than the US FDA in authorizing and adopting Covid-19 testing kits, which it did within an impressive two weeks of the first confirmed Korean case, a step now acknowledged to have contrib-uted to lower Covid-19 infections and deaths in that country.[280] Low and late vaccination rates in Japan are ascribed partly to "several months of delay in approval compared with other high-income countries due to the regulatory requirement for a domestic clinical trial involving Japanese citizens and its own review process".[281] Japanese Covid-19 infections were low, but only at the

276. Hilts 2004, xiv; Carpenter 2010, 11, 22.

277. Peltzman 1973; Sarett 1974; Grabowski, Vernon, and Thomas 1978; Wiggins 1981; Gier-inger 1985; H. Miller 1988; Kaitin et al. 1989; DiMasi et al. 1991; Kaitin and Brown 1995; Grabowski, Vernon, and DiMasi 2002; DiMasi, Hansen, and Grabowski 2003; Adams and Branter 2006; J. Evans and Watson 2015; Tabarrok 2017; Chorniy et al. 2021.

278. Shojaei and Salari 2020; Sung et al. 2020; M. Kim and Denyer 2020; March 2021, 1216–21.

279. Bhimraj et al. 2022; Fuleihan 2022.

280. Sung et al. 2020; M. Kim and Denyer 2020.

281. Kosaka et al. 2021, 2234–5. Only 4% of the Japanese population was vaccinated in May 2021 in the run-up to the Tokyo Summer Olympics, compared with vaccination rates in April 2021 of 62% in Israel, 51% in the UK, 43% in the USA, and 28% in Germany.

cost of prolonged social distancing, which inflicted economic damage. Europe, Canada, and the USA spent different periods of time even before submitting vaccines for approval, let alone authorizing them once submitted. For Pfizer, Moderna, and Janssen vaccines, the median total delay (submission plus authorization) was 64 days by the US FDA, 72 days by Health Canada, and 86 days by the European Medicines Agency. The FDA never authorized the Oxford AstraZeneca vaccine, while the EMA did it in 49 days and Health Canada did it in 148.[282] In 2020, the United States and the European Union criticized the United Kingdom for rushing its approval of the Pfizer/BioNTech vaccine for general use without sufficient data, even though the director of the US National Agency of Allergy and Infectious Diseases recanted within a day, telling the BBC, "I have a great deal of confidence in what the UK does both scientifically and from a regulator standpoint. Our process is one that takes more time than it takes in the UK. And that's just the reality. . . . I did not mean to imply any sloppiness even though it came out that way."[283] Within weeks, the US and the EU regulatory agencies granted emergency authorizations for the same vaccine, including for pregnant women, while as late as 2021 the United Kingdom advised against such use. In 2021, there were more than 50 regulatory pathways to accelerated approval across 24 countries, imposing significant hindrances in markets for vaccines. Medical experts urged regulators to harmonize and streamline approval procedures to enable vaccine producers to prepare applications, share findings, compare analyses, and reach doctors and patients without needless regulatory delays.[284]

Even modern, rich countries with high-capacity states, therefore, display weaknesses in regulating markets for preventive remedies against epidemic disease. For one thing, they find it difficult to make clear cost-benefit calculations which balance patient safety, patient access, incentives to innovate, and contagion control. For another, national agencies fail to take account of international evidence on best-practice market regulation. Both these problems result in arbitrary delays and bans, stifling the market, blocking doctor and patient access, exacerbating contagion, and increasing mortality. They are surprisingly reminiscent of similar regulation of markets for variolation and vaccination in eighteenth- and nineteenth-century smallpox epidemics, which, as we shall see, also issued in needless infections, deaths, and sequelae.

282. Lythgoe and Middleton 2021, calculations based on data in table 1. The delay to submission is calculated as the number of days relative to the earliest submission date across the three agencies (the FDA, EMA, and HC), with the earliest agency set to zero. The delay to authorization was calculated as the number of days between the date of submission and the date of authorization.

283. Henley 2020.

284. Forman et al. 2021, 555.

Non-market institutions, as long as they have better information than doctors and consumers, can in principle enable regulation of fake remedies and prophylactics while letting the market itself continue to generate benefits by facilitating transactions in non-fake ones. Of course, non-market institutions did not always have better information than doctors and consumers, as shown by the epidemic nostrums endorsed by governments, religions, and medical associations, by the political, religious, and medical opposition to smallpox variolation in eighteenth-century Europe, and by the many examples of governmental, communal, religious, and corporative groupthink examined in later chapters. Regulating markets is difficult, and the trick is to make sure the regulatory remedy is better than the disease.

5. Did Innovations Make Markets Fail?

It might seem unlikely that the market could play any positive role in developing new medical techniques. After all, an innovative idea is like any type of information—it has public good characteristics. Because information is non-rival and non-excludable, the market will fail to compensate individuals adequately for producing or communicating it, since it can easily spread to others without the producer reaping any reward to cover her costs. So the private benefits of innovating will be lower than the social benefits. Innovations will be under-provided by private individuals transacting in the market. Either an innovation may not be devised at all, since potential inventors cannot profit from their own efforts. Or it may be thought up but—in order that the private inventor can profit—communicated only to a few paying customers, even though at zero additional cost it could benefit society more widely. Because new knowledge is a public good, other institutions than the market—state, community, religion, guild—might be better at encouraging its invention and diffusion. Non-market institutions might enable individuals to reap greater rewards from their ideas, giving them better incentives to think them up. Or non-market institutions might give inventors better incentives to diffuse their innovative knowledge to everyone who might use it.

5.1. THE MARKET FOR SMALLPOX VARIOLATION

It is therefore surprising that the earliest historical innovations to immunize people against infectious diseases were mainly improved and diffused through the market, not the state. Long before Edward Jenner devised vaccination against smallpox using cowpox material in 1796, folk experience had empirically developed a different method, called "variolation" (traditionally termed "inoculation" or "engrafting"). This technique involved transferring material infected with smallpox itself—not cowpox—from a weakly infected person to a susceptible one in order to transmit a mild attack of the disease, which would stimulate the immune system to resist a future severe one.

Even during the poorly recorded "folk" phase of variolation, the records show the market at work. For one thing, the market helped people get raw virus material. People in Europe, Africa, Asia, and the Middle East separately coined the expression "buying the pocks", because to get variolated they had to buy smallpox "lymph" or "dust" from those who had it.[285] In 1671 and 1677, people in the German (now Polish) towns of Breslau and Thorn were "buying the pox" by sending their uninfected children to buy scabs for a couple of gold pieces in order to get infected with a mild case of the disease.[286] In Denmark in 1673, the physician Thomas Bartholin knew "more than a few people who have bought smallpox for themselves".[287] In seventeenth-century Scotland, people got themselves variolated by paying infected people money or goods in exchange for material from their pocks.[288] In seventeenth-century south-west Wales, local people, including schoolchildren, engaged in "buying the smallpox": in 1700, the price was 12 pustules full of pus for 3 pence, about a quarter of the day wage of an agricultural labourer.[289]

Variolation succeeded—usually—because the originating case of smallpox was mild, the dose was small, the transfer was normally to skin rather than respiratory tract, and the lymph or scab was sometimes aged before being transferred, attenuating its virulence. In a small minority of cases, one of these variables was miscalculated and the patient died. The risk of dying from variolation was many times lower than the risk from natural smallpox, as eighteenth-century variolation enthusiasts were quick to point out. The Chinese variolation advocate Zheng Wangyi calculated around 1700 that natural smallpox had a minimum mortality rate of 10–20 per cent, compared with only 4–5 per cent for variolated smallpox.[290] In 1722 the British doctor Thomas Nettleton reported that the mortality rate of natural smallpox was 20 per cent, whereas only 1.6 per cent of those he variolated died. He concluded that one should just apply the logic of the merchant: "State the account of profit and loss to find on which side the balance lies . . . and form a judgement accordingly."[291]

Table 2.2 compares the risks and benefits of variolation, vaccination, and natural smallpox. Variolation involved a risk to the individual (occasionally it induced a serious rather than a mild infection) and to others (someone who

285. Boylston 2012, 311.
286. Klebs 1914, 6.
287. Quoted in M. Bennett 2020, 16.
288. Boylston 2012, 311.
289. Williams 2010, 52–3. According to Bob Allen's (n.d.) London database, in 1700 the day wage of an agricultural labourer in southern England was 12 pence.
290. Chang 1996, 157–8. Zheng Wangyi wrote this sometime between 1680 and 1740.
291. Quoted in M. Bennett 2020, 21.

TABLE 2.2. Natural Smallpox, Variolation, and Vaccination Compared

	Natural smallpox	Variolation	Vaccination
Origin	Probably Near East, India, or China Ancient variola virus may originate in prehistory or antiquity; modern smallpox virus identified in DNA for 1643–55	Independently emerged in China, Near East, India, North Africa First documented China *c*.1550	Invented by Edward Jenner in England in 1796; unpublished precursor experiment by Benjamin Jesty 1774
Raw material	Smallpox virus	Smallpox lymph or dust	Cowpox lymph
Procedure	N/A	Scalpel, needle, thread, insufflation	Mainly needle, sometimes scalpel
Protection	Lifelong (if survived)	Lifelong (if survived)	Complete for 3–5 years; partial for at least 20; re-vaccination after 10–20 years recommended
Risk of infection (%)	95	N/A	N/A
Risk of death (%)	10 to 20	1.6	0.0002
Risk to community	High probability of infection spreading to susceptible	Low but non-zero probability of infection spreading to susceptible	Nil
Adverse reactions	High probability of severe fever, pain, abscess, delirium, other serious symptoms	Low but non-zero probability of fever, pain, abscess	Minor soreness around injection point
Risk of complications	High probability of disfiguration, non-trivial probability of blindness or lameness	Low but non-zero probability of all complications of natural smallpox (disfiguration, blindness, lameness)	None
Restrictions	Confinement to prevent community spread	Confinement to prevent community spread	None
Other	N/A	Entire susceptible community should have procedure simultaneously	None

Sources: Lahariya 2014, 493 (in turn adapted from Bhattacharya, Harrison, and Warboys 2005); M. Bennett 2020, 12, 15, 21; Krylova and Earn 2019; Duggan et al. 2016.

had not already contracted smallpox might catch it from a variolated individual with active skin lesions). But it also involved a benefit to the individual (life-long smallpox immunity, conditional on surviving inoculation) and to others (reduced contagion once their contacts were variolated).

Advocates of immunization in the eighteenth century initially focused only on the benefits and costs to the individual. But gradually they realized that immunization generated both positive and negative externalities—benefits and costs beyond those that the individual personally incurred. The distinguished Swedish doctor and political economist David Schulz von Schulzenheim wrote a treatise in 1767 presenting the arguments for variolation in Sweden, based on the English example. In it, he acknowledged that variolated persons caused negative externalities to non-variolated ones through risks of unintended contagion. But he pointed out that the externality went both ways: "By Inoculation it is said that our Neighbour is injured by spreading the Small Pox. But I do not find that I ought to lose my Life, because my Neighbours will not use the same precaution."[292]

We do not know who invented variolation. The original idea cannot be traced to any specific date, place, or person. Variolation might have been practised in India as early as 1000 (though the evidence is shaky), and was reliably described in China from around 1550, Wales by around 1600, the Ottoman Empire by around 1675, North Africa by 1700, Libya by 1706, and Bengal by 1731.[293] In Britain, information about variolation arrived around 1700 in separate correspondence from China and the Ottoman lands.[294] British and European journals published items about variolation between 1714 and 1717, beginning with an article in the *Philosophical Transactions of the Royal Society* by Emanuele Timony, a Padua-trained Greek doctor practising in Constantinople, who said variolation had arrived there from Georgia and Circassia about 40 years earlier, in the 1670s.[295] In America, variolation arrived in 1706 when a Boston clergyman learned of it from an enslaved African in his household, who probably came from what is now southern Libya.[296] The fact that variolation appeared in multiple societies across the world—China, India, Turkey, Africa—with no record of its origins suggests that it had no single inventor. Its earliest communication took place through multiple, idiosyncratic, and often obscure channels. In the words of Schulz von Schulzenheim in 1767, variolation was just another example of the fact that "the principal Remedies Physic has to

292. Schulz von Schulzenheim 1767, 130–1.
293. Herbert 1975, 540–1; M. Bennett 2008, 500; Chang 1996, 130–1, 143–6.
294. Silverstein 2009, 292–3.
295. G. Miller 1957, 55–9, 287–8.
296. G. Miller 1957, 92–6; Boylston 2012, 309–10; Herbert 1975, 540–1; M. Bennett 2008, 500.

boast of, are Fruits of the Experience of the simple multitude, and not Labours of the Brain generated in Study"—a maxim that would be greatly weakened a generation later when Edward Jenner invented vaccination.[297]

Knowledge of variolation was rooted in folk practice and, as we shall see, took a long time to be accepted by Western medical practitioners and governments. But even before that happened, the market drove its diffusion and improvement.[298] For one thing, as during its folk origins, a market arose for the raw virus material, helping customers find suppliers. In eighteenth-century Orkney, for instance, a commercial variolator bargained with parents and children, offering alcohol and sweets in exchange for smallpox "matter".[299] In the Sudanese city of Sennar in the later eighteenth century, "upon the first hearing of the small pox anywhere" both Black and Arab mothers would seek out an infected child and bargain with its mother for pocks to treat their own children.[300] In the Tigre region of Ethiopia in 1810–21, when smallpox approached,

> The people of the country and villages collect their children and those who have not had it into one gang, for the purpose of having them inoculated. Everyone carries a piece of salt [the main local currency], or a measure of corn: they then march together to the neighbouring town, or wherever the disorder may have made its appearance. Here they pick out a person, who is thickest covered with sores, and procure a skilful person or Dofter [lay priest] who takes a quantity of matter from him into an egg-shell, and then by turns he cuts a small cross with a razor on the arm, puts in it a little of the matter, and afterwards binds it up with a piece of rag. The salt and other articles which they carry are given to the Dofter, and he divides it with the person from whom the matter is taken.[301]

Long after the invention of vaccination, the market for variolation matter survived. In Morocco in 1855, for instance, "when smallpox (*djidri*) is discovered, the parents of the child to be inoculated buy one or two sores through a small gift to the young infected person".[302]

The market not only helped people get the raw material for variolation. It also diffused and improved the technique. Commercial variolators set up businesses and competed for customers by offering innovations. The earliest documentary reference to variolation dates from China in 1567–72, when commercial

297. Schulz von Schulzenheim 1767, 134.
298. M. Bennett 2020, 55.
299. B. Smith 1998, 401.
300. Quoted in Herbert 1975, 547–8.
301. N. Pearce 1831, 297–8.
302. Quoted in Amster and El Aoued 2021, 91.

variolators were already in operation.[303] From then into the nineteenth century, Chinese society accommodated at least two types of commercial variolator: *douyi* (medical variolators treating better-off customers in towns) and *doushi* (religious variolators treating poor customers in the countryside).[304]

Professional, paid variolators were also well known in parts of eighteenth-century India. In 1767, an East India Company physician reported that a caste of variolators (*tikadārs*) earned their livelihoods in Bengal, Bihar, and eastern Uttar Pradesh by visiting each locality annually: "The Operator takes his fee, which from the poor is a *pund of cowries*, equal to about a penny sterling, and goes on to another door, down one side of the street and up the other, and is thus employed from morning until night, inoculating sometimes 8 or 10 in a house."[305] Commercial variolation was practised in Dinajpur (modern Bangladesh) in 1808 by local Hindu and Muslim cultivators, at Serampore around 1822 by low-ranking Brahmin astrologers, at Dacca in the 1840s by garland makers and barbers, and in Punjab in the 1860s by a wide array of lower-class healers, including barber-surgeons and low-status Ayurveda and Unani-Tibb medical practitioners.[306] So successful was commercial variolation in India that vaccination found it hard to compete, since the *tikadārs* "were well positioned in the medical market-place in Bengal and offered a procedure that, with its ritual trappings and record of success, was familiar and acceptable".[307] As late as 1850, among 35,000 Bengali villagers 81 per cent had been variolated, exceeding the 68 per cent of villagers *vaccinated* in the 1960s.[308]

China and India, with their well-established groups of professional variolators, were far ahead of Europe in smallpox immunization. Then in the eighteenth century, England developed its own lively variolation market. From the 1750s onwards, commercial variolation became so widely available in provincial England that groups of teenagers from the same village would walk into town on market day and get a commercial variolater to inoculate them collectively so that they would all fall mildly ill at the same time but then be immunized so they could safely migrate into towns to seek jobs.[309] Adult villagers also used the town market to seek out variolation from, as licensed medical professionals complained, "some operator, too often as crude and thoughtless as themselves".[310]

303. Boylston 2012, 311.
304. C.-L. Liu 2016, 91.
305. Dharampal 1971, 158 (quotation); Greenough 1980, 346.
306. R. Nicholas 1981, 29–30; Minsky 2009, 170.
307. M. Bennett 2020, 256.
308. Bhatnagar 1952; Greenough 1980, 347; Marglin 1987, 11.
309. M. Bennett 2020, 46.
310. Quoted in M. Bennett 2020, 43.

Competition was vigorous. Customers shopped around for lower prices and shorter procedures. Providers advertised their education and training, professional experience, number of variolations performed, and even percentage of fatalities.[311] The best-known commercial variolator in England was the Suffolk apothecary Robert Sutton, whose son had contracted severe smallpox from being variolated by a neighbour in 1756. Sutton saw a gap in the market and systematically remedied it. He tempted customers by offering a simplified procedure, minimal scarring, residential care packages, nurses with good reputations, and lower prices than many medically supervised variolation procedures.[312] Sutton's eight sons all set up as commercial variolators. They were businessmen rather than educated professionals—in the words of one educated lady, the most entrepreneurial of the Sutton sons was "a fellow of very quick parts [but] as ignorant as dirt both with regard to books and the world".[313] Robert Sutton's "system" remained local until the 1760s, when his son Daniel (the one who was "ignorant as dirt") expanded the business throughout Essex and nearby Kent. By 1768, he had extended the franchise so widely that 62 accredited Suttonian variolators were operating all over England and as far afield as America, France, Ireland, and the Netherlands.[314] Robert Sutton and his sons developed an identifiable, pre-packaged, easily diffused, and successful system, which enabled them to benefit from "vertical integration and brand marketing".[315]

Robert Sutton's procedure was so influential that out of 73 European publications on variolation that appeared in 1768, nearly two-thirds related to the Suttonian system. That was the year in which the largest-ever number of publications on variolation appeared, and the 48 that referred to Robert Sutton's procedure were published in seven languages: 15 in English, 10 in French, 9 in German, 6 in Dutch, 3 each in Italian and Latin, and 2 in Russian.[316] In the second half of the eighteenth century, many of the commercial variolators who inoculated aristocrats and other members of the elite in Russia, Livonia, Austria, and the German lands were from Britain, often trained by the Sutton franchise.[317] The German writer Goethe recalled that when he was growing up in Frankfurt in the 1750s and 1760s, "among us, inoculation was still viewed as very problematical . . . German doctors were hesitant about using a procedure that seemed to pre-empt nature. Consequently, speculating Englishmen came

311. M. Bennett 2020, 45.
312. M. Bennett 2020, 43–4.
313. Quoted in M. Bennett 2020, 44.
314. M. Bennett 2020, 44.
315. M. Bennett 2020, 43–4.
316. Dimsdale 2017.
317. Penschow 2022, 42–6, 56–8, 64.

over to the Continent and, for a considerable fee, inoculated the children of persons they found to be well-to-do and unprejudiced."[318] In Ireland, as in England, commercial variolation spread widely during the eighteenth century. In County Mayo, for instance, a Gaelic-speaking priest earned a living as an itinerant inoculator for 30–40 years.[319]

Irish variolators joined English ones in spreading the practice to other countries, as in the Spanish town of Ferrol, where the Irish immigrant Timoteo O'Scanlan made a comfortable living in the 1770s as a commercial variolator of government administrators, army officers, noblemen, financiers, merchants, and other medics, but also immunized poor people for free.[320]

Scotland was another society that produced numerous commercial variolators, even in remote regions. In Shetland in the 1780s and 1790s, for instance, the tailor, joiner, blacksmith, and clock mender Johnie Williamson developed a particularly successful approach to variolation with unusually low fatalities, earning a living as an itinerant inoculator by selling his services to ordinary Shetlanders.[321] Scottish commercial variolators spread the practice overseas, as with the Edinburgh medical graduate Adam Thomson, who in the 1730s devised a new approach to preparing patients for the procedure, which he applied in Scotland before moving his business to Philadelphia in the 1740s.[322]

5.2. VACCINATION AND THE MARKET

Then, in 1796, vaccination was invented. As table 2.2 shows, it improved on variolation by using less dangerous cowpox rather than smallpox material, killed incomparably fewer patients than the 1–2 per cent who died from variolation, and caused no cross-infection to the non-jabbed. We do know who invented it—Edward Jenner, a modest country doctor.

Jenner struggled to profit from his invention precisely because ideas are public goods. To persuade people to get vaccinated, Jenner needed to explain his idea, and once he explained it no one would pay. The familiar market failure arising from innovations being non-excludable and non-rival thus struck Jenner in classic form. In the end, Jenner's reward was non-material: he became world-famous, Napoleon idolized him, and he set an eternal model for researchers. But his monetary reward—a belated parliamentary prize organized by noble patrons—did not come from the market.

318. Quoted in Penschow 2022, 43.
319. M. Bennett 2020, 46.
320. M. White 2020, 786, 790.
321. B. Smith 1998, 402–3.
322. M. Bennett 2020, 56.

Once vaccination became known, however, the market drove its diffusion and improvement. As with variolation, the market helped people get the raw material for vaccination. In 1800, for instance, the Philadelphia wine merchant John Vaughan received a sample of cowpox vaccine from his brother in Maine, who had in turn procured it from their father, a merchant banker in London; John then supplied the cowpox material to many American vaccinators and personally financed vaccination publications via his business connections.[323] In Havana in 1804, a doctor offered a fee to a Puerto Rican lady to take lymph from her recently vaccinated son and maidservants, which he then used to vaccinate local children.[324] In China after 1805, commercial vaccinators paid wet nurses to travel with them along with their infant charges to transmit cowpox vaccine from arm to arm.[325] In Canton in 1878, a vaccinator would take a child with him to supply the lymph, charging the patient 50 cents to a dollar, plus a fee of 25 cents to the child.[326] Cantonese commercial vaccinators paid paupers to bring their children to be vaccinated or hired children directly to provide a constant supply of fresh lymph to use on fee-paying patients.[327] In Punjab in 1873, arm-to-arm vaccinators could often procure lymph only by offering payment to parents of poor children.[328]

The market diffused vaccination, like variolation, because it enabled commercial providers to make a living. Hardly had Jenner invented vaccination than surgeons, physicians, apothecaries, female freelancers, and completely untrained entrepreneurs were charging fees to provide it—no wonder Jenner himself never made a profit.[329] As soon as the French government approved vaccination in 1800, a Paris doctor opened a clinic where he vaccinated the poor for free but charged private patients fees, which, in an astute marketing ploy, he promised to refund if the procedure failed. Other aspiring French vaccinators learnt from this entrepreneur and soon set up profit-making vaccination businesses in over 100 provincial towns throughout France and Flanders.[330] In Boston by the summer of 1800, a doctor was charging private patients 5 dollars per vaccination, and establishing over a dozen franchise arrangements throughout New England in return for 25 per cent of the revenues.[331] Another Boston doctor remarked in October 1800, "If I had matter [vaccine] enough I could make a mint of money in a bit of time. . . . Everyone here is in a rage

323. M. Bennett 2020, 280–2.
324. M. Bennett 2020, 302.
325. Leung 2008, 8.
326. Leung 2008, 12.
327. Leung 2008, 12, 14.
328. Minsky 2009, 179–80.
329. M. Bennett 2020, 83–93, 98–102.
330. M. Bennett 2020, 154–6.
331. M. Bennett 2020, 273.

to have the cow-pox"; by the following month he was writing that even the limited amount of fresh vaccine he had got his hands on "would maintain me and a wife in a snug way".[332]

In China, commercial vaccinators started selling their services in the market in the same way as commercial variolators had since the 1560s. The first Chinese vaccinator, Qiu Xi, learned the technique from an English East India Company surgeon and was employed by the Macao merchant guild to vaccinate locals.[333] After doing that job for 10 years, he set up a family business and founded a dynasty of commercial vaccinators, which survived into the late nineteenth century.[334] He also published a vaccination textbook (shown in figure 2.6), which went through multiple editions. Qiu Xi adeptly marketed vaccination by using the language of acupuncture and traditional Chinese medicine, securing endorsements from celebrated literati, officials, and businessmen.[335]

As early as 1815, one British surgeon in China remarked:

> It is in no way unfavourable, either to the chances of disseminating or preservation of the practice, that it has become a source, both of reputation and emolument to the Chinese, who have engaged in it, and who conduct it extensively throughout the city of Canton and country around, as well as at the station specified.[336]

According to one American medical missionary in Canton in 1865:

> There are now so many persons devoted exclusively to the business, and interested in the preservation of the virus, that there is no danger of its ever being lost. Several persons have made fortunes from the practice, and those first engaged in it have obtained an enviable fame among their countrymen as great benefactors of the race.[337]

By 1870, Canton had an estimated 50–60 professional vaccinators, and about half the city's children were vaccinated.[338] Chinese commercial vaccinators competed for customers by introducing micro-innovations, some based on the venerable Chinese tradition of variolation.[339] The market thus enabled vaccination to spread in China, become embedded in society rather than facing cultural rejection, and bring esteem and profit to commercial practitioners.[340]

---

332. Quoted in J. Putnam 1906, 221–3.
333. Leung 2008, 10–11, 20–1, 24.
334. Leung 2008, 10–11, 20–1, 24.
335. Leung 2008, 15–16, 24–5; Leung 2011, 10; Leung 2020b, 1354.
336. Quoted in Leung 2008, 11.
337. Quoted in Leung 2008, 11.
338. Leung 2008, 12.
339. Leung 2008, 17–20; Leung 2011, 10–11.
340. Leung 2020b, 1354.

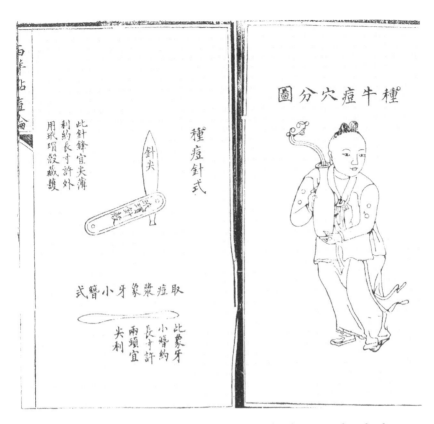

FIGURE 2.6. Illustration from Qiu Xi's vaccination textbook, *Xiyang dian dou lun* (On Western vaccination). This illustration appears in the 1828 edition. Throughout the book, illustrations show the meridian points on the human body at which the smallpox lymph was to be inserted, the knife to be used to cut the arm, and the ivory spoon to extract the lymph. *Source*: Leung 2008, 16.

Throughout the world after 1796, a myriad of individuals and organizations helped diffuse vaccination. As we shall see in later chapters, these included enlightened rulers, local communities, religious organizations, medical associations, doctors, charities, philanthropists, and parents—especially mothers—who vaccinated their own children. These individuals and organizations often acted through non-market institutions—state, community, religion, medical association. Even so, they often used the market at the same time, charging fees to paying customers, which cross-subsidized unpaid vaccinations for the poor.[341]

341. M. Bennett 2020, 144.

The market for immunization could not solve the basic problem that innovations are a public good. No known inventor was ever rewarded for the idea of variolation, and Edward Jenner never earned a profit by inventing vaccination. But once those ideas were invented, the market facilitated their diffusion and use. The market enabled those with a demand for smallpox dust or cowpox serum to find those with a supply of it. The market enabled commercial variolators and vaccinators to find customers, and people desiring immunization to find someone with the raw material and expertise. Market competition created incentives for commercial providers to devise micro-innovations, which enabled them to appropriate profits from the idea of inoculation by improving quality, reducing risks, increasing supply, and lowering prices, which in turn attracted new customers. In short, the market helped diffuse and improve an innovation that successfully limited contagion in one of the most serious diseases in history, long before either the disease or the technology behind the procedure was understood by medical science.

6. Conclusion

Was William Laud right when he declared in 1637 that epidemics are caused by "the carelessness of the people, and the greediness to receive into their houses infected goods"?[342] The market does make exchange easier—for both goods and pathogens. Epidemics are transmitted along the same roads, waterways, sea lanes, and flight paths as trade. But the routes used for market exchange are also used by states, communities, religions, guilds, and families to move people and goods for their own purposes. Soldiers, vagrants, beggars, refugees, pilgrims, journeymen, servants, harvesters, settlers, brides, and migrating tribes transmitted epidemics—alongside long-distance merchants, local traders, and the consumers they provisioned and infected.

The market for grain, cattle, fish, game, and furs opens the gate to zoonoses—infectious diseases that jump from animals to humans. But trade in such goods also brings benefits. What was its net effect on human well-being? The market for food is hard to condemn. The trade in grain and foodstuffs carried pathogens and their animal vectors. But it also mitigated famine, sustained towns, and raised real incomes.

The market also helps people fight contagion. Historically, societies with well-functioning markets for labour, land, credit, goods, and services achieved faster economic growth. Such growth generated resources people used to control contagion. These resources made it possible to buy better food, housing, hygiene, medical remedies, and immunization. They also supported families through social distancing, market withdrawal, and flight from disease,

---

342. Quoted in Slack 1985, 22.

reducing contagion and death. There is no guarantee that the resources generated by market-led growth will be used to control contagion, since that depends on who controls their allocation. But if the resources are not there, they certainly will not be available to deal with epidemics.

The market also helped improve and diffuse the first medical innovations that actually prevented epidemic disease—variolation in China after the 1560s, vaccination in Europe after 1796, and global immunization against other infectious diseases, most recently Covid-19. The market alone could not reap all the benefits of immunization because of positive externalities—spillover benefits which immunized individuals do not themselves enjoy, requiring coordination by the state, community, or religion. But the market played a big role in making medical innovations better, cheaper, and more plentiful. It does so to this day.

The market cannot do everything. For one thing, it is embedded in the wider institutional framework of every society. It works well only when not corrupted by other institutions. When states, communities, religions, or guilds grant monopolies to privileged groups, the market fails. It also fails when faced with the negative externalities of contagion, the positive externalities of immunization, and the public goods of information and sanitation. Epidemics create situations where market prices do not reflect the actual costs and benefits of people's choices.

The market creates failures for other institutions to solve—at least in principle. But it also creates part of the solution. Market-led economic growth generated more resources for other institutions—state, community, religion, and guild. Rising market incomes enabled people to donate more to communal poor relief, religious charities, and guild chests, making market withdrawal more affordable for others. Above all, markets generated resources which the state could extract as taxes. The rising per capita GDP generated by market-led economic growth hugely enhanced fiscal capacity.[343] The nascent market economies of late medieval Italy and Flanders, early modern England and the Netherlands, and nineteenth-century America and Germany had the highest fiscal capacity in their world. Much of this capacity, then as now, was wasted on war, vanity projects, and buying off powerful elites so rulers could retain power. But some was used to fight epidemics—as we shall see in chapter 3.

---

343. Besley and Persson 2009; Dincecco 2015; Ogilvie 2023.

3

The State

> [The three-member Council committee is] to consider diligently all possible ways to preserve public health and avoid the corruption of the environment.
> —LARGE COUNCIL OF THE VENETIAN REPUBLIC, 30 MARCH 1348[1]

> You have been inoculated with less fuss than a nun taking an enema. . . . We French can hardly be inoculated at all, except by decree of the *Parlement*.
> —VOLTAIRE WRITING TO CATHERINE THE GREAT OF RUSSIA, 1768[2]

"State" is our word for a political territory. But the state is also an institution—a set of practices imposing obligatory rules over people in a territory, claiming priority over the rules of other organizations, and backed by legitimate coercion.[3]

Institutions making these claims have taken many forms—kingdoms, principalities, city-states, republics, constitutional monarchies, dynastic composite states, empires, parliamentary democracies. They also emerged gradually and unevenly across the centuries. They did not follow the same trajectory in different continents or even in different societies on the same continent. In many developing economies, historical and modern, the state's claims to monopolize legitimate coercion have been limited in principle and in practice by the entitlements and powers of other institutions. But virtually every society in history possesses an institution that asserts such claims. This is the "state" analysed in this chapter.

1. Quoted in Cipolla 1976, 11.
2. Quoted in Lentin 1974, 56.
3. For overlapping definitions to this effect: Weber (1922) 1978, 54–5; Tilly 1990, 1–2.

Not all states were (or are) centralized. Nor do all states follow a unidirectional path from less to greater centralization. On the one hand, state centralization can increase, as fragmented regions coalesce or rulers bring outlying provinces under a central yoke. But on the other, empires collapse, nation-states divide, city-states survive, provinces and cities retain or extend devolved governance.

Most states impose rules and coercion at multiple levels—imperial, territorial, provincial, local—but the entity that does so remains the state. So this chapter also looks at lower levels of formal, rule-governed collective action. Local government, as we shall see, turns out to be crucial in the history and practice of contagion control. Where local collective action is informal and governed by norms rather than formal rules, it is taken to be part of the institution of the "community", discussed in chapter 4. Some overlap between state and community nonetheless remains, since rules and norms are different ends of the same spectrum.

So how did the state affect epidemic contagion between the Black Death and Covid-19? "State capacity"—the ability of the state to implement its aims— is widely used to analyse how the state affects the economy and society.[4] The commonest quantitative measure of state capacity is *fiscal* capacity—central state tax revenues—which gives governments resources to implement their aims. But the ability of the state to achieve its aims also includes the *legal* capacity to impose its policies across society and the *bureaucratic* capacity to administer those policies effectively.

Greater state capacity (usually measured as fiscal capacity) is broadly associated with higher per capita GDP across countries and over time, as we saw in chapter 2.[5] An expanding literature argues that this link is causal, with historical increases in state capacity leading to better economic and social outcomes.[6] Since 2020, the state-capacity literature has extended this perspective to pandemics.[7] Fiscal capacity gives the state resources to deal with contagion externalities, provide public goods, and address cross-border spillovers. Legal capacity enables it to impose sanitary regulations, social distancing, and immunization across the entire society. Bureaucratic capacity gives it the ability to administer public health measures effectively and fairly. Together, these capacities enable the state to project power beyond territorial frontiers to deal with cross-border externalities of pandemics.

4. See, e.g., Besley and Persson 2009; Besley and Persson 2011; Besley and Persson 2013.

5. Besley and Persson 2009; Dincecco 2015; Dincecco 2017; Dincecco and Onorato 2018; Dincecco and Katz 2016; N. D. Johnson and Koyama 2017. On how to improve our measures of fiscal capacity, see Ogilvie (2023, 29–35).

6. Besley and Persson 2009; Dincecco 2015; Dincecco 2017; Dincecco and Onorato 2018; Dincecco and Katz 2016; N. D. Johnson and Koyama 2017.

7. Serikbayeva, Abdulla, and Oskenbayev 2021; Besley and Dann 2022.

But some studies pose tough questions about state capacity.[8] The link between state capacity and good social outcomes is only a rough association. It might not be that state capacity improves economic growth, but rather that economic growth fuels state capacity. Or underlying variables could be causing both economy and state to grow. Can we really take for granted that state capacity causes good economic and social outcomes?

Fiscal, legal, and bureaucratic capacity give the state the ability to achieve its purposes, but what shapes these purposes? What ensures they will benefit society at large rather than state personnel or powerful social elites? What prevents state capacity from being used for harmful purposes—fiscal capacity lavished on war and domestic oppression, legal capacity used to impose laws that benefit elites (feudal landlords, slave owners), bureaucratic capacity deployed to favour special interests (venal office holders, guilds, business cartels)? Does anything guarantee that the state will use its capacity to benefit the whole society rather than pursue the narrow interests of the powerful? State capacity is a powerful weapon. But what decides how it is used?

Epidemics make these questions even more salient. As we shall see, the state interacts with epidemics in harmful as well as beneficial ways. Throughout most of history, fiscal systems were highly regressive and still are so in many developing countries today.[9] States spend money on war and palaces in addition to—or instead of—health and welfare. Regressive fiscal extraction can lessen citizens' capacity to avoid contagion themselves and to comply with public health measures. State legal capacity can legitimize harmful measures such as the eighteenth-century French ban on smallpox variolation lamented by Voltaire in the epigraph to this chapter. State bureaucratic capacity can implement bad public health policies very effectively. Projecting state power outside territorial frontiers can result in warfare or colonial domination, which exacerbate epidemic contagion.

The state capacity literature argues that these problems have been solved by three features that states developed between the Middle Ages and the twentieth century: higher fiscal capacity, centralization, and parliaments.[10] These features ensured, according to this view, that state capacity benefited society. Higher fiscal capacity provided the state with more resources, which enabled it to pursue a wider range of beneficial policies, including contagion control. Greater centralization gave the state the ability to implement policies uniformly, transmitting the benefits of anti-contagion measures to all

---

8. For critical reflections: Cingolani 2013; Kiser and Karceski 2017, esp. 85–7; Koren and Sarbahi 2018; Geloso and Salter 2020; Suryanarayan 2021; Geloso and Makovi 2022; Ogilvie 2023.

9. Kiser and Karceski 2017, 78–9, 83, 85–7; Alfani and Di Tullio 2019, 145–80.

10. Besley and Persson 2009; Besley and Persson 2013; Dincecco 2015; Dincecco and Katz 2016.

citizens. Stronger parliaments checked authoritarian excesses and calibrated state action to citizen preferences, directing state action towards public health. As the centuries passed, this literature concludes, states increasingly developed these three features and thus became "effective states" exercising their capacity to benefit citizens in pandemics.

This chapter investigates how closely these ideas correspond to state behaviour during epidemics across the past seven centuries. It focuses on five key market failures which epidemics generate and state capacity might correct: the negative externalities of infectious waste; the negative externalities of interpersonal contagion; the positive externalities of immunization; the public good of epidemic information; and the cross-border externalities of pandemics.

State capacity addressed these market failures in some places and times, but not others. Fiscal capacity could be used negligently, corruptly, or for purposes that spread contagion. Centralization could be excessive, inefficient, or both. Parliament was probably better than any of the alternatives, but was not a magic bullet: representative bodies were often steered by narrow interests that resisted or corrupted public health policy; what mattered was not just the presence of a parliament but its internal interests and workings.[11] On their own, fiscal capacity, centralization, and parliamentary representation did not guarantee that the state acted to benefit society at large.

What made the difference? Beyond sheer state capacity, three further characteristics were important. First, state motivation was essential in deciding how the state allocated its capacity. Many states do not use their capacity to benefit their citizens. Rather they use it extractively—to benefit the ruler, state personnel, or the interest groups that keep the state in power. Second, political realities played a major role—what domestic interests did the state have to navigate and mediate in order to govern? Finally came knowledge— even with fiscal capacity, motivation, and the agreement of domestic interests, does the state in a particular time and place actually have adequate scientific understanding and technical ability to tackle the complex problems posed by epidemic contagion? Motivation, politics, and knowledge are central to state action in general—and perhaps even more so in epidemics.

1. Getting Rid of Garbage

Individuals do many things perfectly innocently that make them get diseases themselves and infect others. One is to pollute. We produce garbage and sewage from our houses, effluent from our farms and industries, carcasses of animals we kill, and our own corpses when we die. Such waste often hosts non-human sources of infection such as bacteria, viruses, and their insect and

11. Ogilvie and Carus 2014, 418–28.

animal carriers. When I dispose of infectious waste carelessly, it inflicts costs beyond those that I myself incur. In principle, the state can deal with these externalities by regulating waste disposal.

1.1. GARBAGE—A BRIEF HISTORY

Governments have long tried to enforce sanitation. Sometimes this was just to prevent public nuisances. But often it was also to control disease. Long before the invention of germ theory in 1861, or even before most doctors accepted the idea of contagion, ordinary people and their governments thought waste was associated with disease and tried to improve public sanitation.[12]

It might be thought that states started issuing sanitary measures because of great pandemics like the Black Death. In fact, they started much earlier, and mainly to control endemic rather than epidemic disease.[13] As early as 100 BCE–100 CE, the *Arthashastra*, an Indian Sanskrit treatise on political science and economic policy, gave clear instructions about waste disposal:

> No one shall throw dirt on the streets or let mud and water collect there. . . . No one shall pass urine or faeces in (or near) a holy place, a water reservoir, a temple or a royal property, unless it is for unavoidable reasons like illness, medication or fear. No one shall throw out dead bodies of animals or human beings inside the city. Corpses shall be taken out of the city only by the prescribed route and the gate for corpses, and cremation or burial done only at the designated places.[14]

For millennia, political authorities have debated and experimented with public measures to prevent disease by regulating waste: in Indian, Greek, and Roman antiquity, in the Byzantine and Arabic worlds during the early medieval period, and in Spanish and Italian cities from the eleventh century onwards.[15] Most aspects of public hygiene that are important for governments in modern epidemics were already a focus of statecraft at least 2,000 years ago.

Less is known about enforcement mechanisms, but they clearly predated the Black Death. In Middle Eastern cities from the ninth century onwards, public hygiene was monitored and regulated by a market inspector called the *muhtasib* or *mustasaf*. These official inspectorships were copied—sometimes under the same titles—in adjacent Christian states in Spain, the Latin kingdom of Jerusalem, and Frankish Cyprus.[16] Across western Europe from the

12. Coomans 2019, 97; Coomans 2022, 1067; Zaneri and Geltner 2022, 6.
13. Geltner 2020, 4–5.
14. Quoted in Tumbe 2020, 58–9.
15. Glick 1972, 61, 70–1, 74.
16. Glick 1972, 71, 78–81.

eleventh century on, urban, princely, and papal states increasingly regulated waste disposal, street cleaning, industrial zoning, animal rearing, hospital location, corpse disposal, and maintenance of canals, wells, fountains, and sewers—all in the name of paternal care for citizens' health.[17] In thirteenth-century Bologna, the municipal government created the office of the *fango*—dirt master—to monitor waste disposal, water supply, and sewerage, compile citizens' complaints, inspect defects, monitor compliance, and impose penalties for violations.[18] Governments in many other Italian states focused on refuse disposal between 1200 and 1500, extending it into rural areas, where *camparii*—field masters—were appointed to regulate waste management and water infrastructure.[19]

The same development can be observed in the Netherlands. By 1280 Ypres had appointed a "mud official" who was responsible for monitoring waste disposal and punishing environmental offences, followed in the early fourteenth century by the Ghent *coninc der ribauden* (lit. "king of the ribalds", later *moorkoning*, or "dung king") and the Deventer "brink brigade" (named after the central market square, the Brink). In the fifteenth century came the Antwerp *moosmeiers* (dung carriers), the Bruges *meuderaars* and *moerknechten* (dungers, dung-fellows), the Brussels *moddermeiers* (scavengers), the Utrecht *slijkburgers* (waste burghers), the municipal cleaners in Louvain and Haarlem, and the Groningen *hovelingen van de schutten* (courtiers of the pounds).[20]

When the Black Death arrived in 1348, one of the first things high-capacity states in central and northern Italy did was to issue (or reissue) sanitary regulations. In Pistoia, for instance, even before plague actually reached the city, the municipal government issued its famous 23 "Ordinances for Sanitation in a Time of Mortality", which closely echoed numerous previous ordinances directed at preventing disease through sanitation.[21] Public waste management to prevent epidemic mortality was not new. But the new pandemic concentrated people's minds.

In the three centuries after the Black Death, both plague epidemics and public sanitary measures proliferated. Local governments were most active. Local public sanitation to combat epidemics began to be recorded in other parts of Europe, more and earlier in rich and urbanized Italy and Flanders, less and later in poor and sparsely populated central and northern Europe.[22] From the mid-fifteenth century onwards, north-eastern French towns openly imitated their

---

17. Zaneri and Geltner 2022, 6–7.
18. Zaneri and Geltner 2022, 7–8.
19. Zaneri and Geltner 2022, 26.
20. Coomans 2018, 80; Coomans 2019, 86–8.
21. Geltner 2020, esp. 6–7.
22. Glick 1972, 77–8; Zaneri and Geltner 2022, 26–7.

neighbours in the southern Low Countries in expanding public sanitation—
cleaning streets, getting rid of human waste, mandating and inspecting latrines,
constructing public privies—to combat epidemic contagion, especially after
the devastating plague of 1457–59.[23] In fifteenth- and sixteenth-century Dutch
towns, urban magistrates sanitized city streets and canals and ordered the safe
disposal of household refuse and medical waste.[24] From the 1490s onwards,
Scottish burghs were employing "clengeris" (cleansers), whose job was to
clean, burn, or fumigate plague-infected property, clear middens off streets,
bury the dead, and distance their own bodies from the rest of the community
for the duration of the plague.[25] In 1600, the municipal government of York
enacted new public hygiene measures, explicitly motivated by the view that
dirt bred disease, especially in hot weather.[26] In the 1645 Leith plague, the
magistrates sought to limit contagion by ordering citizens to remove "their
middens of mucke and dead swine affe the Streete", employing eight "foul
cleagners" to move the dead, bury them, and clear their houses, and requiring
twelve women who survived the plague to "mucke out and reid" houses before
the cleansers fumigated them.[27] By around 1650 most English towns were tackling plague contagion by a programme of cleaning public streets and squares.[28]

Measures to provide clean water and sewerage, which were crucial in the
fight against waterborne diseases such as typhus, cholera, dysentery, and influenza, developed more gradually than those to clear away visible garbage. The
Dutch draper and self-taught microscope maker Antoni van Leeuwenhoek
discovered microbes (he called them *dierkens*, or "little animals") in the 1670s
in drops of water, and within a few years members of the English Royal Society
were speculating that air might also be full of invisible creatures which could
cause "general infections of men or animals".[29] But as we shall see in chapter 6,
for a long time the medical and scientific establishment rejected the idea of
contagion and thus the notion that epidemics could be caused by invisible
little animals in the water. This made it hard to argue that governments or
communities should build expensive public infrastructure to provide clean
water and sewerage.

In the course of the eighteenth century, some town governments began
to display sporadic concern about clean water supplies, but mainly focused

23. N. Murphy 2013, 141–2.
24. Coomans 2021, 223–30; Coomans and Weeda 2020, 82–3.
25. Oram 2007, 28.
26. Palliser 1973, 46.
27. Quoted in Rosie 2020.
28. Slack 1985, 45–7, 200, 207–8, 276–7.
29. Quoted in Robertson 2022, 3.

on taste and turbidity rather than the revolutionary notion that water might carry infection and should not be contaminated. Clean water regulations were slowly introduced in some late eighteenth-century English cities, but only in better-off neighbourhoods, with poorer districts receiving little municipal attention.[30] Extensive public construction of water and sewerage infrastructure did not spread widely until the second half of the nineteenth century, even in England, the United States, and Germany, the richest and highest-capacity states in the world.[31] But when governments took action, the results were striking. American cities such as New York and Philadelphia pioneered municipal water systems starting in 1798, reducing cholera morbidity and mortality in the 1832 epidemic; by 1873, those American cities that introduced municipal water systems enjoyed lower cholera mortality than in nearby rural areas.[32] Investments in sewerage and water infrastructure, it is estimated, caused around 30 per cent of the decline in mortality in England and Wales between 1861 and 1900,[33] and approximately the same magnitude of decline in infant mortality in Massachusetts between 1880 and 1915.[34]

These developments in public health infrastructure are sometimes ascribed to the rise of knowledge, particularly contagionism and germ theory.[35] But the medical orthodoxy of miasma theory made nearly identical policy recommendations. It held that disease was caused by foul odours in particular locations (e.g. from sewer gases and dirty water), and could thus be prevented by improving sanitation, sewerage, and clean water supplies. If anything, sanitary policies were the speciality of the miasmatists rather than the contagionists until the end of the nineteenth century, as we shall see in chapter 5. It was not mainly scientific and medical knowledge of microbes, therefore, that led to the growth of state provision of sanitation, sewerage, and clean water.

What mattered much more were changes in how the state operated internally and how it responded to outside pressure. But what were these changes? What characteristics made it more likely that a state would implement sanitary measures? Did public sanitation depend on the developments stressed in the state capacity literature—fiscal capacity, centralization, and parliaments?

30. Hardy 1984, 257–8.
31. Hardy 1984; John Brown 1988; John Brown 1989a; John Brown 1989b; Aidt, Davenport, and Gray 2023.
32. L. Anderson 1984, 215–16.
33. Chapman 2019.
34. Alsan and Goldin 2018.
35. As argued by Troesken (2015, 38).

1.2. TAXES AND DIRT

Fiscal capacity was not the main determinant of sanitary regulation. The health inspectors that proliferated in Islamic cities after the ninth century and in European ones after the eleventh were paid by governments, but their salaries consumed a tiny share of municipal spending. Conversely, much richer local governments of later eras had plenty of fiscal capacity but most did not use it to pay for clean water, sewerage, and waste disposal until well into the nineteenth century.

The Grand-Duchy of Florence, for instance, had high per capita incomes and fiscal capacity—probably one of the highest in the early modern world. In the sixteenth century, the Florentine government paid *votapozzieri* (sewer-emptiers) to empty cesspits, dumping liquids into the river and selling solids to nearby farmers for manure. But in the early seventeenth century, the state withdrew from funding sewerage. Instead, it devolved the problem to urban landlords, who sold waste directly to farmers. The result was irregular waste disposal, river contamination, and riverbank damage. The Florentine government then restored the official *votapozzieri* but refused to pay them, shifting the fees onto landlords. But this resurrected the negative externality: why should an individual landlord pay to dispose of waste whose contagion risks mainly hit others? Florentine landlords passed on the charge to tenants, who in turn ignored the externality and failed to pay, causing cesspits to overflow and spread contagion to the city.[36]

Early twentieth-century Japan is another example of a state with considerable fiscal capacity—at least enough to fight a colonial war to capture and occupy Korea in 1910. But the Japanese state did not devote fiscal capacity to paying for waste disposal, even though newly occupied Seoul experienced severe epidemics. The Japanese colonial government blamed the "backward" Korean waste management system, whereby merchants collected human waste from houses every day free of charge, profiting by using it to manufacture fertilizer. The colonial state instead granted monopolies to Japanese sanitation companies to collect human waste in return for a monthly fee paid by each household. This led to manure shortages, higher prices, and lower profits, as well as declining sanitation and rising disease. Many poor Koreans were unable or unwilling to pay the fee, and the monopolistic Japanese companies collected only once every 10–20 days, so "shit piles up like mounds in and around people's houses".[37] The Japanese state had plenty of fiscal capacity for conquering and occupying colonies, but used it to serve the interests of political beneficiaries rather than to improve public hygiene.

36. Henderson 2019, 69.
37. Quoted in T. Henry 2005, 656–7.

This is not to say that fiscal capacity was unimportant for dealing with sanitary externalities. In England between 1845 and 1884, for instance, local governments made rising investments in water provision, which were associated with a significant reduction in infant and early childhood mortality. In 1872, it passed the Public Health Act, after which existing investments in clean water provision interacted with new investments in sewerage, amplifying the mortality benefits.[38] In early twentieth-century America, too, city governments that introduced filtration and chlorination of public water supplies experienced a noticeable reduction in diarrhoeal diseases, a huge reduction in typhoid mortality, and positive interactions between the declines in non-typhoid and typhoid infections.[39] Where governments allocated revenues to clean water and sewerage, citizens reaped non-trivial improvements in mortality. Fiscal capacity clearly mattered. But what made governments decide to spend their revenues in this way? Not all governments did so, even when they had the fiscal capacity. Other factors—notably state motivation and political realities—decided whether fiscal capacity was allocated to sanitary measures as opposed to other state purposes.

1.3. IS CENTRAL OR LOCAL GOVERNMENT DIRTIER?

In principle, public goods such as sanitation can benefit from both centralization and devolution. The central state can bang local heads together, counteract corruption and rent-seeking by local elites, and overcome cross-border spillovers where each locality seeks its own interests at the expense of others. But devolution also helps. Local government is better informed about local conditions (e.g. disease prevalence), responds more readily to local preferences (e.g. about public goods), and has multiple means of controlling its citizens (e.g. punishing risky waste disposal).

How did these countervailing pressures work out in practice? One study of the Black Death concludes that local autonomy was the key to epidemic control. Mid-fourteenth-century plague mortality, it argues, was significantly and substantially lower in cities that were autonomous instead of being governed by centralized princely governments.[40] Autonomous cities, the argument goes, "were in a better position to adopt swift and efficient measures against the pandemic than those governed by remote kings and emperors"—inspecting food and drink, regulating burials, and disinfecting victims' houses and possessions with vinegar and sulphur.[41]

---

38. Aidt, Davenport, and Gray 2023.

39. D. Anderson, Charles, and Rees 2022; M. Phillips et al. 2020; Beach et al. 2016; Ferrie and Troesken, 2008; Cutler and Miller 2005; Condran 1987.

40. Wang and Rodrígues-Pose 2021.

41. Wang and Rodrígues-Pose 2021, 1 (quotation), 3.

Does this study provide definitive evidence in favour of local autonomy? Probably not. It provides no direct evidence that autonomous governments adopted sanitary measures more than others. Nor does it show that sanitation was effective against the Black Death—food and drink inspections cannot have been, and it is unlikely that vinegar or sulphur did much good.[42] More fundamentally, its data on mortality and state classification may be too fragile to sustain the argument. The mortality data, other scholars have pointed out, derive from undocumented studies, fail to evaluate source quality, over-represent huge cities, are biased towards France, and conflate plague and non-plague deaths.[43] The state classification underplays the authoritarianism of urban elites, overestimates the inclusiveness of guild and citizenship rights, and ignores gradations between autonomous and non-autonomous government.[44] Sadly the data may not be robust enough to support the happy conclusion that local government helped you survive the greatest pandemic the world had yet experienced.

This does not mean that local governments were unimportant for disease-related sanitation, even if there is no strong evidence that sanitary measures helped to limit the Black Death. We have already seen how municipal governments in the early medieval Islamic world, late medieval Italy and Flanders, and many parts of early modern Europe allocated funding and attention to controlling disease. But central governments also mattered, especially when infectious waste spread beyond local boundaries. A leaky local latrine, as one German petition pointed out in 1873, not only infected its own immediate surroundings but created "typhoid ovens" and cholera "breeding grounds" that unleashed epidemics far downstream.[45] Only central governments had

42. Wang and Rodrígues-Pose (2021, 3) refer to Geltner (2020, which argues that urban sanitary measures long predated the Black Death) and to CitiesX (2018, which is a non-academic YouTube video about Venice). No evidence is provided that sanitary measures were adopted disproportionately in autonomous cities or were effective against the Black Death.

43. Wang and Rodrígues-Pose (2021, 2, 4) use the Black Death mortality data of Christakos et al. (2005. The latter derive much of their data from Biraben (1975), who does not provide references and concentrates on France. This precludes checking sources or assessing their reliability. For a discussion of the Christakos et al. data, see Roosen and Curtis (2018).

44. Wang and Rodrígues-Pose (2021, 3) acknowledge that "autonomous" cities were actually quite authoritarian: they denied citizenship rights to many inhabitants; they excluded women, servants, and minorities (such as Jews and Muslims); and they linked political participation to patronage by religious and noble authorities and membership of exclusive associations such as guilds. See Ogilvie (2021, esp. 189–90) on how putatively "inclusive" urban institutions could actually give rise to more "exclusive" outcomes because of their domination by local elites, whereas authoritarian rulers (especially negligent ones) could turn a blind eye to interstices within which non-elite urban inhabitants could flourish.

45. Quoted in John Brown 1989a, 6.

the authority to prevent local infectious waste from spreading downstream in river water or across country with night-soil carriers. Whether central states actually used their authority to do so is another question. States could fail in this as in other anti-contagion measures, as we shall see shortly.

Historical epidemics show that the key to controlling disease through sanitation was neither the greatest possible devolution to local government nor the highest possible degree of state centralization. Both in theory and in practice, controlling infectious waste required subsidiarity, whereby problems—including externalities—are addressed at the lowest level consistent with their resolution.[46]

1.4. HOW CLEAN ARE PARLIAMENTS?

What about the contention of the state capacity literature that parliaments will ensure that state capacity is directed to provide beneficial services to citizens? Were public sanitary measures that limited epidemics adopted mainly because of parliamentary pressure? The historical evidence suggests that parliamentary representation may, on average, have been associated with higher levels of public sanitary infrastructure. But parliaments were neither necessary nor sufficient for public sanitation, and sometimes acted to block it. What mattered was not so much whether there was a parliament but how it worked internally and how it responded to external pressures.

The Dutch Republic was the richest economy in early modern Europe, had by far the highest fiscal capacity, and also had unusually strong and active parliaments, with representative bodies at the central and provincial levels, and powerful town councils at the local level. It is also renowned for its private and collective focus on sanitation and hygiene from the early modern period onwards.[47] But even the most parliamentary government in early modern Europe failed when influenced by entrenched interests. In Leiden around 1600, for instance, the highly representative town council switched from providing public cesspits to having human waste flushed directly into the town canals, triggering recurrent severe epidemics. The council implemented this measure in response to lobbying by an oligarchy of local property owners, who saw this as a way to keep down their own costs.[48] Another dismaying example is provided by Mumbai local government during the 1896 plague epidemic. The municipal council of Mumbai was quite representative by contemporary standards, in the sense that Indians who satisfied a property qualification could

46. Føllesdal 1998.
47. Van Bavel and Gelderblom 2009.
48. Van Oosten 2016.

vote and stand for election to the council. But the council was dominated by property owners who opposed any sanitary improvements that might increase their taxes or infringe on their property rights. This hindered sanitary improvements that might have reduced infestations of rats that hosted plague fleas.[49]

This is not to say that representative government had no benefits. Even the oligarchical town councils and "parliamentary estates" of medieval and early modern polities were usually better than alternative forms of pre-modern governance. But the sheer presence of a representative body in government was not a magic bullet. What mattered was the specific structure of that representative body, the pressures exerted on it by its constituencies, and the incentives these structural features created to prevent contagion.

During the later nineteenth century, as we saw earlier, many European city governments gradually controlled cholera and typhoid by building sewerage and clean water infrastructure.[50] But the precise organization of municipal governance was crucial, as emerges from comparing Germany, England, and the United States.[51] England and the USA had higher per capita incomes than Germany and potentially greater fiscal capacity. In 1880, piped water was available in 47 per cent of English cities, compared with only 12 per cent of German ones.[52] But sanitary reform spread faster in German than in English or American cities. Municipal governance made the difference, in a surprising way. German cities allocated political power to a rich minority, who demanded clean water both to supply their factories and to create a less contagious environment for their own families.[53] American and English cities gave more power to middle-income voters, who resisted policies that would increase their tax bills to pay for social benefits that would accrue mainly to the very poor and the very rich. In America in particular, the "messy democracy of New England town meetings or urban ward politics" hugely increased the transaction costs of providing local public goods to reduce epidemic contagion.[54] The more authoritarian form taken by German town governments enabled them to move faster and more effectively than the more "democratic" forms in England or the United States. The structure of representative government, not its mere presence, made the difference.

49. M. Harrison 2012, 180.
50. John Brown 1988; Baldwin 1999, 128–9; Alfani and Melegaro 2010; Alfani 2022, 27, 32–3; Aidt, Davenport, and Gray 2023.
51. John Brown 1988, 316.
52. Gallardo-Albarrán 2020, 736.
53. John Brown 1988, 310.
54. John Brown 1988, 318.

2. Keeping People Apart

We also spread contagion by interacting with one another—working, shopping, selling, partying. When I meet people in person while infected, it leads
to costs that I myself do not incur. In principle, these negative externalities can
be curbed by governments. Indeed, by the later eighteenth century Enlightenment thinkers such as Adam Smith declared uncompromisingly that "those
exertions of the natural liberty of a few individuals, which might endanger the
security of the whole society, are, and ought to be, restrained by the laws of
all governments; of the most free, as well as of the most despotical".[55] Smith
was referring to financial conduct, though he applied the same principle to
infectious disease, as we shall see. Yet not everyone before or after *The Wealth of
Nations* took the same view. When did social distancing regulations arise? Were
they undertaken by both free and despotic governments, as Smith advocated?
Or did some states mandate social distancing and others not?

2.1. THE ORIGINS OF SOCIAL DISTANCING

Government action to limit social interaction during epidemics left little historical record before the Black Death. Lack of state capacity was probably not
the main reason, since we saw that local governments already had the capacity to impose sanitary regulations before the 1340s (and pursue even costlier
projects like warfare, which strongly affected public health, though not in a
good way). More likely, the lack of social distancing regulation before the
Black Death was because Europe and the Middle East had not experienced a
devastating pandemic since the Justinianic plague of the 540s. Lesser epidemics had of course occurred, but in the absence of sweeping, protracted, and
lethal pandemics there was less need for such intervention, and perhaps also
no institutional memory of it.

But almost as soon as the Black Death arrived in the late 1340s, governments started to regulate social interactions. From 1348 onwards, many Italian
states appointed plague officials and health boards whose task was to control
epidemic disease, often through what we now call "social distancing".[56] These
new government measures started out simple. But as waves of plague recurred
in the centuries after the Black Death, they developed into elaborate, multilay-
ered interventions. To prevent epidemics from moving into their territory from
outside, Italian states carried out health checks at political frontiers, rivers,
harbours, and mountain passes, and imposed quarantines requiring foreign
travellers to be isolated for a period in centralized units called *lazaretti* before

---

55. A. Smith 1776, 2:79.
56. Cipolla 1976, 11.

interacting with locals; we discuss these later when we look at cross-border externalities. To keep infection from crossing between localities inside their territory, governments isolated infected villages or towns, sometimes closed off whole regions using sanitary cordons, and required travellers to observe quarantines in isolation units. To stop infection from passing between individuals or households inside the same locality, governments issued stay-at-home orders, closed markets, and interned infected persons and their contacts in *lazaretti* or pesthouses.[57]

The fact that Italian governments began to devise social distancing measures soon after the Black Death arrived indicates that they believed they had sufficient state capacity to implement them—or planned to develop it as soon as possible. But even precocious Italian states devised such regulations gradually and took generations to develop the bureaucratic capacity to implement them consistently. Thus, although temporary shacks and sheds were soon built to intern the infected, the first permanent pesthouse was not erected until 1423 (in Venice).[58] In central and northern Italy, government anti-plague measures reached their apogee between 1550 and 1600, by which time states in this zone of Europe had managed to render themselves almost free of endemic plague, with epidemics flaring up only when plague was reintroduced from outside.[59]

But this happy state of affairs lasted for just a generation, before an ancient and ubiquitous aspect of state capacity—war—brought plague back to this wealthy zone, with its high state capacity and exceptional public health regulations. In 1629, German and French armies fighting the War of the Mantuan Succession crossed into northern Italy and moved south. The series of plagues this unleashed in the 1630s killed an estimated 30–35 per cent of the population of central and northern Italy. This was much higher plague mortality than that suffered in the seventeenth century by societies such as England and France, whose governments were much more backward in adopting social distancing against epidemics. The only other parts of Europe that suffered as terrible plague mortality in the seventeenth century were the German lands, also because of their involvement in continual warfare.[60] Even though Italian states continued to operate at full capacity to control the epidemics of the 1630s, the dark side of state capacity in the form of war overwhelmed the bright side in the shape of public health measures.[61]

57. Cipolla 1976, 12–30; Slack 1985, 45–6; Alfani and Melegaro 2010; Alfani 2013b; Alfani and Murphy 2017, 327–8; Alfani, Bonetti, and Fochesato 2023, 2.

58. Stevens Crawshaw 2012, 3.

59. Alfani and Murphy 2017, 329; Alfani, Bonetti, and Fochesato 2023, 2.

60. Alfani and Murphy 2017, 327–8; Alfani 2023a, 14–15.

61. See Henderson (2019), for instance, for a moving account of Florentine state capacity during the 1630–31 plague.

Other European governments imitated Italian social distancing regimes, but much later, with a clear contrast between southern and northern Europe. It was not until after 1450 that municipal governments in France implemented social distancing measures in response to plague outbreaks.[62] Austria was even later, with Vienna modelling itself on Venice in 1540 by appointing its first municipal "master of sanitation" and its first health council.[63] England was sluggish, too, as shown by the fact that as late as 1543, the King's Council wrote to the London aldermen to exhort

> such of you as have travelled in outward parts to set forth such devices to be put in execution . . . as you have seen there observed and kept; so as we may be seen to have learned that point of civility, and to have among us as charitable a mind for preservation of our neighbours, as they have.[64]

It was not until after the devastating English plague of 1563 that the queen's Padua-educated physician Cesare Adelmare suggested policies long prevalent in central and north Italian cities, "providing against plague and other calamities which aggravate poverty in London".[65] As late as the 1590s, the English traveller Fynes Moryson could still remark in astonishment that the Italians "are carefull to avoyde infection of the plague and to that purpose in every citty have Magistrates for Health".[66] The Southern Netherlands and Germany were also backward, as reflected in a 1633 letter from the Milan Health Board to its counterpart in Florence remarking how in Germany and Flanders "they are unmindful of the plague".[67] These contemporary comments referred to the full range of plague measures, of course, but social distancing was implied by expressions such as "preservation of our neighbours", "avoyde infection", and "unmindful". The Scandinavian societies were even more backward, with only occasional quarantine regulations in the sixteenth century, no compulsory urban health boards until 1857, and no isolation hospitals or pesthouses until the 1870s.[68] As late as the early seventeenth century, and in some cases for centuries longer, government epidemic measures in Europe covered a wide spectrum, with Italy by far the most advanced, England, Germany, and Scandinavia very backward, and France, Spain, and Flanders somewhere in between.[69]

62. Biraben 1976, 86–9, 102–5, 139–41, 174; Cipolla 1976, 11–15; D'Irsay 1927, 170, 176; Slack 1985, 46.

63. Velimirovic and Velimirovic 1989, 817.

64. Quoted in Slack 1985, 203.

65. Quoted in Slack 1985, 207–8.

66. Quoted in Cipolla 1973, 16.

67. Quoted in Cipolla 1976, 19.

68. Sköld 1996b, 509–11.

69. Slack 1985, 47.

These qualitative impressions are consistent with a quantitative analysis of the timing of key epidemic policies, especially social distancing. Table 3.1 shows the results of one scholarly study of plague measures in three major European zones: the Italian peninsula, the German lands, and England.[70] The study restricted itself to plague measures implemented by the state (both local and central) which are still recognized as "effective" according to modern epidemiological policy. It arrived at a list of 12 distinct measures. These progressed from defensive measures through active ones to institution-building, and finally to coordination beyond the local region. The findings in table 3.1 show clear differences across the three European zones. Overall, the north of Europe (Germany and England) was more than a century behind the south (Italy) in controlling travel, collecting information, enacting plague legislation, and cooperating across regions. The north not only trailed in implementing the measures pioneered in the south. It also failed to adopt certain measures at all, or adopted them in milder form. England and Germany disinfected less systematically, favoured home isolation over centralized internment, set up fewer plague agencies, enacted less plague legislation, and held back from allocating public funds to plague control.

England, as table 3.1 shows, caught up with Italy only after 1600. From the later sixteenth century, English local governments started to adopt some social distancing measures from continental European cities.[71] Almost all the action was undertaken by local rather than central government until around 1600, when the central state issued a series of important plague laws. These had five distinctive features that bred success—mostly because they harnessed the incentives and capacities of local governments, communities, and religious parishes. First, in 1604 the local regulations implemented by many but not all English towns were brought together into a national statute, whose provisions applied across the whole country. Second, measures previously adopted only in towns were extended into the countryside, even into tiny villages. Third, the regulations were funded through taxation, which was mandated centrally but levied locally, legally obliging local parishes to compensate their inhabitants for complying with stay-at-home measures. This was essential, since the poor "of necessity must be by some charitable course provided for, lest they should wonder [sic] abroad and thereby infect others".[72] Fourth, the central state mandated local risk-pooling, obliging adjacent parishes and sometimes entire counties to fund social distancing and compensate locked-down households in severely afflicted parishes.

70. Dinges 1994.
71. Slack 1985, 45–7, 200, 207–8.
72. Quoted in Champion 1993, 47.

TABLE 3.1. Chronology of Plague Measures in Italy, Germany, and England, 1375–1700

Plague measures		Country			Delay	
		Italy	Germany	England	Italy: Germany	Italy: England
DEFENSIVE PLAGUE MEASURES						
1.	Systematic control of access to the town	1485	1580	1600	95	115
2a.	Ship passports	1455	N/A	1640	N/A	185
2b.	Health passports	1570	1665	N/A	95	N/A
3.	Regular victim counts in the town	1400	1620	1585	220	185
ACTIVE PLAGUE MEASURES						
4.	Supervised separation of infected and contacts from healthy, in private dwelling	1525	1590	1595	65	70
5.	Establishment of plague hospitals	1460	1545	1555	85	95
6.	Provisioning of poor incarcer-ated persons using public funds	1460	N/A	1635	N/A	175
7.	Systematic disinfection/ destruction of possessions of plague victims	1375	N/A	1600	N/A	225
INSTITUTIONALIZATION						
8.	Temporary establishment of a "plague agency"	1460	1580	N/A	120	N/A
9.	Establishment of a permanent "plague agency"	1505	1580	N/A	75	N/A
10.	Comprehensive plague legislation	1455	1575	1580	120	125
SUPRA-REGIONAL COORDINATION						
11.	Regular information exchange with neighbouring territories	1550	1680	N/A	130	N/A
12.	Regular coordination of measures with neighbouring territories	1620	1700	N/A	80	N/A
Median year / mean arrears		1460	1585	1598	108	127

Source: Dinges 1994, 23 (policy definitions), 25–6 (country definitions), 42 (dates).

Notes: Date = middle year of period when measure reached its culmination. "Italy" = cities and territories of northern and central Italy; exemplifying the measures prevailing in southern France, Barcelona, and the northern margin of the Mediterranean. "Germany" = northern and southern Germany, excluding the Habsburg core provinces; exemplifying the measures prevailing in the Netherlands and Switzerland. "England" = England (not Great Britain). Delay = number of years elapsed between the date the policy was undertaken in Italy compared with Germany or England.

Finally, the new national legislation made stay-at-home orders much stricter but minimized internment of diseased, suspected, and convalescent in pest-houses (though partly because England had few existing hospitals).[73]

Neither central state nor local government in England could have created this social distancing system by itself. The central state had the fiscal capacity to fight expensive wars but lacked motivation to allocate central taxes to local social distancing measures. It was, however, able and willing to order local and county governments to allocate their funds to that purpose—a systematic, if variable, feature of the growth of state capacity in early modern Europe more widely.[74] Not only did the central state order each town or village government to levy plague rates, but by around 1600 it became increasingly willing to order plague rates to be levied from local authorities within a 5-mile (8 km) radius of a plague-struck locality, or even from the entire surrounding county.[75] During the 1604 epidemic, for instance, five-sixths of the funds spent to monitor and support infected households in Nantwich came from a plague rate levied on the surrounding county of Cheshire.[76] The Privy Council and the county authorities could oblige a local government that received transfers from neighbouring communities to reciprocate by setting up a local sanitary cordon to protect other communities from spillovers. In the 1636 epidemic in Presteigne, for instance, the county authorities threatened to stop bread deliveries from surrounding Radnorshire and Herefordshire if the town inhabitants "do wander abroad as heretofore they have done".[77] Local, county, and central governments had to work together and substitute for one another's deficiencies in order to make sure social distancing worked.

Some components of the English social distancing measures appeared elsewhere in early modern Europe. Italian states also based their early success on local government, ordered inhabitants into home lockdown, and spent huge sums to help citizens obey the regulations—as early as 1575–76 in Vicenza, Padua, and Palermo;[78] in 1630–31 in Bologna and Florence;[79] and in 1731 in Venetian-ruled Split.[80] What was distinctive in England was the interaction between central state and the lowest levels of local government, which standardized practice across urban governments, extended it to village councils, made it legally compulsory, banged local heads together, mandated

---

73. Slack 1985, 210–12; Columbus 2022.
74. Ogilvie 2023, 32.
75. Slack 1985, 266–7, 281; Tronrud 1985, 23.
76. Slack 1985, 279.
77. Quoted in Slack 1985, 268–9.
78. Alfani 2013a, 96.
79. Rose 2019, 162–3 (Bologna); Henderson 2019, 17, 136 (Florence).
80. Andreozzi 2015, 128.

inter-communal risk-pooling, and compelled cooperation among local, pro-vincial, and central government.

The social distancing measures devised by governments to deal with plague between 1350 and 1600 were adopted across the world in the centuries that followed, and were used to tackle smallpox, cholera, influenza, and many other contagions. Indeed, they were resurrected in surprisingly familiar form during Covid-19. Government social distancing measures took two main forms— general measures to create distance between everyone, and specific measures to isolate the sick from the well.

"General" social distancing measures were deployed by states to decrease contact between people whose disease status was unknown but who were statistically likely to include some diseased individuals. They took many forms. Some involved curfews, either of the whole population or of low-status subgroups such as women, children, immigrants, workers, or particular ethnic groups. Others ordered the closure of public places attracting large crowds in close proximity—markets, shops, taverns, theatres, churches, restaurants, schools, trams, metros, or trains. Finally, there were bans on leisure events such as games, dances, concerts, plays, and films, which required people to spend prolonged periods indoors at close quarters. Such enjoyable events were banned mainly because of fears of contagion, but they were also often portrayed as immoral and hence likely to attract supernatural retribution in the form of worse epidemic outcomes.[81]

These general behavioural measures varied in both design and enforcement, and were more effective for airborne diseases such as influenza and smallpox than for waterborne cholera and typhoid. Bubonic plague, typhus, and yellow fever, with animal and insect vectors, occupied a middle ground, since fleas and mosquitoes are attracted by humans and can pass from person to person in crowds. Given the variation in design, enforcement, and epidemiology, it is hard to assess the effectiveness of generalized social distancing measures for all diseases, but they were probably quite effective against airborne epidemics such as influenza. In the 1918 Spanish flu epidemic, for instance, American cities that implemented such social distancing measures most comprehensively reduced transmission rates by 30 to 50 per cent.[82] Likewise, American cities in which multiple social distancing measures were implemented early in the epidemic experienced 50 per cent lower peak death rates, shallower epidemic curves, and 20 per cent lower cumulative excess mortality.[83]

81. For a survey of social distancing measures during the 1918–19 influenza pandemic in the USA, see Tomes (2010, esp. 52–5).

82. Bootsma and Ferguson 2007.

83. Hatchett, Mecher, and Lipsitch 2007; the gap in cumulative mortality was less statistically significant than the gap in peak death rates.

The second type of social distancing measure was much stricter in both conception and enforcement. This involved much more specific and targeted rules to distance the sick from the rest of society. There were two main approaches—stay-at-home orders and centralized internment. Both approaches were developed by European states between 1350 and 1600 in the attempt to control plague epidemics. As smallpox emerged as a major epidemic threat in the seventeenth century, both home isolation and centralized internment were redeployed to deal with the new threat. In England, the smallpox "lodges" in rural communities were often small, housing individuals or families, but on the European continent, smallpox patients were often interned in large plague *lazaretti*, and in late nineteenth-century America they were confined in huge isolation hospitals.[84] When cholera broke out of India between 1816 and 1830, European states again redeployed the old plague and smallpox measures, and new states—such as Russia—adopted the centralized internment approach with military-style cholera "barracks". By the time of the 1918–19 influenza pandemic, by contrast, most governments were abandoning centralized isolation, though there were some emergency internments, which evoked vigorous protest. States abandoned centralized measures partly because of such popular resistance, partly because forced incarceration appeared increasingly incompatible with civil rights in democratic societies, and partly because infections were so numerous that existing infrastructure was in any case inadequate. During the epidemics of the twentieth and twenty-first centuries, most states favoured curfews, closures, bans on mass gatherings, and—when things got desperate—used home lockdowns. Centralized internment became largely a thing of the past.

2.2. LOCKING UP OR LOCKING DOWN?

Until the early twentieth century, however, most states used centralized internment and home lockdown side by side. But different states adopted a different balance between the two. In general, home lockdown was favoured in northern and western Europe, while centralized internment was commoner in the south and east of the continent, as well as in parts of the non-European world.

The European north–south divide—at least as far as England and Italy are concerned—emerged as early as the seventeenth century, as table 3.2 shows. One reason was that England did not have many existing hospitals that could be requisitioned for plague isolation, and English governments, communities, guilds, and religious organizations were unwilling to spend capital to build new pesthouses.[85] But even where a pesthouse was available in an English

---

84. Leavitt 1976, 557.
85. Van Steensel 2016.

TABLE 3.2. Centralized Internment during Plagues, 1485/1666

Place	Date	% of total population interned in pesthouses	% of quar- antined interned in pesthouses	% of plague deaths occurring in pesthouses	% of pest- house inmates who died
Milan	1485				34
Venice	1575–77	5.9			73
Padua	1575–77				50
Padua	1630			24–30	
Bologna	1630			24–30	
Venice	1630			15	
Florence	1630–31	13.8		43–71	55
Carmagnola	1630–31	20.8			28
Preston	1630–31		4.6		
Pistoia	1630–31				49–60[a]
Worcester	1637			25[b]	
Genoa	1656				70
Rome	1656–57			43–71	64[c]
London	1665	0.15			
Norwich	1665–66			10[d]	

Sources: Cohn and Alfani 2007, 197; Henderson 2019, 184, 187, 209; Henderson 2020, 271; Stevens Crawshaw 2012, 190–1; Weiner 1970, 42; Malanima 1998, 110–18; Alfani, Bonetti, and Fochesato 2023, 3; Slack 1985, 277; Davies and Saunders 2004, 35; France 1938, 61–2; Risse 1999, 210.

Notes:
[a] 60% for townspeople; 49% for inmates from rural areas.
[b] Described as "exceptional".
[c] From 24 June to 24 August 1656, mortality was 53% for men and 78% for women.
[d] Described as "more usual".

town, home lockdown greatly exceeded central internment. In Preston in 1630–31, for instance, less than 5 per cent of those placed under quarantine were interned in pesthouses, whereas in Florence and Carmagnola that year, internees made up 13.8 and 20.8 per cent of the entire urban population. In seventeenth-century Norwich only 10 per cent of plague deaths occurred in pesthouses, compared with 24–30 per cent in Padua and Bologna and 43–71 per cent in Florence. Worcester, with 25 per cent of plague deaths occurring in its pesthouse in 1637, was described as "exceptionally high".

In England, even when pesthouses were available, home lockdown was quantitatively more important. Figure 3.1 shows this pattern for the parish of

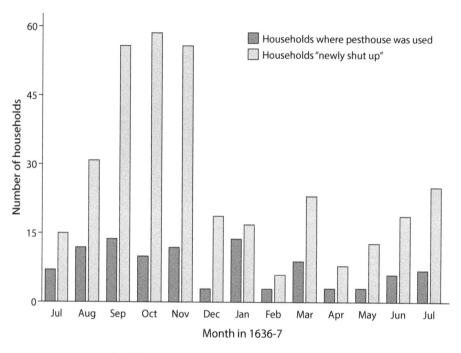

FIGURE 3.1. Home lockdown compared with pesthouse internment, London parish of St Martin-in-the-Fields, July 1636–July 1637. *Source*: Based on Columbus 2022, 17.

St Martin in the Fields in 1636–37. This parish had greater opportunities for central internment than most places in England because it was located in London, which had many more hospitals per capita than other English towns, though fewer than Italian ones. Yet in every month between July 1636 and July 1637, home lockdown vastly outweighed pesthouse internment in this parish.

Each approach to separating the sick from the well had its own costs and benefits. Centralized internment benefited from economies of scale through in-house surveillance, provisioning, and care. But it suffered from higher capital costs, lack of pesthouses in small towns and villages, stronger popular resistance, more internal cross-infections, and higher concern about spillovers into the surrounding neighbourhood. In the case of plague—though not smallpox, for which pesthouses were often used in the eighteenth century—centralized internment was based on the false assumption that the disease was transmitted person to person rather than via rats and their fleas. Home lockdown, by contrast, benefited from lower capital costs, easier extension into smaller towns and villages, weaker popular resistance, and lower risk of cross-infection. Its disadvantage was that surveillance, care, and provisioning could not reap scale economies by being carried out in a single location.

These differences partly explain why the balance between home lockdown and centralized internment differed across societies. Italian states used centralized internment to a greater extent because they had an existing infrastructure of hospitals before the Black Death, their welfare systems were more focused on centralized provision than out-relief, they were highly urbanized so could reap economies of scale, and they had higher initial state capacity in the medieval period, which eased internment, segregation, and surveillance. The English state favoured home lockdown because England had few existing hospitals, its welfare system was based mainly on out-relief, it was less urbanized so needed a solution for rural areas, and it had lower state capacity until around 1600, so was less able to enforce internment. Yet Italian states sometimes used home lockdown for citizens with less direct contact with the disease, when the scale of epidemics exceeded hospital capacity, or in rural settlements. Conversely, English local governments sometimes used centralized internment, building a few large pesthouses in urban centres during early modern plagues and many tiny ones in rural settlements during eighteenth-century smallpox epidemics. Even then, however, English smallpox pesthouses were found only in southern and Midlands parishes, which were larger on average than northern ones, could afford the capital costs, offered generous poor relief to induce paupers into internment, and were more trade-oriented so expected greater commercial benefits from keeping themselves smallpox-free.[86]

Which approach to social distancing was better? Revealed preference suggests that individual citizens strongly favoured household isolation over centralized internment. The rich and powerful used their wealth and privilege to stay out of pesthouses, while the poor and powerless evaded them whenever possible.[87] In the 1578 Milan plague, for instance, a Dominican monk complained that women in particular tended to conceal infections because of their horror of pesthouse internment.[88] In the 1665 Delft epidemic, two women were sentenced to the house of correction for trying to escape from the pesthouse.[89] In the Russian cholera epidemic of 1892–93, internees told doctors of "the terror they felt when they entered the cholera barracks, from which they thought there was only one exit—the grave".[90] In the 1910–11 plague in northeast China, thousands of families discarded relatives' corpses on streets, in gutters, in pits, under snow, or on frozen rivers for dogs to eat, in order to avoid pesthouse quarantine.[91] In the 1918–19 flu pandemic in Alaska, many Inuits were

86. Davenport, Satchell, and Shaw-Taylor 2018, 84; Davenport 2020a, 64–7, 74–80.
87. Alfani, Bonetti, and Fochesato 2023, 3, 5, 9; N. Murphy 2013, 154.
88. Carmichael 1998, 145.
89. Curtis and Han 2021, 60; Curtis 2021a, 9.
90. Quoted in Frieden 1977, 548.
91. Hu 2010, 310–11, 324.

rounded up from their cabins and placed in a single large building, putatively to increase the efficiency of their medical care, to which a number "responded to what they apparently perceived as incarceration in a deathhouse by hanging themselves".[92] In 1926, a description of the ideal Chinese plague isolation hospital took for granted that internees would seek to abscond:

> The danger of patients escaping must always be kept in mind. . . . [T]he plague compound should be surrounded by a solid high wall and carefully watched. As far as practicable, any possibility of escape should be counteracted by the design and management of the wards, so as to avoid those sad instances recorded in other localities where patients were shot down by the guards while trying to escape.[93]

In China in 2022, when the Shanghai police tried to enforce centralized internment against Covid-19, people resisted even when officers threatened retribution against their families.[94]

One reason for resistance was that conditions in internment were often horrific—so much so that one sixteenth-century Italian described a lazaretto as a *beccaria* (slaughterhouse).[95] If you were not already mortally ill, the pesthouse made it much more likely. In the 1575–76 Venetian plague, the stench and groans of the 8,000 patients in the Old Lazaretto were described as resembling Dante's inferno. One ward was packed with beds containing corpses, whose stench was so appalling that it had to be evacuated, disinfected, and have all the beds burnt.[96] In the Milan pesthouse in 1629, a public health official "went into a dead faint for the stinking smells that came forth from all those bodies and those little rooms".[97] In the Bologna lazaretto in 1630, a visiting cardinal declared, "Here you are overwhelmed with intolerable smells. Here you cannot walk but among corpses. Here you feel naught but the constant horror of death. This is a faithful replica of hell."[98] During the Prato plague of 1630–31, the state-appointed governor of the Hospital della Misericordia, which had annual revenues equal to that of the entire Prato municipal government, refused to provision the pesthouse, creating such acute hardship that in March 1631 the surviving inmates staged a mini-rebellion "because the hospital's superintendent refused to send food".[99] Employees in Florentine pesthouses in 1630–31 stole bed sheets, bed covers, and food, worsening the already

92. Crosby 2003, 250.
93. Quoted in Benedict 1993, 73.
94. Z. Zhang and Gardner 2023, 5
95. Stevens Crawshaw 2012, 144.
96. Stevens Crawshaw 2012, 143; Risse 1999, 205.
97. Quoted in Risse 1999, 207.
98. Quoted in Risse 1999, 208.
99. Cipolla 1973, 82.

wretched conditions in the isolation wards and creating even stronger incentives for people to avoid internment.[100] Even the well-organized and lavishly funded Monticelli pesthouse in Florence during the relatively mild plague epidemic of 1633 had four to five patients to a bed, crammed together in an atmosphere of fetid air and "abominable filth".[101] The one pesthouse where mortality outcomes in the 1630 plague suggest that conditions were better than the poor would have experienced in their own homes was that of the small north-west Italian town of Carmagnola, which was so generously funded that it caused a local fiscal crisis; Carmagnola may thus be the exception that proves the rule.[102] Home lockdowns, when supported by supplies of food and water, typically provided much better living conditions.

Pesthouses were particularly dangerous places for socially vulnerable groups such as women and Jews. In the 1578 Milan plague, women did anything they could to avoid the pesthouses, where they feared sexual abuse while alive and public nudity when they died.[103] In the Carmagnola pesthouse in 1630, women's mortality was significantly higher than men's, either because they received inferior care or because they themselves were required to tend the sick.[104] In the Florentine lazaretto of San Miniato in 1630, a nurse reported that a number of female inmates had been raped.[105] In the Rome San Bartolomeo lazaretto, in the first two months after its opening on 24 June 1656, approximately equal numbers of men and women were admitted, but female mortality was 78 per cent, compared with only 53 per cent for the men.[106] For Jews, too, risks were intensified by pesthouse internment. In the 1680 Bohemian plague epidemic, one Jewish memoir described how being consigned to the manorial lazaretto

> would involve grave danger, for the fact would become known to the inhabitants of the villages, who are mostly wicked men, thieves and murderers, lying in wait for the blood and the property of Jews. Even in the cities they love to oppress and rob them in their houses, how much greater then was the danger of their coming to murder us in the forest.[107]

100. Henderson 2019, 267.
101. Quoted in Henderson 2019, 199.
102. Alfani, Bonetti, and Fochesato 2023, 18–19.
103. Carmichael 1998, 145.
104. Alfani, Bonetti, and Fochesato 2023, 15; the mortality gap prevailed among those interned while still healthy, suggesting that it was pesthouse conditions that were particularly bad for females.
105. Risse 1999, 208.
106. Risse 1999, 210.
107. Quoted in Jeremy Brown 2022, 81.

Not just women and Jews, but many ordinary people suffered physical and psychological abuse in centralized internment. In Russia in 1892–93, as we shall see, the cholera barracks were pervaded with systematic brutality that violated inmates' physical integrity and denied them spiritual and emotional consolation.[108] Home lockdowns were safer for all, but especially for the weak and vulnerable.

Pesthouses were also dangerously infectious. Often they inadvertently mixed together infected and uninfected people in the same space, increasing mortality for the uninfected. Diagnosis was difficult in any case before the discovery and acceptance of germ theory after 1861, as we shall see in chapter 6. During epidemics, governments had to deal with huge numbers of cases, so most health boards sent suspected and infected to the same places, or sent suspected plague patients to ordinary hospitals when specialized pesthouses were unavailable.[109] In Amiens before 1544, the pesthouse housed only those obviously infected with plague, but from that year onwards it interned suspects and contacts alongside those who definitely had plague.[110] In the 1555 Venetian epidemic, when the prior of the Old Lazaretto was unable to keep internal order because of his own illness, plague patients and body-clearers mixed with staff from the prior's residence.[111] In the 1645 plague, the Scottish burgh of South Leith built "ludges" (pesthouses) to isolate the infected, but it was nothing unusual when its session clerk David Aldinstoune wrote in 1646 that the parish had been "visited with the plague of pestilence in such sort that the number of the dead exceeds the number of the living; and amongst them it cannot be discerned who are clean and who are foul".[112] Even in large, rich, and sophisticated cities such as Florence, where the suspected and convalescents were interned separately from the truly infected, misdiagnoses meant that healthy suspects were often cooped up with ill suspects and falsely convalescent.[113] Small wonder that one of the doctors employed by the Florentine Health Board in 1630 remarked that "everybody feared the *Lazaretto* and burial there more than death itself".[114] As late as the 1910 plague epidemic in north-east China, quarantine internment stations spread plague to the many uninfected people interned there by ignorant officials.[115] Home lockdowns avoided such institutionally transmitted cross-infections. Centralized intern-

108. Frieden 1977, 548.
109. Risse 1999, 203.
110. N. Murphy 2013, 155.
111. Stevens Crawshaw 2012, 145–6.
112. Quoted in Oram 2007, 22 (spelling modernized). On the Leith "ludges", see Rosie (2020).
113. Henderson 2019, 215–16
114. Quoted in Henderson 2019, 227.
115. Benedict 1993, 69.

ment was not a death sentence, but sometimes came uncomfortably close, as with the mortality rates of pesthouse inmates shown in table 3.2, which averaged 53 per cent, ranging from a minimum of 28 per cent in the small town of Carmagnola in 1630–31 to 73 per cent in the great city of Venice in 1575–77.

It might be argued that plague patients objecting to centralized internment were simply refusing to recognize the negative externalities their infection imposed on others. Did centralized internment at least reduce contagion in the surrounding community? Here, the balance is less clear. Home isolation, if poorly enforced, could create multiple nodes of community infection. But a pesthouse, unless carefully sited and policed, created a concentrated pool of infection that could spill over into the wider community. In the Florence plague of the 1630s, *lazaretti* spread plague into the surrounding community via admission and discharge of patients, delivery of provisions, and frequent escapes by desperate inmates.[116] In Gothenburg in 1875, the smallpox pesthouse in the old Kronan poorhouse formed a node of infection which erupted into a severe smallpox epidemic in the wider community.[117]

Plague lazarettos, smallpox pesthouses, cholera barracks, lepers' asylums, quarantine stations, and isolation hospitals attracted popular hostility precisely because those living nearby knew that contagion sometimes spilled out into the neighbourhood. In seventeenth-century China, lepers' houses located near population centres suffered violent attacks and were sometimes burnt down by vigilantes.[118] One reason the total capacity of all London pesthouses taken together was only 600 during the Great Plague of 1665–66 was that well-off Londoners opposed building of additional facilities near their own residences for fear that they would operate as nodes of contagion.[119] In England in the 1870s, the general public resisted construction of smallpox hospitals on the grounds that they increased infection in the surrounding neighbourhood.[120] In Milwaukee during the 1894–95 smallpox epidemic, the crowded southside neighbourhood was the main seat of smallpox in the city, for which its residents blamed the local isolation hospital, pressing for this "pesthouse" to be moved outside the city limits because it was a "menace to the health of citizens".[121] As late as the 1940s, local governments in China accused lepers' asylums of stoking hostility in nearby neighbourhoods by failing to keeping their inmates inside.[122]

116. Cipolla 1973, 52–3; Henderson 2019, 193.
117. Sköld 1996b, 511.
118. Q. Liang 2009, 65.
119. Columbus 2022, 9.
120. Sköld 1996b, 511.
121. Quoted in Leavitt 1976, 557–8.
122. Q. Liang 2009, 163, 203, 289n145.

Governments were fully aware of the risk that pesthouses and isolation units would export infection. But they seldom had the capacity or the incentive to take measures to isolate a pesthouse from the surrounding community. A few early modern pesthouses were constructed on islands or riverbanks, if appropriate sites were available—as in Venice with its lagoon islands or Regensburg with its natural Danube island.[123] A few cities created artificial islands by diverting streams, while others at least tried to locate the pesthouses in the east so the prevailing western winds would not blow their miasmas towards other, usually richer, neighbourhoods.[124] But most pesthouses were established in large, densely populated metropolises, which had the fiscal and bureaucratic capacity to build, provision, and operate them; few small towns or villages could afford such establishments. In cities like Florence, Milan, and Paris, pesthouses tended to be located in the middle of ordinary residential neighbourhoods, into which they diffused infection. Even when rivers made water isolation possible, the authorities did not always take advantage of it. In Paris, the Seine possessed a drainage stream which always contained running water so could have been used to provide a natural barrier to infection. But when the Hôpital Saint-Louis pesthouse was planned and built in 1607–12, it failed to take advantage of this feature. The Saint-Louis pesthouse was not built on an artificial island or even in the east of the city to take advantage of prevailing winds. Indeed, the walls that were supposed to ensure its isolation from surrounding neighbourhoods were penetrated by a church and by three gates that were not even equipped with external masonry.[125]

It was not until the last few decades of the nineteenth century that governments took serious action to move some pesthouses from the midst of urban neighbourhoods to riparian or marine locations. By the 1870s, Chinese lepers' asylums were being increasingly set up on rivers, as in Canton, where "several anchorages are set apart on the river for boats in which they [lepers] are accommodated", although capacity constraints in the main lepers' asylum also played a role.[126] In England, it was not until the 1880s that smallpox pesthouses began to be moved to riverbanks or mid-river boats.[127]

As far as controlling epidemic mortality was concerned, which approach to social distancing was better? For the Black Death, we cannot say—both because the morbidity and mortality evidence is so fragile and because the first social distancing measures were only gradually devised, implemented, and improved in the century and a half after 1350. We know that Black Death

123. Jetter 1970, 115.
124. Jetter 1970, 115.
125. Jetter 1970, 115–17.
126. Q. Liang 2009, 108.
127. Sköld 1996b, 511.

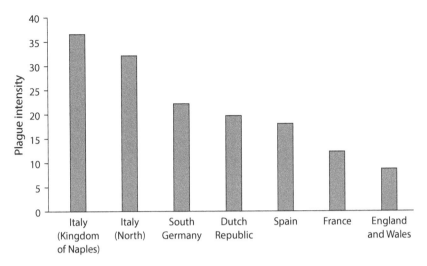

FIGURE 3.2: Plague intensity in western Europe during the seventeenth century, calculated as the cumulative number of victims throughout the century as a percentage
of the population as of 1600. *Source*: Based on Alfani 2020b, 202.

mortality varied greatly from one place to another. But for the reasons discussed earlier when we looked at public sanitation, the quality of the data is
insufficient to demonstrate statistically significant differences between different
institutional regimes.[128]

We do, however, have cross-country comparisons of plague mortality during the seventeenth century, the next most lethal phase of the second plague pandemic. Figure 3.2 shows, for seven European societies, the
"plague intensity", defined as the cumulative number of plague victims across
the seventeenth century as a percentage of each society's population in 1600.
England, which relied mainly on home lockdowns, had a plague intensity
below 10 per cent, while Italy, which relied more on centralized internment,
lay above 30 per cent.[129] This does not mean home lockdown was better than
centralized internment. Many other things differed between Italy and England
in the seventeenth century—climate, geography, urbanization, religion, occupational structure, warfare, welfare provision, and the broader institutional
framework. Plague mortality may have been higher in Italy because of longer

128. For an attempt to establish such differences, see Wang and Rodríges-Pose (2021). For
criticisms of the data on both mortality outcomes and institutional regimes, see Roosen and
Curtis (2018).

129. Alfani 2020, 202. Another striking difference is that the figures for northern Europe
reflect multiple plague outbreaks across the century, while the Italian figures are for a single
outbreak (northern Italy 1629–30, southern Italy 1656–57).

summers, more campaigning armies, higher urbanization, more religious processions, more large and multigenerational households, falling fiscal capacity, lower local welfare expenditures, or any combination of those factors. Locking people up in pesthouses may have played little role.

What we can say is that centralized internment was not the only way for governments to contain epidemic contagion. Even in the early modern period, state-mandated home isolation was a feasible option. It was widely used for almost the whole population in early modern England, and for rich and privileged citizens even in Italy. Reliance on household lockdown rather than centralized internment in the early modern period did not hike up plague mortality in England to anything like the Italian level in the seventeenth century. Conversely, Italian pesthouses do not appear to have been very effective in reducing plague mortality in the seventeenth century. According to some studies, indeed, there is little evidence that they were effective even during the two centuries after the Black Death.[130]

The empirical findings on centralized internment show that throughout much of the history of plague, smallpox, cholera, and influenza epidemics, the state had sufficient capacity to intern those suspected of being infected. But it typically lacked capacity, motivation, or both to ensure that the citizens it interned were also correctly diagnosed, humanely treated, and prevented from exporting contagion to the surrounding community. As a consequence, both inmates and neighbours voted with their feet—often literally—in evading, resisting, and sometimes attacking internment hospitals. By the early twentieth century, most modern states were using their capacity to bring about social distancing through mechanisms that avoided centralized incarceration.

2.3. SOCIAL DISTANCING AND STATE CAPACITY

What characteristics made it more likely that a state would implement effective social distancing during epidemics? Did success depend on the developments stressed in the state capacity literature—fiscal capacity, centralization, and parliaments?

Government social distancing measures required a minimum fiscal capacity simply because of the enormous costs of provisioning poor people so that they would not go out to work, beg, find food, and infect others. In Italian pesthouses, as we have seen, provisioning was always a major problem: either inmates were deprived of sustenance or they were fed and warmed and the state coffers imploded. In early modern England, supporting the poor in household lockdown always amounted to at least double the normal annual

---

130. Stevens Crawshaw 2012, 10.

income of the urban corporation, and sometimes five or six times the normal level.[131] As one London parish lamented during the Great Plague of 1665, social distancing could not be maintained without comprehensive and expensive home support: "All have liberty lest the sick poor should be famished within doors, the parish not being able to relieve their necessity".[132]

But modern levels of fiscal capacity were neither necessary nor sufficient for public social distancing measures. Early state social distancing demonstrates that it was not necessary. Eleventh-century China had low fiscal capacity, for instance, yet in 1089 the prefect of the city of Hangzhou funded the establishment of a public infirmary, creating a model for the eleventh-century system of Chinese public infirmaries, which sought to segregate the seriously ill and minimize the spread of infection.[133] Nor was fiscal capacity sufficient for state social distancing measures. The sixteenth- and seventeenth-century Ming state had enough fiscal capacity to subsidize ineffective medicines and the Imperial Academy of Medicine, but allocated none of it to quarantines or social distancing.[134] London had the highest fiscal capacity in England, but the royal physician Theodore de Mayerne described its plague policies as completely inadequate.[135] A minimum threshold of fiscal capacity was clearly necessary for states to implement social distancing and especially to provision the locked-down poor. But above that threshold level, political will played a more important role in deciding whether fiscal capacity would actually be allocated to social distancing measures.

What about state centralization? The central state is often essential since it alone has the coercive power to compel recalcitrant local authorities to adopt health measures, oblige better-off local inhabitants to subsidize local quarantines, resolve internal conflicts inside local governments, force less infected localities to pool risks with more infected ones, and (as we shall see) take account of cross-border externalities among different localities and regions. In the 1630–31 Cambridge plague epidemic, for instance, town, university, and county authorities found it so difficult to cooperate that ultimately the Royal Council had to intervene, mandating regular meetings of town and university, supporting plague rates and watchmen, recommending new quarantine tactics, and building forty "booths" outside the town where the infected could be isolated with attendants.[136] In the 1690–92 epidemic in the Kingdom of Naples, likewise, municipal officials concealed plague cases for fear of trade bans and

131. Slack 1985, 281.
132. Quoted in Slack 1985, 282.
133. Leung 1987, 136.
134. Leung 1987, 141–2; M. Harrison 2012, 11.
135. Slack 1985, 219.
136. Slack 1985, 220.

failed to enforce travel restrictions so as not to offend local bigwigs. The central state had to appoint a vice-regal official with absolute power to impose anti-contagion measures, ride roughshod over local objections, and requisition local tax funds to relieve the poor during lockdown.[137] In the United States in 1898, similarly, state governments argued that they should regulate quarantine because they were better informed about local businesses, but the surgeon general pointed out that local officials were tempted to yield to vested interests by weakening quarantine, leading to local epidemics, counter-measures by other localities, and stoppages in inter-state commerce. The only way to prevent this downward spiral was for quarantine to be controlled by the federal government, which was more insulated from local interests and could bang local heads together.[138] The same problem arose in Italy during the Covid pandemic in 2020, when clashes between different layers of government severely compromised national capacity to coordinate pandemic management. Only after several crucial months elapsed, during which the central Italian state more or less kicked regional governments into submission, did social distancing and other aspects of Covid contagion control improve.

But maximum state centralization was not the key to effective social distancing, either. Local governments collected more and better information, fostered multiplex ties with local citizens, and reflected local preferences about public goods, improving local motivation and compliance. From the Black Death onwards, local governments often moved decisively to implement social distancing, sometimes compensating for central neglect or intransigence. In 1377, hardly a generation after the Black Death, the first quarantine in recorded history was devised by the local government of Ragusa (modern Dubrovnik), a small city-state that had until recently been part of the vast Venetian empire.[139] In early modern England, the rapid transition from tardy social distancing during the two centuries after the Black Death to a well-funded and pervasive system of lockdowns and quarantines after 1600 was almost wholly thanks to effective local government, in cooperation with communities and church parishes.[140] During the Covid pandemic, too, lower levels of government played a major role in social distancing across the world. In Brazil, for instance, President Jair Bolsonaro's erratic stance at the centre was counteracted by more well-directed and effective policies at the provincial and local level.[141]

137. Fusco 2017, 106, 108.
138. M. Harrison 2012, 127–9.
139. F. Carter 1972, 113; Alebić and Marković 2017.
140. Slack 1985, 45–7, 200, 207–8.
141. Barberia and Gómez 2020.

In practice, therefore, neither extreme devolution nor maximum centralization was the key to effective governmental social distancing measures. Rather, what was needed was subsidiarity—dealing with problems at the most immediate level consistent with their resolution. In the most successful cases, central and local government operated independently in the spheres in which they were most effective. Sometimes centre and locality cooperated, sometimes they clashed, but both were beneficial, since the two levels of government curbed and compensated for each other's failures.

What about the role of parliaments? The central and north Italian city states were not exactly parliamentary, but they did benefit from representative government in the form of city councils. The degree of representativeness in these councils and the extent to which they curbed the executive varied greatly. Nonetheless, the consultation they enabled between government and governed may have contributed to the effective development of social distancing measures in central and northern Italian states from the Black Death to 1600. Similarly, the development of effective social distancing measures against plague in early modern England probably owed something to the growing effectiveness of its parliamentary government, although one must ask why this did not emerge until the second half of the sixteenth century. The single most important contribution of the English Parliament to anti-contagion measures took place from the 1560s onwards, with the promulgation of welfare laws and plague ordinances obliging local governments to levy plague rates from better-off citizens, extending them into the countryside, and mandating epidemic risk-pooling across local boundaries. This does not mean that the English Parliament never did anything harmful. In the Great Plague of 1665–66, it twice failed to pass the necessary legislation because of the narrow self-interest of the House of Lords in seeking exemptions for its own members. Local authorities had to step into the parliamentary vacuum with highway watches, gate guards, inn inspections, travel tracing, boat quarantines, home lockdowns, and even building a few pesthouses.[142]

But the fact that pre-modern parliaments sometimes failed to act to limit epidemics is not to say that alternative forms of governance were better for social distancing overall. As in the case of public sanitation, so too with social distancing measures, even the oligarchical representative bodies of early modern polities were usually better than alternative political systems. Nonetheless, the sheer presence of a representative body was not a magic pill. What mattered was which interests were represented in that body, how much influence they had over its decisions, and how strong incentives they had to control contagion.

142. Slack 1985, 223–5.

3. Getting Jabbed

The bright side of living in society is that we do not just inflict negative externalities on our fellow citizens, creating costs for others on top of the costs we ourselves incur. We also create positive externalities, where some action of mine creates a benefit for others on top of the benefits I myself enjoy. When I keep bees, I get honey but my neighbours get their orchards pollinated. When I get vaccinated, I immunize myself but also protect everyone I meet. If my keeping bees or getting immunized creates benefits for others, society would like me to do more of it than if I were acting altogether selfishly. In principle, non-market institutions can make everyone better off by inducing me to get immunized.

3.1. VARIOLATION AND THE STATE

Immunization, as we saw in chapter 2, started centuries before Jenner invented vaccination. People were practising smallpox variolation in China at latest from 1560, in the Ottoman lands and north Africa from around 1670, and in England and the USA soon after 1720. Markets, as we have seen, helped spread variolation among paying customers. But not everyone could afford it, and many neglected it out of ignorance, indifference, or fear. For them, the individual benefit was not worth the cost. In principle, this is where the state could have stepped in, creating incentives for people to create social benefits by getting immunized.

In practice, governments did this late, feebly, or not at all. Ordinary people in Ming China had practised variolation since the mid-sixteenth century, but the Manchu Qing dynasty that took over in 1644 ignored the practice until 1679. Even then, it acted flaccidly in replacing "smallpox apartheid" with variolation—at first it only introduced the practice in the Qing court to protect the ruler, later only among the military, and even in the eighteenth century it did not undertake any formal intervention in society at large but just provided informal recommendations.[143] In Europe, too, the state did little to reap the positive externalities of variolation—in many cases quite the contrary. England became the epicentre of variolation after 1720, but through government inaction. The most important thing the English state did for variolation was to refrain from banning it. In other European societies, the state was more active— and not in a good way. In France, the state required all new medical techniques to be approved by the Paris Faculty of Medicine, which banned variolation until 1768.[144] In Spain, the state granted veto power to medical associations

---

143. Hanson 2011, 109–10, 122–3.
144. G. Miller 1957, 187–94

and Catholic clergy until the 1770s. This was not from lack of knowledge but rather from a failure of politics, since in 1774 the Enlightenment-influenced minister of state Campomanes demanded in outrage, "What excuse could we have not to give the population such important aid?"[145]

Even states that encouraged variolation did so ineffectively. The Swedish state banned variolation until 1756, and even then bowed to monopolistic medical associations, as we shall see in chapter 6, excluding the commercial, religious, and philanthropic variolators who increased supply and reduced cost in England.[146] In eighteenth-century Prussia, as in China, the monarch personally favoured the practice, encouraged it for his family and soldiers, but did not deploy state capacity to diffuse it among ordinary citizens.[147] In Russia, likewise, Catherine the Great introduced the practice only in her own charitable establishments and among her own enserfed peasants.[148]

Central state capacity thus failed—or at best stayed inactive. But local governments stepped into the breach. In England from the 1760s on, parish councils in the Midlands and south organized "general inoculations" of all paupers or even all susceptible inhabitants, funded by local taxes.[149] Local authorities saved welfare funds by paying to variolate the poor rather than treating smallpox victims, burying the dead, and caring for orphaned survivors. Burying 25 smallpox victims, it was pointed out, cost nearly as much as variolating a parish of 545 inhabitants.[150] Collective variolation was seldom mandatory, but was often a tacit condition for getting welfare support.[151] Local paupers were rewarded after a general inoculation, as in Quainton and Stoney Stratford in the 1770s, when they were given a lavish feast and entertained with "people adorned with ribbons . . . maurice dancing, ringing of bells, [and] bull-baiting".[152]

But England also illustrates the weaknesses of local government. Local initiatives varied widely. General inoculations were almost never undertaken outside the south and Midlands. Northern parishes were poorer, so could not afford the fees for variolation or the welfare payments to induce paupers to accept it. They were less commercialized, decreasing their susceptibility to economic disruption if a natural smallpox epidemic occurred, the opportunity costs of failing to control contagion, and thus their motivation to undertake expensive anti-contagion measures.[153]

145. M. Bennett 2020, 152, 200; Ramírez 2018, 140–1.
146. Sköld 1996a, 249–53.
147. M. Bennett 2020, 53–4, 177–8.
148. M. Bennett 2020, 54.
149. Davenport 2020a, 76.
150. Razzell 1977, 91.
151. M. Bennett 2020, 46–7; Davenport 2020a, 67–8, 76; Vialls 1999, 266.
152. Quoted in Leadbeater 2020, 41.
153. Davenport 2020a, 64–5, 74–7, 79–80.

Local governments often depended heavily on persuasion, information, and funding from philanthropists or local elites. In Chester in the 1780s and 1790s, the pioneering physician John Haygarth established a Smallpox Society to campaign for variolation.[154] In 1788 the well-off vicar of Luton personally funded general inoculation and promised to continue his support in future years.[155] In Scotland in the 1790s, general inoculations on remote islands were sponsored by affluent parishioners.[156] Where links to civil society were weaker, so too was local government action.

Local governments took the initiative in promoting variolation in many societies throughout the world, even after the invention of the superior technique of cowpox vaccination. In the eastern Transvaal in the eighteenth century, when news of a smallpox epidemic arrived, a tribal headman would travel to the epidemic locality, collect pus from a sufferer, bring it back to his kraal, infect a 10-year-old boy, and then use the boy's pus to variolate everyone in the kraal.[157] In early nineteenth-century Ethiopia, the ruler of the Tigre region officially ordered all his subjects to get variolated.[158] Later in the nineteenth century, as soon as smallpox arrived, local chieftains in Ethiopia ordered general inoculation, giving rise to a reported variolation rate of 20 per cent by 1912.[159] In Burkina Faso in 1926, "the village chief declared that each time a case of smallpox appeared, the whole population must be inoculated with smallpox pus".[160] In the northern territories of the Gold Coast as late as 1932, the Isala tribe went so far as to impose compulsory variolation.[161] In 1949, according to a contemporary observer, "Compulsory inoculation was practiced in northern Ghana, virus taken from a person suffering with the disease being placed in an incision in the wrist and rubbed in".[162] In nineteenth- and early twentieth-century southern China, the leaders of adjacent Hakka villages drew up a roster of children in need of variolation ("the smallpox children"), engaged a commercial variolator, and shared expenses across inhabitants of all villages involved.[163]

The problem with local governments was that they were local. They mainly cared about local inhabitants and local finances. But the advantages of variolation crossed local boundaries. Variolated locals who emigrated conferred

154. Davenport 2020a, 67.
155. M. Bennett 2020, 46–7.
156. Davenport 2020a, 80.
157. Herbert 1975, 550.
158. Pankhurst 1965, 347.
159. Herbert 1975, 548.
160. Quoted in Schneider 2009, 209.
161. Bader 1986, 81.
162. Quoted in Bader 1986, 81.
163. C.-L. Liu 2016, 117.

benefits on their destinations. Non-variolated immigrants inflicted local costs, but were hard to persuade to be variolated without offering them local welfare support. Dealing with these cross-border externalities required action by the central state, which was seldom forthcoming.

The role of the state in variolation was not determined by sheer state capacity but rather by how that capacity was directed. England had one of the highest-capacity states in eighteenth-century Europe, but its central government took no step—apart from inaction—to reap the social benefits of variolation. France and Spain were also high-capacity states, and the Spanish state allocated higher absolute amounts to non-military purposes than the English one.[164] But Spain and France used their state capacity to oppose variolation, harming society at large. What mattered was not state capacity but state motivation and the political pressures it had to manage in the wider society—as in France and Spain, where the Church and monopolistic medical associations opposed variolation in their own interests.

Nor was centralization the answer. On the contrary. Where state institutions acted to reap the social benefits of individual variolation, they were local. In England, Ethiopia, Burkina Faso, Ghana, and southern China, local governments covered the costs of variolation, provided individual inducements, or imposed compulsion. Inevitably, however, such initiatives did not cover all of society, depended on local conditions, stopped at the borders of parish or village, and could not reap all the benefits of immunization to society beyond the local area.

3.2. VACCINATION AND GOVERNMENT

Vaccination with cowpox posed an even starker cost–benefit analysis, as we saw in chapter 2. In pre-modern Europe before immunization, 95 per cent of people in Europe caught natural smallpox. The disease killed an estimated 10 per cent of people in rural areas and 20 per cent in towns. Someone who caught it infected 50 per cent of their social contacts. Vaccination led to fewer breakthrough infections and had a much lower mortality rate (0.0002 per cent) than variolation (at 1.6 per cent). Vaccination caused no risk of serious cross-infection, unlike variolation, which could transmit smallpox to a non-immunized contact. The one down side was that while successful smallpox variolation protected the patient for life, cowpox vaccination gave complete protection only for 3–5 years, partial protection for 10–20, and for best results required re-vaccination.[165]

---

164. Torres Sánchez 2007, 443; Ogilvie 2023, 35–7.
165. M. Bennett 2020, 12, 15, 21; Krylova and Earn 2019.

Vaccination, like variolation, had private benefits, since it protected the individual recipient. And like variolation it also had social benefits, since it protected the recipient's contacts, whose non-infection in turn protected further contacts. Vaccination prevented not only disease and death but economic damage from private market withdrawal and public lockdowns. Vaccinating someone created less value for that person than for society. So individual demand for vaccination was not as high as society would want it to be. In principle, by encouraging individuals to get vaccinated, an institution like the state could make society better off.

With vaccination, as with variolation, local governments moved faster than central states. Soon after its invention in 1796, vaccination was taken up by local authorities—not just in England but all over Europe, even in Spain and France where variolation had been banned for so long. As early as 1801, a local mayor in the Baztán Valley in the Spanish Basque region asked for help from a French Basque village across the border, which sent a physician with a little girl to transmit vaccination arm to arm with the children of Baztán.[166] In 1803, the mayor of Orleans sent two community officers to Paris, accompanied by a local child to be vaccinated so his lymph could be used to vaccinate the children of Orleans.[167] In 1804, the town council of Rota, north of Cadíz, eagerly accepted the offer of the Economic Society of Sanlúcar to provide vaccine for the whole community.[168] During the 1807 smallpox epidemic, the mayor of Mornant, near Lyon, publicly exhorted citizens to vaccinate their children.[169] The central state was just permissive. It did not forbid local governments to vaccinate citizens, unlike with variolation. But it did not itself move quickly to take positive action.

Local governments had lower fiscal and bureaucratic capacity than central states. So they depended more on local elites and civil society to organize vaccination—just as with variolation. The local government of the Württemberg village of Botnang began a vaccination programme in 1801, for instance, but communal opposition erupted when a vaccinated child died of an unrelated illness. The Württemberg court physician intervened, offering to waive his fees for a seriously injured Botnang man if the village let him vaccinate 20 children. The local pastor used this external lever to persuade the community and local council to reverse its anti-vaccination stance, making Botnang one of the first villages in Germany to adopt comprehensive smallpox vaccination.[170] In similar manner, Boston and Philadelphia organized general

166. M. Bennett 2020, 203.
167. M. Bennett 2020, 158.
168. M. Bennett 2020, 217.
169. M. Bennett 2020, 163.
170. Cless 1871, 105–8; Wolff 1998, 110.

vaccinations in 1816, which succeeded by mobilizing members of ward-based committees to go from door to door persuading and assisting every household to get vaccinated.[171]

Local governments had less coercive power than central states, so they resorted to subsidies and cash rewards. The selectmen of the Massachusetts town of Milton offered vaccination in 1809 for a token fee of 25 cents, which over a quarter of its citizens agreed to pay.[172] The English town of Norwich in 1812 not only offered free vaccination for the local poor but promised half a crown to any pauper who could produce a vaccination certificate.[173] These local initiatives prefigure the four principles of successful vaccination inducements in modern pandemics: cash payment, certain receipt, immediate delivery, and sufficient size.[174]

The one coercive lever local authorities had was welfare control. In 1811, for instance, the small Berkshire town of Hungerford ordered all poor inhabitants who refused vaccination to be removed to a pesthouse, and in 1824 went so far as to deprive them of poor relief.[175] In 1819, the mayor of Thetford in Norfolk listed all non-vaccinated inhabitants and threatened them with "public exposure".[176]

Central governments moved much more slowly than local ones to reap the social benefits of individual vaccination. As table 3.3 shows, while the first European states did so within 10 years of the invention of vaccination in 1796, others waited for generations and some for over a century. Of the 33 European states in the table, 18 made vaccination compulsory between 1805 and 1827, after which a quarter of a century passed before Britain legislated in 1853, followed by another 18-year gap before a new surge of legislation between 1871 and 1903. Timing thus varied hugely across states even in the same continent, as did the precise legislative package and the degree of enforcement. What caused these differences?

The state capacity literature, as we have seen, regards parliaments as a key to ensuring that state capacity is used for socially beneficial purposes such as controlling epidemics. The medical history literature, by contrast, tends to take the opposite view. The great medical historian Erwin Ackerknecht, for instance, theorized that parliamentary governments will be less willing to com-

171. M. Bennett 2020, 292.

172. M. Bennett 2020, 286–7, 292.

173. Baldwin 1999, 253.

174. Brewer et al. 2022, 1–2. Such payments can be very effective, even in modern rich societies: in Sweden in 2021 a payment of 200 kronor (about $24) increased Covid-19 vaccination rates by 4.2 percentage points from a baseline of 71.6% (Campos-Mercade et al. 2021, 879–80).

175. Baldwin 1999, 255.

176. Quoted in M. Bennett 2020, 372.

TABLE 3.3. Compulsory Smallpox Vaccination Laws in European States, 1805–1946

Location	Date	Regime type	Source
Germany, Hessen (grand duchy)	1805	Authoritarian	1
Italy, Piombino and Lucca (principality)	1806	Authoritarian	2
Germany, Bavaria	1807	Democratic	3
Germany, Erfurt	1807	Authoritarian	4
Denmark	1810	Democratic	5
Germany, Schleswig-Holstein	1810	Democratic	6
Germany, Waldeck-Pyrmont	1811	Authoritarian	7
Norway	1811	Democratic	8
Russia	1812	Authoritarian	9
Germany, Baden	1815	Democratic	10
Germany, Hessen (electoral)	1815	Authoritarian	11
Sweden	1816	Democratic	12
Germany, Nassau	1818	Democratic	13
Germany, Württemberg	1818	Democratic	14
Germany, Oldenburg (grand duchy)	1819	Authoritarian	15
Germany, Hessen-Homburg	1820	Authoritarian	16
Germany, Hannover	1821	Democratic	17
Germany, Trier	1827	Democratic	18
Britain	1853	Democratic	19
Netherlands	1871	Democratic	20
Germany, empire	1874	Authoritarian	21
Germany, Prussia	1874	Authoritarian	22
Germany, Saxony	1874	Democratic	23
Switzerland	1886	Democratic	24
Hungary	1887	Authoritarian	25
Italy	1888	Authoritarian	26
Austria	1891	Authoritarian	27
Romania	1893	Authoritarian	28
Turkey	1894	Authoritarian	29
Portugal	1899	Authoritarian	30
France	1902	Democratic	31
Spain	1903	Authoritarian	32
Belgium	1946	Democratic	32

Location	Date		Regime type	Source
	Mean	**Median**		
Authoritarian (n = 17)	1852.8	1874		
Democratic (n = 16)	1842.8	1819.5		
All (n = 33)	1848.0	1821		

Sources: [1] M. Bennett 2020, 195, 362. [2] Baldwin 1999, 247, 264. [3] Baldwin 1999, 255; S. Williamson 2007, 104; Kübler 1901, 179. [4] Baldwin 1999, 260. [5] M. Bennett 2020, 195; S. Williamson 2007, 104; Kübler 1901, 174, 188. [6] Kübler 1901, 174. [7] Huerkamp 1985, 623; Rupp 1975, 113. [8] Kübler 1901, 174. [9] M. Bennett 2020, 228; S. Williamson 2007, 104 [10] Mühlhoff 2021, 5; Kübler 1901, 179. [11] Kübler 1901, 179. [12] Baldwin 1999, 257, 263; M. Bennett 2020, 197, 365; Kübler 1901, 173, 187. [13] Kübler 1901, 179 (1818); Rupp 1975, 112 (1820). [14] Mühlhoff 2021, 5; S. Williamson 2007, 104–5; Kübler 1901, 179. [15] Baldwin 1999, 261. [16] Rupp 1975, 111. [17] Baldwin 1999, 260; Kübler 1901, 179; Rupp 1975, 107. [18] Baldwin 1999, 262. [19] Baldwin 1999, 259; M. Bennett 2020, 375. Compulsion repealed 1898. [20] Blume 2006, 628. [21] Baldwin 1999, 261, 263; Mühlhoff 2021, 23. [22] Baldwin 1999, 261. [23] Huerkamp 1985, 625. [24] Kübler 1901, 341. Compulsion soon abolished in many cantons. [25] Kübler 1901, 377; Statista 2018. [26] Rolleston 1933, 189; Kübler 1901, 377; Statista 2018. [27] Kübler 1901, 376. [28] Kübler 1901, 377. [29] Kübler 1901, 379. [30] Garnel 2014. Conditional on serum quality (1899); condition fulfilled (1911). [31] Baldwin 1999, 266. [32] Devos 2021.

Notes: Democratic = government subject to meaningful constitutional or parliamentary checks; authoritarian = lacking such checks.

promise individual and business interests to ensure epidemiologically beneficial outcomes, while authoritarian states will ride roughshod over obstacles.[177]

The 33 European countries in table 3.3 support neither view. Democratic governments passed compulsory vaccination laws a bit earlier on average than autocratic ones (1843 compared to 1853). This might seem to support the state capacity literature. But each regime type showed huge internal variation. In a simple linear regression, the difference between the two regime types was not statistically significant and explained less than 2 per cent of variation in the date of compulsory vaccination laws. Whether a state was German played a much bigger role, despite the absence of German political unification until 1871. In a multiple regression, German states imposed compulsory vaccination 42.5 years earlier than non-German ones, while regime type remained insignificant.[178] The irrelevance of regime type is consistent with the history

177. Ackerknecht 1948.
178. The adjusted R-squared was 0.2496, i.e. the multiple regression including regime type and the German variable explained 25% of the variation in the date of vaccination laws across European countries.

of vaccination in particular European countries. In France, for instance, compulsory vaccination was imposed not under the authoritarian first Napoleon but rather in 1902 under the democratic Third Republic.[179] Democratic Britain imposed compulsory vaccination in 1853, repealed it in 1898, and further weakened it in 1907. In democratic Switzerland, too, soon after compulsory vaccination was enacted in 1886, many cantons democratically repealed the mandate.

A sophisticated variant of the Ackerknecht argument was proposed by Werner Troesken, who estimated a regression of smallpox mortality rates against GDP per capita across 28 countries in 1900 and found the U-shaped relationship shown in figure 3.3.[180] Very poor and very rich countries had the highest smallpox mortality, while middle-income ones had the lowest. Troesken argued that this arose from the Ackerknechtian pattern whereby authoritarian states were good at reducing epidemic mortality because they forced through public health measures such as vaccination mandates. However, such states were bad for economic performance because other forms of state compulsion damaged the economy. Democratic states, Troesken argued, were good for economic performance because they did not restrict productive decisions by individuals, but bad for reducing epidemic mortality because they guaranteed individual rights against public health measures. The countries at the far left of the curve in figure 3.3 had both low state capacity (hindering public health measures) and poorly functioning markets (hindering economic performance), resulting in low per capita incomes and high smallpox mortality. The countries in the middle had greater state capacity, which facilitated both compulsory vaccination and coercive economic policy, resulting in low smallpox mortality but also poor economic performance. The countries at the far right of the curve had democratic state institutions that reduced economic coercion (increasing per capita GDP) but also hindered coercive public health measures (increasing smallpox mortality).[181] Troesken based this intuitive account of the U-shaped cross-country relationship mainly on the case of the United States, where a high degree of representative democracy did often block vaccination laws.

Does effective public health policy indeed require authoritarian government, which harms economic dynamism? Fortunately not. The regression analysis underlying figure 3.3 explains smallpox mortality using just one variable—per

179. Baldwin 1999, 330–3.

180. Troesken 2015, 99. The regression explains 25.6% of the variance in smallpox mortality in 1900, and the coefficients on both GDP per capita and its square are statistically significant at conventional levels.

181. Troesken 2015, 97–9.

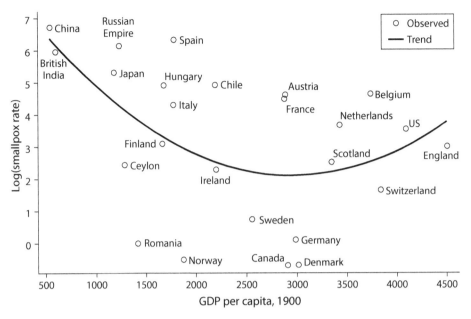

FIGURE 3.3. Smallpox mortality versus GDP per capita, 28 countries, 1900.
Source: Based on Troesken 2015, 97.

capita GDP. Rich countries are on average more democratic than poor ones.[182]
But rich and poor countries also differ in many other ways. Rich countries are
more urbanized, and natural smallpox mortality was twice as high in towns as
in the countryside. Rich countries had larger service sectors, more trade, more
labour migration, and better transport, opening them up to flows of people and
goods carrying epidemic disease.[183] Higher smallpox mortality may result from
these variables as well as, or instead of, democratic government.

Moreover, even if the higher smallpox mortality in rich countries derived
partly from democratic freedoms, this does not mean that all forms of democratic government are bad for public health. In the case of the USA, the source
of Troesken's intuition, what blocked vaccination laws was not so much that
the political regime was democratic. Rather, American democracy had two
special features that enabled a small minority with very strong opinions opposing vaccination mandates to overpower a large majority with less deeply held
preferences favouring mandates. First, the USA had a distinctive form of feder-
alism, which made it possible for individuals to sort themselves into very small
communities of like-minded individuals, and gave those communities massive political power. Second, the American Constitution obliged public health

182. Dasgupta and Weale 1992, 128, 130; Prados de la Escosura 2022b, 61–4.
183. M. Bennett 2020, 96.

authorities and school officials to obtain explicit legislative authority before enacting compulsory vaccination orders.[184] In a wider perspective, there were many democratic states that lacked these idiosyncratic American features and readily passed vaccination laws. The characteristics of the state that mattered for public health consisted not so much of authoritarianism versus democracy but rather of specific political configurations.[185]

What light do vaccination laws shed on the three features of state capacity emphasized in the literature? Fiscal capacity did not play a major role. In 1805 when the first vaccination laws were passed, the highest fiscal capacity in Europe was found in the Netherlands (with per capita state revenues equivalent to over 20 days' wages for an urban unskilled worker), followed by France (14.3 days), England (13.5), Portugal (12.7), and Prussia (12.3).[186] Yet these five states passed relatively late vaccination laws: the Netherlands in 1871, France 1902, England 1853, Portugal 1899, and Prussia 1874. The average date of national vaccination laws for these high-fiscal-capacity states was 1880, compared with 1848 for the whole sample of 33 European states in table 3.3. Fiscal capacity estimates are unavailable for the nine German, Italian, and Scandinavian states that passed national vaccination laws between 1805 and 1811, but their fiscal capacity was unquestionably much lower than that of the five great European military powers (the Netherlands, France, England, Portugal, and Prussia). The tenth European state to pass a vaccination law was Russia (in 1812), where per capita fiscal capacity was 6.2 days' wages, less than half that of England and less than one-third that of the Netherlands. Fiscal capacity was not clearly associated with national vaccination laws.

Nor was state centralization. In 1800, England and France were highly centralized by any standard, and Prussia was highly centralized compared with most other German territories. Yet none of these three centralized states passed national vaccination laws until after 1850, France not until after 1900. In all three, moreover, local governments played a leading role in public vaccination campaigns. In Britain, as we have seen, local governments organized general vaccinations before 1810, long predating the national Vaccination Act of 1853.[187] In Prussia, many local governments made vaccination practically compulsory in their districts between 1810 and 1825, openly risking disapproval by the central government, which failed to legislate until 1874.[188] In France, national legislation was passed in 1902 but was so poorly enforced that in a 1913 epidemic the Marseille local government sent out vaccination squads to

184. Troesken 2015, 99.
185. Baldwin 1999, 331–8.
186. Freire Costa, Henriques, and Palma 2022, table 1; Karaman and Pamuk 2010, 615.
187. M. Bennett 2020, 104, 372; Baldwin 1999, 253; Batniji 2021.
188. Kaiserlichen Gesundheitsamte 1888, 103–7.

immunize over 90,000 people in working-class neighbourhoods.[189] In some of the most centralized states in Europe—as also in federal states such as the USA—it was local government that took the initiative in reaping the social benefits of vaccination.

Nor were parliaments the key to mandatory vaccination, as we have seen. In the German south and in parts of Scandinavia, states with strong parliaments passed early vaccination laws between 1807 and 1816. But Britain, with the "mother of parliaments", passed such legislation only in 1853 and repealed it in 1898, while highly parliamentary Switzerland passed a national law only in 1886, which was promptly repealed by popular democratic movements in several cantons. The highly democratic United States never passed compulsory vaccination and had only 10 states with vaccination laws as late as 1930. Parliamentary government could go both ways when it came to public health. Standard measures of state capacity thus do not explain whether a state was likely to make individuals take account of the social benefits of their private immunization decisions.

4. Getting Informed

Information is one way we limit infection. If we know an epidemic is around, how fast it is growing, what its risks are, and what we can do about it, we can make better decisions about avoiding and controlling it. But information is a public good—non-rival and non-excludable. Non-rival means that my consumption of a fact does not prevent you from consuming it. Non-excludable means that you can often consume a fact even if you have not paid for it. Because I find it hard to get anyone to pay me for information, I will produce and diffuse less of it than would benefit society at large. Non-market institutions may be better than markets at producing and diffusing information. The state, for instance, may benefit us all by providing information that no one can profit from by selling on the market.

4.1. STATE INFORMATION

Since the Black Death at latest, states have been collecting information about epidemics. In March 1348, as we saw in the chapter epigraph, the Republic of Venice established a prototype public health board whose task was "to consider diligently all possible ways to preserve public health and avoid the corruption of the environment"—that is, to compile information about the epidemic and how to circumvent it.[190] In Florence, too, the state paid doctors in 1348 to carry

189. Baldwin 1999, 266.
190. Cipolla 1976, 11.

out post-mortems on Black Death victims "in order to know their illness more clearly".[191] From 1452 to 1755, the Milan Health Board kept Books of the Dead, which not only registered all plague deaths but required that "university-trained physicians—not parish priests, other clerics, or gravediggers—evaluated the corpses, gathered the reports of symptoms, and pronounced the cause of death".[192] From 1457 to 1590, the Barcelona city council sought to calm panic and deter citizen flight during epidemics by ordering parishes to deliver a precise count of plague deaths, "so that the truth of the matter may be known, because many untrue things are said about the number of dead".[193] In the 1540s the Danish state ordered the Copenhagen local authorities to draw up lists of epidemic deaths, which were regularly produced, though they survive only in scattered examples.[194] In Mexico in the 1576 epidemic of cocoliztli (probably an indigenous haemorrhagic fever transmitted by rodents), the Spanish viceroy convened doctors to investigate the causes of the disease, and ordered them to carry out post-mortems.[195] Sixteenth- and seventeenth-century Italian health boards systematically collected information in order to provide early warnings for public health policies.[196] In 1622, the Manchu state created a "smallpox investigation agency" to which any suspected infection was to be reported, after which agency officials would diagnose and isolate the patient to prevent contagion. In 1644, when the Manchus conquered China, where smallpox was much commoner, they strengthened this government information-collection system.[197]

The English state, as we have seen, lagged behind many other parts of Europe in anti-contagion measures until around 1600. So little English-language literature on epidemics existed that the government relied on trans-lations from Italian and French.[198] But the English state did pioneer a specific public information source, the Bills of Mortality, which assisted contagion control in London from the early sixteenth century on.[199] In 1519 Cardinal Wolsey, the Lord High Chancellor, ordered periodic tallies of the number of deaths in the capital to ensure that the royal court had advance warning of epi-demics. City office holders supported it. "Ancient matrons", sometimes assisted by surgeons, were paid to visit houses and report plague cases. Parish clerks

191. Quoted in Park 1985, 3–4.
192. Cohn and Alfani 2007, 178.
193. Quoted in R. S. Smith 1936, 84–5.
194. P. Christensen 2003, 420.
195. Wieser 2023, 161.
196. Cipolla 1976, 12–30; Palmer 1982, 94–5; Slack 1985, 45–6; Alfani and Melegaro 2010; Alfani 2013b; Alfani and Murphy 2017, 327–8.
197. Chang 2002, 180–1, 189.
198. Slack 1985, 201–26; Mauelshagen 2005, 261.
199. Hull 1899, lxxx–xci.

drew up lists of vital statistics. From 1593 onwards, the Bills of Mortality were printed in broadsheet form. During an epidemic, you could buy a copy of that week's Bill of Mortality from the official clerk of London.[200] Other English local governments followed suit, as when the corporation of York ordered every parish to provide a weekly certificate of mortality on the London model in 1604, a year when 30 per cent of York inhabitants were dying of plague.[201] People eagerly consumed all this information, so much so that in 1610 the state considered censoring it for fear that the bills were damaging trade and causing panic "to the public hurt". Fortunately, however, the English government decided against censorship on the grounds that formal information was better than informal rumour and actually calmed market sentiment.[202]

The societal benefits of collecting epidemiological information were explicitly recognized in the 1660s by John Graunt, famous to this day as a pioneer of epidemiology and demography, the inventor of the concept of excess mortality. Graunt was a London haberdasher and draper. But he was also a self-taught mathematician and data nerd, who applied his mathematical interests, honed in the shop, to the Bills of Mortality. He used plague deaths to analyse change over time, geographical variation, gender differences, and associations between plague and other variables. Graunt's social status as a modest tradesman was explicitly lauded by Charles II, who in 1662 recommended his election to the Royal Society, urging "that if they found any more such Tradesmen, they should be sure to admit them all".[203] This was because in 1662, Graunt published a book analysing the data from the London Bills of Mortality. He introduced it by acknowledging that the bills had previously been used just by individuals to calibrate their own decisions to withdraw from the market during epidemics: "a Text to talk upon in the next company, and withal in the Plague-time, how the Sickness increased or decreased, that the Rich might judge of the necessity of their removal, and Trades-men might conjecture what doings they were likely to have in their respective dealings". But Graunt pointed out that collecting information like this had wider advantages: "I thought that the Wisdom of our City had certainly designed the laudable practice of taking, and distributing these Accompts, for other, and greater uses, than those above-mentioned".[204] In summing up his findings, Graunt asked why we should care about all these nerdy details anyway: "To what purpose tends all this laborious buzzling, and groping?" His charming answer was that "there is much pleasure in deducing so many abstruse, and unexpected

200. Morabia 2013.
201. Palliser 1973, 54, 56.
202. Slack 1985, 245.
203. Quoted in Sutherland 1963, 539.
204. Graunt 1662, preface, 1.

inferences". But he also argued that analysing information was necessary for "good, certain and easie Government".[205] Graunt was clear that epidemiological information was important for the governance of society.

The London Bills of Mortality were not a pure state initiative. Multiple institutions and individuals supported their success. Collecting the information relied on local government, church parishes, guilded surgeons, and individual women (even though females were denied any formal role in government, church, or guilds). Diffusing the information relied on market institutions to sell the weekly bills, the pamphlets based on them, and Graunt's book analysing them. Graunt himself used "the Mathematiques of my shop-Arithemetique" to process the raw data into "information", which was incidentally useful for both individuals and the government. But he neither sold his information on the market nor was paid by the state to produce it, though he was rewarded retrospectively by market sales of his book and by royal endorsement of his election to a voluntary scientific association—a mark of great intellectual esteem. Nor is there any actual evidence that the beautifully tabulated information and quantitatively informed analyses that Graunt produced were used by governments of the time.[206] It is therefore hard to regard the Bills of Mortality in general or John Graunt's analysis in particular as a pure product of state capacity.

But the afterlife of the London Bills of Mortality reveals how they helped civil society influence subsequent state policy. Throughout the eighteenth century they served a purpose that no one expected in the 1660s—to support arguments in favour of smallpox variation, not just in England but all over Europe. In 1722, the English physician James Jurin used the bills to calculate that the death rate from natural smallpox was 1 in 7 (over 14 per cent), compared with a death rate from variolation, based on the evidence he collected from his correspondents, of just 1 in 49 (2 per cent).[207] The Bills of Mortality were also used to support anti-contagion measures in France since, as d'Alembert pointed out in his 1765 treatise advocating the legalization of variolation, France did not have any such lists and hence had to rely on English evidence.[208] In 1761, the Berlin churchman and public health pioneer Johann Peter Süßmilch used the London Bills of Mortality for 1728–57 to support his calculations that natural smallpox had an 8 per cent death rate, compared with 0.3 per cent for variolation. This, he argued, meant that a ruler should spare no costs in widely diffusing information about variolation, "out of love for his people and country, and especially for the sake of [increasing] population and his own advantage".[209]

205. Graunt 1662, 73–4.
206. Morabia 2013.
207. Berti 2021, 12.
208. G. Miller 1957, 228–9.
209. Süßmilch 1761, 2:440.

But all this information and knowledge was not enough in itself to sway state policy. Neither the Prussian king nor Berlin local bureaucrats nor the Prussian medical establishment was yet willing to act on such epidemiological information, for reasons we shall explore in chapter 6.[210]

In the event, it took centuries for governments to develop the capacity to collect systematic epidemiological information—and even longer to process it into intelligible public health advice, a job they still perform imperfectly. A generation or so after Graunt, the polymath Gottfried Wilhelm Leibniz exhorted German states to set up health councils to apply quantitative analyses of mortality statistics to health planning.[211] A century later, between 1779 and 1827, the Austrian court physician Johann Peter Frank wrote a nine-volume work on "medical policing", outlining how the state should collect information to drive public health surveillance.[212]

Despite such exhortations, the systematic public collection of epidemiological information developed only gradually. Where it emerged, it was not solely, or even mainly, because of central government. It continued to rely on a broad set of organizations—local government, communities, religious organizations, guilds, voluntary associations—as well as the initiative of enthusiasts like John Graunt. For a surprisingly long time, compiling data on infectious diseases was dominated by individuals, such as J. C. Moore for smallpox in 1817, William Farr for influenza in 1847, John Snow for cholera in 1854, and August Hirsch for influenza in 1881.[213] Formal state infectious-disease notification systems did not appear until the later nineteenth century—Japan in 1875,[214] Italy in 1881, Britain in 1890.[215] In the United States, Michigan was the first state to introduce it, in 1893, although the obligation did not spread to all American states until 1925, and it is still a matter for states rather than the federal government.[216] Globally, it was not until around 1948 that the World Health Organization was established and not until 1965 that it set up an epidemiological surveillance unit to compile information about communicable diseases.[217]

Ever since the Black Death, therefore, the state has itself been collecting information about epidemics. But for many centuries it relied heavily on civil society organizations and private individuals to do the information collection, analyse the resulting data, and even make policy recommendations.

210. Penschow 2022, 63.
211. Thacker and Stroup 2013, 22.
212. Frank 1779–1827.
213. Beveridge 1991, 225; Simonsen et al. 2016, 381.
214. Jannetta 1987, 151.
215. Thacker and Stroup 2013, 22.
216. Thacker and Stroup 2013, 25–6.
217. Thacker and Stroup 2013, 26.

The twentieth century saw a huge growth of government information collection, cross-border information sharing, and the establishment of international organizations for disease notification and medical communication. But
even after this expansion of government information collection and diffusion, a
fundamental problem remained. Did all this public information actually reduce
epidemic contagion? Would contagion have been higher if states had not collected and communicated it? What were the incentives of states to diffuse
accurate information or to act on it themselves?

What matters is not just whether epidemiological information is collected
and diffused, but how it is used. Public information is not always used well, as
we shall see shortly. During the 2020 Covid pandemic, for instance, a study
of 76 countries found that state information campaigns about epidemic contagion had ambiguous effects. In countries where trust in government was
already high, public information campaigns decreased infections and deaths.
But where trust in government was low, public information campaigns had
no impact.[218]

Why do the governed not always trust the information provided by the
government? Why does state information not always improve epidemic outcomes? History provides some answers. States, like markets, can fail, even
when it comes to public goods like information.

4.2. STATE IGNORANCE

One problem is ignorance. The state will improve on the information people
collect for themselves only if it compiles, processes, and interprets the facts
accurately. When it comes to epidemics, many states are unable or unwilling
to undertake that work. Throughout history, as we have seen, states typically got information about epidemics by working with non-government
organizations and individuals. Even nowadays, few states have in-house capacity to collect, process, and interpret information well, because their personnel
lack expertise.

States started seeking expert advice on disease well before the Black Death.
Since about 1250, a central or north Italian state often employed a *medico
condotto*. This public medical officer was supposed to treat the poor for free
and advise on public health measures, though also to give tips on how best to
torture prisoners.[219] When the Black Death arrived, some individual physicians issued public advice "for the safety of the men of the city" and quickly
published treatises on the new pestilence.[220] During this greatest of all known

218. Farzanegan and Hofmann 2021.
219. Park 1985, 89–93; Henderson 1992, 145–6.
220. Quoted in Henderson 1992, 146.

pandemics, therefore, conduits already existed for information exchange between experts and the state.

But these conduits should not be romanticized. When Florence set up its first plague commission in 1348, not a single medical professional was invited to serve.[221] Hardly any Italian state health boards included medical experts for the three centuries after the Black Death.[222] English local governments behaved similarly, as in 1603 when Bristol set up a plague committee with no medical members.[223] Early modern German plague regulations seldom referred to medical advice before the late seventeenth century.[224] Even in northern Italy, where after the 1530s doctors increasingly served on health boards, governments often ignored their advice.[225]

Identifying disease was beyond the capacity of most governments, with or without medical advice. Plague created surprising uncertainty despite its distinctive buboes, as in Florence in 1630 when health officers could not decide if the new infections were really plague, so they failed to act until the epidemic was out of control.[226] Nearly three centuries later, during the 1905–7 plague epidemic, officials in north-east China were ignorant about the nature of the disease, quarantine and prevention, and any language enabling them to communicate with Russian officials across the border.[227] When the epidemic returned in 1910, many Chinese government personnel were ignorant of plague symptoms and too illiterate to comprehend written information, so they often misdiagnosed plague as other diseases (or vice versa).[228] Poor government information exacerbated contagion in two ways: uninformed officials often interned the healthy, fostering cross-infections, and official ignorance undermined popular confidence, encouraging evasion of public health measures.[229]

Medical professionals themselves were deeply divided about the nature and cause of infectious disease. Until germ theory was formulated in 1861, most European doctors held to the ancient view that disease arose from individual patients' "humours", which interacted idiosyncratically with unhealthy "miasmas" emanating from particular locations. A minority espoused the heterodox view that disease was caused by "contagion" from infected humans, animals, or objects, but they were often censored or persecuted by their professional associations, as we shall see in chapter 6. Official medical advice to governments

---

221. Park 1985, 97.
222. Park 1985, 98n42; Cipolla 1976, 21–2; Palmer 1978, 74–5.
223. Udale 2023, 125.
224. D. Christensen 2004, 203.
225. Cipolla 1976, 22.
226. Cipolla 1973, 41–2.
227. Hu 2010, 302.
228. Hu 2010, 318.
229. Benedict 1993, 69.

was often based on ancient ideas that epidemics were caused by miasmas, humours, or psychological weaknesses such as "fear" and "panic".[230]

Governments were unable to judge between contagionist and non-contagionist advice and often guessed wrong. In 1852, the Danish government followed "miasmatic" medical advice and dismantled the quarantine system, unleashing a terrible cholera epidemic the following year.[231] Even after 1884 when the German physician and microbiologist Robert Koch discovered that cholera was caused by "the comma bacillus", government policy responses frequently ignored any scientific understanding of the disease.[232] During the 1918 influenza pandemic, many governments based policy on non-scientific notions, as when the Chicago public health commissioner refused to implement any social distancing measures on the grounds that "worry kills more people than the epidemic."[233] This echoes some political leaders during Covid-19, with their claims that the epidemic was mainly caused by "coronaphobia".[234]

Ignorance led governments to blame epidemics on particular social groups. As we saw in chapter 2, poverty increased an individual's probability of catching a disease. So governments blamed epidemics on poor people. In Spain in 1556, the court physician ascribed pestilence to the "vile, coarse and base poor who crowded together and lived in narrow and tight quarters like suckling pigs".[235] In the 1585 Edinburgh plague, one of the first steps the authorities took was to expel all "vagabonds, strange and idle beggars, and disordered people".[236] In Madrid in 1598, a royal medical official ascribed epidemics to "the corruption that comes from [poor people's] breath, dirty sweat, and corrupted sores of their own making, alters and corrupt[s] the air, generating diseases and typhus and at times even plague".[237] In the 1910–11 Chinese plague epidemic, local governments in Yingkou ensured that "all the beggars and poor people from the various districts were seized by the patrol police and sent to the poorhouses so as to prevent them from polluting the streets and accelerating the spread of disease". The local government of Liaoyang ordered the police to "expel all the coolies living in small hotels", since "this plague mostly spreads from the lower classes".[238]

Ignorance and political expedience led governments to blame epidemics on foreigners. In the Milan plague of 1576–78, the resident German community was

230. Underwood 1948, 166.
231. Bencard 2021, 4–5.
232. Lacey 1995, 1412.
233. Quoted in Barry 2005, 65.
234. Quoted in Robinson 2020.
235. Clouse 2013, 145.
236. Quoted in Oram 2007, 24 (spelling modernized).
237. Quoted in Clouse 2013, 164.
238. Quoted in Hu 2010, 317.

blamed because it "did not adequately inspect [its] churches and women".[239] As plague approached the French town of Angers in 1598, the municipal government expelled "foreign" beggars.[240] When plague returned in 1626, it ordered "poor foreigners and vagabonds present in this town to empty the said town and suburbs within 24 hours after the publication of these presents, on pain of a whipping".[241] During the 2003 SARS epidemic in Shenzhen, Chinese public health officials blamed the disease on migrant workers.[242] At the beginning of the Covid-19 pandemic in February 2020, the governor of Italy's Veneto region said on television that "China has paid a high price for this epidemic they have been having because we have all seen them eating live mice and the like."[243] Later in 2020, the president of the United States publicly described Covid-19 as "the Chinese virus".[244]

Ethnic minorities also suffered from state ignorance, as well as governments' domestic political calculations. During the Black Death, governments condoned or encouraged mass violence against Jewish communities by popular mobs, religious bodies, and occupational guilds.[245] Between 1347 and 1351, over 1,000 town governments in the German Rhineland, Spain, France, and eastern-central Europe supported violent attacks on Jewish minorities, who were blamed for causing the plague.[246] These pogroms were particularly virulent in the Holy Roman Empire of the German Nation, where different levels of state authority—emperor, territorial princes, city-states, ecclesiastical states, noble micro-states—competed to extract resources from different social groups: "Where the rents from Jewish moneylenders were contested and no one ruler had secure access to the future stream of revenue associated with moneylending, Jewish communities were much more vulnerable to mob violence and to predation from local rulers".[247] Government attacks on minorities during epidemics recurred throughout the following centuries. The Jews continued to be particular official targets. In the Rome plague epidemic in 1656, for instance, the papal state locked the Jews into the city ghetto, where crowding sent mortality through the roof.[248] In the Baltic plague epidemic

239. Midura 2021, 39.
240. Quoted in Lebrun 1971, 308.
241. Quoted in Lebrun 1971, 314.
242. Leung 2020a, 258.
243. Vista Agenzia Televisiva Nazionale 2020.
244. Rogers, Jakes, and Swanson 2020.
245. Kacki 2020, 3; Alfani and Murphy 2017, 329–30; Jedwab, Johnson, and Koyama 2019, 391; Finley and Koyama 2018, 257.
246. Cohn 2007.
247. Finley and Koyama 2018, 257.
248. Henderson 2019, 75.

in 1711–12, the Danish king ordered the royal Health Commission to keep a special watch over Jews.[249]

But states also targeted other ethnic groups. In the Cape Town plague epidemic of 1901, for instance, the government forcibly rounded up all Black Africans in the city's poorest neighbourhoods and marched 6,000 of them under armed guard to internment on a former sewage station, which it transformed in 1902 into one of the first segregated black townships.[250] In Rio de Janeiro in 1904, the state and its health administrators blamed smallpox and yellow fever epidemics on Black, mixed-race, and immigrant residents, whom they portrayed as "dangerous, unsanitary, and immoral".[251] In Guangzhou in 2020, the Chinese authorities used Covid-19 as a pretext to evict African residents from their apartments and herd them into quarantine.[252]

Government ignorance also led to persecution of females. State officials and medical professionals theorized that women attracted God's ire, spread epidemics deliberately, or contained "humours" that were inherently contagious. Such ideas were used to justify harsh measures against female sex workers, who were locked down, incarcerated, or ejected during epidemics—in Valencia in 1395 and 1489–90,[253] in Saint-Flour in 1402,[254] in Abbeville in 1493,[255] in Great Coggeshall in 1578,[256] and in Sluis in 1605.[257] But ignorant state authorities blamed even virtuous females. In the Geneva epidemic of 1571, the government prosecuted, banished, or burnt alive a large number of women, whom it claimed had deliberately spread the plague.[258] In the Milan plague of 1576–78, the state restricted movement and gathering for all suspect groups, but imposed an overall ban only on women (and children).[259] In the Amsterdam plague of 1602, the government banned women from attending funerals, claiming that "their presence increased the dangers of contaminated air rising from the graves".[260] In the Florence plague of 1630–31, the government forbade all females to leave their houses and kept them locked down long after the general quarantine was lifted for males, on the grounds that women's "moist and corruptible" humours exhaled infection. When plague

249. Bencard 2021, 2.
250. Echenberg 2002, 446–7; A. White 2018, 135–9.
251. Cantisano 2022, 616.
252. Fifield 2020.
253. Quoted in Agresta 2020, 380–2.
254. N. Murphy 2013, 152.
255. Curtis 2021a, 11; N. Murphy 2013, 152.
256. Slack 1985, 29, 101.
257. Curtis 2021a, 11.
258. Monter 1971, 184.
259. Carmichael 1998, 144; Midura 2021, 33n40.
260. Quoted in Curtis and Han 2021, 67.

returned in 1633, the Florentine authorities again imposed a female-specific lockdown.[261]

Why were governments ignorant? What made them fail to collect or accept accurate information about epidemics? Lack of state capacity was one limiting factor. Successful information provision did not always require government spending to employ experts directly. But if the state did not employ experts, it needed to encourage civil society and individual researchers to collect, analyse, and interpret epidemiological information. Many governments took centuries to develop the capacity to accept and act on expert information from citizen experts and civil society.

Scientific and technical knowledge was another thing that states lacked. It is often argued that the problem with government management of epidemics before the later seventeenth century was the backwardness of science. Only between 1670 and 1820 did an "epidemiological transition" take place, it is claimed, during which scientific knowledge was progressively applied to disease.[262] This is over-optimistic, as chapters 1 and 6 discuss. Until the late nineteenth century, there was a very weak scientific consensus about the contagiousness of disease. Scientific opinion was divided, medical experts disagreed, and both state and civil society were at odds about how to interpret the limited available evidence. State ignorance about epidemics reflected a lack of very basic knowledge of contagion, anti-contagion techniques (hygiene, pest control, social distancing), and information collection. This gave rise to legitimate disagreements about what the problem was, how to collect and diffuse information about it, and what to do then. When scientific knowledge became available after the later seventeenth century, governments did not know how to decide which components of that knowledge were correct and what actions they implied. Even nowadays, as we shall see in chapter 6, social and institutional features hinder acceptance of scientific medicine. Knowledge alone is no magic pill.

Why? Two additional aspects of governance play an important contributory role: motivation and political realities. First, the state will collect and process information better than the market only if it is motivated to act in the interests of society. States often have other interests—notably their own political, fiscal, and military survival—which do not necessarily coincide with those of society at large.[263] Second, the survival even of a non-democratic state relies on political realities—the need to navigate and mediate among powerful groups and institutions in society, which may view epidemic control measures as damaging their interests.

261. Henderson 2019, 250–3, 280.
262. Omran 1971.
263. See Ogilvie 2023, 46–7.

These pressures—state motivation and political realities—can be seen at work in the stance of many states towards immunization. Governments were initially ignorant about immunization. But ignorance was not the only problem. When information became available, the state often ignored or censored it. This was partly because of state failure—the inability on the part of state personnel to understand new knowledge. But it was also because the state was pursuing other purposes which it prioritized over public health. One of these was political. The state censored new knowledge to satisfy politically important interest groups that benefited from monopolizing old knowledge. When the Manchus conquered China in 1644, they failed to obtain information about smallpox variolation from their new Han Chinese subjects and adopted it only in 1679, after a generation of rampant infection.[264] In Europe after around 1720, as we have seen, private individuals imported information about variolation from other continents, and some local governments in England acted on it. But many European states rejected the information and banned the practice, including high-capacity states such as Sweden (until 1756),[265] France (until 1768),[266] and Spain (until 1774).[267] During such bans, governments often blocked citizens' access to information, as in 1754 when the Spanish state forbade the translation of a book on variolation, which it claimed was "prejudicial to the public health".[268]

The political concerns of states to pander to influential interest groups hindered smallpox variolation even in those European states that did not prohibit it altogether. In German states such as Prussia, the spread of variolation even among aristocrats and the elite continued to be hindered not so much by ignorance on the part of the ruler as by opposition to new knowledge by institutions that monopolized old knowledge: the religious authorities and a conservative medical establishment. In Electoral Saxony, Electress Maria Antonia was able to get the royal children variolated only thanks to encouragement from her cousin Friedrich II of Prussia, to whom she wrote in 1763, "It was your words that encouraged me, and persuaded the Prince-Elector to permit it. . . . [M]y doctors, and above all the priests here, did not want to allow it."[269] The wider societal importance of persuading rulers to relax their political support for doctors and priests emerges from later passages of Maria Antonia's letter, in which she wrote, "I owe you the preservation of my children, and Saxony owes you the lives of about a thousand children whose parents followed my

264. Chang 2002, 178–9, 197.
265. Sköld 1996a, 249–53.
266. G. Miller 1957, 234–40
267. M. Bennett 2020, 152, 200; Ramírez 2018, 140–1.
268. Quoted in M. Bennett 2020, 200.
269. Quoted in Penschow 2022, 53.

example . . . since it was a kind of authorisation. . . . [A]ll the nobility here soon followed my lead."[270]

State opposition to vaccination followed a similar pattern. In Japan in 1818, the scholar Baba Sadayoshi met an English merchant-ship captain who informed him of smallpox vaccination, offering him vaccine samples and a book on how to perform the procedure, but Baba could not accept them because of strict Tokugawa state laws that prohibited unauthorized transmission of such materials.[271] In the Kingdom of Madagascar (Imerina) during the 1833–35 smallpox epidemic, the royal court forbade vaccination on the grounds that Europeans were using it deliberately to infect the Malagasy people.[272] In Nigeria in 2003, the governments of the three northern states of Kano, Zamfara, and Kaduna halted polio immunization on the grounds that the vaccine had been "corrupted and tainted by evildoers from America and their Western allies".[273] In 2022 the Florida state governor called for a grand jury to investigate Covid-19 mRNA vaccines because they made recipients "more likely to get infected", and in 2023 the Lee County Republican Party asked the state governor to ban Covid-19 vaccines "because we have foreign non-governmental entities that are unleashing biological weapons on the American people".[274] Knowledge alone was not enough, where other state priorities and political realities intervened.

4.3. FAKE NEWS AND FALSE CONFIDENCE

Information is a public good—except if the state falsifies it, when it becomes a public bad. Even states that get accurate information and understand its implications may conceal or corrupt it because of their other interests, exacerbating contagion.

What interests make governments spread fake news about epidemic disease? One major concern is to avoid trade embargos. In the 1575 epidemic, the Venetian government concealed the existence of plague in the city for as long as possible and then downplayed its severity in order to avoid trade bans.[275] In the 1593 Nottingham plague, a local citizen was prosecuted for "slandering our town with the sickness, which will be to our decay".[276] In 1601, the Glasgow town council was accused of concealing plague from other Scottish towns and going so far as to issue mendacious health passes.[277] In the 1657 epidemic

270. Quoted in Penschow 2022, 53.
271. Walker 1999, 139–40, 143.
272. G. Campbell 1991, 432.
273. Quoted in Jegede 2007, 0418.
274. Quoted in Lee 2023.
275. Alfani 2013a, 95.
276. Quoted in Stevenson et al. 1899, 238.
277. Oram 2007, 26.

in Lower Saxony, the town governments of Hildesheim and Braunschweig concealed evidence of plague and downplayed infections to protect trade links.[278] In the 1679 Vienna plague, the first infections were identified by the physician Paul de Sorbait in January, but the government was so concerned about the threat to trade that it pressed the Sanitary Council to conceal the epidemic until July, giving plague seven months to spread unchecked.[279] In České Budějovice (Budweis) in 1680, plague deaths involving visible buboes were widely observed, but the municipal government refused to close infected dwellings "since the real plague is not fully known yet". Even after six monks died of plague, the government insisted that "we do not recognize the pestilence to be here, even though some Capuchins died from the heat".[280]

In 1720, one of the last plague epidemics in western Europe broke out in Marseille when information was falsified by two state authorities in succession. First, a plague-struck merchant vessel from Sidon (in modern Lebanon) reported eleven deaths at Livorno, where the port officials sought to prevent trade disruption by declaring the infection to be merely "malignant and pestilential fever".[281] Then the vessel sailed onwards to Marseille, where the municipal Sanitary Commission sought to protect trade by concealing the epidemic for three crucial months between May and August, allowing it to spread unchecked.[282]

State concealment continued throughout nineteenth-century epidemics. In the 1828–29 Bucharest plague, for instance, the authorities muzzled a doctor who diagnosed the disease, "as they knew the inconveniences to which they would be subjected, if placed in strict quarantine".[283] In nineteenth-century Hamburg, the authorities concealed cholera to maintain commercial confidence, as in 1832 when they refused to make any official announcements of cholera cases, or in 1848 when the Senate file on the epidemic is entitled "File Concerning the Epidemic of So-Called Asiatic Cholera which Took Place in Hamburg in 1848, against which No Quarantines, Hospitals or Otherwise Important Preventive Measures Were Taken".[284] In the 1896 Mumbai plague epidemic, the town government declared the disease was not true plague, hoping to avert quarantines and trade bans.[285] In the Portuguese city of Oporto, plague cases were reported in March 1899 but were concealed by

278. D. Christensen 2004, 464.
279. Mauelshagen 2005, 242–3.
280. Quoted in Holasová 2005, 13–14.
281. Quoted in M. Harrison 2012, 28.
282. M. Harrison 1992, 138.
283. Quoted in J. E. Alexander 1830, 104.
284. R. Evans 1992, 167 (quotation), 169.
285. M. Harrison 1992, 138.

the authorities for fear of trade bans, enabling the epidemic to spread widely before the official report was made in June.[286]

Fear of local market withdrawal was another reason governments concealed and falsified information about epidemics. In England in 1603, Thomas Lodge advised magistrates that "if by chance, or by the will of God, the city becometh infected, it ought not incontinently to be made known: but those that have the care and charge of such as are attainted ought in the beginning to keep it close, and wisely conceal the same from the common sort".[287] In Prato in 1630, the town council asked for authorization to prepare a pesthouse against the approaching plague, but the Florence municipal Health Board refused for fear of unleashing local panic.[288] In Bologna in June 1630 plague had been raging for five weeks, but the municipal government threatened the death penalty for anyone who spoke of *peste*, "so it is not surprising that it has not been declared more openly".[289] In Braunschweig in 1657, the city council deliberately undercounted plague deaths to avoid alarming citizens.[290] In the Kingdom of Naples in 1690–92, town governments obstinately sought "to conceal the obvious truth" about plague, for fear of internal alarm and disruption.[291] In Lübeck in 1832, 1848, 1850, 1853, and 1856–59, the government concealed cholera and declared no quarantines for fear of public agitation.[292] In Sydney in 1900, the authorities first denied there was plague at all and then sought to minimize its severity to avoid local panic.[293] In the 1918–19 flu pandemic, governments all over the world routinely lied to their own citizens, claiming that the disease had not arrived, was something other than influenza, was not a serious infection, was a rumour spread by "panic" and "hysteria", or was already past its worst.[294]

States nowadays still falsify information about epidemics, seeking to maintain business confidence. In January 2020 when Covid-19 appeared in Wuhan, the Chinese state concealed the virus and punished anyone who spread warnings, even privately. When the young ophthalmologist Li Wenliang reported the SARS-like outbreak to colleagues in a closed WeChat group, the Public Security Bureau summoned him, threatened him, and compelled him to confess publicly to making false statements. Nonetheless, he continued to

286. M. Harrison 2012, 189.
287. Quoted in Slack 1985, 256.
288. Cipolla 1973, 41–2.
289. Henderson 2019, 26.
290. D. Christensen 2004, 329.
291. Quoted in Fusco 2017, 97, 99 (quotation), 103.
292. R. Evans 1992, 168.
293. M. Harrison 1992, 141.
294. Barry 2005, 65; Tomes 2010, 53.

speak out, because "we needed to be ready for it mentally. Take protective measures . . . I think a healthy society should not have just one voice."[295]

Government concealment and falsification may be more common in authoritarian states. But democratic states also indulge in it. Scientific advice is seldom categorical. Governments often choose those perspectives that suit their interests. Scientific advisors often tell governments what they wish to hear. During the Covid-19 pandemic, the UK government acted on what it described as scientific advice. But key elements of this advice were questioned by non-government scientists at the time and turned out to be inaccurate. In March 2020, for instance, the government claimed to follow scientific advice when it let large leisure events such as major football matches and horse-racing meetings go ahead with hundreds of thousands of spectators. By 2023 the former prime minister and England's chief medical officer admitted this had been a mistake.[296] From March to July 2020, likewise, UK government health authorities advised citizens not to use face masks and banned mask advertisements as "likely to cause fear", despite clear advice from the British Medical Association and a majority of doctors that face masks helped control infection and save lives.[297] For many months, the UK government claimed that Covid-19 was transmitted by fomites (viruses on objects), which could be removed by hand washing, rather than, as the *British Medical Journal* advised in August 2020, by airborne transmission, which required social distancing and ventilation.[298] In August 2020, the UK government claimed to be acting on scientific advice when it spent £500 million to subsidize people to eat out in restaurants, even though this soon turned out to have significantly increased Covid-19 infections, accelerated the pandemic into its second wave, and created no lasting economic benefit for restaurants.[299]

Democratic states, like authoritarian ones, even engage in outright concealment of information about epidemics. In June 2021, for instance, the administration of Governor Ron DeSantis ordered the Florida health department to remove online information about Covid cases, deaths, and vaccinations. Officials falsely announced that public Covid data did not exist, and that, even if it had existed, the public were not allowed to know it. As a former state congressman points out:

295. Quoted in A. Green 2020, 682.

296. Triggle, Foster, and Reed 2023.

297. Sample 2020; Blackburn 2020.

298. N. Wilson et al. 2020. Peer-reviewed articles had already demonstrated the importance of airborne transmission by the summer of 2020: see Buonanno, Morawska, and Stabile 2020; Y. Liu et al. 2020; Ma et al. 2020.

299. Fetzer (2022, 1210) estimates that 8% to 17% of all new Covid-19 infections in August 2020 were caused by the "eat-out-to-help-out" government subsidy.

Our school leaders were struggling to make informed decisions about how to mitigate the spread of Covid, whether it be masking or social distancing policies, or other strategies. They needed data, they needed information, but the state made it unavailable, then said it didn't exist. All Floridians have a constitutional right to public records and receive them in a timely manner. And what's interesting about the governor's arguments about Covid is he repeatedly talks about giving people the choice over masks and vaccinations, but without critical public health data how are they able to make informed choices?[300]

Not until October 2023 did a legal battle mounted by a coalition of open government advocates, media outlets, and opposition politicians compel the Florida state administration to admit that it did collect Covid-19 information and to resume making it available to citizens.

It might be argued that state falsification of information about pandemics was not all bad. As we saw in chapter 2, market exchange played a major role in economic growth, generating resources essential for contagion control. By falsifying information, might governments have prevented market withdrawal that could choke off economic activity? Perhaps we can conclude that states falsified information about epidemics out of justified concern for their citizens' well-being? On the other hand, one must ask whether the state actually had better information than market participants themselves, or could use it more effectively. Much evidence suggests not. Many governments found it difficult to obtain information about epidemics, and even those that got accurate information understood it poorly because of lack of expertise in interpreting disease symptoms, transmission mechanisms, and mortality risks. Thus when the government falsified information to maintain market confidence and suppress public "fear", nothing guaranteed that it was more accurately informed than market participants.

4.4. TAXES AND LIES

The state also had its own reasons for falsifying epidemic information. Among these, fiscal concerns took pride of place. In 1598, for instance, Carl Emanuel I of Savoy concealed the Turin plague epidemic to safeguard the revenues he derived from the Fair of Asti. According to a contemporary account, the 1598 fair "had already opened, [and] he had ordered the merchants of Turin, indeed had forced them, to all come and bring there their merchandise, in order to be able to obtain from them that sum of money, which in various

300. Quoted in Luscombe 2023.

ways he usually obtains at the present time".[301] Carl Emanuel did not do this to protect the economic position of poor citizens. On the contrary. After the epidemic ended in 1600, Carl Emanuel cut off food rations to the poor: "Since the city is drained of money because its revenues and income have ceased and is burdened with many debts, it would be better if it withdrew the rations that it still gives because no better alms can be given than paying off debts."[302]

Governments seldom stopped pursuing their fiscal interests during pandemics—on the contrary. In Bohemia during the 1680 plague, the town council of České Budějovice (Budweis) continued to compel merchants trading salt and other goods to pass through the town to pay their staple taxes into the town coffers, even though it spread contagion.[303]

Such state behaviour was normal during every major epidemic in history. Pre-modern tax systems were strongly regressive, as we saw in chapter 2, so the poor were much more heavily taxed, relative to their incomes, than the rich.[304] In medieval and early modern Europe, the state allocated 50–90 per cent of its expenditures to warfare or servicing military debts.[305] Governments devoted very few resources to civilian purposes.[306] The Grand-Duchy of Florence was one of the most enlightened states in early modern Europe and displayed unusual concern for its citizens in the great plague of 1630–31, yet in the 1625–50 period almost four-fifths of government expenditures were devoted to warfare and elite consumption.[307] Even in rich Western economies, until the 1930s only a tiny share of state expenditures went to welfare relief.[308] When states concealed epidemics on fiscal grounds, it was to benefit the elite, not to secure public revenues either for contagion control or for other activities that might benefit ordinary citizens.[309]

4.5. THE FIRST CASUALTY OF WAR

It is a truth universally acknowledged that "the first casualty when war comes is truth".[310] State concealment of epidemics often had military motives. Military falsification of medical emergencies became ever more common as public

---

301. Quoted in Alfani 2013a, 99.
302. Quoted in Alfani 2013a, 100.
303. Holasová 2005, 22–3.
304. Kiser and Karceski 2017, 78–9, 83, 85–7; Alfani and Di Tullio 2019, 145–80.
305. Hoffman 2015; Alfani and Di Tullio 2019, 167.
306. Lindert 1998, 144 and passim; Alfani and Di Tullio 2019, 166–74; Ogilvie 2023, 35–40.
307. Litchfield 2008, para 351: of total state expenditures, 47% were devoted to military purposes, 15% to the ducal court, 13% to the ducal family, and 4% to palace building, leaving just 21% for all other purposes.
308. Van Bavel and Rijpma 2016, 171.
309. Ogilvie 2023, 35–40.
310. Quoted in Barry 2005, 64.

information sources proliferated in the early modern period. During the Seven Years' War in North America, for instance, military commanders concealed smallpox outbreaks even from their own subordinates, as in 1759 when smallpox raged through the forts along the Ohio Valley without the rank and file being warned.[311] In 1770 during the Russian–Turkish war, plague broke out among Russian troops in the Moldovan town of Focşani. The Russian General von Shtoffeln ordered army doctors to conceal it, allowing it to spread across wide tracts of eastern Europe and Russia. For the entire first year of the epidemic, the Russian government refused to admit the presence of plague on Russian territory, the two official newspapers in Saint Petersburg and Moscow printed nothing about it, and foreign diplomats in Russia got all their information from newspapers abroad. Ultimately the epidemic killed not only General von Shtoffeln himself but thousands of soldiers and over 100,000 ordinary people.[312]

The 1918–19 influenza pandemic was also covered up for military reasons. Governments of all countries involved in the First World War, including the USA, Britain, and Italy, concealed the epidemic from citizens, censored press coverage, and ordered health officials to lie to the public. When rampant disease and death could no longer be completely hidden, governments downplayed the risks, ascribing infection to overactive imaginations, war-weariness, anxiety, depression, "hysteria", "neurasthenia", and "sheer panic". Only in neutral states such as Spain could the press write freely about the epidemic—the reason it became known as the "Spanish" flu.[313] Concealment extended far beyond the European theatre of war. When influenza reached India in August 1918, a Scottish doctor in the Punjab lamented that "no information had been received, either from other stations [in India] or from England which would help in diagnosing the disease".[314] In Ghana, the colonial government provided almost no information to the inhabitants; the one article it asked newspapers to run was published late, appeared on an inside page, and falsely claimed the disease was mild.[315] The Ghanaian colonial government also failed to warn neighbouring states, delayed drafting the notification, opposed the expense, and sent the telegram only after four days of debate.[316]

State capacity is still deployed to conceal epidemic information. Polio epidemics re-emerged in Syria in 2013 partly because military authorities blocked information transmission.[317] In 2020, the Syrian state actively stifled Covid-19

311. Apthorp 2011, 85, 87.

312. Melikishvili 2006, 24–5; Lammel 2021, 90.

313. Barry 2005, 64; Honigsbaum 2013, 166, 175–9, 182, 184; Flecknoe, Wakefield, and Simmons 2018, 63; Galletta and Giommoni 2020, 6–7; Devos et al. 2021, 256–7; Basco, Domènech, and Rosés 2021, 2, 6–7.

314. Quoted in Arnold 2019, 193.

315. Patterson 1983, 492–3.

316. Patterson 1983, 494.

317. Abbara et al. 2020, 192–3.

reports.[318] Small wonder that in the Covid pandemic, analysis of 76 countries in 2020 found that in those with low trust in government, public information campaigns to communicate risks of contagion had no beneficial effects.[319] In such countries citizens rationally ignored information provided by governments that were known to falsify it.

Unsurprisingly, government concealment increased epidemic mortality. When central and northern Italian states concealed information about plague in 1630, they fuelled an epidemic that ultimately killed a third of the population.[320] When the Viennese government concealed plague for seven months between January and July 1679, contagion spread into the surrounding countryside and as far afield as Bohemia (the Czech lands), killing thousands.[321] When the Marseille Sanitary Commission denied the existence of plague and officially redefined plague deaths as "fever" for three crucial months between May and August 1720, nearly 10,000 inhabitants fled the city, carrying plague into the surrounding Provençal countryside, where it killed nearly 90,000 people; of the 80,000 who stayed in the city, nearly half died.[322] When British military commanders in Ohio concealed smallpox among their troops in 1759, the resulting epidemic killed eight times as many soldiers as died in battle, and raged through the indigenous population.[323] When the imperial government concealed plague in the Russian army in January 1770, the epidemic spread into Romania, Moldavia, Wallachia, Transylvania, Poland, Ukraine, and across much of Russia, killing one-third of the population of Moscow.[324] When the Bucharest government concealed plague in 1828–29, the resulting epidemic killed half the town's inhabitants and spread into Wallachia, Moldavia, Bulgaria, and Rumelia.[325] When the government of British India concealed the fourth cholera pandemic, it travelled with pilgrims to the Middle East, killing one-third of the 90,000 Mecca pilgrims in 1863, before spreading to Africa, Europe, North America, and Russia over the ensuing years.[326] When warring states censored information about influenza in 1918–19, they helped spread the pandemic across the globe.[327]

For states, concealing information about epidemics seemed advantageous. Governments rightly feared that foreign trade would stay away, locals withdraw

318. Abbara et al. 2020, 192–3.
319. Farzanegan and Hofmann 2021.
320. Alfani and Murphy 2017, 316–7.
321. Mauelshagen 2005, 242–3.
322. M. Harrison 1992, 138.
323. Apthorp 2011, 85, 87.
324. Melikishvili 2006, 24–5; Lammel 2021, 90.
325. J. E. Alexander 1830, 104.
326. Lacey 1995, 1412.
327. Ferrari 2020, 111.

from the market, state revenues shrink, and enemies exploit the crisis. But they ignored the harm to their citizens, the damage beyond their borders, and the future repercussions of letting an epidemic spiral out of control.

4.6. NEW IDEAS AND OLD STATES

A big problem in any epidemic is lack of scientific knowledge. Accurate explanations of disease and reliable techniques to control it are still imperfect, as Covid-19 showed, and in the past they were much worse. Producing and diffusing new knowledge suffer from market failures, as we saw in chapter 2. Like any kind of information, innovations are non-rival and non-excludable. Non-rivality may deter people from inventing new ideas, since they cannot reap market profits. Non-excludability may motivate inventors to keep new knowledge secret to profit personally, even though diffusing it would benefit society. In principle, the state can create better incentives than the market—for example, by offering patents, prizes, or salaries for researchers.

State support for science and innovation relies on fiscal, legal, and bureaucratic capacity. It also depends on two additional factors we have already discussed: motivation and political realities. The state had to believe that a new idea or technique would serve its interests before it would devote resources to solving the market failure. The state also had to exercise the art of the politically possible, navigating and mediating the interests of social groups and institutions threatened by new ideas.

Constraints on state capacity, lack of motivation, and political realities have for centuries limited government action to support medical research. States in central and northern Italy started granting patents (temporary monopolies) to encourage inventions as early as 1421. But these mainly rewarded industrial rather than medical innovations. Medical patents were sometimes granted, but typically for what would now be called "alternative" remedies. The first English medical patent, for instance, was awarded in 1698 for Epsom salts. Governments also sometimes awarded medals and prizes to inventors, but seldom for medical discoveries. Two brilliant exceptions were the medals awarded in 1802 by the British Parliament and 1804 by Emperor Napoleon of France to Edward Jenner for inventing vaccination.

From the twelfth century onwards, governments also helped fund universities. These provided salaries for scholars, partly compensating for the failure of markets to reward scholarly research. But that was an unintended by-product. The main reasons states supported universities were to train their own future bureaucrats and to please the Church by educating priests. Medical and scientific research, to the extent that university teachers undertook it, was a side benefit. Government-funded research universities and medical institutes arose only in the nineteenth century and only in some societies.

Variolation against smallpox, the earliest and most important innovation for controlling epidemic disease, was invented without state involvement. Between 1550 and 1700, variolation emerged anonymously in multiple societies—in Asia, Africa, and the Middle East—without recorded state support. After around 1700, knowledge of variolation spread to Europe and North America, again through individual contacts: an East India merchant in China writing to a London physician in 1700; an enslaved African speaking to his clergyman master in Boston in 1706; a Greek-Italian physician in Constantinople writing to a London physician in 1714; an aristocratic English lady speaking to old Greek women in Constantinople in 1718.[328] After around 1720, as we saw in chapter 2, variolation was improved and diffused in England, America, and the European continent by a plethora of individual parents, physicians, philanthropists, welfare administrators, and commercial variolators.[329]

The British government did provide a primitive regulatory framework. Markets do not provide optimal incentives for experimentation with new ideas, since innovators may not adequately consider ethical issues, randomization, or self-selection into control or treatment groups. Generally, it takes some form of regulation—by the state or a professional body—to provide a codified framework to govern experimentation. As early as 1721, the British government granted a few physicians permission to experiment with variolation in Newgate Prison, offering a pardon to condemned prisoners for participating. It considered ethical issues, seeking legal advice from the Attorney and Solicitor Generals about "Whether His Majesty may by Law Grant his Gracious Pardon to two Malefactors under Sentence of Death upon Condition that they will suffer to be try'd upon them the Experiment of Inoculating the Small pox". Within three days, the legal advice returned:

> The Lives of the persons being in the power of His Majesty, he may Grant a Pardon to them upon such lawful Condition as he shall think fit; and as to this particular Condition We have no objection in point of Law, the rather because the carrying on this practice to perfection may tend to the General Benefit of Mankind.[330]

A generation later, in 1751, the state of Geneva went further, and permitted the city hospital to experiment with variolation, using "subjects entirely dependent upon the Directors, and principally upon bastards"—though without offering the children any reward.[331] The British and Genevan governments thus provided

328. Silverstein 2009, 292–3; Herbert 1975, 540–1; M. Bennett 2008, 500.
329. M. Bennett 2020, 54.
330. Quoted in Silverstein 2009, 296.
331. Quoted in Silverstein 2009, 300.

a regulatory framework to address the ethical issues raised by experimenting with variolation.

They did not, however, provide regulatory guidance to address randomization and self-selection (nor, indeed, do modern governments). This is not because such problems were unrecognized at the time. In fact, precisely those issues were raised in 1723 by Isaac Massey, an opponent of the innovation, who pointed out that variolated people were richer, healthier, and medically better tended than random members of society. Non-variolated people might have enjoyed just as low mortality as variolated ones if they had been "treated with equal Care with those that are inoculated; but to form a just Comparison, and calculate right in this Case, the Circumstances of the Patients, must and ought to be as near as may be on a Par".[332] As it turned out, variolation did reduce smallpox mortality even among the poor, debilitated, and medically neglected. But criticisms by opponents like Massey would have been more easily countered had there been a code of practice governing scientific randomization.

It might be argued that clinical randomization is a key issue in which markets fail and governments should play a role. But even in modern, high-capacity states, according to a 2023 survey, "There are sparse recommendations on randomization in current regulatory guidance, with little mention of recently developed methods which might outperform current practice."[333] Efforts to provide systematic recommendations reflecting modern statistical knowledge emanate less from state agencies such as the European Medicines Agency, the US Food and Drug Administration, or even the International Council for Harmonisation of Technical Requirements for Pharmaceuticals for Human Use. Rather, they come from scientists in academia and industry, as shown by initiatives such as the Randomization Working Group at the University of Aachen.[334]

Did early regulation of the ethical aspects of variolation experiments play a role in the permissive stance of the British state towards later commercial variolators? Or did underlying features of the British state foster both early regulatory approval for experimentation and a more permissive stance to later market provision? In either case, even in Britain the role of the state was to create a framework for individual experimentation and diffusion, not to reward medical innovation directly. The British government showed no interest in schemes to reward variolators for carrying out research and development. Its central contribution was to refrain from prohibition, unlike governments across most of the European continent.

332. Quoted in Hasselgren 2020, 2840.
333. K. Carter et al. 2023, abstract.
334. The website of the Randomization Working Group can be found at https://randomization-working-group.rwth-aachen.de/?page_id=28.

Vaccination turned out to be even more important than variolation in controlling smallpox contagion, as we saw in chapter 2. Yet state action played little role in its invention or diffusion. Edward Jenner thought up vaccination in 1796 without government involvement. As the practice diffused after 1796, the state played a permissive role but did not solve the market failure. In 1802, Parliament awarded Jenner a £10,000 "premium" for having invented vaccination six years earlier.[335] This reward did not operate to address either the public-good characteristic of new ideas or the need for regulation to solve ethical and randomization issues. Before 1796, the government did not know vaccination existed, so could not promise any reward for inventing it. In 1802 when Jenner got the reward, he had already incurred years of research and development costs with no expectation of government support. Parliament did not award the prize spontaneously, but rather in response to lobbying from aristocratic, scientific, medical, and philanthropic individuals and organizations. Indeed, the parliamentary committee rejected the suggestion that the prize should be £20,000, and another five years passed before Parliament granted Jenner a further premium, this time of £20,000. The government reward thus provided no incentive for Jenner to incur the costs of innovation and, of course, did not address ethical or randomization issues at all.[336]

The British state at least permitted private persons to experiment with vaccination, which enabled them to improve it, diffuse it, and ultimately save many thousands of lives. Other European states initially banned the procedure, partly on the grounds that it had not been tested. Information about vaccination was published in the Swedish newspaper *Stockholms posten* on 3 November 1798, just a few months after Jenner published his results in English, and several Swedish physicians were keen to try it out. But the Swedish state refused them permission, followed up in 1800 by outright prohibiting the procedure, and took another two years to repeal the ban.[337] Only as evidence of its astonishing success emerged from England did other states begin to permit the procedure, though it took them much longer to encourage or mandate it, as we saw earlier.

In these first path-breaking innovations to limit epidemic contagion, therefore, the state played a modest role. In England, the government adopted a permissive stance. But it did not deal with the problem that inventing and experimenting with a new medical idea has positive externalities for society at large, few of which accrue to the individual inventor. Nor did it do much to provide a regulatory framework to ensure innovators adequately considered ethical issues, randomization, and self-selection into control or treatment

335. M. Bennett 2020, 66.
336. M. Bennett 2020, 89–92, 119.
337. Sköld 1996a, 253–4, 258.

groups. Immunization, the most path-breaking epidemiological innovation in history, was facilitated not by state initiative but by government quiescence.

5. Cross-Border Externalities

"No one is safe until everyone is safe." This mantra was intoned so often during the Covid-19 pandemic that it sometimes seemed purely phatic—to establish a congenial social atmosphere rather than to convey meaning. But the fundamental logic is deeply serious. It is based on the idea of the negative externality, which comes back repeatedly whenever we think about epidemic disease. Inside each society, it refers to the sad fact that I can take an action perfectly innocently that inflicts costs on others in addition to those I myself incur. Internationally, it refers to the idea of a *cross-border* externality—when uncompensated costs spill over political frontiers.[338] Individuals in one state take decisions that make them get an infectious disease, one consequence of which is to infect individuals in another country.[339] Or one state decides on a policy—such as abolishing quarantine or vaccination—based on the risks to its own citizens but not on the risks to citizens of other states.[340]

The market failure caused by an externality is likely to be even greater when the uncompensated harm crosses political borders. Agreeing on compensation is much costlier between different legal systems, languages, and cultures. Civil society institutions—communities, religions, medical associations, kin networks—are likely to fail in cross-border situations, because they tend to be geographically circumscribed and lack coercive power. So the case for state action is correspondingly greater. In the case of epidemics, five types of cross-border externality come into play: information sharing, travel regulation, environmental pollution, vaccination diplomacy, and war.

5.1. INFORMATION SHARING

Disease does not heed political frontiers, so information about an epidemic in one polity is important for controlling contagion in others. In principle, the state is well placed to share information across borders. It can address the public-good problem leading information to be under-provided by market mechanisms. It can also address the international externality problem leading disease information to be under-provided by individual states because its benefits can be reaped by other states. Finally, the state can reap economies of

---

338. This was the sense in which the expression was used by the Secretary General of the United Nations in his statement to the Global Health Summit in May 2021 (Guterres 2021).

339. Jit et al. 2021, 2.

340. Kanbur 2001, 3.

scale because it already employs diplomats to communicate with other states on matters other than pandemics.

In the two centuries after the Black Death, the central and northern Italian states did just this. By the late medieval period, most of them had set up "reciprocal correspondence" arrangements among their government health boards.[341] By the early modern period, state capacity was high enough that swift mutual warnings about plague epidemics had become the norm among central and north Italian polities. In October 1629, as we have seen, a German army marched into northern Italy, bringing plague to Lake Como. The news arrived on 21 October in Milan, whose government swiftly informed its counterparts elsewhere in central and northern Italy. Within five days, most Italian states were taking measures to prohibit travel from infected areas.[342] State capacity in early modern Italy was clearly sufficient for government information sharing.

But state motivation was often lacking. Many states refrained from sharing information with others during epidemics for fear of harming the home polity. Even in precocious Italy, state concealment of epidemics was so notorious that all governments employed secret informers to spy out what was really happening in other states.[343] In 1575, Venetian ambassadors abroad employed "all possible duplicity" to conceal the plague in their state in order to stave off trade embargos.[344] In August 1630, the Florentine state health officers notified other states of a few "fever" deaths but claimed that, "having been investigated and discussed by the physicians, it is held to be certain that, although the disease is contagious, it is not the plague". Over the next two months, the Florentine state repeatedly dismissed plague deaths as "rumours" and claimed that plague victims had died of "poor and inadequate food" or "petechial disease with blisters".[345] The ensuing plague epidemic of 1630–1, as we have seen, spread throughout central and northern Italy where it ultimately killed 30–35 per cent of the population.

But perhaps it was only pre-modern governments that refused to share information? Sadly not. States—even high-capacity ones—behaved the same way in the era of international health organizations. In 1863–75, for instance, the government of British India concealed mounting evidence of a cholera epidemic, concerned that an international quarantine would threaten Indian exports and anger Indian Muslims desirous of making the hajj pilgrimage. The British government's refusal to share information with other states

341. Cipolla 1976, 47–50.
342. Cipolla 1973, 20–1.
343. Cipolla 1976, 58.
344. Quoted in Alfani 2013a, 95.
345. Quoted in Cipolla 1976, 54–5.

permitted the disease to spread with pilgrims to the Middle East, directly fuelling the fourth cholera pandemic across the globe.[346] In Africa between 1978 and 1987, likewise, cholera spread across many countries partly because governments failed to report cases to the World Health Organization for fear of trade embargoes by other states.[347] In 2002, the Chinese government refused to share information with other states about the SARS epidemic, enabling the epidemic to spread.[348] Chinese state concealment of Covid-19 cases as early as November or early December 2019 may have worsened the ensuing global pandemic.[349]

In all these cases, state capacity was sufficient to censor information about emerging infections. This suggests that state capacity was also sufficient to share such information had these governments been so motivated. They were not.

5.2. TRAVEL RESTRICTIONS

Travel restrictions are a major way states deal with cross-border externalities of epidemics. The potential benefit is clear. Individuals decide to travel based on risks to themselves but not others. Their state of origin decides on policy based on risks to its own citizens but not foreigners. The destination state can take into account both sets of uncompensated risks, through sanitary cordons, border checks, and quarantines.

But there are also potential costs. The state must have fiscal, bureaucratic, and legal capacity to control travel and trade. It must also be motivated to do so. States can indeed be motivated to reduce their subjects' mortality, as with the early modern European mercantilist doctrine that maximizing population size benefited rulers. Such mercantilist policies provided one impetus for the sanitary cordon the Austrian Habsburg state operated from around 1740 to 1870 on its border with the Ottoman Empire to keep out plague, though the health cordon piggybacked on the existing military frontier.[350] Outside such exceptional military situations, a state's motivation to impose travel and trade restrictions to reduce mortality was often blunted by the fact that travel restrictions stringent enough to reduce contagion will also be strict enough to harm economic activity, reducing fiscal capacity and enraging domestic interest groups.[351]

346. M. Harrison 1992, 118–19; Low 2008, 270–1.
347. Lacey 1995, 1414.
348. Huang 2004.
349. Davidson 2020; Shangguan, Wang, and Sun 2020.
350. Mandić 2022, 46–7.
351. Jit et al. 2021, 2.

Even ancient rulers restricted travel during epidemics. Nearly three and a half millennia ago, around 1350 BCE, the governor of Byblos (in modern Lebanon) responded to an epidemic by declaring, "I will not permit the men of the town of Sumur to enter into my city. There is a pestilence in the town of Sumur."[352] The earliest *systematic* regulation of travel on public health grounds appears in the records millennia later, in the aftermath of the Black Death.[353] In the centuries after 1350, central and north Italian states not only mandated internal social distancing, but also developed health controls at harbours, river docks, mountain passes, and political frontiers.[354] Formal quarantines—where incoming travellers were detained for a standard period before admission—were first introduced in 1377 in the city-state of Ragusa (modern Dubrovnik), and by the 1420s had been adopted in most central and northern Italian states.[355] International quarantines were supported by pesthouses to intern foreigners, as in the case of the New Lazaretto erected by Venice in 1468.

But it was not until the seventeenth century that state measures to restrict epidemic contagion using border checks, sanitary cordons, and quarantines really proliferated. Central and north Italian states imposed sanitary cordons on land and quarantines on the sea during the seventeenth century, seeking to stop the north Italian plague from passing to southern Italy in 1629–33 and the south Italian plague from passing to the north in 1656–57.[356] From the early seventeenth century, Venice christened itself the "Barbican of Europe", because its government used systematic information collection, military control of maritime and land routes, and strict quarantine inspections to exclude plague from the Ottoman lands, where the authorities imposed little control.[357] This period also saw the inception of Habsburg attempts to build a sanitary cordon along its 1,900-kilometre military frontier with the Ottoman Empire, though the full panoply of guards, fortifications, and quarantines only developed after around 1740.[358]

State efforts to limit cross-border externalities using international quarantines moved to a higher level during the nineteenth century, when cholera broke out of its endemic heartland in West Bengal and made its way to the Middle East, Europe, and soon around the globe, transmitted by trade, war, religion, and migration. Most states imposed border checks, sanitary cordons, international quarantines, ship inspections, and health passes to try to control

352. Gestoso Singer 2017, 226–7.

353. Alfani 2022, 19–20.

354. Cipolla 1976, 12–30; Slack 1985, 45–6; Alfani and Melegaro 2010; Alfani 2013b; Alfani and Murphy 2017, 327–8.

355. Carmichael 1983, 513.

356. Henderson 2019, 27.

357. Andreozzi 2015, 117–18.

358. M. Harrison 2012, 36–7; Mitchell and Ingrao 2020; Mauelshagen 2020, 128–9.

the transmission of cholera. Yet between 1816 and 1923, no fewer than six waves of cholera erupted, each afflicting a wider swathe of the globe.

Of course, the series of pandemics that spread across multiple societies from the fourteenth to the twenty-first century might have been even worse without state travel restrictions to contain cross-border spillovers. But clearly these measures were inadequate to prevent the repeated eruptions of global pandemics. Why was this?

Insufficient state capacity was certainly one reason. But the key inadequacy was not fiscal. Quarantines and travel restrictions did not require much direct state spending. Quite the contrary. They were the epidemic-control tactic of choice for poor and underdeveloped states, because they cost so much less than sanitation infrastructure or domestic social distancing. As the French ambassador to Russia remarked in 1831 during the first European cholera epidemic, "Quarantinism was the response of weak and unstable regimes, able at best to concentrate efforts at certain points, but hampered in sustaining any massive intervention into the lives of their subjects by fears of possible unrest".[359] Quarantine continued to be favoured by most Mediterranean states throughout the nineteenth century "because it entailed a relatively small financial outlay, which was usually more than matched by the charges levied".[360] Fiscal capacity was not the reason states failed to contain cross-border externalities of contagion.

Bureaucratic capacity, by contrast, was always a serious problem. For one thing, state officials were often negligent. Plague entered Exeter in 1625 in a bale of infected wares which careless guards failed to keep out.[361] In Prato in 1630, the plague watchmen were caught gambling with cronies and "paying little attention to their service", while the guards manning the sanitary cordon in the surrounding mountains proved incapable of reading a health pass.[362] In Florence in 1630, an outsider without a valid health pass was turned back at one city gate but got in through another which the guards had left unattended.[363] Plague returned to Florence in 1633 because a whole series of guards at multiple Italian state frontiers let an infected woman and her son travel back from Livorno, a distance of 150 kilometres.[364] Plague arrived in the Kingdom of Naples in 1690 because local health officials in Polignano inspected a ship from plague-stricken Albania, ordered it to depart, but did not monitor compliance, so the ship remained for a further five days, unloading merchandise on the sly,

359. Baldwin 1999, 532.
360. M. Harrison 2012, 94.
361. Slack 1985, 112.
362. Quoted in Henderson 2019, 29.
363. Henderson 2019, 29.
364. Henderson 2019, 278.

sending its sailors ashore, and spreading contagion throughout Apulia.[365] In the 1731 Split plague, the quarantine pesthouse became a node of contagion for the city because the travellers, refugees, military recruits, and local plague patients it supposedly isolated were constantly breaking the rules by traipsing in and out.[366] In 1891 the SS *Deccan*, carrying Indian hajj pilgrims, brought epidemic cholera to Jeddah because incompetent inspectors in British India let it depart with the disease already spreading on board.[367] In 1910, plague spread in northeast China because quarantine inspectors were "hasty", "careless", and "shoddy", while higher officials explained that negligent subordinates could not be dismissed for fear of "troubles and hindrances".[368] This sounds like lack of state capacity. But it was also lack of state motivation. These states had plenty of capacity for war, palace building, and colonial conquest. By denying resources to adequate monitoring of borders against epidemic infection, states revealed their priorities.

Corrupt officials often vitiated cross-border travel checks. In 1630, plague gained access to Florence via the nearby village of Trespiano when the steward of the pilgrims' hospice took a bribe from a traveller, who duly infected the steward, his family, and all the other villagers, who in turn transmitted the plague to the city of Florence, unleashing the worst epidemic since the Black Death.[369] In seventeenth-century England, town guards routinely accepted bribes to let people smuggle in goods from infected places.[370] Near Split during the 1731 plague epidemic, officers and soldiers were well known to facilitate the illicit movement of people across the border with the Ottoman lands to serve their own personal advantage.[371] Around the Black Sea in the early nineteenth century, bribery was notoriously widespread among Russian quarantine guards, health passports were sold openly in the streets, and travellers could pay small sums to avoid quarantine altogether.[372] In British India in the 1890s, health inspectors accepted money to turn a blind eye to cholera symptoms on outgoing vessels carrying pilgrims to the Middle East.[373] Venality may reflect lack of fiscal capacity. But it also reflects lack of state motivation to allocate resources to official pay and training.

States also had motivations that heavily outweighed controlling contagion. For one thing, governments frequently yielded to pressure from powerful

365. Fusco 2017, 97.
366. Andreozzi 2015, 130.
367. M. Harrison 1992, 132.
368. Quoted in Hu 2010, 319–20, 326.
369. Henderson 2019, 33–4.
370. Slack 1985, 316.
371. Andreozzi 2015, 131.
372. Robarts 2010, 286–8; Robarts 2017, 233.
373. M. Harrison 1992, 132.

interests. In Naples in 1656, the vice-regal state relaxed travel rules for nobles and the rich, allowing plague to spread; in 1690–92, by contrast, it enforced quarantine even for powerful families, controlling the plague much more successfully.[374] In Marseille in 1720, plague gained entrance because the city's top magistrate used his political influence to exempt his own ship from quarantine.[375] The 1866 Indian cholera epidemic spread partly because the government of British India opposed ship quarantines to placate domestic business and religious interests.[376] The Manchurian plague of 1910–11 spread partly because the Harbin circuit intendant collaborated with cartelistic merchant associations to relax sanitary cordons.[377]

States weakened cross-border controls that conflicted with their own military purposes. In Bremen between 1623 and 1628, plague spread because military considerations led the King of Denmark to suspend inspections of imported grain and block closure of trade fairs.[378] Plague spread from Germany to Italy in 1629 partly because German military commanders did not enforce travel controls: "The German soldiers roam without health passes and they stay wheresoever they will."[379] Throughout the nineteenth century, efforts by states in Europe, the Ottoman Empire, and the eastern Mediterranean to systematize cholera and plague quarantines, prevent a race to the bottom on epidemic controls, and agree on how to contain cross-border contagion externalities were often blocked by individual states—even ones such as Britain with enormous capacity—seeking their own political advantage.[380] In 1906, the third International Conference of American states met at Rio de Janeiro to ratify the Washington Convention regulating quarantine measures to prevent cholera, plague, and yellow fever from passing among south, central, and north American countries. But Latin American states were suspicious of American "sanitary imperialism", a number of them insisted on retaining measures that violated the convention, and Brazil refused to send any delegate at all.[381] Lack of state capacity did not explain these failures. Rather, the "good" state capacity of the travel restrictions was outgunned by the "bad" state capacity of military and political imperatives.

A deeper reason why government regulations failed to control cross-border contagion was that they were imposed by individual nation-states. As a result, they suffered from two forms of behaviour by which governments tend to seek

374. Fusco 2017, 101–2.
375. Ermus 2020.
376. M. Harrison 1992, 119, 130.
377. Nathan 1967, 14.
378. Mauelshagen 2005, 239–40.
379. Quoted in Cipolla 1973, 15–16
380. M. Harrison 2012, 73–7, 141–53.
381. M. Harrison 2012, 133–5.

their own benefit at the expense of global well-being—whether measured in terms of pandemic control or in terms of facilitating international movements of people and goods.

The first problem was what economists call "race-to-the-bottom" behaviour. In the competition to attract more trade or favour their own business groups, each state has an incentive to undercut the trade of others by weaking its anti-epidemic measures—either in its own ports or in foreign ports its traders use. If a nation imposes a stringent quarantine policy, it would hamper trade, creating an incentive for a rival nation to impose a weaker quarantine policy. The nation with the stricter quarantine would lose trade, its fiscal revenues would fall, and it would lose support from domestic business interests. The undercutting nation with the milder quarantine policy would gain trade, its government would collect more taxes, and it would enjoy domestic business support. In this quarantine competition, each state would reason that its quarantine measures would be undercut by other nations and by illegal trade by infected ships from the non-quarantined nations, and would therefore decide not to incur the enforcement expenses and loss of trade associated with quarantine. So all countries would abandon their quarantine policies, even though all would benefit if only they could agree not to race to the bottom.

The second problem with quarantines imposed by individual nation-states arises because of what economists call "strategic trade" behaviour. According to this logic, each nation has an incentive to claim that rival nations are operating inadequate quarantines. It can then use such claims—true or false—as a justification for imposing its own quarantines in order to disrupt the trade of rival states in an effort to capture some of their trade. Inexorably, all nation-states would end up imposing quarantines against one another as weapons in a trade war. This would seem logical for the individual nation-state but harm the international trading system.

Race-to-the-bottom behaviour generated international quarantines that were too permissive, while strategic trade generated international quarantines that were too restrictive. Both forms of behaviour seemed advantageous to individual states but harmed contagion control and global trade. In principle, both problems could be solved by international agreements. From the 1860s onwards, consular commissions and international conferences were convened by various European, Middle Eastern, and north African powers to address these problems. In some zones of the world, for some periods, international agreements did succeed in controlling these two forms of opportunistic behaviour by individual states, though the agreements were seldom comprehensive or lasting.[382]

382. M. Harrison 2012, 69–72, 78–9, 141–72.

In the nineteenth and twentieth centuries, a number of international institutions emerged for coordinating responses to pandemics, as we have seen. It might be imagined that these solved the problem that individual governments care only about their own citizens and not those of other states. But the mere establishment of such international institutions was not enough. Rather, each state's own motivations and need to navigate domestic political pressures played an important role. International institutions could propose measures to solve cross-border contagion. But they seldom possessed enforcement capabilities. They continued to rely on national governments, which in turn relied on compliance inside their own societies. The extraordinary variation in the degree of compliance with World Health Organization Covid-19 pandemic guidelines provides a vivid illustration of how national interests can countervail against the mere existence of international health agencies.[383]

5.3. ENVIRONMENTAL DIPLOMACY

Microbes cross borders through natural as well as human vectors. This creates a cross-border externality involving the biophysical environment. The government of a particular state has an incentive to prevent environmental contagion at home, but not beyond the frontier. Contaminated water, for instance, is a major vector of gastrointestinal epidemics such as typhoid, dysentery, and cholera. In the words of a Romanian living in the Danube delta city of Sulina in 1894:

> [Rivers] belong to everyone, and riparian inhabitants do not have the right to pollute the water, which is used by other municipalities downstream, to kill fish living in the water, to poison the water with toxic waste from certain industries, to infect it with the secretions and excretions of the sick, rich in germs capable of spreading disease.[384]

Cross-border externalities can arise even inside a nation-state, if a river flows through different provinces or localities, each of which cares only about local pollution, not its downstream effects. But at least the central government is entitled to bang together the heads of local governments to make them take account of non-local costs and benefits of polluting rivers. In practice,

---

383. See the WHO's diplomatic description of this problem: World Health Organization, "Statement on the Fourteenth Meeting of the International Health Regulations (2005) Emergency Committee regarding the Coronavirus Disease (COVID-19) Pandemic", News, 30 January 2023, https://www.who.int/news/item/30-01-2023-statement-on-the-fourteenth-meeting-of-the-international-health-regulations-(2005)-emergency-committee-regarding-the-coronavirus-disease-(covid-19)-pandemic.

384. Quoted in Ardeleanu 2023, 14.

however, cross-border externalities can be severe even inside the same nation-state. In the USA in the 1890s, for instance, the Chicago local authorities sought to cleanse the city's water source by diverting sewage discharge from Lake Michigan into the Chicago River. Chicago sewage then flowed downstream into the Mississippi River, allegedly increasing typhoid cases in Saint Louis, Missouri. Saint Louis sued in a federal court to stop Chicago from discharging sewage into the Chicago River. The judgment fell in favour of Chicago, but at least Saint Louis had a federal court to which it could appeal.[385] Similar cross-border externalities prevail inside India, where the Ganges has for centuries transmitted epidemics via sewage, water burials, and animal waste. The Covid-19 pandemic decreased industrial pollution of the Ganges but increased epidemiological pollution, because the river was used to dispose of huge numbers of human corpses. Even the modern Indian state fails to coordinate or coerce local governments, communities, and religious organizations to limit pollution in the interests of all.[386]

Cross-border contagion is even less tractable for international rivers, which can often be kept healthy only through sanitary diplomacy. The regulation of the Danube illustrates the possibilities and limits of such diplomacy. The Danube is 2,850 kilometres long and flows through 10 modern countries (Germany, Austria, Slovakia, Hungary, Croatia, Serbia, Bulgaria, Romania, Ukraine, and Moldova). Its watershed extends into another 9 countries, and its Black Sea outlet is shared between modern Romania and Ukraine.[387] For many centuries, therefore, the Danube has been shared among multiple states, whose use and abuse of its waters have literally spilled over onto one another's inhabitants. Across the centuries, upstream decisions on navigation, trade, industrial waste, domestic sewage, fishing, locks, dams, shoreline erosion, and flooding turned the Danube into the main route for epidemics to spread to south-eastern Europe, particularly Romania and Ukraine.[388] As one Romanian expert put it in 1894, the Danube received "colossal quantities of putrescible matter from Europe even before it reached Romania's borders".[389] In turn, ships contracted cholera, typhoid, and gastroenteritis in the Romanian port of Sulina and carried the diseases back upriver to other ports, as with the typhoid epidemic that was transmitted from Sulina to Hamburg in 1895.[390]

The problem of cross-border contagion along the Danube was not solved by bilateral sanitation diplomacy, which foundered on the rock of international

385. Troesken 2015, 53.
386. Sigdel, Carlton, and Gautam 2023.
387. Olson and Krug 2020.
388. Ardeleanu 2023, 3.
389. Quoted in Ardeleanu 2023, 14.
390. Ardeleanu 2023, 11.

resentments. It needed the European Commission of the Danube, an agency put together by several great powers. The commission provided political pressure and—crucially—funding to persuade the Romanian authorities to build a modern water treatment plant in Sulina.[391] By 1911, after decades of teething problems, water quality in Sulina became so good that a local newspaper remarked that "dysentery, typhoid fever and other water-derived diseases have almost completely disappeared".[392] In 1913 the city was spared a cholera outbreak despite the arrival of over 1,000 Turkish refugees bearing cholera from the Second Balkan War.[393]

The Danube delta illustrates the benefits of sanitary diplomacy, but also its limitations. For one thing, the imposition of a German waterworks model derived from the Rhine city of Worms, which had not been tested in Danube conditions, proved inadequate, and it took nearly two decades and huge expenditure to convert it to a new ozonization system that actually did the job. For another, the Danube commission simply funded a mitigation system in the worst-affected locality rather than negotiating with upstream polities to control pollution. The costs of the mitigation system were shared by the powers funding the commission but were not imposed on the upstream polluters and thus did not deter continued discharge of infected effluent. The troubled military and political situation of the first half of the twentieth century blocked cross-border cooperation, with the USSR-dominated Danube commission refusing to cooperate with the United Nations and its agencies, while the western bloc re-established the Danube commission in exile in Rome. It was not until the late 1950s that cooperation between the "communist" and "capitalist" Danube states tentatively resumed, and not until after 1989 that true sanitary diplomacy again became possible.[394] State motivation and political realities thus mattered more than state capacity in tackling cross-border contagion along the Danube, even though the river traversed many high-capacity states.

5.4. VACCINE DIPLOMACY

Epidemics do not stop at political frontiers. Even a state with no altruistic sentiments towards foreigners has reason to prevent epidemics abroad to protect its own citizens. One way to achieve this end is vaccine diplomacy, where donor countries deliver vaccines to recipient countries to serve foreign policy objectives and—it is hoped—global health goals. The state has advantages over other institutions in spearheading international immunization campaigns. Its

---

391. Ardeleanu 2023, 8–10.
392. Quoted in Ardeleanu 2023, 14.
393. Ardeleanu 2023, 13.
394. Ardeleanu 2020, 321–2.

fiscal capacity can draw on an entire country's resources, and it monopolizes legitimate coercion, helping it exert pressure on other states.

But here again, motivation matters. A state may see greater advantage in devoting resources to vaccinating its own citizens who pay taxes and vote, ignoring the long-term benefit of eradicating foreign disease reservoirs which can reinfect the home polity. Recipient countries themselves may resist vaccination efforts from foreign powers which they perceive as seeking political or commercial domination.

In the decade after smallpox vaccination was invented in 1796, several European states supported international expeditions to take vaccination to other countries. The English Mediterranean Mission visited Gibraltar, Minorca, Malta, Sicily, Naples, and Marmaris in 1800–1, carried out hundreds of vaccinations, provided live vaccine, and established several vaccine institutes. But this mission was devised and implemented by a private network of doctors, philanthropists, and diplomats. The state merely facilitated the mission in the context of naval and diplomatic manoeuvring.[395] At most, this vaccination mission was a hybrid enterprise between private actors and a permissive state.

The Russian Buttats Expedition of 1802, by contrast, received direct state support. Originally, the tsar intended an expedition of public vaccinators to travel from province to province in European Russia and then to Russian imperial dominions in Asia, immunizing and setting up vaccine institutes as it proceeded. In the event, the expedition journeyed slowly, covered only seven provinces, ran into vaccine hesitancy, and completed just 6,000 vaccinations before limiting itself to despatching vaccine and instructions to more distant provinces. In 1805–6, the tsar sent a follow-up mission to China, which consolidated and extended vaccination east of the Urals but failed to gain entry to the Celestial Empire.[396]

France adopted a different approach in its conquered territories during the Napoleonic Wars. French puppet states in Hessen and Piombino-Lucca were the earliest in Europe to impose vaccination mandates, as we saw in chapter 2.[397] In the decade up to 1815, France set up vaccine committees, disseminated information, and despatched vaccines to client polities in northern Italy, the German Rhineland, the Netherlands, and the Illyrian Provinces along the Dalmatian coast, seeking to persuade subject peoples of the enlightened benevolence of France over its dominions.[398] In so doing, it exploited the inability of occupied territories to resist, championing vaccination abroad to a greater degree than at home in France, where domestic resistance delayed a national vaccination mandate until 1902.

---

395. M. Bennett 2020, 126–9.
396. M. Bennett 2020, 231–3.
397. M. Bennett 2020, 195, 247, 264, 362.
398. Baldwin 1999, 252; M. Bennett 2020, 168–71.

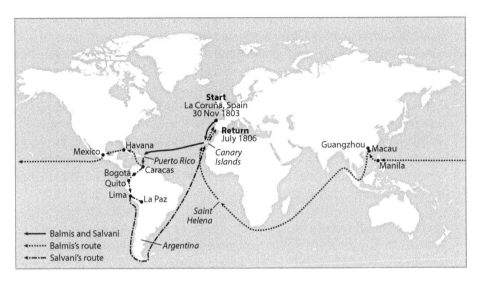

FIGURE 3.4. Route of the Spanish Royal and Philanthropic Vaccine Expedition, 1803–12. The expedition was despatched by King Charles IV of Spain to take smallpox vaccine and vaccination practices to the Americas, the Philippines, Macau, and Canton. *Source*: Based on Franco-Paredes, Lammoglia, and Santos-Preciado 2005, 1287.

Spain deployed the most impressive vaccine diplomacy, with the Royal and Philanthropic Vaccine Expedition of 1803, inspired by Enlightenment guilt over the epidemics unleashed overseas by Spanish conquests.[399] This expedition, whose route is shown in figure 3.4, aimed to vaccinate the inhabitants of the Canary Islands, Colombia, Ecuador, Peru, Mexico, the Philippines, and China, to disseminate epidemiological knowledge, and to establish local vaccine commissions to carry on the work. It vaccinated up to a million people in Spanish America, saved thousands of lives, transmitted vaccination knowledge across the world, and established local organizations, some of which carried on vaccinating for generations.

These early vaccination expeditions vividly illustrate how governments can project their power across political frontiers to prevent contagion. State capacity was clearly essential, but the states that practised vaccine diplomacy in the early nineteenth century did not have high capacity by modern standards. Moreover, Britain had higher state capacity than France, Russia, or Spain, but its vaccination expedition had the least state involvement. State motivation was more important.

But these expeditions also illuminate many of the problems with vaccine diplomacy. For one thing, the expeditions were viscerally interlinked with other state interests, particularly warfare, military occupation, and colonial

399. Franco-Paredes, Lammoglia, and Santos-Preciado 2005; M. Bennett 2020, 214–16, 295–357.

domination. For another, they seldom achieved deep or lasting acceptance in the donor societies. All were hindered by suspicion about their motives (often justified), jurisdictional conflicts, entrenched elites, medical privileges, religious shibboleths, and community resistance.

Vaccine diplomacy has flourished to this day, achieving notable successes but also encountering many of the same obstacles as in the early nineteenth century. From 1913 onwards, rich countries in North America and Europe sought to introduce vaccination into many less developed countries, often in cooperation with their own civil society organizations such as the Rockefeller Foundation and the Pasteur Institute.[400] The Cold War was paradoxically one of the most productive eras of vaccine diplomacy, during which the USA and the USSR cooperated in developing and delivering polio vaccines in the 1950s, hugely limiting the spread of polio in many societies beyond their borders. During the 1960s, similar international diplomacy diffused smallpox vaccination, eradicating the natural disease entirely by 1970.[401] In the past century, individual rich countries, philanthropic foundations, and the World Health Organization have worked together to provide vaccines and other preventive measures against yellow fever, hookworm, malaria, tuberculosis, measles, meningococcal meningitis, enteric bacteria, leishmaniasis, and AIDS/HIV in many poor countries.[402] But even during this seeming golden age, donation and absorption of vaccines across international borders suffered from the same problems as ever. On the donor side, they were hindered by geopolitical suspicions and national self-interest, such as tying donations to political and business benefits. On the recipient end, they suffered from postcolonial suspicions, religious resentments, and domestic vaccine hesitancy.[403]

Such problems dog vaccine diplomacy to this day. During the Covid-19 pandemic, international vaccine donations were more generously funded than in the nineteenth and twentieth centuries. But they were also comprehensively hindered by geopolitical and institutional obstacles. Almost as soon as Covid-19 vaccines were developed, vaccine-producing polities such as China, Russia, Cuba, the United States, the United Kingdom, and the European Union started using them for diplomatic competition, "playing favourites for geopolitical reasons, making decisions with limited transparency, and competing for the favour of public opinion and governments in different countries".[404] This does not mean there were no benefits. Without Covid-19 vaccine diplomacy, poor countries would have had even lower vaccination rates, their vaccine

---

400. Hotez 2001, 862.
401. Hotez 2001, 864; Hotez 2014.
402. Hotez 2001, 862–3.
403. Hotez 2014; Hotez and Narayan 2021.
404. Greer et al. 2022, 240.

manufacturing capacity would have been even smaller, and global inequality in vaccination would have been even higher. But Covid-19 vaccine diplomacy in the 2020s encountered eerily similar problems to smallpox vaccine diplomacy more than two centuries earlier. Donor countries delivered less funding than promised, institutions in recipient countries resisted vaccination, there was no credible plan to ensure that the donated vaccines actually reached large enough numbers of ordinary people, the number of vaccines distributed was small relative to requirements, and the number effectively dispensed was even smaller. Even the most international and charitably motivated campaign, the WHO's COVAX programme, suffered from unambitious targets and limited delivery. A year after its establishment, COVAX had despatched 70 million vaccines out of its unambitious target of 2 billion, just 3.5 per cent of those required.[405] Many donor countries used the programme to sell their own vaccines, extract political advantage from recipients, and earmark donations to specific recipients for soft-power purposes. Some countries sought to discredit the vaccines provided by others. In 2021, for instance, Russia used social media to impugn the integrity and safety of Western vaccines. Chinese media and health officials propagated conspiracy theories claiming that American and European mRNA vaccines had not been sufficiently tested, were linked to deaths of elderly people, and might be part of biological warfare.[406] These failures of vaccine diplomacy threatened to exacerbate the Covid-19 pandemic, increasing "the odds that the evolution of the virus defeats the very effective vaccines used in rich countries".[407]

Vaccine diplomacy, with all its imperfections, achieved striking successes historically and still does so to this day. States have sometimes proved able and willing to help limit contagion outside their borders by deploying their own fiscal resources and their monopoly of legitimate coercion. Where they succeeded, it was typically by cooperating with civil society organizations such as philanthropic foundations on the donor side, as well as communal and religious organizations on the recipient side. Where they failed, they fell foul of adverse incentives at home and abroad. Donor states begrudged resources to vaccinate foreign citizens and used vaccines to serve their own geopolitical and commercial ends. Recipient states were reluctant to accept foreign vaccines for fear of geopolitical domination and domestic resistance. Non-epidemiological interests of donor and recipient states hindered outcomes that could have benefited all. This is not to discount the importance of vaccine diplomacy, but rather to identify the historical mistakes. Successful vaccine diplomacy makes the domestic political case for limiting foreign contagion, minimizes donor state

---

405. Kampfner 2021.
406. Hotez and Narayan 2021, 2338; Shih 2021.
407. Greer et al. 2022, 241.

self-seeking, and collaborates with non-governmental organizations inside both donor and recipient societies.

5.5. WAR AND DISEASE

"War is not an adventure. It is a disease."[408] The famous children's author who wrote this during the Battle of France in 1940 meant it as a metaphor. But it is also a fact. Directly, war spreads disease by moving masses of soldiers, camp followers, captives, and refugees across different spheres of immunity under insanitary conditions.[409] Indirectly, war exacerbates epidemics by diverting funds away from civilian purposes such as contagion control measures, public health information, and medical research.

War is by far the most ubiquitous cross-border enterprise practised by states. Military activity consumed the great majority of state expenditures in high-capacity states until well into the nineteenth century.[410] War and trade often used the same transportation routes, as we saw in chapter 2. But war had different targets, so it often moved disease into "inland civilian regions which were otherwise little exposed to long-distance contact".[411] In 1323, the earliest documented European influenza epidemic spread via the Catalan army invading Sardinia and the papal army campaigning against Milan.[412] In 1345–46, as we have seen, the Black Death came from Mongolia to the Black Sea with a Tartar army,[413] was fostered there by insanitary conditions during the siege of Caffa,[414] and moved onwards to the Middle East and Europe in military galleys as well as merchant ships.[415] In 1348, an army besieging Baghdad spread plague to the civilian populations of Mesopotamia and Iran,[416] and in 1349–50 Muslim and Christian armies spread plague to civilians throughout Spain.[417] In fifteenth-century France, epidemics of plague, typhus, and dysentery were carried by English and French armies during the Hundred Years War.[418] In the Ottoman lands between 1463 and 1479, war with Venice unleashed a series of intense plague outbreaks.[419] In the Netherlands during the 1566 iconoclasm and

408. Saint-Exupéry (1942) 1986, 46.
409. Smallman-Raynor and Cliff 2004.
410. Hoffman 2015; Ogilvie 2023, 35–40.
411. Duncan-Jones 1996, 135.
412. Bauch 2020, 57–8.
413. Dols 1977, 52–3; Benedictow 2004, 50.
414. H. Barker 2021, 119.
415. H. Barker 2021, 123.
416. Borsch and Sabraa 2017, 67.
417. Dols 1977, 66.
418. Park 1985, 89.
419. Varlik 2015, 152.

the 1568 Dutch Revolt, plague and other epidemics spread with troop movements and military grain transports.[420] During the Thirty Years War (1618–48), plague killed 30–35 per cent of central and northern Italians and 40 per cent of Germans.[421] In eighteenth-century Russia, the Great Northern War and the Russian–Turkish War killed more soldiers than died of enemy fire and spread across the civilian population, triggering the two worst plague epidemics of the century.[422] In 1757, a cholera epidemic broke out in the army of the Afghan ruler Ahmad Shah Durrant, which was invading northern India, forcing him to retreat from the holy city of Vrindavan.[423] In 1776, the War of American Independence exacerbated a smallpox epidemic which was, as John Adams wrote to his wife, "ten times more terrible than Britons, Canadians and Indians together".[424] In 1817, British troops carried cholera from Bengal to the rest of India, whence it spread across the globe.[425] In China in the 1860s, troop movements during the Muslim Rebellion triggered a plague epidemic that killed up to 80 per cent of the inhabitants of some Yunnan counties.[426] In 1870–71, the Franco-Prussian War sparked off the worst smallpox pandemic of the century, killing half a million Europeans.[427] In nineteenth-century Africa, European and indigenous armies triggered numerous smallpox epidemics.[428] At the end of the First World War, mass troop movements helped spread the 1918–19 influenza pandemic that killed 50–100 million people across the globe.[429] Military priorities dominated public health, as admitted in 1919 by the English chief medical officer when he observed that "the relentless needs of warfare justified incurring the risk of spreading infections".[430]

Wars spread epidemics not just during active campaigning but when soldiers returned home. Smallpox may have become established in Europe in the eleventh and twelfth centuries with Crusading armies returning from the Levant.[431] The Black Death came to Morocco 1348 with Marinid soldiers returning from Tunisia.[432] Plague came to Devon in 1589 with soldiers returning from Portugal,

420. Rommes 2015, 52–3.

421. Alfani and Murphy 2017, 327; Henderson 2019, 23–4; Outram 2001.

422. Lammel 2021, 82; Melikishvili 2006, 22.

423. Tumbe 2020, 27.

424. Quoted in M. Bennett 2020, 269–71.

425. Jannetta 1987, 157; R. Evans 1992, 160; Arnold 2020, 573.

426. Benedict 1988, 125.

427. Baldwin 1999, 263; Krylova and Earn 2019, 12.

428. Dias 1981, 358–9, 368–9; Koponen 1988, 666.

429. N. P. Johnson and Mueller 2002; Taubenberger and Morens 2006; Aassve et al. 2021, 840; Arnold 2019, 191; Harris 2018, 605, 610–11; Chandra, Christensen, and Likhtman 2020, 414; Galletta and Giommoni 2020, 2, 7–8; Flecknoe, Wakefield, and Simmons 2018, 63.

430. Quoted in Gorsky et al. 2021, 208.

431. Snowden 2019, 97.

432. Dols 1977, 65.

and a contemporary described how "the diseases which the soldiers brought home with them did grow more grievous as they carried the same farther into the land".[433] Plague came to Provence in 1629 with regiments coming back from the Italian theatre of the Thirty Years War.[434] A typhus epidemic spread across France in 1812 with the Napoleonic army retreating from the Moscow campaign.[435] The 1918–19 influenza pandemic was brought by soldiers returning from Europe to India,[436] Africa,[437] and the Ottoman Empire.[438]

Prisoners of war were another conduit. The Black Death came to Yemen when its captured king, Mujahid, returned from imprisonment in Cairo.[439] Plague spread across Russia and eastern Europe in 1770 because soldiers fighting in the Russian–Turkish War captured prisoners who then infected them.[440] Smallpox raged across Prussia in 1870 because Berliners came to Spandau to gape at diseased French prisoners.[441] Influenza spread rapidly in Anatolia in 1918 because, as one British captive described, prisoners of war "were confined to houses and being very badly treated, naturally the disease spread very rapidly under this condition of close confinement".[442] In the autumn of 1918, according to a report to the League of Nations, "'Spanish influenza' was brought into Russia from the west (an exceptional case) by the prisoners of war returning from Germany, and very quickly spread over the whole country".[443] Covid-19 spread in Syria in 2020 among the 90,000 prisoners captured and incarcerated during the civil war.[444]

Refugees incubated epidemics because of forced displacement and irregular living conditions. During the Thirty Years War, plague raged in Bremen among displaced peasants flooding in from the countryside to shelter from imperial troops between 1623 and 1628.[445] Typhus spread in Civil War York in 1643–44 among villagers seeking protection from marauding soldiers.[446] The Baltic plague epidemic of 1700–21 was escalated by civilian refugees from

433. Quoted in Slack 1985, 85.
434. Kettering 2001, 38.
435. M. Bennett 2020, 241.
436. Mills 1986, 4–5; Arnold 2019, 181–2, 191; Arnold 2020, 573–4, 577; Prabhu 2021.
437. Doyle 2000, 443; Patterson 1983, 485; Chandra, Christensen, and Likhtman 2020, 415; De Kadt et al. 2020, 2; Prabhu 2021.
438. Yolun and Kopar 2015, 1103.
439. Dols 1977, 47.
440. Melikishvili 2006, 24.
441. Baldwin 1999, 263.
442. Quoted in Yolun and Kopar 2015, 1104.
443. Quoted in Ewing 2021, 251.
444. Abbara et al. 2020, 194.
445. Mauelshagen 2005, 239–40.
446. Galley 1995, 452.

the Great Northern War.[447] The 1860s Yunnan plague epidemic in China circulated among people displaced by the Muslim Rebellion.[448] The 1918 influenza pandemic spread in Belgium via French refugees fleeing from the Germans.[449] Iran and Turkey suffered some of the world's highest Covid-19 infections in 2020 by sheltering 5.5 million refugees from the Syrian civil war.[450]

Military quartering almost always spread epidemics to civilian hosts. The 1629–31 Tuscan plague epidemic initially spread from German soldiers quartered in civilian dwellings, where they emitted "unbearable odours due to the rotting straw whereon they sleep and die".[451] Typhus spread in Bristol in 1641 from billeted Royalist soldiers, "so that the houses where they quartered are like gaols for nastiness".[452] Plague circulated in Burgundy in 1649 via soldiers who "have to be fed to prevent them wandering or else, if they fall ill, spoiling and infecting the town with epidemics."[453] Plague diffused in Romania in 1770 through Russian soldiers quartered in civilian households in Iași.[454]

Army deserters spread disease to civilians. Upper California suffered its worst ever epidemics in 1769 and 1777 when Spanish troops deserted to live in indigenous communities.[455] Plague spread in Manchuria in 1920 when soldiers deserted to shelter in underground hovels, where they spread contagion to the civilian population, 25 per cent of whom died in the resulting epidemic.[456] The influenza pandemic diffused across Eastern Anatolia in 1918 partly via contacts among the French occupying army, deserting soldiers, prisoners of war, and civilians.[457]

Most spectacularly, state action escalated epidemics by bringing together separate spheres of immunity. This already occurred with the Ottoman conquest of Syria and Egypt in 1516–17, which intensified plague epidemics in the Middle East by facilitating ecological exchanges on a widening scale, connecting the Mediterranean basin with the Black Sea region and its hinterland, the Caucasus and Central Asia, the Red Sea, and the Indian Ocean.[458] An even more catastrophic example was the Columbian Exchange in the centuries after 1492, when Europeans arrived in the New World bringing diseases against

447. Frandsen 2010, 20, 24.
448. Benedict 1988, 125.
449. Quoted in Devos et al. 2021, 259.
450. Abbara et al. 2020, 192–3.
451. Quoted in Cipolla 1973, 15–16.
452. Quoted in Slack 1985, 121.
453. Quoted in Brockliss and Jones 1997, 255.
454. Melikishvili 2006, 24.
455. Cook 1943, 22–7.
456. Nathan 1967, 66.
457. Yolun and Kopar 2015, 1104.
458. Varlik 2015, 161–2.

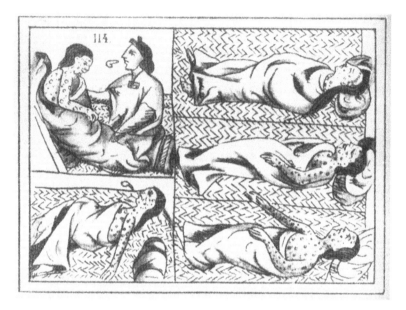

FIGURE 3.5. Aztec drawing of smallpox victims, Tenochtitlan, Mexico, 1520. Tenoch-titlan was the largest city in the pre-Columbian Americas, with a population of *c*.215,000 inhabitants in 1519. Its residents described this epidemic as *hueyzahuatl* (great leprosy) and *totomonaliztli* (pustules), but it was almost certainly smallpox. The disease covered the sick with sores from head to foot, prevented them from caring from themselves, and disrupted supply chains, so that vast numbers died of starvation as well as disease. On the top left of this image, a female healer cares for a male victim. On the bottom left, a female victim cries in pain while trying to move. The drawing comes from the Florentine Codex, an encyclopaedic work about the people and culture of central Mexico compiled by Bernardino de Sahagún (1499–1590), a Spanish Franciscan missionary who arrived in Mexico in 1529. The book was researched, compiled, and written by Sahagún in partnership with Nahua men who had been his students, and took thirty years to complete (1545–77). The published book, *Historia general de las cosas de Nueva España*, is 2,400 pages long, consists of parallel text in Nahuatl and Spanish, and contains 2,468 illustrations by Nahua art-ists, including this one. *Source*: Wikimedia Commons.

which indigenous peoples had no immunity. These included measles, typhus, influenza, and above all smallpox, as illustrated by the sixteenth-century Aztec drawing of smallpox sufferers in figure 3.5.[459]

The mortality caused by the Columbian Exchange is poorly documented, regionally various, and vigorously debated, but estimates range from 20 to 95 per cent of the pre-Columbian population.[460] In Spanish America by the end of the colonial period, all indigenous populations that encountered

459. Crosby 1972.
460. Livi-Bacci 2006; J. Williamson 2010, 241; Arroyo Abad, Davies, and Van Zanden 2012, 151.

Europeans were smaller than half their pre-Columbian size; some were extinguished completely within two generations.[461] Similar epidemics arose out of military expeditions to Australia, as in 1788 when the British fleet brought more than 1,000 convicts and hundreds of soldiers to Sydney Cove, unleashing a smallpox epidemic that killed many indigenous people.[462] In nineteenth-century Africa, European and indigenous armies brought together separate spheres of immunity, spreading and worsening innumerable epidemics.[463]

Some go so far as to argue that epidemics were a form of "biological weapon" deployed by European states to conquer other continents.[464] Occasionally, European military figures did act in this way, as in 1763 when the British commanding officer in America, Sir Jefferey Amherst, wrote, "Could it not be contrived to Send the Small Pox among those Disaffected Tribes of Indians? We must, on this occasion, Use Every Stratagem in our power to Reduce them." Several British army officers indeed deliberately gave smallpox-infested blankets to native Americans, who duly caught and spread the disease.[465] But there is no evidence that such practices were used systematically—indeed, this example is so shocking partly because it is so rare. States seldom used disease deliberately in this way, even against enemies.

But they did not need to. Even without deliberate biological warfare, state-sponsored military expeditions triggered catastrophic epidemics on other continents. Because they struck immunologically naïve populations, the resulting mortality—at least during the Columbian Exchange—sometimes exceeded that of the Black Death in Europe centuries before.[466] Even if the cross-border externalities of state action were not deliberate, they were unquestionably lethal.

6. State Overkill

Much discussion of state anti-contagion measures emphasizes their benefits or laments their absence. Less analyses the costs. The benefits of public epidemic measures may fail to arise because the state lacks capacity, technology, motivation, or domestic consensus. But there are costs to state action during epidemics, and it may be good if those do not arise either.

The historical record reveals many instances of what might be called "state overkill". Some episodes of overkill arose when a state imposed excessive

461. Newson 1985, 41–2.
462. M. Bennett 2020, 331.
463. Doyle 2000, 437–43.
464. Diamond 1997.
465. Quoted in Fenn 2000, 1555.
466. M. Harrison 2012, 17.

epidemic control measures because of an inaccurate estimate of the benefits. Governments do not have perfect information. They can underestimate the benefits of epidemic control measures—as we saw earlier with state failure. But sometimes they err in the opposite direction, overestimating the societal benefits of epidemic controls and underestimating their costs. The genuine difficulty in calculating the balance between costs and benefits could easily give rise to authoritarian overkill. More often, however, there was no governmental cost–benefit analysis. Instead, the state used an epidemic as a pretext for imposing extraordinary coercion that benefited the governors at the expense of the governed. Scrutinizing situations in which states behaved in this way can make sense of popular resistance to public health measures—such as that discussed in chapters 4 and 5—which might otherwise seem incomprehensible.

Strict social and physical distancing policies imposed high costs—both economic and personal. Many plague treatises referred to the widespread revulsion against social distancing. One popular medieval Dutch plague treatise, for instance, provided a recipe for a prophylactic drink that bestowed a year's immunity, so that the drinker no longer had to avoid society but "is free to go as he pleases".[467] In 1556 the English clergyman James Balmford began his *Short Dialogue concerning the Plagues Infection* by tackling the economic and personal implications head-on:

> I will propound certain doubts: and will first begin with that which I know doth most trouble most men, especially of the poorer sort. To wit, they think it most extreme cruelty, to be barred from going abroad to seek relief or maintenance for them and theirs, except they either had sufficient of their own, or their wants were supplied. . . . [And] those, who are not so poor, but that they may keep their houses at their own charges, till they be cleansed. . . . They think it an hell to be so long shut up from company and their business: the neglecting whereof is the decay of their state.[468]

Many voices down the centuries confirm the "hell" of being "shut up from company and their business". In the Scottish burgh of Irvine in 1500, for instance, the town government limited trade so comprehensively that Adam Multrar publicly announced at the market cross that "since the council was taking measures injurious to his livelihood as a travelling merchant, he was quitting the town".[469] In Seville in 1582, local merchants protested that a Health Board ban on trade with plague-infected cities would cause "intolerable harm and injury", especially since it applied to wares such as wine and vinegar which did

467. Dorst 2019, 12, 16 (quotation; my translation).
468. Balmford 1603, 8–10 (spelling modernized).
469. Oram 2007, 29–30.

not carry infection.[470] In Milan in 1630, merchants complained that plague-related travel restrictions caused losses "to all connected with this trade".[471] In 1766, British merchants in Livorno complained to the Privy Council that quarantine charges "amounted to as much as one fifth of the value of their cargoes", not to mention the value of goods perished or lost during detention.[472] In the Black Sea region in the early nineteenth century, Russian quarantine regulations brutally restricted commercial activities which were essential for the local economy.[473] In 1836, Russia imposed a strict quarantine involving arbitrary detention of trade and shipping; local traders suffered and foreign ship-captains complained that Russian gunboats, using sanitation as a pretext, "boarded, visited, detained, examined and annoyed every vessel passing up the Danube".[474] In the 1910–11 Manchurian plague, local merchants vociferously objected to government epidemic controls on the grounds that they strangled business.[475] In North Korea during the Covid-19 pandemic, government border closures and other pandemic edicts stifled so much of the informal trade that was essential to ordinary livelihoods that the number of malnourished people rose by 10 per cent between 2020 and 2023.[476]

It might be argued that traders and consumers who opposed epidemic measures were simply seeking their own self-interest without considering contagion for others. They did not know any better than governments whether the costs of epidemic measures outweighed the benefits for society at large. No doubt this was often true. But the economic costs of epidemic measures nonetheless existed—and could themselves indirectly damage epidemic control. For one thing, restricting economic activity choked off the tax revenues that financed border guards, quarantine officials, plague cleaners, pesthouses, and sustenance for the poor to comply with home lockdown, all of which were crucial for epidemic control. Beyond formal fiscal capacity, well-off citizens were important emergency donors to local exchequers during epidemics, as in the burgh of Ayr when over half of the town's expenditures in the 1515 plague were financed personally by a certain William Nesbit, "furnisher of the sick folks upon the moor in time of the pest".[477] Against this background, it would not be surprising if governments sometimes miscalculated the relative costs and benefits of restricting economic activity during epidemics.

470. Quoted in M. Harrison 2012, 15.
471. Quoted in Cipolla 1976, 43.
472. M. Harrison 2012, 43.
473. Robarts 2010, 286–8; Robarts 2017, 233.
474. Quoted in Ardeleanu 2020, 33.
475. Nathan 1967, 14.
476. *Economist* 2023.
477. Quoted in Oram 2007, 39n132 (spelling modernized).

Many cases of state overkill, moreover, arose not from miscalculation but from deliberate government strategy. States were not averse to using an epidemic as a pretext for imposing authoritarian measures in order to augment their capacity to control their citizens. A vivid illustration is provided by the extraordinary measures the Russian state put in place during the 1892–93 cholera epidemic, arbitrarily arresting citizens without evidence of infection, forcibly interning them in isolation barracks, placing them under armed military guard, subjecting inmates to extreme violence and degradation, and birching or executing the recalcitrant. As one Russian physician later recounted,

> Many patients . . . had heard that some sort of *sanitaire* in leather gloves with an iron hook roamed the streets; if he saw someone who looked sick—or just a bit drunk—he would seize the unfortunate one with the hook, throw him like a dog into a cart, and carry him to the cholera hospital. There they would shower him with lime, cram it into his mouth, eyes and ears . . . throw his bare body into a pitch coffin, nail down the lid, and without confession or Holy Communion throw him into a grave quite disrespectfully. And they would not even place a cross over the grave, so that no one would know where the unfortunate martyr was buried.[478]

State anti-contagion measures display excessive authoritarianism in many other historical epidemics in earlier and later centuries. When the Manchu dynasty took over Han China in 1644, according to an early Qing account, "Residents of the capital who had smallpox [in their family] were ordered to leave their homes and exit the city to avoid its contagious spread. Some were so afraid of the authorities along the roads that they abandoned their children."[479] Other accounts describe how non-infected Chinese families were evicted on sheer suspicion, poor families could not in any case afford to leave, and families with infected offspring killed them to avoid forcible expulsion from their family homes.[480] In 1656–57, the Genoese state interned plague suspects in the Consolazione Monastery, where lazaretto conditions were so horrific that it came to be called "Sconsolatione" (Desolation).[481] In the 1656 Rome plague, a traveller from Terracina who arrived at the city gates but could not find his health pass was shot on the spot; when he was undressed for burial, his executioners found the mislaid pass inside his boot.[482] In the 1731 Split plague epidemic, two brothers from the village of Knin were executed by firing squad for moving between family homes with a few cattle—despite the fact that the

---

478. Quoted in Frieden 1977, 548.
479. Quoted in Hanson 2011, 109.
480. Chang 1996, 182–3; Hanson 2011, 109; Leung 2020a, 258.
481. Henderson 2019, 185.
482. Gentilcore 2012, 161.

Governor General in charge of plague measures in Split kept open the long-distance cattle trade to provision Venice itself.[483] In the 1801 Egyptian plague epidemic, the French authorities

> exercised the greatest severity in the application of sanitary measures [which] harass the people and frighten them. When someone fell ill, the doctor visited him, and if he was recognized as stricken with plague, he was immediately transferred to quarantine without any of his family being able to see him afterwards. . . . [If] any passerby was imprudent enough to touch the door of the house or to overstep the boundary drawn around it, he was immediately arrested by the guards and sent to quarantine.[484]

In 1835, the Habsburg sanitary cordon against plague along the 1,900-kilometre Ottoman border was enforced so harshly that, as described by an English traveller, "If you dare to break the laws of the quarantine, you will be tried with military haste; the court will scream out a sentence to you from a tribunal some fifty yards off . . . and after that you will find yourself carefully shot and carelessly buried".[485] In 1856, the Portuguese colonial administrators in Goa used violence to "vaccinate an immense number of people" and to stamp out the indigenous practice of variolation, of which the colonial administrators disapproved.[486] In the Naples cholera epidemic of 1884, the Vatican newspaper reported:

> The conduct of the authorities contributes mightily to the terror of the citizenry. As soon as a person is found to suffer the least disorder of the stomach, his home is invaded by municipal guards, police and doctors. . . . [W]hile it is possible to admire their energy, everyone condemns their behaviour. The guards and doctors act with such lack of concern and with such highhandedness . . . [487]

In the 1904 smallpox epidemic in Rio de Janeiro, sanitary police imposed a military-style "Torture Code", during which they forcibly invaded homes and shops, destroyed furniture and wares, ejected residents for days, sprayed noxious chemicals, demolished tenements, and violently enforced compulsory vaccination, imprisoning those who resisted or sentencing them to forced labour in distant locations.[488] In 1905 a Portuguese businessman who filed a court appeal against the forcible disinfection of his residence against yellow

---

483. Andreozzi 2015, 131.
484. Quoted in Kuhnke 1990, 76.
485. Kinglake 1844, 2.
486. Quoted in Bastos 2009, 152.
487. Quoted in Snowden 1995, 140–1.
488. Machado 2021; Cantisano 2022, 618–19.

fever was warned by his lawyer that "violence will be inflicted on you": the next day an "army" of inspectors, sanitary agents, policemen, and street gang members hired by the authorities broke into his house to disinfect it by force.[489] In the 1917 Goan smallpox epidemic, a Portuguese colonial official threatened to march the entire population of a village—"men, women and children"—into the nearest town to be vaccinated.[490] In the 1926 Moroccan typhus epidemic, the French authorities raided the rural tribes "day and night", arrested all natives entering through town gates, and conducted them to the lazaretto to be forcibly deloused. In Marrakesh, armed troops surrounded the Jemaa el-Fnaa square and vaccinated 10,000 people at gunpoint.[491]

It might be thought that such excesses are limited to historical regimes that lacked modern "state capacity". Not so. Similar behaviour emerged during Covid-19. In Cuba in 2020, for instance, Human Rights Watch reported that government security forces were using Covid-19 rules on test-taking and mask-wearing as a pretext for "arbitrary arrests, abusive prosecutions, and detention in unsanitary and overcrowded cells conducive to the spread of Covid-19".[492] In the western Chinese city of Urumqi in November 2022, hazmat-suited guards blocked residents from escaping a burning building in order to enforce government zero-Covid policies.[493] In North Korea, according to a defector's report in December 2023, "North Koreans starved to death during the Covid-19 pandemic. . . . [O]fficial anxiety about the spread of the virus led the authorities to completely isolate communities where even a single case was suspected—leaving local people cut off from food supplies."[494] Such behaviour was not exceptional. Calculations based on the Human Rights Watch *World Report* show that in 2022, 16 out of 101 governments in the world were still using Covid-19 rules as a pretext for restrictions on assembly, bans on peaceful demonstrations, strike-breaking, arbitrary imprisonment, censorship, journalist persecution, denial of food and medical care, separation of children from parents, internment in isolation hospitals, overriding parliament, travel prohibitions, border closures, AI facial recognition tracking, sexual abuse, or capital punishment.[495]

489. Quoted in Cantisano 2022, 628.
490. Quoted in Bastos 2009, 160.
491. Quoted in Amster and El Aoued 2021, 121.
492. Human Rights Watch 2020.
493. Reuters 2022.
494. Parry 2023.
495. Human Rights Watch 2023, 29–30 (Angola), 57 (Azerbaijan), 111, 113 (Cambodia), 149, 153–4, 156 (China), 171, 175 (Cuba), 287 (Hungary), 309 (Iran), 345 (Jordan), 461 (North Korea), 504 (Russian Federation), 515 (Rwanda), 545 (South Korea), 593 (Thailand), 617, 621 (Turkmenistan), 693 (Vietnam), 707 (Zimbabwe).

States also used epidemic measures as a pretext to persecute groups that they viewed as politically, economically, or socially undesirable—foreigners, Jews, women, and ethnic minorities. During an epidemic in 430 BCE, the Athenian state targeted the Peloponnesians for allegedly poisoning wells.[496] In the fourteenth-century Black Death, as we have seen, many European states used the plague as a pretext for pogroms against Jews.[497] In the 1529 plague, the Venetian state gave the Health Board power to punish all the local beggars.[498] In the 1630 Florence plague, the state refused entry to "all Jews, beggars, rogues and gypsies, although they had very clean passes . . . because it was not the time to make the body of the city worse with such malign humours, the most inclined towards putrefaction".[499] In the 1636 plague, the Windsor parish authorities ordered the expulsion of anyone living in lodgings before it "shut them up in theire houses as . . . infected & dangerous".[500] In the 1708 Denmark plague scare, the Political and Commercial Committee ordered special inspections and restrictions against Polish Jews.[501] In early nineteenth-century Romania, the state used plague scares as a pretext to deport Roma (gypsies) from Bucharest and intern beggars in monasteries.[502] In 1832, the British government used the cholera epidemic as a justification for illegally imprisoning 15,000 vagrants.[503] In 1860, the government of the Japanese domain of Ōno used a smallpox epidemic as a pretext to expel beggars.[504] In Rio de Janeiro in 1904, the state used a military-style sanitation and vaccination campaign as a pretext to arrest and expel vagrants, prostitutes, and political agitators.[505] In north-east China during the 1910–11 plague epidemic, the Epidemic Prevention Bureau instructed local officials to move hundreds of women out of cities into villages "so as to isolate plague viruses".[506] In 2020, the Chinese government used Covid-19 as a pretext to evict and quarantine African residents.[507]

Governments manipulated epidemic measures to extract benefits for themselves. During early fourteenth-century epidemics, the Egyptian state used the crisis situation to empower its notorious "Returns Office" (*diwan al-murtag'at*) to force peasants to return to their deserted villages so they could deliver the

---

496. Duncan-Jones 1996, 115.
497. Cohn 2007; Jedwab et al. 2021, 5.
498. Cipolla 1976, 32.
499. Quoted in Henderson 2019, 71.
500. Quoted in Newman 2012, 828.
501. Frandsen 2010, 72.
502. Robarts 2017, 231.
503. Durey 1979, 35, 38; Alfani 2022, 31.
504. Ehlers 2011, 182.
505. Cantisano 2022, 622.
506. Quoted in Hu 2010, 317.
507. Fifield 2020.

required taxes and coerced labour services.[508] In Syria during the Black Death, the state forced absconding peasants to return to their villages, resume cultivation, and pay taxes.[509] During the 1438 Cairo plague, the sultan attached control of all inheritances to the public treasury and sold to the highest bidder the privilege of confiscating the inheritances of Jews and Copts.[510] In Peru after the 1718–23 epidemic, the viceroy used the death of one-quarter of the indigenous population as a justification for drawing up new censuses, increasing coerced labour dues, and extending them to new groups.[511] In Egypt in the 1820s, villagers evaded and resisted vaccination, which they viewed as a government plot to create permanent bodily scars marking children for future conscription into the detested troop levies and naval drafts.[512] After Russia annexed the Danube delta in 1829, it imposed quarantine regulations that diplomats and merchants viewed as a pretext for strangling Danubian shipping in order to prevent the ports of Brăila and Galați from becoming commercial rivals of Russian-ruled Odessa.[513] In 1864, the Ottoman authorities at Basra were demanding "four or five times the proper fee . . . as Quarantine fees from vessels. . . . [T]hese fees are looked upon as exactions, and therefore cannot fail to contribute their mite towards preventing the increase in trade and shipping".[514] In early twentieth-century Niger, ordinary people believed that the government was using vaccination registers to organize conscription and coerced labour levies.[515] Government manipulation of epidemic measures for state advantage encouraged resistance and exacerbated contagion.

State personnel used epidemic regulations to exploit ordinary people for their own private advantage. In Verona in 1580, according to Michel de Montaigne, the state health passport regulation was "probably kept up for the purpose of cheating travellers out of the fees which they exact for the health certificates".[516] In the 1587 Beijing plague, imperial soldiers used the epidemic as a license to extort money from civilians.[517] In the 1630 Lombardy plague, the Busto Arsizio health officers cunningly abused their official positions "to fill their purses".[518] In 1667 the English ambassador complained that Portuguese quarantine officers imposed "unreasonable" plague restrictions so as to extort

508. Darrāğ 1961, 63.
509. Darrāğ 1961, 62.
510. Dols 1977, 180.
511. A. Pearce 2001, 69–70; Dueñas 2010, 60.
512. Kuhnke 1990, 114, 116–17.
513. Ardeleanu 2020, 36–8.
514. Quoted in M. Harrison 2012, 159.
515. Schneider 2009, 208n44.
516. Quoted in Bamji 2017, 445.
517. Brook 2020, 373.
518. Quoted in Cipolla 1976, 36.

payments from ships.[519] In the 1699 Milan plague, merchants complained about "the extortions and abuses practised by the Health Officers in time of contagion".[520] In Mexico after the Matlazahuatl typhus epidemic of 1736–38, the price local oligarchs were willing to pay to buy the official post of *alcalde mayor* increased in districts with public granaries, since these enabled an *alcalde* to manipulate food supplies to his own advantage.[521] Around the Black Sea in the early nineteenth century, venal Russian quarantine officials sold quarantine passports openly in the streets of Crimean towns.[522] In the 1830s the quarantine commissar in the Wallachian town of Kalarasi forbade relatives to bring food to quarantined family members, so he could compel them to buy provisions from him at monopoly prices.[523] In the 1876 plague epidemic along the Persian-Ottoman land border, unscrupulous officials extorted money from anyone trying to cross the frontier.[524] In Brazil in the 1880s, an engineer administrator in the Public Health Council denounced resistance to tenement demolition as an obstacle to public health, covertly advancing the interests of his own construction company.[525] In the 1910–11 plague epidemic in north-east China, quarantine officials abused their powers by peeping at women's bodies during household inspections, persecuting personal enemies, and diverting epidemic funds to their own pockets.[526]

States used public health measures as a pretext to escalate regulation of non-health-related activities. In Amiens, the authorities used the 1494 plague to justify a ban on gambling, and the 1523 plague to prohibit a particular type of popular dance.[527] In the sixteenth-century Low Countries, local governments instrumentalized epidemics to impose social disciplining over eating, drinking, fighting, women's bodies, gender segregation at funerals, school attendance, religious observance, baking, wood collection, food selling, and sexual behaviour.[528] In Milan, the 1576–78 plague provided a pretext for the government to expand bureaucratic capacity, public documentation, miscellaneous edicts, "tickets" for myriad everyday activities, and regulation of the moral, social, and sexual lives of citizens.[529] In seventeenth-century Italy, plague epidemics were used to justify a proliferation of officials, committees, paperwork,

519. Quoted in M. Harrison 2012, 27.
520. Cipolla 1976, 38.
521. Garfias and Sellars 2020.
522. Robarts 2010, 288.
523. Robarts 2010, 289.
524. M. Harrison 2012, 163.
525. Cantisano 2022, 616.
526. Hu 2010, 318–19.
527. N. Murphy 2013, 151–2.
528. Curtis 2021a, 9–11.
529. Midura 2021, 21–2, 28, 33–4, 39–40, 46.

and information collection, expanding the capacity of the state to monitor citizens' lives.[530] As one seventeenth-century Venetian grumbled, the Health Board had been established to control plague, but instead it tried to "take care of all and sundry problems of the city".[531] In 1690–92, the bishop of Monopoli inveighed against the despotic ordinances which Neapolitan state health officials issued "for every single thing under penalty of life".[532] From the 1740s to the 1870s, the Habsburg imperial state enforced its sanitary cordon against the Ottomans with extreme harshness, not just to serve military purposes but also to control trade, migration, crime, brigandry, disorder, vagrancy, and "prohibited activities" widely defined—a sort of "homeland protection" *avant la lettre*.[533] In Gujurat in 1897–98, the British colonial government imposed arbitrary anti-plague measures which the inhabitants viewed "as a pretext for the exercise of control over society, indeed as a direct attack on it".[534] In the United States towards the beginning of the Covid-19 pandemic in March 2020, the Trump administration used Title 42 of the United States Code on Public Health as a pretext to summarily expel more than 980,000 children and adults seeking refuge at the US border, counter to the objections of the Centers for Disease Control and Prevention, one of whose senior officials later testified to a House Select Subcommittee that "the bulk of the evidence at that time did not support this policy proposal".[535] In North Korea in 2023, the regime used Covid-19 controls as a pretext for summarily apprehending and imprisoning street sellers and pullers of delivery carts, whose informal trading had long been a thorn in the side of state regulation of economy and society.[536]

It might be argued that all these authoritarian measures simply constituted a beneficent deployment of state capacity to achieve the socially optimal degree of contagion control. But given the state ignorance discussed above, did the state actually know how much contagion control was socially optimal? Moreover, as we have seen, governments had other incentives than achieving optimal social outcomes—warfare, princely display, bureaucratic venality, pandering to influential domestic interests.

Even if the state had known and cared about how much contagion control was socially optimal, authoritarian enforcement was often counterproductive. In many cases it created incentives for concealment, which in turn exacerbated contagion. In England in 1603, as Balmford pointed out, the "impatience" felt

530. Bamji 2017, 462.
531. Quoted in Cipolla 1976, 36.
532. Quoted in Fusco 2017, 105.
533. Quoted in Mandić 2022, 46–9, 50.
534. Chaturvedi 2006, 169.
535. Hampton et al. 2021; Montoya-Galvez 2021 (quotation).
536. *Economist* 2023.

by those prevented from attending to their business by government isolation measures "is the cause why so many smother the plague in themselves and their families, so long as they can to the hazarding of life".[537] In Hameln in 1664 when a Jewish girl developed a plague bubo, the duke of Low Saxony had established such a reputation for brutal state overkill that the instinctive response of the Jewish community was concealment. As the girl's mother wrote in her diary,

> "If this gets out," they said, "and His Excellency the Duke hears that there is such a thing in his city, God forbid, what a catastrophe it will be!" . . . My brothers-in-law, our master and teacher R. Avraham Segal, Reb Lipman, and Reb Leyb immediately sat down to consult with their wives to see what could be done: where to hide the maid and the girl; how to keep it from the authorities.[538]

In the 1835 plague epidemic, the Egyptian government forcibly ejected families of alleged victims from the city, placed them in quarantine so they could not work or eat, and carted off their household effects by night. As a result, "if someone were afflicted, he would not mention it for fear of being removed from his home".[539] In the 1904 Thai epidemic, British Indians concealed infections in order to avoid the razing of plague-struck buildings, as had occurred during earlier Mumbai epidemics.[540]

State overkill also led to evasion of rules. In Beijing in 1644–45, when the new Manchu Qing dynasty ordered the ejection of any family with a smallpox-afflicted member, families evaded the regulations by abandoning or killing their infected offspring.[541] In Hameln in 1664, the Jewish community evaded state overkill by disguising a plague-infected child and her maid as beggars and sending them away to a nearby village to mingle among itinerant festivalgoers, even though by doing so they might (and perhaps did) infect those around them.[542] In early nineteenth-century Black Sea epidemics, the brutal Russian quarantine regulations led merchants to pay the officials to look the other way, regarding such bribes as a cost of doing business.[543] In the 1835 plague epidemic, Egyptian government authoritarianism created incentives for the populace to respond by "throwing their dead into the streets so that no one could identify them".[544] In the 1899–1900 Indian plague epidemic, the Mysore sanitary commissioner criticized the compulsory segregation

537. Balmford 1603, 10 (spelling modernized).
538. Quoted in Jeremy Brown 2022, 79.
539. Quoted in Kuhnke 1990, 80.
540. Puaksom 2007, 324–5.
541. Chang 1996, 182–3; Hanson 2011, 109; Leung 2020a, 258.
542. Jeremy Brown 2022, 79.
543. Robarts 2010, 286–8; Robarts 2017, 233.
544. Quoted in Kuhnke 1990, 80.

measures used in Bangalore, because they created a motive "for destruction of plague corpses in houses, stealthily burying them in backyards and throwing them into streets".[545]

Authoritarian overkill also evoked active opposition. In Milan in 1630, the arbitrary imposition of plague-related travel restrictions led merchants to mount concerted resistance to the whole public health campaign.[546] The brutality displayed by the Russian state during the 1892–93 cholera epidemic was so excessive that peasants and workers staged anti-cholera riots, attacked isolation barracks, "emancipated" cholera patients, and murdered cholera doctors.[547] In all these cases, the state's use of arbitrary coercion in the name of contagion control evoked concealment, evasion, and resistance, which ended up exacerbating rather than controlling contagion.

The state can use its capacity to coerce citizens to behave in ways that benefit society at large by limiting the contagion spillovers they impose on others—through hygiene, social distancing, immunization, and cross-border action. But it can also use its capacity to coerce citizens in ways that either reflect a mistaken calculation of societal benefits or, more frequently, seek benefits for the state at the expense of society at large. To the extent that this coercion exceeds that required for contagion control and needlessly oppresses the governed, it represents a net cost for society. It may also result in acts of evasion and resistance which reduce or entirely negate the benefits of public anti-contagion measures. The costs of state action to limit epidemic contagion may not only outweigh the benefits but actually diminish them by stifling the consent of citizens which is required for effective government.

7. State Capacity

Three features of the state are widely held to ensure that state capacity benefits society at large: fiscal capacity, state centralization, and parliamentary representation.[548] In containing infectious waste, mandating social distancing, providing immunization, diffusing information, and managing cross-border contagion, the state did sometimes act to deal with externalities, public goods, and information asymmetries. But the three features of state capacity stressed in the literature did not play a straightforward role.

Fiscal capacity was largely irrelevant, at least beyond quite a low threshold. Some medieval states with low fiscal capacity by historical standards

---

545. Quoted in Tumbe 2020, 99.

546. Cipolla 1976, 43.

547. Quoted in Frieden 1977, 548.

548. Besley and Persson 2009; Besley and Persson 2013; Dincecco 2015; Dincecco and Katz 2016.

successfully pioneered anti-contagion measures, while some early modern states with much higher fiscal capacity failed to allocate it to controlling epidemics. Before the twentieth century, states used most of their fiscal capacity for military purposes, and as their fiscal capacity grew so too did their military involvements. Warfare spread epidemics directly through troop movements, refugee flows, prisoners of war, deserters, quartering, and colonial encounters between distinct pools of immunity. It also exacerbated epidemics indirectly by diverting state resources, distorting information, and overruling public health measures in pursuit of military ends.

State centralization, too, was often irrelevant or counterproductive in controlling contagion. Instead, what mattered was subsidiarity—tackling epidemics at the most immediate level consistent with their containment. In practice, local governments frequently moved earlier and more effectively than central states. Local governments pioneered sanitary measures as early as the tenth century, social distancing at latest by the Black Death, variolation and vaccination long before central states mandated or even permitted it, and public information about epidemics for local citizens long before central states were willing or able to allocate resources to that purpose. The wars that so often triggered and exacerbated epidemics were conducted by centralized states like England and France just as they were by decentralized states like the Holy Roman Empire of the German Nation or the Spanish composite monarchy.

Nor were parliaments a magic bullet. Some states with strong parliaments and representative councils did indeed address epidemic contagion successfully—medieval Italian city-states, early modern England, and Golden Age Holland. But even then, the representative body did not invariably play a positive role—as in early modern England, where one of the most powerful parliaments in Europe blocked crucial anti-plague measures, or in the Netherlands, where highly representative town councils corrupted sanitary measures in favour of powerful interest groups. In nineteenth-century Europe, authoritarian governments imposed vaccine mandates no later on average than constitutional ones. Furthermore, state military activities that exacerbated pandemics were pursued by parliamentary states like England, the Netherlands, and the south-west German territories, as well as by absolutist states like France, Austria, Spain, Prussia, and Russia. This is not to say that representative government had no benefits. Even the oligarchical pre-modern town councils and parliaments were usually better than alternative forms of governance. But the findings of this chapter have shown that what mattered was the specific structure of the representative body and the incentives it created to prevent contagion, not its mere presence.

What does history say about whether democratic or authoritarian states are better at controlling epidemic contagion? This question haunted public debate in the peak years of the Covid-19 pandemic and rumbles on in its aftermath.

On the one hand, the success of China in controlling Covid in its first two years evoked lavish praise of authoritarian states.[549] On the other, democratic polities firmly maintain, as the Organization for Economic Cooperation and Development declared in 2021, that "the healthy functioning of democratic systems . . . [is] key to societies' capacity to absorb shocks".[550]

Historical epidemics show that authoritarian and democratic states differ in both their capacities and their incentives. An authoritarian state may be better able to enforce policies restricting individual decisions on business, mobility, or sociability because of facing fewer constitutional limits. It may also have better incentives to do so because it does not need electoral support from groups opposed to restrictions, whereas democratic governments are electorally exposed. On the other hand, an authoritarian state is less able to collect accurate information because of citizens' fear and mistrust, and has less incentive to implement policies that benefit the entire society as opposed to the ruler or oligarchy in power.

A democratic state, by contrast, has less capacity to implement policies restricting individuals because it has to respect civil rights and the rule of law. It has less incentive to do so because of the need to be electorally responsive to citizens, even those who refuse to take account of the external costs of their actions. But a democratic state enjoys better information and greater consent from its citizens, because a lower level of state oppression makes them on average less fearful and suspicious. A democratic state also has better incentives to implement policies that benefit ordinary people as opposed to rulers and oligarchs.

The performance of the two types of state differs between non-epidemic and epidemic periods. In non-epidemic periods, the democratic state is likely to be unambiguously better at formulating policies and developing enforcement mechanisms that benefit aggregate social well-being, because individual citizens are the best judges of their own interests when externalities are minor. In epidemic periods, the authoritarian state is likely to gain ground, since it has the capacity to formulate policies that take externalities into account and will normally have stronger mechanisms to enforce all its policies, good or bad. But both authoritarian and democratic states will find that their own flaws prevent them from implementing policies that impose the efficient penalty on individual choices that spread contagion. The democratic state will set the penalty too low because of citizen pressure. The authoritarian state may set it too high or too low, depending on the interest of rulers in maximizing fiscal receipts, military power, or public order rather than aggregate citizen well-being.

549. Gao and Zhang 2021.
550. OECD 2021, 23.

Down the centuries, successful anti-contagion measures were not usually associated with authoritarian government. Admittedly, as we have seen, data weaknesses make it impossible to maintain that Black Death mortality was significantly lower in "autonomous" cities (though also not in non-autonomous ones). But in the centuries after the Black Death, the earliest quarantining and social distancing measures were introduced by Italian city-states that were highly democratic by the standards of the time—indeed, sometimes outright republican in form. In the post-1500 period, the first states to use governmental powers systematically to coordinate responses between different localities and to align individual with collective interests by providing welfare support to the poor in lockdown were England and the Low Countries, again democratic by the standards of the time. Smallpox epidemics show the same lack of association between authoritarian government and anti-contagion measures. In the later eighteenth century, New England controlled smallpox contagion so strictly that this "most democratical region on the face of the earth", according to one contemporary, had "voluntarily submitted to more restrictions, and abridgments of liberty, to secure them against this terrible scourge, than any absolute monarch could have enforced".[551] In the nineteenth century, vaccination mandates were not clearly associated with authoritarian regimes, as we have seen. Although the USA found it difficult to implement public health policy nationally because of specific constitutional features, many democratic European countries implemented mandatory vaccination early, and many authoritarian ones did it late. There was no significant association, as we saw, between authoritarian regimes and the date at which vaccination mandates were enacted.

Historical pandemics show that state capacity, if appropriately directed, has powerful tools to limit contagion. Democratic governance can help it do that, but is not a magic pill. Even when states try to limit contagion, they often fail. All states can exacerbate epidemics when they pursue narrow political or military ends rather than the welfare of all citizens, although they are less likely to behave in this way if they are democratic rather than authoritarian. In epidemics, as in most other spheres, any type of state capacity can be used for harmful as well as beneficial purposes.

8. Conclusion

Historical epidemics cast doubt on the idea that state capacity was always beneficial for controlling contagion. But this does not mean that state action was (or is) unimportant for managing the market failures caused by epidemic contagion. It does mean we have to look closely at the characteristics that

551. Quoted in M. Bennett 2020, 271.

made a state more or less likely to deal with epidemics well. The history of epidemics over the past seven centuries alerts us to key features. These provide a corrective to optimistic assumptions that fiscal capacity, centralization, and parliaments are all that are needed for state capacity to create societal benefits.

First, fiscal capacity is needed to provide resources to control contagion. But it must be measured more comprehensively than merely in terms of money revenues collected by the central state. This measure excludes state resources collected at lower levels of government. Fiscal capacity, moreover, is a cost. What matters for public health is not so much the total resources available to the state but how they are spent. Before the modern era, the state devoted the majority of spending to military activities. These almost always exacerbated contagion. State spending on civilian purposes also included many socially useless things, such as building palaces and elite consumption. Of the small amount of civilian spending allocated to epidemic control, the most resource-intensive—but also the most beneficial—consisted not of direct contagion-control measures but rather of supporting the poor to comply with social distancing and immunization.

Second, epidemic control did not require maximum state centralization. Rather, it required subsidiarity—tackling problems at the most immediate level consistent with their resolution. Local governments could take advantage of local information, mobilize local sentiment, take account of local preferences concerning public goods, and respond nimbly to new opportunities such as variolation or vaccination. Central governments could resolve local conflicts, coordinate efforts across multiple local government authorities, and use their deeper fiscal pockets to supplement the funds of hard-hit local governments. Local and central anti-contagion measures succeeded best when they worked in tandem.

Subsidiarity had a cross-border component. There was a limit to what any single state could do. Each national government in the world, just like each local government in a nation, had better incentives to control contagion that directly affected its own citizens than to prevent its citizens from infecting non-locals or non-nationals. Yet each national government in the world, like each local government in a state, was menaced by other governments that behaved in the same way. This meant that every government, at every level, needed cooperation and support from the outside. Historically, control of plague, smallpox, cholera, influenza, and Covid-19 was most successful when states developed cross-border mechanisms for information exchange, vaccine diplomacy, and international quarantine—and failed when they concealed information from other states or pursued narrow local or national advantage in quarantine arrangements.

Third, parliaments were not a magic pill. Representative bodies were only one node in the web that connected state and non-state institutions. In the

Middle Ages and the early modern period, government sanitary measures and social distancing depended on communal, religious, occupational, and familial institutions. Eighteenth-century variolation was organized and financed by local governments supported by clergymen, local elites, pioneering medical professionals, and voluntary associations.[552] Nineteenth-century vaccination was organized, financed, diffused, and rewarded by governments in collaboration with medical bodies, scientific associations, religious organizations, and private charities.[553] The resources, knowledge, and social influence of civil society played a major role in funding, organizing, and persuading public opinion to line up behind public health measures from the fourteenth to the twenty-first century. The key to controlling epidemic contagion was not so much that the state interacted with a parliament. Rather, it was that the state and civil-society organizations not only cooperated and compensated for each other's failures, but also curbed each other's excesses and minimized mutual backscratching.

Fourth, whether the state acted to control epidemics depended on the political realities it had to navigate. Even autocratic states, let alone more representative ones, have always been institutions in which decision-making processes responded to complex ways of aggregating and mediating between the diverse interests of different socio-economic groups, often expressed through institutional privileges. The state faces the delicate task of trading off between policies that, on the one hand, might stop the contagion and, on the other, will still allow the society to carry on ordinary and vital functions (trading, meeting, socializing, and so on). The state always has to mediate among the different interests of the governed, if it wants to stay in power.

Fifth, knowledge mattered. State capacity was little use in the face of epidemics if the state lacked basic knowledge of contagion and how to control it. The state might possess adequate fiscal resources, understand subsidiarity, have good relationships with civil society, and yet simply lack the knowledge and technology needed to keep epidemics out of its territory and avoid their spread once they arrived. As we shall see in chapter 6, knowledge of contagion, microorganisms, sanitation, antibiotics, and antivirals was limited before the later nineteenth and in many cases the early twentieth century. The technology of governance, especially information collection and disease monitoring, also took many centuries to develop. Monitoring technologies and organizational capabilities were costly, limited, and inefficient. Even states that wanted to control contagion were often limited in their ability to do this because of lack of knowledge and low levels of technology.

552. M. Bennett 2020, 46–7; Davenport 2020a, 67–8.
553. Cless 1871, 105–8.

Finally, state motivation mattered. Imagine that a state has adequate fiscal capacity, centralization, parliaments, knowledge, and the consent of the governed. It will still undertake optimal measures to control epidemics only if it is motivated to act in the interests of society. Not all governments in history held the view expressed by Adam Smith in *The Wealth of Nations,*

> [that it would] deserve the most serious attention of government . . . to prevent a leprosy or any other loathsome and offensive disease, though neither mortal nor dangerous, from spreading itself among [the great body of the people], though perhaps no other publick good might result from such attention besides the prevention of so great a publick evil.[554]

States, as we have seen in this chapter, often have interests in their own political, fiscal, and military survival that do not coincide with those of society at large when it comes to contagion control, and often profoundly conflict with those interests.

In a nutshell, the key to state action on epidemics did not reside in sheer fiscal capacity, centralization, or parliaments. What mattered was state expenditures on civilian purposes, subsidiarity, links with civil society, political realities, scientific knowledge, and the motivation of the state itself to act in the interests of society at large. All these variables were affected not just by what the state itself did but by other components of the institutional framework, to which we now turn, starting in chapter 4 with the local community.

554. A. Smith 1776, 3:144.

4

The Local Community

They relocked four houses indiscriminately, two of which did not have any bread to sustain them; the rest of the parish was discouraged by the others [from going out], prohibiting them from frequenting the churches, the streets, work, and everywhere they were threatened.
—VILLAGE PRIEST OF PINZIDIMONTE NEAR FLORENCE, 1631[1]

It is hard to go against an angry mass of people. The doctors are about to compel our Chinese people to be inoculated. . . . Tomorrow . . . all business houses large or small must be closed and wait until this unjust action [is] settled before any one be allowed to resume their business. If any disobey this we will unite and put an everlasting boycott on them. Don't say that you have not been warned first.
—ANONYMOUS CHINESE-LANGUAGE CIRCULAR OPPOSING PLAGUE VACCINATION, SAN FRANCISCO, 1900[2]

"Community" is our word for the collectivity of people living in the same local area.[3] But the local community is also an institution—a set of practices connecting people living in spatial proximity, typically governed by informal norms rather than official rules, and enforced by social pressure rather than legal coercion.

1. Quoted in Henderson 2019, 144.
2. Quoted in Shah 2001, 134.
3. Sometimes "community" is used to refer to any group with a shared characteristic: location, religion, occupation, language, ethnicity. This chapter focuses on the local (geographical) community, chapter 5 on the religious community, and chapter 6 on the occupational community.

This chapter focuses on the *local* community—the network of norm-based practices connecting people living near one another. This is distinct from the local government discussed in chapter 3, whose collective action is formal, governed by law, and enforced by state coercion. It is also distinct from the religious community discussed in chapter 5: religions are still communities, which means that similar issues arise, but they are special cases because they claim authority from spiritual beings. The local community is also quite different from the occupational community of chapter 6: occupational associations are communities, too, but ones specifically focused on collective action in the economic realm.

The community might look too puny to deal with a pandemic—a 90-pound weakling confronting a steroid-pumped colossus. But it has a special superpower: "social capital". This is the name given to the stock of shared norms, information, and trust generated inside small, closely knit groups where people know one another and form multistranded relationships. Social capital enables the community to organize collective action and penalize opportunistic behaviour. Now, such collective action might solely benefit members of that particular community. But an influential literature claims otherwise. Community social capital spills over onto the rest of society, it is argued, benefiting everyone. It also makes other institutions work better, the argument continues, correcting failures of market and state such as those we examined in chapters 2 and 3.[4]

So the humble local community can in theory help a whole society deal with epidemics. It can mobilize its members to organize and comply with norms that control contagion. It can monitor deviance from these norms and impose social sanctions on violations. These community activities not only protect locals but create benefits that extend beyond community boundaries.

But a growing literature has found that the community can also fail.[5] Communal norms, information, and trust are not invincible. Community leaders may be weak or absent, internal conflicts block action, or the community collapse entirely. Epidemics by their nature transcend local horizons, posing challenges that leave local institutions powerless.

The community can thus be bad at doing good things. It can also be good at doing bad things. Like other organizations that foster social capital, the community has a dark side.[6] The local community can be literally parochial. Worse, it can be xenophobic, secretive, oligarchical, and riotous. Community norms can be inward-oriented. Community sanctions can be corrupt. Community

---

4. Coleman 1988; R. Putnam, Leonardi, and Nanetti 1993; R. Putnam 2000; Dasgupta 2000; Rajan 2019; Rajan 2021.

5. Bourdieu 1980; Gambetta 1988; Fukuyama 1999; Field 2008.

6. Ogilvie 2005; Dennison and Ogilvie 2007; Field 2008; Dennison 2011; Ogilvie 2019.

information can be false. Community trust can organize collective resistance to public health measures and persecution of innocent scapegoats. All these activities exacerbate epidemics.

Communal norms, information, and sanctions can thus work in good ways and bad. They can mobilize people to comply with norms such as waste disposal, social distancing, immunization, and disseminating health information. Or they can organize local residents to corrupt, resist, and violate measures that would help control contagion. Social capital inside the local community is a powerful weapon. What decides which way it will be directed?

1. Communal Cleansing

Local sanitation has long been recognized as a good way to control infectious disease. As we saw in chapter 3, local sanitary norms to control epidemics date back many centuries before the theory of contagion was accepted by medical science. This was partly because local sanitation was consistent with the ancient orthodoxy about disease which held that infections were caused by bad "miasmas" or vapours arising from particular locations.[7] By cleaning up those locations and ridding them of bad smells, it was believed, communities could prevent disease.

Local governments took initiatives to regulate waste disposal from the early medieval period, as we saw in chapter 3. But waste disposal is ubiquitous, continuous, and hard to observe. Formal monitoring and enforcement of sanitary regulations are costly. The local community can reduce these costs by using informal norms, information, and sanctions to motivate compliance, detect violations, and penalize offenders.

Informal communal pressure historically contributed to enforcing formal sanitary regulations. In Ghent as early as 1314, the local government ordered the "king of the ribalds" and his minions to enforce formal regulations on waste disposal. But this municipal employee was supposed to cooperate with informal associations called *gebuurten* (medieval Dutch for "surroundings" or "neighbourhoods").[8] In many towns in the late medieval Low Countries, neighbours used peer pressure against those who disposed of infectious waste carelessly and organized informal working groups to maintain wells and cesspits.[9] In Ipswich in the 1470s and 1480s, too, neighbourhoods mounted a grass-roots response to "the most universal death", the popular name they gave to the plague. Epidemics brought an upsurge in neighbourly monitoring of things people thought spread infection—dirty gutters, overflowing drains,

---

7. Coomans 2019, 97; Coomans 2022, 1067; Zaneri and Geltner 2022, 6.
8. Coomans 2019, 88–9, 97–8, 103–4.
9. Coomans 2021, 5.

smelly dungheaps, and stray animals.[10] In Southampton in 1550, urban pigs were widely believed to spread plague, but a jury argued that it could be stopped through informal naming and shaming: "When the thing is at the worst, shame may redress it."[11]

It might be thought that informal communal mechanisms, important though they were in medieval and early modern societies, were superseded by the growth of modern state capacity. Not entirely. Community social capital was still widely used to control epidemics in the twentieth century. In the United States in the 1910s, for instance, the Rockefeller Foundation recognized the importance of peer pressure inside the local community and mobilized it to persuade people to adopt sanitary measures against the hookworm (helminthiasis) epidemics that impaired physical and cognitive health across the American South. The foundation sought to shame parents into upgrading their latrines, as with a letter addressed to parents in Wilmington, North Carolina, telling them that "microscopic examination has given us evidence that Johnny has been eating food that has been contaminated, probably by flies, with human feces". In Mississippi, households that had not yet upgraded their sanitary arrangements were pinpointed on public maps which revealed their identity to the community.[12] External philanthropic organizations thus recognized that they would not succeed in improving public health without mobilizing peer pressure inside local communities.

On the other hand, peer pressure is costly and not always effective. Wells and cesspits are expensive to build, irksome to monitor, and costly to repair, despite their wider social benefits in limiting waterborne epidemics.[13] Owners of disease-spreading animals do not always keep them contained, and rounding up strays is costly.[14] Letter-writing campaigns and mapping latrines consume resources.[15]

Informal peer pressure worked better when it cooperated with institutions wielding ampler resources. One such resource was formal coercion. In the Ipswich plague of 1488, peer pressure did not suffice to prevent 40 citizens from letting their pigs stray, which was believed to spread disease; the offenders had to be summoned formally before the court leet.[16] In Southampton in 1550, "the redress of shame" alone did not deter the mayor from endangering public health by keeping a pig in his garden; getting him to stop

---

10. Quoted in Rawcliffe 2019, 83 (spelling modernized).
11. Quoted in Rawcliffe 2019, 89 (spelling modernized).
12. Quoted in Shubinski and Iacobelli 2020.
13. Coomans 2021, 5.
14. Rawcliffe 2019, 83, 89.
15. Shubinski and Iacobelli 2020.
16. Rawcliffe 2019, 83, 89.

required formal court proceedings.[17] In late medieval and early modern Dutch and Flemish plagues, peer pressure became considerably more effective when local governments promised half of all sanitation fines to people who reported their neighbours.[18] Even the hundreds of neighbourhood associations that supported municipal sanitary officers in medieval Dutch cities were hybrid organizations, starting as grass-roots initiatives in the fourteenth century but after around 1500 gaining semi-official status in the formal administrative divisions of wards and quarters.[19] In the USA during the 1918–19 influenza pandemic, public shaming was used as a method of making people refrain from spitting, coughing, and sneezing in public. But this informal shaming was given teeth by formal government information campaigns and even legislation, such as the Chicago city law enacted in October 1918 which threatened the arrest of anyone who coughed or sneezed without using a handkerchief.[20] Similar findings emerge from modern developing countries—as in Bangladesh slums in 2016, where attempts to harness social pressure and shame to encourage individual handwashing had no more effect than a standard educational health message: people do not always care what their neighbours think.[21]

Communal peer pressure also worked better when supported by external funding and knowledge. Just as external organizations could not improve public health without mobilizing local peer pressure, so too local communities could not improve it without support from outside. In the American South in the 1910s, as we have seen, informal peer pressure on sanitation was supported by formal philanthropic organizations. The Rockefeller Foundation deliberately and strategically reinforced communal peer pressure, as when it "convinced county newspapers to publish a list of heads of families who had brought their latrines up to the standard approved by the State Board of Health. Each family wished to be recorded on the 'honor roll' as early as possible." In one Mississippi county, as we have seen, success was achieved not through communal pressure alone but by the fact that the foundation pinned up a big map in a central spot, marked the location of every local residence, and collected information enabling each household to be highlighted as it updated its latrines. It was only after funding and information had been provided by the philanthropic organization that community peer pressure kicked in, as residents gossiped about the map and "further delay for the other families became embarrassing".[22]

17. Rawcliffe 2019, 83, 89.
18. Coomans 2021, 223–30; Coomans and Weeda 2020, 82–3.
19. Coomans 2018, 131; Coomans 2022, 1061–2.
20. Tomes 2010, 57.
21. Guiteras et al. 2016, 341–3, 348.
22. Quoted in Shubinski and Iacobelli 2020.

Completely informal pressure is seldom observed in the written records.[23] Two things may explain this. Either informal peer pressure is working very effectively, hence does not evoke conflict or violations, and thus does not appear in the records. Alternatively, informal peer pressure is not working at all, so there is no success to record. The most one can say is that there are not many documented examples of informal peer pressure alone limiting contagion, without support from formal institutions.

Communal peer pressure also had a dark side, which we do observe in the records. The local community engaged in vigilante action against groups it regarded as causing epidemics by insanitary behaviour. A popular view in many medieval European communities was that plague was spread by the poor, who should therefore be locked up or kicked out. During the Black Death, Narbonne responded to the plague deaths of a quarter of its inhabitants with communal violence against "many beggars and medicants of various countries . . . carrying (as they said and it appeared) powdered substances which they were putting into rivers, houses, churches and foodstuffs to kill people".[24] In early modern plagues, communities all over Europe targeted paupers, who were viewed as sources of infection.[25] Foreign paupers were even worse than local ones. In the 1545 plague, the Scottish community of Stirling drew an explicit distinction between "our awin puir", who were allowed to remain, and the "strangears" and "otheris", who were kicked out.[26] In the 1579 Norwich plague, locals rioted against Dutch and Walloon "aliens", who were accused of causing contagion by "the corrupt keeping of their houses", as well as by publicly washing their (innovative and competitive) woollen textiles in the river.[27] In early modern London, plague was regarded as arising out of the suburbs outside the walls, which were regarded as pits of moral and actual infection.[28] In the 1641 plague epidemic, an Essex parish whipped up rumours that a vagrant employed to cart away the corpses was actually a plague spreader, spurring a village mob to drive him out.[29] In the 1731 Split plague epidemic, a communal mob threatened to attack caravans and burn merchandise, forcing the Governor General to bar travelling merchants from the local lazaretto, even though this merely encouraged them to circumvent inspection and quarantine.[30] In

---

23. See Ogilvie (2011, 268–70) for similar lack of documentary evidence of peer pressure successfully enforcing contracts in pre-modern long-distance trade.

24. Quoted in Horrox 1994, 222–3.

25. Slack 1988, 447.

26. Oram 2007, 23.

27. Quoted in Slack 1985, 140, 273.

28. Slack 1988, 448.

29. Slack 1985, 101.

30. Andreozzi 2015, 129.

the 1804–5 Swiss yellow fever epidemic, Graubünden communities excluded vagrants because their "dirtiness" was rumoured to spread the disease.[31]

Communal rumours accused foreigners—even if they were not poor—of causing epidemics by deliberately defiling local buildings and water sources. In the 1630 plague in Spain, local communities blamed Italians for using secret ingredients to spread pestilence.[32] In the 1630 epidemic in Volterra, local rumour accused a man from Borgo a Buggiano (75 km away) of causing plague by poisoning the holy water in the cathedral stoup.[33] In Florence, communal gossip alleged that plague patients were being deliberately infected by a man variously described as a Neapolitan or a Sicilian.[34] In nineteenth-century Krakow, the Jewish community accused a recently arrived man of having brought cholera with him, and offered him lavish gifts if he would only depart, taking the disease with him.[35] In the 1858 Japanese cholera epidemic, coastal communities accused English sailors of poisoning wells.[36] In late nineteenth-century Guangxi epidemics, Liujiang communities accused foreigners of poisoning water supplies.[37] When plague struck north-east China in 1910–11, local communities accused the Japanese of employing Chinese traitors to poison the wells, and the American consul general reported that "old men and women, accused of witchery, have been torchered [sic] in the outlying villages until they have confessed that they are secret agents of the Japanese and have cast an evil spell over the communities".[38] In these cases, communal social capital fostered rumours and persecution against those whose only offence was not belonging to the face-to-face network of the community.

Perhaps the most harmful way communities used their social capital during epidemics was to organize resistance to anti-contagion measures, including sanitation. In the 1584 Angers epidemic, for instance, the community of Bressigny refused to use the new plague cemetery at Saint-Sauveur and instead marched "by force and carrying arms" to bury their dead in the public cemetery at Saint-Martin.[39] In the 1623 Groningen plague, neighbourhoods organized collective stone throwing when the government sought to control contagion by employing official corpse carriers instead of letting families bear their own dead to burial.[40] In the 1630 Milan plague, crowds resisted fumiga-

31. Quoted in Besl 1998, 269.
32. Mauelshagen 2005, 259.
33. Henderson 2019, 43, 244.
34. Henderson 2019, 44.
35. Tuszewicki 2021, 221.
36. Gramlich-Oka 2009, 45.
37. Benedict 1988, 140.
38. Quoted in Nathan 1967, 29.
39. Quoted in Lebrun 1971, 305.
40. Rommes 2015, 60; Curtis 2021a, 10.

tion of plague-stricken dwellings and burning of infected clothing.[41] In the 1710–13 Swedish epidemic, parishioners in Holje resisted segregated plague burials, violently forcing their priest to bury victims in the customary grave-yard.[42] In the 1798–99 Egyptian plague epidemic, when the French authorities ordered that plague victims' possessions be sterilized by being aired on the roof for two weeks after death, the order was resisted by the masses, who "in their ignorance, saw in it only a means to learn what each one possessed".[43] In the 1831 Memel cholera epidemic, a mob broke into the isolation hospital and demanded that corpses be buried in the churchyard instead of being segregated for sanitary purposes.[44] In the 1832 Paris cholera epidemic, ragpickers and rag-sellers organized mobs to erect barricades and burn property in opposition to anti-contagion rules centralizing rubbish collection.[45] In the 1884 Naples chol-era epidemic, violent crowds resisted public health teams seeking to disinfect housing, purify the air with sulphur bonfires, or inspect infected possessions.[46] In the 1899 Porto plague, mobs confronted health inspectors and doctors to protest against household inspections, disinfection brigades, and the burning of infected residences.[47] In the 1920–21 Chinese plague, crowds attacked the Harbin plague squads with revolvers and threatened to make inspectors drink their own disinfectant.[48]

Community action during epidemics casts light on key features of informal social capital. First, norm-based action is costly. Sometimes the costs are so high that communal norms fail to control disease-causing behaviour. Informal action tends to work better in cooperation with formal funding, information, and coercion provided by institutions external to the community itself—whether local government or civil society.

Second, community pressure is based on personal relationships. Commu-nal norms are therefore often formulated based on personal characteristics such as poverty, nationality, or ethnicity, instead of people's actual behaviour. Communal sanctions and collective action target persons whose identity-based characteristics are assumed to make them deviate from communal norms, rather than on deviant actions themselves. This triggers vigilante action against minorities and outsiders rather than sanctions against behaviour that violates the norms.

41. Cipolla 1976, 36, 43.
42. Arcini et al. 2016, 114.
43. Quoted in Kuhnke 1990, 75.
44. R. Evans 1992, 164.
45. R. Evans 1992, 164.
46. Snowden 1995, 139–40, 144–9.
47. Echenberg 2007, 122, 127.
48. Nathan 1967, 68.

Third, the particularistic, personalized quality of communal norms can distort communal information. When this happens, the community may accept rumours that particular groups are deliberately harming the majority.

In a fourth and even more harmful shift, informal initiatives can be based on wholly false information, causing the community to organize collective action to resist sanitary measures that would help contain contagion. We return to communal falsification of information below in a broader context.

2. Peer Pressure and Social Distancing

Social interaction, like waste disposal, is omnipresent and continuous, making it hard to monitor and control during epidemics. Informal communal norms can in principle work better than formal rules in enforcing social distancing during epidemics.

Some communities indeed organized collective action to minimize outside contacts during epidemics. In 1610, for instance, the "leading men" of the small Welsh town of Ruthin forbade its inhabitants to visit the fair in plague-stricken Chester 20 miles (32 km) away, mobilizing communal social capital to coordinate market withdrawal.[49] In late eighteenth-century Indonesia, inland communities avoided smallpox by organizing trade with outsiders using "silent barter", in which a group of villagers would go to a certain place and leave trade goods, external traders would then decide if they accepted the goods, in which case they would take the goods, leave their own goods in return, and depart without any face-to-face contact.[50] In the 1910–11 Manchurian plague epidemic, villages would delegate a few reliable members to carry out all marketing activities in the larger towns, buying and selling with maximum speed and avoiding inns where they might pick up infection.[51] Withdrawing from trade fairs, trading silently, and delegating exchange involved economic losses. But catching plague or smallpox involved existential ones. Communal action coordinated collective mechanisms to balance the two.

In other epidemics, communities organized collective action to prevent outsiders visiting the locality at all. In Languedoc during the 1629 plague epidemic, villagers destroyed local roads to prevent travel to or from infected places.[52] In the 1856 Ethiopian smallpox epidemic, peasants posted guards around their villages to keep out travellers from the afflicted city of Harar.[53] In the 1883 Indonesian smallpox epidemic, villages closed off incoming roads to

49. Slack 1985, 256.
50. Boomgaard 2003, 596.
51. Nathan 1967, 11.
52. Lucenet 1985, 137.
53. Pankhurst 1965, 349.

exclude travellers who might bring infection.[54] In the 2014 Guinea Ebola epidemic, Kissi-speaking communities in Guéckédou felled trees and cut bridges to prevent outside contagion, though they wrongly ascribed the infection to urban medical teams.[55] At the beginning of the Chinese Covid-19 pandemic in January 2020, villages in Henan province erected barriers and posted villagers as informal guards against incomers.[56] Communities organized such informal local cordons mainly when governments lacked capacity or motivation to implement more general measures.

But community peer pressure to enforce social distancing was most effective in cooperation with formal regulations—complementing rather than replacing state capacity. Thus peer pressure supported social distancing more successfully when it collaborated with local government. From the fifteenth century on, people in Dutch and Flemish towns reported their neighbours for frequenting public markets if they were infected with plague, but these informal reports were elicited partly because local governments enacted formal rules and promised half the fines to informants.[57] In the 1576–78 Milan plague, people informed anonymously on fellow citizens for endangering public health, but only as part of "a larger bureaucratic protocol" that was enshrined in a print programme of weekly plague edicts and monetary rewards paid by the state for denunciations.[58] In the 1630–31 Florentine plague epidemic, likewise, "secret friends" (spies) and nosy neighbours denounced those who violated social distancing measures, but this was partly because the city government paid the equivalent of 45 days' wages to reward them.[59] In the 1896 Mumbai plague epidemic, spies and informants reported neighbours they thought should be removed to isolation hospitals, but this was effective only because the government rewarded informants and used their reports to guide official search parties (shown in figure 4.1).[60] In Egypt during the 1897 plague epidemic, community leaders in Alexandria played a central role in disease notification, but they were also rewarded by the Health Department and municipal authorities for doing so.[61] Even in China during Covid-19, "civil society organizations took responsibility of isolating residents in every community", but did so in the shadow of state regulations mandating strict social distancing.[62]

54. Boomgaard 2003, 602.
55. Honigsbaum 2019, 207.
56. *Economist*, 2020a.
57. Coomans 2019, 92; Coomans 2021, 223–30; Coomans and Weeda 2020, 82–3.
58. Midura 2021, 33, 43.
59. Henderson 2019, 234 (quotation), 240, 257, 264.
60. Echenberg 2007, 58.
61. M. Harrison 2012, 187–8.
62. S. Zhang et al. 2020, 216.

FIGURE 4.1. Justice of the Peace with plague search party, Mumbai, 1896/97. Informal notifications from nosy neighbours and paid spies were rendered effective by formal government search parties to remove infected residents to isolation wards. *Source*: Wellcome Collection.

Communal shaming also operated in the shadow of formal government regulations. In Milan in 1630, "the whole family of Lorenzo Turate" were found to have violated social distancing orders. When they died of plague, their corpses were paraded in a roundabout procession throughout the entire city, "completely nude, so that everyone could see the true and veritable signs of plague, which could be found on their bodies in abundance". This act of public shaming was deliberately staged, however, by the director of the Health Board to make the masses "recognize their errors".[63] In December 2021, likewise, four Chinese men were accused of importing Covid-19 infections to China by smuggling people across the border. They were paraded through the streets of Jingxi carrying placards displaying their names and photos in an exercise which Weibo users said "reminded them of public shamings from hundreds

63. Quoted in Carmichael 1998, 145–6.

of years ago". But this was no spontaneous communal act: it took place with formal state approval and support.[64]

Communal action to control contagion can also fail. Epidemics often intensify internal fissures, which trigger communal failure. London, for instance, had the worst anti-contagion measures in early modern England because of conflicts inside its elite and divergent interests within the communal oligarchy.[65] Exeter spectacularly failed to control plague in 1626–28 because of disputes between the freemen and the oligarchy of magistrates.[66] Prato exacerbated plague contagion in 1630 by discriminating against the lower-status inhabitants in the suburbs, whom it excluded from the communal pesthouse, fostering a suburban plague reservoir which seeped back inside the walls to infect citizens.[67] In the early seventeenth century, Manchester failed to control plague because it was riven by internal conflicts among the leading townsmen who dominated the court leet, the parish officers selected through communal shoulder tapping, and the lords of the manor; contagion was contained only through intervention by county authorities in 1605 and parliamentary troops in 1645.[68] The Dalmatian city of Split exacerbated its plague epidemic in 1731 when the community inside the walls isolated itself from the suburbs, and the different suburbs isolated themselves from one another, giving rise to violent conflict, abandonment of the infected, and breakdown of collective anti-plague measures. Contagion was brought under control only when the Venetian Governor General allocated state resources to improving living standard in the suburbs (and threatened to fire cannons at suburban curfew breakers).[69] In the nearby village of Podstrana, communal cohesion collapsed entirely in 1731 when the inhabitants took up the "disorder of wine and spirit" and resisted troops despatched by the Governor General to impose plague control.[70] The Gujarat city of Surat failed to control its 1994 plague epidemic partly because of internal conflicts among different castes and religious groups, who could neither agree nor cooperate on social distancing measures.[71] Behind the harmonious façade of the community lurk fissures and conflicts that may be the more bitter for being exacerbated by face-to-face interactions and multiplex local ties.[72]

64. "China: Public Shaming Returns amid Covid Fears", BBC News, 29 December 2021, https://www.bbc.co.uk/news/world-asia-china-59818971.

65. Slack 1985, 206, 214–15.

66. Slack 1985, 264.

67. Cipolla 1973, 123.

68. Slack 1985, 259.

69. Andreozzi 2015, 129.

70. Quoted in Andreozzi 2015, 132.

71. Barnes 2014, 173–4.

72. See Dennison and Ogilvie (2007) on such fissures inside Russian and Czech serf communities.

Even when communal social distancing succeeded, its implementation had a dark side. In the 1630–31 Tuscan plague, as reflected in the chapter epigraph, a shadowy posse in the village of Pinzidimonte incarcerated four families in their houses without food and terrorized everyone else into staying at home, preventing them from going to work, walking in the streets, and even attending church.[73] In the 1680 Bohemian plague epidemic, according to an anonymous Hebrew memoir, "If someone fell sick in one of the villages, he was driven out of his house with all his belongings" and forced into internment in a two-room manorial lazaretto deep in the forest.[74] In the 1731 Split plague, suburban communities incarcerated the infected in a "very small place" and expelled suspected victims into the countryside, where they were confined inside tiny self-built huts and abandoned without food or assistance.[75] In one Guangdong village in 1741, a 43-year-old man called Hu Zuoting was discovered to be infected with leprosy, whereupon the "clans and people of the community feared contamination by him, and made a public and collective decision to expel him".[76] In eighteenth- and nineteenth-century Madagascar, some communities stoned smallpox sufferers, and others buried them alive.[77] During the 1817–25 Indian cholera epidemic, a northern Konkan village convened an informal panel of *bhagats* (men claiming to reveal the use of magic), who determined that the disease had been supernaturally transmitted by a male witch, whereupon a band of villagers beat the accused man to death and threw his body into the sea.[78] More than 100 people openly admitted to taking part in actions like this in various Konkan villages during the epidemic, and all but one were pardoned by British government officials on the grounds that killing witches had been permitted under Maratha law.[79] In nineteenth-century Ethiopia, when smallpox was detected in a household, villagers "surrounded the house in the night . . . set fire to it . . . then thrust the inmates back into the burning dwelling at spear point even though they were their neighbours or relatives".[80] In the 1892 Russian cholera epidemic, six Tomsk villagers murdered a woman they identified as "Cholera" personified, marching into town after the murder shouting, "Give thanks unto God! We have killed cholera, dressed as a woman above, but underneath a man."[81] In South Africa in 1918–19, witch-finders "smelt out" influenza sufferers, whereupon the village attacked

73. Henderson 2019, 144.
74. Quoted in Jeremy Brown 2022, 80.
75. Quoted in Andreozzi 2015, 129.
76. Q. Liang 2009, 65 (quotation), 91.
77. G. Campbell 1991, 432.
78. M. Harrison 2020, 517–18.
79. M. Harrison 2020, 520.
80. Quoted in Pankhurst 1965, 349.
81. Quoted in Frieden 1977, 552.

the victim's kraal, injuring or killing the whole family to stop them from infecting the community.[82] In Maharashtra in 1943 during a cholera epidemic, "the Hindus of a village attacked an Achchut [untouchable] family; tied the hands and feet of an elderly woman, placed her on a pile of wood which was subsequently set on fire. All this because they thought she was the cause of the Cholera in the village."[83] The problem in these cases was too much community and not enough hierarchy, with no one wielding formal authority to enforce the legal rights of individuals or proceed against communal mobs.

Horrific though such communal persecutions were, even more harmful from the perspective of contagion was communal resistance to social distancing measures. Pesthouses, lazarettos, and isolation hospitals, as we saw in chapter 3, were attacked by communal mobs, whose members feared that they would be borne away to incarceration and, as they saw it, inevitable maltreatment, infection, and death. In Florence in 1633, the authorities feared popular resistance to pesthouse confinement so acutely that they held back from implementing isolation measures for several weeks, allowing the epidemic to spread unchecked.[84] In the 1831 cholera epidemic in Stettin, mobs violently resisted removal of cholera patients from their homes into hospital internment.[85] In Russia during the 1892 Astrakhan cholera epidemic, a mob invaded the isolation barracks, "liberated" the quarantined patients, violently attacked the medical staff, and burnt down the buildings.[86] As cholera moved up the Volga, a crowd of peasants in the district of Saratov "rescued" the cholera patients, burnt down the isolation barracks, and murdered a student who tried to reason with them.[87] In the 1894 Hong Kong plague, a crowd of over 1,000 assembled at the Dongwa hospital to protest against household inspections and hospital isolation measures.[88] In the 1894–95 Milwaukee smallpox epidemic, a mob of 3,000 "furious" neighbours armed with clubs, knives, and stones demonstrated against the threatened removal of an infected child to the isolation hospital (shown in figure 4.2), forcing the hospital ambulance to retreat and abandon the attempt. This was followed by weeks of street protests against consignment to the isolation hospital on the grounds that the "people's rights were paramount and should be protected, if need be, at the point of a pistol".[89] In Kanpur in 1900, a plague segregation camp in which females were

82. Quoted in H. Phillips 2008, 35.
83. Quoted in Tumbe 2020, 41.
84. Henderson 2019, 279.
85. R. Evans 1992, 165.
86. Frieden 1977, 544.
87. Frieden 1977, 545.
88. Benedict 1988, 140.
89. Leavitt 1976, 558–9.

FIGURE 4.2. Smallpox troubles in Milwaukee, 1894. During the 1894–95 smallpox epidemic, community mobs in southside Milwaukee neighbourhoods roamed the streets, resisting health workers seeking to implement public health regulations mandating internment of smallpox patients in the local isolation hospital. Note the central role played by female rioters, who, according to the newspaper report accompanying this illustration, played a major role in maintaining the street demonstrations by exploiting police reluctance to use force against women. Original illustration in *Leslie's Weekly Illustrated Newspaper*, 27 September 1894. *Source*: Library of Congress.

forcibly interned was attacked by a mob of mill workers, Muslim butchers, and members of the Chamar caste.[90]

Communities organized popular resistance to the mere presence of pest-houses in their midst. In the 1606 Scottish plague, temporary isolation lodges for the infected were provided on the common muir (moor) of Gogar, west of Edinburgh, for those "infecit with the pest", but the nearby community of Ratho attacked the encampment, destroyed the lodges, and expelled the plague patients.[91] In 1742, a group of Jiangxi villagers burnt down a small isolation colony outside the village, inhabited by lepers, killing two of the most crippled inmates, a deed the vigilante villagers regarded as perfectly justifiable:

We asked them to move somewhere else and they refused. . . . The solution was to burn down their sheds while they were asleep. In so doing, we

90. Tumbe 2020, 97.
91. Quoted in Oram 2007, 25–6.

eliminate this evil [*hai*] from our place and people will now not be contaminated [*chuanran*]. . . . [One of the accomplices said that] even if we burn these *mafeng* [leprous] people to death, I don't think we will be in deep trouble, as we do this to eliminate an evil for the community.[92]

In the 1911 plague in north-east China, a 300- to 500-strong mob gathered in Changtu to block the building of a lazaretto.[93]

Restrictions on travel and trade attracted similar communal resistance. In Milan in 1630, "people, fearing health controls on trade, scream, threaten and are on the verge of rioting. They do not want to admit that it is the plague."[94] In Marseille in 1720, crowds rioted against travel bans and trade restrictions even while the plague spread to kill half the inhabitants.[95] When cholera arrived in Russia in the 1830s, peasant villagers attacked sanitary cordons and murdered those who were trying to build and enforce them.[96] In the 1899 plague in the Portuguese city of Porto, crowds confronted health inspectors and doctors to protest against sanitary cordons.[97] In the 1911 plague in north-east China, crowds of Huangqi villagers organized violence against roadblocks and house-to-house inspections.[98]

Local lockdowns, quarantines, mobility restrictions, and entertainment bans attracted communal resistance. In Salisbury in 1627, crowds of poor people demonstrated in the streets against lockdowns, quarantines, and closures.[99] In Rome in 1656, the community of Trastavere protested so vigorously against quarantine that the Health Congregation had to send in soldiers by night to guard the public workers building a "cage" around the neighbourhood; even then, the inhabitants illicitly slipped out and secretly removed quarantine signs from their infected houses.[100] In the 1731 plague epidemic in the Dalmatian city of Split, a communal mob from the suburbs armed itself and tried to march into the city by force in order to protest against social distancing measures that kept them outside the walls; on one occasion, unknown hands threw a plague guard off the town wall in the middle of the night.[101] In Moscow in 1771, a mob of thousands (depicted in figure 4.3) demonstrated against urban

92. Quoted in Q. Liang 2009, 87.
93. Hu 2010, 324.
94. Quoted in Cipolla 1976, 36, 43.
95. Biraben 1968, 537.
96. R. Evans 1992, 164.
97. Echenberg 2007, 122, 127.
98. Hu 2010, 324.
99. Slack 1985, 258–9.
100. Risse 1999, 193–4.
101. Andreozzi 2015, 129.

FIGURE 4.3. The Moscow plague riot, 1771. From 15 to 17 September 1771, thousands of Muscovites flooded into Red Square to demonstrate against urban quarantines and closures. The mob invaded the Kremlin, razed a monastery, killed an archbishop, and destroyed two quarantine zones before being suppressed by the army. Watercolour by Ernest Lissner, painted in the 1930s. *Source*: Wikimedia Commons.

social distancing measures for two days and could be quelled only by military intervention.[102] In the 1900–1 San Francisco plague, large crowds flooded onto the streets of Chinatown to protest against a municipal quarantine.[103] In the 1929 Inner Mongolian plague, a mob of villagers besieged the Chientiatien headquarters of the Plague Prevention Service.[104] In the 1918 Spanish flu pandemic, Minneapolis crowds insisted on attending football games in the teeth of public health prohibitions, and the St Paul bowling club insisted on resuming meetings at the height of the infection—a case that illuminates the less beneficial side of the social capital generated by twentieth-century American bowling clubs.[105]

102. J. T. Alexander 1980, 177–201; Melikishvili 2006, 25.
103. Echenberg 2007, 221.
104. Nathan 1967, 72.
105. Ott et al. 2007, 805.

Local communities also attacked health workers, whom they viewed as the enforcers of hated social distancing measures. In Dresden during the plague of 1680, the populace harassed, stoned, and violently attacked the plague surgeon and lazaretto employees in the streets as they carried out their official duties.[106] In the 1884 Naples cholera epidemic, health officials lamented the "indescribable resistance opposed by the lower classes [*popolo minuto*] to the measures that were intended for their salvation": crowds violently attacked health workers, who were seen as enforcers of segregation.[107] In the Russian town of Saratov in 1892, an urban mob raided the homes of physicians and anyone suspected of hiding medical personnel.[108] In Khvalynsk, a temporary surgeon who disseminated information about preventive measures and began to organize cholera barracks was hunted down, butchered in the street, and then surrounded by a crowd of peasant women, "who spit in the face of the deceased and railed at his imagined crimes, rejoicing that the poisoner had received proper retribution".[109] In the 1896 Mumbai plague, mobs attacked ambulances and assaulted those rumoured to be assisting in forced segregation.[110] In the Gujarat village of Chaklasi in 1898, a village priest and medicine man called Ranchod Vira assembled a mob of 500–600 armed supporters, proclaimed himself the local king, and declared the area free of British plague measures, including a recently installed quarantine camp.[111] In Delhi around the same time, anonymous placards appeared in a major marketplace urging resistance to plague controls and a commitment to sacrificing lives for the cause, along the lines of the 1857 mutiny.[112] In the 2003 Chinese SARS epidemic, Zhejian villagers broke windows in government offices and violently attacked health officials.[113] In London during the Covid-19 epidemic in June 2021, large crowds abused and jostled England's chief medical officer, whom they blamed for pandemic lockdowns.[114]

Closely knit communities can thus mobilize collective action to support social distancing measures. But they can also mobilize the same sort of action to carry out disproportionate enforcement, vigilante measures, persecution of innocent minorities, and resistance to social distancing. Communal social capital is a powerful weapon. But it can be aimed at bad as well as good targets.

106. Schlenkrich 2002, 51.
107. Quoted in Snowden 1995, 144–9.
108. Frieden 1977, 545.
109. Quoted in Frieden 1977, 545.
110. M. Harrison 2012, 181; Arnold 2015, 117.
111. Chaturvedi 2006, 162, 166–9, 175–7, 180–1.
112. Arnold 1993, 230–1.
113. Srivastava et al. 2020, 3.
114. *Economist* 2021a.

3. Jabbing the Community

Communal social capital also played a role—both positive and negative—in immunization. This already occurred with smallpox variolation. In Germany, as we shall see, variolation was rare until the very end of the eighteenth century because of opposition by churches and monopolization by medical associations. Where variolation was practised, it was often because of an informal agreement between an entire peasant community and wealthy local elites, frequently mediated by a clergyman. In Westphalia in 1785, for instance, the entire community of tenant farmers in a village near Herford agreed with the local landlord to have their 33 children variolated at his expense, after the local pastor mediated the agreement and secured the services of an urban doctor to implement the operation.[115] In Holstein in 1796, the village community of Thürk agreed to accept smallpox variolation after the wealthier farmers agreed to fund the inoculation of the poor, inspired by the persuasion of a rich local landlord.[116]

Informal communal action also played a role in the early implementation of cowpox vaccination. In the summer of 1802, a peasant from the remote French village of La Gleize heard rumours about the new procedure, undertook the long journey on foot to a town, procured vaccine from a health officer, and brought it back to his village, where he personally vaccinated over 100 children, making his house "a sort of centre for inoculation".[117] In 1807, villagers in West Yorkshire spontaneously organized the vaccination of over 1,000 local children using penknives and needles.[118] One of the special strengths of community institutions was explicitly evoked in 1807 when a Lajarasse farmer vaccinated his neighbours arm to arm, succeeding because "in a commune made up entirely of farmers, a person of their own cloth inspires more confidence than all the doctors of the Empire".[119]

But informal communal peer pressure seldom operated in isolation. Rather, it worked best in combination with other institutions. The local government was one, as in La Gleize in 1802, when communal action organized the vaccination, but the vaccine was procured from a local government health officer.[120] The same interplay between community and local government occurred in 1819, when the English town of Thetford managed to stave off a smallpox epidemic partly because the mayor organized lists of those inhabitants who were

115. Penschow 2022, 188.
116. Penschow 2022, 189.
117. Quoted in M. Bennett 2020, 159.
118. M. Bennett 2020, 104.
119. Quoted in M. Bennett 2020, 163.
120. M. Bennett 2020, 159.

susceptible to infection, recorded their vaccination status, and then threatened non-vaccinated inhabitants with exposure to their neighbours.[121]

The central state was another institution that collaborated with community peer pressure. In 1808, for instance, the Austrian government used communal "naming and shaming" during state vaccination campaigns, ordering local newspapers to castigate delinquent parents as "people blinded by prejudice who would rather allow their dependents to die . . . than keep them alive by so simple and safe a means as vaccination".[122] In 1881, the Liouville bill by which the French state sought to introduce compulsory vaccination incorporated an element of public shaming by threatening those who did not vaccinate their household members with having their names posted publicly on the door of the local town hall—the shame was informal but the legislative bill and the town hall door were formal (the legislation failed to pass).[123]

The Church also sometimes interacted with the local community to push for immunization. As already mentioned, the informal communal agreement to carry out a collective variolation in the Westphalian village near Herford in 1785 was initially inspired by the local clergyman, who first convinced the villagers of the benefits of immunization and then arranged for a doctor to come to the village and do it.[124] The same was true of vaccination, as in the Swedish village of Kuddby in 1806, when the Reverend Johan Peter Wallensteen threatened that:

> if any child withheld from vaccination dies of smallpox, it will be buried on the north side of the church with a notice on the grave giving the reason for this; that in the case of such parents the newspapers shall be notified of their crime; a public record of their disgrace will be kept after their death etc. etc. After this, the next vaccination session was announced, and the names read out of those who were expected to attend, together with those who had previously been vaccinated, and I also said that henceforth all vaccinations will be announced in this way. The announcements after this have been obeyed, with a carefulness which cannot be praised enough.[125]

Each sanction named by Reverend Wallensteen involved spiritual disgrace alongside community shame.

Communal social capital, however, was just a weapon. It could be aimed in the exact opposite direction—to oppose immunization. It was already used

121. M. Bennett 2020, 372.
122. Quoted in M. Bennett 2020, 194.
123. Baldwin 1999, 267.
124. Penschow 2022, 188.
125. Quoted in Sköld 2000, 214.

that way against variolation. In the 1754 smallpox epidemic in Braunschweig-Wolfenbüttel, communal opposition by villagers prevented introduction of variolation, despite support by medical experts, educated elites, and the Braunschweig Privy Council.[126] In eighteenth-century New England townships, popular opposition to variolation forced locals to seek inoculation on the black market in illicit clinics located on islands off the coast, where neighbourly peer pressure could not prevent them.[127] During the 1768 Virginia smallpox epidemic, local villagers rioted when a group of private individuals assembled in a country house to get variolated.[128] During a 1774 epidemic in Massachusetts, a crowd with blackened faces besieged a variolation hospital, seeking to destroy "Castle Pox".[129] In the 1797 French smallpox epidemic in the Île-de-France, a variolation scheme was abandoned when villagers organized concerted resistance against medical teams.[130]

Vaccination encountered similar community opposition. Sometimes a community organized informal action against its own members who wanted to vaccinate their families privately or offer the procedure voluntarily inside the community. In the 1774 Dorset smallpox epidemic, for instance, the parish of Yetminster ostracized Benjamin Jesty for testing pre-Jennerian cowpox inoculation on his own family.[131] In England in 1807, one anti-vaccination activist warned Edward Jenner, the inventor of smallpox vaccination, "to immediately quit London, for there was no knowing what an enraged populace might do".[132] In a Württemberg village in 1831, a crowd of peasants chased away a surgeon who tried to collect lymph for vaccination.[133]

Many local communities organized informal opposition to external vaccinators despatched by state or Church. In the 1803 Russian epidemic, peasant communes resisted state physicians who wanted to vaccinate village children.[134] In the 1806 Spanish smallpox epidemic, villagers organized passive resistance to government vaccination campaigns.[135] In a Württemberg village in 1832, a peasant mob attacked a government vaccination officer with stones and pitchforks.[136] In 1837 when the Egyptian government imposed mandatory vaccination, rural communities concealed local children, bribed inspec-

126. Lindemann 1996, 331–2.
127. M. Bennett 2020, 59–60.
128. M. Bennett 2020, 60, 270.
129. M. Bennett 2020, 60, 270.
130. M. Bennett 2020, 153.
131. Anon. 1862, 291; Pead 2003, 2105; Beale and Beale 2005, 81.
132. Quoted in M. Bennett 2020, 119.
133. Mühlhoff 2021, 16.
134. M. Bennett 2020, 236.
135. M. Bennett 2020, 217.
136. Mühlhoff 2021, 16.

tors to turn a blind eye, forged vaccination certificates, and violently attacked the barber-vaccinators.[137] On the Shetland island of Foula around 1850, local inhabitants refused to let a clergyman vaccinator land his boat because of communal rumours that he had come to castrate the men.[138] In the 1894 Milwaukee smallpox epidemic, communal mobs opposed all public health initiatives, causing vaccination to be widely rejected even though it was free of charge and infection was spreading fast.[139] In the 1902 Punjab plague, popular rumours spread about the horrors of vaccination: "The needle was a yard long; you died immediately after the operation; you survived the operation just six months and then collapsed; men lost their virility and women became sterile; the Deputy Commissioner himself underwent the operation and expired half an hour afterwards in great agony."[140]

In the 1902 Madras smallpox epidemic, the indigenous state vaccinator Swamy Naick described how in the Black Town neighbourhood he and his assistants "were most wantonly attacked by a number of Armenians, and other inhabitants who were ignorant of the beneficial effects of the cow-pox, and cruelly assaulted".[141] In the 1904 Brazilian smallpox epidemic, anti-vaccination sentiment was stirred up by rumours that vaccines were produced from the bodies of rats, and the serum would be injected into women's groins. This triggered a 12-day "Vaccine Revolt", during which communal mobs erected barricades, attacked public health vehicles, stoned health inspectors, and destroyed public infrastructure.[142] In the face of such communal resistance, the vaccination programme was cancelled, resulting in several years of high smallpox mortality.[143]

Communal resistance was even more violent when vaccination was attempted by foreigners. Indeed, community institutions were one of the many obstacles to successful vaccine diplomacy alluded to in chapter 2. In the 1804 Madras smallpox epidemic, according to a British surgeon, thousands of angry Trivatore villagers mobbed him, declaring that "rather then [sic] allow me or any ones to be vaccinated in, or near the Village, they would suffer death".[144] In north-eastern Peru in 1805, villagers around Chocope threw out the philanthropic Spanish vaccination expedition with violent threats.[145] In Indonesia in 1847, the Sipirok uprising erupted because of a popular rumour that smallpox

137. Meyer 2022, 442.
138. B. Smith 1998, 403.
139. Leavitt 1976, 561.
140. Tumbe 2020, 94.
141. Quoted in King 1902, 413; M. Bennett 2020, 356.
142. Cantisano 2022, 621–3; Cukierman 2021; Echenberg 2007, 172, 176.
143. Cantisano 2022, 611–12.
144. Quoted in Brimnes 2004, 210.
145. M. Bennett 2020, 313.

vaccination was a Dutch plot to mark Indonesian children so they would join the colonial army, while in other regions popular rumour held that vaccination aimed to render Indonesians weak and cowardly.[146] In the great Indian city of Varanasi in 1899, "a general stampede" broke out among crowds at a fair when rumours spread that a European accompanied by two policeman was a plague inoculator.[147] In the 1900–1 San Francisco plague, the Chinese community organized resistance to the Haffkine vaccine, circulating posters ordering Chinese businesses to close in protest. As reflected in the chapter epigraph, the community warned business owners: "If any disobey this we will unite and put an everlasting boycott on them. Don't say that you have not been warned first."[148] Huge mobs gathered to threaten vaccination officers and destroy shops of Chinatown residents suspected of cooperating with public health officers.[149]

As with sanitation and social distancing, so too with immunization, communal social capital played an influential role in swaying individual and collective decisions. In some cases, social capital could be mobilized by insiders to persuade their neighbours to get immunized. In other cases, community peer effects could be manipulated by local or central governments to fuel state vaccination campaigns. But communal social capital often veered against immunization. Communities used ostracism and violence against their own members, outsiders, and representatives of state and Church to resist variolation and vaccination. How communal social capital affected immunization depended on who got control of it.

4. Communal Whispers and Information Cascades

Controlling contagion requires information—about both disease and diseased. The community should be good at information. It fosters multiplex relationships in which neighbours interact in multiple spheres—economic, social, political, religious, cultural, residential. Multistranded ties mean that community members have multiple means to collect and spread information, reducing its costs.[150]

But the community also reduces the costs of spreading false information. Some communities lack the capacity to compile accurate information about disease symptoms, transmission mechanisms, and preventive measures. Some falsify information to serve other community interests. Many suffer from

---

146. Boomgaard 2003, 609.
147. Quoted in Arnold 1993, 221.
148. Quoted in Echenberg 2007, 221.
149. Echenberg 2007, 223.
150. Coleman 1988, S104–10; Ogilvie 2011, 7–8, 347.

"information cascades"—convergence in beliefs for reasons unrelated to their accuracy.[151]

Community successes in sanitation, social distancing, and immunization sometimes arose from information advantages. When peer pressure helped enforce sanitary measures during fifteenth-century Dutch plagues, it was because information passed readily within closely knit neighbourhoods where people lived in spatial proximity and sharply scrutinized one another's daily actions.[152] When peer pressure helped enforce plague lockdown in Florence in 1630–31, it was because nosy neighbours easily observed and reported one another for violating isolation and curfew regulations.[153] When Thetford managed to contain smallpox in 1819, it was because local residents knew that if they refused to get vaccinated everyone would find out.[154] When public embarrassment caused Mississippi families to upgrade their latrines against hookworm in the 1910s, it was because gossip conveyed information about laggard households across the whole community.[155]

But these successes should not blind us to the fact that the community could be poorly informed even about epidemics that were very close. In 1630, plague sprang up in Florence during the months of spring, but as late as August "all the city was divided between [different] opinions: one that said it was plague and these were called the Frightened Ones . . . others who said that they were ordinary sicknesses, which happened every year, caused by suffering and hardship."[156] Even when the plague reached Trespiano, 5 miles (8 km) north of the city, the news diffused imperfectly:

> This [information] was spread through Florence, but through closed teeth and whispered in the ear to a confidant, with the usual recommendation not to say anything to others; it was not believed, it was mocked, and there was nothing that could be done about it, as usually happens; meanwhile people came every day from Trespiano into the city and mixed freely with everybody, and we swallowed the bait, which in time had its effect.[157]

During the 1896 Mumbai plague, the local health officer described three stages in "popular feeling": first, "when people would not believe in [any] plague measures"; second, when they "believed in all measures except the right ones"; and third, when they "believed in every rumour and would not

151. Burt 2001, 62–3; Ogilvie 2011, 347–9.
152. Coomans 2021, 223–30; Coomans and Weeda 2020, 82–3.
153. Henderson 2019, 234, 240, 257, 264.
154. M. Bennett 2020, 372.
155. Shubinski and Iacobelli 2020.
156. Quoted in Henderson 2019, 51.
157. Quoted in Henderson 2019, 34.

believe in any measure".[158] Communal channels easily convey rumours, but lack quality control.

More baneful even than ignorance are "information cascades" inside closely knit communities, resulting from repeated transmission and amplification of unchecked messages. Experiments in social psychology find that reports we learn through personal contacts are not as reliable as information we get from direct experience. This is because in personal contacts it is polite to share those components of what we know that are consistent with the perceived dispositions of our interlocutors. But people fail to compensate for this tendency and regard reports transmitted through closely knit community ties with more certainty than they deserve.[159] The biased sample of facts shared via contacts within a community becomes "information". A closely knit community creates a self-sustaining system in which the same report is repeatedly transmitted through multistranded interactions among daily contacts. Repetition amplifies people's opinions—both positively and negatively. The collective sanctions often applied within closely knit communities further intensify members' incentives not to deviate from community norms with regard to what information they transmit. As a result, a closely knit community may generate "information" for its members which consists excessively of amplified predispositions.[160] Such "ignorant certainty", amplified within a closely knit community, can reduce the quality of the information disseminated, misdirecting or corrupting communal action.

The 1630 plague epidemic in Milan illustrates this vividly. As early as 1629, local hearsay began to spread rumours that plague was transmitted not through infected persons or goods but by *untori* (anointers), who allegedly smeared mysterious unguents around the neighbourhood.[161] One of the first to be accused was a traveller from Sicily, who was popularly rumoured to be an anointer because "he was dressed in the French fashion and his appearances well supported it [the rumour]".[162] Other alleged anointers also had foreign connections—the son of a Spanish official, travellers from the politically contested region of Valtellina, men dressed in French fashions.[163] Even locals were sometimes rumoured to be working treacherously as anointers for foreign powers, spreading contagion to prepare for a French or Venetian invasion.[164] It was only after informal gossip had widely propagated this "information" about

158. Quoted in Arnold 2015, 115.
159. Burt 2001, 62–3; Ogilvie 2011, 362–3.
160. Burt 2001, 62–3; Ogilvie 2011, 347–9, 362–3.
161. Brivio 2017.
162. Quoted in Brivio 2017, 93.
163. Brivio 2017, 153, 157, 168–9.
164. Brivio 2017, 13, 123, 153, 157, 160, 169.

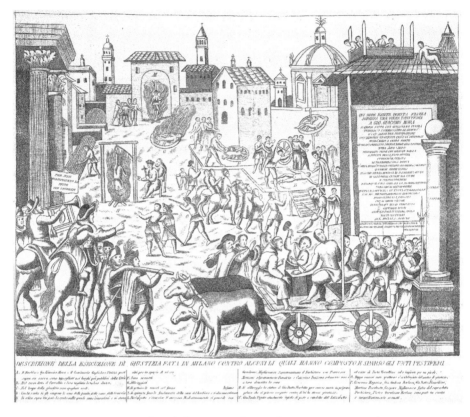

FIGURE 4.4. Torturing alleged plague spreaders, Milan, 1630. Communal rumours spread throughout Milan during 1629–30 that so-called *untori* (anointers) were smearing walls and buildings with grease and potions that caused plague. Informal rumours within the community ultimately triggered state action, in which a large number of people, many of them immigrants or other marginal inhabitants, were executed. Etching from *c.* 1839, attributed to Orazio Colombo, after an engraving by "Bassano" or "Francesco Vallato". *Source*: Wellcome Collection.

the causes of the plague that the Milan government felt constrained to respond by arresting suspects, torturing the accused, and finally executing them (as depicted in figure 4.4).[165] Communal transmission of fake news absorbed popular attention and government resources that could have been devoted to public health measures against a plague that ultimately killed 46 per cent of Milan's inhabitants.[166]

The Milanese anointer scandal was not unique. Information cascades claiming that epidemics are being deliberately transmitted by bad actors have been

165. Brivio 2017, 90–2.
166. Brivio 2017, 90–2 (on the anointers); Kohn 2007, 200 (on mortality).

recorded for millennia. Sometimes such rumours are propagated to pursue private feuds, as in the 1630–31 Florence plague epidemic when neighbours made false accusations of public health violations in order to settle scores against old enemies or earn rewards from the authorities.[167] But often such information cascades focus on "identity-based" characteristics such as religion or occupation. Communal social capital amplifies and transmits rumours that people with these traits are deliberately spreading infection.

Communal information cascades have often targeted religious minorities. In the second century CE, the early Christian author Tertullian drily noted that "if the Tiber overflows to the walls, if the Nile does not rise to the fields; if the sky does not move or the earth does; if there is famine or plague, the cry goes up at once, 'The Christians to the lion!'"[168] In Christian parts of Spain during the epidemics of 1320 and 1333, rumours spread that Muslims were causing the infection through their heretical practices.[169] When the Black Death reached Cyprus in 1348, the Christian Cypriots blamed non-Christians and massacred all the Muslim slaves and prisoners.[170] When the Black Death struck Mecca, conversely, Muslims blamed it on the presence of unbelievers violating the holy city.[171]

All over Europe, as we saw in chapter 3, Christians attacked Jews in response to rumours that they had caused the Black Death. Between 1347 and 1351, over 1,000 local communities in the German Rhineland, Spain, France, and eastern-central Europe carried out mass attacks on their Jewish inhabitants, locked them up in synagogues, rounded them up on islands, or burnt them to death. Many epidemic pogroms were organized formally by institutions such as the state, as we saw in chapter 3. Religious organizations and occupational guilds also contributed to pogroms, as we shall see in chapters 5 and 6.[172] But many attacks on Jews were organized informally by community mobs, counter to the mandates of religion and the commands of the state. In Barcelona on 17 May 1348, for instance, "some people incited by an evil temper, having set their fear of God and our [royal] dominion aside, gathered as a riotous mob and entered into the *call* [quarter] of the Jews of Barcelona. And there they destroyed and despoiled many dwellings and they killed many Jews."[173] Communal pogroms flared up for years and extended across large swathes of Europe, as with the massacre of Jews in 1349 depicted in figure 4.5.[174]

167. Henderson 2019, 234, 240, 257, 264.
168. Quoted in Fredriksen 2006, 601–2.
169. Dols 1977, 288.
170. Dols 1977, 58–9.
171. Dols 1977, 63.
172. See Cohn 2007, 3–36; Finley and Koyama 2018, 257; Jeremy Brown 2022, 241–2.
173. Quoted in Colet et. al 2014, 66.
174. Cohn 2012, 536; Jedwab, Johnson, and Koyama 2019; Agresta 2020, 377.

FIGURE 4.5. Massacre of Jews in a European town during the Black Death, 1349. On the right, a woman restrains a young boy from leaping into the fire, while on the left, a crowd cheers as the local Jews burn. On both sides, men add logs to the fire. Miniature by Piérart dou Tielt illustrating the "Antiquitates Flandriae" by Gilles li Muisis, held at the Bibliothèque royale de Belgique. *Source*: Wikimedia Commons.

Communal information cascades continued to fuel attacks on minority religions throughout the seven centuries following the Black Death. In the Devon town of Barnstaple in 1644, majority Anglican townsmen blamed the plague on local Calvinists, who in turn blamed it on the heretical views of the Church of England.[175] In 1665–66, London Protestants spread rumours that the Great Plague was caused by sectaries, schismatics, Papists, and other "friends of Antichrist".[176] In mid-nineteenth-century Hunan, popular rumour blamed Muslims for using black magic to spread plague to the Han Chinese.[177] In north-east China during the 1910–11 plague, a Catholic villager who accused corpse searchers of plundering the dead was tied up by the "consortia" in his community and "chastised by 100 whips".[178] In India during the Covid-19

175. Slack 1985, 243.
176. Quoted in Slack 1985, 247.
177. Benedict 1988, 140.
178. Quoted in Hu 2010, 321.

epidemic, rumours spread in majority Hindu villages that Muslim neighbours were deliberately infecting food and water supplies in a "corona jihad".[179]

Community information cascades also targeted health officials and medical workers, whose occupational proximity to disease engendered rumours that they were actually causing it. In two Brabant villages in the 1523 epidemic, women working as plague "scrubbers" were accused of "plague spreading" by touching the doors and door handles in the houses of plague patients.[180] In Geneva in 1530, informal rumours circulated that the master of the plague hospital, his wife, the hospital barber-surgeon, his family, and the priest who served as the hospital almoner had formed a coven of plague spreaders; only after this communal rumour had blown up into an information cascade did the town authorities respond by arresting, torturing, and beheading the vilified health-care workers.[181] In Volterra in 1630, rumours spread that a travelling "empiric" who claimed to be an apothecary had caused the plague by poisoning holy water.[182] In Florence in 1630, neighbours spread rumours that a lazaretto physician was poisoning patients with a mysterious powder.[183] In seventeenth-century Salisbury, rumours spread that Ursula Barrett, a specialist plague searcher, was burying people alive and hanging out clothes in the garden to disseminate plague to her neighbours.[184] In 1680, two Saxon villages spread rumours that the Dresden lazaretto surgeon was transmitting plague; community members violently attacked a man on horseback they wrongly suspected of being the surgeon.[185] In the Porto epidemic of 1899, communal mobs blamed the plague on doctors and attacked them as they transported patients to the hospital or the morgue; as one foreign correspondent remarked, "The people believe that the disease is the invention of the doctors, and that patients are taken to the hospital only to be made away with."[186] In the 1918 plague epidemic in northern China, communal mobs rioted to protest autopsies and "anybody wearing a mask was liable to be attacked as a foreign doctor".[187] In the 2014 Ebola epidemic, communal rumours in the Guinea village of Worme blamed the disease on visiting health-care workers, so a village mob killed them and dumped their bodies in a latrine.[188]

179. Quoted in Arnold 2020, 576.
180. Curtis 2021a, 7.
181. Monter 1971, 183.
182. Henderson 2019, 43.
183. Henderson 2019, 44.
184. Slack 1985, 274–5.
185. Schlenkrich 2002, 53.
186. Quoted in M. Harrison 2012, 190–1.
187. "The Plague Situation: A Tour of Inspection", *North-China Herald*, 26 January 1918, 185.
188. Honigsbaum 2019, 207; Srivastava et al. 2020, 3;

Sometimes information cascades arose from rumours that medical providers were profiting financially from communal misfortune. According to popular gossip in sixteenth-century Italian communities, public health officials, health-care workers, plague cleaners, cartmen, and gravediggers were perpetuating plague for their own gain.[189] When plague came to Florence in 1633, a mob of 400 women rioted in front of the pesthouse screaming abuse at the barber-surgeons, whom they accused of skimming off the provisions that were supposed to support poor families during lockdown.[190] In the 1896 Mumbai plague epidemic, many Indians refused to go to hospital because of rumours that they were being taken there to extract body fluids that would be used to protect the lives of Europeans.[191] In West Africa during the 2014 Ebola epidemic, an angry mob marched on the Kenema hospital, actuated by rumours that nurses there were deliberately infecting locals in order to attract foreign aid which would profit local elites.[192]

Communal information cascades also targeted specific anti-contagion measures and those responsible for implementing them. In Dresden in 1680, as we have seen, the plague surgeon and lazaretto employees were attacked in the streets as they carried out their official duties.[193] In nineteenth-century Württemberg, village mothers spread conspiracy theories about vaccination clinics, deterring neighbours from getting their children immunized.[194] In Egypt in the 1830s, rural communities not only resisted vaccination but beat up the barber-vaccinators, imprisoned them, and persecuted them with extra corvée labour obligations. On one occasion, the village of Dai'rut al-Sharif mobilized 200 armed *fallahin* (peasants) within minutes of the arrival of state health officials in the village.[195] Nineteenth-century cholera and yellow fever epidemics in the USA, France, Spain, and Italy saw waves of rumour and violence against public officials, doctors, and hospital workers implementing anti-contagion measures.[196] In the 2014 West African Ebola epidemic, popular rumour held that spraying chlorine disinfectant and taking blood samples spread the disease, triggering violent demonstrations by mobs in Forécariah.[197] Across the globe in 2021, information cascades about face masks, vaccinations, and Covid

189. Cohn 2012, 536.
190. Litchfield 2008, para 335.
191. Arnold 2015, 116.
192. Honigsbaum 2019, 212.
193. Schlenkrich 2002, 51.
194. Mühlhoff 2021, 19; Mühlhoff 2022, 7n20.
195. Kuhnke 1990, 117.
196. Cohn 2012, 544.
197. Honigsbaum 2019, 207.

lockdowns triggered mob attacks on health workers in many communities.[198] Such communal rumours reduced the productivity of health-care workers, diverted resources away from concrete anti-contagion measures, and directly undermined public health.

Communal norms and multiplex relationships thus do lower the costs of collecting and diffusing information during epidemics. But not all this information is true. Communal social capital also lowers the cost of fabricating and transmitting false information, exacerbating contagion even for community members.

5. The Disease outside the Walls

"By eradicating the disease outside the walls, its eradication within is made easier."[199] This admonition, addressed to the town of Prato when it tried to exclude suburban residents from its pesthouse in 1630, arose from a basic flaw with purely communal approaches to contagion. No community is an island. Social capital may help a community control its own contagion. But epidemics by their nature spill over borders—the national frontiers analysed in chapter 3 and the local boundaries acutely present in the mind of every townsman or villager. To tackle contagion, the community had to interact with the world outside its walls.

This arose from the distinctive feature of contagion—its negative spillover effects. As chapters 1 and 2 discussed, contagion is like pollution, causing harm that extends beyond the individual who gets infected. Indeed, as we saw in chapter 3, contagion causes cross-border externalities that spill over beyond state frontiers. The same is true of the local community. Each community has good incentives to control contagion that directly affects its own members, but poor incentives to prevent its members from infecting outsiders. Yet each community is menaced by other communities that behave in the same way. In a pandemic, the local community needs to cooperate with the wider society.

Eyam, a small lead-mining village in Derbyshire that was struck by plague in 1665, vividly illustrates the limits of community contagion control. A famous story describes how Eyam used communal social capital to quarantine the entire village population, sacrificing its own members to save the wider society.[200] During Covid-19 this story went viral, making its way into print journalism, television, and a 34-line poem entitled "Lockdown" by the poet laureate.[201]

198. Devi 2020.
199. Quoted in Cipolla 1973, 123.
200. Bradley 1977; Race 1995; Wallis 2006.
201. Wallis 2006; Wallis 2020.

The historical evidence tells a sadder tale. In actuality, the community of Eyam did not come together in solidarity to impose quarantine upon itself to save the rest of England. Many wealthier villagers fled before quarantine was imposed. As a result, plague deaths were concentrated among the village poor, who could not afford to make a run for it. Among the poorer village households with just a single hearth, 43 per cent suffered plague deaths, compared with only 17 per cent of the better-off households with two or more hearths.[202]

Nor was the Eyam quarantine enforced voluntarily by deploying communal social capital. On the contrary. Villagers who could not afford to flee early were prevented from leaving later by the city of Sheffield 13 miles (21 km) away, which paid constables to keep villagers hemmed up in Eyam in order to protect other settlements—not unlike the military blockade of Wuhan in February 2020 during the Covid-19 pandemic.[203] The community of Eyam could not limit contagion by itself. Action by other communities, including the formal institutions of Sheffield local government, was essential to keep contagion from spreading.

Eyam holds important lessons on epidemics, but not the ones proposed in the Eyam legend. A single community alone cannot contain contagion. This is because of the problem of free-riding. It was in the collective interest of society at large (and thus all communities in seventeenth-century Derbyshire) for plague-struck localities to be quarantined. But each individual village had an incentive to let its members break out, both to escape local contagion and to relieve local food supplies. To control contagion, the community needed support—and indeed coercion—from other institutions.

Preventing plague from spreading out of Eyam depended on external sources of support. Eyam was able to sustain its quarantine in 1665 only because of provisions organized and provided by the Earl of Devonshire, who arranged for supplies to be left at the boundary of the village.[204] This reflects another limitation on the capacity of the community to control contagion. A community hard hit by epidemic disease needs to provide welfare support to its poorer members in order to align individual with collective incentives to comply with quarantine. But precisely during an epidemic, a community can ill afford such support. External resources are needed. In early modern English epidemics, as we saw in chapter 3, the central state supported local governments and parish vestries by coordinating efforts across multiple communities, mandating inter-communal risk-pooling, and supplementing depleted funds of hard-hit localities.

202. Wallis 2006, 51n14.
203. Wallis 2006, 31.
204. Wallis 2006, 31.

External institutions can also provide a formal framework to channel informal peer effects into supporting rather than subverting anti-contagion measures. This can be seen in the divergent success of two adjacent south-west German territories, Baden and Württemberg, in controlling smallpox epidemics. Both states decreed compulsory vaccination at nearly the same date—Württemberg in 1815, Baden in 1818.[205] Both made local communities responsible for implementation. But the two states channelled communal action in very different ways. The Württemberg vaccination programme was radically decentralized, allowing noisy minorities inside each community to entrench anti-vaccination peer pressure, leading to high vaccine hesitancy. The Baden programme, by contrast, mandated public mass vaccination events in each community. No individual or family had to act as a first mover, undertake individual effort, or incur individual cost. Instead, people acted jointly with a wider group of neighbours to comply with the law publicly. Conversely, refusing to show up on vaccination day involved publicly opposing an emerging communal consensus that getting one's children vaccinated was a normal act of good communal citizenship. The Baden state requirement for public mass vaccinations ensured that peer effects reflected the community as a whole rather than a noisy minority. This resulted in much higher vaccination rates and much lower smallpox mortality in Baden than in Württemberg.[206] Formal state rules, even apparently trivial ones, could channel community peer effects in ways that benefited rather than harmed contagion control.

6. Conclusion

Do the ways communities behaved during historical pandemics hold wider lessons? If the community undertook informal action that benefited contagion control during the Black Death or nineteenth-century smallpox epidemics, does that imply that the community should act likewise in the present day? Might the intervening growth of other institutions like the state and the market make community action redundant in the modern world?

History provides some answers. In some ways, the state and the market have expanded so much since the Black Death, and even since the nineteenth century, that the institution of the local community is inevitably less important. Even in the medieval and early modern world, communal institutions tended to be stronger precisely where state and market institutions were weaker.[207] As state, market, and other institutions have become more powerful and all-encompassing, the importance of the local community has waned.

---

205. Baldwin 1999, 260–1, 330–3; M. Bennett 2020, 196–7, 365; Mühlhoff 2021, 5.
206. Mühlhoff 2021, 19, 33; Mühlhoff 2022, 7, 9–10.
207. Dennison 2023.

In many ways, however, the community has characteristics that are still important in all societies. The community can do things that market and state cannot, in epidemics as in other situations. It has an almost unparalleled capacity to generate a sense of membership, alert neighbours to shared motivations, bring individuals together in repeated interactions that engender reciprocity, and cultivate multistranded relationships among its members. These features foster shared norms, ease information flow, and facilitate collective action. They do generate "social capital". Informal community norms, information, and collective action can in principle solve some of the market and state failures that arise during epidemics.[208]

Historical epidemics provide examples of beneficial community action. To tackle contagion, we have seen, the local community displayed striking success in creating interpersonal trust, fostering shared norms about neighbourly behaviour, organizing collective action to prevent disease transmission, and conveying information about individual choices likely to transmit infection. Sanitation, social distancing, and immunization were greatly enhanced when the local community directed its social capital to these ends.

But history also provides rich evidence of how the community can fail—not just when its special features break down, but when these features go into overdrive. Epidemics strain all institutions, and the community is no exception. Epidemics destroy solidarity in some communities, leaving an institutional vacuum that stifles local action to prevent contagion. Epidemics create incentives for emigration by rich and powerful citizens, weakening communal leadership.

Above all, the community has a dark side, which epidemics could unveil. In controlling contagion, many communities organized vigilante action, persecuted minorities, or harassed health-care providers. To protect the interests of locals, community institutions falsified or concealed information about epidemics, exacerbating their spread. The community often mobilized informal norms and information transmission to resist anti-contagion measures. Even the best-functioning community institutions, moreover, operate on too small a scale to manage the degree to which local contagion decisions spill over beyond local boundaries.

In historical epidemics, the local community was best able to deploy its unique advantages when it was supported by outside institutions, but also curbed by them. The community worked better when it secured support from adjacent communities, local governments, the central state, religious bodies, civil society organizations, and wealthy philanthropists. Conversely, these other components of the institutional framework beneficially curbed the

208. Rajan 2021.

weaknesses of the local community in failing to control contagion, transmitting fake news, and actively opposing public health measures.

Historical epidemics hold no universal lessons for the community any more than for the market or the state. This is partly because the local community, like every other institution, did not operate in isolation. Rather, it was embedded in a wider framework of other institutions, which both facilitated its activities and constrained them. This framework consisted of both market and state, as we have seen in earlier chapters. But it also consisted of a whole range of additional institutions. An important component of this wider framework was a different type of community—religion, to which we now turn.

5

Religion

Even by the rule of charity all men are bound in conscience not to do anything that by common judgement and experience may bring a manifest peril and danger to their brethren or neighbours. . . . This thing being both so charitable and godly, and also very like to be profitable for this afflicted city.

I shall not scruple to call [smallpox inoculation] a diabolic operation, which usurps an authority founded neither in the laws of nature or religion, which tends in this case to anticipate and banish Providence out of the world, and promotes the increase of vice and immorality.

Religion is the name we give to a set of beliefs about spiritual beings who are not observable to the ordinary senses but whom believers think can influence human existence.[3] But religion is also an institution—a system of rules, customs, and practices governing the relationship between humans and such spiritual beings. Religious institutions are the observable manifestations in society of spiritual beliefs that prevail unobservably inside people's minds.

Religion thus has a unique selling point. It gets inside people's heads to a greater extent than other institutions. Religion often imposes formal rules

---

1. Grindal 1843, 8:271.
2. Quoted in Silverstein 2009, 299.
3. See the discussion in Seabright 2024, 15–16, 88–104.

requiring its adherents to act in the world, and in that sense resembles other institutions. It would be much less possible for religious beliefs to be operationalized in society if they did not have institutional levers to pull. Conversely, other institutions also foster morals, ethics, norms, beliefs, narratives, habits, and even spirituality. But they do so mainly as a by-product of their worldly purposes. For religion, by contrast, inward phenomena are supposed to be central. Religion, much more than other institutions, bases its aims, authority, and capacity to influence human action on beliefs about spiritual phenomena experienced only inside people's minds. This is what makes it distinctive.

But what are the inward services that religion supplies and people demand? And how does religion relate to epidemics? For one thing, religion provides epistemological services. It specializes in explaining unobservable actions and agents. This is particularly relevant to disease, whose occurrence is catastrophic for human life but whose causes are almost as invisible as it is possible to get. The only shock that is nearly as catastrophic and inexplicable is the kind of weather that causes harvest failure. But harvests are only partly about weather, and mostly about things you can see. Disease is caused by things that ordinary senses cannot directly observe. Epidemics enormously increase people's demand for explanations of the invisible. Religion specializes in the invisible and provides such explanations—right or wrong. How people explain epidemics to themselves affects what they do about contagion.

Second, religion provides consolation. A major thing religion does is to tell people a story that makes sense of suffering—the problem of "theodicy".[4] When something dreadful happens, like an epidemic, people want to understand why. Why do people fall ill? Why do they die? What happens afterwards? How can we endure existence when it can be cut off by random disaster? Why is life so terrifying? Different religions provide different forms of emotional guidance. Some offer a core narrative of fatalism, as we shall see: spiritual beings move in mysterious ways so human suffering is part of a plan that makes sense in nonhuman terms. Others offer an opposing narrative of struggle, according to which suffering is a mechanism by which divine beings move believers to take positive action. Epidemics enormously increase people's demand for consolation in a time of dread. Religion supplies such consolation. How people emotionally cope with disease and death affects sanitary behaviour (e.g. burial practices), social distancing (e.g. religious assemblies and pilgrimages), and immunization (e.g. vaccination), which are central influences on contagion.

Third, many religions offer ethical guidance. Religion often provides a narrative showing what actions are right or wrong. Different religions do this differently. Monotheistic religions of the book, like Christianity, Judaism, or Islam, lay down abstract rules of right and wrong. Polytheistic, non-book-based

---

4. Leibniz 1710; Weber 1920, 1:571–2; Adair-Toteff 2016, 157–76.

religions like Hinduism or Buddhism provide more personalized and context-specific guidance. Other religions, especially local or animistic ones, define "right" simply as acting in accordance with what the spirits want. But when crises such as epidemics arise, religion provides guidance on how to behave ethically in situations in which, as we have seen many times, there are difficult trade-offs to be made among individual, group, and societal interests. Ethical prescriptions on altruism affect the willingness of believers to observe sanitary rules, comply with social distancing, get immunized, or make charitable donations to help the poor with the costs of complying with contagion controls.

To supply its epistemological, emotional, and ethical services, a religion has to take worldly action. It must attract individual believers, who will join the religion to consume—and then help produce—its spiritual services. Any religion must secure support (or at least toleration) from other components of the institutional framework—resources from the market, compulsion from the state, cooperation from the community and the guild, socialization from the family. Religions originate their worldly activities to serve spiritual ends. But the worldly side of religion often develops its own logic, becoming an end in itself.

The Janus face of religion, with one side contemplating the inner spirit while the other attends to the outer world, raises questions about how religion interacts with epidemics. When a religion directs action during an epidemic, what weight does it place on its spiritual compared with its worldly interests? When people turn to religion in epidemics, do they seek spiritual or worldly services? Does the intellectual content of the religion matter, as opposed to its ability to amass followers, resources, power, and social capital? Do all religions provide similar services, or does the theological content of the faith play a role? How and why does religion induce people to act counter to their ostensible epidemiological or economic interests? Do established religions behave differently from radical sects in their moral recommendations or the worldly actions they take in epidemics?

Religions, like epidemics, change over time. This raises further questions. Is religion less important in providing explanations, consolation, and moral guidance now than before the growth of science? Is religion less influential now that the market and the state dominate the institutional framework? Or has it retained importance precisely because these other institutions do not address its unique selling points?[5] Does the role of religion in historical epidemics hold lessons for modern ones?

Religion is widely believed to improve human welfare. This implies that it should improve human outcomes during epidemics. It should motivate the faithful to sacrifice individual desires out of concern for their fellow believers,

5. As suggested, for instance, by Seabright (2024).

or even the wider society, by engaging in social distancing and immunization. Religion should organize worldly activities to mitigate contagion. Some religions did indeed behave like this, prescribing hygienic behaviour, providing spiritual or practical support for anti-contagion measures, or mandating rituals with unintended contagion-limiting effects.

But religion, like any institution, has a dark side. It operates in ways that do not seek the worldly well-being of even its own adherents, let alone society as a whole. Its users may be more interested in satisfying the spirits, religious personnel, elite believers, or external sponsors. It may prioritize increasing its adherents, enhancing its material resources, or securing political influence. Such motivations can lead users of a religion to ignore epidemic contagion. Religions may prescribe unhygienic rituals, fatalistic neglect of social distancing, puritan opposition to immunization, or anti-scientific rejection of medical explanations. To serve the interests of the religion, its members may even mandate worldly activities such as mass gatherings, processions, pilgrimages, missions, crusades, and holy wars, which exacerbate contagion. What decided how a religion was likely to act during epidemics?

1. Cleanliness and Godliness

Hygiene reduces epidemic contagion by limiting contact between people and organisms that cause human disease—viruses, bacteria, fungi, protozoa, worms, and their insect and animal carriers. Keeping clean relies mainly on decisions taken by individuals. But like many individual choices, hygiene generates costs and benefits for other people which the individual herself does not incur—the externalities discussed in earlier chapters. The external benefits of individual hygiene should not be undervalued. In rural Bangladesh in 1991, maternal handwashing reduced children's diarrheal infections by up to 90 per cent, while availability of running water had no effect.[6] In modern developing economies in the decade before 2020, individual hand hygiene, by reducing gastrointestinal disease, increased disability-adjusted life years, childhood cognition, human capital investment, work productivity, and per capita GDP.[7] In 2016, the expected benefit from non-handwashing individuals adopting handwashing at appropriate times was estimated at $23 billion in India (1.2 per cent of GDP) and $12 billion in China (0.12 per cent of GDP).[8]

Whether individuals keep clean is shaped by the institutions around them. Market, state, and community affect the costs of taking hygienic decisions—for instance, by making clean water and sewerage available. Religion, by contrast,

6. Derosas 2003, 112.
7. Guiteras et al. 2016, 321–2; Kresch, Lipscomb, and Schechter 2020.
8. Townsend, Greenland, and Curtis 2017, 77–80.

operates by shaping individuals' preferences, norms, and beliefs. Some religions prescribe particular conduct deliberately to reduce disease. More often, however, religions influence hygiene inadvertently, through precepts and rituals prescribed for other reasons—to please the spirits, placate the clergy, or bond the congregation.

1.1. RELIGION AND PURITY

For millennia, religions have insisted that spiritual and bodily purity are linked. Christian faiths are not alone in declaring that cleanliness is next to godliness. Most religions connect worldly with spiritual hygiene. Most prescribe rules and rituals governing the washing of bodies, preparation of food, cleaning of houses, management of water, feeding of infants, treatment of corpses, and other contacts between humans and pathogens.

Nearly every religion, consequently, claims to be cleaner than all the others. Catholicism emphasizes its reverence for the immaculate Virgin, Eastern Orthodoxy its code against defilement, Protestantism its mandates on baptism, Islam its ritual handwashing, Hinduism its *suddhatā* (purity), Judaism its food hygiene and bathing, Buddhism its path of self-purification. Many African and indigenous American religions emphasize ritual purity.

The claim to be cleaner than all other religions cannot be true for all religions. But is it true for any? Such theories are hard to evaluate empirically, since they require comparative information on infectious disease outcomes, confounding variables, and causal relationships between religious directives and believers' behaviour. As a result, most of them are not borne out empirically.

But in one case, Judaism, there is some empirical support. As table 5.1 shows, mortality studies find evidence of higher Jewish survival rates in a number of historical epidemics. But Judaism did not create an advantage in all diseases, and when it did the causal mechanisms are unclear. Lower Jewish mortality, where it existed, was associated with multiple activities, not all related to hygiene—or even necessarily to religion at all.

Many tales tell of Jews' miraculous immunity to bubonic plague. But they are only stories. One such tale claims that Jews survived plague better because the Torah commanded them to remove leavened bread from their houses for seven days in early spring, ridding dwellings of stored grain which hosted plague rats.[9] Unfortunately, there is no evidence. No mortality data survive for the Torah period (450–350 BCE) or for many centuries thereafter, so no one knows if Jews survived plague better than non-Jews.[10] Moreover, deep cleaning at particular times of year is mandated by most religions—Catholicism on

9. Blaser 1998, 245–51.
10. Jeremy Brown 2022, 65; Woods 2007.

TABLE 5.1. Jewish Mortality Advantage, Possible Causes, and Quality of Evidence

Date	Place	Disease	Causal mechanism	Quality of evidence on: Mortality	Quality of evidence on: Cause	Source
450–350 BCE	Middle East	Plague	Household hygiene (Passover cleaning of grain stores)	None	None	a
c.1350	Europe	Plague	Food hygiene, handwashing, burials, water, medical care, lifestyle	None	None	b
1630s, 1650s	Italy	Plague	Hygiene, medical care, social isolation (ghettos)	None	None	c
1500–1930	Central Europe/Baltic	Infant diseases	Breastfeeding, childcare, handwashing, food hygiene	Good	Indirect	d
18th century	Surinam	Infant diseases	n.g.	Good	Indirect	e
1787	Padua	Infant diseases	n.g.	Good	Indirect	f
1819/1967	160 populations	Infant/child diseases	n.g.	Good	Indirect	g
19th century	Italian towns/cities	Infant diseases	Lifestyle, handwashing, ritual bathing, food hygiene, housecleaning	Good	Indirect	h
1849/1867	Venice	Cholera	Lifestyle, handwashing, ritual bathing, food hygiene, housecleaning	Fair	Indirect	i
1867–70	Amsterdam	Cholera	No advantage (shared water and sewerage)	Good	Indirect	j
1867–70	Amsterdam	Infant diseases	Breastfeeding, birth intervals, food hygiene	Good	Indirect	j
1867–70	Amsterdam	Respiratory	Dietary rules, social isolation	Good	Indirect	j
1867–70	Amsterdam	Diarrhoeal	Breastfeeding	Good	Indirect	j
1867–70	Amsterdam	Smallpox	Social isolation, modern medicine, vaccination	Good	Indirect	j

Sources: [a] Blaser 1998, 245–51.[b] Jeremy Brown 2022, 247–53.[c] Jeremy Brown 2022, 247–53; Derosas 2003, 110. [d] Botticini, Eckstein, and Vaturi 2019.[e] R. Cohen 1991, 61–2. [f] Derosas 2003, 111.[g] Schmelz 1971.[h] Derosas 2003, 111. [i] Derosas 2003, 110. [j] Riswick, Muurling, and Buzasi 2022.

Notes: Central Europe/Baltic = Austria-Germany and Poland-Lithuania. 160 populations = regions of Russia, Poland, Prussia, Bavaria, Westphalia, Serbia, Bohemia, Moravia, Italy, Switzerland, the Netherlands, USA, and Canada, plus cities of Vilna, Lvov, Krakow, Warsaw, Lodz, Budapest, Berlin, Much, Vienna, Florence, Trieste, Rome, Turin, Milan, Amsterdam, London, New York, Saint Louis, Providence, Detroit, Montreal. n.g. = not given.

Palm Thursday, Zoroastrianism on the first day of spring, Eastern Orthodoxy in the first week of Great Lent (*c.*1 April), Hinduism just before Diwali (after the monsoon season). Plague-carrying rodents live on any food waste, which would be cleared away during any careful cleaning. But the deepest problem is that we have no evidence of either the outcome (plague mortality) or the cause (religious cleaning).

What about the Black Death? A widely held view holds that Jews survived the worst pandemic of all time because they had cleaner food, water, hands, and funeral practices. Again, though, these are stories, not facts. Jews may have been cleaner, but there is no evidence they died less from plague.[11] Indeed, contemporaries stated that they did not. The Cistercian monk Pierre Ceffons from Clairvaux, for instance, pointed out that the Jews cannot have caused the Black Death, since they "have died just as much as the others".[12] Pope Clement VI likewise exonerated the Jews from causing plague in 1348, declaring:

> It cannot be true that the Jews, by such a heinous crime, are the cause or occasion of the plague, because through many parts of the world the same plague, by the hidden judgment of God, has afflicted and afflicts the Jews themselves and many other races who have never lived alongside them.[13]

The earliest Jewish eyewitness to live through the Black Death, Isaac ben Todros of Avignon, described how the plague "first and foremost affected our people, and after them, spread to the Christians . . . This is the accepted explanation".[14] In 1346, a Russian source described plague deaths in southern Russia as similar for all groups: "The mortality was great among the Bessermens, and among the Tartars, and among the Armenians and the Abkhazians, and among the Jews, and among the European foreigners [*fryazy*], and among the Circassians, and among all who lived there, so that they could not bury them."[15] The little surviving quantitative evidence tells the same story, as in Marseille where Black Death mortality was 50 per cent for Jews and 55 per cent for others.[16] Any Jewish plague advantage was small to non-existent.

In the seventeenth-century plague epidemics, Jews are again held to have died less than Christians. Again, however, the evidence shows no systematic mortality gap. In Venice in 1630–31, Jewish mortality was 14 per cent compared with 33 per cent in the city at large.[17] But Leon Modena, Venetian rabbi in 1630–31, stated explicitly that although the Venetian Jews had been fortunate,

11. Blaser 1998, 251–3; Jeremy Brown 2022, 257–8.
12. Quoted in Schabel and Pedersen 2014, 149.
13. Quoted in Horrox 1994, 222.
14. Quoted in Jeremy Brown 2022, 255.
15. Quoted in Benedictow 2004, 50.
16. Jeremy Brown 2022, 258.
17. Derosas 2003, 110.

"it was not so in the communities of Verona and Padua, for God's hand struck them, and less than one-third survived".[18] Modern scholarship confirms that in Padua in 1630, the ghetto was initially spared (probably because of social isolation rather than hygiene), but as soon as plague entered, 59 per cent of Jews died, identical to Christians in the rest of the city.[19] In Rome in 1656, Jewish plague mortality was at least twice as high as for Christians—16–20 per cent in the ghetto, compared with 8 per cent in the city at large.[20] Jews may have been hygienic, but during plague epidemics that did not help them.

After about 1500, European Jews did have lower mortality in one respect. Fewer of them died in childhood. Between 1500 and 1930, infant and child mortality in Germany-Austria and Poland-Lithuania was lower among Jews than other faiths.[21] Similar findings emerge from over 160 populations across the world from the eighteenth to the twentieth century, as table 5.1 shows. By the mid-nineteenth century, Jewish mortality advantage extended beyond infant deaths to other infectious diseases. In Amsterdam in 1867–70, predominantly Jewish neighbourhoods had lower than average mortality for diarrhoeal diseases, respiratory diseases, and even smallpox. The only exception was cholera, possibly because it depended on water and sewer infrastructure, which individual Jewish household decisions could not affect.[22] In Venice in the 1860s, by contrast, Jews did have better cholera outcomes, suggesting that some specific Jewish characteristics outweighed the factors spreading cholera among Venetian Catholics.[23]

But what were those characteristics? Confounding variables are a first issue. Can we be sure that mortality differences among religious groups are caused by religious affiliation, as opposed to other characteristics? Many studies do not—often cannot—control for other characteristics. A few others do. The study of Amsterdam in the 1860s, for instance, controls for neighbourhood wealth, rental values, tax revenues, housing density, birth rate, and hospital presence.[24] So at least in some times and places, Jewish groups displayed lower mortality independently of other characteristics.

The precise mechanisms involved, however, are still unclear. Table 5.1 shows the wide range of speculative explanations that have been advanced. Some relate directly to hygiene: spring cleaning, food preparation, handwashing, burial practices, water sources. Others relate to demographic and familial

18. Quoted in M. Cohen 2021, 136.

19. Bell 2020, 59.

20. Jeremy Brown 2022, 257 (ghetto mortality 800 out of 4,100, either original population or survivors); Alfani 2013b, 417 (overall mortality 80 per 1,000, superseding earlier estimates of 187 per 1,000).

21. Botticini, Eckstein, and Vaturi 2019, 2638–9, 2641, 2663–4, 2669–70, 2674.

22. Riswick, Muurling, and Buzasi 2022.

23. Derosas 2003, 110.

24. Riswick, Muurling, and Buzasi 2022.

patterns that indirectly improve child-care hygiene: prolonged breastfeeding, low female labour force participation, low illegitimacy. Still other mechanisms have nothing to do with hygiene: communal poor relief, moderate lifestyle, low alcohol consumption, social isolation in ghettos, respect for medical authority, and greater willingness to vaccinate. Qualitative evidence shows Jewish communities differing from others in many of these respects. But no study has clearly identified the specific causal mechanisms. Explanations of the Jewish mortality advantage often boil down to the tautological claim that "Jews enjoyed a lower infant mortality because they were Jews."[25]

A final stumbling block is the role of religious belief. What, after all, is "religion"? Is it what God wants, or what your grandmother says? Let us assume that we can be sure both that a particular religion enjoys better disease outcomes and that these outcomes are caused by particular forms of behaviour, such as individual hygiene. Can we be sure that such behaviour is caused by religious belief? Or is it maintained within a religious community through the formal commands of its political leaders, the informal peer pressure of neighbours and relatives, or the authority of its medical professionals? It is conceivable, for instance, that food hygiene, handwashing, bathing, breastfeeding, and careful child-care arise not from Jewish religious precepts but from communal norms concerning marriage, family structure, fertility, legitimacy, and labour force participation by married women. Respect for medical authority may result not from religious precepts but from social stratification inside closely knit Jewish communities, in which educated professionals exercised unusual influence over ordinary people. Thus even when we observe significant mortality gaps across religions, and even when these can be definitively linked to individual decisions involving hygiene, we cannot be sure that differences in epidemic outcomes arise from religious beliefs rather than non-religious mechanisms that operate within closely knit groups regardless of what they formally believe about the spiritual world.

1.2. RELIGION AND FILTH

Religion also has a dark side—or at least a dirty one. As table 5.2 shows, many religions mandate practices that intensify contact between believers and pathogens. These are not arcane practices applying to just a few of the hyperfaithful. Rather, they involve central and widespread human activities—eating, drinking, washing, bathing, breastfeeding, dealing with animals, and touching the ground.

Table 5.2 mainly reflects modern medical literature. It excludes rare or extinct diseases such as bubonic plague and smallpox, which caused many

---

25. Derosas 2003, 125.

TABLE 5.2. Unhygienic Religious Practices and Associated Infections

Religious practice	Religions	Associated infections (mostly modern)
Diet:		
Ritual meals, esp. funeral	African religions	Cholera
Holy Communion (bread and wine)	Christianity	Gastrointestinal and respiratory disease (incl. Covid-19)
Ritual eating of human corpses	Papua New Guinea religions	Prion infection (kuru)
Ritual raw mollusc consumption	Afro-Brazilian Candomblé and Umbanda	*Angiostrongylus cantonensis*-related eosinophilic meningitis
Ritual drinking of holy water	Hinduism	Cholera, gastrointestinal disease
Ritual geophagy (earth-eating)	Christianity, Islam, Hinduism, Hoodoo	Gastrointestinal disease, parasitic infections, parotiditis
Breastfeeding taboo/ aversion	Catholicism	Diarrhoeal disease (incl. cholera), lifelong immune function
Skin injury:		
Self-flagellation	Shia Islam, Catholicism	HTLV-1 (human T-cell leukaemia virus), hepatitis C
Blood brotherhood and blood rituals	Islam, African religions	Multiple blood-borne infections
Tattooing	Samoan Christianity	Sporotrichosis, blood-borne infections
Tongue and cheek piercing	Hinduism, Buddhism	Blood-borne infections
Water contact:		
Ritual bathing and dipping in rivers	Hinduism	Diarrhoeal disease (incl. cholera), respiratory infections (incl. Covid-19)
Sprinkling of holy water	Christianity, Buddhism	Bacterial infections of skin and lungs (esp. pneumonia)
Ritual ablution, nasal irrigation	Islam	*Naegleria fowleri* meningoencephalitis
Baptism (esp. whole-body)	Christianity	Schistosomiasis
Miscellaneous:		
Ritual animal sacrifice	Islam, Judaism, many folk religions	*Mycobacterium bovis*, orf, brucellosis, cutaneous anthrax, Rift Valley fever
Ritual side-rolling (angapradakshinam)	Hinduism	Cutaneous larva migrans

Sources: Pellerin and Edmond 2013; Gajurel and Deresinski 2021; Young 2011, 47–66; Fildes 1986.

Notes: Associated infections relate mainly to present-day societies and thus exclude bubonic plague and smallpox. Other blood rituals: group circumcision, skin scarification, bloodletting, female genital mutilation.

Multiple blood-borne infections = HIV, hepatitis B and C, *Clostridium tetani*, *Chlamydia trachomatis*, *Neisseria gonorrhoeae*, syphilis, *Trichomonas vaginalis*, herpes simplex virus.

historical epidemics. But many of the religious practices reach far back in the history of particular faiths. If they spread diseases nowadays, they almost certainly spread them in past centuries. This means they had the capacity to affect epidemics such as bubonic plague and smallpox which are now extinct or easily controlled.

Breastfeeding aversion provides a good example of a religiously mandated activity that was historically associated with differences in infectious disease outcomes. A moral aversion to breastfeeding, sometimes expressed as a social taboo, is widely observed in Catholic populations, both historical and modern. Catholicism historically banned sexual intercourse during breastfeeding, deterring married women and their husbands from undertaking prolonged nursing even if they wanted to. Catholic teachings also inculcated unusually prudish norms, making it socially unacceptable for women to breastfeed except in complete privacy. Sometimes, Catholicism mandated the binding of women's breasts to constrain female sexual display, damaging lactation capacity.[26] In sixteenth- and seventeenth-century Europe, Catholic mothers were widely reported to be less likely to breastfeed than Protestant ones.[27] In nineteenth-century Brabant, a Catholic region of the Netherlands, priests actively proselytized against breastfeeding, portraying it as shameful and contrary to female modesty.[28] In nineteenth-century Germany, breastfeeding was taken for granted in Protestant zones of the north but reviled in Catholic regions of the south. In the 1880s, for instance, a medical researcher in Catholic Upper Bavaria reported that "a woman who came from northern Germany and wanted according to the customs of her homeland to nurse her infant herself was openly called swinish and filthy by the local women. Her husband threatened that he would no longer eat anything she prepared, if she did not give up this disgusting habit."[29] Across pre-modern Europe, the prevalence and duration of breastfeeding was on average higher in northern, Protestant societies than in southern, Catholic regions.[30] Modern analyses still find that breastfeeding is significantly lower where the proportion of Catholics is higher, a result that holds across 37 Western countries, and also within countries: across 94 French departments, 26 Irish counties, and 13 Canadian provinces.[31] Lower frequency and duration of breastfeeding are in turn associated with higher infant infections and deaths, with the negative externalities for society arising

26. Thorvaldsen 2008.
27. Bernard, Cohen, and Kramer 2016, 6.
28. Walhout 2010, 81.
29. Quoted in Knodel and Van de Walle 1967, 119–20.
30. Thorvaldsen 2008.
31. Bernard, Cohen, and Kramer 2016.

from damage to human capital investment, cognition, labour productivity, and per capita GDP discussed earlier.

For most other religious practices in table 5.2, such clear historical evidence is lacking. Modern medicine views these religious practices as "unhygienic", in the sense that they increase contact between believers and pathogens. But there are few studies demonstrating that they actually cause disease. Whether specific religious practices, insanitary though they may have been, significantly increased contagion needs the same sceptical scrutiny as claims that other religious practices were distinctively hygienic and significantly reduced contagion.

First, we must investigate whether a particular religious group experienced worse disease outcomes at all. Second, we must control for other characteristics, such as poverty, poor housing, bad infrastructure, and low education, that may be associated with religion but also affect disease. Third, we have to identify specific causal mechanisms—religions impose many rules, and each affects different diseases in different ways. Finally, even if particular religious directives result in unhygienic practices that increase contagion, there is still the question of where belief comes in. Do these practices result from theological mandates? Or do they reflect the prescriptions of religious leaders, medical authorities, or peer effects inside small face-to-face communities? Do I take Communion, bathe in the Ganges, get a tattoo, or wean my baby because it is what God said? Or do I act that way so the others don't criticize?

2. Religion and Distancing

Before immunization, antibiotics, and antivirals, epidemics were hard to stop once they got going. The dominant approach was to limit interpersonal contact. But social distancing is a public good. Left to my own devices, as we saw in chapter 2, I will avoid others only to the extent that it reduces my private risk of contagion. I will not take account of external benefits of social distancing unless some other institution gives me an incentive to do so. Chapter 3 showed how this incentive could be provided by state coercion, and chapter 4 how it could be supplied by community social capital. Religion has other instruments that can motivate social distancing—the epistemological, emotional, and moral authority discussed above.

2.1 KEEPING THE FAITHFUL APART

Privileged access to the spiritual world means a religion can sometimes persuade believers to act independently of their narrow self-interest. Religions extracted charitable donations from the faithful, for instance, which could support poor people through lockdowns or fund isolation hospitals.

Religious organizations sometimes provided resources to help with the logistics of social distancing. Occasionally, as with Bishop Grindal in 1564, religious figures directly exhorted the faithful to comply with state or community social distancing measures.

Many religions tell believers that they should donate to religious charities for spiritual and moral reasons, and such exhortations understandably intensify during epidemics. Charity provides general care for the needy, but during epidemics it has the incidental benefit of helping them engage in social distancing, since it spares them from the need to work or beg.

Religions certainly provided charitable relief in epidemics, as in other disasters. During the Black Death in Egypt, Islamic pious endowments provided care for the diseased poor and safe burial for victims.[32] In Europe, too, poor people who caught plague during the Black Death were given succour either directly by the Church or, more often, by individual believers via religious institutions. In late medieval England, for instance, religious bequests made up an estimated one-quarter of the value of testators' estates. Testators also left legacies to establish or support hospitals, and this particular type of charitable bequest hugely expanded in the aftermath of the Black Death. In the London Hustings Court, before 1348 about 5 per cent of all testators bequeathed funds for hospitals, rising to 15 per cent in the decade after 1350, with the value of the average bequest increasing by nearly 40 per cent. Across England as a whole, 70 new hospitals were established between 1350 and 1390.[33]

The foundation of hospitals made a direct contribution to social distancing, since in epidemics they could be used to isolate the infected from the rest of society—indeed, this was almost all they could do, as until the 1890s medical science could neither cure plague nor prevent it. Hospitals were not all established by religious institutions, but even those set up by guilds or private donors often owed their existence to religious impulses. In the richest zone of Europe, central and northern Italy, hospitals began being established from the year 1000 onwards. As table 5.3 shows, they did not start out as primarily medical institutions but rather as hostels providing shelter ("hospitality") to poor members of specified groups.[34] Between 1000 and 1250 only 8 per cent of Florence hospitals were aimed mainly at sick people, rising to 21 per cent between 1250 and 1349. But even during this period before the Black Death, hospitals established for other purposes were becoming "medicalized". They gradually moved away from sheltering all members of the target group to focusing on sick members, they began to employ medical staff, and they provided more in-house

32. Dols 1977, 238.
33. Gottfried 1983, 85–7.
34. Park 1985, 102; Henderson 2006, xxxi.

TABLE 5.3. Primary Target Groups of Florence Hospitals at Time of Foundation, 1000–1350

Primary target group	1000–1249		1250–1349		1000–1349	
	No.	%	No.	%	No.	%
Pilgrims and travellers	8	66.7	6	20.7	14	34.1
Sick	1	8.3	6	20.7	7	17.1
Poor	1	8.3	5	17.2	6	14.6
Religious	1	8.3	2	6.9	3	7.3
Artisans	0	0.0	3	10.3	3	7.3
Foundlings	0	0.0	1	3.4	1	2.4
Old	0	0.0	0	0.0	0	0.0
Women	0	0.0	0	0.0	0	0.0
Unknown	1	8.3	6	20.7	7	17.1
Total	12	100.0	29	100.0	41	100.0

Source: Henderson 2006, 14.

care, particularly during epidemics.[35] During the recurrent plagues that struck Europe in the century and a half after the Black Death, existing hospitals created isolation wards, and new lazarettos or pesthouses were established to segregate the infected. In many of these establishments, religious organizations provided administration and care. During the 1630 plague epidemic, for instance, Prato had a lazaretto and a convalescent home which were administered and provisioned by the Veneranda Compagnia del Pellegrino, an association of religious laymen.[36]

Religion thus contributed to social distancing by building and running isolation hospitals. But the contribution was inevitably small. Not all hospitals were religious in any case, and not all provided isolation for epidemic patients. Florence's hospitals, almost certainly the largest and most numerous in Europe, contained perhaps 3,000 beds in 1300, accommodating just 2.7 per cent of the urban population. This was lavish compared with London, where in 1500 hospitals provided beds for less than 1 per cent of the population, or in Ghent where hospital provision was more meagre still.[37] Even in generous Florence, hospitals could not remotely provide isolation for the 60 per cent of inhabitants dying of plague in 1348–51 or the 14 per cent in 1630–1. Hospitals—religious or non-religious—made a very modest contribution to

35. Park 1985, 102–3; Risse 1999, 214–16; Henderson 2006, 25–9; Henderson 2019.
36. Cipolla 1973, 84–5.
37. Van Steensel 2016, 19.

social distancing even in the great, wealthy cities that had them. Furthermore, the vast majority of the population until the nineteenth century lived in small towns and villages that lacked hospitals altogether.

Nor did religious hospitals always operate to control contagion. In sixteenth-century Angers, for instance, the friars who ran the Saint Jean hospital resisted admitting plague patients, and the prior of Papillaie refused to let priory premises be used for an isolation hospital.[38] In Florence in 1630, the Church authorities opposed the city government when it tried to requisition the abandoned buildings of the church and convent of San Miniato al Monte to house a lazaretto.[39] In Prato in 1630, several monasteries and convents refused to accommodate a pesthouse and imposed onerous conditions on any use of their buildings, ultimately delaying the establishment of plague isolation facilities for months, during which the pestilence spread rapidly.[40] In the 1731 Split plague epidemic, the prior of the lazaretto insisted that it be reserved solely for commercial purposes and refused to let the building be used to accommodate or isolate the sick.[41] The 1848 cholera epidemic in Alexandria spread out into the city partly because two pilgrims died of suspected cholera in the lazaretto, whose authorities forbade the chief physician and his medical colleagues to carry out a post-mortem because the deceased were Muslim women.[42] Religious authorities could thus divert hospitals, even ones explicitly intended for epidemic isolation, to serve religious purposes rather than contagion control.

A special feature of medieval Catholicism was the lay religious association. These arose in the form of confraternities, "companies" (in Italy), or "parish guilds" (in England).[43] In some Italian cities, such lay religious associations were significant sources of poor relief even in normal times—as in late medieval Florence, which had an estimated 50–100 confraternities averaging 100 members apiece, mainly from the middling sort and respectable poor. About half offered medical benefits to members' families, implying that 15,000 people—about one-third of the population of Florence—were entitled to some sort of pre-paid confraternal insurance.[44] Such charitable support made market withdrawal, social distancing, and other contagion-control measures more affordable for the less well-off, though such confraternal support was almost certainly far less important anywhere else in the world than in Renaissance Florence.[45]

38. Lebrun 1971, 304, 308.
39. Henderson 2019, 194.
40. Cipolla 1973, 53–7.
41. Andreozzi 2015, 128.
42. Kuhnke 1990, 60.
43. Rosser 2015; Park 1985, 106–8; Henderson 1989.
44. Park 1985, 108.
45. Van Steensel 2016; Van Bavel and Rijpma 2016.

FIGURE 5.1. Cellites at work during the plague in Leuven, *c.* 1578. The Congregatio Fratrum Cellitarum seu Alexianorum ("Cellites" or "Alexians") was a voluntary lay Catholic association. These sixteenth-century Cellites are painted dressed in their black cloaks and hoods burying victims of the plague epidemic in a continuous stream in the graveyard of St Jacob's Church in Leuven (Louvain), in what is now Belgium. About half the population of the town died in this epidemic. The painting shows the continuation of daily life and its negative externalities, including a chamber pot being emptied from a high window, immediately onto the heads of a strolling couple. Artist unknown, held in the Museum M, Leuven, Belgium. *Source*: Wikimedia Commons.

Confraternities also helped provide logistical support for social distancing in the wider urban population. From 1345 on, confraternities of Cellites or Alexians proliferated in the Low Countries, where they tended the sick poor and arranged safe burials during plague epidemics (as illustrated for the town of Leuven in figure 5.1).[46]

In central and northern Italian plagues, likewise, lay religious bodies such as the Florence Misericordia (shown in figure 5.2) provided comprehensive administrative, logistical, and financial support for social distancing, both

46. Coomans 2021, 247–9.

FIGURE 5.2. Misericordia members caring for plague victims, Florence, 1630–31. The Venerabile Arciconfraternita della Misericordia di Firenze was a voluntary lay Catholic association, founded in 1244. This engraving, based on a seventeenth-century painting, shows Misericordia members dressed in black habits with black felt hats, carrying people who are sick and dying of the plague. Note the fence (*right*) constructed during the epidemic to separate the Misericordia from the wider city, excluding potentially infected members of the public and protecting uninfected citizens from Misericordia members who had daily contact with plague victims. Nineteenth-century engraving by Enrico Pratesi, based on a painting attributed to Luigi Baccio del Bianco (d. 1657) and located in the Sala di Compagnia of the Misericordia headquarters in Florence. The Pratesi engraving was incorrectly labelled as representing the Black Death of 1348, whereas in fact it portrays the Florence plague of 1630. *Source*: Venerabile Arciconfraternita della Misericordia di Firenze. With gratitude for their advice and assistance.

when people were ordered into home lockdown and when they were interned in isolation centres. The Misericordia recorded names of those infected with plague and their social contacts. They carried the infected to hospitals and pesthouses. They conducted contacts—the "suspects"—to isolation centres. They drew up sanitary surveys. And they devoted the Misericordia's own financial resources to employing porters and paying for provisions to be delivered to patients and suspects during isolation.[47] All these religiously motivated

47. Henderson 2019, 95–104.

activities provided substantial support for social distancing measures imposed by state and community.

Religious organizations also contributed to the growth of so-called "out-relief". This was welfare support in people's own dwellings rather than in centralized institutions such as poorhouses, hospitals, and pesthouses. Out-relief had always existed, but in the sixteenth century it expanded as a central and systematic feature of welfare provision. During this period, especially in north-west Europe, it became increasingly common for welfare institutions to provide food, drink, and cash payments to the poor during plague epidemics with the deliberate intention of helping them comply with social distancing measures in their own dwellings. In England by the later sixteenth century, the "parish"—an organization combining elements of religion, community, and local government—conducted almost all the dirty work of identifying, isolating, supplying, tending, and burying plague victims.[48]

Quantitatively, however, the size of purely religious charity was small. Before the twentieth century, the total value of social transfers in three of the world's richest economies (Italy, Flanders, and England) from all sources—religious and non-religious—are estimated at less than 1 per cent of GDP, occasionally rising to 2–3 per cent in exceptionally rich societies such as the Low Countries. Only between 1930 and 1980 did the value of social transfers rise to modern levels of 20 per cent of GDP, even in rich economies, and the institution responsible for that increase was not religion but the state.[49] During the Black Death and the two centuries thereafter, social transfers amounted to less than 1 per cent of GDP, and only part of this was provided or even administered by religious institutions. After around 1500, social transfers rose in some societies, especially the richest ones. But a larger share of both the transfers and their administration was provided by other institutions, particularly the state and the local community. In a quantitative perspective, religious charity during epidemics made only a limited contribution to supporting social distancing, and did so mainly in cooperation with other institutions.

A final way religion could support social distancing was through direct moral exhortation. As reflected in the chapter epigraph, Bishop Grindal preached in 1564 that "all men are bound in conscience not to do anything that by common judgement and experience may bring a manifest peril and danger to their brethren or neighbours"—a clear exposition of contagion externalities four centuries before the term was invented.[50] By 1603, Anglican "plague prayers" declared uncompromisingly that violation of social distancing was a presumptuous offence against God and "a public and manifest detriment to

48. Slack 1985, 270–2.
49. Van Bavel and Rijpma 2016; Lindert 2004.
50. Grindal 1843, 8:271.

the state".[51] Jewish religious institutions also directly mandated social distancing during epidemics. In the Polish cholera epidemic of 1831, the Poznań rabbi Akiva Eger instructed the faithful "not to have large gatherings in the synagogue in a small space", to pray in groups of only 15 people, to limit the Rosh Hashanah service to just five hours, and to break the religious fast if the attending physician so instructed:

> If a person ignores this directive, they are personally liable for any outcome, not just for themselves, for their action might, God forbid, damage another person. In the end they will have to give an account of how their actions might have brought death to themselves and to others, on this, the most holy and auspicious of all days.[52]

Yet as we shall see later in this chapter, in the same epidemics senior clergy of both Anglicanism and Judaism preached—and practised—the exact opposite. In the sixteenth- and seventeenth-century English plagues, many Church of England clergymen exhorted the faithful to resist social distancing and subordinate it to religious ends.[53] In Poznań in the summer of 1831 as Rosh Hashanah and Yom Kippur approached, even Akiva Eger found himself constrained to expand synagogue gatherings to 50 and grant exceptions to senior religious officials, who would otherwise resist social distancing on High Holidays.[54]

Most religious support for social distancing was indirect, arising out of activities that religions undertook for other reasons, such as charity. Most practical religious support was provided by voluntary lay bodies, confraternities, and pious philanthropists, not the Church itself or even its personnel. There were exceptions, such as individual religious leaders who instructed the faithful to observe social distancing so as not to cause harm to others. But, as we shall see later, most religions continued to insist on religious assemblies that violated social distancing during epidemics, regardless of whether "their action might, God forbid, damage another person".

2.2. SHOULD YOU TRY TO EVADE GOD'S WILL?

Religion could also exhort the faithful to refrain from social distancing during epidemics. One widely held view is that they did so theologically, by preaching fatalism. This involved telling believers that epidemics were God's will, true faith required passive submission, and the deity or other spiritual beings

---

51. Quoted in Slack 1985, 230.
52. Jeremy Brown 2022, 128, 129 (quotation).
53. Slack 1986, 205–6.
54. Jeremy Brown 2022, 128.

would punish them if they took action to resist infectious disease. Did religions actually hold these theological beliefs? Did people follow them in daily life?

Christianity has portrayed Islam as the prime example of epidemic fatalism for the past half millennium or more. The Christian Greek refugees' son Theodore Spandounes wrote in 1509 of the Ottoman lands that "the plague is very common in these parts; but the Turks take no precautions against contagion because they firmly believe in the inescapability of destiny, for good or ill".[55] Christians later applied this trope to all Muslims and it endures into the modern day. According to this stereotype, Islam holds that disease should be fatalistically accepted as God's will; it therefore tells Muslims that it is impious to investigate or combat the causes of epidemics or to seek to escape by travelling away. Disease is not transmitted by contagion in any case, according to this portrayal of Muslim teaching, so there is no point in social distancing.[56] Conversely, the story continues, Christianity preaches that disease is not God's will, it is our Christian duty to combat it by discovering and uprooting the causes, we should avoid epidemics through flight, and disease is contagious and can thus be controlled through social distancing.[57]

A closer look, however, reveals diversity inside religions and much overlap among them.[58] Islamic theology has always encompassed diverse opinions on whether disease should be accepted, avoided, or viewed as contagious.[59] In a famous account of the 638–39 plague of 'Amwās, the Muslim Arab military council was deeply split on whether the army should march away to escape the epidemic. Some argued that the Prophet prohibited fleeing a plague-stricken land, since that implied avoiding God's decree; those holding this interpretation insisted that the army was bound in faith to stay in the plague zone. The caliph, however, responded with the following parable: "Suppose you come to a valley where one side is green with pasture and the other is bare and barren; whichever side you let loose your camels, it would be the will of God. But you would choose the side that was green."[60] He argued that by leaving the plague-struck zone, "we are running from what Allah had ordained to what Allah has ordained".[61]

This divergence of views about whether one should avoid plague was still current among Islamic scholars seven centuries later, during the Black Death.[62] Islamic debate over distancing oneself from pestilence continued to rage in

55. Quoted in Boyar 2018, 220.
56. Dols 1977, 109, 285–98.
57. Slack 1985, 49–50; Slack 1988, 438.
58. Stearns 2009, 1366.
59. Varlik 2015, 82, 208; Shabana 2021, 11–12.
60. Quoted in Dols 1977, 22.
61. Quoted in Mehfooz 2021, 7. See also Shabana 2021, 9–10.
62. Dols 1977, 292.

the centuries that followed—as during the 1419 Cairo plague, when one imam argued that pious forebears had accepted plague as God's will, while the sultan and many other notables took the opposite view and advocated avoiding it.[63] In 1511–20, the well-known Ottoman religious scholar İdris-i Bidlisi wrote a treatise discussing the necessity for pious Muslims to flee the plague.[64] Later in the sixteenth century, the Ottoman jurist Ṭāshköbrüzāde published a plague treatise recommending flight, conditional on respecting one's civil responsibilities, familial ties, and obedience to community leaders.[65] In the 1834–35 Alexandria plague epidemic, the coexistence of fatalism with activism emerged when the Egyptian ruler Muhammad Ali admonished the city irritably:

> The failure of the populace to observe the health regulations is a consequence of their ignorance. As I have said before, such observance is within the bounds of Islamic law and is required for the public good. This is a sign of God's wrath, and fleeing from divine wrath to divine mercy is not contrary to the law. . . . Is it not proof of God's mercy that our fleet and the workers of our arsenal have been preserved from the evils of the epidemic?[66]

As late as the 2020–21 Covid-19 pandemic, Islam still encompassed a diversity of views about epidemic prevention in general and social distancing in particular.[67]

This diversity of Muslim opinion about avoiding epidemic disease also influenced practical behaviour. When the Black Death arrived in the Middle East in the 1340s, pious Muslims frequently fled plague-struck localities.[68] In the 1419 plague, the sultan and notables did not accept the pestilence passively but led a mass exodus into the desert to beseech God to end the epidemic.[69] Writing before 1574, the influential senior mufti Ebu Su'ud Efendi described how "at the very first rumor of plague, in Istanbul or elsewhere, holders of religious office ran for their lives, abandoning their communities just when the latter were most in need of spiritual support".[70] In the 1580s a Venetian diplomat reported that Ottomans no longer believed that God prohibited escaping epidemics, "because experience had taught them the opposite"; the şeyhülislam (head of the Islamic "learned class") had just left Constantinople (Istanbul) to avoid plague.[71] In the 1604 Constantinople plague, a Venetian diplomat reported that even the senior Muslim clergy left town to avoid plague:

63. Dols 1977, 248–9.
64. Boyar 2018, 220–1.
65. Dols 1977, 299.
66. Quoted in Rue 2016, 32.
67. Shabana 2021, 13–18.
68. Dols 1977, 292.
69. Dols 1977, 248–9.
70. Shefer-Mossensohn 2011, 30.
71. Quoted in Boyar 2018, 221.

All that have means have retired to gardens outside the city, each attempting to distance himself from the danger as much as possible. In particular, even though in other times they have not taken the trouble to do it, the Mufti and the other doctors of law have departed to their gardens, not withstanding that this goes against one of the principal points of their law.[72]

During the Adrianople (Edirne) plague epidemic of the 1670s, a resident English clergyman described how even pious Islam permitted trade-offs:

The best sort of people fled to other places, as the Turkes likewise themselves did from Adrianople to their houses here, for that same is a story that they are not afraid of the plague, because their fortunes are wrote in their forehead; for all fled, but such as were poor, or had offices about Court, and could not get away.[73]

Wide differences in views within Islam still prevailed in Cairo in 1831, when some religiously minded Muslims viewed the cholera epidemic as divine retribution and opposed fleeing it, but many more sought to escape it through market withdrawal or leaving the city altogether, including hundreds of peasant labourers, who fled back to their villages.[74] During historical epidemics, therefore, many Muslims did not adopt a fatalistic stance but instead undertook practical social distancing measures, even if only to safeguard themselves and their families.

Christians also held diverse views. Some Christian thinkers advocated positive action against epidemics, in accordance with the stereotype of Christian dynamism in the face of pestilence.[75] Others, however, explained disease as God's providence, rejected the concept of contagion, and condemned the idea of distancing oneself from epidemics.[76] In 1400, a striking eyewitness account reversed the trope contrasting the fatalistic Muslim with the dynamic Christian. The sultan of Tlemcen (in modern Algeria) dispatched a group of couriers to travel the 444 kilometres to carry messages to the sultan of Fes (now Morocco). On arriving, they discovered that an epidemic was raging and decided not to approach the city for fear of contagion. The sole Christian in the party objected, declaring, "Fleeing will not save them. There is no doubt that what God has decreed is what will be."[77]

Attitudes to social distancing differed even inside particular Christian confessions. Some devout Catholics regarded disease as God's punishment for human sin. In 1424, Johannes de Saxonia wrote a treatise on plague, listing

72. Quoted in S. White 2010, 553.
73. Quoted in Boyar 2018, 221.
74. Kuhnke 1990, 53.
75. Slack 1985, 49–50; Slack 1988, 438.
76. Curtis 2020, 283, 290.
77. Quoted in Stearns 2009, 1369.

nine reasons why "so few attempted the recommended prophylaxis", among them the belief that the length of everyone's life and time of his death has already been fixed. He also described how in one plague in Montpellier, "When many men desired to die, the pope gave to the dying absolution from punishment and guilt and thus they hoped immediately to be translated to heaven; for this reason they did not want physicians to prolong their lives."[78] But there were also Catholic voices arguing against the idea that one should refrain from preventive measures because disease and death were already predestined. In 1603, for instance, the Roman friar Scipion Mercurio explicitly castigated such views and argued that "God has ordained that health is recovered through medicine".[79]

Protestants were also split on the issue. In 1580, for instance, the Puritan mayor of Norwich declared that plague regulations were unimportant, "seeing God hath appointed and limited unto every man a certain tenure of life".[80] In 1585, the radical Scottish Presbyterian minister James Melville described the plague epidemic as deliberately intended by God—"a good work" designed by the Almighty to "draw us nearer and nearer unto him".[81] In 1603, an English Puritan pamphleteer urged magistrates not to confine the infected, and exhorted the faithful to violate the plague orders, claiming that "the infection is not general, but unto those whom [God] will have it touch".[82] Other devout Protestants, by contrast, vigorously opposed such fatalism. In 1613, for instance, the London minister Robert Hill warned firmly that "if you meane to be freed from the plague, you must use meanes to keepe yourself from it".[83] According to a Spanish Catholic writing in 1609,

> The Puritans say that [plague] should not be avoided, that it is good fortune to die of the plague, and that although they are close to it, it will not attack any but those already singled out by God, let them take what measures they may. That this is infallible and that it is false madness to try to guard against it.

But, he added wryly, "with all that, I think a great many of them leave London".[84] Popular pamphlets in early modern England reflected widely divergent views: some told of the devout being saved from plague by faith in Providence; others

78. Quoted in Amundsen 1977, 417.
79. Quoted in Palmer 1982, 89.
80. Quoted in Slack 1985, 231.
81. Quoted in Oram 2007, 15 ("a guid wark" designed by God to "draw ws neirar and neirar vnto him").
82. Quoted in Slack 1985, 235.
83. Quoted in Wrightson 2011, 100.
84. Quoted in Slack 1985, 231.

recounted how pious people lay down on corpses to show that Providence would protect them and promptly caught plague and died.[85]

Judaism likewise encompassed diverse views on the propriety of flight and social distancing during epidemics. The Talmud appeared to prescribe fatalism: disease was a divinely ordained consequence of sin, so a believer should not try to prevent or flee an epidemic. But as early as 323, the Babylonian Jewish sage Rav Yosef pointed out that even sinless innocents could fall victim to disease, so faithful Jews were ethically justified in trying to avoid it.[86] From the fifteenth century on, Jewish responsa and law codes covered the entire spectrum from echoing the Talmudic view that all deaths are deserved to advising on the ethical acceptability of avoiding epidemic contagion.[87] Meanwhile, the ordinary behaviour of faithful Jews largely reflected common sense: those who could fled, and those who could not stayed at home and observed social distancing.[88] The early modern period saw Jews increasingly taking the view that Jewish law was to be decided not by ancient literature but by observation of what Jews were actually doing now—that is, fleeing epidemics or social distancing in place.[89] As the Polish rabbi Moshe Isserles put it in 1565, "The custom of Israel is Torah"—in other words, regardless of any theoretical religious discourse, the law is determined by the way that Jews act.[90] Stating this tenet explicitly may be specific to Judaism. But many religions followed it in practice.

Most religions involved a diversity of views on social distancing during epidemics, in which religious leaders more often advocated extreme fatalism, while ordinary believers adjusted to practical realities. This did not mean that an extreme view pronounced by a powerful religious authority figure would have no effect. But the fact that different authorities preached differing views created interstices within which ordinary believers could find religious support for ordinary prudence. The exhortations about submitting to God's will promoted by many Muslim, Christian, and Jewish clergy could have exacerbated contagion had the faithful obeyed them. Where religious elites held the levers of worldly power, this probably sometimes happened. But even where religious fatalism prevailed, the diversity of views inside each religion created theological space for sensible people to act otherwise. Yet it created space only for individual flexibility, not for moral exhortations to take account of harm to others. When religious leaders opposed social distancing, they choked off

85. Slack 1985, 242.
86. Jeremy Brown 2022, 41–2.
87. Jeremy Brown 2022, 46–8.
88. Jeremy Brown 2022, 46–8.
89. Jeremy Brown 2022, 52–3.
90. Quoted in Jeremy Brown 2022, 51–2.

the possibility that religion would motivate believers to take account of the external costs of contacts with others during epidemics.

2.3. THE ICONS AND THE CROWD

Religions might be internally divided on the theology of social distancing. But when it came to religious gatherings during epidemics, they were virtually unanimous. Almost every religion insisted that religious assemblies must continue during epidemics, regardless of contagion risks. Even in normal times, assemblies of the faithful were crucial for religions to motivate members, foster community, collect resources, communicate teachings, and maintain their public profile. In epidemics, such gatherings became even more important, since they enabled the religion to be seen to intercede with the spirits on behalf of believers.

Religions frequently held mass assemblies to beseech spiritual intervention to end epidemics. During the Black Death, almost all religions mandated mass expressions of piety to persuade deities to bring the infection to an end.[91] The Piacenza notary De Mussis, for instance, recounted how in 1348,

> a warning was given by a certain holy person, who received it in a vision, that in cities, towns and other settlements, everyone, male and female alike, should gather in their parish church on three consecutive days and, each with a lighted candle in their hand, hear with great devotion the mass of the Blessed Anastasia.[92]

When the Arab-Berber Maghribi scholar and explorer Ibn Battutah arrived in Damascus in the summer of 1348, he described religious anti-plague assemblies ranging from mass street processions to private gatherings, such as the one to which he was invited by a pious notable who had vowed a feast to God if a day passed without plague deaths.[93] In the 1395 Valencia epidemic, the Church organized a mass procession to the chapel of Our Lady of Mercy to "beseech divine mercy for the said plague".[94]

After the sixteenth-century Protestant Reformation, the Church of England sought to ban plague-averting public processions, only to transform them into plague-averting indoor church services, even more likely to transmit contagion.[95] In the 1563 epidemic, the same Bishop Grindal who admonished Londoners to avoid needless sociability to protect their neighbours also exhorted

91. Slack 1988, 436.
92. Quoted in Horrox 1994, 25–6.
93. Dols 1977, 61.
94. Quoted in Agresta 2020, 371.
95. Slack 1985, 37.

them to attend all-day anti-plague assemblies consisting of seven sermons in a row delivered in an indoor service.[96] In the 1576 Mexican epidemic of cocoliztli (haemorrhagic fever), the Catholic Church organized a procession of the image of the Virgin of Remedios around Mexico City, which local clergy described as the "only remedy" that demonstrated any effect.[97] In the plague epidemics of 1593, 1625, and 1666, Puritans in the Church of England campaigned for mass fasting events to be held every week to avert the pestilence.[98]

Religions acted this way with open eyes. Their leaders were perfectly aware that mass gatherings spread contagion. In the 1469 Brescia plague, Church and magistrates recognized the infection risk but still went ahead with the Corpus Domini procession, "since from the said solemnity and devotion to it liberation and health are to be hoped for rather than greater infection".[99] In the 1478 Abbeville epidemic, those suffering from plague were allowed to participate in Mass in the central church of Saint-Sepulchre on the grounds that the Eucharist had the power to heal the sick and dispel the miasmas that caused disease.[100] In the 1576–78 Milan epidemic, Cardinal Carlo Borromeo organized mass processions to petition God against the plague in the teeth of repeated medical warnings, and explicitly forbade the city health office to prevent the faithful from participating.[101] In the 1630 Prato plague, the town clergy repeatedly organized processions, despite full awareness of the danger of infection.[102] In 1630 the town of Montelupo was so seriously infected that it was placed under quarantine by the Florentine state, but the town priest insisted on organizing a plague procession and inviting neighbouring communities to participate.[103] In the 1630 Volterra plague, the health commissar Luigi Capponi asked the bishop to reduce the number of religious assemblies, whereupon the bishop not only refused to comply but formally accused Capponi of heresy. The health commissar was protected from prosecution only through intervention by the grand duke and magistracy of Florence. The bishop of Volterra and all the Tuscan clergy then complained to the Pope, who duly excommunicated all the officers of the Florence Health Board.[104]

Protestant religious leaders also demanded that the faithful attend religious gatherings, even when state, community, and medical experts ordered

96. Slack 1985, 229.
97. Quoted in Wieser 2023, 162.
98. Slack 1985, 237.
99. Quoted in Palmer 1982, 96.
100. N. Murphy 2013, 150.
101. Palmer 1982, 97; Mauelshagen 2005, 249; Midura 2021, 36.
102. Cipolla 1973, 43.
103. Henderson 2019, 155.
104. Cipolla 1976, 37; Palmer 1982, 98; Mauelshagen 2005, 251.

otherwise.[105] In the 1603 London plague, the English Calvinist divine Henoch Clapham exhorted "the meaner sort of people" to flock in crowds to funeral gatherings in direct contravention of the Lord Mayor's orders limiting attendance to six persons.[106] In the 1603 Norwich plague, the city's many Puritan ministers insisted that the city fathers hold general assemblies for fasting and prayer, despite public health warnings.[107] In 1644 the Church of England clergyman Lionel Gatford criticized those who stayed away from church during epidemics, claiming that "very few, if any of those who have been infected with the plague . . . could say, and say truly, and upon certainty, that they caught the infection . . . by frequenting the house of God".[108]

Religious pressure to attend religious gatherings during epidemics swayed individual decisions, as in the case of the mother-in-law of the Puritan diarist Adam Martindale. In 1645, Manchester suffered a plague epidemic, during which death rates increased to many times their normal level. Martindale's mother-in-law shared a church seat with a woman who died of plague the next night. But as Martindale wrote in his diary, this was an occurrence "which I have heard my mother-in-law say never put her into any fright, but being satisfied she was in her way of duty she confidently cast herself upon God's protection and was accordingly preserved".[109]

People were not ignorant of the risks of religious gatherings. From the Black Death onwards, mass religious events were observed to spread contagion. When the plague arrived in the north-west Russian town of Pskov in 1352, the local government pleaded with the archbishop of Novgorod to come and hold an event to bless the town against the epidemic. The archbishop duly travelled the 210 kilometres to Pskov. Unsurprisingly, he contracted plague in the city and died on the return journey. His followers then organized a procession to conduct his corpse home, spreading plague to Novgorod, Chernigov, Kiev, Ladoga, Suzdal, Smolensk, and other cities throughout Russia, where the epidemic raged for the next two years.[110]

This was no isolated event, as we have seen. Even in advanced Florence, with high state capacity and a finely developed public health office, when plague returned in 1633 after a two-year gap, the authorities felt constrained to permit religious processions. Admissions to the lazaretto immediately surged, despite the fact that only Church and state dignitaries directly participated,

---

105. Mauelshagen 2005, 249.
106. Quoted in Slack 1985, 233–4.
107. Slack 1985, 231.
108. Quoted in Slack 1985, 243.
109. Martindale 1845, 53–5. In August 1645 the Manchester Collegiate Church registered 310 burials, compared with only 12 in August 1646.
110. Melikishvili 2006, 20.

with the populace limited to socially distanced observation on street corners.[111] In the 1656 Rome epidemic, the Clerics Regular of the Mother of God defied the papal closure of churches and insisted on disseminating leaflets to attract worshippers to their thirteenth-century plague-averting votive image of the Virgin Mary. They even kept open a side door through their convent so that worshippers could touch, kiss, and crowd around the image. This spread contagion to such an extent that ultimately the authorities could devise no other solution than to remove the image to a different, more controllable church and suppress the convent altogether.[112] In the 1680 epidemic in the Bohemian town of České Budějovice (Budweis), even after six Capuchin monks died of plague and neighbouring authorities imposed a ban on the town, devotions continued to be held in the monastery church.[113]

Muslim and Christian religious organizations were not the only ones to entice adherents by organizing assemblies claiming to protect against epidemics. In Calcutta during and after the 1817–25 cholera epidemic, Hindu temples associated with the cholera goddess Kali competed for visitors and donors by circulating chain letters promising protection from cholera to all who visited. To compete in their turn, temples associated with the rival cholera goddess Ola Bibi (Lady of the Flux), staged their own attractions, such as displaying a young woman as a living avatar of Ola Bibi herself. Fearful crowds, including Muslims, Christians, and Chinese people as well as Hindus, thronged both temples and crowded the streets leading to them.[114] As late as the twentieth century, Chinese Buddhists organized similar gatherings during epidemics, which they portrayed as spiritual punishment of the community for immoral behaviour. In the Chinese village of Chiqiao in 1926 and 1940, for instance, a Buddhist monastery conducted sacrifices, recitations, and prayers performed by a monk, followed by a mass procession through the village streets to beg the Plague God to grant peace on the community.[115]

All major religions thus shared the view that mass spiritual supplication was more important than social distancing. Where multiple religions coexisted in the same locality, this shared view was displayed in shared assemblies, a pattern observable across more than six centuries of epidemics. A first example comes from the summer of 1348, when the Black Death reached Damascus. The visiting scholar Ibn Battutah described a desperate mass procession of the Damascus populace, with the majority Muslim population marching alongside Christians holding aloft the Gospel and Jews holding up the Torah, beseeching

111. Henderson 2019, 280–3.
112. S. Barker 2017, 43–4; S. Barker 2006, 259–60.
113. Holasová 2005, 14.
114. Tumbe 2020, 231; M. Harrison 2020, 513–4.
115. H. Harrison 2015, 46.

their respective deities to mitigate the plague. The Muslims expected the Christian prophet Jesus Christ to descend to the white minaret at the East Gate to do battle with the Islamic version of the devil.[116] This was no unique occurrence. In late fourteenth-century Damascus, as plague deaths increased to hundreds daily, the Arab historian Ibn Kathir described how Muslims, Christians, and Jews participated in a collective plague procession:

> It was proclaimed in the land that the people should fast for three days. And they went out on the fourth day, and it was Friday at the Mosque of the Foot (*al-Qadam*) and they implored God and they asked him to lift the plague from them. Most of the people fasted and the people slept in a group and arose at night like they do during the month of Ramadan. The people awoke on Friday, on the twenty-seventh. The people went out on the day of gathering from all sides, and the Jews, and the Christians, and Samaritans, old men and old women, and children, and the poor, the amirs, the great and the judges after the morning prayer. They did not cease to beseech God the Most High there.[117]

Similar shared religious gatherings recurred in religiously mixed societies into the modern day. In Ottoman Rumelia (modern Bulgaria), villages with mixed Catholic, Orthodox, and Muslim populations organized joint ceremonies to the Plague Goddess. All villagers regardless of religion assembled inside a circle of carts, leaders of all three religions performed a common liturgy and common prayers to protect the village from the epidemic, and then the villagers collectively threw specially baked unleavened bread mixed with honey into the centre of the enclosed religious space.[118] At the beginning of the Covid-19 pandemic in March 2020, Jewish, Christian, Muslim, Druze, and Baha'i religious representatives met outside the Jerusalem town hall "to pray to the Almighty God that this pandemic may stop".[119] Such joint events temporarily subsumed interfaith rivalry to summon joint spiritual intercession against epidemics, despite the known risks of contagion.

Mass religious gatherings during epidemics were not brought to an end by the discovery of germ theory in the second half of the nineteenth century. John Snow discovered water transmission of cholera in 1854 and Robert Koch identified the *Vibrio cholerae* bacterium in 1884. But during the 1892–93 cholera epidemic in the Russian city of Simbirsk (modern Ulyanovsk), a physician described how local priests organized a huge procession to avert the disease:

116. Borsch and Sabraa 2017, 84–5.
117. Quoted in Cuffel 2012, 127.
118. Robarts 2017, 229.
119. Quoted in Jeremy Brown 2022, 234.

Prayers began at 7 A.M. on July 12, an extremely hot day, and continued until 4 P.M. A large crowd followed the icons around the city limits, many of them succumbing to the heat, many drinking water directly from wells and the river. After July 12, the number of cholera victims rapidly increased, and the city was forced to open temporary cholera barracks; but the passage of crowds of worshippers with icons from one house to another, often from sick to well, somehow failed to deliver the city from infection![120]

Alexandre Yersin isolated the *Yersinia pestis* plague bacterium in 1897. But during the 1910–11 plague in Fujiadian, the local Catholic church continued to hold normal religious services and refused to send the infected to lazarettos, instead tending and burying them by stealth. Of the 300 church members, 81 per cent died of plague, including the French and the Chinese bishops.[121] The influenza virus had not yet been identified by 1918, but contagion theory had been solidly established. Nonetheless, religious assemblies were organized by many churches during the 1918–19 influenza pandemic. In 1918, a Catholic priest in New Orleans protested against church closures since the epidemic meant "people had all the more reason to go to church to ask for divine help".[122] Calvinist churches in South Africa adopted the same attitude, excoriating state orders to close churches on the grounds that they prevented "a communal approach to the Lord when people are suffering His trials and punishments". "Closed churches", they declared, "fill us with greater fear than the bacillus catarrhalis". Such Calvinist insistence on church attendance remained adamantine, even while 6 per cent of the South African population died of influenza in just six weeks.[123]

Many religions behaved the same way during the Covid-19 pandemic. In March 2020, the Muslim missionary movement Tablighi Jamaat held a mass gathering in New Delhi, after which many of the 8,000 attendees tested positive.[124] Those returning from New Delhi in turn infected more than 1,000 people across 22 of the 34 provinces of Indonesia.[125] Christian churches in the USA, Germany, and South Korea also held mass events in 2020–21 which turned into superspreader events.[126] In 2020, ultra-Orthodox New York Jews continued to hold religious gatherings, contributing to disproportionately high infection levels, since, as one observer put it, "The idea of praying alone, they do not really know how to do that."[127]

120. Quoted in Frieden 1977, 546–7.
121. Nathan 1967, 13; Hu 2010, 321.
122. Quoted in Tomes 2010, 54.
123. Quoted in H. Phillips 2008, 35.
124. Ellis-Petersen and Rahman 2020.
125. *Economist*, 2020b.
126. J. Baker et al. 2020, 359–60; Barlow 2021.
127. Quoted in *Economist*, 2020c.

Why do so many religions behave in this way, not just in the Middle Ages, but into the present day when scientific medicine is supposed to be omnipresent? In many cases, religions seek worldly advantage by holding gatherings to attract and retain adherents, combat internal religious indifference, and compete against the lure of other belief systems. But in many cases, such behaviour reflects a genuine belief on the part of both leaders and followers that collective religious assemblies will move the spirit world to extinguish the epidemic. The tension between natural and supernatural explanations plays a role in how religion affects other aspects of epidemic contagion.

3. A Diabolic Operation

Immunization illustrates this tension vividly. Religions upheld immunization where it was anchored in their explanatory systems and business models. Variolation enjoyed these religious advantages in China, India, Africa, and the Middle East, but not in Europe, where it was widely denounced as non-Christian. Cowpox vaccination, by contrast, was an innovation and thus not deeply rooted in the epistemology or business model of any religion. Both types of immunization evoked accusations of evading God's will and violating religious epistemology, but sometimes secured toleration through involvement of religious personnel, adjustment to local culture, or political considerations. Nonetheless, theological fundamentalism could and often did trump such worldly considerations.

3.1. VARIOLATION AND INFIDEL CALCULATIONS

Some religions not only permitted smallpox variolation but actively commended and sanctified it. Across large swathes of the Middle East, Asia, and Africa, the practice had deep cultural roots and religious personnel directly participated in it.

In China from the sixteenth century onwards, variolation was embedded in rural folk religion,[128] and in nineteenth-century south Chinese Hakka villages the operation was carried out under the aegis of the Smallpox Goddess.[129] A majority of Chinese commercial variolators were *doushi*, religious masters who learned the practice through secret oral transmission and treated poor customers in rural areas.[130] In eighteenth-century Tibet, a pioneering Buddhist variolator described how monasteries set up immunization centres: "In the Iron Dragon year (1760), the existing white smallpox in Kokonor became

128. C.-L. Liu 2016, 91.
129. .C.-L. Liu 2016, 117.
130. C.-L. Liu 2016, 91.

SITALA.
GODDESS OF SMALLPOX

FIGURE 5.3. (*Left*) Śītalā, the Hindu goddess of smallpox and epidemics, India, nineteenth-century watercolour. (*Right*) Sopona [Shapona], West African god of smallpox. Carved bone figure adorned with glass, hair, metal, and string, 1960s. *Sources*: (*Left*) Wellcome Collection; (*right*) © Smithsonian National Museum of American History.

known and heard, so I sent people to collect smallpox scabs. Then I inoculated my master cook Zhidar. Then this lineage spread to Tibet, China and Mongolia and this practice has been continuously practised to the present day."[131] Religious personnel similarly presided over smallpox variolation in parts of India. In eighteenth-century Bengal, Bihar, Uttar Pradesh, and Bangladesh, some commercial variolators were religious figures, and even lay vaccinators operated under the aegis of Śītalā, the goddess of smallpox and epidemics (shown in the left-hand image in figure 5.3).[132] In nineteenth- and twentieth-century West Africa, likewise, hereditary priests called *féticheurs* administered variolation to worshippers in shrines of the Yoruba smallpox deity Sopono (shown in the right-hand image in figure 5.3). In Accra as late as 1920, at least one female fetish-variolator was still at work during a smallpox epidemic.[133]

131. Quoted in Yongdan 2021, 65.

132. R. Nicholas 1981, 30; Brimnes 2004, 207.

133. Herbert 1975, 548; Bader 1985, 370 (Sopono first recorded 1885); Bader 1986, esp. 79–84 (variolation); Fenner 1988, 219.

In Europe and North America, by contrast, variolation was introduced only after around 1720, and many Christian confessions denounced it as a primitive pagan practice.[134] In the 1721 Boston smallpox epidemic, a hell-raising Puritan newspaper inveighed against the pro-variolation clergyman Cotton Mather, and a Puritan mob attacked his house with grenades. One of their key accusations was that Mather had learned the practice from an enslaved African. Mather and his medical collaborator defended cross-cultural learning, asking "why 'tis more unlawful to learn of Africans, how to help against the Poison of the Small Pox, than it is to learn of our Indians, how to help against the Poison of a Rattle-Snake".[135] But this defence merely inflamed their Puritan critics, who continued to excoriate the procedure as fundamentally non-Christian.

In Europe, too, variolation was widely denounced as primitive and profane. In 1722, the Reverend Edmund Massey preached at Holborn that variolation was the Devil's invention, and hence "let the Atheist, the Scoffer, the Heathen and the Unbeliever inoculate and be inoculated".[136] That same year, Doctor William Wagstaffe, a physician at St Bartholomew's Hospital and a fellow of the Royal Society, apostrophized variolation as an ignorant and unchristian procedure practised by "the Native Turks, stupid as they are, notwithstanding their favourite Doctrine of Fatality".[137] In 1724, the Stamford apothecary Francis Howgrave attacked variolating surgeons as "learned mimics of a few ignorant Greek women"—even though the Greeks in question were actually a Christian minority within predominantly Muslim Ottoman society.[138] In 1751, a senior Canterbury clergyman declared publicly that variolation was "the off-spring of atheism".[139] In Sweden in 1756, opponents of variolation expressed astonishment that "the discovery of a simple and illiterate People, should be encouraged by a wise Nation".[140] In 1764, four years before France finally legalized variolation, a physician at the Hôtel Dieu declared that "the methods that are used to establish inoculation are founded on infidel calculations and false principles".[141] Not just clergy but many educated men in Christian countries were deeply reluctant to accept knowledge from non-Christian belief systems.

Christian authorities often argued that variolation violated God's will. This view was widespread even in England, the epicentre of European variolation. In 1722, as reflected in the chapter epigraph, the London clergyman Edmund Massey devoted an entire sermon to "the Dangerous and Sinful Practice of

134. Brimnes 2004, 199.
135. Quoted in Herbert 1975, 541–2.
136. Quoted in Grant 2019, 66.
137. Grant 2019, 66 (quotation), 67, 75.
138. Quoted in M. Bennett 2008, 500.
139. Quoted in Grant 2019, 100.
140. Schulz von Schulzenheim 1767, 134.
141. Quoted in Rusnock 2002, 86–7.

Inoculation", arguing that God alone was entitled to decide about disease: "I shall not scruple to call that a Diabolic Operation, which usurps an Authority founded neither in the Laws of Nature or Religion, which tends in this case to anticipate and banish Providence out of the World, and promotes the encrease of Vice and Immorality."[142] As late as 1766, when King George III's son got variolated, a Newcastle vicar refused to pray for the boy's recovery because the procedure had placed the royal child "in the hands of Man, not of God".[143]

A more sophisticated variant of Christian opposition to variolation went beyond the epistemological to the normative, arguing that God deliberately sent disease to improve people's behaviour. Variolation was evil because it circumvented this moral project. In the Boston smallpox epidemic of 1721, for instance, the Reverend Samuel Grainger declared that variolation was a wicked evasion of the message God conveyed by sending smallpox. The faithful should instead embrace disease as God's admonition to undertake "national repentance and reformation".[144]

Christian religious opposition failed to stifle variolation in England, but had concrete legal effects across the European continent. In Lutheran Sweden, according to a 1756 account,

> Amongst the theological Arguments perhaps the most important is, that Inoculators take upon them a Right that belongs to God alone, in being the Authors or Cause of a Distemper in People at pleasure. . . . It is further mentioned, that we ought to leave every thing in the Hands of God, and be contented with Good or Evil, and not of ourselves tamper with our small Understanding.[145]

In Spain, many Catholic clergy publicly declared that variolation contravened God's will, an argument that helped sustain a state ban on the procedure until 1774.[146] In France from the 1720s onwards, the leading opponent of variolation was the conservative Catholic physician Philippe Hecquet, who argued that preventing smallpox violated the natural order laid down by God.[147] Such epistemological claims enabled the French Catholic Church to keep vari-olation illegal across France until 1768.[148] Even after it was legalized, parish priests in Brittany systematically blocked the practice into the 1790s.[149] In

142. Quoted in Silverstein 2009, 299.
143. M. Bennett 2020, 61.
144. Quoted in Silva 2011, 149.
145. Schulz von Schulzenheim 1767, 104–5.
146. M. White 2020, 793–5.
147. G. Miller 1957, 191–2.
148. Herbert 1975, 547; Silverstein 2009, 299.
149. Rusnock 2002, 76.

the German city of Dessau as late as 1792, both the Lutheran clergy and the Jewish rabbi opposed variolation for interfering with "God's rights".[150]

In European countries where religious opposition secured legal bans, even families who wanted to immunize their members could not do so. Europeans who were rich enough travelled to England to get the operation—just like well-off British citizens in 2023 travelled to France or the USA to pay for Covid-19 vaccinations, which the UK government prevented them from buying domestically (though not even for religious reasons).[151] Eighteenth-century Dutch elites travelled to London to be variolated, as in the early 1750s when the Dutch Count of Bentinck sent his two sons to London for the procedure.[152] European diplomats took advantage of their English postings to get their families variolated legally, as in 1725 when the Austrian Habsburg ambassador's daughter was inoculated in London,[153] or in 1755 when the Danish ambassador got himself immunized during his residence in London.[154]

Where Christian communities did accept variolation, direct involvement of religious personnel helped. In the 1721 Boston epidemic, acceptance of variolation relied hugely on proselytizing by the Puritan clergyman Cotton Mather.[155] In England, religious opposition was soothed by Bishop Madox of Worcester, who in 1752 delivered a sermon systematically addressing theological concerns.[156] In The Hague in 1754, variolation achieved greater acceptance when the pastor of the French church published a defence against religious criticisms.[157] In Livonia in the 1760s, the partial acceptance that variolation achieved was almost entirely due to the Lutheran pastor Johan Georg Eisen, who promoted it among the peasantry in the teeth of clerical opposition.[158] In Saxony between 1778 and 1797, the Lutheran pastor Johann Wilhelm Frotscher developed such a reputation for skilled variolation that he was called upon to help medical professionals and was said to have variolated over 1,000 people during his 19 years of practice.[159] In Leeds in 1789, the introduction of "general inoculation" (communal variolation) proved impossible until the incumbent clergyman preached that God approved—though he also swayed parents by pointing out that if all children were simultaneously variolated in

150. Quoted in Maehle 1995, 208.
151. Davis 2023.
152. Chais 1754, 42–3.
153. G. Miller 1957, 173n4.
154. G. Miller 1957, 173n4; Schulz von Schulzenheim 1767, 38–9n1.
155. Herbert 1975, 540–1.
156. M. Bennett 2020, 35.
157. M. Bennett 2020, 38, 179.
158. M. Bennett 2020, 224, 226.
159. Penschow 2022, 175.

springtime, the family could avoid losing labour at harvest time, when they might have to nurse offspring through natural smallpox.[160]

Although some religious opponents of variolation were mainstream believers, a disproportionate share were from the extremes: unbending authoritarians within the established Church and radical sectarians on the fringes. In Boston in 1721, the opponents of variolation were the radicals, opposing the "ministerial elite", which included Cotton Mather and other moderate clergy.[161] In France after 1724, the undisputed standard-bearer of the war on variolation was Philippe Hecquet, an ardently conservative member of the extreme Jansenist faction within the Catholic Church.[162] In the Netherlands in the 1750s, rural fundamentalists adamantly rejected variolation, while urban leaders of the established Calvinist Church endorsed it.[163] In eighteenth-century Russia, conservative rural priests opposed variolation, while urban Orthodox leaders accepted it.[164]

Variolation opened up a chasm inside Christianity between the religious extremes and the moderates. On both the conservative and the radical ends of the spectrum, religious fundamentalists rejected variolation as contradicting God's epistemological and moral dictates. In the middle, moderate clergy and believers accepted the idea that both disease and prevention were part of Creation.

3.2. A PRACTICE EMANATING FROM THE IMPURE HAND OF AN UNBELIEVER

Vaccination evoked many of the same religious responses. Acceptance was greater where the procedure could not be portrayed as foreign, involved religious personnel, and avoided provoking fundamentalists. But there were also differences between vaccination and variolation. Vaccination had been invented in a Christian society, so was more acceptable to European Christian confessions, just as variolation was more acceptable in non-European religions because it had originated in those cultures. On the other hand, vaccination was alien to all cultures because it was rooted in science, so it attracted religious opposition even in Christian societies. Vaccination also competed with variolation, so non-Christian religious variolators sometimes opposed it because it challenged their business models. Finally, state support was much

160. Davenport 2020a, 72.
161. Silva 2011, 146–8.
162. G. Miller 1957, 191–2.
163. M. Bennett 2020, 179.
164. M. Bennett 2020, 226.

stronger for vaccination than for variolation, so religious attitudes were tempered by relationships with governments.

Non-Christian religions often opposed vaccination as a Christian imposition. Islamic leaders sometimes forbade it, as in 1804 when a British doctor started vaccinating children brought to him by anxious mothers, and the Persian sheikh of Bushehr (in modern Iran) banned it as "a practice emanating from the impure hand of an unbeliever".[165] In Egypt in the 1820s, *fallahin* (peasants) objected to vaccination, which they thought mixed blood from Muslim and Christian arms.[166] In Indonesia in the 1820s, Muslims, Hindus, and animists opposed vaccination as a practice that circumvented sacred intentions—but so too did Indonesian Christians, suggesting that opposition was not primarily anti-Christian.[167] In Algeria during the French military conquest after 1830, rumours spread that vaccination was a Christian conspiracy to mark Muslim children for later abduction and religious conversion.[168] In the south-west Indian princely state of Travancore in 1914, Muslim households were said to reject vaccination because of "religious superstition".[169]

Among Hindus, vaccination was opposed as a Christian imposition, but also a British one. In 1802, Hindu leaders in Madras opposed vaccination because, according to a British report, they "apprehended that the English government intended to introduce something which would tend to prejudice their religion, and other Hindu systems of worship".[170] In nineteenth-century Benares, Hindu priests prophesied "that India would expel the British through the leadership of a black child with white blood. Vaccination, the priests charged, was how the English intended to find that child to kill him."[171] Religious opposition to vaccination in India was exacerbated by the fact that some of the professional variolators (*tikadārs*) in regions such as Bengal were members of Brahmin castes, who sought to protect their own livelihoods by claiming that this new form of immunization was contrary to Hindu law.[172]

In Africa, too, some religions opposed vaccination. Nineteenth-century Yoruba fetish-priest variolators opposed vaccination because it threatened their entitlement to claim the possessions of anyone who died of smallpox; members of the cult defended this entitlement with extreme violence, murdering at least one team of vaccinators.[173] In francophone African colonies in

165. Quoted in M. Bennett 2020, 265.
166. Kuhnke 1990, 115.
167. Boomgaard 2003, 609.
168. Amster and El Aoued 2021, 243–4.
169. Quoted in Nair 2019, 377.
170. King 1902, 413.
171. Quoted in Marglin 1987, 20.
172. Bhatnagar 1952, 186–8; Greenough 1980, 347.
173. Fenner 1988, 888.

1931, according to one report, "The numbers of those not vaccinated remains high, especially among infants as a result of the hostile propaganda of witch doctors [*féticheurs*]."[174] In Nigeria, it was 1953 before officials reported the practical demise of "active opposition to vaccination particularly by local vested interests such as a gerontocratic oligarchy of 'juju' priests, fetish men and witch doctors".[175]

Latin America likewise saw religious opposition to vaccination, especially when it encroached on traditional religious practices and revenues. In Rio de Janeiro from the 1870s onwards, resistance to vaccination emanated partly from Afro-Brazilian syncretist religions devoted to faith healing, under the auspices of Omulu, the feared and respected spirit god of smallpox. Many Afro-Brazilian religious leaders charged fees to perform ceremonies to protect against smallpox, so they exhorted adherents to reject vaccination.[176]

In non-Christian societies, however, support from cultural "influencers" could turn the tide in favour of vaccination. A notable example was China, where vaccination became widely accepted partly because local practitioners integrated it into traditional Chinese beliefs. The pioneering Cantonese vaccinator Qiu Xi, whose entrepreneurial vaccination business we discussed in chapter 2, indigenized the procedure using terminology and practices from traditional medicine.[177] He applied the language of acupuncture, used the time-honoured concept of the liberation of *taidu* (foetal toxin), injected the vaccine at the appropriate meridian points, followed the long-established pattern of inoculating boys on the left arm and girls on the right, and provided traditional Chinese recipes for dishes patients should consume after being vaccinated.[178] In the 1820s, Java kickstarted mass vaccination by securing support and involvement from *penghulus* (village priests and experts in Islamic law), achieving almost 50 per cent vaccination rates by the 1860s.[179] In nineteenth-century Punjab, priest variolators at Śītalā shrines were among the most important early vaccinators, simply shifting over from using smallpox crusts taken from humans to vaccinia crusts taken from cows or buffaloes, redeploying their existing technical skills and knowledge for their work as employees of the vaccination establishment, continuing to incorporate Śītalā worship and convalescent care, and indigenizing vaccination to suit Punjabi cultural practices.[180]

174. Quoted in Schneider 2009, 208.
175. Quoted in Schneider 2009, 209.
176. Cukierman 2021, nn66–68; Cantisano 2022, 626.
177. Leung 2008, 15–16, 24–5; Leung 2011, 10; Leung 2020b, 1354.
178. Leung 2008, 16–17.
179. Bosma 2019, 40.
180. Minsky 2009, 174–5, 189.

Christians also held anti-vaccination views. The procedure was invented in a Christian society, but it relied on science rather than religion, so some members of nearly every Christian denomination denounced it. The mainstream Catholic Church supported vaccination. But Catholicism also sheltered extreme anti-vaccination sentiment and was sometimes captured by it. In nineteenth-century Germany, Catholic territories supported vaccination much more than did Protestant ones, but nationally the Catholic Centre Party was taken over by anti-vaxx extremists and became one of the most virulent opponents of smallpox immunization.[181] In nineteenth-century France, the Catholic clergy were split, with rural priests preaching against the practice, while urban Church leaders supported the Napoleonic vaccination campaign.[182] With vaccination as with variolation, therefore, religious opposition was particularly common among extreme authoritarians in the established Church and extreme radicals on the fringes.[183]

The Russian Orthodox Church followed the same pattern, with many rural priests and Old Believers implacably opposing vaccination, while the leaders complied with the tsar's support for the procedure.[184] In the Russian countryside, Orthodox priests widely described vaccination as "unheard-of freemasonry" that completely contravened God's will, a belief so difficult to uproot that physicians and reformers mass-produced colourful religious books called *lubki* (shown in figure 5.4), seeking to win over peasant sentiment.[185]

Protestant confessions fostered many variants of vaccine rejection. In nineteenth-century Sweden, grass-roots Lutherans believed that vaccination clinics were wickedly cheating divine justice.[186] The Swedish pastor Liljekvist claimed that vaccination caused masturbation, hysteria, sexual perversion, haemorrhoids, scrofula, humpbackedness, osteonecrosis, and a wide array of other ailments.[187] In nineteenth-century South Africa, many rural Calvinists refused to pollute their children with vaccination even during the terrible smallpox epidemic of 1805.[188] In Württemberg, many Lutheran clergy fomented popular resistance to state vaccination mandates.[189] As in other Christian confessions, so too within Protestantism, anti-vaccination sentiment was weaker in the established Church and stronger in the non-established sects—among Baptists in Sweden, Pietists in Württemberg, Nonconform-

181. Baldwin 1999, 292, 306.
182. M. Bennett 2020, 164–5.
183. Baldwin 1999, 279.
184. M. Bennett 2020, 236.
185. Quoted in M. Bennett 2020, 236.
186. Baldwin 1999, 275.
187. Baldwin 1999, 284.
188. M. Bennett 2020, 335.
189. Cless 1871, 22.

FIGURE 5.4. Illustration from a popular booklet promoting vaccination to nineteenth-century Russian peasants. On the left, a mother with infant and toddler watches smallpox-struck neighbours leaving their house with a cradle containing a dead child. The healthy mother says, "Thank God I listened to good people and so saved my children through cowpox. Disease and pox kill other children. Mine frolic and they are not pocked, and know no illness. No, they frisk and spin their tops! God save the gentlemen who save the people from their ruin." *Source:* Gubert 1896, 502–3.

ists and Quakers in Britain.[190] In Sweden, the mainstream Lutheran clergy advocated and personally carried out vaccinations, but there were also sectarians, such as the Bottnaryd farmer's wife who wrote an influential pamphlet claiming that she had been called to be a prophet and to proclaim the message that "the continued existence of smallpox epidemics was proof that God still ruled the world and that he was angered by the practice of vaccination".[191] The German state of Württemberg made vaccination compulsory at the unusually early date of 1815, but widely failed to enforce compliance, partly because its extreme Pietist sects adamantly proselytized against the practice.[192]

Religious opposition had less influence on popular sentiment when at least some clergymen supported vaccination. Just three years after the invention of vaccination in 1796, both Anglican and Catholic clergymen in English and Welsh villages were preaching sermons to allay parishioners' concerns, printing leaflets to distribute at baptisms, persuading local surgeons to vaccinate the poor free of charge, vaccinating hundreds of their parishioners with their own hands, offering vaccination on preaching tours, and forwarding raw vaccine

190. Baldwin 1999, 292.
191. Sköld 1996a, 259n54.
192. Cless 1871, 18; Baldwin 1999, 305.

to colleagues.[193] Geneva became an epicentre of vaccination on the European continent as early as 1800, partly because its Calvinist clergy instructed parents on the benefits of vaccination at infants' baptisms.[194] In Austria in 1801, the first vaccinations of ordinary members of the population were carried out in the village of Brunn am Gebirge after the local Catholic priest preached in support.[195] In Palermo, according to an eyewitness account of the 1801 smallpox epidemic, "It was not unusual to see in the mornings of the public inoculation at the Hospital a procession of men, women, and children, conducted through the streets by a priest carrying a cross, come to be inoculated".[196] Vaccination first arrived in most rural Scottish parishes in 1803 after the General Assembly of the Church of Scotland endorsed the practice, and a number of Church ministers began operating as rural vaccinators.[197] In Sweden, many Lutheran clergy personally vaccinated their parishioners and fostered links with lay Lutherans who persuaded the hesitant.[198] Some, like the pastor of Kuddby in 1806, deployed religious sanctions, threatening that "if any child withheld from vaccination dies of smallpox, it will be buried on the north side of the church with a notice on the grave giving the reason".[199] In 1808, along similar lines, Austrian Catholic priests obeyed state instructions to move funerals for smallpox victims into the night hours and refuse to ring the bells, in order to inflict public shaming for "the crime the parents have committed against their children" by failing to vaccinate them.[200]

Church–state relations also affected religious attitudes to vaccination. We already saw how the French Catholic Church and the Russian Orthodox Church officially supported vaccination under pressure from the state.[201] The Spanish Catholic Church behaved differently in Spain compared with its empire. At home in Spain, the Church was less reliant on active state support so showed little enthusiasm for propagating vaccination or even silencing anti-vaccination clergy. In Spanish America, by contrast, the Church depended greatly on royal favour, motivating it to disseminate vaccination actively, especially among indigenous communities.[202] In 1804, the Catholic Church in Caracas organized public vaccination sessions in Easter week,[203] while the

193. M. Bennett 2020, 104–5.
194. M. Bennett 2020, 133, 147.
195. M. Bennett 2020, 130.
196. M. Bennett 2020, 136–7 (quotation), 146–7.
197. Macdonald 1997, 303.
198. Sköld 1996a, 259; Sköld 1996b, 418–19, 498.
199. Quoted in Sköld 2000, 214.
200. Quoted in M. Bennett 2020, 194.
201. M. Bennett 2020, 164–5, 236.
202. M. Bennett 2020, 321–2.
203. M. Bennett 2020, 295, 303.

bishop of Oaxaca sent out a pastoral letter endorsing vaccination and offering indulgences to parishioners who agreed to be vaccinated.[204]

Nearly all religions were internally divided on whether to support or oppose immunization. For every religious leader mobilizing a deity in favour of immunization, another authoritative voice in the same religion argued against. Most religions had some members claiming that epidemic disease was God's will, but others declaring that prevention was also God's will. Thus theology did not play a clear role in religious attitudes to immunization. What increased religious support was when immunization had indigenous cultural roots, was administered by religious practitioners, and was favoured by the state. Support was also affected by whether religious voices came from mainstream believers or extreme sects on the authoritarian or radical fringes. The behaviour of a religion with regard to anti-contagion policies was thus driven not so much by a consistent set of epistemological and moral principles as by the position of that religion within the overall framework of worldly society.

4. Religion and Sinful Science

Religious institutions shaped responses to epidemics in a wider way—through controlling knowledge. A major thing religion seeks to do, after all, is to provide an explanation for the invisible and advice on how to cope with it. Controlling knowledge—both raw information and tools for its interpretation—was central to this mission.

4.1. NATURAL AND SUPERNATURAL KNOWLEDGE

Even before the nineteenth-century divergence between religion and science, religions tended to reject non-religious knowledge and explanations. This affected approaches to all diseases, infectious and non-infectious, endemic and epidemic. But in epidemics this rejection became particularly harmful.

Medical thinkers down the centuries were so conscious of the threat from religion that they immunized their scientific ideas by incorporating a judicious admixture of religious ones. Medieval Muslim medical writers ensured that their treatises included prayer and penance alongside purely medical recommendations.[205] The Andalusian physician ash-Shaqūrī wrote a layman's guide to plague during the Black Death, but was careful to preface it with lengthy passages explaining why medical knowledge was compatible with Islam.[206] The same was true in medieval Catholicism, whose theologians debated vigorously

---

204. M. Bennett 2020, 309.
205. Dols 1977, 98–9.
206. Dols 1977, 99–100, 323–4.

whether it was impious to follow medical advice.[207] The medieval Catalan religious thinker Francesc Eiximenis went so far as to warn Valencian patricians against letting their children study liberal arts, as academic knowledge would cause them to lose religious faith or even become "Saracens".[208]

The idea that disease was contagious might seem obvious today, but it proved an apple of discord until the later nineteenth century, both among theologians and—as we shall see in chapter 6—among physicians. Many Islamic authorities, for instance, viewed contagion as contradicting basic sharia dogma which denied the existence of infection.[209] In Granada just a decade after the Black Death, the Muslim statesman, physician, and poet Ibn al-Khatib wrote a treatise *On the Plague*. He courageously argued that the disease was transmitted through contagion, which he claimed was "established by experience [and] by trustworthy reports on transmission by garments, vessels, ear-rings; by the spread of it by persons from one house, by infection of a healthy seaport by an arrival from an infected land, [and] by the immunity of isolated individuals".[210] The existence of contagion, he concluded, was thus confirmed "through experience, research, sense perception, autopsy [i.e. personal observation], and authenticated information".[211] Al-Khatib sought to anticipate religious objections by adding that "one may not ignore the principle that a proof taken from [Muslim religious] tradition (*Hadith la ʿadwa*), if observation and inspection show the contrary, must be interpreted allegorically".[212] Notwithstanding these arguments, the Muslim religious authorities viewed contagion theory as a violation of religious dogma, harassing al-Khatib for heresy and ultimately executing him (though probably not just for his unorthodox ideas about disease).[213] Later Muslim scholars formally denied the existence of contagion in order to avoid open confrontation with religious dogma, even while often advancing theories that implied contagion.[214] Islamic religious proscriptions did not completely block medical or popular belief in contagion, but pushed such views underground, hindering transmission of medical knowledge.[215]

In Europe, the early modern scientific revolution transformed academic views about nature but did not give rise to a sudden or radical separation between Christian and scientific thinking. Rather, it stimulated attempts to

207. Palmer 1982, 88.
208. Balaguer i Perigüell 1997, 19.
209. Dols 1977, 109.
210. Quoted in Byrne 2012, 182.
211. Quoted in Dols 1977, 93.
212. Quoted in Ober and Alloush 1982, 423.
213. Dols 1977, 94; Ober and Alloush 1982, 423.
214. Dols 1977, 82, 110; Ober and Alloush 1982, 422.
215. Dols 1977, 94–5.

bring theology and natural science into closer consilience.[216] Unfortunately, this often took the form of religion trying to shape science in its image rather than vice versa. Both Catholic and Protestant theologians sometimes took this project to extremes by persecuting innovative medical thinkers, as in Geneva in 1553 when Michael Servetus was burnt at the stake for correctly discovering that blood travelled from the left to the right ventricle via the lungs but rashly postulating that this was so that it could be infused with the Holy Spirit, which Calvin regarded as denying the Trinity. The Geneva Calvinists not only murdered a medical scientist in his prime (Servetus was only 42) but forced his medical publications underground for many decades.[217] Lest it be thought that this was merely because of primitive early-Reformation sectarianism, the same attitude threatened scientific medicine during the Scottish Enlightenment, when the greatest living Scottish medical thinker, William Cullen, was threatened with dismissal from the University of Edinburgh in the 1760s for alleged atheism.[218]

The continued domination of religious over scientific explanations of epidemics, even in rich and advanced north-west Europe, is borne out by a corpus of 104 handwritten "chronicles" or "ego-documents" written in the Low Countries between 1500 and 1850. These consisted of informal personal accounts in which non-medical persons of the middling sort—farmers, local officials, tax collectors, merchants, artisans, members of literary clubs—discussed what they thought caused epidemic disease. The corpus shows the chroniclers searching for patterns in the facts to make sense of prevailing epidemics and anticipate future ones, increasingly using tables, lists, and even statistics to do so. But their beliefs about the causes of epidemic contagion did not result in a rejection of religion, a shift towards "scientific" explanations and remedies, a move towards regarding God's intervention as indirect rather than direct, or a belief that divine and natural phenomena were separate spheres. Explanations of epidemics in terms of "natural" causes became more elaborate, but well into the nineteenth century they continued to be combined with, and subordinated to, explanations in terms of religion.[219]

Religious views of epidemics continued not just to dominate scientific explanations but often actively to reject them, well into the modern era. In South Africa in 1918, for instance, the Dutch Reformed Church officially attributed the influenza epidemic to the sin of "worshipping science".[220] One senior South African clergyman wrote in 1919 that both the influenza and the Great

216. J. Henry 2010, esp. 42–3.
217. J. Henry 2010, 41.
218. McCullough and Chervenak 2021, 57–8.
219. Dekker 2023, 229–31, 237, 243.
220. Quoted in H. Phillips 2008, 34.

War were an expression of God's implacable hostility to scientific reasoning: "Is not it as if the Almighty is toying with the murder resulting from sinful science? Humans may kill in thousands, but God can kill in tens of thousands!"[221] A similar stance emerged in Inner Mongolia during the 1928–30 plague epidemic, when communal and religious leaders organized a seven-hour anti-plague procession, during which villagers sacrificed animals to the gods, women entered sacred trances, and medical practitioners were demonstratively ostracized.[222] During the 2020–21 Covid-19 pandemic, a quantitative study found a significant and substantial association, controlling for other individual characteristics, between belief in an engaged God and mistrust in the Covid-19 vaccine as an expression of modern scientific attitudes.[223]

Religion thus does often try to establish close relationships with—indeed, control over—scientific explanations of medical phenomena, including but not limited to epidemic contagion. For much of human history, this might not seem to be a terribly serious matter. After all, as we shall see in chapter 6, until the discovery of germ theory in the second half of the nineteenth century most medical knowledge was wrong. On the other hand, if religion had managed to reshape the scientific method and ban the practice of proposing hypotheses and evaluating them experimentally, regardless of how they related to theological doctrines, it would have been difficult to invent and evaluate germ theory at all. Furthermore, once scientific medicine emerged, religious rejection of science amplified religious opposition to anti-contagion measures, including vaccination.

Many religions opposed scientific approaches in general, scientific explanations of disease, and scientific advice on contagion control. For one thing, they routinely exerted pressure on medical researchers to bring their explanations into line with religiously approved views and move away from hypotheses about sensitive topics such as contagion or immunization. For another, many religions objected to the whole scientific project because it challenged the epistemological explanations that are part of what religion offers its adherents. Third, many religions explicitly exhorted the faithful to reject scientific and medical advice on epidemic contagion.

4.2. A BROOM IN THE HANDS OF THE ALMIGHTY

Religions not only opposed scientific explanations but put forward their own, ascribing disease to divine rather than natural causes. Sometimes, religions blamed disease on unspecified spiritual offences. In Aleppo in 1348, the Islamic

221. Quoted in H. Phillips 2008, 34.
222. Nathan 1967, 72.
223. Upenieks, Ford-Robertson, and Robertson 2022.

writer Al-Wardi argued that no medical or policy measures against plague could succeed because God had sent it as a punishment for human miscon-duct and as an opportunity for Muslims to renounce their sins.[224] In Denmark in 1349, likewise, the king summoned councillors to a meeting in Lödöse to "consider religious countermeasures to God's epidemic punishment for their sins".[225] In Mexico in the 1520s and 1530s, Christian missionaries explained epi-demics as God's punishment for the transgressions not just of the indigenous people who were being wiped out but of humanity at large—"our sins".[226] In England in 1578, the Puritan divine Laurence Chaderton recommended moral cleansing to prevent plague: "It is not the clean keeping and sweeping of our houses and streets that can drive away this fearful messenger of God's wrath, but the purging and sweeping of our consciences from . . . sin."[227] In the 1663 epidemic in the French town of Alet, the Jansenist bishop claimed that God sent plague "to punish all sorts of sins, but especially those which are public and scandalous".[228] In Essex in 1666, the clergyman and diarist Ralph Jos-selin expressed amazement that only five plague deaths had struck his own parish of "Colne, sinful Colne".[229] In the 1700 Shetland smallpox epidemic, the presbytery described the epidemic as "God's just judgement by reason of our sin".[230] In the 1892–93 Russian cholera epidemic, preventive measures such as washing hands and boiling water were thwarted by local priests, who warned parishioners not to yield to "those young people who are seized with arrogance and who, in their blindness, seek to overcome cholera", which was caused by human sinfulness.[231]

This is not to say that all religious authorities believed that epidemics were caused by sin. As early as the fourteenth century, the Cistercian monk Pierre Ceffons argued that the Black Death could not have been caused by present-day sins since people had been just as wicked in the past, and "when this [pestilence] ends, the world will be as evil as it is [now]". Moreover, he added, the rich and powerful commit more sins than the poor and weak, yet "kings, princes, counts, dukes, knights, and prelates are not dying any more than they used to". Furthermore, good people were dying alongside evil ones, while many very wicked people were surviving. Ceffons, despite having dedicated

224. Vanneste 2010, 38.
225. Benedictow 2004, 160.
226. Quoted in Wieser 2023, 166.
227. Quoted in Palmer 1982, 97.
228. Quoted in Brockliss and Jones 1997, 68.
229. Quoted in Slack 1985, 108.
230. Quoted in B. Smith 1998, 395 (quotation), 399.
231. Quoted in Frieden 1977, 546.

his life to religion, declared himself decisively in favour of natural rather than supernatural causes of plague.[232]

But Ceffons' hard-headed reasoning was unusual. Most religious people continued to ascribe epidemics to human sinfulness, and many were quite certain what those lethal sins were. Inadequate religious observance was one. As early as the Justinianic plague of 541, the emperor himself declared that plagues were caused by "God's righteous anger" at impiety and blasphemy.[233] During the Black Death, Islamic scholarly literature described plague as divine punishment for lack of ordinary piety.[234] In sixteenth-century Mexico, the conquistador Francisco de Aguilar ascribed the 1520 smallpox epidemic to God's wrath against indigenous paganism: "Our God was served, as the Christians were very much tired by the war, to send them smallpox, and among the Indians came a great pestilence."[235] In 1579, Cardinal Borromeo wrote his famous "Letter to the People of Milan", in which he blamed the plague on pagan celebrations of Carnival, which were "provocations to God".[236] In 1603, an English Puritan pamphlet claimed that plague had been attracted to London by "atheistical politicians".[237] Early modern Islamic authorities routinely explained plagues as divine retribution for people's failure to devote attention and resources to religious matters.[238] In South Africa in 1805, a Congregationalist mission leader interpreted a smallpox epidemic as God's punishment for indigenous people's failure to attend church.[239] In Bengal in 1817–25, epidemic cholera was ascribed to inadequate veneration of the cholera goddesses Ola Bibi and Kali.[240] In France in 1832, clergymen and religious newspapers blamed the cholera epidemic on lack of piety. One French priest declared balefully that "the wrath of the God of justice is growing and soon each day will count its thousand victims; the crime of the destruction of the archdiocese is far from being expiated", while a Catholic newspaper pointed out gleefully that "Paris alone was struck, the city of the Revolution, the cradle of political storms, the center of so many vices, the scene of so many attacks".[241]

Alcohol consumption caused epidemics, according to both Muslims and Christians. In 638–39 when the plague of 'Amwās struck an Arab army campaigning in Syria, theologians claimed it was because Syrian Muslims violated

---

232. Quoted in Schabel and Pedersen 2014, 142–3.
233. Quoted in Sarris 2022, 333.
234. Benedictow 2004, 64.
235. Quoted in Wieser 2023, 166.
236. Quoted in Midura 2021, 36.
237. Quoted in Slack 1985, 233.
238. Schama 1987, 46–8; Akasoy 2007, 395.
239. T. Smith 1825, 2:177–8.
240. M. Harrison 2020, 513.
241. Quoted in Delumeau 1978, 136–7.

Islam by drinking wine.[242] In 1364, the Muslim medical jurist Ibn Abi Hajalah argued that the fundamental reason for plague in general and the Black Death in particular was that God was punishing people for consuming alcohol.[243] Although alcohol consumption was a particular concern under Islam, Christians also blamed excessive drinking for all sorts of epidemics. In the 1490 Ghent plague, a town ordinance explicitly included drinking among the activities whose restriction would prevent future epidemics.[244] In 1627 when the owners of an unlicensed Salisbury alehouse died of plague, the Puritan alderman John Ivie remarked, "It pleased God to give me power to suppress all, saving that one house; then the God of power did suppress that house in his judgment."[245] In the Netherlands in the 1830s, preachers ascribed cholera epidemics to sinful behaviour, particularly alcohol abuse; some regarded gin as more dangerous even than cholera.[246] In South Africa as late as 1918, the Dutch Reformed Church's official mouthpiece ascribed the influenza epidemic to God's wrath at sins such as drunkenness.[247]

Sexual sins were also blamed for epidemics by many religions. In 1364, a Muslim medical jurist declared that plague was caused by adultery.[248] In Ghent in 1490, the aldermen issued a plague ordinance regulating sexuality and the corruption of youth, since "it is to be feared that these sins have caused the rising of plagues in this land, and will continue to do so, worse and worse, when they are not adequately prevented".[249] In Venice in 1497, a Franciscan friar told the doge in a Christmas sermon in San Marco that ridding the city of the raging epidemic

> will need a remedy for the causes of the plague, which are the horrendous sins committed, the schools of sodomy. . . . And worse, when some gentleman comes to this city you show him the nunneries, not nunneries but public brothels. Most Serene Prince; I know that you know all this better than me. Take action, take action, and you will deal with the plague.[250]

In Valencia in 1519, a Dominican preacher blamed the plague on sodomy, whipping up such popular outrage that the Criminal Justice executed several alleged sodomites, while a mob burnt another alive in the Plaça del Tossal.[251] A 1579

242. Dols 1977, 23–4.
243. Dols 1977, 114.
244. Coomans 2021, 236–7.
245. Quoted in Slack 1985, 262.
246. Jensen 2023, 131
247. H. Phillips 2008, 34.
248. Dols 1977, 114.
249. Quoted in Coomans 2021, 236–7.
250. Quoted in Palmer 1982, 96.
251. Agresta 2020, 394.

Leiden by-law targeted adultery, "as it fiercely evokes the wrath of God over the land and its people, who are increasingly punished with war, conflict, plague and other depravities".[252] In France in 1832, a Catholic newspaper claimed that cholera "stops on the hearth of corruption, swoops down like a vulture on the city of disorder, surprises it in the midst of its pleasures and harvests there with preferences those unbridled men who indulge in excessive passions and brutal pleasures".[253] In the AIDS epidemic of the 1980s, many American Christian and Jewish groups portrayed the epidemic as divine punishment for homosexuality; among African Muslims in 2010, such views were so widespread that they triggered violent attacks on AIDS clinics.[254] In the 2013 Ebola epidemic in West Africa, both Islamic and Christian religious authorities portrayed the disease as God's punishment for adultery and homosexuality.[255]

Women caused epidemics, according to many religions. In the epidemics that raged in Cairo in the reign of al-Mustanṣir (r. 1036–94), women were persecuted as notorious carriers of disease.[256] In 1348, the Piacenza notary De Mussis ascribed the Black Death to sinful behaviour, singling out for special censure "the overweening vanity of great ladies, which so easily turns to voluptuousness".[257] In the 1438 Cairo plague, Muslim judges, jurists, and scholars blamed the epidemic on women's conduct and persuaded the sultan to forbid females from going into the streets. Inspectors enforced the ban, and women who left their houses received death threats. Rules were relaxed to let veiled female slaves and old women to go to market, and other women sometimes to visit the baths, but otherwise females were forbidden to leave their houses even to attend their own children's funerals.[258] In the 1517 Rouen plague, a local Catholic cleric warned the magistrates that to prevent plague they needed to correct the vices of the inhabitants, especially the indecent dress of "foolish women".[259] In the 1576 Milan plague, a Capuchin friar alleged that an infirmarian in the lazaretto had died of plague because he seduced a young girl: "Intercourse with a woman costs you your life."[260] In 1608, a treatise by a Han author described how women of the Miao tribe in the Chinese south-west brewed up a poison called *gu* that directly caused disease and indirectly subverted epidemic appeasement rituals.[261] In 1644 the English divine

252. Quoted in Coomans 2021, 237.
253. Quoted in Delumeau 1978, 137.
254. Kowaleski 1990; Roehr 2010, 1168.
255. Manguvo and Mafuvadze 2015, 2.
256. Cortese and Calderini 2022, 227.
257. Quoted in Horrox 1994, 23–4.
258. Dols 1977, 114–5; Cortese and Calderini 2022, 195–6.
259. Quoted in N. Murphy 2013, 151.
260. Quoted in Carmichael 1998, 156.
261. Hanson 2011, 83.

Lional Gatford blamed a plague in Oxford on women's extravagant fashions.[262] In Rome in the 1656 plague epidemic, the Jewish rabbi and physician Jacob Zahalon declared authoritatively that plague was caused by women's menstrual blood.[263] In 1665–66, Anglican clergymen blamed the Great Plague of London on women's cosmetic and clothing choices.[264] In 1807, the newly revised edition of a Jewish encyclopaedia published in Zółkiew (now in western Ukraine) stated that smallpox was caused by "menstrual blood that has entered a child's circulation", echoing a long-held view among Jewish thinkers since at least the seventeenth century.[265] In nineteenth-century Lublin (in present-day Poland), ordinary Jews believed cholera to be "a tall, shrivelled, scabrous woman who, on arriving in the city, had announced her presence to one of the Jewish community officials. When the same official saw her leaving, the epidemic abated."[266]

It might be argued that religions, in blaming epidemics on women, were simply reflecting prevailing cultural norms. Up to a point. Negative views of women were indeed widespread in traditional societies, and are still widespread in modern ones. But their practical implementation relied on institutions. One of these was religion. Religious institutions enabled individuals to coordinate on a set of beliefs, establish a hierarchy of values, and impose sanctions on deviations from those beliefs and values. Religions achieved such coordination, and provided incentives to comply, partly by creating benefits for a dominant group of members. The dominant group in almost every religion is male, for economic and social as well as cultural reasons.[267] Religiosity is still strongly associated with low female status. Thus a recent cross-national analysis of over 97 societies found that higher strength of religion was associated with lower female well-being, that no religion was an exception to this pattern, and that female well-being was reduced not by theological content but by "the intensity of religious belief and the frequency of religious participation".[268]

Cultural norms certainly included negative views of women in most societies. But the role of religion is to ensure that believers coordinate on a particular subset of possible norms and do not deviate from them. Religious institutions issued rules barring women from being fully integrated into religious practice,

262. Slack 1985, 243.
263. Jeremy Brown 2022, 108.
264. Slack 1985, 247.
265. Jeremy Brown 2022, 116.
266. Tuszewicki 2021, 221.
267. Social scientists do not have a definitive explanation for why males are dominant in most religions. Hypotheses include lower female economic productivity because of physical weakness and reproductive responsibilities; religiosity as a response to insecurity; and the fact that religion is a formal institution and hence characterized by hierarchy. See the survey by Seguino (2011).
268. Seguino 2011, 1317.

holding religious leadership roles, enjoying economic and political autonomy, and achieving full moral and ethical stature. Religious institutions then penalized individual believers who deviated from these rules. The key point is that such religious rules about women would not be required if everyone automatically obeyed them because of prevailing cultural norms. Religious institutions thus did not simply reflect the wider culture. They created a coherent subset of norms, a code of rules committing members to observe them, and a system of sanctions penalizing those who did not. Of course, religion was not the only institution to blame epidemics on women. State, community, guild, and family did likewise. The distinctive feature of religion was that it placed supernatural and moral authority behind the idea that women were morally defective and epidemics could be blamed on them.

A final religious explanation for epidemics was different. It blamed neither sin nor sinner. Instead, it blamed the victim. Poor people, according to many religions, caused epidemics. We have already seen that both the state and the local community blamed disease on the poor and sought to address epidemics by expelling paupers and beggars. But religion elevated this widely held attitude into a formal belief supported by spiritual authority. Hardly a generation after the Black Death, the Franciscan monk Francesc Eiximenis wrote in his 1383 *Government of the Republic* that the poor were "like useless limbs on the body . . . that damage the living". When he moved to Valencia, Eiximenis presented his book to the governing council (as depicted in figure 5.5), and in 1395 the city duly sought to contain a plague epidemic by persecuting its beggars.[269] In early modern England, likewise, preachers welcomed plague as "a broom in the hands of the Almighty with which he sweepeth the most nasty and uncomely corners of the universe". An epidemic was particularly serviceable because it killed those "of the baser and poorer sort, such whose lives were burdensome, whose deaths are beneficial to society".[270] In the 1656–57 Genoa plague, Friar Antero Maria di San Bonventura asked without irony, "What would the world be, if God did not sometimes touch it with the plague? How could he feed so many people? . . . [C]ontagion is the effect of divine providence, for the good governance of the universe."[271] The widely held observation that the poor were disproportionately afflicted with disease was thus widely formalized by religious authority figures, who integrated it into their explanations. According to this view, epidemics were deliberately brought into being by the almighty father in order to husband his resources, purify his household, and rid it of useless limbs and mouths.

269. Quoted in Agresta 2020, 383.
270. Quoted in Slack 1985, 239–40.
271. Quoted in Alfani 2013a, 106.

FIGURE 5.5. Francesc Eiximenis presents his 1383 book *Government of the Republic* to the Council of Valencia. The six jurats composing Valencia's governing body kneel each side of the city's gothic gate. Eiximenis is on the right, and the guardian angel of Valencia is on the left. From the title page of Francesc Eiximenis's *Regiment de la Cosa Pública* (1499, originally published 1383). *Source*: Wikipedia.

When religious leaders blamed epidemics on the poor, they were throwing religious authority behind the widely held fallacy that association implies causation. As we saw in chapter 2, poor people suffered more from epidemic disease than their more fortunate fellows. This positive correlation made people infer a causal link, rather than recognizing that both poverty and disease could be caused by underlying factors. Such religious explanations may also have arisen from what economists call "statistical discrimination". People have imperfect information about one another. So they use current and past statistical information on groups to infer their other characteristics, such as their tendency to be infected. If a particular group—such as the poor— tend to be more infected initially, each individual pauper is assumed to be infected. This causes non-poor people to discriminate against them, resulting in a vicious equilibrium, in which non-infected poor people are treated as if they are infected, pushing them back into the circumstances which made their infection more probable to begin with. We saw in chapters 3 and 4 how such statistical discrimination was operationalized by the state and the community to oppress the poor during epidemic episodes. Both the fallacy that association implies causation and the tendency to use statistical discrimination when information is lacking are widespread in human cognition, and it is not surprising that they made their way into religious explanations. The special contribution of religion, however, was that it threw spiritual authority behind these explanations of epidemics, which, though intuitively attractive, were mistaken.

Religions did deliver on their tacit promise to the faithful by providing explanations of epidemic disease. These explanations were typically couched in terms of spiritual and moral causes—understandably, since that was the special realm of religion. If a false explanation of contagion fit the religion's explanatory framework, it was likely to be adopted, regardless of empirical support, since religious explanations explicitly specialize in unobservable actions and agents. Because the actual mechanisms involved were unobservable, religious institutions had to focus on observable conduct (inadequate religious observance, alcohol consumption, adultery, homosexuality) or personal traits (female gender, poverty), which they could credibly claim attracted sacred disapproval. The view that epidemics were caused by spiritual rather than natural vectors entailed counter-measures, which themselves were spiritual rather than practical. Since disease is caused by microbes and is diffused by human decisions about hygiene, social distancing, and immunization, religious explanations could not supply counter-measures that actually worked. But they could divert moral and material resources away from explanations and measures that might be more effectual.

4.3. DIVINE PLAGUE PROTECTION KITS

Religious institutions sometimes went further, and threw their authority behind preventive remedies that were fraudulent. As we saw in chapter 2, such fake prophylactics not only deceived the faithful and increased their personal risk of infection. They also created "moral hazard": a reduced incentive to guard against risk when one believes one is protected from its consequences. Religious guarantees for fake prophylactics made people falsely believe they were protected against contagion and hence could afford to take more risks. This in turn amplified the risks to others and exacerbated societal contagion.

The problem of moral hazard was already recognized more than eighteen centuries ago. Between 160 and 180 CE, the Mediterranean world was struck by the Antonine plague. During this epidemic (possibly smallpox), the religious leader Alexander of Abonouteichos advertised and sold a sacred remedy consisting of a line of oracular verse, which, if written over one's doorway, would protect against pestilence. The Roman writer Lucian wrote an exposé, pointing out:

> In most cases it had the contrary result. By some chance it was particularly the houses on which the verse was inscribed that were depopulated! Do not suppose me to mean that they were struck on account of the verse— by some chance or other it turned out that way, and perhaps too people neglected precautions because of their confidence in the line, and lived too carelessly, giving the oracle no assistance against the disease because they were going to have the syllables to defend them.[272]

Alexander of Abonouteichos, it is clear, used his religious authority to propagate this sacred yet fraudulent preventive remedy. Not only was it medically useless but it created moral hazard, giving people confidence to live carelessly, taking risks in the belief that they were insured against contagion.

Religious leaders propagated similarly false anti-contagion measures throughout subsequent epidemics. During and after the Black Death, for instance, Christian plague treatises almost always included disquisitions on the astral causes of the pestilence, recommending that people purchase horoscopes to guide their behaviour in protecting themselves from the disease.[273] In the 1607 London plague epidemic, a Puritan divine dispensed advertisements throughout the city for his spiritual plague preventives, attracting furious denunciations from the Royal College of Physicians.[274] During the 1858 Japanese cholera epidemic, Shinto shrines made huge profits because the faithful paid religious entrepreneurs who claimed to "expel evil for money", got priests to offer prayers to ward off contagion, and visited shrines to beseech protection.[275]

More than eighteen centuries after the Antonine plague, religious leaders still throw their spiritual and supernatural authority behind false epidemic protection measures. In the 2021 Covid-19 pandemic, for instance, the head

272. Quoted in Duncan-Jones 1996, 119.
273. Dols 1977, 91–2.
274. Clark 1964, 1:214.
275. Gramlich-Oka 2009, 53, 57.

of a south London church allegedly sold, for the price of £91, "divine plague protection kits" consisting of a piece of red yarn and a small bottle of cedar-hyssop oil, which he claimed would protect against Covid and had already cured "at least ten people". When prosecuted for causing harm and risk of death to users who believed the claims, he defended himself by appealing to the freedom-of-religion defence.[276]

It might be argued that religions can also filter out false knowledge. Some religions certainly do prohibit ideas that do not fit their explanatory framework, and some of these ideas are indeed false. Medieval Islamic authorities, for instance, forbade the inclusion of astral causes of disease in plague manuals, because astrology was incompatible with Islam.[277] But there is no guarantee that the knowledge religion bans will be false or, as we have seen, that the knowledge it propagates will be true. Religious authority does not provide a good way of monitoring the quality of knowledge.

4.4. PIOUS LIES

Religion interacted with knowledge about epidemics in a final, paradoxical way. Religious leaders told lies to make followers believe the truth about epidemic contagion. In India in 1802, for instance, a group of Brahmins sought to combat Hindu anti-vaccination sentiment by forging a Sanskrit text purporting to show that using cowpox to immunize against smallpox was an ancient Indian tradition.[278] Around the same time, the Catholic Church in Spanish America sought to deceive indigenous people into accepting vaccination by portraying it as a sacrament and associating it with Easter, communion, and godparenthood.[279] In the 1850s, a group of Lutheran clergymen and school-teachers in the Württemberg Jagst district tried to induce young adults to get vaccinated against smallpox by falsely announcing that the state now required everyone over 14 to be re-vaccinated. This lie was widely accepted, giving rise to a vaccination rate 33 per cent higher, and smallpox mortality 50 per cent lower, than elsewhere in the country.[280]

The fiery Swedish Lutheran pastor Johan Peter Wallensteen, whom we have met before, openly admitted that he used religious lies to control epidemic contagion. In 1806, Wallensteen decided to persuade his parishioners to vaccinate their children. At first he deployed rational argument and appealed to parental affection, but to no avail. So he mobilized religious lies:

276. Quoted in Burgess 2021.
277. Dols 1977, 91–2.
278. Shoolbred 1805, 54–5.
279. M. Bennett 2020, 313, 322.
280. Mühlhoff 2021, 14.

With regard to enforcement, I had always found the language of power to be most efficient. I used it in this matter too, for the excellent objective and the effectiveness of this method justified its use. . . . After one and a half years of troublesome efforts I got permission from the Royal Office to present vaccination as compulsory. After reading from the pulpit, I would strike both hands with all my strength on the pulpit, stamp, shout loudly as if enraged, reminding the congregation how often they have heard what I am talking about, not only from the county governor and all such enlightened people, but also from God and the King, that they now have heard the King's gracious approval for all this, so I no longer ask, but order, and if obedience does not follow, the resister shall be forced to comply with help from the police etc.[281]

Wallensteen backed up his false announcements with religious authority, threatening to bury any unvaccinated children on the side of the churchyard where outcasts and sinners were typically interred. He concluded that his pious fraud had succeeded, in the sense that all the official vaccination recommendations "have been obeyed, with a carefulness which cannot be praised enough".[282]

It might be thought that the end justified the means. But though pious frauds about vaccination were apparently successful in Jagst and in Kuddby, clerical chicanery did not always achieve its ends. In north-eastern Peru in 1805, for instance, Catholic missionaries led the indigenous people of Chocope to believe that vaccination would cause them to "be made immaculate". The Chocope people found the simplicity of the procedure so disappointing that they denounced the vaccinators as the Antichrist and drove them out of the village.[283]

Such pious frauds also raise a fundamental question about the role of religion in controlling contagion. Religious endorsement enjoyed a cognitive authority which, even when it avoided outright falsehoods, was based on faith rather than evidence. Religious authorities are seldom experts in scientific knowledge. So their exhortations on contagion are based on faith and supernatural authority. They also reflect worldly interests such as the desire to please the state. The most serious problem, however, is that the same motivations can direct religious exhortations in the opposition direction, diffusing false ideas that exacerbate contagion. Should religious lies be endorsed merely because they sometimes have beneficial effects, given that they can also lead to malign outcomes?

281. Quoted in Sköld 2000, 214.
282. Quoted in Sköld 2000, 214.
283. Quoted in M. Bennett 2020, 313, 322.

5. The Kingdom of God Has No Borders

Cross-border externalities are a final way in which religion affects epidemic contagion. As we have seen, this particularly virulent type of spillover arises when people in one polity take decisions that impose costs or benefits on those in another polity which the original decision-makers do not consider. Thus when an epidemic arrives, one society can impose a quarantine or vaccination mandate which reduces contagion not just locally but also outside its borders in ways from which that society does not benefit. Conversely, one society can conceal an epidemic, increasing contagion abroad in ways from which that society or its citizens do not suffer any cost. When benefits or costs spill over in this way, they are not considered by the society that originates them, which therefore produces fewer benefits and more costs than would be best for humanity at large.

Religion does not exactly have borders, and it seldom precisely follows political frontiers. But it is an institution which takes decisions that can have repercussions for those who are not its adherents. Historically, religion has operated outside its own borders through three activities that project the faith but also project contagion: pilgrimages, missions, and wars.

5.1. PILGRIMS AND PLAGUES

Most religions mandate or even directly organize pilgrimages—journeys by the faithful to sacred locations, often in distant places. For many centuries, Islam, Catholicism, Judaism, and Hinduism have despatched large numbers of the faithful to new places on pilgrimage.[284] Protestantism suspended the practice temporarily during the sixteenth and seventeenth centuries, but oversaw its resurgence after around 1700 among high Anglicans, Methodists, and Pentecostals.[285] Pilgrimages moved not just the faithful but their diseases, bringing people and microbes together in new and virulent combinations.

As soon as written records of medieval Christian pilgrimages survive, we learn of epidemics attacking pilgrims en route. In 1184, for instance, the Muslim pilgrim Ibn Jubayr recorded how on his journey home to Valencia from Mecca he boarded a ship in Acre bound for Sicily with 50 Muslim pilgrims and 2,000 Christian pilgrims among the passengers: "Two Muslims died— God have mercy on them. They were thrown into the sea. Of the (Christian) pilgrims two died also, and then were followed by many."[286]

---

284. Dols 1977, 63; Denecke 1986.
285. Goh 2021.
286. Quoted in Broadhurst and Irwin 2019, 349.

Epidemics did not dampen but rather inflamed the practice, since many religions expanded their supply of pilgrimage destinations to address the demand for health miracles. Long before the Black Death, a major motive for pilgrimage was already the quest to obtain sacred help with chronic illnesses and disabilities. But when the great plague arrived in the 1340s, many shrines moved into the new market by promising plague-specific protection.[287] Plague shrines sprang up in Sicily, Pisa, Florence, Tolentino, Loreto, and Siena in Italy; in Canterbury and Hereford in England; and in numerous sites through-out France, Switzerland, the Low Countries, and other European lands.[288] By the early modern period, two-thirds to three-quarters of all recorded miracles in France related to the cure and prevention of disease—often specifically directed at plague.[289]

The medieval and early modern Catholic Church explicitly advised the faithful to go on pilgrimage to petition God against plague. In the 1426 Gouda plague epidemic, for instance, a man fell ill, prayed "in vain to all other saints", was visited by a vision of Mary, and recovered while dressing to depart on pilgrimage to Delft.[290] In Basel in 1439, a plague epidemic inspired citizens to undertake mass pilgrimages to Marian shrines in the Black Forest and the canton of Schwyz.[291] In Antwerp in 1490, a woman with nine gigantic buboes was advised by her confessor to make a pilgrimage to Amersfoort, where she was miraculously cured.[292]

Plague pilgrimages, however, helped spread plague. The tiny Swiss village of Einsiedeln in canton Schwyz suffered from recurrent epidemics brought by pilgrims to its Marian shrine, requiring the local graveyard to be extended several times. In 1519, a pilgrim travelling back from Jerusalem reported that "deaths are high in Einsiedeln, with corpses being carried on wooden sleds, seven per sled".[293] In 1611, a Lucerne peasant made a pilgrimage to Einsiedeln, caught plague in the church, and brought it back to his home village, where it killed him, his wife, their four children, and more than 60 fellow villagers.[294] Pilgrims travelling home from many other shrines are recorded as bringing plague with them. When plague returned to Florence in 1633, it came with Alessandra Vivuoli and her 18-year-old son, who had travelled to Livorno to worship a miraculous image of the Madonna, where Alessandra caught plague

287. Osheim 2012.

288. Osheim 2012; Coomans 2021.

289. Brockliss and Jones 1997, 72–3.

290. Quoted in Coomans 2021, 234.

291. Landolt 2012, 47.

292. Coomans 2021, 234.

293. Quoted in Landolt 2012, 48.

294. Landolt 2012, 56.

and brought it home to Florence. There it killed her son, her husband, and two other family connections, before spreading throughout the city.[295]

The Muslim hajj was a general-purpose rather than a plague-specific pilgrimage, but it too spread disease. As early as the ninth century, the famous medical scholar and translator Qusta Ibn Luqua wrote his *Health Guide for Pilgrims to Mecca*, which not only gave advice on health for any traveller but provided specific warnings for hajj pilgrims. Despite the religious sensitivity of the concept of "contagion", the *Health Guide for Pilgrims* implicitly referred to its existence, and elsewhere Qusta explicitly defined contagion as "a spark which jumps from a sick to a healthy body, whereby the same illness as exists in the sick body arises in the healthy body".[296]

Despite this long tradition of medical warnings about contagion risks, the hajj continued to be held. In 1348–49 it went ahead as usual in the teeth of the Black Death, and an estimated 50 per cent of the Mecca pilgrims died.[297] Throughout the late medieval and early modern periods, pilgrims repeatedly brought epidemics to the holy city and transmitted them to fellow pilgrims, who then carried them home across the world. After 1800, the hajj emerged as a major conduit for the globalization of epidemic disease.[298] Cholera had long been endemic in India, but the expansion of steam shipping hugely reduced travel costs, increasing hajj participation by Indian Muslims. On at least 40 occasions between 1831 and 1912, cholera spread from India to the Hijaz region around Mecca, whence it was transmitted globally by returning pilgrims.[299] In Egypt, at least half of the 10 cholera epidemics between 1831 and 1902 were traced to pilgrims returning from the Hijaz.[300] In Tanzania, severe cholera epidemics were brought back from Mecca in 1821, 1836–37, 1858–59 and 1869–70, killing around half the inhabitants of major urban centres.[301] In the Russian Empire, cholera epidemics were unleashed in the 1820s and 1830s when Muslim pilgrims brought the disease back from the hajj, resulting in 250,000 Russian cholera deaths between 1823 and 1831.[302] But it was the 1865 hajj that arrested world attention, since cholera killed 30,000 pilgrims on the spot in Mecca and then travelled much faster than any of the earlier hajj-related cholera epidemics, thanks to railways and steamships, unleashing

295. Henderson 2019, 278.
296. Quoted in Bos 1992, 6, 157.
297. Dols 1977, 63; Borsch and Sabraa 2017, 86.
298. Low 2008, 269–70, 274.
299. Low 2008, 270.
300. Kuhnke 1990, 49.
301. Koponen 1988, 661–2.
302. Robarts 2017, 225.

a worldwide epidemic that claimed over 200,000 lives.[303] During the 1894 hajj, cholera killed an estimated 15 per cent of that year's 200,000 pilgrims, and the survivors carried infection back home to many lands.[304] Overall, between 1850 and 1931, there were 21 cholera epidemics in Mecca which played a central role in the global cycle of recurrent cholera pandemics.[305]

Hindu pilgrimages also disseminated epidemics, including cholera, small-pox, and plague. Since medieval times, Hindu pilgrimages to the Ganges had led to a close association between holy days and cholera epidemics.[306] In 1782–83, cholera appeared in the holy city of Hardwar, killing 20,000 pilgrims in just eight days.[307] In 1877, Hardwar saw an even more lethal cholera epidemic, during which 250,000 Hindu pilgrims visited the city and over half succumbed to the disease.[308] Smallpox spread in the same way—as in nineteenth-century Bengal, where pilgrims picked up the disease at their favoured Puri shrines in Orissa and brought it home, where it spread across the countryside.[309] As late as 1994, a lethal plague epidemic arose in the Gujarati city of Surat, trig-gered by the annual Ganesh festival, which attracted crowds of pilgrims from Maharashtra.[310]

In Japan, Shintoism urged the faithful to make pilgrimage to particular shrines. During epidemics, Shinto authorities strongly encouraged the faithful to undertake pilgrimages specifically to ask for protection against infection. In the 1858 Japanese cholera epidemic, for instance, many village representatives made pilgrimages to Shinto shrines at community expense to obtain protec-tion for their fellow villagers.[311] In the 1918–20 influenza pandemic, pilgrims flocked to Shinto shrines to pray for protection and recovery. Many contracted influenza at the Ise Shrine in Mie prefecture and brought it home with them to their villages.[312]

By encouraging pilgrimages, religions did not intend to foster epidemics. But both religious leaders and ordinary believers valued the benefits of pil-grimages enough to go on conducting them regardless of the epidemiological

303. M. Harrison 2012, 139–50. The figure of 30,000, 30% of total pilgrims, is reported by Lacey (1995, 1411) and Harrison (2012, 139). Low (2008, 269–70) reports a lower estimate of 15,000 pilgrim victims.

304. M. Harrison 1992, 135.

305. Lacey 1995, 1414.

306. Gómez-Díaz 2008, 95.

307. Gómez-Díaz 2008, 96; Tumbe 2020, 27.

308. Echenberg 2008, 106.

309. R. Nicholas 1981, 35–6.

310. Barnes 2014, 174.

311. Gramlich-Oka 2009, 53.

312. Noy, Okubo, and Strobl 2020, 8.

fallout. Indeed, religions deliberately recommended pilgrimages in times of epidemic—including for the infected. Partly this was because they believed that pilgrimage saved souls, which was important when mortality was high. But it was also because pilgrimages were big business, bringing taxes to rulers, deals to long-distance merchants, and custom to local retailers, all of whom rewarded religious leaders for continuing to hold them. Religions may also have incentives to urge the faithful to undertake perilous actions such as going on pilgrimage, refusing vaccination, rejecting social distancing, and doffing face masks in order to bind believers more closely to the faith and signal to others that outside options have been demonstratively rejected.

5.2. MEDICAL MISSIONARIES

Religious missions represented another type of cross-border religious enterprise with epidemiological repercussions. Missions moved believers across geographical boundaries and created mission stations at which people lived in close spatial clusters. Missions served to communicate ideas across cultures, confirm religious conviction, attract new adherents—and transmit microbes.

Some missions helped control the resulting epidemics by communicating knowledge about disease, sanitation, immunization, and scientific medicine. In nineteenth-century Asia, for instance, Protestant missions organized small-pox vaccination and advocated medical hygiene. In Thailand, the American missionary Dan Beach Bradley pressed for ship quarantines to limit cholera transmission and published articles in Thai-language newspapers explaining how sanitation and medicine could limit contagion. He campaigned for smallpox vaccination, and during the 1835 epidemic personally inoculated 3,500 patients, demonstrating the technique before excited crowds. Although Bradley espoused the incorrect miasmatic theory of disease, he provided an effective antidote to the religious approach of the Thai state, which promoted ceremonial activities directed at the symbolic and supernatural destruction of illness.[313] In late nineteenth-century China, likewise, Protestant medical missionaries distributed vaccination tracts, instructed on vaccine preservation, trained Chinese vaccinators, established vaccination departments in hospitals, and supplied fresh lymph to local vaccinators.[314]

In Africa, too, Catholic missionaries advocated immunization and often carried it out personally. In Ethiopian epidemics between 1850 and 1880, for instance, the Catholic missionary Guglielmo Massaia became known as "the smallpox doctor" by vaccinating hundreds of people every day.[315] During

---

313. Puaksom 2007, 314–16.
314. Leung 2008, 11, 25, 28; Leung 2020b, 1357–9.
315. Pankhurst 1965, 350.

the 1885 smallpox epidemic on Lake Tanganyika, one of the Catholic White Father missionaries inoculated hundreds of people with pus taken from small-pox patients, and in the 1900 smallpox epidemic in Katanga another missionary used arm-to-arm variation on local inhabitants for lack of vaccine.[316]

But the same features that made missions good at transmitting ideas also made them good at transmitting diseases. In eighteenth-century Mexico, the Catholic Church found it hard to establish religious, moral, and social discipline in widely scattered indigenous settlements, where converts were surrounded by neighbours observing their original cultural and religious prac-tices. So missionaries worked to congregate people into large, centralized villages, first by persuasion and then by force. In these villages, crowding, poor living conditions, and mandatory religious gatherings spread epidemic contagion.[317]

In eighteenth- and early nineteenth-century California, likewise, indigenous people ordinarily lived in settlements of fewer than 100 inhabit-ants, where each family occupied a separate hut. Catholic missions sought to eradicate indigenous religion by assembling people in larger mission cen-tres of 1,000–2,000 inhabitants, who were expected to reside in collective dormitories or compounds and attend mass religious celebrations. In these missions, indigenous people encountered European clerics, soldiers, and set-tlers, contracting epidemic diseases against which they had no immunity and dying at higher rates even than the non-missionized indigenous population.[318] Spanish missionaries knew that mission centres fostered epidemics, and even sometimes implemented social distancing measures, as in the Jesuit missions of eighteenth-century Paraguay.[319] But they preferred firm believers with high mortality to backsliders who survived.

Missions moved proselytizers and believers across borders to serve reli-gious ends. Missionaries genuinely believed this created spiritual benefits for converts as well as new adherents for the faith. In some cases, missionary activity transmitted knowledge of sanitation, quarantine, and vaccination, helping to limit contagion. In others, however, missions merely transmitted disease without countervailing knowledge of how to contain it. This raises a stark question. Did the number of people missions saved by transmitting vaccination and modern sanitation in Asia and Africa outweigh the converts missions killed by transmitting European diseases to indigenous people in Spanish America? Almost certainly not.

316. Herbert 1975, 550.
317. Newson 1985, 58–60.
318. Cook 1943, 3–34.
319. Livi-Bacci 2006, 222–3.

5.3. HOLY WAR AND THE COMMON CROWD

Religions also project faith and contagion across borders through warfare. As we saw in chapter 3, wars create cross-border contagion externalities by moving multitudes of humans to new locations, where they exchange microbes with new human hosts, often in crowded and unsanitary conditions.

The Crusades inspired by the medieval European Church in the Holy Land are only the most notorious of the many wars down the centuries waged by and for religion. As table 5.4 shows, the eight major Crusades between 1098 and 1272 involved recurrent epidemics of typhoid, dysentery, and plague, alongside insect-transmitted infections such as malaria and nutrition-related diseases such as scurvy.

As early as the First Crusade (1095–99), Albert of Aachen described how after the Crusader invasion in 1098,

> a plague of most severe mortality happened in the city of Antioch, by which a very great and countless multitude of the Christian army, as many noble leaders as of the common crowd, were taken. . . . [T]his severe plague grew more widespread and serious, and death began to diminish the Christian army to such an extent that for six months scarcely a day dawned but a hundred, or fifty, or thirty at least, gave up the ghost. . . . [O]ver one hundred thousand were laid waste by death, without a weapon being wielded.[320]

In 1167, between the Second and the Third Crusades, Frederick Archbishop of Tyre contracted dysentery on crusade against Egypt: "He began to suffer from a dangerous attack of dysentery by drinking the water of the Nile, and his illness increasing, he was forced to return home [to Tyre] before Alexandria was surrendered to the king."[321] In 1203 during the Fourth Crusade (1203–4), when the Christian fleet arrived at Acre the Crusaders were afflicted by a serious epidemic (possibly cholera) that struck fast and killed thousands of people each day: "The plague attacked so swiftly and unexpectedly that whoever began to feel ill could, most certainly, expect to be dead within three days."[322] In 1250 at the end of the Seventh Crusade, the Egyptian campaign of King Louis IX of France was so seriously affected by dysentery and other diseases that many soldiers were ill by the time the king finally left Egypt with

---

320. Quoted in Edgington 2007, 343–4.
321. Quoted in Babcock and Krey 1943, 2:337.
322. Quoted in Andrea 1997, 86–8.

TABLE 5.4. Religious Conflict and Disease during the Crusades, 1095–1272

Crusade	Date of crusade	Location of epidemic	Date of epidemic	Disease (hypothesized)	Notes
First	1095–99	Antioch	1098–99	Malaria, typhoid, scurvy	Over 40 French Crusaders buried daily at height of epidemic, 1,500-strong German contingent almost completely annihilated
Second	1147–49	Attalia	1148	Plague, dysentery, typhoid fever	High mortality in Louis VII's Crusader army, many thousands of pilgrims die
Third	1189–92	Acre	1189–91	Severe scurvy, other diseases	High mortality in Crusader army besieging Acre
Third	1189–92	Antioch	1190	Unknown	High mortality in Crusader army besieging Antioch
Fourth	1198–1204	Zadar	1202	Unknown pandemic	Pestilence and many deaths among townspeople immediately before Crusader army sacks city
Fifth	1217–21	Damietta	1218–19	Severe scurvy, ophthalmia, other diseases	High mortality in Crusader army besieging Damietta; one-sixth of the pilgrims die; 90% of 80,000 besieged Damietta inhabitants die
Sixth	1228–29	Brindisi	1227	Plague, "fever"	Many deaths among Crusaders gathering to sail to Acre
Seventh	1248–54	Al Mansurah	1250	Severe scurvy, typhoid, other diseases	Severe epidemic and nutritional disease forces Crusader army to retreat to Damietta, causing collapse of Seventh Crusade
Eighth	1270–72	Carthage	1270	Dysentery	Many deaths among Crusaders

Sources: Smallman-Raynor and Cliff 2004, 76; J. Phillips 2017, 156–7; Curta 2019, 550.

his defeated army. As soon as the Crusader army arrived in Frankish Acre, according to John of Joinville,

> I succumbed, and all my people too, to a continual fever which forced me to take to my bed; and there was never a day all that time on which I had anyone to help me or lift me up. I felt that only death awaited me, from a sign that was constantly close to my ear; for there was no day on which twenty or more dead were not carried to the church, and from my bed, as each was carried in, I heard the chant of *Libera me, Domine.*[323]

The epidemics transmitted by crusading armies did not kill just pilgrims, lords, soldiers, camp followers, and enemy combatants. They also inflicted horrific mortality on multitudes of ordinary people who happened to live along the route. During the Fourth Crusade (1203–4), the epidemic that struck Acre after the Crusader fleet arrived killed widely, far beyond the ranks of the Crusaders themselves:

> That summer, during those days which, because of the wickedness of the heat we call "dog days", a very serious epidemic broke out, and the human mortality rate was so great that more than two thousand corpses are said to have been buried on one day. . . . The pestilence pervaded the city and its environs for quite a while. As a result, a majority of Acre's citizens and the pilgrims pausing there were carried off by the corruption of the contagion. . . . [Even] those who survived, as if they had accepted the answer of death, awaited it every single moment, languid and drawn.[324]

The Fifth Crusade (1217–21) likewise brought epidemic disease, which wreaked civilian mortality alongside army deaths. The siege of Damietta in 1218–19, for instance, gave rise to an epidemic that killed one-sixth of the Crusaders themselves, but nine-tenths of the 80,000 besieged city-dwellers.[325]

Within three generations of the last major Crusade (the Eighth, 1270–72) came the Black Death.[326] As we saw in chapter 1, this great pandemic was transmitted from Mongols to Europeans in the context of a military conflict with a strong religious component. In the 1340s, the desire to strengthen Islam in his territory was one reason the Mongol emperor Khan Janibeg sent an army to chivvy Italian trading communities around the Black Sea, the Sea of Azov,

323. Joinville, Wailly, and Hague 1955, 129.
324. Quoted in Andrea 1997, 86–8.
325. Smallman-Raynor and Cliff 2004, 76.
326. The Eighth, though often described as the final Crusade, was followed by other papally mandated Crusades, notably the Alexandrian Crusade of 1365 (see Van Steenbergen 2003) and the Savoyard Crusade of 1366–67 (see Cox 1967, 179–84, 205–39), as well as by a number of subsequent minor crusades.

and the Don River. The Black Death emerged in the Mongol army during or after the siege of Caffa in 1346 and crossed the Black Sea in 1347 to Constantinople, whence it was carried by refugees to Asia Minor, the Middle East, and Europe.[327] Religious motivations, alongside political and commercial forces, played into the complex encounters between Mongol armies and European merchants, which combined to create a perfect epidemiological storm in the Black Sea region in the 1340s.

A century and a half later, the Reconquista wars between Christians and Muslims in Iberia brought a new wave of epidemics fuelled by religious conflict. One Castilian commentator described how "when the army was reviewed at the beginning of the year 1490, the generals noticed that 20,000 men were missing from the rolls, and of these 3,000 had been killed by the Moors and 17,000 had died of disease".[328] Some 28 per cent of the Castilian army, which had an estimated size of 60,000 in 1491, had thus died of disease the preceding year.[329]

The Thirty Years War was not solely or even predominantly religious in nature, but religious issues helped to motivate, power, and sustain it. Even the deeper struggle over state capacity and the imperial constitution also involved competition for control of the wealth, entitlements, and regulatory legitimacy of the Church.[330] Religion thus contributed to both the beginning and the maintenance of a European "civil war", which brought with it the worst plague epidemics since the Black Death, particularly in the cockpits of conflict in the German and Italian lands. In just the 17 years from 1622 to 1639, this war involved approximately 450 local epidemic outbreaks, mainly bubonic plague and typhus fever.[331] The plague epidemics of the 1630s, as we saw in chapter 3, killed an estimated 30–35 per cent of the population in Italy and Germany and non-trivial percentages in Switzerland, the Netherlands, France, England, Iberia, and other European polities.[332]

Religion also triggers conflict inside societies. Even when internal religious animosities do not issue in open violence, they exacerbate epidemics by diminishing the social cohesion needed to control contagion. In the nineteenth-century Ottoman Empire, for instance, cholera and plague quarantines were resisted by Muslims resentful of Christian minorities and their

---

327. Wheelis 2002; Benedictow 2004, 44, 49–54, 60–1, 64, 69, 130, 181, 183, 212, 227; Slater 2006, 271–2, 274–7; M. Harrison 2012, 3; Benedictow 2021, 164, 178–9, 187, 248, 431, 451; Favereau 2021, 248–9, 256; H. Barker 2021.

328. Smallman-Raynor and Cliff 2004, 83.

329. Ladero Quesada 1967, 279.

330. On the multiple causes of the war, which included but were not restricted to religious belief and religious extraction, see Ogilvie (1992) and P. Wilson (2008, esp. 503–14).

331. Smallman-Raynor and Cliff 2004, 86–93.

332. Alfani and Murphy 2017, 316–17; Alfani, Gierok, and Schaff 2022.

medical practices.[333] In 1841, an Istanbul gravedigger called Mehmed gave open utterance to this hostility:

> Not one of the patients who come from all the barracks to that [Christian] hospital in Topçular gets better. The Frank [western Christian] doctor looks after the patient for five or 10 days and then poisons and kills him. . . . Does an infidel show mercy to a Muslim? They want all Muslims to die. Is there no Muslim doctor, that the sons of the *umma* of Muhammad do not die at their appointed time?[334]

In twentieth-century America, too, religious fissures undermined efforts to control contagion. Across 438 American cities in 1918–19, greater religious fractionalization was associated with significantly higher influenza mortality, controlling for other city characteristics.[335]

Religions motivated wars between societies and conflicts within them. They did not deliberately set out to spread contagion through such conflicts, but nor did they take epidemic risks into account in choosing to pursue them. Religious conflicts unleashed epidemics both directly through open warfare and indirectly by undermining the social cooperation needed to contain them.

6. Conclusion

The unique selling point of religion is that it coordinates relations between humans and spiritual beings. This gives it huge epistemological, emotional, and moral authority inside believers' minds—arguably more than any other institution. But religion also exists in the world. To serve its spiritual ends, it seeks adherents, power, and resources. This means it inhabits real polities and real economies, where it competes and collaborates with worldly institutions— market, state, community, guild, family, and many others. Historical epidemics repeatedly display this Janus head, in which religion turns one face to God and the other to Caesar.

In principle, religion could help with epidemic control by throwing its epistemological authority behind explanations that held that disease was contagious, sanitation and social distancing could control it, immunization could prevent it, and science could explain it. In practice, this did sometimes happen. Some adherents of some religions came to accept contagion theory, sanitation, quarantine, variolation, vaccination, and scientific medicine. Some missionaries in the nineteenth century sought to project scientific medicine across religious and political borders. But for most religions the epistemological

---

333. Boyar 2018.
334. Quoted in Boyar 2018, 240.
335. Clay, Lewis, and Severnini 2019, 47–8.

acceptance of scientific medicine, contagion theory, and immunization took generations, and for many it took centuries.

Some religions have still not found it possible to incorporate such ideas into their epistemology. Historically, many religions have insisted on explanations of disease in terms of supernatural influences—God's will, the wrath of the spirits, astrology, sin. As a consequence, many religions could not accept that epidemics might be controlled by sanitation, social distancing, immunization, and scientific medicine. Moreover, because such explanations contravened religious epistemology, many religions used their worldly power to muzzle contagion theorists, preach against scientific medicine, lobby against immunization, and organize resistance to social distancing. On balance, religious explanations of the invisible damaged contagion control much more than they benefited it.

What about emotional consolation in the face of suffering and disaster? In principle, the coping mechanisms supplied by religion could help with epidemic control by recommending cautious deathbed and burial practices, suspending religious assemblies and pilgrimages, and sustaining social solidarity to support poor citizens engaging in social distancing or immunization. In practice, some religions did behave in this way. Some religious personnel instructed the faithful to avoid plague deathbeds, bury epidemic victims separately, and even suspend religious gatherings. More importantly, many religions explicitly exhorted the faithful to help the unfortunate. This could include supporting the poor during home isolation, provisioning them in hospitals, and organizing immunization programmes both at home and abroad.

But the motivation to undertake these activities depended crucially on the religion's epistemological acceptance of at least certain aspects of contagion theory and immunization. Such acceptance, we saw, was slow and far from universal. Moreover, many religions regarded deathbed gatherings, burial within the religious community, religious assemblies, processions, and pilgrimages as being so crucial to religious consolation that their emotional benefits outweighed their epidemiological costs. On balance, religious activities to supply consolation to the faithful probably also exacerbated epidemics more than they helped control them.

What about the moral guidance which religion supplies? Ethical prescriptions are particularly important in epidemics, because contagion externalities imply difficult trade-offs between individual and societal interests. In principle, the moral guidance supplied by religion can motivate believers to undertake individually costly actions, such as complying with social distancing or getting immunized, in return for moral approval. It can also increase people's willingness to undertake philanthropic activities to help the poor do these contagion-controlling things. In practice, the ethical prescriptions issued by religions did sometimes move the faithful to obey public health measures, get immunized, and help the unfortunate.

But again this ran into the problem that the normative component of religion is viscerally interlinked with its epistemological system. Why would a religion exhort the faithful to support social distancing or immunization if it did not accept contagion theory or scientific medicine? Many religions viewed science as fundamentally opposed to religion and thus inherently immoral, so they used their spiritual authority to exhort the faithful to resist quarantine, home isolation, variolation, or vaccination. Furthermore, many religions regarded it as morally essential to engage in activities such as religious assemblies, processions, pilgrimages, missions, crusades, and religious wars, which served the moral (and worldly) purposes of the religion but also exacerbated contagion. On balance, therefore, the ethical guidance supplied by religion almost certainly exacerbated epidemics more than it benefited contagion control. This resulted both from the indissoluble link between religious epistemology and morality and from the fact that the main aim of religion was to pursue sacred and spiritual purposes which were orthogonal to the worldly welfare of humanity.

It is not at all surprising that religions should often fail to help people cooperate to limit epidemics. This was inevitable, given that the basic purpose of religion is to manage relationships between people and spiritual beings. A religion competes against other religions and against unbelief not mainly by offering worldly benefits, even to believers, let alone to society as a whole. Rather, it offers explanation, consolation, moral guidance, and a promise of rewards in return for belief. The religion amasses resources and power by offering services to the faithful and, if need be, to allied groups and institutions. Hence even the worldly activities of religions during epidemics are directed not at reducing contagion but rather at securing more adherents, resources, and power for that religion—even if purely to serve its spiritual ends.

This evidence casts a sobering light on the widely held view that scientific beliefs replaced supernatural ones between the Middle Ages and the present day, leading to the decline of epidemic morbidity and mortality. Scientific beliefs certainly emerged and spread during this period. But for many centuries—and in many societies into the present day—scientific beliefs coexisted with supernatural explanations and were often dominated by them, including among people who were literate and came from the middling strata of society. More important still, for science to be used to limit epidemic contagion, what mattered was not just scientific beliefs but the incentives created by the institutional framework of society. The successful application of scientific beliefs to anti-contagion measures depended not so much on the beliefs themselves but on their acceptance or rejection by powerful institutions—the religious ones discussed in this chapter and the medical ones discussed in the next.

6

Medical Guilds and Associations

> You stand indicted . . . for that you by inoculating, and causing to be inoculated, and by means of certain secret medicines and modes of practice, unknown to this College [of Physicians] and to all other practitioners, not having the fear of the College in your heart, do presume to preserve the lives of his Majesty's liege subjects.
>
> —SATIRICAL PAMPHLET ON THE ROYAL COLLEGE OF PHYSICIANS' ATTACKS ON THE COMMERCIAL VARIOLATOR DANIEL SUTTON, 1767[1]

> The American College of Surgeons (ACS) has published "COVID-19 and Surgery," a comprehensive evidence-based resource to guide surgeons through challenges of the ongoing pandemic. This organized response by a professional society has roots dating back to surgical guilds and efforts by surgeons to advance pragmatic solutions during the Black Death.
>
> —JOURNAL OF THE AMERICAN COLLEGE OF SURGEONS, 2020[2]

"Guild" is our word for an association of people practising the same occupation. But it is also an institution—the system of rules, customs, and practices by which such associations regulate their occupations. Occupational associations exist nowadays, but they trace their existence millennia back in history under a variety of terms—"guilds", "fellowships", "brotherhoods", "fraternities", "colleges", "faculties", "societies", "companies", "associations". This chapter uses "guild" as a shorthand term for all these occupational associations, while distinguishing among the different types that proliferated down the centuries.

1. Anon 1767, 2.
2. Hakes et al. 2020, 774.

A guild gives its members the exclusive right to practise a specific economic activity in a specific territory. The same is true of many modern occupational associations, including those in the medical professions. The guild or association (sometimes in cooperation with state, local community, or religion) controls entry to the occupation, barring it to non-members and deciding who can become members. Internally, it regulates supply, price, costs, business practices, training, quality, innovation, and technology. Guilds and occupational associations also often engage in politics, religion, culture, and sociability. These non-occupational activities still have occupational repercussions, since they motivate the association's members to follow internal rules, help the association monitor compliance, and legitimize the association in the eyes of state, local community, religion, and popular opinion.[3]

Social scientists view the guild or occupational association as a "social network"—a closely knit group whose members engage in repeated transactions across multiple spheres. As we saw in chapter 4, such networks are believed to generate a "social capital" of shared norms, information, sanctions, and collective action, facilitating cooperation that is impossible if everyone acts independently. Such social capital, it is argued, creates benefits not just for network members but for society at large.[4]

Guilds and occupational associations certainly justified their exclusive privileges on the grounds that they benefited society as a whole.[5] Medical associations were no exception, as in the case of the Paris physicians who in 1352 secured an exclusive charter from the Crown "for the public utility of our subjects",[6] the English physicians who in 1421 petitioned Parliament for exclusive privileges "to the worship of God and comyn profit",[7] or the Norwich doctors' guild which described itself in 1605 as "very mete and necessary for the better order to be had and maintained in the said mystery or science and the Common good of this commonwealth".[8] Modern medical associations describe themselves in similar ways. The American Medical Association declares that "throughout history, the AMA has always followed its mission: to promote the art and science of medicine and the betterment of public health."[9] The British Medical Association describes itself as "the trade union and professional

3. Ogilvie 2014b; Ogilvie 2019, 18–23; Ogilvie 2021.
4. Coleman 1988; R. Putnam, Leonardi, and Nanetti 1993.
5. Ogilvie 2019, 3–5.
6. Quoted in Vanneste 2010, 55.
7. Quoted in Vanneste 2010, 57.
8. Quoted in Pelling 2014, 7 (spelling modernized slightly).
9. American Medical Association, "About", accessed 10 June 2024, https://www.ama-assn.org/about.

body for doctors in the UK", adding that "we look after doctors so they can look after you".[10]

Social capital can be deployed in harmful ways, however, as we saw in chapter 4.[11] A closely knit network can use its norms, information, and sanctions to organize collective action that benefits its members at the expense of society. Occupational associations do what is best for their members. They limit entry, sometimes imposing conditions relating not just to skill but to wealth, gender, ethnicity, citizenship, religion, parentage, practitioner quotas, or collective approval. These entry barriers inflict harm on many capable but excluded applicants. They also harm society at large. The right to restrict entry of outsiders and limit competition among insiders enables the members of an occupational association to act as a cartel. This gives the association an incentive to limit supply, creating scarcity and increasing prices. Lack of competition reduces members' incentive to monitor training carefully, maintain quality honestly, and experiment with disruptive innovations, since consumers cannot go elsewhere. The occupational association is thus a Janus-faced institution that creates harm as well as benefits.[12]

Guilds and occupational associations have been central institutions in most societies since antiquity, and continue to regulate many professions to this day.[13] They were formed not just by craftsmen but also by many service professionals, including physicians, surgeons, and pharmacists.[14] This chapter focuses on such associations of medical practitioners, since they were important in historical epidemics and are still active in modern ones. This is not to say that modern professional associations are identical to pre-modern guilds. Indeed, the medieval and early modern guilds, brotherhoods, colleges, faculties, companies, and societies were not all identical to one another. But there are core activities that are shared by most occupational associations, historical and modern. These include regulating entry, supply, price, skill, quality, knowledge, and technology in that occupation. These core activities are central to how particular professions operate and hence to their wider societal impact.

Not all medical practitioners were members of professional associations. Medical services have historically been provided by a multiplicity of practitioners beyond the formally certified professionals in their guilds and associations. Medical historians often refer to this diverse array of practitioners

10. British Medical Association, "About Us", accessed 19 May 2024, https://www.bma.org .uk/about-us/about-the-bma/how-we-work/bma-mission.

11. Sobel 2002; Ogilvie 2005.

12. Ogilvie 2011; Ogilvie 2019.

13. On the long history of European guilds from the tenth to the nineteenth century: Ogilvie 2011, 1–2, 19–40; Ogilvie 2014b; Ogilvie 2019, 8–16. On modern occupational associations: Strauss 1963; T. Johnson 1972. On occupational licensing: Kleiner 2000.

14. Ogilvie 2019, 10–11; Pelling 2014; Deneweth and Wallis 2016; H. Murphy 2019.

as constituting the "medical marketplace".[15] But this should not be taken to mean that the market was the sole or even the dominant institution governing the work of non-guilded medical providers. As discussed in this book, other institutions, including state, community, religion, and family, also facilitated and constrained medical services both in normal times and during epidemics. During epidemics, as we shall see, other institutions came into greater prominence when many guilded doctors used their market power to withdraw their services in order to avoid risks of infection and death.

Nonetheless, formally licensed medical practitioners, and the associations that licensed them, are of particular interest in analysing how institutions cope with epidemics. This is partly because of power and partly because of economics. From a political point of view, formal medical associations enjoyed legal privileges, which gave them market power and enabled them to put pressure on competitors, patients, and even the authorities. From an economic point of view, medical activities are widely held to have special features—skilled training, quality requirements, and technical knowledge—which can give rise to market failures. Occupational associations are sometimes seen as the solution to those market failures.

Medical associations, as we shall see, did engage in activities that helped address epidemic contagion. They provided training and quality controls, requiring their members to provide good advice and expert assistance for individuals, communities, and governments. They monitored and certified medical knowledge, including ideas and innovations that might help control infectious disease. Medical guilds did this in medieval and early modern epidemics, and medical associations do it in modern ones, as we saw during Covid-19.

But as we shall see, medical associations also had a dark side. This arose from their legal privileges as cartels of privileged producers. The entry restrictions they imposed reduced the supply of medical expertise even in normal times, and exacerbated that scarcity during epidemics, when demand shot up. Limits on competition enabled members of medical associations to withdraw their services without losing their livelihoods to competitors, further aggravating scarcity of medical services. Medical guilds mandated training for the privileged candidates they agreed to admit, but denied it to many capable applicants who could not afford the entry fees or had the wrong gender, ethnicity, religion, citizenship, or parentage. During epidemics, this prevented women, Jews, immigrants, and other excluded groups from filling gaps in the ranks of licensed practitioners caused by mortality or market withdrawal.

Medical associations also faced incentives to regulate the occupation in the interests of their members rather than patients or society at large. They

15. See R. Porter (1985) for one of the first uses of the term; see Jenner and Wallis (2007) for a thoughtful survey.

monitored quality but also sheltered culpable members from condign punishment. They accredited medical training but also sold accreditation corruptly. They monitored the safety of medical technology but also blocked disruptive innovations that threatened their members' business models. They certified medical knowledge but also censored scientific concepts such as contagion theory, chemical medicine, variolation, vaccination, and other ideas they rejected as heterodox.

Modern medical associations are not immune to these problems. They do what is best for their members. To this end, they limit supply, increase prices, restrict access to training, and protect culpable members. Some comply with political pressure, pander to professional groupthink, or corruptly administer medical licensing, training, and pharmaceutical prescriptions. Where modern medical associations behave in those ways, they harm epidemic outcomes in ways similar to those of their pre-modern predecessors.

This is not to downplay the differences between modern medical associations and pre-modern medical guilds. For one thing, members of modern medical associations get access to training through more meritocratic avenues than masters of pre-modern medical guilds—even if access is still often needlessly rationed. Second, they learn scientific approaches to disease, which differ fundamentally from the untested orthodoxies espoused by members of pre-modern medical guilds. Finally, modern medical associations are embedded in a wider institutional framework in which they are monitored and curbed by governments, markets, universities, the media, the internet, and popular opinion. Modern medical associations are thus more meritocratic, scientific, and scrutinized than their pre-modern predecessors. Where these associations' activities are informed by expertise, science, and external scrutiny, their effects on medical outcomes are much less harmful, even when they still act as cartels.

Medical provision creates the potential for market failures during epidemics, as we shall see. But so do medical associations. Indeed, when medical associations abuse their cartel privileges they create a new market failure.

1. A Brief History of Medical Associations

Medical practitioners have formed professional associations from the Middle Ages to the modern day. They did so in many societies across the world, as we shall see. But the surviving records and the current state of scholarship mean that we know far more about such associations in Europe than in any other continent.

Table 6.1 shows data on the number of such organizations recorded in pre-modern Europe. They typically described themselves as "guilds", but physicians in particular increasingly formed associations called "societies", "companies", "colleges", or "faculties". These last two, despite the nomenclature, were not

TABLE 6.1. Medical Guilds in Europe, by Date of Foundation or First Record, 1252–c.1900

Occupation	1200–49	1250–99	1300–49	1350–99	1400–49	1450–99	1500–49	1550–99	1600–49	1650–99	1700–49	1750–99	1850–99	1900–49	Total
(Barber-)surgeons	1	4	4	8	6	7	8	6	4	4	2		2	1	57
(Barber-)surgeons and bathmasters				1	1	1	1								4
Apothecaries	1	2	1	2	1	2	3	4	7	2	2				27
Bathmasters		1		4	1	1		1	1	3		3			15
Physicians		1		4	2		5	5	4	9					30
Physicians and (barber-)surgeons		2	1			1		1							5
Physicians, (barber-)surgeons, and apothecaries		1							1						2
Grand total	2	11	6	19	11	12	17	17	17	18	4	3	2	1	140

Published sources: Belton 1882, 22–3; Brent 1860, 41; Brockliss 2010, 75; Brockliss and Jones 1997, 173–4, 176, 178–80, 182–3; Brohm 1999, 336; Broomhall 2004, 28; Bruijn 2009, 37; Bullough 1959, 448, 454; Cipolla 1976, 6; Corvi 1996, 167; De Meyer 1842, 12, 18–19; Depping 1837, 189; Duffin 2010, 138, table 6.2; Falck 1975, 279; Ferragud i Domingo 2002, 133–4; Fors 2016, 487–8; Garcia-Ballester, McVaugh, and Rubio-Vela 1989, 8–9, 39; Gelfand 1993, 1122, 1124–6; Gründer 1859, 221–2; Haugland 2015, 169; Heffner 1864, 23, 56, 85; Horn 1993, 256; Hybel and Poulsen 2007, 279; Kluge 2007, 133; Kuronen and Heikkinen 2019, 15; Lipson 1915, 303; Marzocchi 1967, 398; McVaugh 1993, 237; Mickwitz 1936, 45; Mitsel'Makheris 1960, title; Ouin-Lacroix 1850, 315; Pancier 1936, 410; Parrish 2015, 4; Pelling 2014, 19–21, 24, 27–9, 31–2, 35–40; Portas 2003, abstract; E. Porter 1998, 18–19, 73n172; Riera Blanco 1994, 214; Rodocanachi 1894, 2:387; Rosen 2008, 70; Sandvik and Straand 1996, abstract; Schütte 2017, 204–6, 208–9; Sherstneva 2011, abstract; P. Smith 2004, 196–7; Wallis 2002, 93, 100n46; Wischnitzer 1928, 440; Wikipedia contributors, "Bader," Wikipedia, die freie Enzyklopadie, accessed 17 May 2024, https://de.wikipedia.org/wiki/ Bader; Wikipedia contributors, "Histoire du métier d'apothicaire," Wikipédia, l'encyclopédie libre, accessed 17 May 2024, https://fr.wikipedia.org/wiki/Histoire_du_m%C3%A9tier _d%27apothicaire; "College of San Cosme and San Damián (Pamplona)—Colegio de San Cosme y San Damián (Pamplona)," Second Wiki, last updated 26 November 2020, https:// second.wiki/wiki/colegio_de_san_cosme_y_san_damic3aln_pamplona.

Archival sources: The archival sources used are those listed in the "Archival Sources" section of the bibliography.

Notes: Includes only those organizations explicitly described as "guilds", "crafts", "occupations", "fraternities", or "brotherhoods". Excludes the new types of corporative medical association which became especially common among physicians under the terms "collegia", "faculties", "societies", "companies", or "associations". These were sometimes elite subgroups inside the old guilds, but increasingly formed new bodies; see discussion in text.

so much educational organizations as guild-like bodies to regulate entry and competition, as we shall see.[16]

Medical guilds, as the table shows, first emerge into view in Europe around 1200. They were thus not an institutional response to the Black Death, since they predated it by a century and a half. By the time the great pandemic erupted in the late 1340s, at least 19 such associations had been recorded over the preceding 150 years in various parts of Europe. The Black Death did not bring medical associations into being, but it may have encouraged their proliferation, since another 19 appeared in the half-century after 1350. However, this may simply reflect the general proliferation of guilds in most urban occupations in the late medieval period.[17] Nor were medical guilds (or guilds in general) only a medieval phenomenon. New medical guilds continued to appear steadily across Europe from 1350 until around 1700. New mentions of medical guilds slowed down after 1700, but this does not mean that existing ones declined or disappeared. Instead, medical associations had been established in most European societies by 1700, though a trickle of new organizations continue to appear in the records, extending into the first half of the twentieth century.

As table 6.1 shows, guilds were formed in Europe by four main groups of specialized medical practitioner: physicians, surgeons (also called barber-surgeons or plain barbers), bathmasters, and apothecaries. Physicians were the richest and grandest of these groups. They claimed exclusive rights to practise internal medicine and based their claims to superiority on university training in knowledge handed down from antiquity.[18] Occasionally they formed a joint guild with other practitioners, but increasingly they began to set up separate associations called "colleges" or "faculties"; these, as we shall see, behaved in very similar ways to guilds. As early as 1271, for instance, the Paris "Faculty" of Physicians' petitioned the Crown for the right to reserve medicine to themselves, and exclude surgeons, apothecaries, herbalists, and other "operators" (among whom they singled out Jews):

> Since certain manual operators make or possess some confections but totally ignore their cause and reason, nay do not even know how to administer

16. The Latin term "collegium" was a widely used synonym for "guild", handed down from classical antiquity (Ogilvie 2011, 14, 20–1; Ogilvie 2019, 9). The best documented collegia of antiquity, those of Roman Egypt, excluded outsiders, arrogated to their members exclusive rights to sell in particular localities, fixed minimum prices, set maximum production quotas, and restricted competition, although such behaviour is not explicitly documented for medical guilds in Roman Egypt (see Alston 1998, 175; Cotter 1996, 83–4; Van Nijf 1997, 13–14).

17. See Ogilvie 2011, 1–2, 19–40; Ogilvie 2019, 8–16.

18. In northern and central Europe, physicians were university trained, while surgeons, apothecaries, and bathmasters were apprenticeship trained, so physicians regarded themselves as superior. In Italy, physicians were always university trained, surgeons could be either university or apprenticeship trained, and the barbers formed a distinct, apprenticeship-based occupation (Park 1985, 8, 58–62; Savoia 2019, 29).

them and the relation which medicines have to disease, especially in all particular respects, since those matters are reserved exclusively to the industry of the skilled physician, yet these manual artisans thrusting their sickle into alien crops participate, as we are assured by dependable testimony, in certain cases rashly and to public scandal, in this likewise incurring sentence of perjuries and excommunication; therefore we strictly prohibit that any male or female surgeon, apothecary or herbalist, by their oaths presume to exceed the limits or bounds of their craft secretly or publicly or in any way whatsoever, so that the surgeon engage only in manual practice and as pertains to it, the apothecary or herbalist only in mixing drugs which are to be administered only by masters in medicine or by their license.[19]

Claims to enjoy exclusive legal privileges over particular spheres of medical activity have remained characteristic of all medical associations from the medieval period into the present day.

The second group of professionalized medical practitioners consisted of the surgeons. Unlike their modern counterparts, who perform operations by cutting into patients' bodies, surgeons historically monopolized external medicine, as opposed to the internal medicine monopolized by the physicians. The term "surgeon" came from the fact that external medicine involved minor surgery, as well as treating wounds, broken and sprained limbs, contusions, ulcers, skin diseases, and hernias. Surgeons also often provided physical services that are no longer part of mainstream medicine, including bloodletting, shaving, hair-cutting, and other aspects of personal grooming and bodily care. So they were also often called "barber-surgeons" or even just "barbers".[20] In some European cities, there was a division between a "college" of surgeons (who were trained academically) and a "guild" of barbers or barber-surgeons (trained through apprenticeship). Both regulated entry and limited competition, but they also waged vicious demarcation battles. On the one hand, the academic surgeons were constantly pressing for restrictions on the barber-surgeons for encroaching on their monopoly by carrying out medical activities that went beyond their craft training. But on the other, the barbers constantly demanded that the surgeons not poach on barbers' shaving business, a conflict still being waged in Spanish towns as late as 1787.[21] In other cities, academically trained surgeons became members of the college of physicians, while apprenticeship-trained surgeons worked under license

---

19. From the translation in Thorndike 1975, 84.

20. Knox 1984, 100–4.

21. On surgeons' complaints against barber-surgeons, see Bullough (1958, 36–9) and Vanneste (2010, 64–7). On barber-surgeons' complaints against surgeons, see Mackay (2006, 101).

either from that college or from a barber-surgeons' guild.[22] Because surgeons and barber-surgeons provided general medical advice and treatment for such a wide variety of ailments, their associations clashed constantly with those of the physicians, bathmasters, and apothecaries.

The bathmasters enjoyed much lower status than the barber-surgeons but provided many of the same services, especially those involving bodily care. The main thing they did was to keep public baths, where they provided hot and cold bathing, which served for therapy as well as hygiene. But bathmasters also provided services such as hair-washing, hair-cutting, shaving, massaging, cupping, and other bodily advice and treatments.[23] Bathmasters occasionally formed joint organizations with the barbers and surgeons but usually set up their own separate guilds. This arose mainly from ferocious demarcation disputes, in which the barbers and surgeons increasingly sought to distinguish themselves from the lowly bathmasters and sometimes managed to eject them from their guilds altogether.[24]

Apothecaries made up a fourth professionalized medical occupation. In some cities, they formed joint associations with spicers, grocers, or herbalists, since their prescriptions largely overlapped with the latter's remedies. In other places, the apothecaries set up their own independent corporative organizations. Apothecaries specialized in pharmacological activities, compounding internal potions and external ointments. But they also often provided medical advice and treatment to their customers, encroaching on the spheres that physicians, surgeons, barbers, and bathmasters claimed to monopolize.[25] Conversely, the apothecaries objected to encroachments by these other medical practitioners, who often compounded potions and ointments for their patients. Pharmaceutical expertise gradually became more academic, leading apothecaries to claim (and sometimes actually obtain) greater education and prestige. In some places, this led them to form organizations—such as the Society of Apothecaries in Britain—which no longer called themselves guilds but still regulated entry and competition in similar ways.[26]

Overlapping spheres of activity created constant friction among the associations of physicians, surgeons, barbers, bathmasters, and apothecaries. Where state or Church supported physicians or where universities were powerful, the colleges and faculties of physicians more easily subjugated the

22. In most towns north of the Alps, all surgeons were members of the barber-surgeons' guild and none were admitted to the college of physicians, though occasionally a subgroup of elite surgeons formed their own college of surgeons. See the discussion in Savoia (2019, 29).

23. Knox 1984, 101–2; Savoia 2019, 43.

24. Savoia 2019, 44.

25. Bullough 1958, 39.

26. Berridge and Edwards 1981, 114.

other medical practitioners; where this framework was lacking, the guilds of surgeons, barbers, bathmasters, and apothecaries enjoyed greater autonomy.[27] But despite disputes over professional demarcations, all these associations agreed on one thing. This was to oppose the unlicensed medical practitioners who were not members of any guild, college, faculty, or association but nonetheless crept into every unsupervised crevice of the medical marketplace. The licensed members of medical associations vilified these outsiders as mere "empirics" precisely because they feared them as serious competitors. Women, Jews, and Muslims were barred from almost all European guilds, colleges, and universities, so they were not even allowed to undertake medical training, though some widows of guilded medical practitioners were allowed to practise under an inherited license from a deceased husband.[28] But even many Christian males could not get into medical associations. As we shall see, this was not necessarily because they lacked medical skill. It was often because they could not afford the high entry fees, could not get local citizenship rights, got their training in a different town, belonged to a religious minority, had the wrong parentage, were tainted by "dishonourable" ancestry, threatened to be too competitive, would excessively expand the number of local practitioners, or were unacceptable to existing guild members for other reasons.[29] Many of those discriminated against by the medical associations used their skills illegally, setting up as empirics, mountebanks, and charlatans and finding eager customers, especially among poorer social groups who could not afford the high fees of the guilded practitioners.

Medical guilds also existed outside Europe. But we know much less about them. The *Milinda pañha*, a Buddhist text whose earliest sections date from 100 BCE, records a guild-like association of *vaidya* (medical practitioners) in north-west India, specializing in snakebite treatment.[30] The Hindu text of the *Sukra niti sara*, variously dated between the fourth and the nineteenth century, lists 64 guilded occupations, among them wound surgery and compounding of medicines.[31] As early as 718, Japan had 75 medical guilds, which supplied the government with personnel every year, and an unspecified number providing specialists for the state pharmaceutical bureau.[32] In the late sixteenth or early

27. Bullough 1958, 39; Bullough 1970, 164.

28. On women in European guilds, see Ogilvie (2019, ch. 5); the treatment of female medical practitioners by guilds is discussed in detail later in the present chapter. On Jews and their exclusion from the practice of medicine in Europe from the late medieval period onwards, see Bullough (1970, 166).

29. For a detailed discussion of the many identity-related barriers to guild admission, see Ogilvie (2019, ch. 3 (on entry barriers in general) and ch. 5 (on barriers against women)).

30. Nalapat 2012, 94.

31. Nalapat 2012, 83.

32. R. Miller 1978, 157.

seventeenth century, a guilded Egyptian doctor wrote a commentary on a poem about guilds, illustrating his points with anecdotes about physicians, surgeons, barbers, and drugs, and lamenting that some guilds were not limiting entry strictly enough.[33] Seventeenth-century Ottoman cities had guilds of physicians, surgeons, oculists, and pharmacists,[34] and nineteenth-century Egyptian cities had guilds of barber-surgeons, which as late as the 1870s were among the most traditional in their mastership admission ceremonies.[35] So little is known about these Indian, Japanese, Ottoman, and Egyptian organizations, however, that our knowledge of what medical associations did, both during epidemics and in normal times, relies mainly on evidence from Europe.

In Europe, the medieval and early modern periods were the heyday of traditional guilds, including those of medical practitioners. Guild-like associations existed in Greek and Roman antiquity under the name of "collegia" and left tantalizing hints during the so-called Dark Ages (*c*.400–*c*.1000 CE). But occupational guilds appeared most noticeably in the European documentary sources, and probably in reality, between around 1000 and 1500. After around 1500, guild strength diverged across European societies. Guilds and other occupational associations started weakening in the Low Countries and England during the sixteenth and seventeenth centuries, even though they were not formally dissolved until the eighteenth or nineteenth. In France and its client states, by contrast, guilds were forcibly abolished in the aftermath of the 1789 French Revolution. But in many societies of Iberia, Scandinavia, and central Europe, guilds survived in full strength well into the nineteenth century, with the last guilds in Europe disappearing only in 1883.[36]

The so-called "colleges", "faculties", "societies", "companies", and "associations" of physicians, surgeons, and apothecaries coexisted with traditional "guilds" of medical practitioners but long outlived their abolition and in some cases survive to this day. Beginning in the later eighteenth century and accelerating throughout the nineteenth, new medical associations were established in many societies that no longer had guilds or (as with the USA, Canada, Australia, and New Zealand) had never had them. Because these new associations took new forms, they are not included in table 6.1. The two dominant forms taken by modern medical associations are, on the one hand, corporations governed by public law as separate legal entities and, on the other, independent professional associations or federations; but there are also a number of others.[37]

33. Baer 1964, 3, 38, 49.
34. Baer 1970, 29, 32.
35. Kuhnke 1990, 19; Baer 1964, 63.
36. Ogilvie 2014b; Ogilvie 2019, ch. 9; Ogilvie 2021.
37. Bautista and Lopez-Valcarcel 2019.

The scientific, economic, and political structure of the medical professions has changed in many ways since most of the traditional medical guilds gradually dissolved in the period between the French Revolution and the 1880s. But modern medical associations still engage in many of the same activities as the pre-modern guilds. They regulate entry, limit competition, certify training, investigate malpractice, advise governments, and make authoritative pronouncements on medical knowledge. The discussion that follows assesses how the features shared by pre-modern and modern medical associations have interacted with epidemics over the past seven centuries.

2. Corporatism and Quality

One obvious way medical associations contribute to controlling epidemics is by monitoring the quality of medical expertise supplied to individuals, communities, and governments. Modern medical associations regard this as a historical model for their role during modern epidemics. In 2020, as illustrated in the chapter epigraph, the *Journal of the American College of Surgeons* published the guidebook *COVID-19 and Surgery*, which it traced back to the "pragmatic solutions" proposed by medical guilds during the Black Death.[38]

The reason professional associations might be good institutions for ensuring quality arises from a standard source of market failure: asymmetric information between producers and consumers. Producers, with their expert training and superior information, know whether they are providing a good- or a bad-quality product—for example, good or bad medical advice. But consumers, whether individuals or governments, lack information and expertise to be sure that the medical advice on offer is good or bad. So they are only willing to pay a price for medical advice that is the average between the value they place on good advice and the value they place on bad advice. Given that uninformed consumers will pay only the average price, medical providers will sell only bad advice and will leave the market when they have good advice to sell, since they cannot get a good price for it. As providers of good medical advice leave the market, the average quality of medical advice declines, with the result that consumers' average willingness to pay decreases, leading to even more producers of good medical advice leaving the market, followed by the departure of even more consumers, in a vicious circle. As George Akerlof showed in his analysis of "The Market for Lemons", asymmetric information between producers and consumers about product quality can create an adverse selection problem which drives out good products, causing the market to shrink and, in the extreme case, collapse.[39] In the medical case, practitioners, patients, and

38. Hakes et al. 2020, 774.
39. Akerlof 1970.

society at large suffer when information asymmetries about quality choke off the production, consumption, and exchange of medical services. This potential market failure creates a demand for non-market institutions to correct the information asymmetry between producers and consumers.[40]

2.1. RUDE AND UNSKILFUL MEN

Medical associations took action to ensure quality, both in normal times and during epidemics. They did so in four main ways: licensing, training, quality monitoring, and controls on internal competition.

Licensing of practitioners was a first major way medical associations could ensure quality. This was one justification they themselves adduced to support their monopoly over practising the occupation. As early as 1260, for instance, a group of Paris surgeons demanded guild privileges from the king, because "there are some males and females who undertake surgeonry who are not deserving to do so and put people in peril of death".[41] In Florence during the 1412 plague epidemic, the guilded doctor Niccolo Falcucci warned:

> We should not call just any empiric or wisewoman a surgeon, even though he lances boils, stitches up wounds, and does similar work. We should rather bar them everywhere from this kind of operation and shun their treatments, since they practice wrongly. And if they perform successful cures, it is not thanks to their competence but to luck.[42]

Training requirements were a second way medical associations could guarantee quality. This, too, was one reason they gave for needing to have a collective monopoly over their profession.[43] In 1271, the Paris physicians justified their exclusive control over medical practice in and around the city on the grounds that:

> Some not yet advanced in the art of medicine and quite ignorant of the causes of medical procedure by shameful and brazen usurpation assume to themselves at Paris the office of practice, administering, without consulting skilled persons, to all comers and rashly any medicines whatever . . . which out of their own heads they wretchedly administer to simple men and so by their treatments, made not according to art but rather by chance and fortune, have criminally handed over many to the suffering of death, . . .

---

40. On institutional solutions to the market failures caused by information asymmetries between producers and consumers, see Ogilvie (2019, ch. 6, and 2021).

41. Depping 1837, 419 (quotation; my translation); Lespinasse and Bonnardo 1879, 208–9.

42. Quoted in Park 1985, 70.

43. Amundsen 1977, 406–7.

which also is no small peril to all residents of Paris and further tends to the disgrace and grave infamy of all skilled in medicine.[44]

In 1475, likewise, the Florentine doctors' guild distinguished those who had completed guild training from "those who begin to practice medicine on their own authority, based on simple and fallible experience".[45]

A third way medical associations could ensure quality was by directly inspecting their members' activities. In London between 1620 and 1640, for instance, the apothecaries' guild prosecuted members who broke its regulations, destroying bad drugs and making the offending master admit they were "false".[46] Offences were numerous: about one-third of the senior guild members were punished at one point or another, and half the offences the guild punished related to quality violations.[47] In seventeenth-century Bologna, the apothecaries' guild even inspected the medicines produced by non-guilded "charlatans", although partly to ensure the charlatans paid the guild an annual fee for permission to go on prescribing.[48]

The final way medical guilds could help maintain quality was by limiting internal competition. This, they believed, reduced the incentive for guild members to make false promises in order to entice away one another's patients. In Florence in 1699, for instance, the physician Anton Bertini lamented that the excessive growth in the number of doctors in the city had created such competition that "there are now doctors who degrade the practice through subservience, sycophancy, and buffoonery".[49] In Istanbul in the 1760s, likewise, the doctors' guild complained that admitting entrants from the lower social strata generated too much competition, giving doctors incentives to engage in malpractice and deception against "naive" patients.[50]

Epidemics intensified the salience of medical advice for everyone. Patients were desperate for help. Unlicensed healers flooded in, seeking to profit from the surge in demand. And medical associations intensified their claim to be the sole guardians of quality. In Moorish Granada shortly after the Black Death, the physician ash-Shaqūrī sternly warned laymen against getting plague treatment from anyone but a recognized doctor: "The men of religion and reason, who were appointed to deal with the affairs of the Muslims, should prevent the people of ignorance and adventure from harming the people by giving

---

44. Translated in Thorndike 1975, 83.
45. Quoted in Park 1985, 67.
46. Wallis 2002, 93, 100.
47. Wallis 2002, 89.
48. Gentilcore 1995, 300.
49. Quoted in Cipolla 1976, 86.
50. Boyar 2018, 235.

them medicines and bleeding them without consulting the doctors."[51] In Florence around the same time, the doctors' guild complained that high plague mortality had attracted "idiots and mechanicals" into medical practice, and warned darkly that "it frequently happens that patients treated by such pretenders are harmed and injured rather than helped and cured".[52] In 1586, the officers of the London Grocers' Company (the guild that included the apothecaries) wrote to the Royal College of Physicians expressing concern about non-guilded encroachments on the production and sale of "plague treacle", the popular term for theriac, an ancient wonder drug believed to be a universal preventive against all illnesses, including plague. The guild officers

> [had] of late perceavid in our Companie great abuse in the sale and utterance of certaine Triacle commonly sould by the name of Jeane Triacle [Genoa Treacle] which we find by search to be corrupt and unwholsome for the bodies of man or children being indeed made and compounded by certein rude and unskilful men.

The College of Physicians announced that Christian charity required it to lay down an official recipe for plague treacle and grant a monopoly over its production to a single specific apothecary.[53] In 1612, the College of Physicians excoriated so-called "Italian plague treacle" brewed from opium and vipers' flesh, insisting that "London treacle" was just as effective and need not contain vipers, although the college did not require any evidence that it actually prevented plague.[54] The smallpox epidemics of the eighteenth century also increased demand for medical advice and prophylactics, attracting nonguilded practitioners whose presence provoked counter-attacks by the medical associations. In 1767, as reflected in the chapter epigraph, the College of Physicians attacked the commercial variolator John Sutton for offering smallpox immunization, which they claimed did not comply with the careful analysis of patient "humours", ritual preparations, and dietary regimes prescribed by licensed physicians, as well as being unacceptably cheap and competitive.[55]

Quality control during epidemics casts light on how medical associations sought to remedy information asymmetries between practitioners and patients. But it also illuminates a deeper issue. The "quality" of medical advice is notoriously hard to measure, even in the era of modern scientific medicine. It was even more so in the pre-modern period, when medical doctrines commanded neither complete consensus among practitioners nor strong confidence on the

51. Quoted in Dols 1977, 108.
52. Quoted in Park 1985, 37.
53. Clark 1964, 1:159–60; Jacques 1992, ch. 3, p. 4 (quotation).
54. Slack 1985, 31.
55. Anon 1767, 3–4.

part of those who espoused them.[56] Before the discovery that microorganisms caused disease, which only gradually emerged after the 1870s and was still not universally accepted as late as 1900, many medical views on quality were completely bogus. Bloodletting, opium, vipers' flesh, "humours", and ritualistic variolation diets did not actually prevent infectious diseases. A pre-modern medical association might, if it had the right incentives, monitor the quality of a careful and clean act of bloodletting, the official recipe for plague treacle, meticulous compliance with a variolation diet, or the accurate mapping of a specific patient's symptoms onto the system of "humours" handed down from antiquity. But it could not monitor the quality of the underlying doctrines and practices. In that respect, modern medical associations differ from pre-modern guilds, in the sense that their quality regulations are much more often informed by experimental science than by groupthink. But to the extent that "quality" is defined in terms of "compliance with professional orthodoxy" rather than scientific understanding of disease, its maintenance by medical associations does not actually benefit patients, although it might profit the members of those associations.

2.2. TO PRESERVE THE WHOLE, AS WELL AS TO CURE THE INFECTED

Medical associations could also provide high-quality advice and expertise to improve public health measures during epidemics. From the Black Death onwards, governments approached medical associations for advice on diagnosing plague and limiting contagion. In 1348 when plague arrived in Paris, for instance, King Philip IV asked the "Faculty" of Physicians for assistance in formulating anti-contagion policies, commissioning it to write a treatise, which it quickly issued under the title *Compendium de epidimia*.[57] Two and a half centuries later, in the 1500 plague epidemic, the provost of Paris again asked for help, which the Faculty of Physicians agreed to provide on condition that the provost provide better policing of the unlicensed "empirics" who were encroaching on its monopoly over medical services.[58]

Among plague treatises, however, the *Compendium de epidimia* was exceptional in being authored by a medical association. Most plague treatises were not, as table 6.2 shows.[59] The Paris *Compendium* was the only one of

56. That is, medical knowledge was not "tight" in the terminology used by Mokyr (2002, 6, and 2005, 313).
57. Kibre 1953, 1–6; Henderson 1992, 146; Hong and Park 2017. For an English translation of this treatise, see "The Report of the Paris Medical Faculty, October 1348" on the website of Professor Martha Carlin at the University of Wisconsin-Milwaukee (https://sites.uwm.edu/carlin/the-report-of-the-paris-medical-faculty-october-1348/; and references cited therein).
58. Kibre 1953, 1.
59. A. Campbell 1931, 9–32.

TABLE 6.2. Plague Treatises Written between 1348 and 1350, by Place, Author Type, and Intended Audience

Year	Country	Author	Intended audience
1348	Lerida	Physician	The lords and council of Lerida
1348	Perugia	Physician and university lecturer in medicine (in consultation with college of masters)	The authorities of Perugia
1348	Naples	Individual member of university faculty of medicine	Not known; later communicated to university
1348	Paris	Entire faculty of medicine (collectively)	King of France
1348	Italy (?)	Unknown master	Not known
1348	Montpellier	Master of medicine and liberal arts	Not known
1349	Almeria (Muslim)	Poet, theologian, and physician	Not known
1349	Montpellier	Non-standard medical practitioner	Medical *studium* and whole university
1349	Not known	Not known	Not known
1349	Göttingen	Physician, bishop, "learned in astrology"	Not known
1349	Strasbourg	Five named "masters of medicine" and "servants of the city"	Not known; possibly the city of Strasbourg
*c.*1350	Carinthia	Not known	Not known
*c.*1348	Granada (Muslim)	Senior official; writer on history, literature, mysticism, philosophy, and medicine	Popular audience; possibly sultan
1348–50	Belluno	Physician	Not known
1349–50	Not known	Not known	Not known
1350	Liege, Montpellier	Practitioner of medicine and astrology	Not known

Source: A. Campbell 1931, 9–32.

the 16 Black Death treatises authored by a guild. A second treatise was written by an individual physician who was also a member of a medical faculty and acknowledged that he had consulted "the college of masters". The other 14 treatises—88 per cent of the total—were authored by a motley array of authors: two individual physicians; one individual member of a medical faculty; one "master" of an unknown discipline (possibly medicine); one master of medicine and liberal arts; one Muslim poet, theologian, and physician; one non-mainstream medical practitioner; one physician who was also a bishop and astrologer; a group of five named "masters of medicine and servants of the city of Strasbourg"; one Muslim vizier who was also a writer on history, literature, mysticism, philosophy, and medicine; one practitioner of medicine and astrology; and three miscellaneous authors of unknown background. Even though this was the medieval heyday of guilds, and medical practitioners had been forming associations for at least a century and a half, published medical advice during the Black Death came mainly from individuals whose occupational background extended far beyond medicine into theology, astrology, philosophy, poetry, and service to the state, as well as men of unknown expertise.

Medical publications on epidemic disease became more plentiful as the early modern period progressed. But even in the sixteenth century, as table 6.3 shows, non-medical writers played an important role, especially during serious epidemics. Across the sixteenth century as a whole, Italy saw an estimated 3.4 plague treatises published every year. This shot up to over 39 annually during the 1575–78 plague epidemics. Before and after that four-year period, nine out of ten treatises were authored by physicians. But during the four-year crisis, over half were authored by non-physicians. As in the Black Death, so too in sixteenth-century plagues, licensed physicians did not dominate the market for published expertise, at least while epidemics were in progress—unsurprisingly, since it would be another four centuries before medicine had any knowledge of what caused plague and thus what might prevent it.

What about direct advice? Did medical guilds step in to provide practical expertise during epidemics? Certainly not when the Black Death first erupted. In Perugia in the spring of 1348, "a number of doctors conducted anatomical dissections", but their guild was not involved.[60] In Florence in June 1348, the government requested post-mortems on plague victims "in order to know more clearly the illnesses of the bodies", but it asked specific named doctors, not the medical guild.[61]

Nor did governments approach individual doctors to help with anti-plague measures during the Black Death or for centuries thereafter. When Florence set up its plague commission in 1348, it did not include a single medical professional, let alone any delegate from the doctors' guild.[62] This was normal for Italian health boards for the next two centuries.[63] Milan took a novel step when in 1534 its duke reformed the Health Board to include a president and five officers, of whom two were elected by the College of Physicians.[64] In Venice, no doctor was appointed to the Health Board until 1541, and that first

60. Quoted in Fabretti 1850, 68.
61. Quoted in Park 1985, 97.
62. Park 1985, 97.
63. Park 1985, 98n42.
64. Cipolla 1976, 21–2.

TABLE 6.3. Physicians as Authors of Plague Treatises, Sixteenth-Century Italy

Society and period	No. of years	Unadjusted plague publications			Adjusted plague publications			Adjusted plague publications authored by physicians		
		No.	%	No. per annum	No.	%	No. per annum	No.	%	No. per annum
Italy 1500–74	75	134	35.9	1.8	119	35.3	1.6	106	89.1	1.4
Italy 1575–78	4	170	45.6	42.5	157	46.6	39.3	69	43.9	17.3
Italy 1578–99	22	69	18.5	3.1	61	18.1	2.8	56	91.8	2.5
Italy 1500–99	100	373	100.0	3.7	337	100.0	3.4	231	68.5	2.3

Source: Cohn 2010c, 25–6. Based on a keyword search of titles listed in "Edit 16", Italian census of all known sixteenth-century publications compiled from over 1,500 Italian libraries.
Notes: Unadjusted plague publications ($n = 373$) = printed publications dating from sixteenth century with "plague", "contagioso morbo", etc., in their titles. Cohn gives $n = 378$, but this table uses $n = 373$ since the sub-totals for periods add up to that number. Adjusted plague publications ($n = 337$) = unadjusted figure minus "texts where *peste* refers to heresy rather than disease, translations and republications of Arabic, Greek, and Roman classics, tracts written before the sixteenth century, works by foreign authors, and tracts on contagion which did not concern plague" (Cohn 2010c, 26).

medical member was chosen as an individual rather than a representative of his guild.[65] Even when doctors were members, health boards did not necessarily respect their advice. In 1598, for instance, the Cremona College of Physicians complained that "the two physicians appointed to the Board are not held in proper consideration by the other members. The latter either do not call the two physicians to the meetings, or, if the two physicians are present, do not want to take their votes into account."[66] In the medieval Low Countries, too, medical professionals played no recorded role in municipal or government health measures during the two centuries after the Black Death. In principle, doctors could have provided a conduit between academic medicine and public health measures, but in practice there is no evidence that they did so before 1500.[67]

It was the seventeenth century before medical associations, as opposed to individual doctors, were formally requested to contribute to public health policy.[68] The first signs of this new role for medical associations appears in

65. Palmer 1978, 74–5.
66. Quoted in Cipolla 1976, 22.
67. Dorst 2019, 32–3.
68. Cipolla 1976, 23.

the central and north Italian plague of 1630. In Florence that year, the Health Board asked the College of Physicians to produce a booklet explaining everything people needed to know about plague.[69] In Bologna, the health magistrate ordered all doctors to meet in their guild halls to discuss plague control and treatment.[70] In Milan, the Health Board summoned more than 50 physicians and surgeons to provide their professional opinions on how to deal with the epidemic.[71]

The same occurred in England, where in March 1631, the Royal Council wrote to the College of Physicians asking for "political" as well as "natural" recommendations on managing plague.[72] Throughout the 1630s, the Royal Council urged the College of Physicians to provide up-to-date medical input for the "Advice" section appended to royal plague orders. The college's advice was initially worthless, merely prescribing what we now know to be useless nostrums such as "plague treacle". But over time the guild improved its guidance, making recommendations on overcrowding, poverty, and quarantine, "to preserve the whole, as well as to cure the infected".[73]

Even in the seventeenth century, however, medical practitioners and their guilds were often strikingly inactive in public anti-contagion policies. In the Bristol epidemic of 1603, the city's Common Council set up a plague committee, but appointed only merchants and craftsmen, with not a single medical member.[74] In the 1636 epidemic in Newcastle-upon-Tyne, which had the highest mortality rate of any early modern English plague, the Barber-Surgeons' Company was all but silent. It held two meetings in May and June 1636, one of them "because of the sickness". Then the minutes broke off, the company did not meet again until December, and during the entire epidemic it provided no recorded advice to individuals, community, or local government.[75] Medical advice likewise played no official role in the severe plague of 1656 in Rome, where the government re-established its "Congregation of Health for the liberation of the city of Rome from contagion", but manned it entirely with cardinals, recruiting not a single medical professional.[76]

Practical assistance from guilds also arose quite late. In England it was not until 1583 that the King's Council asked the College of Surgeons to nominate

69. Cipolla 1976, 8.
70. Rose 2019, 162.
71. Cipolla 1976, 8.
72. Quoted in Slack 1985, 219.
73. Quoted in Slack 1985, 218.
74. Udale 2023, 125.
75. Quoted in Wrightson 2011, 47.
76. Quoted in Gentilcore 2012, 156.

physicians, apothecaries, and surgeons to help with plague quarantines.[77] Another generation passed before in 1609 the government again asked the college to recruit surgeons to supervise the plague measures in London.[78] In central and northern Italy it was not until the 1630–31 epidemic that governments commonly asked medical guilds to recruit experts to serve in pesthouses.[79] In Denmark it was not until the 1710–12 plague epidemic that the Crown formally required the Copenhagen barbers' guild to assist the new royal Health Commission.[80]

Nor were medical guilds always willing to help. In 1630, for instance, the grand duke of Tuscany called on the Florence College of Physicians to provide personnel to implement plague control measures. The college drew up a list of 80 physicians and 86 surgeons present in the grand duchy's 29 towns, but did not do anything to confirm that they would actually serve.[81] It recruited hardly any volunteers from among its own members, instead merely offering to examine any outside doctors the Health Board might propose.[82] The same was true in north-west Europe. In the London plague of 1609, the College of Surgeons nominated just six of its members to supervise anti-plague measures—a tiny contribution in a city of 200,000.[83] By the time of the Great Plague in 1665, London had grown to 400,000 inhabitants, but the College of Surgeons nominated just 10 or 11 volunteers to assist with plague containment.[84] In the Baltic plague of 1710–12, the Danish Crown asked the Copenhagen barbers' guild to assist the Health Commission but had to threaten to take away its guild privileges unless it obeyed.[85]

Medical associations did sometimes contribute expertise during epidemics, but played a surprisingly minor and grudging role. Small wonder that, as we saw in chapter 3, European governments increasingly sought to develop their own bureaucratic capacity to implement anti-contagion measures. Medical associations were hardly used to provide epidemic advice or services before around 1540, and their contribution to government epidemic measures seemingly peaked between 1630 and 1710. Even then, they and their members were hardly eager to serve during epidemics—for reasons we shall examine shortly.

77. Slack 1985, 214.
78. Slack 1985, 215.
79. Cipolla 1976, 8.
80. Frandsen 2010, 335.
81. Henderson 2019, 107–8.
82. Cipolla 1973, 25.
83. Slack 1985, 215. For London's population *c.*1600, see Finlay (1981, 51).
84. Slack 1985, 246. For London's population on the eve of the Great Plague, see Davies and Saunders (2004, 35).
85. Frandsen 2010, 335.

2.3. PROFESSIONAL PROBITY

Occupational associations also claimed to guarantee quality in a more wide-ranging way by fostering a corporate ethos of professional probity. In epidemics, such probity could be especially important, since accurate diagnoses, careful disease notification, and meticulous immunization records are essential for contagion control. In many cases, medical associations did declare that their members would diagnose, certify, and notify the true state of epidemic infections, thereby serving the common good and the public interest.[86]

But we should not romanticize the practical success of this high-minded rhetoric. For one thing, guilded doctors misdiagnosed disease to benefit themselves. In northern and central Italy, for instance, health boards required physicians to report all plague cases so that contacts could be traced and isolation orders issued. But guilded physicians often failed to comply when pressed by high-status patients.[87] In Pavia during the 1630 epidemic, for instance, guilded doctors deferred to powerful patrons by covering up cases of unquestionable plague infections.[88] In Milan in the 1629–32 plague, physicians of the college were widely known to conceal infections among their wealthy patients.[89] In Florence in 1630–31, guilded surgeons accepted bribes to misdiagnose plague patients, enabling them to avoid pesthouse incarceration, and guilded physicians issued false death certificates so that families could bury relatives normally instead of yielding them up to safe interment in a plague pit.[90] In October 1630, a Florence surgeon who venally declared a wealthy innkeeper's widow and her servant to be plague-free, a deliberately false certification that gave rise to multiple infections among their contacts throughout the city, was left unpunished by his guild and even kept his job with the Health Office.[91] In the 1656 Rome plague epidemic, which would go on to kill over 18 per cent of the city's population, Doctor Giovanni Pescia of the honourable College of Physicians courted popularity by proclaiming far and wide that the disease was "nothing like plague".[92] Another Rome physician, Girolamo Rota, conspired with two accomplices to sell plague suspects false health declarations, recording the payments in a register entitled "The Book of Plague Delights".[93] In the 1742–43 Messina plague epidemic, the guilded physicians placated the dominant classes by

---

86. Amundsen 1977, 406–8.
87. Cipolla 1976, 9.
88. Cipolla 1976, 35.
89. Cipolla 1976, 9.
90. Henderson 2019, 108, 116, 263.
91. Henderson 2019, 268–9.
92. Cipolla 1976, 9; Gentilcore 2012, 157–8 (plague mortality).
93. Gentilcore 2012, 161.

declaring the city to be uninfected to a very late date, facilitating a lethal epidemic that killed 71 per cent of inhabitants.[94] In Württemberg during nineteenth-century smallpox epidemics, the guilded surgeons stored vaccines poorly, administered them carelessly, documented them deficiently, forged vaccination certificates, and issued false exemptions, contributing to a dangerously low vaccination rate and a dangerously high infection rate.[95] In the 1894 Milwaukee smallpox epidemic, members of local and national medical associations were prosecuted for deliberately failing to report smallpox cases.[96] In the 1918 influenza epidemic in Saint Paul, Minnesota, it was widely recognized that "physicians are not reporting their cases, to prevent [patients'] homes from being quarantined."[97]

Licensed members of medical associations behave in the same way to this day. In 2023, for instance, a licensed Utah doctor was charged with accepting payments from parents in return for administering saline shots so that their children would falsely think they were being vaccinated against Covid-19, destroying over $28,000 worth of government-provided vaccines, and issuing nearly 2,000 fraudulent vaccination certificates.[98] These activities not only violated medical probity but also created moral hazard, giving thousands of minors the false belief that they were protected against Covid-19 and imposing wider contagion risks on their unsuspecting contacts.

It might be argued that there are always some medical practitioners who cover up infectious diseases for powerful patients, falsify health passes, and issue fraudulent vaccination certificates, and that their professional associations are uninvolved in their malfeasance. But that is the point. A major justification for the exclusive entitlements of medical associations, historical and modern, is that they certify their members' probity and penalize violations of professional standards. Indeed, the cartel privileges enjoyed by members of occupation associations are widely assumed to operate as a commitment device to induce members to refrain from misconduct for fear of losing their cartel profits. During epidemics, medical probity plays an unusually important role in disease notification and certification. If a society trusts that its medical associations are guardians of probity, it may believe itself to be insured against violations of epidemic regulations. The historical evidence—including from recent epidemics—suggests that such trust may not always be justified.

94. Restifo 1992, 1117 (physicians); Ciappara 2021, 74 (plague mortality).
95. Gross 1999, 263; Mühlhoff 2021, 20–1, 23–5; Mühlhoff 2022, 7.
96. Leavitt 1976, 563 incl. n33.
97. Ott et al. 2007, 806–8.
98. US Attorney's Office District of Utah 2023.

3. Monitoring Medical Knowledge

Medical associations also affected epidemic contagion by monitoring and certifying medical knowledge. Their justification for doing so was closely related both to quality certification and to defending their cartel privileges, as in 1271 when the Paris physicians threatened penalties against non-members (especially Jews), "since there are some who simultaneously seek knowledge and the mode of knowing, which is very inconvenient, since their error, not small even in the beginning, is very great in the end".[99] In principle, a medical association had clear advantages in certifying existing knowledge and evaluating new ideas. Its members were trained experts, the association could reap economies of scale and scope in compiling and diffusing knowledge, and it based its cartel privileges partly on claiming to be the sole font of medical expertise, so it enjoyed general trust. A medical association could use these advantages to ensure that the best available advice was supplied to patients and society.

But a medical association could also have harmful effects on knowledge. For one thing, compiling, inventing, and disseminating knowledge is costly: why would a cartelistic professional association incur these costs when it would enjoy its privileges even if it did not do so? For another, any closed network with shared aims has a strong incentive to maintain internal harmony, which can result in groupthink—reaching a consensus without reasoning critically, evaluating alternatives, or considering disruptive views. Moreover, demarcation conflicts between different medical associations—physicians, surgeons, pharmacists—harmed exchange between adjacent bodies of knowledge, confrontation of theory with empirical practice, experimentation with ideas and techniques from other specialties, and invention of practices that combined ideas and techniques from different medical fields.[100] Finally, any professional association does what is best for its members, giving it an incentive to reject new ideas that threaten their business model.

3.1. NEITHER DOCTOR NOR MEDICINE WAS OF ANY USE

For at least five centuries after the Black Death, medical practice was professionalized but ignorant. Most medical advice consisted of lifestyle advice and straightforward remedies for simple complaints. As far as epidemic disease was concerned, such advice was largely worthless. Medical practitioners did not know that microbes caused infection. They and their associations had no

---

99. Translation in Thorndike 1975, 84–5.

100. On inter-guild demarcations as a barrier to innovation, see Ogilvie (2019, 497–9); on their effect on medical knowledge in particular, see Bullough (1958, 39–40).

idea what caused or prevented disease, so they could not genuinely certify knowledge or assess information about how to control its spread.

Plague, for instance, was inexplicable to the art of medicine until 1894. When the Black Death arrived in Constantinople, the Byzantine emperor John VI Cantacuzenos described bubonic plague as "incurable" and added that "no physician's art was sufficient".[101] The Florence humanist Giovanni Boccaccio observed the same, writing that when plague came, the physicians "could form no just idea of the cause", so they could not recommend "a true method of cure".[102] A generation later, Marchionne di Coppo Stefani described how during the Black Death:

> Neither doctor nor medicine was of any use, either because the diseases were not yet known or because doctors had never studied them, and there did not appear to be any remedy. . . . [T]hey felt [the patient's] pulse with their faces turned away and inspected his urine from afar, holding strong-smelling substances to their noses.[103]

Ignorance did not deter licensed medical practitioners from proclaiming that plague was caused by the stars, the wind, bad smells, individual sins, or scapegoats such as Jews, beggars, women, or gypsies. Nor did the eminent medical authorities hold back from disseminating advice, as noted by the chronicler Matteo Villani: "All over the world, doctors found no remedy or true cure for this pestilential disease, whether in philosophy, medical theory, or astrology. Some, driven by greed, went about seeing patients and prescribing treatment, but the failure of such measures showed their art to be feigned and not true."[104] Physicians' explanations of the plague in terms of celestial bodies attracted sardonic comment, as in the 1360s when Petrarch drily observed:

> [The doctors] maintain that Mars and Saturn are coming together somewhere among the stars and that conjunction—to use their word—after the year's end [1361] will last for a full two years. Quite astonishing that from the beginning of things stars have never been in these locations as long as they have travelled their courses throughout the heavens! . . . We do not know what is happening in the heavens, but impudently and rashly they profess to know. . . . For they are going to say this and any nonsense at all rather than confess their own ignorance. Theirs is not only ignorance but blindness and total madness, which many times in the past was evident to everyone, but never more clearly than during this present plague.[105]

101. Quoted in Vanneste 2010, 36.
102. Quoted in Gasquet 1908, 55–6.
103. Quoted in Park 1985, 35.
104. Quoted in Park 1985, 4.
105. Quoted in Carmichael 2008, 23–4.

Honest medical practitioners, by contrast, admitted that they possessed no useful knowledge about how to prevent plague. The surgeon Guy de Chauliac, who survived the Black Death in Avignon, openly acknowledged that "in preserving [from plague] there was no better than, before the infection, to flee the country".[106] In the Egyptian epidemics of 1476 and 1491, the distinguished physician Sihāb al-Manṣūrī declared, "For every disease there is medicine to cure it except for madness, plague and old age."[107] In the 1576 Neapolitan plague, the great physician Giovan Filipo Ingrassia wrote that the only useful plague prophylactics were "pills made of three ingredients called *cito, longe* and *tarde* [swiftly, far, and tardily], namely run swiftly, go far, and return tardily".[108] In France in 1620, Jean de Lampérière wrote a plague treatise stating that "the same difficulty to which mathematicians are reduced for the squaring of the circle and with which chemists find themselves obstructed in their quest for transmuted gold, the same difficulty faces doctors who try to find the remedy for the plague".[109] The Jewish physician Abraham Catalano spent the entire 1630 plague epidemic in the Padua ghetto watching as neighbours and family members died of the disease and wrote starkly that all physicians' remedies were useless:

> If you are told by a physician that "no disease will touch your tent" if you take the drugs Elettuario, Conservi and Preservativi, do not believe him, for they are useless and offer no protection. I have seen many whose habit was to take drugs for their entire lives, yet they died in agony, while many others who never took a single drug ever fell ill, and if they did become sick they quickly recovered. The plague does not distinguish between those who take drugs and those who do not.[110]

During the 1710–12 Baltic epidemic, when the Danish Crown asked the Copenhagen doctors' guild to explain what caused and transmitted plague, the guild officially declared that "no human mind can ascertain what its proper nature and qualities consist of".[111]

A group portrait of the Amsterdam surgeons' guild, shown in figure 6.1, offers a chilling illustration of the impotence of the medical profession in the face of plague. The guild commissioned Aert Pietersz to paint the portrait in 1601 but, as the guild memorandum book recorded, "A great plague arose within this city, because of which this work stood still for more than a year."

106. Quoted in Vanneste 2010, 39.
107. Quoted in Dols 1977, 109.
108. Quoted in Cipolla 1973, 23.
109. Quoted in Brockliss and Jones 1997, 82.
110. Quoted in Jeremy Brown 2022, 88.
111. Translated in Bencard 2021, 2.

FIGURE 6.1. Group portrait of the Amsterdam Surgeons' Guild (*The Anatomy Lesson of Dr. Sebastiaen Egbertsz de Vrij* by Aert Pietersz), 1601–3. This group portrait was commissioned by the Amsterdam surgeons' guild and displayed in their headquarters until the guild was abolished in 1798. The renowned Amsterdam surgeon and praelector of the guild, Doctor Sebastiaen Egbertsz de Vrij, stands in the centre behind the body that is being dissected, holding a pair of scissors in his right hand. On the far right, a man holds a piece of paper on which is written the names of all the master surgeons of the guild in the year 1603. The guild masters look neither at the anatomist nor at the body, but rather in the direction of the spectator. The composition celebrates not just the skill of the anatomist but the corporate identity of the Amsterdam Surgeons' Guild. *Source*: Wikimedia Commons.

By the time the picture was completed in 1603, 5 of the 28 attending surgeons from 1601 had died of plague, and one appeared in the portrait only because the painter visited him on his deathbed to capture his likeness.[112] Eighteen years later, the eminent guild member carrying out the dissection at the centre of the painting himself also died in a plague epidemic.[113]

As smallpox overtook plague in Europe from the seventeenth century onwards, licensed medical practitioners revealed themselves to be ignorant about how to diagnose, prevent, or treat it. Gideon Harvey, a famous member of the Royal College of Physicians, declared openly in 1696:

> Motherly Women, Nurses and Midwives, by their petty inspection of Diseases of their Family, and of those whom they neighbourly go to visit, do attain to so distinguishing a knowledge in the Measles, Small-pox, Red-gum, Rash, Blasts, spotted, viz. Red and Purpre Fevers, that they very frequently

---

112. "De anatomische les van Dr. Sebastiaan Egbertsz", Amsterdam X Museum, accessed 19 May 2024, http://am.adlibhosting.com/amonline/Details/museum/38538 (quotation; my translation); Baljet 2000, 5–6.

113. Baljet 2000, 4.

hitting right, doth embolden them in point of judgment, to demand a priority of a whole herd of Doctors.[114]

In 1721, Lady Mary Wortley Montagu lamented the "Ignorance of Physicians" when she envisaged introducing them to the idea of variolation.[115] This was not unjust. Many eminent members of European medical associations vehemently opposed variolation throughout the eighteenth century, as we shall see, and continued to make authoritative declarations reflecting their ignorance of smallpox. To give just one example among many, Friedrich Casimir Medicus, Palatine court physician, Enlightenment scholar, president of the Palatine Physical-Economic Society, and distinguished member of the Mannheim Academy of Sciences, published a book in 1763 declaring that smallpox was an unspecific "inflammatory fever", that it was dangerous only because of popular "fear", and that it could be eradicated by treating people with "a rational cure" involving cold water.[116]

Medical ignorance extended to cholera when it reached Europe and the Middle East from India after 1816. In 1833, the German physician and medical writer Doctor Böhr lamented openly that "we know of absolutely no other disease in which the utter powerlessness of the healing art is so displayed as in cholera".[117] In 1852, the Copenhagen medical establishment expressed uncertainty about whether cholera was caused by bad smells or poor diet, though it was quite certain (wrongly, as it proved) that contagion played no role.[118] During the 1853 English cholera epidemic, the editor of the *Lancet* asked, "What is cholera? Is it a fungus, an insect, a miasma, an electrical disturbance, a deficiency of ozone, a morbid off-scouring of the intestinal canal? We know nothing; we are at sea in a whirlpool of conjecture."[119] In the 1858 Japanese cholera epidemic, the chronicler Kinton Dōjin made the matter-of-fact observation that people adopted magical and religious remedies because "even the wisdom of famous doctors cannot explain the cause of the disease".[120] When cholera broke out at Mecca in 1865, killed one in three pilgrims, and then spread across the world causing 90,000 deaths in Russia, 50,000 in North America, and 165,000 in the Austro-Hungarian Empire, the medical profession was still at a loss, ascribing the epidemic variously to noxious vapours, atmospheric electricity, monsoon winds, and (accurately but unsupportedly)

114. Harvey 1696, 1–2.
115. Quoted in Murdoch 2015, 515.
116. Maehle 1995, 211 (quotations); Popplow 2012.
117. Böhr 1833, 178.
118. Bencard 2021, 4–5.
119. Wakley 1853, 393.
120. Quoted in Gramlich-Oka 2009, 51.

unobservable organisms.[121] The medical profession remained so divided on the cause and prevention of cholera, and even whether it was contagious, that in 1873 the Berlin authorities declared outright that the state always had to "take certain measures and secure their implementation . . . irrespective of whether they correspond to one theory of cholera or another".[122] As we saw in chapter 3, it was not until 1884 that the German physician and microbiologist Robert Koch discovered that cholera was caused by what he called "the comma bacillus", and even then his new knowledge encountered many professional obstacles before it was accepted and acted upon.[123]

With influenza, likewise, licensed doctors and their professional associations were at a loss to understand the cause or prevention of the disease. Their knowledge had hardly advanced beyond the remedies recommended by Giovan Filipo Ingrassia to the ruler of Sicily after the 1558 influenza epidemic:

> prayers for forgiveness of sins; purification of the air by burning fires; removal of stagnant water in general; removal of stagnant water that was green and smelly at the drapery ("Panneria") under the church of Santo Spirito; covering the stream of the tanners; cleaning water troughs of waste usually filled with dead dogs, cleaning public roads, purging stench with perfumes and big fires, covering wells, canals and aqueducts to stop fetid vapours polluting the air, and provisioning the population with good bread and meat.[124]

More than three and a half centuries later, as American doctors were beginning to realize the magnitude and severity of the Spanish influenza in October 1918, the *Journal of the American Medical Association* acknowledged that "the 'influence' in influenza is still shrouded in mystery".[125] In December 1918, a published report of the preceding week's meeting of the American Public Health Association described how, "in discussing the causes of influenza, the doctors one and all have, with becoming humility, recognized and freely expressed the fact that the cause is unknown".[126] In the aftermath of the pandemic in 1919, a former president of the American Medical Association declared frankly:

> So far as the prevention of the respiratory diseases is concerned, we do not know anything more than our ancestors knew a hundred years ago, and we may as well admit it. I say that in the face of the greatest pestilence that

121. M. Harrison 2012, 139–40, 148.
122. Quoted in R. Evans 1992, 169.
123. Lacey 1995, 1412; M. Harrison 2012, 172.
124. Cohn 2010c, 242.
125. Quoted in Crosby 2003, 271.
126. Price 1918, 367.

has ever struck our country we are just as ignorant as the Florentines were with the plague described in history.[127]

Virology was then in its infancy, the bacterium-based vaccines touted by licensed doctors during the influenza pandemic were useless, and it was not until the 1930s that vaccines against viral diseases began to be developed.[128]

The knowledge that medical associations defended, therefore, was not characterized by consensus, and when it was characterized by confidence, that confidence was gravely misplaced. During all major epidemics from the Black Death to the Spanish flu, medical practitioners and their professional associations did not understand what caused the infection and thus what might prevent or control it. In many cases, as we have seen, they were admirably open about their ignorance. But in many others they made authoritative pronouncements.

3.2. THE OPINIONS OF MANY OF THE FIRST MEN

Medical associations did not seek to deny the existence of a terrible epidemic during the Black Death, since the appalling scale of disease and death was undeniable. Although doctors did not know how to diagnose it, they did openly declare that it was serious, as described by the contemporary chronicler Jean de Venette: "This sickness or pestilence was called an epidemic by the doctors. Nothing like the great numbers who died in the years 1348 and 1349 has been heard of or seen or read of in times past."[129]

During the recurrent plague epidemics that followed the Black Death, however, medical associations often made official pronouncements on whether a particular disease was plague. Surprisingly often, these were wrong—whether because ignorance caused genuine misdiagnosis or because political and economic pressures swayed medical associations to downplay the risk. When plague appeared in Padua in early 1576, for instance, the Public Health Department asked the College of Physicians if the disease was plague. The college issued a vehement denial. As a consequence, the city took no public health measures, allowing the epidemic to grow so fast that it killed 10,000 of Padua's 36,000 inhabitants by the summer of 1577.[130] In October 1629 as the plague approached Milan, the College of Physicians engaged in learned debate about whether it was truly plague and, according to one health officer, "caring little for the public health, kept saying there was no question of plague".

127. Anon. 1918, 2100.
128. Schwartz 2018, 1455–7.
129. Quoted in Vanneste 2010, 36.
130. Whitteridge 1977, 72.

This false announcement by the city's medical association was soon followed by a calamitous epidemic that killed 46 per cent of the population over the ensuing three years.[131] In Florence in August 1630, the grand duke asked the College of Physicians to assess "the true essence and quality of this sickness". The college declared that although it was "a contagious pestilential disease, it was not plague", a spectacularly incorrect diagnosis that allowed the disease to spread until it killed 14 per cent of the city's population.[132]

It might be thought that these misleading pronouncements by medical associations during sixteenth- and seventeenth-century plague epidemics reflected the primitive state of medical science in that early era. But medical associations continued to issue similarly authoritative but inaccurate public declarations throughout the eighteenth and nineteenth centuries. In Philadelphia in 1797, 13 members of the Academy of Medicine issued a signed declaration claiming that yellow fever was not contagious, and one of them went on to denounce quarantine as a "medieval institution". In fact, yellow fever was indirectly contagious, in being transmitted from one human sufferer to another via an insect vector (mosquitoes); so quarantine could actually help slow its transmission.[133] In the 1848 cholera epidemic, the Hamburg College of Medicine denounced "the release of public notices about cholera as alarmist and advis[ed] people that remaining calm was the best prophylactic against infection".[134] In Copenhagen in 1852, as we have seen, the medical establishment declared that cholera was not contagious, dismantling the 20-year-old cholera quarantine system. Despite the ensuing cholera epidemic of 1853, the Copenhagen medical officer and distinguished member of the Danish College of Health, Børge Anton Hoppe, continued to declare authoritatively that cholera contagion was impossible.[135]

That same year in England, the Royal College of Physicians was asked to provide "some plain directions—to offer to the public some instructions during the prevalence of cholera".[136] In a circular printed in the *Lancet*, the college officially declared "that the fear of infection may be practically disregarded".[137] One practising physician wrote a letter to the *Lancet* adducing evidence to the contrary.[138] The response was a long tirade from a member of the college, expressing "astonishment at the reflection cast on the Cholera Committee of the Royal College of Physicians", referring to "the opinions of many of the first

131. Cipolla 1976, 9 (quotation); Henderson 2019, 24.
132. Henderson 2019, 52 (quotation); Percoco 2013, 137.
133. Quoted in M. Harrison 2012, 56.
134. R. Evans 1992, 168.
135. Bencard 2021, 375–7.
136. Parkin 1853, 422.
137. E. Wilson 1853, 422.
138. E. Wilson 1853, 422.

men whose great experience, skill, and talent are well known in every quarter of the civilised world", and appealing to the authority of the physicians and surgeons of the Hôtel-Dieu in Paris, who in 1832 "asserted that cholera was not contagious, and signed a resolution to that effect".[139] Given that the eminent college member himself admitted "that the question at issue is far from being satisfactorily decided", one might have expected him—and the College of Physicians—to have refrained from making confident public pronouncements and deploying collegiate authority to stifle medical debate.[140]

Medical associations issued false public declarations outside Europe as well. In 1846, for instance, the French Academy of Medicine declared that its investigations in Egypt had demonstrated that bubonic plague was not contagious. This declaration was made at the exact time when the scientific basis for this conclusion was being falsified by empirical findings in Egypt, the Himalayas, western Arabia, the Kurdish highlands, and the Chinese hinterland of Yunnan.[141] But the view was widely accepted in Egypt, including by French-influenced government medical advisors, greatly hindering plague prevention. In 1889, a committee of the British Royal College of Physicians, probably yielding to political pressure from West Indies governors and the Colonial Office, endorsed the erroneous view that quarantine would be useless against yellow fever because its incubation period was uncertain.[142]

In the United States, associations of medical practitioners mounted concerted resistance against attempts to set up a national quarantine system to overcome the cross-border externalities created by differences in quarantine regulations among American states. In 1870 Congress formally established a bureau within the Treasury called the Marine Hospital Service (MHS), later to become the Public Health Service (1912), then to evolve into the Health Services Administration (1973), and finally to merge into the present-day Bureau of Primary Health Care within the Health Resources and Services Administration (1981). The federal government gave the MHS broad powers to advise state-level public health administration during epidemics, resolve inter-state quarantine conflicts, and regulate inter-state disease transmission. But an 1898 bill to grant the MHS additional powers was opposed by the New York Academy of Medicine and the American Public Health Association, which believed it encroached on the autonomy of medical professionals. The Florida physician and health officer Joseph Porter inveighed openly against

139. Gooday 1853, 513.
140. Gooday 1853, 513.
141. Kuhnke 1990, 71.
142. M. Harrison 2012, 104.

the MHS as an "army of [federal] sanitarians that, like the locusts in the field, eat up our substance and usurp our liberties".[143]

Even after the existence of microbial infection was widely accepted by scientists, medical associations continued to make authoritative declarations advising the public that there was little risk of contagion from diseases such as influenza, even though these were already displaying their infectiousness. During the Russian flu of 1889–90, which attacked 60 per cent of the American population in urban areas, the *Medical Record* declared that "the disease is undoubtedly due to some microorganism which floats in the air, and which infects the human system, but is generally killed in so doing, for influenza is but slightly if at all contagious".[144] During the influenza pandemic in September 1918, the *Journal of the American Medical Association* declared that the Spanish influenza "should not cause any greater importance to be attached to it, nor arouse any greater fear than would influenza without the new name". The *JAMA* article added, presumably in response to government pressure, that the disease "has already practically disappeared from the Allied troops".[145]

The corporate ignorance of medical associations was much more harmful than the individual ignorance of particular doctors or the untrained ignorance of patients, since it came with the authoritative imprimatur of collective professional expertise. False declarations by medical associations observably delayed or dismantled measures such as quarantine and social distancing. They swayed practising doctors to give patients poor advice—for instance, not to observe "seclusion" when they were suffering from influenza. Ignorant announcements by medical associations also created moral hazard, creating a false sense of security which led patients to take fewer precautions than they would if they had not been authoritatively assured that there was no epidemic or that it was not transmitted in particular ways.

3.3. CONTAGION AND GROUPTHINK

Why did medical associations make false declarations about epidemics? Sometimes it was medical ignorance or—to put it more politely—weak confidence and low consensus in medical knowledge.[146] Before 1894, there was room for legitimate medical disagreement about the contagiousness of plague because no one yet understood its idiosyncratic transmission via rats and rat fleas. Yellow fever was a puzzle until 1881, when it was discovered that it was transmitted

---

143. Quoted in M. Harrison 2012, 127.

144. Tomes 2010, 50 (quotation); Berche 2022 (morbidity).

145. Quoted in Crosby 2003, 73.

146. Confidence and consensus are the defining characteristics of "tight" knowledge; on this, see Mokyr (2002, 6) and Mokyr (2005, 313).

between humans via particular species of mosquito, though it took until 1927 to identify the virus responsible. Cholera, too, remained mysterious even after Snow's experiment with water supplies in 1854 and Koch's identification of the bacillus 30 years later, because the disease seldom passed through person-to-person contact but rather through water contaminated with faecal matter, which could be carried long distances without visible vectors. Even smallpox, typhus, and influenza were susceptible to having their contagiousness questioned because microbes were hard to see or explain.

Low confidence and low consensus gave rise to legitimate disagreements. This meant that medical practitioners were more easily swayed to shade their professional speculations in the direction of policies they held for non-scientific reasons. Nineteenth-century British publications on cholera, for instance, were significantly more likely to reject the idea that the disease was contagious if their authors had ties to commerce, which would be harmed by quarantines and other social distancing measures. As scientific consensus about the microbial causes of cholera tightened after around 1850, the association between anti-contagionism and commercial interests became statistically insignificant.[147] The same situation was replicated at the beginning of the Covid-19 pandemic in 2020, when scientific consensus about the new disease was still weak. Too little medical consensus was—and still is—one source of false declarations by medical associations and their members.

But too much consensus can also be a problem. Groupthink—when a group of individuals reaches a consensus without critical reasoning or evaluation of alternatives because of a desire for harmony with other members—is a notorious Achilles heel of social networks, including professional associations.[148] Until the mid- to late nineteenth century, most medical associations in Europe clung to "miasmatic" and "humoral" theories of disease handed down from antiquity. These held that diseases were transmitted by miasmas, or bad airs, attached to particular locations, which interacted with the balance of humours inside each patient. This medical orthodoxy rejected contagion theories, according to which diseases were transmitted by infected humans, animals, or objects with which sufferers had been in contact. In the best case, opposition to contagion theory might merely cause a medical association to be lukewarm in supporting social and physical distancing. But medical associations often went further, publicly denouncing contagionist ideas, vilifying those who espoused them, and dismantling or defunding quarantines, home isolation, inspections, contact tracing, and curfews.

Miasmatic and contagionist recommendations sometimes overlapped. Improving slum housing, for instance, was supported by miasmatists as a good way of ridding neighbourhoods of harmful miasmas and by contagionists as a

---

147. See the discussion in Petroff (2023, 5–35).
148. Burt 2001, 62; Ogilvie 2011, 362–3.

good way of enhancing physical and social distancing. But epidemics gave rise to many situations in which the two explanatory approaches conflicted, and scarce resources could be allocated to only one set of recommendations. Miasmatic theory typically hindered the adoption of social distancing measures and some-times resulted in their complete dismantling. In the 1630–31 plague epidemic in central and northern Italy, for instance, distinguished members of physicians' guilds publicly declared that contagionism contravened expert medical theory, so that unpopular social distancing measures should be abandoned.[149] In the 1782 influenza epidemic, the London College of Physicians received 17 replies to its appeal for views on the transmission of influenza, of which 6 argued for contagion, 5 argued for "atmospheric" (i.e. miasmatic) explanations, and 6 refused to commit themselves. So the college issued a non-committal report which failed to recommend any anti-contagion measures, even the mild ones such as the "seclusion" recommended by contagionist physicians.[150]

The damage to public health that could result from the miasmatic ortho-doxy was pointed out by the physician and medical writer John Haygarth, who in the later eighteenth century campaigned for variolation and social distanc-ing to eradicate smallpox in Chester, built isolation wards as physician to the Chester Infirmary, firmly supported smallpox vaccination when Jenner discov-ered it, and in retirement in Bath set up the first vaccination clinic in England. Haygarth was horrified when British physicians began around 1800 to revert to miasmatic views and to ascribe epidemics to a "morbid constitution of the atmosphere, independent of contagion". Despite having retired, he decided to bring out his unpublished treatise on influenza, expressing open concern that a return to the miasmatic view would discourage epidemic prevention, since "the morbid constitution of the atmosphere cannot possibly be corrected or controuled by man".[151]

Haygarth was right to be worried. Contagionism had gained ground among British medical practitioners during the eighteenth century, but by 1800 mias-matic views were indeed making a comeback.[152] From around 1820 until the 1850s or even later, miasmatic views were widely adopted by physicians and increasingly informed the official pronouncements of medical associations.[153] In 1846, the French government asked the national Academy of Medicine to advise on whether plague quarantines against Egypt, Syria, and Turkey were still needed, whereupon the academy issued a miasmatic report declaring plague to be non-contagious.[154] In 1848, the London College of Physicians

149. Cipolla 1976, 9.
150. Delacy 1993b, 53, 64.
151. Quoted in DeLacy 1993a, 108.
152. DeLacy 1993a, 110.
153. Ackerknecht 2009, 14.
154. Ackerknecht 2009, 16.

advised that cholera was not contagious, shortly before John Snow showed that cholera contagion existed and was transmitted by contaminated water.[155] In Denmark, as we have seen, the resurgence of miasmatic theory led the College of Health to advise dismantling cholera quarantine in 1852 and reallocating the funding to miasmatic measures. A year later, cholera appeared in an airy, dry, and well-sanitized Copenhagen neighbourhood with no miasmatic features, infected 6–7 per cent of the city's population, and killed 3.6 per cent of it between June and December 1853.[156] In British India, miasmatic views dominated the colonial medical establishment, which resisted the idea that cholera was contagious and opposed all proposals for quarantines and sanitary cordons.[157] In France as late as 1884, so many physicians still espoused the miasmatic view that one-quarter of the 145 reports on cholera received by the French academy opposed the idea that the disease might be contagious.[158]

The positions adopted by medical associations were often influenced by non-medical considerations, sometimes admirable in themselves but uninformed by science. In the eighteenth century, contagionist views were held by doctors on the "left", who believed in the scientific improvement of society, while miasmatic views were held by conservatives, who believed in ancient wisdom handed down from classical antiquity.[159] In the nineteenth century, political alignments shifted, with miasmatic views held both by doctors on the left, who wanted to clean up slums, and by those on the right, who opposed restrictions on trade. Between 1800 and 1850, it was these political alignments rather than advances in science that swung medical associations against contagion theory, inspiring them to dismiss policies of social and physical distancing to prevent plague, yellow fever, cholera, and typhus.[160] The anti-contagionism of individual doctors and medical associations brought about the relaxation or abolition of quarantine legislation in England (1825, 1849, 1880s), the Netherlands (1825), France (1828, 1832, 1849, 1853), Austria (1841), and Russia (1847).[161] The situation gradually improved with the identification of waterborne cholera infection in the mid-1850s, the articulation of germ theory in the 1870s, and the discovery of viruses in 1892. But even as scientific medicine discovered definitive evidence that key epidemic diseases were contagious, medical associations clung obstinately to miasmatic orthodoxy; a generation of powerful senior doctors had to die before contagionism became accepted as a general principle.[162]

155. Ackerknecht 2009, 14.
156. Bencard 2021, 375–7.
157. Ackerknecht 2009, 14.
158. Ackerknecht 2009, 14.
159. Delacy 1993b, 63; Ackerknecht 2009, 16–19.
160. Ackerknecht 2009, 14–16.
161. Ackerknecht 2009, 16.
162. Ackerknecht 2009, 14–16.

The debate between miasmatic and contagionist views of infectious disease illustrates some broader features of how medical associations dealt with knowledge. Medical knowledge was incomplete and ambiguous during the centuries following the Black Death; in many respects, especially with regard to emerging pathogens, it remains so to this day. Yet for much of that period, medical associations followed an internal logic whereby they reached a collective view that reflected groupthink, often dominated by the loudest voices or swayed by pressure from politics and business. When medical associations nonetheless issued recommendations with a spurious claim to authority, they perverted the behaviour of individuals and governments. Medical science began to nibble at the edges of microbiology, epidemiology, and immunology in the second half of the nineteenth century, but medical associations remained enamoured of discredited ideas about infectious disease for much longer, and deployed those notions in their policy advice. Modern medical science is still opening up new frontiers in studying the human immune system, population epidemiology, and microbial transmission mechanisms. Modern medical associations are fortunately much more responsive to advances in medical science than they were throughout much of human history. But the past seven centuries of epidemics suggest that modern medical associations should avoid, not emulate, the mistakes their historical predecessors made in certifying knowledge.

3.4. RATHER BE SICK BY THE DOCTOR'S PRESCRIPTIONS, THAN IN HEALTH IN REBELLION TO THE COLLEGE

Medical associations also monitored new knowledge—though not always in a good way. When smallpox variolation was introduced to Europe and North America around 1720, many medical associations opposed it. This was not because variolation required a belief in contagionism. Many advocates of variolation held miasmatic or humoral theories of disease and did not think of smallpox as something you caught from other people. They simply accepted the evidence that variolation, for some reason, worked. Early variolation supporters did not view the procedure as a way of achieving herd immunity (which would have implied a belief in contagion), but rather focused on the benefits to the inoculated individual.[163] Variolation thus did not intellectually contradict the body of ancient knowledge which medical associations sought to monopolize and defend. The reason variolation sparked off opposition by medical associations was that it was an innovation—new knowledge—that challenged the entrenched notions and business models of their members.

---

163. Eriksen 2013, 526–9, 533; Esfandiary 2023, 237.

England, as we saw in chapter 2, became the undisputed epicentre of European variolation after Lady Mary Wortley Montagu introduced "ingrafting" to elite circles in the early 1720s. But she herself expected English doctors to reject this new knowledge. As early as 1717, she had written privately to a female friend:

> I am going to tell you a thing that I am sure will make you wish yourself here. The small-pox, so fatal, and so general amongst us, is here entirely harmless by the invention of ingrafting. . . . I am patriot enough to take pains to bring this useful invention into fashion in England; and I should not fail to write to some of our doctors very particularly about it, if I knew any one of them that I thought had virtue enough to destroy such a considerable branch of their revenue for the good of mankind. But that distemper is too beneficial to them not to expose to all their resentment the hardy wight that should undertake to put an end to it. Perhaps, if I live to return, I may, however, have courage to war with them.[164]

In the event, the London College of Physicians greeted variolation with caution but did not reject it out of hand. In 1718, Lady Mary had persuaded an English doctor in Constantinople to variolate her son according to local practice. During the 1721 London smallpox epidemic, she dragged the same doctor out of retirement to immunize her daughter. He agreed, conditional on the outcome (though not the procedure itself) being inspected by several members of the London College of Physicians. After the college members inspected Lady Mary's daughter, one of them got his own child variolated. The president of the college, Sir Hans Sloane, began to support the practice, though in his private rather than official capacity.[165]

The college itself did not prohibit the procedure, though for some years it adopted a discouraging stance. As Lady Mary described in a 1725 letter:

> I am sorry to inform you of the death of our nephew, my sister Gower's son, of the small-pox. I think she has a great deal of reason to regret it, in consideration of the offer I made her, two years together, of taking the child home to my house, where I would have inoculated him with the same care and safety I did my own. I know nobody that has hitherto repented the operation; though it has been very troublesome to some fools, who had rather be sick by the doctor's prescriptions, than in health in rebellion to the college.[166]

164. Quoted in Esfandiary 2023, 238–9.

165. Silverstein 2009, 294–5; Esfandiary 2023, 241.

166. Montagu 1837, 2:174–5 (letter from Lady Mary Montagu to the countess of Mar, undated, probably 1725).

The college might have disapproved but, unlike its counterparts in France or Spain, it did not have the power to veto new medical knowledge. As a result, individual physicians, commercial variolators, local governments, clergymen, and charitable institutions in England began to experiment with variolation, as we saw in earlier chapters. By 1755 their success was so widely recognized that the college declared formally:

> The College being informed that the Success of inoculating the Small Pox, and it's [sic] reputation in this Country, having lately been Misrepresented among Foreigners, came to the following Resolution. That in their Opinion the Objections made at first to it have been refuted by experience, and that it is at present more generally esteemed and Practised in England than ever, and that they Judge it to be a Practice of the Utmost benefit to Mankind.[167]

The "misrepresentation among Foreigners" which provoked this declaration was a torrent of anti-variolation medical publications in France, where the procedure was banned until 1768. In France, the 1707 Edict of Marly formally granted to each local "faculty" (medical association) the legal entitlement to decide not only who was allowed to practise medicine within its jurisdiction but—crucially—what medical techniques he was allowed to use.[168] The Paris Faculty of Medicine, which in 1720 comprised just 82 doctors and admitted only 2 new members annually, had regulatory rights over almost every legal question touching on medicine across the entire country, including which medical techniques were permitted. It prided itself on its conservative motto, *veteris disciplinae retinentissimae* (the most retentive of the old discipline), and was said to be "not so much an enemy of progress as such, but only admitted that progress which came from its own members".[169] After the mid-seventeenth century, the faculty refused to permit the "old discipline" to be tainted with new medical knowledge. It rejected William Harvey's theory of the circulation of blood because it came from England, the use of antimony as a drug because it came from Paris's arch-rival Montpellier, and the prescription of quinine to treat malaria because it came from America.[170] This does not mean that no new medical knowledge and practices were introduced in eighteenth-century France. But where they were adopted, it was tentatively and illicitly by heterodox physicians, surgeons, apothecaries, and unlicensed "empirics". Because such practitioners were excluded or condemned by the physicians' corporations, which forced them to operate in the informal sector, they found

167. Quoted in G. Miller 1957, 170.
168. Rusnock 2002, 73.
169. Raynaud 1862, 19.
170. Rusnock 2002, 74; Raynaud 1862, 19.

it hard to develop new medical techniques, diffuse them formally, or improve them through clinical experimentation.

As soon as knowledge of variolation began to spread out of England, the Paris Faculty of Medicine erupted in opposition. In 1723, it voted to prohibit the procedure throughout France, and for the next 45 years it pursued a zealous campaign against the mere idea, let alone its practical implementation.[171] This corporate anti-variolation crusade was directed by Philippe Hecquet, a senior member and former dean of the faculty, who had a track record of opposing all medical innovations, instead advocating "theological medicine" and "natural" remedies such as bloodletting, water drinking, and the consumption of baked apples. Smallpox, Hecquet argued, should be left to the wisdom of God and Nature, which cared for human beings in the best of all possible ways with no need for intervention by sinful humans.[172] Because the Paris Faculty of Medicine opposed it, variolation was banned nationally by the Parlement of Paris.

Things began to change only in the 1760s, and then grudgingly. Spurred by a lethal smallpox epidemic in 1760, the Paris faculty ordered that variolation should be considered by a "balanced" committee, six of whose members opposed variolation while the other six supported it. The committee then wasted more than a year collecting expert opinions from physicians across Europe, while the French smallpox epidemic raged unchecked. A majority of the international medical opinions endorsed variolation, but the Paris committee could not agree to accept them. Instead, it issued two diametrically contradictory reports—six members remained completely opposed, while the other six favoured tolerating variolation, though not in big cities for fear of spillover infections. In 1763, the Paris Faculty of Medicine as a whole voted 57 per cent in favour of variolation, with 29 per cent opposed and 14 per cent abstaining; but the conservative minority succeeded in blocking approval for another five years.[173] Opposition came partly from the challenge to members' business models, partly from religious concerns, and partly from resentment that variolation was a piece of knowledge developed outside the corpus of the profession. This is reflected in a 1764 pamphlet by the eminent physician Pierre-Louis Le Hoc attacking the pro-variolation arguments of those who "announce the ignorance of a profession that they scorn because they do not know it, have not studied it, and have not fathomed it".[174] Even in 1768, when the French ban on variolation was relaxed, the Paris Faculty of Medicine would only call the practice "admissible", adamantly refusing to provide any

---

171. G. Miller 1957, 187–8.
172. G. Miller 1957, 192.
173. G. Miller 1957, 234–40.
174. Quoted in Rusnock 2002, 87.

positive endorsement for immunization against the most lethal epidemic of the age.[175]

It might be thought that the stance of the Paris faculty reflected French culture or French science, not the incentives created by its powers as the national medical association. But this would be wrong. Many strands of French culture—even of French medical culture—were enthusiastic about the new knowledge. Variolation was strongly supported by French Enlightenment philosophers such as Voltaire, by individual French aristocrats, and by the Royal Chamber of Medicine, which admitted physicians trained outside the Paris faculty.[176] The main rival to the Paris faculty was the Montpellier Faculty of Medicine, which although it did not formally endorse variolation had several members who advocated the procedure.[177] Furthermore, popular demand for variolation in France was huge. Even while the legal ban was in force, desperate French customers were paying illicit variolators to perform the operation on them in rented premises in out-of-the-way locations.[178] As soon as the ban was lifted, British commercial variolators poured into Paris, though they took care to avoid faculty attention by operating only on the outskirts of the city.[179] Yet the continued coolness of the national medical associations continued to impede French variolation. As late as 1776, a French publication estimated that only 15,000 people were being variolated annually in France, compared with 200,000 annually in England, even though France had almost three times the population.[180] What mattered was not French culture, or even French science. It was French institutions—the entrenched power of the dominant medical corporations, together with the adamant disapproval evinced by the Catholic Church, discussed in chapter 5.

In the eighteenth-century German lands, too, the failure of variolation resided neither in German culture nor in German science. Rather, it lay in the formal institutions through which medical innovations had to secure approval before practitioners and patients could use them. Medical associations in the German lands imposed two separate obstacles to variolation. First, many German medical associations pushed for outright bans on variolation or formally advised governments against it. In 1798, for instance, when King Friedrich Wilhelm of Prussia ordered the College of Medicine and Sanitation to consider variolation, the college issued a negative report pooh-poohing the notion of

175. G. Miller 1957, 234–40.
176. G. Miller 1957, 187–94; Silverstein 2009, 299.
177. Rusnock 2002, 75.
178. G. Miller 1957, 237.
179. M. Bennett 2020, 39–43, 151.
180. Harper 2021, 408.

ever eradicating smallpox and recommending against any measures to encourage variolation.[181]

The second problem in many German societies was that even once variolation was legalized, medical associations insisted on monopolizing it. In Prussia as late as the 1790s, private individuals were permitted to variolate only members of their own families, so that clergymen who inoculated their parishioners could actually be charged with encroaching on the privileges of the physicians and surgeons.[182] Some German medical associations even barred inoculation by non-local doctors, as in 1774 when a Prussian government minister invited the Dresden-based English variolator William Baylies to Berlin to demonstrate Suttonian variolation, but the Berlin medical establishment got the Upper Medical Council to send Baylies a formal letter warning him that as a foreigner he was not allowed to engage in variolation without a royal permit. It took the passage of another year and the personal intervention of the Prussian king to enable Baylies to demonstrate the Suttonian variolation technique in Berlin.[183] In states such as Braunschweig-Wolfenbüttel, not only was variolation monopolized by the medical associations but costs were further increased by requiring that a surgeon make the incision while a physician supervised.[184] Each group of medical practitioners used its guild or college to make the case that non-members were too ignorant to be trusted with variolation, undermining popular confidence in the practice.[185] As late as 1792, the Halle professor Johann Christian Wilhelm Juncker conducted a vigorous campaign to spread variolation more widely in Prussia but insisted that it remain the monopoly of the physicians. For one thing, it was part of their "privileges". Secondly, he claimed, other practitioners such as surgeons could not carry it out safely. Above all, however, the physicians deserved monetary compensation for permitting smallpox to be prevented, since "with natural smallpox being rendered far less common, physicians lose something in their practice [so] it is both just and wise to try to find a replacement for them through the variolation business".[186] By monopolizing variolation, German medical associations restricted its supply, increased its costs, and blocked the transmission of technical improvements, many of them devised, as we saw in chapter 2, by non-medically-trained commercial inoculators such as John Sutton.

The differing trajectories of knowledge about variolation in Britain, France, and Germany vividly emerge from the number of publications on the subject in the three societies, shown in figure 6.2. In Britain, publications peaked

181. Maehle 1995, 213.
182. Penschow 2022, 176.
183. Penschow 2022, 65–8.
184. Albrecht 2005, 133.
185. Albrecht 2005, 136.
186. Maehle 1995, 203, 205; Juncker 1792–96, 99 (quotation).

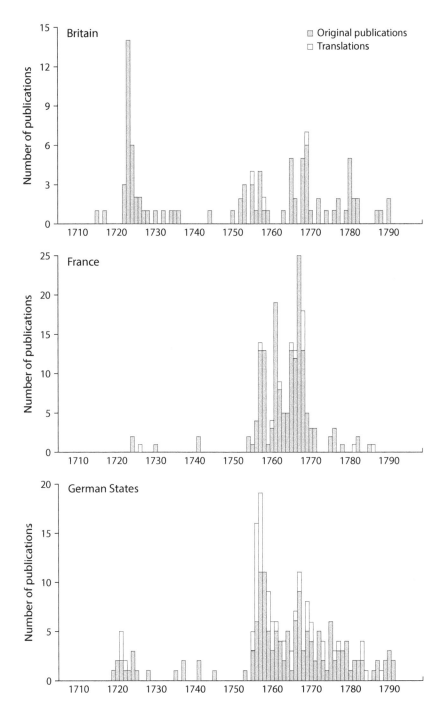

FIGURE 6.2. Number of publications on variolation in Britain, France, and Germany, 1714–90. Publication titles (*n* = 459) compiled from Krünitz (1768) and Olberg (1791). *Source*: Based on Maehle 1995, 201–2.

in the early 1720s when variolation was first introduced from the Ottoman lands, tailing off as the procedure was increasingly accepted and diffused. In France, there were almost no publications on variolation until 1755, when the Enlightenment explorer, geographer, and mathematician Charles-Marie de La Condamine began to campaign for it, which unleashed a spate of controversy until 1768, when the procedure was finally legalized. In Germany, variolation publications started proliferating in the 1750s around the same time as La Condamine unleashed his campaign in France, but continued at a fairly high level through the following decades as different German states debated whether to legalize variolation and which medical associations should be allowed to monopolize the practice.

Not popular or scientific culture but the monopolistic privileges of medical communities also blocked knowledge of variolation elsewhere in Europe. In Sweden, the Medical Board (part medical guild, part government body) agreed to authorize variolation in 1756, explicitly influenced by medical endorsement of the practice in England. But Sweden followed the corporative German model rather than the liberal English one. So when the Swedish state legalized variolation it did not follow the English practice and open the procedure to commercial, philanthropic, community, and religious practitioners to spread the knowledge widely and begin to improve on it. Instead, Sweden made variolation the monopoly of licensed physicians and prohibited it to virtually everyone else, thus excluding surgeons, apothecaries, midwives, clergymen, parents, and other lay persons.[187] This corporative monopoly not only limited the diffusion of information about variolation and made ordinary people overestimate the risks involved but, as we shall see shortly, restricted its supply and increased its costs, further stifling its diffusion.[188]

In Spain, as in France, medical innovations had to be approved by medical associations, which implacably blocked variolation.[189] The royal physician Jose Amar y Arguedas adamantly opposed the innovation and published a book against it in 1774, bemoaning the fact that the procedure was so straightforward that it could be undertaken by unlicensed practitioners instead of professional doctors.[190] Even when the Count of Campomanes, an Enlightenment-influenced statesman and economist, wrote a book urging variolation to be made available to the Spanish population, the stance of the Spanish medical associations relaxed only grudgingly.[191]

187. Grant 2019, 205; Sköld 1996a, 251–2; Sköld 1996b, 315–26.
188. M. Bennett 2020, 39.
189. Ramírez 2018, 140–1.
190. Poska 2022, 8.
191. M. Bennett 2020, 152, 200; Ramírez 2018, 140.

In Russia, likewise, the national Medical College opposed variolation as part of its mission to maintain the profits of "official" doctors against unlicensed competitors.[192] During the smallpox epidemics of the 1760s, the pioneering Livonian pastor Johan Georg Eisen tried to promote variolation among the peasantry, but the Russian Medical College not only denied his application for funds but refused to approve the procedure at all. Variolation gained support in Russia only when it was taken up by the tsarina, and even then the procedure was adopted only sporadically inside noble estates and charitable institutions, rather than spreading freely in the wider population.[193]

Even in Britain, medical associations tried to restrict improvements to knowledge about variolation in order to protect their members' business models. In 1766–67, the rising fame and falling fees of commercial variolators such as the Sutton family prompted the London Royal College of Physicians to spread false information vilifying the Suttonian method as too standardized and simple. (It was also much less costly than the procedure offered by physicians, which involved a huge panoply of dietary and other pre- and post-operative rituals, which the Suttons had shown to be needless.) So notorious did the fake news spread by the college become that a journalist published a satirical pamphlet under the title *The Tryal of Mr. Daniel Sutton, for the High Crime of Preserving the Lives of His Majesty's Liege Subjects.* As reflected in the chapter epigraph, this pamphlet presented a mock indictment against the commercial variolator,

> for the high crime of preserving the lives of his Majesty's subjects by means of inoculation, and particularly by modes of practice and the exhibition of certain medicines unknown to this College, and to all others who practise the art of healing . . . [W]e shall prove, beyond all possibility of doubt, that in twenty thousand, whom the Prisoner hath inoculated, not one single patient hath died, whose death could be fairly attributed to inoculation. . . . Gentlemen, it were needless to expatiate on the heinousness of these crimes.[194]

Fortunately, the London College of Physicians did not have the legal power either to veto new knowledge as in France or Spain or to monopolize it as in Sweden or Germany. So the London college could not put commercial variolators out of business and instead merely tried to smear the Suttons' reputation. This was rendered ineffectual by the commercial variolators' thousands of satisfied customers, the voices of a comparatively free press, and the

192. Pasichnyk 2018, 77–99; M. Bennett 2020, 226.
193. M. Bennett 2020, 226.
194. Anon. 1767, 3–4.

unwillingness of the British state to support claims by guilds or "colleges" to block innovations in the name of their own corporative privileges.[195]

3.5. PROHIBITED FROM PROVIDING VACCINATION WITH COWPOX

Vaccination, too, was new knowledge. It also met obstacles from medical associations, but weaker ones. Why was this? A first reason was that vaccination was inherently less risky than variolation, as we saw in table 2.2. The risk of death from vaccination was nearly nil, compared with 1.6 per cent for variolation; the risk of side-effects from vaccination was nearly nil, compared with occasional adverse reactions to variolation; vaccination posed no risk to the community, whereas variolation could spread smallpox to susceptible contacts. The only way vaccination was riskier was that it provided complete protection only for 3–5 years, with re-vaccination recommended after 10–20 years, whereas variolation provided lifelong immunity. Because vaccination was less risky than variolation, it did not fall foul of the Hippocratic mandate, "First, do no harm."

A second reason medical associations did not oppose vaccination so strongly was that variolation had already done a lot of the heavy lifting in persuading people that immunization was realistic and beneficial. This persuasion had not shifted opinion merely inside the medical profession. It had also changed views across the wider institutional framework—within governments, local communities, religions, and families. Members of medical associations were influenced by the wider social framework within which they operated, much more of which had already been convinced of the existence and benefits of immunization.

A third reason vaccination was more easily accepted than variolation was that it was invented in an era in which science was becoming more widely accepted, even though, as we shall see, confidence and consensus concerning medical knowledge remained incomplete into the late nineteenth century (and to some extent to this day). But by around 1800, both in the population at large and among medical practitioners, science had begun to be perceived in its modern sense as "the systematic study of the structure and behaviour of the physical and natural world through observation, experimentation, and the testing of theories against the evidence obtained", rather than merely its traditional sense as "knowledge of any kind". When vaccination was invented in 1796, medical associations were not yet acting in a fully scientific context, but they had a broader epistemic base than they had when variolation had been introduced to

195. Brunton 1990, 124.

Europe nearly 80 years earlier. Even though medical science around 1800 was still characterized by lack of consensus about many aspects of infectious diseases in general and epidemics in particular, scientific practices were beginning to diffuse in the medical profession. Consequently, more members of medical associations were beginning to understand the benefits of these practices and were developing a more tolerant attitude towards them. This did not mean that scientific medicine was dominant in 1800. As the debate within medical associations about contagion theory during the nineteenth-century cholera epidemics would show, it would take nearly another century for scientific approaches to infectious disease to become dominant in the medical profession.

A final reason medical associations opposed vaccination less than variolation was institutional. Vaccination was invented in a society—England—and a period—the later 1790s—when the institutional powers of occupational associations were gradually breaking down. In England, the Dutch Republic, and the Southern Netherlands in the course of the early modern period, guilds had gradually weakened, so much so that there was little pressure for their legal abolition. In other parts of Europe, guilds endured for longer, not only in law but in their ability to enforce their privileges. In France, guilds had to be coercively abolished in the wake of the French Revolution, and the 1791 Loi d'Allarde that did away with the French guilds had evoked considerable opposition across French society. In parts of Germany, Italy, Switzerland, and other adjacent polities, French military regimes imposed guild abolition during the Napoleonic era, albeit against considerable social resistance. It was mainly in Iberia, Scandinavia, and parts of German-speaking Europe that guilds were still powerful in 1796, and thus still capable of mounting opposition to new knowledge.[196]

English guilds were typically liberal compared with those in most other European countries, and the same applied to English medical associations.[197] In England as early as 1542–43, Henry VIII had issued the so-called "Quacks' Charter", not only denying the petition of the surgeons' guilds for a stricter monopoly but positively "permitting persons being no surgeons to minister medicines outwards, to cure sores by herbs and ointments, or stone or ague by drinks, without being sued by surgeons for so treating the sick".[198] State enactments such as this did not mean that English medical practice was completely open and free, since in principle medical practitioners still had to be licensed by bishops into the eighteenth century, though in practice most rural regions relied on informal providers licensed by neither guild nor Church.[199]

196. Ogilvie 2019, 555–9.
197. Ogilvie 2019, 557–8.
198. Grant 2019, 205; Spector 1952, 514–15 (quotation).
199. Guy 1982, 528–9, 535.

However, state enactments and legal decisions and laws cumulatively deprived medical guilds and colleges in England of much of the monopoly power over knowledge, techniques, methods, and practice that they enjoyed in most other parts of Europe. By the eighteenth century, the London Colleges of Medicine and Surgery "had far less power than equivalent bodies in continental Europe, and there was a general disposition to allow new remedies to compete in the medical marketplace".[200] English physicians, surgeons, and apothecaries still had distinct professional organizations, but their privileges and activities were beginning to merge without provoking the demarcation disputes common in earlier periods or in many other European societies well into the nineteenth century. Academically trained physicians in England were becoming more interested in clinical training, surgeons and apothecaries were seeking greater scientific education, and all medical practitioners were becoming more receptive to new ideas and practices.[201]

In the years after its invention in 1796, vaccination was widely adopted in England partly because the medical associations mounted little opposition to it—despite the rabid anti-vaccination stance of some of their eminent members.[202] In 1806–7, 10 years after Edward Jenner invented vaccination, the London College of Physicians was still ambivalent enough to seek views from both proponents and opponents, as well as from the London College of Surgeons and its sister guilds in Dublin and Edinburgh. Most of these associations took a positive stance, although the College of Surgeons remained rather unenthusiastic. But in the end, British medical associations did endorse vaccination.[203]

Across the European continent, as in England, vaccination benefited from the weakening of medical guilds at the end of the eighteenth century. In France, introducing vaccination was eased by the 1791 abolition of guilds and other corporative restrictions. The first smallpox vaccination in Paris was carried out in the summer of 1800 by a mixed party of French and English doctors, cooperating despite the war between their countries.[204] Prussia abolished its guilds in 1808 and did not make vaccination the monopoly of medical associations, instead permitting the establishment of numerous private vaccination clinics.[205]

In other parts of Europe, however, the knowledge and practice of vaccination became the legal monopoly of medical associations. The German Grand-Duchy of Hesse was the first state in Europe to impose mandatory

200. M. Bennett 2020, 96–7.
201. M. Bennett 2020, 95–6.
202. M. Bennett 2020, 91, 118.
203. M. Bennett 2020, 118–19.
204. M. Bennett 2020, 149.
205. Rupp, Leist, and Benedum 1974, 4.

vaccination, in 1807, but also one of the earliest to grant a legal monopoly over the procedure to licensed doctors.[206] The German state of Württemberg was another early adopter of a vaccination mandate, in 1818, but also made vaccination the monopoly of medical associations. The academically trained physicians lobbied to exclude the guild-trained barber-surgeons from the increasingly lucrative business, and in 1814 secured legislation that imposed penalties on surgeons who "do not possess the required knowledge and take it upon themselves to provide smallpox vaccination and to issue certificates concerning the arising illness which cannot be regarded as reliable".[207] In claiming that surgeons did not have the requisite knowledge, the physicians relied on a supposed distinction between "authentic" cowpox (which putatively prevented smallpox) and "inauthentic" cowpox (which allegedly did not), even though there was no actual evidence of any such distinction.[208] The surgeons' guilds fought back, complaining "that they had been prohibited from providing vaccination with cowpox and thereby a part of their income had been diminished".[209] The profitable monopoly over vaccination in nineteenth-century Württemberg then became a matter of perpetual conflict between surgeons' guilds and physicians' associations, with the only basis for agreement being the importance of excluding the clergymen, midwives, enlightened intellectuals, peasants, shepherds, and myriad private individuals who had initially begun to provide vaccination, especially in rural communities that were unsupplied by any licensed medical practitioner.[210] Serious difficulty in getting access to a doctor was one of the main contributory factors behind low initial take-up of vaccination by ordinary people in early nineteenth-century Württemberg.[211]

The still-strong corporative privileges of the Spanish and Spanish American medical associations likewise enabled them increasingly to exclude informal practitioners, especially women. This was a serious constraint, since as we shall see in chapter 7, women constituted the shock troops of early vaccination in many societies, including Spain and its colonies. In many regions of the Spanish-speaking world, corporative restrictions on the profitable entitlement to administer vaccinations restricted supply, since there were not enough experienced medical professionals with credentials to obtain licenses as vaccinators.[212] Such corporative entitlements also reduced access to immunization by increasing

206. Rupp, Leist, and Benedum 1974, 4.
207. Quoted in Wolff 1998, 131.
208. Wolff 1998, 128, 134.
209. Quoted in Wolff 1998, 131.
210. Wolff 1998, 125–33.
211. Mühlhoff 2022, 5.
212. See Poska (2022, 18) on Spain; Few (2015, 187) on Spanish America.

prices, because demand exceeded supply—which of course was a major reason the medical associations wanted to monopolize vaccination.

Non-European medical associations also organized collective action to restrict access to vaccination. In Bengal, groups of professional variolators called *tikadārs* opposed vaccination because it competed with their rival immunization technique. According to an account of 1805, "There are persons employed in the inoculation [variolation] of smallpox, some of whom are Brahmins and others of inferior castes, but all agreeing in this, that they omit no means to bring the new practice [vaccination] into discredit."[213] The Governor General of India sought to compensate the losers from innovation by suggesting that "the Hindus who had considerable practice in the inoculation [variolation] for small pox might be induced to relinquish their former profession and to adopt vaccination and they be granted pensions for life".[214] The state had to compensate entrenched interest-groups to make it possible to introduce beneficial new knowledge—a vivid actualization of the "political Coase Theorem", whereby beneficiaries of existing institutions may need to be bought off to enable innovations that will benefit society at large.[215]

Medical associations have largely adopted an enlightened and scientific stance towards knowledge of vaccination since 1796, even if many of them sought to monopolize the practice. But the record of medical associations in disciplining members who spread false knowledge about vaccination has been less impressive. Even in nineteenth-century England, as already mentioned, the London College of Surgeons was distinctly ambivalent about vaccination and sheltered virulent anti-vaccination sentiment.[216] John Birch was a governor of the college and became one of the most influential British campaigners against smallpox vaccination.[217] He published pamphlets claiming that smallpox was deliberately brought into being by Providence, that the disease could be cured by electricity, and that vaccination was not only ineffective but harmful. According to Birch, because smallpox vaccine was made of cowpox lymph it caused people to develop bestial features, such as those in pictures he circulated portraying imaginary victims putatively deformed by vaccination, similar to those shown in figure 6.3. Birch's conduct in spreading false information about smallpox and vaccination was not constrained by the College of Surgeons. On the contrary, he used his authority as an eminent member of his medical association as a bully pulpit to disseminate misinformation. His medical association took no disciplinary steps against him.

213. Quoted in Bhatnagar 1952, 186.
214. Quoted in Bhatnagar 1952, 187–8.
215. Acemoglu 2003; Ogilvie 2007, 665–7; Ogilvie and Carus 2014, 407, 482, 484.
216. M. Bennett 2020, 118–19.
217. Royal College of Surgeons 1812, 5.

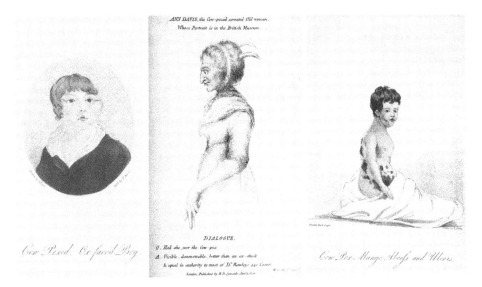

FIGURE 6.3. Anti-vaccination images in England, 1805 and 1806. (*Left*) "Cow Poxed, Ox Faced Boy" (1805). (*Centre*) "Cow-poxed, cornuted Old Woman" (1806). (*Right*) "Mange Girl" (1805). These are a few of the many images circulated by anti-vaccination pamphleteers in many countries, purporting to show that smallpox vaccination infected humans with animal diseases or bestial lineaments. *Source*: Wellcome Collection.

The same still happens now. Most medical organizations are reluctant to proceed against members who use their medical authority to spread false information about epidemics and vaccination. In the autumn of 2021, for instance, 67 per cent of American medical boards who responded to a survey reported an uptick in complaints against their licensees for spreading Covid-19 misinformation, but only 21 per cent had taken any disciplinary action against a member for that reason.[218] American medical boards were widely deterred from taking disciplinary action against licensees because of fears of litigation and threats from powerful political figures to deprive the boards of their licensing privileges.[219] In the United Kingdom in 2023, the General Medical Council (which licenses doctors) went so far as to mount a legal defence of one of its members against accusations of publicly spreading misinformation about Covid-19 vaccination.[220] It is a worrying indictment of medical licensing

218. Rubin 2022, 904.
219. Tahir 2022.
220. Good Law Project 2023; letter from the Good Law Practice to the General Medical Council of 20 April 2023 (redacted) can be seen at https://drive.google.com/file/d/1Poylxb8ok2ywuuz0_bVDWulxtYM3YUpd/view.

associations if they prioritize their own privileges and the protection of their members at the expense of public concerns about the reliability of medical knowledge.

4. Entry Barriers and Supply Shortages

A basic activity of any occupational association is to control entry, and medical associations are no exception.[221] This was true not just of medieval and early modern medical guilds but also of the colleges, faculties, academies, societies, and other associations that were established by medical practitioners, outlived the abolition of traditional guilds, and survive in various forms to this day. Medical entry barriers not only increased incomes for doctors and prices for patients in normal times. They also affected contagion control during epidemics.

4.1. WE SHOULD NOT CALL JUST ANY EMPIRIC OR WISEWOMAN A SURGEON

Each medical association claimed for its members the exclusive entitlement to practise in a particular geographical area, and to decide who was allowed to become a member of the association. A medical guild regulated entry to the occupation by imposing a mandatory career track of apprenticeship, journeymanship, and mastership, each with strict conditions for admission. Most required apprenticeship, a minimum number of years of unpaid (or low-paid) on-the-job training with a guild master. After that, many medical guilds also mandated journeymanship, a minimum number of years of day-labouring for guild masters, usually at capped wages, often involving compulsory "wandering" or "tramping" from town to town. Getting admitted to apprenticeship and journeymanship was necessary (but not sufficient) for becoming a master of the guild—a large share of apprentices did not complete their mandatory apprenticeship period so did not graduate to journeymanship, and an even larger share of journeymen had to keep on working for a series of employers without ever finding guilds that would admit them to mastership. Only a master, who had obtained the full guild license, was permitted to practise a guilded occupation independently. Limiting entry was one form of behaviour which European medical guilds shared with those on other continents. In Ottoman Egypt around 1600, for instance, the guilded physician who authored one of the earliest surviving commentaries on Egyptian guilds lamented that in these degenerate times guilds were accepting members too

221. Ogilvie 2014b; Ogilvie 2019, 83–171.

easily and that his readers should be worried about the excessive numbers of new entrants.[222]

Regulating entry went far beyond making sure practitioners were properly trained. Medical associations excluded many people from even starting apprenticeship by imposing identity-based entry conditions that had nothing to do with the capacity to learn medical skills—gender, ethnicity, religion, local citizenship, legitimate birth, kinship, parentage, ancestry, wealth, property, and the ability to pay admission fees. They then imposed further stringent requirements before a journeyman could become a master, often requiring him to wander from place to place for a minimum number of years working for one master after another at legally capped wages. In Augsburg in 1549, for instance, barber-surgeons were required to complete a two-year apprenticeship but then work as journeymen for five years before they were eligible to apply for mastership.[223] In Württemberg in 1819, both barber-surgeons and apothecaries were required to wander as journeymen for three or four years after completing their apprenticeship training.[224]

Some guilds refused to consider journeymen for mastership if they had not been subjected to local scrutiny. In Speyer in 1591, for instance, the barber-surgeons' guild required four years' roaming as a journeyman followed by half a year's "probationary period" working for a local master before a young man could apply for mastership. In Mainz in 1592, there were only two years of apprenticeship but six years of tramping as a journeyman followed by two years' local probation before one could apply for mastership.[225] Some medical guilds refused even to consider an applicant for mastership who had not been trained locally—as with the Poitiers apothecaries' guild, which in 1628 demanded that a journeyman had to undergo four years' training in the town itself, even if he already had 10 years' training in a guild in another town.[226] Even then, a fully qualified journeyman had to satisfy additional strict requirements before the guild let him set up in independent practice, which the guild again made conditional on identity-based attributes that had nothing to do with medical knowledge or skill—including further fees and acceptability to existing members of the association.[227]

The arbitrary nature of this career path, which had less to do with skill than with restricting entry, is illustrated by the fact that different medical guilds in pre-modern Europe imposed widely differing periods of training.

222. Baer 1964, 49.
223. Stuart 1999, 106.
224. Kluge 2007, 196.
225. Wesoly 1985, 52.
226. Heckscher (1931) 1994, 149.
227. On guild entry conditions, including those for medicine, see Ogilvie (2019, ch. 3 and 5).

Across a sample of 21 barber-surgeons' guilds in Germany, France, the Netherlands, Germany, and Italy between 1355 and 1784, the mandatory minimum apprenticeship period averaged 2.86 years, but ranged from a maximum of 10 years to a minimum of zero.[228] It might be thought that at least mandatory medical training should have become longer as the centuries passed and the skills and knowledge required presumably became more demanding. But this did not happen. Quite the contrary. Across the same sample of 21 surgeons' guilds, the average apprenticeship term declined from 3.5 years in the 1268–1500 period to just 2.6 years in the 1500–1829 period.[229]

Nor was training open to all. Rather, it was restricted to those who could satisfy identity-based requirements that had nothing to do with the capacity to learn medicine. Women, as already mentioned, were completely ruled out by the medical "colleges" and "faculties", because until the mid- to late nineteenth century females were excluded by universities and medical schools. Surgeons' and apothecaries' guilds typically banned females from independent practice, though the fact that they often permitted untrained widows to operate under a deceased husband's license shows that the concern was not about skill but about restricting entry.[230] Even using a female pharmaceutical supplier could attract guild censure, as in 1632 when the London College of Physicians reproved a particular Dutch physician for buying his medicines from a female apothecary.[231] Gender barriers were enforced, as in Chateaubriand in 1732 when a woman practising medicine was prosecuted even though she presented numerous attestations from distinguished patients whom she had cured, or in Frankfurt am Main in 1745 when the surgeons' guild petitioned the authorities to punish 12 illicit female "encroachers" who were enticing away their patients.[232] Women only started being allowed to study medicine, let alone practise it legitimately, in the course of the nineteenth century. Even then, they were often excluded from full membership in medical associations for much longer. In the United Kingdom, for instance, it was 1876 before the first woman was licensed to become a doctor and 1892 before women were admitted to the British Medical Association.[233]

Local citizenship requirements were another obstacle. Although guilds admitted non-locals to mastership, they typically required that they first obtain (and pay for) local citizenship rights before applying for guild membership.

228. Ogilvie 2019, 371 (table 7.5); for the data, see https://sheilaghogilvie.com/wp-content/uploads/guilds-databases/Ogilvie-Guilds-Qualitative-Database-1-Nov-2018.xlsx.
229. Ogilvie 2019, 374 (table 7.7).
230. Bullough 1958, 39; Ogilvie 2019, 291–4.
231. Connolly 2017, 50–1.
232. Ogilvie 2019, 293.
233. Jarral 2016.

Citizenship requirements could hinder admission even of the most skilled non-local practitioners, as in sixteenth-century Bologna where the College of Physicians rejected the brilliant surgeon Giovanni Battista Cortesi because his father had been born outside the city.[234] The Italian physician Cesare Adelmare was prosecuted by the Royal College of Physicians in London in 1554 for "practising medicine against the law of the realm". It was fortunate for subsequent English plague policy that Adelmare managed later to satisfy the college's entry barriers, since it was he who in the 1563 London epidemic drafted a "project" for chief minister Burghley mapping out public health recommendations based on the advanced Italian model.[235]

Medical associations also restricted entry by imposing ethnic and religious barriers. Muslims and converts from Islam were often excluded from medical associations in European societies, as in Lleida in 1600 when the doctors' guild required entrants to prove they were not Moors but rather sons of "old Christians and of good manners, trades or arts".[236] Jews and converts from Judaism were excluded by virtually all European medical faculties and guilds, thereby denying to patients Jewish medical knowledge, even though (or perhaps precisely because) it was believed to be more advanced than that of Christian doctors.[237] In the late fourteenth century, the Montpellier Faculty of Medicine went so far as to prohibit the sale of medical texts to non-Christians, with the result that the famous Jewish physician Leon Joseph of Carcassone spent 10 years trying to get copies of key publications, ultimately procuring them in 1394 by paying double the normal price.[238] Other medical associations went further, as with the Cologne physicians' guild, which after 1393 ostracized any Christian doctor who consorted with Jewish colleagues and after 1630 obliged existing members to swear never even to work with a Jew.[239]

Medical associations continued to impose ethnic barriers in Europe and America well into the twentieth century. In twentieth-century France, "the most antisemitic of all professional associations was without question that representing French doctors—the Confederation des Syndicats Medicaux—together with its student affiliates". From the 1920s until the outbreak of the Second World War, the confederation systematically lobbied against admission

234. Savoia 2019, 46–7.
235. On Adelmare's prosecution by the College of Physicians, see "A Dalmaris, Caesar" (in Physicians and Irregular Medical Practitioners in London 1550–1640 Database (London, 2004), British History Online, accessed 19 May 2024, https://www.british-history.ac.uk/no-series /london-physicians/1550-1640/a-dalmariis-caesar); on his 1563 plague "project" delivered to Lord Burghley, see Slack (1985, 207–8).
236. Quoted in Esteves i Perendreu 1996, 78.
237. Ogilvie 2019, 103–7; Bullough 1970, 166; Roth 1953, 843.
238. Roth 1953, 835.
239. Schütte 2017, 308–9.

of Jews to university medical faculties and their employment in the French medical profession.[240] In the United States from the 1860s until the 1960s, the American Medical Association preserved internal harmony between its northern and southern members by agreeing that Black physicians could be denied membership in state, county, and municipal medical societies in southern and many border states. This exclusion not only professionally isolated Black physicians but restricted their access to training, limited their professional and business contacts, and denied them admitting privileges in most hospitals, preventing them from obtaining board certification and professional advancement. The AMA reiterated this "local autonomy" principle in order to oppose motions prohibiting racial discrimination by member medical societies on no fewer than 12 occasions between 1939 and 1968. It did not repeal its exclusion of Black southern physicians from membership in its subsidiary medical societies until it was legally compelled to do so by the civil rights legislation of the 1960s, and did not acknowledge or apologize for its racial barriers to membership until 2008.[241]

Medical associations also imposed a variety of entry barriers relating to parentage and "honourable birth". Like most guilds, medical associations charged lower entry fees to masters' sons and gave them priority in getting access to the rationed number of examination slots. Partly as a result of these favourable admission conditions, a non-trivial share of entering masters were sons of existing masters, as in the Dijon apothecaries' guild between 1693 and 1790, where 30 per cent of those admitted to mastership were masters' sons.[242]

In German-speaking central Europe, medical associations increasingly excluded those who had not been born "legitimately" to married parents. In Cologne, the barber-surgeons' guild imposed no legitimacy requirement in 1397, but introduced one in 1469 in an effort to overcome discrimination against barbering as a "dishonourable" occupation, which had barred barber-surgeons from representation on the town council.[243] In 1500, the Mainz barber-surgeons' guild ejected an apprentice when it discovered that he had been born out of wedlock.[244] Some medical guilds went further and excluded applicants whose own children were born "too early", as in 1677 when the Dresden barber-surgeons' guild used the fact that an applicant's wife had given birth less than nine months after the wedding to prevent him from becoming a master. Even after the man heroically directed the town pesthouse during the 1680 plague epidemic when no guilded surgeon was willing to serve, falling victim

240. Caron 1998, 41 (quotation), 42–52.
241. Ward 2003; Washington et al. 2009; R. Baker 2018.
242. Shephard 1986, 124.
243. Stuart 1999, 105.
244. Wesoly 1985, 59.

to plague himself and barely surviving, the guild continued for many years to deny him full corporate privileges.[245]

Association with "dishonourable" occupations was often used to exclude applicants or block career progression. In fifteenth-century Nantes, for instance, the apothecaries' guild excluded anyone whose father practised a "vile" occupation (as defined by the existing guild members).[246] In 1583, the Padua College of Physicians mounted long and bitter resistance to admitting the eminent Fabricius of Aquapendente, who had been teaching in the university for more than 20 years, but who was opposed by the college on the grounds that he was a lowly surgeon and anatomist.[247] In 1613, all the barber-surgeons of the German Middle Rhine towns signed an agreement forbidding their members any "secret or public association" with a range of dishonourable persons, including quack healers, executioners, old women, Jews, itinerant salve-smearers, and retailers of theriac and worm-seed (plague remedies prescribed by guilded surgeons and physicians, as we shall see).[248] In 1719, the Wangen barber-surgeons' guild rejected the apprenticeship application of an executioner's son on the grounds of his father's "dishonourable" occupation, refused to recognize the state ruler's official legitimation of the boy, and exercised such virulent opposition to letting him be trained that the town government declared that it would not dare to overrule the guild.[249]

Medical associations also charged high fees for membership. If you could not afford the fee, you could not get into the association and hence could not get a license to practise. In Frankfurt am Main in 1586, the barber-surgeons' guild charged a mastership fee of 10 florins, equivalent to two and a half years' wages for a journeyman barber-surgeon.[250] Amsterdam had one of the most liberal guild systems in Europe, but in the seventeenth century its surgeons' guild charged an admission fee equivalent to nearly 40 per cent of the annual income of an average Amsterdam family and over 200 days' wages for a journeyman of the time.[251] In France by the 1780s, the fee to get into the physicians' corporation in Paris was 7,000 livres (over 13 years' wages for a master mason), in Lyons and Reims 3,000 livres (over 5 years' wages), and in Avignon and Montpellier 1,000 livres (2 years' wages).[252]

245. Schlenkrich 2002, 26.
246. D. Nicholas 1995, 1124; Leguay 1981, 267.
247. Whitteridge 1977, 72.
248. Quoted in Göttmann 1977, 153.
249. Stuart 1999, 237.
250. Wesoly 1985, 240–1.
251. D. Phillips 2008, 49; Lourens and Lucassen 2000, 23; Allen, n.d., Amsterdam wages file.
252. Brockliss and Jones 1997, 482. Allen's (n.d.) Paris wages file gives 41 sous as the day wage of a master mason in 1780. There were 20 sous per livre, and the standard length of the

A final way medical associations restricted entry was to impose *numerus clausus* restrictions. Sometimes the association would cap the number of young men admitted to training, as in Valenciennes, Middelburg, and Vlissingen in 1600, when the apothecaries' guilds admitted only one apprentice each year.[253] Other medical associations limited the number of those allowed to present themselves for examination, as with the Lleida doctors' guild in 1600, which refused to examine more than two candidates annually,[254] or in Thouars in 1617, when the apothecaries' guilds allowed a maximum of three applicants to be examined each year.[255]

Many medical associations simply capped the number of men permitted to practise medicine at all in that locality. They fixed numbers at a low level with the explicit aim of limiting competition, as in Mechelen in 1647 when the apothecaries' guild reduced its existing numerus clausus because of "the excessive number of actual apothecaries";[256] in Helmstedt in 1646, when the barber-surgeons' guild reduced its cap in order to keep out a threateningly competitive surgeon from Hamburg;[257] or in Wolfenbüttel in 1664, when the barber-surgeons' guild used its numerus clausus to reject an applicant from Heinrichstadt who would "diminish their livelihood which was already meager".[258] In 1720, the Paris Faculty of Medicine maintained its numerus clausus at just 82 members, all of whom had to be previously trained internally to the faculty.[259] Medical associations strictly maintained their numerus clausus, despite complaints that this restricted the supply of practitioners unreasonably. In Helmstedt in 1646, for instance, the town council vainly objected to the numerus clausus of just three surgeons imposed by the surgeons' guild, pointing out that "six to eight barber-surgeons could earn a living in the town without any difficulty".[260]

Table 6.4 shows 16 European medical guilds for which quantitative information is available on the ratio between the guild's numerus clausus and the local population. The ratio ranged from a high of 1.59 surgeons per 1,000 inhabitants in Helmstedt in 1646 (caused not by rising surgeon numbers but by drastically falling wartime population) to a low of 0.08 per 1,000 inhabitants in Vienna in 1716. The average was 0.66 medical practitioners per 1,000

---

pre-industrial working year is taken to be 250 days: 7,000 livres is therefore 13.65 years' wages for a master mason, 3,000 livres is 5.85 years' wages, and 1,000 livres is 1.95 years' wages.

253. Bolt 2021, 3.
254. Esteves i Perendreu 1996, 78.
255. Boissonnade 1900, 2:94.
256. Quoted in Bolt 2021, 1.
257. Brohm 1999, 194–6.
258. Quoted in Brohm 1999, 196.
259. Raynaud 1862, 19.
260. Quoted in Brohm 1999, 194–6.

TABLE 6.4. Guild Caps on the Number of Medical Practitioners, European Towns, 1515–1716

Town	Society	Date	Guild	Numerus clausus	Town population	Practitioners per 1,000 inhabitants	Source
Flensburg	Denmark	1515	Barber-surgeons	4	6,000	0.67	a
Stettin/Szczecin	Germany	1553	Barber-surgeons	10	13,000	0.77	b
Vienna	Austria	1564	Apothecaries	10	20,000	0.50	c
Stockholm	Sweden	1571	Barber-surgeons	6	8,000	0.75	d
Stettin/Szczecin	Germany	1611	Barber-surgeons	10	12,000	0.83	e
Helmstedt	Germany	1646	Barber-surgeons	3	1,892	1.59	f
Mechelen	S. Netherlands	1647	Apothecaries	6	20,000	0.30	g
Wolfenbüttel	Germany	1650	Bathmasters	3	9,000	0.33	h
Wolfenbüttel	Germany	1650	Barber-surgeons	6	9,000	0.67	h
Zierikzee	N. Netherlands	Pre-1672	Apothecaries	8	6,000	1.33	i
Zierikzee	N. Netherlands	Post-1672	Apothecaries	3	6,000	0.50	i
Dresden	Germany	1677	Barber-surgeons	10	15,000	0.67	j
Dublin	Ireland	1692	Physicians	14	60,000	0.23	k
Darmstadt	Germany	1701	Barber-surgeons	6	5,000	1.20	l
Vienna	Austria	Pre-1716	Barber-surgeons	9	113,000	0.08	m
Vienna	Austria	Post-1716	Barber-surgeons	12	113,000	0.11	m

TABLE 6.4. (*continued*)

Town	Society	Date	Guild	Numerus clausus	Town population	Practitioners per 1,000 inhabitants	Source
Means							
Physicians (*n* = 1)						0.23	
Apothecaries (*n* = 4)						0.66	
Barber-surgeons (*n* = 10)						0.73	
Bathmasters (*n* = 1)						0.33	
Total (*n* = 16)						0.66	
Median (*n* = 16)						0.67	

Sources: [a] Hybel and Poulsen 2007, 282n92; Bairoch, Batou, and Chèvre 1988, electronic database. [b] Blümcke 1884, 38; De Vries 1984, 273. [c] Noggler 1936; Scheutz 2018, 118. [d] Ojala 2014, 329; Söderberg, Jonsson, and Persson 1991, 1. [e] Blümcke 1884, 1. [f] Brohm 1999, 194–6; Wikipedia contributors, "Helmstedt", *Wikipedia, die freie Enzyklopädie*, accessed 17 May 2024, https://de.wikipedia.org/wiki/Helmstedt#Einwohnerentwicklung (linear interpolation between 1639 (1,645 inhabitants) and 1700 (3,800 inhabitants). [g] Bolt 2021, 1; De Vries 1984, 272. [h] Brohm 1999, 196; Wikipedia contributors, "Wolfenbüttel", *Wikipedia, die freie Enzyklopädie*, accessed 17 May 2024, https://de.wikipedia.org/wiki/Wolfenb%C3%BCttel#Einwohnerentwicklung. [i] Bolt 2021, 1; Bairoch, Batou, and Chèvre 1988, electronic database. [j] Schlenkrich 2002, 26; De Vries 1984, 272. [k] Brockliss 2010, 75; De Vries 1984, 271. [l] Hessisches Staatsarchiv Darmstadt, E 10, 1151, "Zahlenmäßige Festlegung der Chirurgen und Barbiere in Darmstadt auf sechs", Deutsche Digitale Bibliothek, https://www.deutsche-digitale-bibliothek.de/item/AO5X63TDCCZXCSNSICWIWRWB4GYUHH4O?lang=de; Bairoch, Batou, and Chèvre 1988, electronic database. [m] Ehmer 1997, 175–7; Ehmer 2000, 206.

inhabitants. To place these figures in context, in 2018 the equivalent ratio in Europe ranged from a low of 2.8 practitioners per 1,000 population in the United Kingdom to a high of 6.0 in Belgium. Across the 96 countries recorded by the WHO in 2018, the ratio was below 0.66 per 1,000 in only 22 (16 of them in Africa).[261] The numerus clausus imposed by pre-modern medical guilds resulted, therefore, in a ratio of medical providers to population that was less than one-quarter the lowest ratio in Europe in 2018, resembling the poorest quartile of countries in the world that year. The fact that medical guilds felt the need to impose legal caps indicates unmistakably that medical demand in pre-modern European towns could have supported a higher supply of doctors if medical associations had not limited entry.

Medical associations enforced these barriers in practice. Ostracism was one method, as in 1270 when the Venetian barber-surgeons' guild agreed that practitioners who were not members of the guild "shall be neither advised nor supported by the members",[262] or in eighteenth-century England where the College of Physicians prohibited its members from engaging in joint consultations with "illicit" practitioners not licensed by the college.[263] Medical associations enforced their entry barriers by bringing lawsuits, as in cases prosecuted by the fourteenth-century Florence doctors' guild,[264] the sixteenth-century Lüneburg surgeons' guild,[265] or the seventeenth-century Dublin surgeons' guild.[266] Medical associations pressed governments to enforce their entry barriers, as in notorious lobbying campaigns by the thirteenth-century Paris Faculty of Medicine,[267] the fourteenth-century Barcelona doctors' guild,[268] the fifteenth-century Vienna physicians' and apothecaries' guilds,[269] or the seventeenth-century Groningen surgeons' guild.[270]

Medical associations profited financially from their right to limit entry, levying fees and outright bribes in return for granting licenses. They charged outsiders for exemptions, as in 1678 when the Amsterdam surgeons' guild levied a yearly fee from a non-member for permission to heal eyes, pull teeth, and make poultices,[271] or in England in the 1780s when the College of

261. "Physicians (per 1,000 People)", World Bank, accessed 19 May 2024, https://data .worldbank.org/indicator/SH.MED.PHYS.ZS.

262. Quoted in Mickwitz 1936, 32.

263. DeLacy 1993b, 46.

264. Park 1985, 18.

265. Bodemann 1883, xl.

266. Whelan 2012, 31.

267. Brockliss and Jones 1997, 173.

268. García-Ballester, Mcvaugh, and Rubio-Vela 1989, 20.

269. Schütte 2017, 222–3.

270. Huisman 1989, 68–9.

271. P. Smith 2004, 197.

Physicians levied fees from non-member "licentiates" for permission to practise.[272] When a guild expanded its numerus clausus, it required new masters
to pay compensation to existing ones, as in 1716 when the Vienna barber-
surgeons' guild increased its numerus clausus from nine to twelve, and the
three new masters had to pay the nine existing ones 3,600 florins (equivalent
to 9,600 days' wages for a Viennese master craftsman at that time) to compensate them for the loss of some of their cartel profits.[273] In the Southern
Netherlands before 1789, surgeons' guilds charged sufficiently high examination fees that rural applicants could not afford them; sometimes the guilds
simply sold licenses to applicants for cash payments instead of requiring any
training or examination.[274]

Some twenty-first-century medical associations do likewise, rationing supplies of medical practitioners and accepting huge payments in return for licensing dubious medical schools, which in turn accept bribes from unqualified
applicants.[275] The ability to extract such payments is a strong indication that
the entry barriers imposed by medical associations were, and are, a binding
constraint on the supply of medical practitioners.

4.2. MAKING THE COST OF THAT ART SO MUCH DEARER TO THE DAMAGE OF THE WHOLE PEOPLE

The entry barriers imposed by medical associations created a shortage of providers. They had this effect even in normal times. In Coventry in 1391–96, the
barbers' guild was described as creating scarcity and raising prices, "making
the cost of that art so much dearer to the damage of the whole people".[276]
In Gerolzhofen in 1445, citizens complained that the bathmasters' guild was
reducing its working days, even though provision was already insufficient for
the growing number of inhabitants.[277] In Florence in 1468, the government
complained about "the lack of doctors well versed in the art of medicine".[278] In
London in 1542–43, a Royal Act was passed permitting persons to administer
medicines even if they did not have membership in the "Company and Fel-
lowship of Surgeons". The justification was stark:

272. DeLacy 1993b, 46.
273. Ehmer 2000, 206. For the number of days' earnings implied by 3,600 florins, see Allen's
(n.d.) Vienna database (1716 wage of "mason" is 22.5 kr., "mason's handman" is 15 kr., "grape-
picker" is 8 kr.).
274. Schepers 1985, 316.
275. Chatterjee 2010, 1679.
276. Quoted in Lipson 1915, 1:303.
277. Heffner 1864, 23–4.
278. Quoted in Park 1985, 58.

It is now well known, that the Surgeons admitted [to the Company] will do no Cure to any Person, but where they shall know to be rewarded with a greater Sum or Reward than the Cure extendeth unto; . . . although the most Part of the Persons of the said Craft of Surgeons have small Cunning, yet they will take great Sums of Money, and do little therefore, and by Reason thereof they do oftentimes impair and hurt their Patients, rather than do them good.[279]

Ordinary Londoners also thought the surgeons' guild restricted supply and overcharged customers, as in the complaint of one sixteenth-century Londoner to the effect that the barber-surgeons were so few and so costly that the poor could rarely obtain care and were constrained to resort to "sow-gelders, horse-gelders, tinkers, and cobblers".[280] In the Dutch Republic in 1593, a non-guilded surgeon petitioned for a special license from the state on the grounds that the medical guilds were neglecting "the needs of the poor and miserable".[281] In 1625, the inhabitants of Leipzig complained that the guilded barber-surgeons were inadequate for the medical needs of the town and needed to be supplemented by additional healers.[282] In Angers in 1715, with a population of 27,000, people complained that the College of Physicians insisted on maintaining its numerus clausus even though the town had only five *docteurs-régents* (qualified doctors) in post, two of them very old.[283] In 1732, the itinerant Dutch surgeon Johan Herman Francken complained that the physicians' guilds pressed town councils to suppress non-guilded healers: "Much rather would they see the miserable ones [patients] smother in their pains than to brook a stranger—whose curing abilities are well-known—to be crowned with greater fame than they."[284]

Even in normal times, therefore, medical associations deliberately restricted supply. In epidemics, such shortages became calamitous. Many doctors withdrew from the market. This was understandable, given the morbidity, case fatality, and population mortality rates for epidemics shown in table 1.2. The best way to avoid dying of an epidemic disease was to avoid getting it to begin with. Small wonder that doctors withdrew from the market when epidemics raged. Even the influenza epidemic of 1918–19, with a comparatively low population mortality rate of 2.5 per cent, led to massive market withdrawal by doctors, as described by the secretary of the Minnesota State Board of Health,

279. Quoted in Raithby 1811, 3:396.
280. Quoted in Tymms 1853, 39.
281. Huisman 1989, 71.
282. Schütte 2017, 213.
283. Lebrun 1971, 202.
284. Quoted in Huisman 1989, 68.

who tried to recruit physicians to fight the epidemic but reported that "a number who we have called for have made excuses and have not come at all".[285]

It is understandable that some doctors should withdraw their services to save their own lives. What is analytically important is that medical associations did not remedy such shortages but exacerbated them. Guilds and professional associations justified their legal monopolies, as we have seen, partly by claiming to serve the common weal. Entry barriers, they claimed, ensured that medical practice would be reserved to a select group of honourable men who would abjure self-seeking and make personal sacrifices to serve the public good. In times of epidemic, however, this honourable ethos did not always hold, and even the public authorities were unable to enforce this supposed social contract. Medical associations did not ameliorate supply shortages during epidemics. On the contrary. Their entry barriers curtailed the number of practitioners even in normal times, as reflected in the contemporary complaints discussed above. Those entry barriers remained in force during the epidemic, which prevented doctor numbers from responding to rising demand from patient morbidity or falling supply from doctor deaths. To make matters worse, the legal monopoly of a medical association enabled its members to refuse to practise during an epidemic without losing business to competitors.

Market withdrawal by medical practitioners during epidemics was a serious problem. In Venice during the Black Death, so many physicians left town that craftsmen and untrained adolescents had to step in.[286] In the Italian city of Belluno in 1348–50, "each one was physician for himself, and no dealers in medicines were found".[287] In the 1399 Auxerre plague, all the doctors fled, and the town had to bring in an outsider from Nevers.[288] In the 1520 Beauvais epidemic, all the members of the surgeons' guild refused to treat anyone with plague, and the town had to ask the Franciscan monks to help instead.[289] In the 1574 Lyons plague, all but two of the town's surgeons deserted their posts.[290] In the 1583 Angers plague, the head doctor of the hospital left town as soon as the epidemic began, and the other senior doctors refused to treat patients; ultimately the mayor could get a doctor to serve only by offering "extraordinary wages of 50 *écus* per month" (equivalent to 600 days' wages for a Paris journeyman).[291] In the 1632 Loudon plague, all four physicians departed and

285. Quoted in Ott et al. 2007, 804.
286. Gasquet 1908, 35.
287. Quoted in A. Campbell 1931, 30.
288. Biraben 1976, 127.
289. N. Murphy 2013, 146.
290. Brockliss and Jones 1997, 179–80.
291. Lebrun 1971, 304. Allen's (n.d.) Paris wages file gives ten sous per day as the wage of a "worker (helper)" in Paris in 1583. At 120 sous per *écu*, 50 *écus* was 6,000 sous, or 600 days' wages for a Paris worker in 1583.

refused to return until the epidemic subsided.[292] In the 1651 Barcelona plague, the licensed physicians and surgeons fled, and substitutes promised by the king never arrived.[293] In the 1656 Rome plague, physicians, surgeons, and barbers had to be formally prohibited by the Health Congregation from leaving the city.[294] In London during the Great Plague of 1665–66, the entire College of Physicians fled, along with its president, abandoning the populace to apothecaries and the "chemical physicians" whose innovative but heterodox medical ideas the college had long sought to suppress.[295]

Even when guilded practitioners did not leave town, they were able to withdraw from the market because their privileges meant they could not legally be supplanted by bolder interlopers. In Venice during the Black Death, many doctors "shut themselves in their houses".[296] In Florence during the recurrent epidemics after the Black Death, few doctors stayed in town, and even those often refused to care for plague patients.[297] Marchione di Coppo Stefani described how in Florence during the Black Death those few physicians who could be found "wanted vast sums in hand before they entered the house".[298] During the Black Death in Avignon, according to the surgeon Guy de Chauliac, "It was unprofitable for leeches and shameful, for they were not hardy to visit, for dread of infecting."[299] In the 1538 Rouen plague, the College of Physicians refused to nominate any of its members to serve; the town council had to get an order from the *parlement* ordering the college to assign a small quota of members to provide plague advice under threat of punishment.[300] In the 1596 Saint-Omer plague, guilded physicians and surgeons provided advice to the government but flatly refused to diagnose or care for the infected.[301] In the 1628 Lyon epidemic, the guilded surgeons refused to practise, so the town was reduced to hiring untrained boys, who were supposed to learn surgeonry directly on plague patients.[302] In the 1636–37 plague epidemic, Malaga was so ill served by its guilded physicians and surgeons that it appealed publicly for animal doctors to serve in their stead.[303] In the 1680 plague in České Budějovice (Budweis), the town physician flatly refused to treat any patients

292. Biraben 1976, 130.
293. Biraben 1976, 130.
294. Gentilcore 2012, 157.
295. Gelfand 1993, 1126; Mauelshagen 2005, 241, 254.
296. Quoted in Gasquet 1908, 35.
297. Park 1985, 82–3.
298. Quoted in Vanneste 2010, 37.
299. Quoted in Vanneste 2010, 38 (spelling and punctuation modernized).
300. N. Murphy 2013, 148.
301. Biraben 1976, 130.
302. Biraben 1976, 132.
303. Biraben 1976, 134.

other than members of the city council and high-ranking persons; the town council minutes recorded that "the doctor refuses to get involved in any way in the situation". All but one of the barber-surgeons likewise refused to see plague sufferers, so that the town had to offer an exorbitant salary to attract a foreign journeyman barber-surgeon from Bamberg, who turned out to be so inexperienced that he had to seek advice from a local army doctor.[304]

Guilded doctors even neglected patients needing care for other conditions during epidemics. In the 1631 Florence plague, for instance, no guilded surgeon was willing to help "a woman in labour [who] had been in the process of giving birth for fourteen hours with the creature dead and half outside the mother". Not a single guilded doctor would even attend to certify that the woman was not infected with plague so a priest could give her extreme unction. The only medical practitioners willing to attend were midwives, who were legally forbidden to either carry out surgery or certify the woman's non-infectious condition.[305]

Medical associations also refused to contribute to contagion control during epidemics. In the 1583 London plague, for instance, the College of Physicians was asked to provide volunteers to support the quarantine effort, but did so very slowly and sent very few.[306] In the 1600 Saint-Malo plague, the entire surgeons' guild refused to make any contribution to the public health measures organized by the local government, and the city had to offer "much gold" to recruit an outsider.[307] In the 1625 London epidemic, the College of Physicians first temporized and then provided only two volunteers, for a city of 200,000–400,000 inhabitants.[308] In the 1630 Florence epidemic, the College of Physicians refused to send any of its members even to care for plague victims privately for fees.[309] In the Great Plague of London in 1665–66, the College of Physicians did send a team of 10 or 11 members to help fight the epidemic, but the entry barriers of the college meant that there were no more than 30 qualified physicians in a city of over 400,000 inhabitants during an epidemic that killed 60,000 people; even the surgeons, apothecaries, and black-market "empirics" could not remotely compensate for this inadequate medical provision.[310] Indeed, the powers of the College of Physicians, its severe entry barriers, and its enduring reluctance to provide advice and assistance during epidemics are regarded as major reasons London implemented anti-contagion

304. Holasová 2005, 15–16, 22.
305. Quoted in Henderson 2019, 116.
306. Slack 1985, 214.
307. Biraben 1976, 131.
308. Slack 1985, 246. London's population was *c*.200,000 in 1600 and *c*.400,000 in 1650 (De Vries 1984, 270).
309. Cipolla 1973, 25–6.
310. Slack 1985, 246.

measures later and less effectively than other English urban centres.[311] In the 1713–14 Vienna epidemic, the government promulgated a law requiring physicians to gather first-hand information about the plague, but the Medical Faculty outright refused to perform post-mortems on plague victims, so the government had to pay a surgeon to examine the corpses.[312]

In Italian cities, as we saw in chapter 3, central pillars of contagion control were public lazarettos, where the infected and their contacts were isolated until certified to be plague-free. This required medical experts to diagnose infection and recovery. But medical associations often refused to provide the required experts. In the 1630 Florentine plague epidemic, as we have seen, the College of Physicians refused to supply members to serve in the lazaretto; the most it was willing to do was examine any outside doctors the health board could find to serve.[313] In the 1630 Bologna plague, the Health Office asked for physicians to attend in the lazaretto but the College of Physicians refused, instead suggesting that the lazaretto surgeon shout the patients' symptoms from the window, whereupon a college physician would shout back his advice from a safe distance.[314] In the 1630 Pavia plague, physicians outright refused to provide advice or assistance in the public pesthouse.[315] In the 1656–57 Rome plague, "high fees and special prizes were not enough to induce doctors to go and tend people in the pesthouses and they had to be compelled to do so by public authority".[316]

The late seventeenth-century Dresden plague provides a vivid illustration of how guilds exacerbated medical scarcity during epidemics. When plague broke out in Dresden in 1680, the local government needed medical practitioners to serve in the town lazaretto to help diagnose and isolate plague patients, in order to prevent them from infecting the rest of the town. But the Dresden barber-surgeons' guild flatly refused to provide any volunteers. So the ruler of Saxony recruited four journeymen surgeons who were willing to work in the lazaretto. One of them was Johann Gregor Gutturff, who had completed all the requirements for mastership but had been rejected by the Dresden guild because he had impregnated his wife (a guild master's daughter) before marriage. Gutturff agreed to take responsibility for directing the lazaretto, and the other three journeymen agreed to serve in it, in return for the ruler's promise that after the plague was over they would be granted guild mastership if they survived. Shortly after being appointed, Gutturff and another of

311. Slack 1985, 215.
312. Velimirovic and Velimirovic 1989, 822.
313. Cipolla 1973, 25; Cipolla 1976, 78; Henderson 2019, 108–9.
314. Cipolla 1973, 26.
315. Cipolla 1976, 35.
316. Cipolla 1973, 25–6.

the journeymen surgeons in the lazaretto contracted plague. The substitute recommended by the surgeons' guild refused even to visit the lazaretto, so the authorities had to resort to a former wound doctor from Halberstadt with no knowledge or experience of bubonic plague. Wound doctors were less well trained and lower in status than surgeons, so much so that both the recovered Gutturff and the guilded town physician later stated that it was questionable to entrust such healers with the treatment of those suffering from the plague.[317] When the plague passed, the ruler of Saxony found himself unable to fulfil his promise to grant guild mastership to the journeymen who had served in the lazaretto, because the surgeons' guild adamantly refused to let them in. Late in 1681, three of the journeymen wrote to the ruler, reminding him of their loyal plague service and contrasting it with the guilded surgeons, who had turned their back on the city in its peril. Only when the Saxon ruler threatened to rescind its charter did the Dresden surgeons' guild grudgingly admit just one of the journeymen—the former lazaretto director—leaving the other three to go on vainly petitioning. As late as 1700–20 years after the epidemic—the former lazaretto director and another of the four lazaretto journeymen, who had finally got special state permission to practise independently, complained that the Dresden guild was still excluding them from its assemblies.[318]

So reluctant were medical associations and their members to contribute to epidemic contagion control that, as the Dresden example illustrates, governments sometimes resorted to granting emergency licenses to non-guilded medical practitioners.[319] Students who had not completed their medical education, journeymen who had not been admitted to mastership, animal doctors, quacks, charlatans, and even women were sometimes hired during epidemics when guilded medical practitioners were unwilling to provide advice and care. In Orvieto during the Black Death, when no physician would serve even when offered the huge salary of 50 florins annually, the town hired a student who had not yet finished his medical education.[320] From the 1560s onwards, major towns in Brittany filled gaps created by the scarcity or withdrawal of guilded practitioners by appointing "plague surgeons" (who were often outright quacks) and offering them special licenses letting them go on practising after the epidemic without guild or college membership.[321] In the 1581 Chartres epidemic, when the surgeons' guild refused to nominate members to advise or care for plague victims, the town government declared that any outsider

317. Schlenkrich 2002, 39–40.
318. Schlenkrich 2002, 55–6.
319. Cipolla 1976, 87–93.
320. Biraben 1976, 125–6.
321. Brockliss and Jones 1997, 246.

who volunteered would be granted guild mastership after the epidemic.[322] In the late sixteenth century, many French town hospitals began to circumvent the scarce and expensive practitioners of the physicians' and surgeons' corporations by appointing journeymen, who in exchange for serving six years in the high-risk hospital environment were promised mastership that bypassed guild requirements.[323]

Some epidemic-struck communities went so far as to recruit females. In the 1509 plague, the Vierzon town government hired a woman to provide medical services during the epidemic.[324] In sixteenth-century Dutch epidemics, females provided medical care during epidemics because professional medical expertise from guilded male doctors was unaffordable for the urban poor and unavailable in most smaller towns and villages.[325] In the 1630 Florence plague, guild-certified doctors were so scarce that the Public Health Office offered jobs in the lazaretto to 16 non-guild practitioners, half of them women. One of these, Margherita di Giovanni Lombardi, "takes blood and cuts the buboes like a surgeon and merits a higher salary".[326] This may have been the same woman who was still practising during the 1633 epidemic in one of the plague convalescent centres,

> [where] there was a surgeon to treat the men, and for the women there was a woman called Margherita, wife of a coachman, who served as a housekeeper in that convalescent centre, a woman who was truly very diligent, treated [patients] with such accuracy that cannot be properly described, and because the surgeon was sick, it fell to her to treat the men as well, which she performed with such honesty, that is worth recording.[327]

The medical guilds fought back furiously against such encroachments, even in the worst epidemics. In the 1458 Amiens plague, the physicians complained to the town council against "several barber-surgeons, foreign persons, and others, who are meddling and interloping into the science and estate of medicine".[328] In the sixteenth-century Venice plagues, the Health Board issued a handful of special licenses to non-guilded practitioners to provide medical services, but the College of Physicians furiously rescinded them.[329] In the 1630 Florence epidemic, the College of Physicians refused to nominate volunteers to serve in the lazaretto but vehemently opposed the appointment of a surgeon who

322. Biraben 1976, 133.
323. Brockliss and Jones 1997, 25.
324. Biraben 1976, 134.
325. Deneweth and Wallis 2016, 523–4, 543, 546, 550; Curtis 2021a, 6–7.
326. Quoted in Henderson 2019, 113–14.
327. Quoted in Henderson 2019, 200.
328. N. Murphy 2013, 148.
329. Cipolla 1976, 8.

"intended to provide treatment in his own strange way, giving patients medicines by mouth, and not using any irons to cut buboes and swellings".[330] During epidemics in seventeenth-century Brittany, medical corporations refused to care for plague victims but strenuously challenged the special licenses granted to non-guilded plague doctors.[331] In seventeenth-century Paris, the medical colleges and guilds refused to volunteer members to serve in plague hospitals but objected noisily when the town promised guild mastership to journeymen surgeons and apothecaries who agreed to serve.[332]

It might be argued that in a world before scientific medicine it did not matter if medical guilds restricted supply and increased prices, since medical practitioners did not know how to prevent or treat infectious diseases anyway. But the fact that something is mostly useless is no justification for artificially increasing its price or limiting its supply. Only if remedies were known to be unquestionably harmful would it improve social welfare to restrict their supply. But if medical remedies were known to be unquestionably harmful, the socially optimal solution would be to prohibit them, not to allow their producers to reap monopoly profits from selling them at artificially high prices. In reality, of course, pre-scientific medical knowledge was so poor that virtually no medical remedies—licensed or not—were known to be unquestionably harmful, so it cannot be argued that medical guilds improved social welfare by restricting access to them. The most that can be said is that before scientific medicine, most medical remedies were ineffective. People were therefore not made better off by guilds that compelled them to pay artificially high prices for ineffective remedies from guilded practitioners. Quite the contrary. Paying artificially high prices for useless remedies means that sufferers had fewer resources to pay for food, shelter, warmth, nursing, or the ability to avoid contagion by stopping work—health inputs which, as we saw in chapter 2, did actually improve people's survival during epidemics.

Moreover, as we have seen, there were a few medical remedies that were actually effective in preventing epidemic contagion. One of them was small-pox variolation, available as a professional treatment in China since the mid-sixteenth century, as a folk prophylactic in multiple continents in the seventeenth, and as a medical procedure in Europe and North America from around 1720 onwards. Yet medical associations limited the supply of variolation and increased its price in at least three ways.

First, by increasing prices for other, ineffective medical services, medical guilds reduced disposable incomes that could be allocated to effective ones like variolation, even if it was just informally "buying the pox". Second,

---

330. Quoted in Henderson 2019, 200.
331. Brockliss and Jones 1997, 246.
332. Brockliss and Jones 1997, 252.

by restricting the supply of legal variolation to zero, medical associations in societies such as Spain and France ensured that people either could not get variolated at all or had to incur the costs and risks of procuring the procedure illicitly on the black market.

The third way medical associations limited the supply of variolation and increased its price was by turning the procedure into a monopoly for their members. As we have seen, this happened in a number of eighteenth-century European societies. One of them was Sweden, where the state approved variolation in 1756 but made it the monopoly of physicians and a handful of specially licensed surgeons.[333] This legal monopoly for medical practitioners suppressed the commercial, religious, communal, and philanthropic providers who diffused and improved variolation in England, as well as reducing its price by 500 per cent between the 1760s and the 1780s.[334] In Sweden, by contrast, physicians reported illicit private variolators to the authorities for undercutting their profitable monopoly. In 1769 the district physician in Älvsborg complained to the authorities that he himself had completely failed to persuade the common people of the benefits of variolation while—surprisingly!—an itinerant shoemaker was illegally operating a successful variolation practice which charged lower prices.[335] In 1778, a district physician sought to put the former apothecary turned black-market variolator Anders Elg out of business by falsely accusing him of malpractice and reporting him to the authorities.[336] Even where voluntary inoculators were allowed to practise, as in Gothenburg in 1773, they complained that the physicians deliberately kept the variolation lymph for themselves and refused to release it to the volunteers.[337]

Of course, no legal monopoly is perfect, and the market for variolation in eighteenth-century Sweden was no exception. Illicit encroachers, including teachers, farmers, shoemakers, apothecaries, medical students, and surgeons, operated in the black market created by the legal monopoly of the physicians. The difference in price between the monopolistic physicians and the illicit commercial variolators was striking. In 1767, the official price charged by a monopolistic physician for each variolation was 12 coppers, equivalent to five or six days' earnings for a worker or peasant. By contrast, a former teacher turned illegal variolator in the district of Älvsborg in 1769 charged just

---

333. Sköld 1996b, 319.

334. According to Brunton (1990, 144–5), the price of variolation in England averaged 5 shillings per head in the 1760s but 1 shilling per head in the 1780s. According to Allen's (n.d.) London database, an agricultural labourer's wage in both southern and northern England was 12 pence (1 shilling) a day in both the 1760s and the 1780s.

335. Sköld 1996b, 321.

336. Sköld 1996b, 321–2.

337. Sköld 1996b, 316.

1½ coppers, equivalent to less than a day's earnings for a common man.[338] Their corporate monopoly over variolation therefore enabled the guilded physicians to impose a price six times as high as the black-market rate. Inevitably, this limited access by ordinary people to this essential method of limiting smallpox contagion.

The Swedish physicians' association also restricted access by limiting the number of non-medical variolators.[339] Table 6.5 shows the occupational background of all recorded Swedish variolators during two periods, the first running from the legalization of variolation in 1756 to the introduction of the cheaper and safer English Suttonian method in 1767, the second running from then until the beginning of vaccination, around 1800. In the earlier period, physicians made up 65 per cent of all active variolators and administered 91 per cent of all variolations; surgeons (some or all legally licensed) made up another 23 per cent of variolators and administered another 8 per cent of variolations. Together, physicians and surgeons constituted 88 per cent of all recorded variolators in this period and administered 99 per cent of known variolations.

After the Suttonian method was introduced in 1767, the physicians became less able to defend their legal privileges. Between then and 1800, they accounted for only 45 per cent of variolators and administered just 58 per cent of variolations. Surgeons declined to just 13 per cent of variolators and 12 per cent of variolations. All formally licensed medical practitioners taken together accounted for just 58 per cent of variolators and 70 per cent of variolations in this later period. But their place was not taken by the multitude of freelance commercial practitioners who increased supply, enhanced quality, and reduced the cost of variolation in England. Rather, it was filled by clergymen and parents. Clergy-related variolators accounted for 8 per cent of the total before 1767 and 6 per cent afterwards, but increased their share of variolations from 1 per cent to 23 per cent of the total. Before 1767 there was no record of parents variolating their own children, while after 1767 they made up 28 per cent of named variolators, though they administered only 1 per cent of variolations.

These findings are confirmed by the annual reports by Swedish physicians and clergymen between 1750 and 1800, which mention only 15 active variolators who were not formally licensed medical practitioners; many of them variolated only a few children apiece. This state of affairs is ascribed to the medical monopoly of variolation, the limited number of physicians, and the resulting prevention of any extension of the practice of variolation.[340] The best available estimates suggest that between 1750 and 1800, just 50,000 individuals

---

338. Sköld 1996b, 295.
339. Sköld 1996b, 325.
340. Sköld 1996a, 251n24.

TABLE 6.5. Medical Monopolization of Variolation in Sweden, 1756–1800

	Number of variolators				Number of variolations			
	1756–67		1768–1800		1756–67		1768–1800	
Occupation	No.	%	No.	%	No.	%	No.	%
Physicians	26	65	56	45	944	91	8,100	58
Surgeons	9	23	16	13	83	8	1,700	12
Medical students	0	0	2	2	0	0	6	0
Apothecaries	0	0	1	1	0	0	800	6
Clergymen and Church-related	3	8	7	6	6	1	3,163	23
Miscellaneous	2	5	7	6	3	0	79	1
Parents	0	0	35	28	0	0	90	1
Total	40	101	124	101	1,036	100	13,938	101

Source: Own calculations, based on Sköld (1996b, 323–4), who describes his numbers as "approximate".

Notes: In 1756–67, Sköld gives a total of 41 variolators and 1,038 variolations, but columns in fact add up to 40 and 1,036. The 2 miscellaneous variolators consisted of 1 teacher and 1 farmer. In 1768–1800, Sköld gives a total of 13,090 variolations, but the column adds up to 13,938. The 7 miscellaneous variolators consisted of 1 shoemaker, 5 farmers, and 1 farmer's wife. Rounding of figures means percentages do not always add up to 100.

were variolated across the entirety of Sweden.[341] By contrast, in England by 1770, the Suttons' collective alone had variolated over 300,000 clients, and tens of thousands more had been variolated by other commercial providers, local poor rate vestries, philanthropic organizations, and individual physicians and surgeons.[342]

Vaccination turned out differently. When it was approved in Sweden in 1804, the physicians' associations again demanded a monopoly. To make up for their loss of the profitable variolation monopoly, the Medical Board initially reserved state vaccination funding to the licensed physicians. But it did not grant them an outright monopoly. Then, in 1813, the physicians also lost their exclusive claim to state vaccination funding. Vaccination then diffused widely in the hands of clergymen, bell-ringers, midwives, independent women, and many other individuals. The only prerequisite was that any non-physician vaccinator had to obtain a state certificate attesting to their competence.[343]

341. Sköld 1996a, 253.
342. Williams 2010, 138.
343. Sköld 1996a, 258; Sköld 1996b, 412–14.

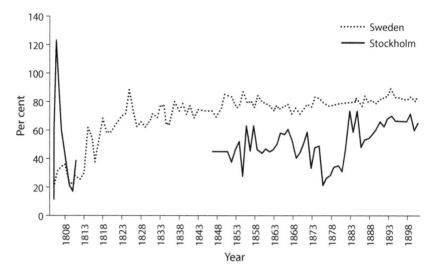

FIGURE 6.4. Vaccination rate in Stockholm compared with the rest of Sweden, 1804–1900. Vaccination rate = number of vaccinations per 100 births during the preceding year. In Stockholm vaccination was monopolized by physicians. *Source*: Based on Sköld 1996b, 473.

The exception was Stockholm, where the physicians enjoyed a complete monopoly over vaccination between 1806 and 1852. Unsurprisingly, as can be seen in figure 6.4, vaccination rates were lower in Stockholm than in the rest of Sweden, except in the single year 1805. The physicians' monopoly over vaccination in Stockholm almost certainly reduced its supply, just as their monopoly over variolation across the entirety of Sweden had limited supply during the preceding half-century.[344]

Table 6.6 shows the institutional features of smallpox immunization in Sweden from 1756 to 1900, along with the immunization rate. Where immunization was monopolized by physicians, as in all of Sweden for variolation and in Stockholm for vaccination, provision was restricted. It was allowed only in centralized and inconvenient locations, it involved costly periods of medically unnecessary supervision, and the outcome was a low immunization rate. Outside Stockholm, non-medical vaccinators were allowed to operate, which greatly increased the flexibility and attractiveness of the procedure. Children were allowed to be vaccinated at home, and the family was not required to pay for costly and unnecessary medical supervision. Despite the absence of legal compulsion, vaccination rates outside Stockholm were high.

344. Sköld 1996b, 472–4.

TABLE 6.6. Institutional Features of Variolation and Vaccination Systems, Sweden, 1756–1900

Institutional feature	Variolation	Vaccination	Vaccination
	all of Sweden	Stockholm	areas outside Stockholm
Monopoly	Only physicians allowed	Only physicians allowed	No monopoly, mostly laymen (state certificate of competence required)
Location	Institute (Stockholm); homes (rest of Sweden)	Inoculation centre	Homes
Care and charge	14 days	14 days (1802–40); 1–2 days (1840 on)	No care
Records	No records kept	No records kept	Records from all parishes annually
Legal compulsion	None	Strong	Slight
Immunization rate	Low	Low	High

Source: Sköld 1996b, 475.

Corporative medical monopolies almost certainly restricted supply directly, and may have indirectly deterred uptake by increasing costs and inconvenience. The physicians' associations may also have deterred acceptance of both variolation and vaccination by portraying them as more difficult and dangerous than they really were. Such portrayals helped to justify the physicians' entitlement to monopolize the procedures, but also increased the perceived risks among the general public, deterring some who would otherwise have had their children immunized.

Medical associations, by limiting entry, created artificial scarcity and increased prices of medical services. There is little evidence that their monopoly privileges and anti-competitive measures were justified either as a recompense for undertaking a high-risk occupation or as a way for doctors to commit themselves to a corporate ethos that they would not abandon their patients in crises. During epidemics, demand for medical provision rocketed but supply plummeted, as members of medical associations used the cushion of their cartel privileges to withdraw from the market without economic penalty. Of course, the cartel privileges of medical associations were only one determinant of medical supply during epidemics. But there would certainly have been more practitioners if the medical associations had not limited entry. Furthermore, the limited number of licensed practitioners would have had more incentive to contribute to epidemic control if their corporate privileges had not insulated them from competition.

5. Conclusion

Occupational associations are often adduced as historical exemplars of closely knit social networks that generate beneficial social capital. Such institutions can indeed benefit society if they use their norms, information, sanctions, and collective action to solve problems—such as those posed by epidemic disease—that prove intractable for market, state, community, religion, or family. Occupational associations are well suited to provide these benefits, since they offer the collective professional expertise that is essential for solving societal problems involving technical challenges. Epidemics create precisely those circumstances.

But closely knit networks can use their social capital to benefit their own members at the expense of society at large. Occupational associations were no exception. Some medical associations did undertake activities that helped control epidemic contagion, although mainly when asked to do so by the authorities. They provided training and quality control, which had the potential to ensure expert anti-contagion advice and professional assistance to support public health. They also monitored medical knowledge and medical innovations, both of which were important for controlling epidemic contagion.

But medical associations were neither necessary nor sufficient to provide training, quality, and information. They were not necessary since there was a vast "medical marketplace" of practitioners whom patients wanted to consult but whom the medical associations rejected for reasons—gender, religion, ethnicity, citizenship, wealth, parentage, collective acceptability—that were unrelated to skill or merit. Nor were medical associations sufficient for tackling epidemic challenges. They and their members often refused to serve during epidemics because the work was dangerous and their corporate privileges sheltered them from competition.

Medical associations also had a dark side for epidemic control. Their entry restrictions reduced the supply of medical advice and assistance. They created these shortages even in times of normal demand. In epidemics, these shortages became lethal, as patients, communities, and governments desperately demanded medical advice and expertise which was not forthcoming. Medical associations' limits on competition further constricted supply during epidemics, since their members could refuse to serve during high-risk periods without losing their livelihoods to competitors.

Most seriously of all, many medical associations deployed their social capital in ways that exacerbated epidemic contagion. They made authoritative but unjustified pronouncements about infectious diseases. They opposed innovative knowledge about epidemic prevention, hindering measures such as quarantine, social distancing, and immunization which helped control epidemics but threatened the associations' legal monopoly over medical expertise and their members' business models. It might seem surprising that medical associations took so many actions that exacerbated epidemic contagion. But it made perfect sense. Occupational associations did what was good for their members, subordinating the interests of the wider society.

Modern medical associations also serve their members' interests by rationing training, limiting supply, and increasing prices. Some protect their members even when they engage in professional transgressions such as falsifying vaccination records, concealing infections, or using their professional standing to spread false information. Nor are medical associations wholly immune to professional groupthink, commercial inducements, or political pressure. As in the case of pre-modern medical guilds, these activities by modern medical associations are facilitated by their privileged position as cartels of medical practitioners. To the extent that they exploit this privileged position, modern medical associations can harm epidemic outcomes just as their pre-modern predecessors did.

Fortunately, modern medical associations also differ from their pre-modern predecessors in crucial ways. Even though they needlessly ration training, access to that training is more meritocratic and less based on identity-related characteristics unrelated to ability. So members of modern medical associations are recruited from a wider pool, giving them better human capital and personal qualities on average than the members of pre-modern medical guilds, who were admitted from a much narrower social base. Furthermore, medical training is now based on scientific approaches to disease, so members of modern medical associations possess expertise that significantly surpasses most folk remedies, in contrast to the ancient orthodoxies espoused by pre-modern medical practitioners and tenaciously defended by their associations. The wider institutional framework also monitors modern medical associations to a much greater extent. Governments, markets, universities, the media, the internet, and public opinion scrutinize the activities and pronouncements of medical associations. This can be uncomfortable and even counterproductive at times, but it also curbs the abuses of market power to which pre-modern medical associations were prone. Modern medical associations are therefore informed by expertise, science, and external scrutiny to a much greater extent than pre-modern medical guilds, reducing the harm they cause and enhancing their benefits. True medical expertise is crucial for defeating epidemics, historical and modern. But as history suggests, in ensuring that such expertise is made available to patients and society medical associations have both great strengths and serious weaknesses.

In a broader perspective, the activities of medical institutions in historical epidemics provide grim counter-evidence to the optimistic idea that the spread of scientific knowledge alone suffices to bring epidemics under control. Scientific knowledge relevant to understanding epidemics certainly advanced with the spread of microscopes, variolation, vaccination, germ theory, experimental approaches, and the identification of microorganisms responsible for infectious diseases. But alongside these scientific advances many medical professionals clung to non-scientific ideas about medicine, including belief in astrology, alchemy, miasmas, humours, and anti-contagionism. Those who espoused immunization or contagion theory often did so for unscientific reasons. Even when scientific knowledge was available, what mattered for epidemic disease was not so much the knowledge itself but the incentives for its adoption. These were—and are—shaped by the institutional framework of society, including the professional associations of medical practitioners.

7

The Family

The poor are most harmed by the plague because of the confined living conditions in houses vulgarly called stables, where every room is filled with large families and where stench and contagion prevail.

—MILANESE PRIEST DURING PLAGUE EPIDEMIC, 1630[1]

Children, on guard at compound doors, give the signal, when they see the inspectors coming along a street, and then all the sick, who can move or be moved, are hidden away, in cupboards, etc., etc. or in the yards under heaps of fuel, until the police have gone by. Though every care possible seems to be taken of the sick and, separately, of contacts, the populace do all they can to spoil the work of the Sanitary Inspectors.

—NEWSPAPER REPORT ON PLAGUE EPIDEMIC, MUKDEN (SHENYANG), NORTH-EAST CHINA, 1911[2]

Does the family belong in this book? Is it really an institution? The family is the name given to a set of people related by blood and marriage—a kinship group. But it also refers to the system of practices surrounding how that group of relatives resides, reproduces, nurtures, consumes, and produces. In that sense, the family is an example of "the humanly devised constraints that structure political, economic, and social interaction"—an institution.[3]

The family, however, is less formal than other institutions. Its constraints are norms, customs, and traditions, not formal codes or rules. You can violate

---

1. Quoted in Cipolla 1976, 35.
2. "The Plague: Mukden, Feb. 13", *North-China Herald*, 24 February 1911, 419.
3. North 1991, 97.

familial norms and not go to jail. But people disapprove of you. That is, the family constrains your behaviour mainly through expectations and peer pressure. Most institutions rely on such influences to some extent. But the family relies on them a lot. Most familial behaviour responds to the conduct and expectations of others, transmitted through past experiences or current peer effects. Expectations are often self-sustaining, so where you end up depends on where you start. As a result, the family can take very different forms in not very different societies.

Another reason the family differs across societies is that, to an even greater extent than other institutions, it does not work on its own. It constantly interacts with market, state, community, religion, guild, and the whole institutional framework. The allocation of activities among institutions differs hugely from one society to the next. So the family takes different forms in different societies.

Historical differences in family forms, many argue, have big effects on how the family interacts with epidemics. Most of these arguments focus on contrasts between nuclear-family systems and extended-family systems. Social scientists are particularly fascinated by a family form called the "European Marriage Pattern" (EMP). This is the name given by the great demographer John Hajnal to a family system characterized by three key features: late first marriage (over age 24–25 for women), frequent non-marriage (10–20 per cent of both sexes), and mainly nuclear-family households (over 75–80 per cent).[4] These three characteristics are often associated with a wider penumbra of practices: formation of new households at marriage, small household size, low household complexity, numerous coresident unmarried servants, weak kin links, and little kin-based welfare support. Some also think the EMP gave rise to successful economic growth, high migration, high female autonomy, and a strong willingness to cooperate outside the family (so-called prosociality).

This "European" or "Western" family form is contrasted with a non-European or "Eastern" system characterized by extended families or clans, complex households, early first marriage, low non-marriage, new couples joining parental households, large household size, strong kin links, few life-cycle servants, and generous kin-based welfare.[5] Some scholars argue that these strong-kinship family systems reduced economic growth, restricted migration, depressed women's status, and stifled prosociality.

More accurately, the European Marriage Pattern should be called the "Western European Marriage Pattern". The original idea, reflected in figure 7.1, was that this marriage pattern prevailed mainly north and west of an imaginary line running through Europe from Saint Petersburg to Trieste—a zone encompass-

4. Hajnal 1965; further elaborated in his 1983 work.

5. Caldwell 1976; Laslett 1977; R. M. Smith 1979; R. M. Smith 1985; Laslett 1988a; Solar 1995; Dennison and Ogilvie 2014; Dennison and Ogilvie 2016.

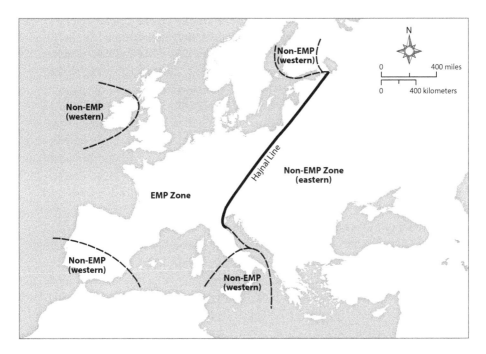

FIGURE 7.1. The original Hajnal Line between the European Marriage Pattern and other family systems in pre-modern Europe. The solid line is the Hajnal Line according to Hajnal's original 1965 formulation. To its west prevailed the EMP, characterized by late female marriage (mid- to late twenties), high percentages of women remaining permanently unmarried, and high proportions of nuclear-family households. To its east prevailed areas of early female marriage, low female lifetime celibacy, and high proportions of extended- or multiple-family households. The dashed lines mark areas of western Europe where the EMP was believed not to prevail. *Source*: Based on Hajnal 1965.

ing England, the Low Countries, Scandinavia, France, Germany, Switzerland, Austria, and central and northern Italy. By contrast, extended-family systems— in different variants—prevailed in most of southern, eastern-central, eastern, and south-eastern Europe.[6] Most other continents of the world, it is thought, were long dominated by early female marriage, low rates of female celibacy, and the extended family or "clan". But this is mostly based on projecting twentieth-century patterns backward in time. We do not actually know enough about non-European demography before around 1900 to be sure about historical family patterns in most societies outside Europe.

Many more data have been compiled on marriage age, lifetime celibacy, and extended-family households in different parts of Europe since Hajnal's

6. Hajnal 1965; Hajnal 1983.

path-breaking 1965 article and since his elaboration in 1983. In 2014, a compilation of 4,705 demographic observations found significant and substantial differences in the prevalence of these three core EMP indicators across 39 European economies between 1500 and 1900.[7] Some years later, Nathan Lazarus visualized these data, as shown in the maps in figure 7.2. The patterns revealed by the 2014 data compilation were broadly consistent with Hajnal's proposition that marriage and household structure differed between western, eastern, and southern Europe. Unsurprisingly, however, the picture that emerged from the 2014 data compilation was much more complex than could have been realized by Hajnal half a century earlier.

The richest countries in early modern Europe—the Netherlands and England—certainly had the EMP, though not in an extreme form. But so too did some of the poorest, such as Scandinavia, Iceland, and Bohemia (which was subject to serfdom until 1781, and in many respects until 1848). There were also very wealthy zones of Europe such as central and northern Italy where the EMP did not prevail, and extended- and multiple-family households made up on average more than a third (34.4 per cent) of the total.[8] These findings suggest that the family did not influence economic outcomes autonomously. Instead, the family was just one component of a society's institutional framework, which might or might not be associated with high per capita GDP and rapid economic growth. Uncertainty remains about whether the family as an institution affects economic and social outcomes independently of the surrounding institutional system.

Huge uncertainty also remains about when the EMP came into being, even in Europe. Some think it arose in the thirteenth century or even earlier, others not until after 1540, and some think it might have emerged right after the Black Death. The EMP is quantitatively testified from around 1540 onwards. But whether it existed before that date is hotly debated. In sober fact, the evidence is too fragile to know for sure when exactly the EMP first arose, even in Europe.[9] Whether it existed outside Europe in earlier centuries is even more of a mystery.

Regardless of the form it takes, the family organizes so many aspects of life that it inevitably interacts with contagion. Small households with little generational complexity may limit the "secondary attack rate" of an epidemic inside closed groups, which is higher than the "reproduction rate" of that epidemic in society at large. Weak kin obligations may limit deathbed and funeral gatherings for epidemic victims, reducing the risk that mourners will become infected. Strong female autonomy may reduce contagion by empowering

---

7. Dennison and Ogilvie 2014.
8. Dennison and Ogilvie 2014, 654 (table 1).
9. See the discussion in Dennison and Ogilvie (2014) and Edwards and Ogilvie (2022a, b).

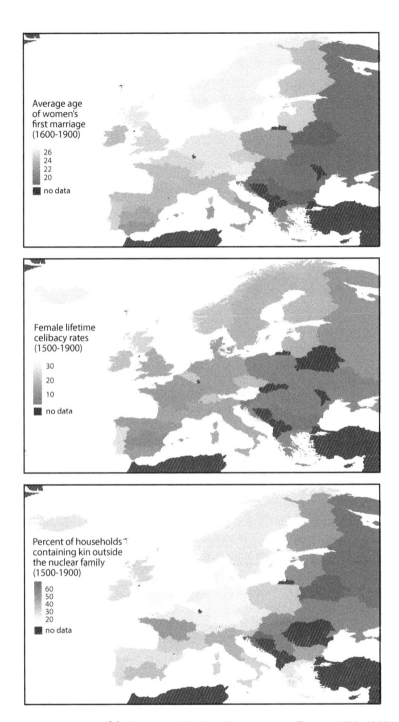

FIGURE 7.2. Intensity of the European Marriage Pattern across Europe, 1600–1900: (*top*) female age at first marriage; (*middle*) female lifetime celibacy; (*bottom*) percentage of non-nuclear households. Maps are based on 2,622 observations of female age at first marriage, 1,172 observations of female lifetime celibacy, and 911 observations of household structure. *Source*: Maps based on those of Nathan Lazarus in 2020 (https://github.com/NathanLazarus/DennisonOgilvieMap), in turn based on data in Dennison and Ogilvie (2014, 654, table 1). With gratitude to Nathan Lazarus for permission to use his maps.

knowledgeable wives and mothers to make family health decisions. Neolocal marriage, low age of leaving home, and life-cycle servanthood may increase contagion by encouraging migration. Weak kinship ties may foster prosocial values motivating people to care about those beyond their own families, and hence to comply with anti-contagion measures enacted by the state, community, religion, or guild.

In theory, specific family forms can make us act in ways that contain epidemic contagion—or exacerbate it. But what happens in practice? Does the family interact with epidemics in any universal way? Or are such interactions always contingent—either on informal norms and expectations, or on the wider framework of institutions that constrain how the family acts?

1. Residential Arrangements

Epidemic infection increases with interpersonal contact. This applies even to diseases like plague that have animal or insect vectors, since those often live on or near human bodies and artefacts. But during epidemics the entire population does not mix homogeneously. There are pockets of higher transmission inside households and other sub-communities (schools, hospitals, nursing homes, apartment buildings, residential compounds). This within-household transmission plays an important role in how fast and severely an epidemic spreads.

Epidemic transmission is thus driven both by the "reproduction number" (R^*, the average number of secondary infections produced by a single infected person in society at large) and by the "secondary attack rate" (SAR, the probability that household members contract the disease, given that one household member is infected). The SAR depends on the specific disease, the degree of immunity, cultural differences, and mitigation measures inside the household. As table 7.1 shows, it is seldom 100 per cent. Even for pneumonic plague, the most lethal sort, the maximum estimated SAR is 75 per cent. For the Omicron variant of Covid-19 in 2021 it was 39 per cent.

Epidemiological models predict that with realistic SAR levels, epidemics will spread more strongly when households are larger. Figure 7.3 shows a simulated epidemic wave for three household-size distributions in 2011: Bangladesh, with a mean household size (MHS) of 4.4 and 54 per cent of households containing over six persons; Poland, with an MHS of 2.9 and 23 per cent of households having over six persons; and Germany, with an MHS of 2.1 and 7 per cent of households having over seven persons. For a moderate societal reproduction number R^* of 1.1 and a within-household SAR of 0.25, Bangladesh will have 50 per cent higher infection than Germany and much faster epidemic progression, with the peak occurring 60 days earlier and almost

TABLE 7.1. Secondary Attack Rate (SAR) inside Households, Various Epidemics, 1906/2021

Disease	Date	Place	Note	SAR (%)	Source
Plague	1906–18	Suffolk	Mostly pneumonic[a]	15.0	[1]
Plague	2002	Shimla, India	Hospital, not household	40.0	[2]
Plague	2022	"Recent attacks"	Pneumonic and bubonic	14.0–75.0	[3]
Influenza	1918	Baltimore	–	32.5	[4]
Cholera	1946	Canton	Non-vaccinated	28.0	[5]
Cholera	1946	Canton	Vaccinated	5.0	[5]
Cholera	2012	Endemic areas	–	50.0	[6]
Smallpox	1969	Pirapitinga, Brazil	Non-vaccinated	53.0	[7]
Smallpox	1969	Pirapitinga, Brazil	Vaccinated	0.0	[7]
Smallpox	20th century	Nigeria, Benin, India, Pakistan, Bangladesh	Non-vaccinated	58.4	[8]
Smallpox	20th century	Nigeria, Benin, India, Pakistan, Bangladesh	Vaccinated	3.8	[8]
Covid-19	2021	Norway	Delta variant	19.0	[9]
Covid-19	2021	Spain	Omicron variant	39.0	[9]

Sources: [1] Egan 2010, 8. [2] World Health Organization 2008, 25. [3] IFRC 2022, 3. [4] Fraser et al. 2011, 509. [5] Peterson 1946, 288. [6] Gotuzzo and Seas 2012, 1866. [7] Arnt and Morris 1972, 368. [8] Fenner 1988, 200; Damon 2012, 2117. [9] Dönges et al. 2023, 1.

Note: SAR = probability that household members get infected, given that one household member is infected.

[a] Most cases believed to be pneumonic, but several possibly bubonic; medical advice recommending no contact inside household issued in at least three cases.

twice as many individuals affected per 100,000 population.[10] To place these figures in context, in the early modern period (1500–1900) north-west Europe typically had an MHS of 4.5, similar to modern Bangladesh, while many parts of southern, south-eastern, and eastern Europe had a larger MHS, especially in the countryside.[11]

A household's kin complexity also matters for infection. The presence of non-nuclear kin increases the probability that a household will contain multiple generations with differing immunity, and especially that elderly people will live in close quarters with multiple younger generations. Family systems with

10. Dönges et al. 2023, 12.
11. For MHS in different historical societies, see the essays in Laslett and Wall (1972).

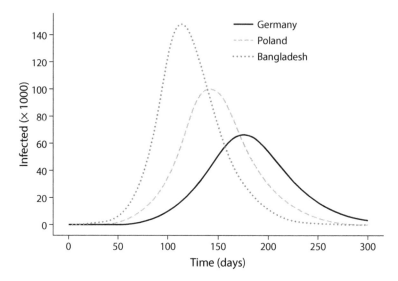

FIGURE 7.3. Simulated effect of household size on epidemic infection. Simulation of a single infection wave of a given epidemic for three countries with different household size distributions in 2011. For all three countries, $R^* = 1.1$ and SAR = 0.25. *Source*: Based on Dönges et al. 2023, 12.

greater multigenerational coresidence are particularly risky for elderly persons in epidemics such as Covid-19, which attack older people more strongly. In the United Kingdom in the first and second Covid-19 waves of 2020–21, living in multigenerational households was associated with significantly increased risk of severe Covid-19, even controlling for location, pandemic wave, age, sex, comorbidities, smoking, obesity, household density, deprivation, and ethnicity.[12] Other epidemics such as smallpox and influenza attack the young more violently, because older people have acquired immunity through previous infection or vaccination. In these epidemics, multigenerational residence is particularly risky for infants and children. In the 1969 smallpox outbreak in the Brazilian village of Pirapitinga, for instance, the SAR was 73 per cent for those in the 0–4 age group (who had never experienced either vaccination or natural smallpox), but just 11 per cent for those aged over 30 (many of whom had been immunized by vaccination or prior infection).[13] For most variants of influenza the overall attack rate is 5–20 per cent among adults, but 40–50 per cent among children.[14]

12. Wing et al. 2022.
13. Arnt and Morris 1972, 369.
14. Hayden 2012, 2096.

These epidemiological considerations underlie the view that, other things constant, epidemic contagion will be lower in family systems where kinship ties are weaker. This is because weak kinship systems (such as the EMP) give rise to more solitary (one-person) households and small nuclear-family households with just one or two coresident generations. Strong kinship systems give rise to fewer one-person households and more extended- and multiple-family ones. The resulting larger household size and greater number of coresident generations increases the probability of epidemic transmission to people of differing immunity. Households with low kin complexity may also have lower diversity of outside contacts (education, jobs, sociability), making them better able to isolate during epidemics.

In historical epidemics, contemporaries recognized that disease passed quickly within households and that larger numbers of people residing in the same living space fostered transmission. During the Black Death in Aleppo, the Muslim author al-Wardi, who would himself soon die of plague, exclaimed: "How amazingly does it pursue the people of each house! One of them spits blood, and everyone in the household is certain of death. It brings the entire family to their graves after two or three nights."[15] During the Black Death in Narbonne, the prominent burgher Andre Benezeit described how one-quarter of the population had already died by 7 April 1348, and declared that "the illness brought about by these things is known to be contagious, for when one person dies in a house, their servants, friends and family are afflicted in the same way by the same disease and within three or four days all lie dead together".[16]

It was not just household size that mattered. Regardless of size, the density of living arrangements relative to the number of rooms and beds also exacerbated within-household contagion. The 1590 Milan plague ordinance, for instance, instructed that "however lowly or poor people may be, they shall not keep more than two or three persons in one bed".[17] In the 1630 plague, as reflected in the chapter epigraph, a Milanese priest commented that "the poor are most harmed by the plague because of the confined living conditions in houses vulgarly called stables, where every room is filled with large families and where stench and contagion prevail".[18] In the early 1630s, the London College of Physicians ascribed urban epidemics to cramped living conditions, though it focused not so much on kinship complexity as on non-related inmates and lodgers, "by whom the houses are so pestered that they become unwholesome".[19] In 1665, William Boghurst included as one cause

15. Quoted in Aberth 2005, 18.
16. Quoted in Horrox 1994, 222–3.
17. Quoted in Cipolla 1976, 34.
18. Quoted in Cipolla 1976, 35.
19. Quoted in Champion 1993, 35.

of the Great Plague of London the "thickenes of inhabitants; those living as many families in a house".[20] In 2020 during the Covid-19 pandemic, the Pew Research Center ascribed high Covid infection rates in some areas to family patterns "where many people live together, [so] the risk of contagion is heightened if anyone in the household falls ill or becomes an asymptomatic carrier of the coronavirus".[21] Among the Orthodox Jewish population in New York, for instance, Covid-19 "swept through families, which tend to be large and live in cramped apartments".[22]

These historical examples confirm the importance of within-household epidemic transmission, but show that it was caused by factors more complicated than the prevalence of large, extended-kinship households. Contemporaries recognized that large and complicated coresidential groups could take many forms, which did not necessarily involve kinship links. Contagion risks were increased by multiple people sleeping in the same bed, multiple families living in the same room, multiple families living in the same house, non-relatives such as lodgers and inmates living in the household alongside biological and affinal relatives, and large families living in small spaces.

Historical demographers have indeed sometimes found large households to be associated with high epidemic mortality. In the north Italian town of Nonantola during the 1630 plague, for instance, there was a positive association between the size of the coresident group and the risk of death, although it became significant only for households with 7 members or more.[23] In the Derbyshire village of Eyam during the 1665–66 plague, household size was a major determinant of contagion, with a susceptible individual almost 100 times more likely to catch plague from an infected member of the same household than from an infected person living elsewhere in the village.[24] In the 1918 influenza pandemic in Baltimore, the attack rate increased with household size, from about 25 per cent for 2- or 3-person households to over 50 per cent for households containing 7 persons or more.[25] In the Brazilian villages of Pirapitinga and Campo Alegra in 1969, households that got smallpox had a mean size of 6.0–6.2 persons, while those that remained uninfected had a mean size of 3.2–3.6.[26] In the Indian city of Surat in 1994, more than 71 per cent of plague patients came from households with 5 people or more.[27]

20. Quoted in Champion 1993, 35.
21. Kramer 2020.
22. *Economist*, 2020c.
23. Alfani and Bonetti 2019.
24. Whittles and Didelot 2016, 6.
25. Fraser et al. 2011, 507.
26. Arnt and Morris 1972, 368.
27. Barnes 2014, 175.

Not all epidemics show contagion increasing with household size in a straightforward way. The English village of Colyton showed no association between household size and plague mortality in the early modern period.[28] In the Great Plague of London in 1665, mortality was higher in smaller than larger households. In the poor parish of Whitefriars during the epidemic period from mid-July to late October 1665, over 34 per cent of all deaths were in small households with just a single hearth. In many cases where plague struck a larger household, it was the servants rather than the family members who caught the disease.[29] In the Oxfordshire town of Banbury in the 1718–19 and 1731–33 smallpox epidemics, mortality was no higher in larger than smaller families.[30] In Italy, there were cities such as Florence where neighbourhoods with smaller than average households were more heavily infected by plague in the 1630–31 epidemic.[31]

Why these contradictory findings? One reason is that households differ in other ways than size, and this affects their susceptibility to contagion. We have to control for these other features before blaming (or praising) the family system. The Nonantola study does control for other household characteristics in 1630—notably, whether a household was lower status (i.e. peasant) or higher status (better off)—so we have greater certainty that plague mortality was caused by living in a larger household rather than being poor.[32] The Eyam study also controlled for wealth, sex, age, and prior infection, so it too can conclude that household size by itself exacerbated contagion in 1665–66.[33] In early modern Colyton, by contrast, not enough is known about the households to control for the effect of their other characteristics on contagion. The same is true for eighteenth-century Banbury, where no other information than size is known for the families with and without smallpox deaths, though the study speculates that the reason a majority of families had just one child die of smallpox regardless of how many siblings it had was that the parish enacted isolation practices as soon as a single smallpox infection was detected in a household.[34] The Surat study also did not control for other household characteristics, so the apparent association between household structure and plague deaths in 1994 may just reflect poverty: large, extended-family households were more common among migrant workers and the poor, who were more likely to catch plague because of poverty and geographical mobility.[35]

28. Slack 1985, 10–11, 346; Schofield 1977, 108–9.
29. Champion 1993, 46.
30. Leadbeater 2020, 43.
31. Litchfield 2008, para 327.
32. Alfani and Bonetti 2019.
33. Whittles and Didelot 2016, 6.
34. Leadbeater 2020, 43–4.
35. Barnes 2014, 162, 174.

A trickier problem is that the nature and direction of the association between household structure and other characteristics—such as wealth—can differ greatly between societies. In some societies larger households were richer, while in others they were poorer. In London in 1665, for instance, the poor lived in smaller and simpler households while the better-off lived in larger and more complex ones; the higher plague mortality in one-hearth households may simply reflect their poverty rather than showing that within-household transmission did not matter. In the Indian city of Surat in the 1990s, by contrast, the poor lived in larger households while better-off groups more often lived in nuclear families; the Surat poor may have caught plague both because of poverty and because of large households. Apparent differences in plague mortality between large and small households were not universal, but were mediated through family practices of each society, with small households being poorer than average in early modern London but richer than average in twentieth-century Surat.

Even inside the same society, household structure could be associated with other household features in diametrically opposed ways in different contexts. This emerges from comparing two communities in Italy in the terrible plague epidemic of the 1630s: the large city of Florence (pop. 76,000) and the small town of Nonantola (pop. 3,500). In Florence, the poor lived in small nuclear-family households or single-parent families, reducing within-household transmission; but poverty made them susceptible to plague because of all the reasons discussed in chapter 2, outweighing the advantage of living in smaller residential units.[36] In the Italian village of Nonantola, by contrast, low-status (mostly peasant) households had a mean size of 5.5 and 8 per cent of them had over 11 members, while high-status households had a mean size of 5.3 and none of them had over 11 members—in this rural environment, household size and poverty coincided, exacerbating contagion.[37] This striking contrast between a city and a village in the same society in the same decade alerts us to the fact that household size and structure themselves were not so much an expression of immutable family norms as a response to the economic and social framework. Thus Nonantola peasants were poor, but they owned dwellings and needed labour to work their farms, encouraging them to have large households. Among Florentine town-dwellers, by contrast, the poor faced high housing costs, they worked for others, and their children often left home early to take jobs in richer households. Furthermore, many of the poor in Florence, as in most pre-modern European cities, were immigrants from the surrounding countryside. For all these reasons, poor households in Florence tended to be smaller than average.

36. Litchfield 2008, para 327.
37. Alfani and Bonetti 2019, 107, 115.

Nonetheless, once all these complications are taken into account there is reason to believe that a family system where households are more often large and multigenerational will have higher within-household epidemic transmission. This has policy implications. Larger average household size dampens the effectiveness of social distancing measures, since in societies with larger households, a larger proportion of infections are transmitted inside households where quarantines do not apply.[38] In a society where households are more often large and multigenerational, offering individuals places to isolate from infection outside the household can reduce the prevalence of an epidemic and speed its decline.[39] The contrasting social distancing measures in England and Italy discussed in chapter 3 may thus have been aptly targeted. Household isolation works well with small nuclear families such as those characterizing much of north-west Europe in the early modern period, including England (with 15.7 per cent household complexity 1500–1900) or northern France (at 16.1 per cent). Household isolation will work less well with large, extended-family households, which were more common in some (though not all) of southern Europe, including central and northern Italy (with 34.4 per cent household complexity in 1500–1900) or central Spain (at 32.1 per cent).[40]

Immunization, by contrast, does prevent infection inside households. Since larger households make a greater contribution to contagion than smaller ones, there may be a case for allocating scarce immunization resources to larger households over smaller ones, or to neighbourhoods or societies with larger mean household size in preference to those where households are smaller.[41] But as the historical findings show, it is important to analyse other household characteristics than size or kin complexity in targeting public health measures.

2. Death Practices

Family institutions also affect interactions between relatives who do not actually live together. Such kin interactions come into play during the mass deaths and burials associated with epidemics. Epidemics give rise to many deaths, and these often draw in people who are still alive (as figure 7.4 illustrates).

Strong kinship links often imply mandatory attendance at deathbeds and funerals. In extreme cases, death gatherings can spread contagion throughout the entire network of mourners. Such superspreader events are widely

---

38. Dönges et al. 2023, 15.

39. P. Liu et al. 2021.

40. For the highly variegated patterns of household kin complexity inside western, eastern, and southern Europe between 1500 and 1900, see Dennison and Ogilvie (2014, 653–8, 666–9).

41. Dönges et al. 2023, 15.

I non essent registrantes
et futuris ministrantes que
viderunt et que audiunt .
et illa que eueniunt in diuerfie

que non viderunt nec faium
per scripturas cognouimus
si nos bene recordemur, que fint
bona ut amenitus, quod ne mali

FIGURE 7.4. Townsmen in Tournai (in present-day Belgium) burying plague victims during the Black Death, 1349–52. The epidemic generated large numbers of victims, requiring many ordinary people to lend a hand, beyond the ranks of the gravediggers who were supposed to have developed biological immunity and professional practices protecting them from contracting diseases from corpses. The painting shows how the work of mass burials brings the living into close quarters with dead bodies and one another. Miniature by Piérart dou Tielt illustrating the "Antiquitates Flandriae" by Gilles li Muisis, held at the Bibliothèque royale de Belgique. *Source*: Wikimedia Commons.

believed to be exacerbated by extended-family systems with strong kinship links. A famous passage from Boccaccio's *Decameron* describes death practices in Florence during and after the Black Death:

> It had once been customary, as it is again nowadays, for the women relatives and neighbours of a dead man to assemble in his house in order to mourn in the company of the women who had been closest to him; moreover his kinsfolk would forgather in front of his house along with his neighbours and various other citizens, and there would be a contingent of priests, whose number varied according to the quality of the deceased; his body would be taken thence to the church in which he had wanted to be buried. . . . But as the ferocity of the plague began to mount, this practice all but disappeared entirely and was replaced by different customs. . . . [I]t was rare

for the bodies of the dead to be accompanied by more than ten or twelve
neighbours to the church, nor were they borne on the shoulders of worthy
and honest citizens, but by a kind of grave digging fraternity.[42]

The same behaviour was reported over 450 years later during an Egyptian
plague epidemic. In 1801, the Somali scholar and chronicler Al-Jabarti quoted
a letter from his friend Shaykh Hasan al-Attar in the Upper Egyptian town of
Asyut. The extremely virulent plague in Asyut had changed normal funeral
behaviour, so that "the most eminent and distinguished person [notable] has
no more than ten people to conduct him to his final resting place, and those
ten are paid for the service".[43]

These reports show two things. Superficially, they appear to reveal that the
strong-kinship family patterns that prevailed in fourteenth-century Italy and
nineteenth-century Egypt implied large funeral gatherings. But at a deeper
level, they show that such kinship norms were malleable. They were certainly
not so deep-seated that people continued to organize superspreader funerals despite the contagion risks. On the contrary. Familial norms adjusted to
changing circumstances. When the expected cost in terms of infection and
death increased, people reduced the size and elaboration of funerals. Only
afterwards—at least in fourteenth-century Florence—did familial behaviour
readjust, once the risk declined.

Turning our attention to weak-kinship societies complicates the link
between kinship and funeral attendance during epidemics. In early modern
England, kinship obligations are supposed to have been weak because of the
EMP.[44] Yet during epidemics, English funerals were large, and relatives of victims felt strong obligations to attend them. During sixteenth- and seventeenth-
century English plague epidemics, victims' funerals were expected to be
attended by large groups of relatives, neighbours, and friends. The 1573 English
plague orders specified dusk burials for victims precisely in the hope that it
would curtail the attendance that daylight events would attract.[15] In the London plague epidemic of 1603, "the meaner sort of people" flocked in crowds
to funerals in direct contravention of the Lord Mayor's orders, which limited
attendance to six persons.[46] In 1613, the London clergyman Robert Hill admonished people to refrain from attending the plague deathbeds of distant kin; if
relatives attended, they should consist only of "they of a family that are bound

42. Quoted in Arcini et al. 2016, 106.
43. Quoted in Kuhnke 1990, 76–7.
44. R. M. Smith 1979; Hajnal 1982, 477; R. M. Smith 1983; Hallam 1985; R. M. Smith 1990a;
R. M. Smith 1990b; Goldberg 1991; Frost 2017, 155–6; J. Bennett 2019a; J. Bennett 2019b.
45. Wrightson 2011, 104.
46. Quoted in Slack 1985, 233–4.

to come".[47] This implies that normal practice in early modern England was for more distant relatives to attend funerals.

Other parts of north-west Europe such as the Netherlands and Scandinavia also developed the EMP and, in some ways, weak kinship links by the early modern period.[48] Yet in seventeenth-century Dutch plague epidemics, people violently resisted public health measures forbidding them to accompany their relatives' bodies to the grave.[49] The EMP prevailed in Sweden at latest by the mid-seventeenth century, yet in the 1710–13 plagues in Scania, which killed almost 15 per cent of the population, relatives continued to gather in houses of plague victims to mourn the diseased and share out their possessions.[50] When Scania plague victims were buried separately in the effort to limit contagion, relatives dug up corpses and reburied them in the ordinary graveyards, despite being part of a nuclear-family, weak-kinship family system.[51] Swedes attended relatives' sickbeds during eighteenth-century smallpox epidemics, too, as in 1787 when "in small towns and in the countryside is it common that neighbours and relatives visit their friends when a disease was in progress, and many people gather unnecessarily".[52] Twentieth-century Ireland also had a predominantly nuclear-family-based system, yet so strong was the Irish tradition of holding "wakes", in which relatives, friends, and neighbours socialized in a deceased person's house before the funeral, that in 1918–19 the practice was officially prohibited by local authorities in Newry and Ballyclare, who feared it would spread influenza.[53]

Nonfamilial institutions also influenced deathbed and funeral gatherings during epidemics, intervening under both strong- and weak-kinship systems. In strong-kinship Ukraine in the 1730s, for instance, medical practitioners and state authorities sought to limit large funeral gatherings during a plague epidemic.[54] In strong-kinship Japan in the 1860s, domain authorities forbade family members to gather at smallpox deathbeds.[55] In strong-kinship Guinea in 2013, the government made it illegal for relatives to assemble at Ebola funerals or touch the body of the deceased, mandating safe medical burials without kin attendance.[56]

47. Quoted in Wrightson 2011, 99–100.

48. Dennison and Ogilvie 2014.

49. Curtis 2020, 287–8.

50. On the EMP in Sweden, see Lundh (2003); on the Scania plague epidemic, see Arcini et al. (2016, 113 (mortality), 132 (death practices)).

51. Arcini et al. 2016, 132.

52. Quoted in Sköld 1996b, 184.

53. Gorsky et al. 2021, 209.

54. Melikishvili 2006, 24.

55. Ehlers 2011, 183.

56. Manguvo and Mafuvadze 2015, 1–2.

Yet the same thing happened in weak-kinship systems. Religious authorities like the London clergyman Robert Hill recommended in 1613 that plague victims be visited only by "honest and aged persons" appointed by the magistrates to inspect the sick and that relatives should stay away.[57] Guilds relaxed their requirement that guild brothers socialize at one another's funerals, as in the 1636 Newcastle epidemic, when funerals of plague victims became more modest because of changing guild enforcement, not because of the weak-kinship norms of the EMP.[58] In Sweden in 1816, the state ordered that no one other than a sole nurse should prepare a victim's body for burial, which should take place in the late evening without a social gathering.[59] What limited kinship death gatherings in England and Sweden was thus not necessarily their weak-kinship system but the interventions of religion, guild, and state.

Historical epidemics do not provide clear evidence that kinship links systematically affected death practices, thereby exacerbating contagion. Both nuclear- and extended-family systems mandated attendance by relatives at deathbeds and funerals, even during epidemics. But the evidence is insufficient to demonstrate that such practices were less common in nuclear-family systems. Under both nuclear- and extended-family systems, norms governing kin attendance at death gatherings did not always adjust to epidemic risks sufficiently to contain contagion externalities. But there is no evidence that such adjustments were less sufficient in extended- than nuclear-family systems. Even if the EMP had weaker kinship imperatives, it might have compensated with stronger imperatives mandating death attendance by friends, neighbours, fellow parishioners, or guild brothers.[60] Finally, family systems might sustain particular kinship norms. But death practices were also shaped by other institutions—state, local community, religion, guild, feudal regimes, and medical authorities. We must remain cautious in assigning responsibility for superspreader death practices to strong kinship links in the absence of more systematic evidence.

3. Women's Status

Epidemic contagion is also affected by women's status inside the family. Many decisions involving infectious diseases are taken on an individual level, as we saw in chapter 2. Such individual decisions are implemented inside the family

---

57. Quoted in Wrightson 2011, 99–100.

58. Wrightson 2011, 104–5.

59. Sköld 1996b, 510.

60. This would be consistent with the suggestion of Dennison and Ogilvie (2014, 687), that weak-kinship family systems such as the EMP were more likely to arise and survive in the presence of strong nonfamilial institutions to take the place of kinship.

by those mainly responsible for household production. These are often wives, mothers, and other female family members. In modern developing economies, for instance, familial vaccination decisions are often taken by women.[61]

Women's autonomy differs across societies, and the family system is sometimes thought to be a key reason. The "girlpower" hypothesis, for instance, holds that pre-modern Dutch, Flemish, and English women enjoyed a uniquely strong position in society, and that this was caused by the prevalence of the EMP. According to this theory, late marriage, high rates of non-marriage, nuclear-family households, life-cycle servanthood, and a narrow age gap between spouses increased women's education, labour-force participation, and voice within marriage, greatly enhancing women's autonomy in society at large. In southern and eastern Europe, and in societies such as China, the argument continues, women's position was much weaker because marriage was universal, women married young, extended- and multiple-family households predominated, fewer girls worked as servants, and much older husbands had greater authority over their young wives.[62]

Women's status was certainly higher on average in England and the Low Countries than in many other parts of Europe between around 1500 and around 1900.[63] But whether this was caused by the EMP or by other features of these societies remains an open question.[64] There are potential advantages for women in both EMP and non-EMP family systems. Under the EMP, late marriage and high rates of non-marriage gave women incentives to gain skills and work experience before and outside marriage, albeit mainly as low-status servants, spinners, seamstresses, and labourers. Such labour market experience could give a woman outside options in the labour force and hence stronger bargaining power if and when she married. The narrowness of the age gap between spouses in the EMP may also have reduced age-related domination of young wives by older husbands.

But non-EMP Mediterranean or east-European family systems also had potential advantages for females. Women might marry young and universally, but this did not prevent their working inside family businesses, and doing so in less subordinate roles than as servants or casual labourers. A wide age gap between spouses, as prevailed in some Mediterranean family systems, gave women less autonomy as young brides but more autonomy in later life. A much younger wife was likely to run the family farm, workshop, or business in an elderly husband's dotage and then act as household head during a long widow-

---

61. Ebot 2015.

62. De Moor and Van Zanden 2010; Voigtländer and Voth 2013; Foreman-Peck and Zhou 2018.

63. De Vries and Van der Woude 1997, 598–601; Ogilvie 2003, 344–51.

64. Dennison and Ogilvie 2014, 672–6.

hood, giving her power as a matriarch. In theory, therefore, the effect of the family system on female autonomy is not clear-cut.

Nor is the evidence. Historically, both EMP and non-EMP family systems displayed a range of outcomes for women. Indicators of women's autonomy such as household headship, labour force participation, and wage rates were not uniformly high in EMP societies or uniformly low in non-EMP ones. Women had a strong position in some EMP societies, notably England and the Netherlands, but much lower autonomy in Nordic, central, and eastern-central Europe, where the EMP prevailed to an equal or greater degree. To explain English, Dutch, and Flemish distinctiveness in female autonomy and economic performance, one cannot invoke the EMP, which England and the Low Countries shared with many other societies in which women were more thoroughly excluded from economic participation, and women's autonomy was lower both inside and outside the family.[65]

Conversely, there were societies where the EMP did not prevail, but females enjoyed considerable autonomy. Large swathes of southern Italy, as well as central and southern Spain, had relatively early female marriage (around age 22, instead of the mid- to late 20s characteristic of the EMP) and parts of central Spain and northern Italy had high percentages of extended-family households (around 33 per cent, instead of the 15 per cent characteristic of the EMP).[66] Nonetheless, Spanish and Italian females migrated seeking jobs as servants and labourers, women of all marital statuses worked for wages, and wives and widows operated independently as self-employed producers.[67] Italy and Spain also gave rise to levels of female headship similar to those in north-west Europe, with females heading 10–11 per cent of village households in fifteenth-century Italy and 20–21 per cent in fifteenth- and sixteenth-century Spain.[68] In its fifteenth-century censuses, Florence had early female marriage (18–20 years), low female lifetime celibacy (less than 1 per cent), and high household complexity (15–21 per cent); but it had 15.5 per cent female household headship, not very different from other late medieval and early modern European urban centres.[69] In comparisons among Florence, Verona, and English cities in the same period, "no simple model linked rates of celibacy,

65. Dennison and Ogilvie 2014, 672–6; Ogilvie and Carus 2014, 406, 462–3; Dennison and Ogilvie 2016, 207–8.

66. Dennison and Ogilvie 2014, 654 (table 1).

67. On the medieval period: Cohn 1998, 115–8; Armstrong-Partida and McDonough 2023. On the early modern period: Zucca Micheletto 2011; Zucca Micheletto 2013; Michaud 2016, 105–6; Sarasúa 2019; Ribeiro da Silva and Carvalhal 2020; Bellavitis and Zucca Micheletto 2018.

68. Ogilvie and Edwards 2000, 971 (table 2).

69. Herlihy 1974, 5, 9; Herlihy and Klapisch-Zuber 1985, 210–14, 334; Klapisch 1972, 273 (female headship in Florence in 1427); Ogilvie 2019, 250 (mean urban female headship rates for premodern European societies).

ages at marriage and household size with the economic independence of women across time or space".[70]

Eastern-central and eastern Europe were subject to the "second serfdom" from around 1500 until the late eighteenth or mid-nineteenth century. A large proportion of the rural population was subject to hereditary servility, the inhabitants of seigneurial towns were subject to a milder form of unfreedom, and only the inhabitants of the few legally privileged "free" or "royal" cities were completely free persons. The marriage and household patterns of serf societies varied. Some, such as Bohemia and Slovenia, practised variants of the EMP. Others displayed variants of an "eastern" family pattern involving early and universal marriage and extended-family households. In some serf societies, including those under the EMP such as Bohemia, female household headship was low, but this was because of seigneurial and communal restrictions rather than the family system, as shown by women's indignant protests when ordered by landlords or village communes to remarry or move into male-headed households.[71] In other serf societies, including those under the eastern (non-EMP) family system, rural female headship was permitted by landlord and commune and therefore attained quite high levels, as with the 15.9 per cent of village households headed by women in seventeenth-century Hungary or the 11.1 per cent in nineteenth-century Russia.[72] Women are found working outside the household for wages in a wide array of European serf societies.[73]

It might be argued that although the EMP was neither necessary nor sufficient for female autonomy, on average there was an association between the two, at least on some measures.[74] However, an association does not imply a causal link. The EMP might cause women to enjoy a higher status via human capital investment, work experience, or spousal age parity, as discussed above. But causation might go in the opposite direction, with higher female status enabling the EMP to arise in the first place. Some scholars claim, for instance, that female autonomy increased when societies moved from arable agriculture (where upper-body strength made men more productive) to pastoral, craft, or service activities (where women's productivity was higher), and that this rise in autonomy made women marry later and less universally, giving rise to the EMP.[75] Others would contend that both the EMP and women's autonomy were favoured by underlying variables such as market development, state

70. Cohn 1998, 122.
71. Ogilvie and Edwards 2000.
72. Ogilvie and Edwards 2000, 971 (table 2).
73. Devroey 2000; Ogilvie and Edwards 2000; Dennison 2011; Wyżga 2022.
74. See e.g. Szołtysek et al. 2017; Van Zanden, Carmichael, and De Moor 2019.
75. This is the hypothesis advanced by Voigtländer and Voth (2013); for theoretical and empirical counterarguments see Edwards and Ogilvie (2022a, b).

capacity, the rule of law, nonfamilial welfare provision, and early liberalization of corporative, communal, and seigneurial institutions—all factors which have been ascribed a causal role in supporting both female autonomy and a late-marriage, weak-kinship family system.[76] What mattered for women's status may not have been the demographic and coresidential features of the family system, therefore, but rather the wider institutional framework, which decided whether women could head households, enjoy secure property rights, conclude contracts, supply and employ labour, offer and obtain credit—and make autonomous decisions about family health.[77] Whether the demographic and coresidential characteristics of the family system influenced women's autonomy independently of the wider social framework remains an open—and important—question.

3.1. AN OLD WOMAN PERFORM'D THE OPERATION

Historical epidemics do show women making familial health decisions affecting epidemic contagion. The most vivid evidence comes from smallpox epidemics, in which mothers often took the initiative in getting children immunized, carried out the procedure personally, and disseminated the practice more widely. The question is whether this was affected by the form taken by family institutions.

Early modern England is a poster child of the EMP and high female autonomy, as we have seen. It was also the European epicentre of early and widespread smallpox variolation. As we saw in chapter 2, this ancient method of smallpox immunization was communicated to England from the Ottoman lands in the early eighteenth century. The most famous figure in this act of cultural learning was Lady Mary Wortley Montagu, the wife of the British ambassador in Constantinople (modern Istanbul), who got her son variolated in 1718 while her husband was absent, and vigorously proselytized about the procedure on her return to England.[78] In 1721 Lady Mary persuaded the retired English physician who had variolated her son in Constantinople to repeat the operation on her three-year-old daughter, the first inoculation on English soil. She followed up this coup by inviting "Several Ladies, and other Persons of Distinction" to observe the young Miss Wortley "playing about the Room, cheerful and well, with the Small Pox rais'd upon her", only to be "perfectly recover'd of them" a few days later.[79] Female agency continued for generations to play a role in variolation of English children of less elevated social

76. Dennison and Ogilvie 2014, 672–6; Dennison and Ogilvie 2016, 207–8.
77. Dennison and Ogilvie 2014, 672–6.
78. M. Bennett 2008, 500.
79. Quoted in Esfandiary 2023, 242.

standing. In 1753, for instance, the 12-year-old Arthur Young, later to become a famous agriculturalist, was taken by his mother to be variolated without his clergyman father's knowledge.[80] The female autonomy exercised by Lady Mary and her dissemination of variolation to other English elite women not only saved the lives of their own children but almost certainly helped spread the procedure across eighteenth-century English society as a whole.

These English examples might appear to confirm that in EMP societies women enjoyed unusual autonomy to take decisions that limited epidemic contagion. But there is a snag. Women also actively implemented variolation decisions in non-EMP societies. After all, the practice itself had been communicated to Europe from the Middle East. Here, various non-EMP family systems prevailed, yet women took the lead in variolation, both as mothers of children and as inoculators themselves. In 1711, for instance, the French writer Aubry de La Mottraye was travelling through Circassia, a region of the North Caucasus characterized by a non-EMP family system. There, he observed variolation being carried out by a female practitioner on a female child under the aegis of the child's mother, with no male involvement:

> I found an Opportunity of being present when it was put in Practice: It was in a Village call'd Deglivad, upon a young Girl [footnote: They oftener inoculate the Small-Pox upon Girls than Boys] of between Four and Five Years old. . . . [A]n old Woman perform'd the Operation; for those of this Sex, who are the most advanced in Age, are believ'd to be also so in Wisdom and Knowledge, . . . and they exercise generally the Practice of Physick. . . . [T]he Mother wrapp'd her Daughter up in one of the Skin Coverings, which, as I have observed, compose the Circassian Beds, and carried her thus pack'd up in her Arms to her own Home. . . . [T]hey assured me, that with this Precaution and Regimen, the Small Pox generally came out very favourably in five or fix Days; about which I took the old Woman's Word. . . . [T]hose Parents who have handsome Daughters, will sometimes ride for that purpose a Days Journey round about, to find some young Child who has [the smallpox].[81]

Women played a dominant role in variolation in Constantinople, too, where the EMP was again not the norm. As Lady Mary Montagu recounted in a 1717 letter to a female friend:

> There is a set of old women who make it their business to perform the operation. Every autumn in the month of September, when the great heat

80. M. Bennett 2020, 46.
81. La Mottraye 1723, 2:74–5.

is abated, people send to one another to know if any of their family has a mind to have the small-pox.[82]

The ensuing operation took place in a largely or wholly female environment:

> They make parties for this purpose, and when they are met (commonly fifteen or sixteen together) the old woman comes with a nutshell full of the matter of the best sort of smallpox and asks what veins you please to have opened.[83]

Variolation was also widespread in northern Africa, where women played a major role, although a non-EMP family system prevailed. In 1790, James Bruce's *Travels to Discover the Sources of the Nile* described women in Nubia (now northern Sudan and southern Egypt) who would tie a piece of cotton around the arm of a smallpox patient and then around the arm of their children, thus transmitting the immunizing agent.[84] In 1798 during Napoleon's expedition to Egypt, the French surgeon general described how upstream, towards the sources of the Nile, "midwives take a small band of cotton, apply it to suppurating smallpox pustules, then place it on the arm of the child they wish to inoculate".[85] In Ghana during the 1920 smallpox epidemic, as we saw in chapter 5, a female "fetishist" in Accra variolated a number of people, despite its having been banned by the British authorities.[86] In 1957, an old woman in the Makeni district of Sierra Leone was still practising variolation, collecting scabs from smallpox convalescents, mixing them with herbs and clay, and using the mixture to inoculate those who desired protection.[87]

Spain had a highly heterogeneous family system, with regions of early and universal female marriage in the centre and south alongside zones of later marriage (though non-nuclear households) in the north.[88] No Spanish region displayed the "pure" EMP in which all three core features—late marriage, high lifetime celibacy, and low household complexity—coexisted. Yet Spanish women were active agents in variolation. In 1757, one of the earliest Spanish-language publications on the practice described the successful inoculation of thousands of recipients by an unnamed woman.[89] In 1785, the *Madrid Gazette* reported that mothers in Galicia were personally variolating

---

82. Quoted in Esfandiary 2023, 238.
83. Quoted in Esfandiary 2023, 239.
84. Bader 1986, 81.
85. Quoted in Kuhnke 1990, 113.
86. Bader 1986, 82.
87. Herbert 1975, 546.
88. Dennison and Ogilvie 2014, 654 (table 1).
89. Poska 2022, 6.

their children.[90] That same year, an enormously popular Spanish translation of an English variolation handbook described how "of late many [mothers] have performed this operation with their own hands; and their success has been equal to that of most dignified inoculators". The Spanish supplement to the handbook described how mothers had been variolating their children for a long time, and it was only now that medical professionals were taking over the operation.[91] Women were active in variolation in the Spanish Empire, too, as in Mexico during the 1795–96 smallpox epidemic, when an experienced female inoculator called Faustina Baleria was employed to help the Tehuantepeque schoolmaster administer variolation.[92]

Italy displayed at least three different family systems between 1500 and 1900.[93] Yet in Italy, too, some of the earliest records of variolation involve women's health decisions. During a smallpox epidemic in Rome in 1754, the Marchesa Bufalini decided to variolate her family and dependents on her rural estate, carrying out the procedure with her own hands.[94] In the Romagna region in 1755, mothers were described as variolating their children without their husbands' knowledge.[95] Rome and Romagna were regions of the centre and north, with marriage age on the low end of the EMP (age 24), lifetime celibacy in the EMP range (12 per cent), but non-EMP levels of household complexity (34 per cent).[96]

In the former Russian Empire, non-EMP family forms prevailed almost universally, with female marriage age around 20, female lifetime celibacy at 2–9 per cent, and 42–61 per cent complex-family households.[97] Yet here, too, women were also involved in practising variolation. In 1771, the young German physician, botanist, and explorer Samuel George Gottlieb Gmelin travelled all over eastern Europe and in "Little Russia" (present-day Ukraine) found that variolation, which he called "smallpox-buying", had existed since "times unimaginable". In Ostrogorskh in the Russian–Ukrainian borderlands he met a 70-year-old woman who had been variolated as a child and was now personally inoculating her granddaughter; Gmelin speculated that the woman had somehow learned the method from the Tartars or Turks.[98] In the 1770s in Livonia (present-day Estonia and Latvia), rural mothers attended a sort of "variolation school" established by the Lutheran pastor Johann Georg Eisen

90. Poska 2022, 7.
91. Quoted in Poska 2022, 7.
92. Poska 2022, 8.
93. Viazzo 2003, 122.
94. Klebs 1914, 59.
95. M. Bennett 2020, 38.
96. Dennison and Ogilvie 2014, 654 (table 1).
97. Dennison and Ogilvie 2014, 654 (table 1).
98. Quoted in Klebs 1914, 7.

with the express intention of teaching them how to carry out the procedure on their children.[99]

In India, until recently women married young, non-marriage was rare, and household complexity was high. Nonetheless, women traditionally played a role in variolation, both symbolically and practically. Chapter 6 already discussed Śītalā, the patron goddess of smallpox, who presided over religious variolation. In nineteenth-century Punjab, at the grander Śītalā shrines variolation was performed by male priests, but in more modest places it was carried out by *mirasis*, poor women from the lowest leatherworking and sweeper castes.[100]

Women thus made variolation decisions for their families and carried out the procedure with their own hands in many societies. There is no evidence that they did so more commonly under the EMP than under other family systems. But even if they had, could we be sure that the family system was responsible? After all, many other institutions influenced the provision and consumption of variolation, as we have seen in earlier chapters—markets, states, communities, religion, and medical associations. All these institutions also influenced women's autonomy and the shape taken by family institutions.[101] There is no support for the idea that the family system was the exogenous cause of either women's autonomy in general or their role in variolation.

3.2. MORE APPROPRIATE FOR WOMEN BECAUSE OF THE GREATER SOFTNESS OF THEIR HANDS

Vaccination, too, owed much to the actions of women. Female initiative contributed greatly to its early success, according to one magisterial study, "probably more so in Britain than elsewhere in Europe".[102] The diffusion of vaccination in Britain in the immediate aftermath of Jenner's 1796 invention certainly owed much to parental love, "with mothers often taking the initiative in appraising it".[103] Although fathers bore formal legal responsibility for children, it was typically mothers who made the decision about vaccination.[104] In early 1799, the London Smallpox and Inoculation Hospital carried out a mass trial of cowpox vaccination on around 200 patients, two-thirds of them children below age seven who were apparently accompanied only by their mothers.[105] Of 3,804 vaccinations carried out at the hospital in 1808–10, over

99. Klebs 1914, 55.
100. Minsky 2009, 168, 170.
101. Ogilvie 2003, 8–14, 320–34, 344–52; Dennison and Ogilvie 2014.
102. M. Bennett 2008, 510.
103. M. Bennett 2020, 95.
104. M. Bennett 2008, 503
105. M. Bennett 2008, 503.

90 per cent were administered to children aged two and under, and the only adults present were mothers, many of whom had brought their children long distances to secure immunization.[106] So typical was this pattern that a male anti-vaccinationist remarked belittlingly in 1808, "Mothers fly to [vaccination] as they have done to Ching's Lozenges for the cure of worms."[107]

Women also practised as vaccinators. The aristocratic Lady Fane took instruction from the London Vaccine Institute, and then vaccinated hundreds of children, either in her own home or going "from cottage to cottage"; by 1824, she reported never having a single failure in 200 vaccinations. But female vaccinators were recruited from lower social strata, too, as in 1808 when a Swanage parson "set old women, school mistresses etc, in neighbouring parishes inoculating with vaccine matter".[108]

In Sweden, too, women were among the first recorded vaccinators.[109] A poor woman called Anna Margareta Borgström, for instance, worked as an "ardent" vaccinator for at least 13 years from 1804 onwards, walking 50–60 kilometres daily in cold weather during October and November in remote areas of Västerbotten to reach her patients.[110] In the district of Halland in 1811, women accounted for 17 per cent of recorded vaccinators,[111] and in the national lists of vaccinators recommended for Swedish state rewards in 1817, 1827, 1837, and 1847, women accounted for 13 per cent of the total.[112]

But similar female empowerment can be seen in societies with different family patterns. In France, the EMP prevailed in the north, while other family systems predominated in the centre and south.[113] In the French context, however, non-EMP family systems did not necessarily entail a low status for women. A recent quantitative analysis of France between 1670 and 1840 found that "greater gender equality and women's agency can occur in the context of active and 'early' marriage".[114] When it came to vaccination, certainly, French women played a central role both inside and outside the family. Between 1798 and 1830, midwives were systematically employed as vaccinators, and ordinary French women exercised agency in both the demand for and the supply of vaccination services.[115]

106. M. Bennett 2008, 511.
107. Quoted in M. Bennett 2008, 506
108. Quoted in M. Bennett 2008, 508.
109. Sköld 1996b, 408.
110. Quoted in Sköld 1996b, 414.
111. Sköld 1996b, 406.
112. Sköld 1996b, 409.
113. Viazzo 2003, 122; Dennison and Ogilvie 2014, 654 (table 1).
114. Perrin 2022, 458.
115. Bercé 1984, 108.

In Italy, at least three different family forms prevailed, none of them the EMP.[116] Yet female vaccinators were recorded in action almost as soon as vaccination arrived in Italy. In 1806 in the Ravenna town of Bagnacavallo, for instance, Zaffira Ferretti was almost certainly involved in the vaccination campaign alongside her father, four years before she got her surgery degree and license to practise from Bologna.[117]

Spain, as we have seen, had at least two distinct family patterns, neither of which precisely complied with the EMP.[118] Yet in the Spanish-speaking world, mothers took decisions about vaccination and carried out the procedure with their own hands. Spanish women advocated the practice and adopted it for their own children, as in 1801 when Xaviera de Mugartegui of Guipuzcoa sought out information about vaccination as "a mother who desires to free her daughter and others from such a cruel enemy as smallpox".[119] Ordinary Spanish women were encouraged to take up the practice, with publications to instruct them. In 1801, for instance, Pedro Hernández published a pamphlet which encouraged women to vaccinate their children and included an image of a mother carrying out the procedure on her son (shown in figure 7.5).[120] The *Madrid Gazette* published a report on Hernández's pamphlet, emphasizing that vaccination was "at the same time so easy and so simple that fathers, mothers, and even wetnurses can execute it with all happiness and without the aid of a doctor and without needing any special preparation".[121]

In Spanish America, Hernández's pamphlet teaching mothers how to vaccinate their offspring was widely disseminated, with 500 copies printed in 1802 in Cuba alone.[122] The Havana Vaccination Board issued mothers with "instructions succinct and simple explaining how to execute [vaccination], the characteristics of the fluid, and the opportune time to take the beneficial pus".[123] In Mexico in 1804, a pastoral letter from the Bishop of Antequera de Oaxaca exhorted women to vaccinate their children and explained that although vaccination could easily be carried out by fathers, mothers, and wetnurses, "really it is an operation more appropriate for women because of the greater softness of their hands".[124]

As it turned out, female vaccination autonomy was indeed curtailed in some societies. But the institution at fault was not the family. Instead, women

116. Viazzo 2003, 122.
117. Logan 2003, 527–8.
118. Viazzo 2003, 122; Dennison and Ogilvie 2014, 654 (table 1).
119. Quoted in Poska 2022, 10.
120. Hernández 1802.
121. Quoted in Poska 2022, 13.
122. Quoted in Poska 2022, 13.
123. Quoted in Poska 2022, 15.
124. Quoted in Poska 2022, 14.

FIGURE 7.5. Spanish mother vaccinating her son, 1802. This illustration by José de Fonseca was inserted at the end of a Spanish pamphlet published in 1802, consisting of an adaptation of a French broadsheet which offered a "how to" manual on vaccination for ordinary people. The Spanish author included illustrations at the end of his pamphlet in order to demonstrate how to implement the procedure. *Source*: Hernández 1802, 75.

were prevented from getting their children vaccinated, and from carrying out the operation themselves, by states, religions, and medical associations. In Persia in 1804, for instance, mothers started bringing their children to a British doctor to be vaccinated, but the sheikh of Bushehr (in modern Iran) forbade it, not because women were displaying unacceptable autonomy but because the practice was "emanating from the impure hand of an unbeliever".[125] In Spain and Spanish America, female vaccinators were swept aside not because they violated gender subordination but because the state granted a monopoly over the procedure to medical associations and public health officials.[126] In Sweden, midwives and other women accounted for one in eight vaccinators until the 1890s, when the physicians excluded them so as to reserve the procedure (and its fees) for themselves.[127]

Nor should female agency be romanticized. It was not always used in good ways—or at least, not always to promote immunization. Many women promoted vaccination, but others opposed it. In early nineteenth-century rural

125. Quoted in M. Bennett 2020, 265.
126. Poska 2022, 9–12, 16–18; Few 2015, 187–8.
127. Sköld 1996b, 409–11.

Styria (Austria), lists of "vaccination refusers" reveal that mothers rejected vaccination for their children systematically more often than fathers. As one father explained in 1824, "My wife doesn't want to have the child vaccinated and I can't bring her to do it." Another father explained in 1830, "To keep the peace at home, because she was really harsh about it, I gave in to her and didn't bring the child for vaccination." As one mineworker's wife put it in 1838, "I am a mother and as such I am entitled to do what I wish with the child."[128]

Female vaccination hesitancy was not restricted to backward rural regions. In London in 1882, Mary Clarke was so horrified at the prospect of having her infant vaccinated that she tore up the floorboards of her dwelling with her bare hands to expose a water tank, in which she deliberately drowned herself and her baby to save it from vaccination.[129] In the 1894 Milwaukee smallpox epidemic, the communal mobs that resisted vaccination, hospital isolation, and other public health measures included many women. As a newspaper reported, "Mobs of Pomeranian and Polish women armed with baseball bats, potato mashers, clubs, bed slats, salt and pepper, and butcher knives, lay in wait all day for . . . the Isolation Hospital van."[130] In the Covid-19 pandemic, women were significantly more likely to express vaccine hesitancy and significantly less likely to get vaccinated.[131] Female agency should therefore be advocated because it is a human right, not because it is good for epidemic control.

Women thus displayed strong agency in the history of variolation and vaccination—for good or ill. But they did so under a wide variety of family forms—the EMP in Britain, Austria, and Sweden; heterogeneous family forms in France, Spain, and Italy; eastern European family systems in Ukraine, Russia, and Livonia; Latin American family forms in Mexico and Cuba; Middle Eastern ones in Persia and Egypt; African ones in Nubia and Ghana; and Indian ones in Punjab. Even if female initiative was indeed more important in Britain than other societies, as some scholarship argues, there is no evidence that this was because of the EMP rather than the well-known autonomy of British women, which foreigners—at least male ones—had been criticizing for centuries.[132]

This draws attention once more to the wider institutional framework. As we have seen in earlier chapters, access to both variolation and vaccination was profoundly shaped by markets, states, local communities, religions, and medical associations. Even if women enjoyed greater autonomy in immunizing their children in some societies than others, it seems likely that it was not only,

---

128. Quoted in Hammer-Luza 2021, 114–15.
129. Williams 2010, 239.
130. Quoted in Leavitt 1976, 559.
131. Zintel et al. 2023; Toshkov 2023.
132. See the survey by Ogilvie (2003, 344–52).

or even primarily, because of the family as opposed to other components of the institutional system, which affected both female agency and immunization.

4. Migration

Human migration is a major vector of epidemic disease, and some family forms are believed to encourage migration more than others. Under the EMP, for instance, many young people left home in their teens and worked as servants or labourers, often migrating to other localities, for a decade or more before marrying in their mid- to late twenties. Couples were expected to set up a new nuclear family after marriage rather than forming a multiple-family household with their own parents or siblings; this "neolocal marriage" norm encouraged new couples to set up house in new locations. High lifetime celibacy freed 10 to 20 per cent of individuals from familial ties that might have deterred migration. Kinship links outside the nuclear family were weak, reducing the kin-based social capital that would be lost by migrating away from one's natal place.

But non-EMP family systems also had features encouraging migration. Early and universal marriage fuelled high fertility, generating numerous offspring who could not be supported on the family farm or workshop, so they migrated away to seek livelihoods elsewhere. Large, multigenerational households made it possible for married males to depart for urban jobs, leaving behind wives and children to run the farm as part of the extended family. Early and universal marriage might curtail life-cycle servanthood, but married or widowed women and men found jobs as servants in urban households, motivating them to migrate from villages into towns. In theory, therefore, the net effect of the family system on the volume of migration is not clear-cut.

Nor is the evidence. Migration was widespread in many pre-modern societies, regardless of the family system. Table 7.2 shows estimates of the magnitude of labour migration, the type of mobility most likely to be influenced by family institutions, rather than the military mobility organized by states or the pilgrimages and crusades organized by religions. The figures in table 7.2 constitute a minimum estimate even of labour migration, since they show only the seven largest labour migration systems in Europe around 1800, those involving at least 20,000 workers migrating every year regularly from a particular catchment zone to a specific destination zone, travelling up to 250–300 kilometres.[133] The total volume of labour migration was much higher, of course, since people migrated in smaller numbers over shorter distances from countryside to town, between towns, and between adjacent rural regions, especially from pastoral villages with low labour demand to arable villages with their

133. Lucassen 1987, 117.

TABLE 7.2. Major Migrant Labour Systems in Europe, *c*.1800

Migrant labour system	Annual no.	Push zone	Pull zone
North Sea	30,000	Westphalia and north-west Germany	German, Dutch, and Flemish coasts
London–Humber	20,000	Ireland, Scotland, Wales, western England	Eastern England
Paris basin	60,000	Massif Central, Alps, western France	Paris and surrounding departments
Mediterranean coast	35,000	Alps, Massif Central, Pyrenees	Provence, Languedoc, Catalonia
Castile	30,000	Galicia, northern Spain, France	Castile with Madrid
Piedmont, Po Valley	50,000	Surrounding northern Italian mountains (Bergamo Alps to Ligurian Apennines)	Po Valley, Milan, Turin
Central Italy with Corsica	100,000	Eastern Italy, Ancona Marche, Frosinone, Neapolitan areas near Rome, Pistoia	Southern Tuscany, Lazio, Corsica, Elba
Total	325,000		
North-west (EMP)	110,000		
South (non-EMP)	215,000		

Source: Own compilation, based on Lucassen 1987, 107–19.

Notes: Includes only those labour migration systems involving an annual minimum of 20,000 labour migrants. Push zone = migrants' zone of origin; pull zone = migrants' destination zone.

seasonal labour peaks. For some epidemics, however, the great long-distance migration systems shown in table 7.2 may have been more important than short-distance labour flows, because they brought together populations from disparate pools of immunity.

Just focusing on these seven great labour migration systems, an estimated 325,000 Europeans were migrating to seek employment in other European regions every year by the later eighteenth century. Of these, about 110,000 were migrating between zones in north-west Europe, where the EMP was the main family system. But nearly twice as many were migrating between zones in the European south, which were dominated by non-EMP family systems involving early and universal marriage, multigenerational households, and strong kinship networks.

The estimates in table 7.2 refer to the period around 1800, but a number of these labour migration systems, in both north-west and southern Europe, had existed at least since the sixteenth century. As the Italian weaver Antonio

Samitaro put it in 1565, "I departed from Venice and then I walked, as young boys do."[134] Many of these labour migration systems were driven mainly by adult males, but some also involved non-trivial numbers of women and children, as in the Po Valley where teams of migrant rice harvesters comprised equal numbers of both sexes,[135] or in eighteenth-century Galicia where women made up one-third of the 30,000 harvesters migrating each year to the Spanish south.[136]

The seven great European labour migration systems shown in table 7.2 give quantitative substance to a more general historical finding. Many historical family systems other than the EMP generated substantial migration flows, both inside and outside Europe. These in turn transmitted epidemic disease. The family systems of sixth-century Central Asian nomads, for instance, took part in mass migrations that are thought to have carried the Justinianic plague to the Roman Empire.[137] The Mongolian family system accommodated long-distance tribal migrations from winter to summer pastoral encampments, which helped bubonic plague emerge from its endemic heartland in Central Asia, bringing it into contact with khanate armies, which in turn transmitted it to European trading settlements on the Black Sea in the 1340s, unleashing the Black Death across Europe and the Middle East.[138] The family system of rural Lombardy generated significant migration into cities, fostering epidemics such as the Milan plague of 1523 in which 42 per cent of victims came from the city parishes most filled with recent immigrants.[139] The eighteenth-century Anatolian and Balkan family systems engendered a swelling stream of male migrants, who travelled to Istanbul to join the notorious *bekâr* (lit., "bachelors"), though many had wives back in their villages. These solitary male migrant workers (shown in figure 7.6) made up about one-fifth of the inhabitants of Istanbul and were widely blamed for spreading epidemics.[140]

A diversity of family institutions also generated migrant flows that carried epidemic disease in the nineteenth and twentieth centuries. The family system of rural Bengal spawned mass migration to the indigo-producing Jessore district of Calcutta, carrying endemic cholera from the countryside into the city, where it flared up into epidemics in 1817–25.[141] Nineteenth-century African family systems produced thousands of small-scale traders travelling in caravans over long distances, bringing smallpox from their places of origin to urban

134. Quoted in Caracausi 2014, 146.
135. Lucassen 1987, 116.
136. Sarasúa 2009, 2–3.
137. Buell 2012, 130–2.
138. Dols 1977, 38, 40–1, 49–50.
139. Cohn and Alfani 2007, 193–4.
140. Hamadeh 2017, 173–5, 184.
141. M. Harrison 2020, 510–11.

VUE DE LA PLACE ET DE LA FONTAINE DE TOP-HANÉ.

FIGURE 7.6. "Bachelors" working as porters and street sellers in Istanbul, 1809. The image shows Tophane Square in Istanbul in which *bekâr* can be seen working as porters and peddlers. These rural migrant labourers made up 20 per cent of the city's inhabitants but were excluded from occupational guilds, respectable neighbourhoods, and urban rights of legitimate residence. When plague broke out in 1812, the sultan blamed the bachelors, tearing down 577 bachelor rooms where the epidemic had already begun to spread, and ordering the demolition of many more, including the insalubrious neighbourhood known as "Melekgirmez" (lit., "Angels do not enter"), where many of the migrant bachelors lived. *Source*: Melling 1809, image 22. See the discussion in Hamadeh (2017, esp. 174, 184).

destinations in societies such as Angola.[142] The nineteenth-century Russian family system begot a stream of migrant labourers travelling to Mongolia and returning with plague, triggering epidemics in places like the Astrakhan city of Vetlyanka in 1878–79.[143] The rural Kenyan family system produced mass migration of labourers into Nairobi around 1900, where they incubated smallpox epidemics.[144] The family system of northern China propagated huge flows of rural migrant workers to booming cities such as Fujiadian and Harbin, spreading the Manchurian plague epidemic in 1910.[145] The family system of northern Nigeria gave rise to smallpox epidemics in 1951 because "bands of labourers

142. Dias 1981, 362–4.
143. Lynteris 2016, 94.
144. Fenner 1988, 358.
145. Gottschang and Lary 2020, 58, 68.

from the remotest northern villages trek to seek work as far south as ports on the coast and Niger Delta".[146] The family systems of rural India generated such copious migration flows that by 1961 one-third of the national population was enumerated outside its place of birth, with countless migrant workers carrying smallpox epidemics back from urban jobs to their home villages.[147]

In many societies, therefore, regardless of the family system, labour migration was non-trivial and observably transmitted epidemic disease. The EMP institutionalized migration by servants and neolocal married couples in northwest and central Europe. But non-EMP family systems institutionalized migration by individuals of various marital statuses in various family groupings in Central Asia, China, India, Africa, and southern and eastern Europe.

Partly this was because migration is shaped not just by the family but also by numerous other institutions. The market conveys signals about labour demand, attracting young people to leave home to seek jobs elsewhere, married couples to leave stagnant villages for growing towns, and entire tribes to migrate seasonally or move nomadically. The state encourages migration for some groups (such as male soldiers) while restricting it for others (such as women). The community welcomes migrants who fill labour shortages and comply with local norms while rejecting those who compete with locals, burden the welfare system, or appear to incubate epidemics. Religion attracts believers from persecuted localities while itself excluding members of other faiths or even ejecting them. Guilds mandate temporary tramping by journeymen labourers while imposing entry barriers against non-local candidates for apprenticeship and mastership. Migration decisions thus respond to the entire framework of institutional constraints at both origin and destination. This can mute or even counteract the effect of family institutions. When migration transmitted epidemic contagion, as often happened, it was the whole institutional framework—not just the family—that influenced the size and composition of the stream of infected people.

The family might, however, have shaped the interface between migration and epidemics. A family system encouraging migration into live-in servanthood might have transmitted contagion less than one involving independently residing migrant labourers, if sanitary arrangements and "social disciplining" of live-in workers reduced risky behaviour. A family system encouraging migration by adult females or entire domestic groups might have limited contagion because of wives' and mothers' beneficent influence on familial hygiene and health decisions. We should not rule out familial effects on the migration–disease nexus until such hypotheses are explored. For now, however, the evidence does not justify concluding that migration, and any epi-

146. Quoted in Schneider 2009, 216.
147. Fenner 1988, 715.

demiological impact it might have had, was encouraged or limited by any specific family system.

5. Amoral Familism

A final effect of the family on epidemics involves values and preferences. Some argue that strong family ties deter individuals from caring about the spillover costs of their choices—such as infecting others with epidemic disease. This is Banfield's famous idea of "amoral familism", the principle that everyone should "maximize the material, short-run advantage of the nuclear family; assume that all others will do likewise". As a result of this attitude, it is argued, people acted "without morality" towards nonfamily members, lacked "political capacity", and failed to cooperate for the common good.[148]

Recent variants of this idea blame amoral familism on extended family, strong kinship, and close-kin marriage. One argues that Europe pulled ahead of China from the medieval period onwards because in ninth-century Europe, "tribal tendencies were gradually undone by the church which, in addition to generalized morality, advanced a marriage dogma that undermined large kinship organizations".[149] In Europe, it is claimed, the Christian Church was instrumental in "shaping reshaping family ties towards the nuclear family, and in diffusing a universalistic value system detached from one's narrow community of friends and relatives".[150] The weak-kin European family system, according to this view, fostered beneficial norms, including "the rule of law, the legitimacy of majority rule, respect for minority rights, individualism, and trust among non-kin".[151]

Another variant of this idea dates the demise of the strong-kinship family and the emergence of prosociality in Europe to an even earlier period. In the fourth to sixth century, it argues, the western Catholic Church began prohibiting close-kin marriage, which weakened kinship networks. Weaker kinship ties brought about a transformation in cognition and values, fostering "greater individualism, less conformity, and more impersonal prosociality".[152] This in turn begot populations that were psychologically "WEIRD": Western, educated, industrialized, rich and democratic.[153] Weaker kinship networks made people in European societies and their global offshoots "cognitively different", so they

---

148. Banfield 1958, 85.
149. Greif and Tabellini 2010, 137.
150. Mokyr and Tabellini 2023, 3.
151. Greif 2006, 311.
152. Schulz et al. 2019, 1 (quotation); Henrich 2020.
153. Schulz et al. 2019, 1 (quotation); Henrich 2020.

developed psychological patterns that favoured individualism, impersonality, and behaviour that served society as a whole rather than just one's own family.

What, if anything, does this imply about epidemic contagion? Do strong family relationships inevitably weaken people's concern for society at large? If you care for your family, does this mean not caring about anyone else?

Of course there are always individuals who create public health risks by acting antisocially, and sometimes they do so to benefit their own families. In the 1484 Leiden plague, Govert die Ketelboeter's daughter sought to scrub out the familial dwelling after several plague deaths, and was fined for exposing the neighbourhood to infected items.[154] In the 1530 Edinburgh plague, a tailor concealed his wife's death and then attended Mass, threatening the safety of the whole community, for which he was condemned to hang (though his sentence was commuted to banishment when the rope broke, signalling God's will).[155] In the 1636 Newcastle epidemic, relatives visited plague death-beds in defiance of exhortations from state, community, and Church.[156] In the 1710–13 Scania plague, families broke public health regulations by gathering in houses of plague sufferers, protesting against segregated burials, and digging up relatives' corpses to reinter them in ordinary graveyards, despite the risks of contagion.[157] In the 1796 Mexican smallpox epidemic, Oaxaca families rioted against officials who sought to limit contagion by isolating infected children from their parents and siblings.[158] In southern Peru in 1807, families fled to the hills for fear the vaccinators would round up their infant offspring.[159] In Rio de Janeiro in 1904, anti-vaccination riots were triggered partly by the legal powers of the family to defend the home as "a space of privacy, honor, and patriarchal authority" against the outside world, in which "anonymity, danger and impersonal laws predominate".[160] As one Brazilian anti-vaccination activist put it, the vaccination of women meant that when the head of household returned from work:

> [He] would be unable to know for certain that his family's honor was still intact, as a stranger would have penetrated the domicile armed with a legal proclamation authorizing him to invade the household and brutalize the bodies of his daughters and his wife. . . . [T]he virgin, the wife and daughter will have to bare their arms and bodies to the vaccination agents.[161]

154. Coomans 2021, 223.
155. Oram 2007, 26.
156. Wrightson 2011, 39–40, 99–105.
157. Arcini et al. 2016, 132.
158. M. Bennett 2020, 299.
159. M. Bennett 2020, 316–17.
160. Cantisano 2022, 614 (quotation), 622–3, 637.
161. Quoted in Cukierman 2021, n16.

In the 1911 Manchurian plague epidemic, many families, "when they know that the plague is in their very midst and a member is down, run off and pawn all the clothes, etc., they can, for fear the authorities may destroy, or, worse still, disinfect it".[162]

But as these examples show, families acted like this not just in strong-kinship societies such as Latin America and China but also in weak-kinship societies such as England, Scotland, the Netherlands, and Sweden. Indeed, Banfield's theory of amoral familism argued that people placed societal inter-ests below those of their own *nuclear* families. Whether the kinship system is weak or strong, the family may lack incentives to take account of the contagion costs its actions impose on people outside the family unless state, community, religion, guild, or other institutions align familial interests with societal ones.

Furthermore, strong family ties can operate in the exact opposite direction, motivating families to reinforce contagion controls in order to safeguard their own members. In seventeenth-century Bristol, for instance, rich neighbour-hoods implemented plague isolation measures more strictly than poor ones, giving rise to higher household clustering of plague deaths but lower overall mortality. This was because urban elites sought to protect their families by allo-cating resources to enforcing plague measures in their own neighbourhoods: "As well as being the areas where they could exert control, the Bristol elite also favoured their own parishes to protect themselves and their families."[163] In nineteenth-century Germany, as we saw in chapter 3, wealthy urban minorities used their influence in municipal government to push through sanitary reform, motivated partly by the desire to decrease epidemic risks for their own fami-lies.[164] In rural Poland in 2020, anthropologists found no evidence of amoral familism blocking epidemic control—for instance, by people stockpiling scarce items for their own relatives. Quite the contrary. At least in some cases, people exerted pressure on non-mask-wearing individuals in supermarkets in order to protect their own family members, incidentally benefiting the rest of the community.[165]

Covid-19 vividly illustrates the way in which "amoral familism" and "family protection" work in opposite directions, with the former hindering contagion control but the latter enhancing it. A study of 63 countries in 2020 found a non-linear relationship between strength of family ties and Covid-19 transmission. These results held even when controlling for other country characteristics, including religious beliefs, rule of law, government pan-demic measures, GDP, human development indicators, health expenditures,

162. "The Plague: Mukden, Feb. 13", *North-China Herald*, 24 February 1911, 419.
163. Udale 2023, 136.
164. John Brown 1988, 310.
165. Burdyka 2020.

geographical features, and demography.[166] On the one hand, strong family ties, especially those running from parents to children, reduced compliance with social distancing mandates. This was the "amoral familism" effect. But on the other, strong family ties towards vulnerable relatives, especially those running from offspring to aged parents, increased compliance with social distancing—the "family protection" effect. The net effect of family on contagion depended not so much on the strength or weakness of family ties, but on the relative force of amoral familism compared with family protection in shaping people's strategies for helping their relatives.

There are two other ways in which strong kin ties can amplify rather than hinder anti-contagion measures. One is what might be termed the "familial coercion" effect. The family has an unparalleled capacity to monitor and coerce its own members. This can be used to limit epidemic contagion in ways that benefit the collectivity even if they harm individual family members. A grim example comes from seventeenth-century China, where the strength of the family protected the community by ejecting diseased family members: "Whenever one is found to have *feng* [leprosy], the family puts him or her into a small boat, with food and clothes, and sets the boat on the river or on the sea."[167] In nineteenth-century Ethiopia, villagers helped their community set fire to dwellings in which their own infected relatives were sleeping, as a collective anti-contagion measure.[168] We do not know whether these families voluntarily coerced their members to prevent contagion to the community, or whether they did so to avoid reprisals by the community against the rest of the family.

In some cases, however, there is clear evidence that anti-contagion measures can be amplified through a "family reprisal" effect. During Shanghai's six-week Covid-19 lockdown in early 2022, for instance, PPE-clad policemen ordered a couple into centralized quarantine. When they resisted, the police threatened retribution against their "family for the next three generations". In this case, there was no family to threaten, as the couple retorted, "We are the last generation."[169] Reprisals against an entire family for misdeeds by individual members is sufficiently common to have been given a specific name in a number of historical (and a few modern) societies—*éraic* in medieval Ireland, *galanas* in medieval Wales, *liánzuò* in early modern China, *yeonjwaje* in nineteenth-century Korea, *Sippenhaft* in medieval (and twentieth-century) Germany, *chleny sem'i izmennika Rodiny* in twentieth-century Russia. It might be argued that kin-based reprisals are used only by low-capacity communities

---

166. Di Gialleonardo et al. 2021.
167. Quoted in Q. Liang 2009, 108.
168. Pankhurst 1965, 349.
169. Quoted in Z. Zhang and Gardner 2023, 5.

and states. But even high-capacity states can deploy family-based reprisals to reinforce anti-contagion measures.

When will strong familial institutions fortify anti-contagion measures? Institutions outside the family are clearly important. The "family protection" effect will be much more potent where families can leverage and amplify anti-contagion measures—home lockdown, centralized quarantine, face-mask mandates, or clean water supplies—put in place by market, state, community, religion, or occupational association. The "family coercion" or "family reprisal" effect will also be much more compelling where nonfamilial institutions can put pressure on the family to constrain its members, whether by ejecting them from the community, subjecting them to communal vigilantism, or blackmailing them into complying with collective interests during epidemics. Even if these familial incentives to reinforce epidemic controls do not depend entirely on community or state, their force will certainly be amplified by them, and the family reprisal effect is entirely dependent on pressure from other components of the institutional framework.

Caring for one's family does not necessarily lead to amoral familism, whether in epidemics or in general. It depends on the wider institutional framework. In both weak-kinship and strong-kinship societies, people do sometimes behave in ways that benefit their own families at the expense of society at large. But in such societies they also undertake contagion-controlling activities to safeguard their vulnerable members or protect the entire family from harm. How families behave in epidemics depends on what other institutions do. Do other institutions abandon the family to its own devices? Do they set up contagion-control measures which families can amplify? Strong family ties can harm epidemic control when they substitute for nonfamilial institutions. But they can enhance it—sometimes in unsettling ways—when they complement measures put in place by other components of the institutional framework.

6. Are Family Forms the Ultimate Cause of Anything?

Even if strong kinship could be shown to be associated with less prosocial behaviour, and thus worse contagion outcomes, could we say for sure the link was causal? Impersonal prosociality arose in Europe, according to these views, because the family system changed, at some point in antiquity or the Middle Ages before good demographic data are available, from an old pattern based on extended families and strong kin ties to a new one based on nuclear families and weak kinship ties.[170] According to this view, this improved family system gave rise to smaller and simpler households, higher female autonomy, different

170. De Moor and Van Zanden 2010; Schulz et al. 2019; Henrich 2020.

migration patterns, and more prosocial cultural and psychological attitudes, all of which benefitted social outcomes, including contagion control.

Proponents of these ideas acknowledge that merely observing the coexistence of weak kinship and prosocial behaviour in modern, rich societies does not establish that causation runs from the family system to good social outcomes. Causation might run in the other direction, or all these outcomes may result from underlying variables. But as we have seen, one set of scholars claims to have identified an outside impetus that kicked off the whole process—the early medieval Christian Church outlawed close-kin marriage.

Unfortunately, the historical evidence does not support this claim. For one thing, historical demographers have established that close-kin marriage was not widespread in western Europe during late antiquity and the early medieval period, either among pagan aristocrats or in more humble social strata, so the Christian ban on close-kin marriage was running in through an already-open door.[171] Second, papal proclamations were not sedulously obeyed out in the various Christian European societies far from Rome; rather, they were reinterpreted and often fundamentally modified by local religious and temporal authorities.[172] Third, medieval historians find no evidence that demographic rules prescribed even by local clergy were systematically enforced; other local institutions, including landlords, rulers, and legal system, decided whether Church rules would be implemented in practice.[173] Fourth, family and kinship varied enormously across the zone of the western Christian Church, from nuclear families and weak kinship in north-west Europe (firmly documented from *c*.1540 onwards) to a wide array of extended- and multiple-family systems with strong kinship organizations in Mediterranean, eastern, and south-eastern Europe (which survived well into the nineteenth or twentieth century). Finally, close-kin marriage in particular and kinship in general varied a great deal across historical periods, European societies, and different social strata in the same society—the existence of a monolithic European family pattern is not empirically substantiated.[174]

Even if weak kinship and good socio-economic outcomes could be shown to be associated, this does not imply a causal link. Weaker kinship might cause good outcomes via the mechanisms postulated in the literature on the EMP, the European non-clan-based family system, or the low-cousin-marriage WEIRD theory. But causation could also go in the opposite direction, with economic and social development weakening kinship links. A third possibility is that both sets of outcomes might be caused by underlying factors. A weak kinship system

171. Shaw and Saller 1984.
172. Dorin 2021.
173. Biller 2001, Donahue 2008.
174. McCants 2021.

and strong cooperation beyond the family may have arisen and survived only within a wider social framework of strong nonfamilial institutions that could substitute for familial labour, insurance, and welfare services that were unavailable to fragile nuclear families and solitary spinsters and bachelors. In societies with weak kinship institutions, these other institutions—market, state, community, guild—provided security, property rights, contracts, labour, credit, insurance, human capital investment, and many of the other services supplied by the family in strong-kinship societies.[175] But they also affected contagion directly, as we have seen in earlier chapters. Disentangling the contagion effects of the family from those of the wider institutional matrix that both shapes contagion and sustains that family system is a crucial challenge that must be tackled before we ascribe an autonomous role to the family in isolation.

7. Conclusion

Contrasts between different types of family institution in how they deal with contagion should not be exaggerated. Most differences are not extreme. They are matters of degree rather than kind. Even where behaviour differs across family systems, we cannot ascribe it to the family in isolation. The family is embedded in a broader institutional framework consisting of markets, states, local communities, religions, occupational associations, and many other components. These affect both how society copes with epidemics and the form taken by the institution of the family. The family takes the form it does in a particular society partly because other parts of the institutional framework substitute for family responsibilities, complement them—or fail to do either.

The size and complexity of households, death practices, women's position, migration, and concern for one's relatives all affect epidemic contagion. But all these aspects of family behaviour are themselves constrained by other institutions. The findings in this chapter suggest caution before ascribing an autonomous role to the family system in determining how a society controls epidemic contagion.

In different societies the family does take different forms, and these are highly resilient to epidemics and other crises. This resilience derives partly from the way the family is embedded in the entire social framework. Family forms interact with epidemics in many ways, but do so in combination with other institutions. The institutional framework as a whole, not the family in isolation, shapes the mutual influences between family institutions and epidemic disease. This finding is explored in detail in the concluding chapter of this book.

175. Dennison and Ogilvie 2014, 674–5, 678, 684, 686–7.

8

Is There a Magic Pill?

> For what is the cause that this pestilence is so greatly in one part of the land
> and not in another? And in the same city and town, why is it in one part, or
> in one house, and not in another? And in the same house, why is it upon one,
> and not upon all the rest . . . ?
>
> —NICHOLAS BOWND, *MEDICINES FOR THE PLAGUE*, 1604[1]

What does history tell us about how human institutions interact with microbes?
We have examined many episodes of infectious disease since the Black Death—at
least seven major pandemics, numerous nationwide epidemics, and countless
regional and local outbreaks. We explored many societies across the world over
seven centuries. We analysed how humans interacted with microbes through six
key institutions—market, state, community, religion, guild, and family. What
can we learn from the hostile yet intimate relationship between human and
microbial populations over the past seven centuries?

Our big investigation breaks down into four tributary questions. The first
looks at what each institution is good and bad at. How does each institution
help individuals agree to take account of the effects their infectious behaviour
has on others? What is its special strength in enabling collections of humans to
deal with collections of microbes? At the same time, what is each institution
bad at? What flaws make it fail to control contagion? Does it have a dark side?
Can it actually make contagion worse?

The second tributary question explores the overall institutional framework in societies facing epidemic disease. How do social institutions interact

---

1. Quoted in Slack 1985, 22.

during epidemics? Does this interaction make it more possible to control contagion, or less?

Our third question is comparative. Did some societies come up with better solutions than others over the past seven centuries? Are there key institutions that a society has to have, or key features that an institution has to have, to tackle epidemic contagion successfully?

The final question is chronological. Did societies learn? Did the experience of terrible epidemics that killed and maimed millions at least spur these victims' societies to devise better ways of mitigating contagion next time? Is institutional learning possible?

This chapter draws together the answers to these questions. It reminds us of why we set out on this journey to begin with, tries to work out where we have got to, and puts forward some ideas about where we might go next. The close yet lethal link between humans and microbes will never be severed—and given the importance of the microbiome to the human immune system, it would be fatal if it were.[2] Over the past seven centuries, we have worked out a series of truces, which have always been broken by either humans or microbes. Does this history tell us anything about what might emerge as a modus vivendi?

1. The Good News and the Bad

Delving into the six key institutions of human societies—market, state, community, religion, guild, and family—brings to light a bright side and a dark one. The good news is that each institution turns out to be effective at dealing with epidemics in some way.

This does not mean going back to the old view that institutions exist because they offer efficient solutions to economic problems. This idea was popular in the early days of institutional economics and was applied to almost every historical institution, even serfdom, slavery, feuds, cartels, guilds, and monopolistic corporations like the East India Company. Economic ideas about historical institutions have since moved on. Many theories about the efficiency of specific historical institutions have been refuted empirically. We now know that institutions rise and survive for multifarious reasons—by benefiting powerful groups, responding to stochastic events, harmonizing with cultural norms, or emerging out of path dependence.[3]

Institutions can exist without making the economy work better. In practice, many institutions do not have any beneficial effect on efficiency, growth, technological progress, or income distribution. In theory, moreover, economic performance is not the only measure of whether an institution is good or bad.

---

2. Lambring et al. 2019.
3. Acemoglu, Johnson, and Robinson 2005; Ogilvie 2007; Ogilvie and Carus 2014.

Institutions can also be measured by other indicators—after all, the whole point of economic growth is to increase human well-being. One indicator is how well a particular institution helps us cope with epidemics. This way of assessing institutions is in no way less important or relevant than the others. Indeed, as we saw in chapter 2, the two measures—epidemiological resilience and economic performance—are viscerally interlinked.

Each major institution in this book—market, state, community, religion, guild, and family—was used during epidemics to do things that helped control contagion. On the other hand, each institution sometimes failed to deliver on its unique selling points. Worse, each had a dark side. People could use it to coordinate activities that exacerbated contagion.

1.1. THE MARKET

It might be asked whether markets even had a bright side during epidemics. Surely this is an oxymoron. After all, the whole problem with contagion is that it involves a market failure. My individual decision to party, work, shop, trade, keep clean, or get immunized not only has costs and benefits for me. It also creates costs and benefits for the rest of society, and markets do not charge me for those costs or reward me for those benefits. So I do more contagion-causing things, and fewer contagion-limiting ones, than I would if market prices were giving me accurate signals about the costs and benefits of my actions. Epidemics are one of the most extreme examples of externalities—market failures—that human societies know. So can we really say that these market failures were mitigated by markets themselves?

We can. There are always infectious diseases around. Typically, they switch from endemic to epidemic phases. They turn into epidemics for many reasons other than market exchange or market failure. Epidemics emerge out of biological changes in microbes, in animal vectors, and in their ecosystems. Epidemics also arise from human activities mediated by non-market institutions—by states, communities, religions, guilds, and families. So there is always a pool of epidemic infection that has nothing to do with markets or their failures but is susceptible to control if human beings allocate resources to controlling it.

Markets are the best institution we know for generating those resources. The richest economies over the past seven centuries also had the best functioning markets—northern Italy and the Southern Netherlands in the medieval period; the Northern Netherlands from 1550 to 1800; England from 1650 to 1850; America, Germany, and much of the industrializing world after that date. Markets enabled these societies not only to achieve high and rapidly growing per capita GDP—that is, better material living standards. They also enabled them to bring about better human development indicators such as education, political representation, civil rights, good health, and extended life expectancy.[4]

This was partly because all those components of human development are what economists call "normal goods": as incomes rise, individuals consume more of them. Higher incomes gave people resources to deploy in private decisions that reduced their own risk of disease. In historical epidemics, as we have seen, higher incomes enabled people to get better food, housing, clothing, hygiene, and care, which improved their ability to survive disease. Higher incomes also made it possible to support families through market withdrawal, flight from disease, social distancing, and pharmaceutical immunization.

When fewer individuals were infected, the number of other people they infected was also lower. This diminished the risks of infection for the whole society. The market thus indirectly reduced contagion externalities by increasing individual incomes. This was not because market failures were absent but because people had the resources to avoid infection themselves, so they inadvertently transmitted fewer microbes to their fellows.

Human development indicators rise with incomes for a second reason. Higher incomes mean higher fiscal capacity for central states and local governments, but also for all other institutions that levy taxes, collect dues, or solicit donations: local communities, religious organizations, occupational associations, extended families. As people's incomes rose, they could better afford these contributions. Market-driven economic growth enriched all these institutions. Such contributions were necessary—though sadly not sufficient—for anti-contagion measures like quarantines, waste management, clean water, immunization. They were also essential in funding welfare support to help less well-off families voluntarily withdraw from markets and comply with social distancing measures. Collective action against contagion requires resources, and markets are the best institution humans have devised to generate such resources.

Markets, however, had a dark side. They facilitated exchange of goods and services that people wanted. But they also facilitated exchange of pathogens, including zoonoses, which we know underlie most emerging epidemics.[5] Plague could indeed come, as William Laud put it in 1637, "by the carelessness of the people, and the greediness to receive into their houses infected goods".[6]

The market also exacerbated epidemic contagion in more complicated ways. First, it failed to transmit signals that made individuals take account of the costs they imposed on others by producing, consuming, or socializing while infected. People withdrew from the market voluntarily, as we have seen,

4. Dasgupta and Weale 1992; Crafts 1997a; Crafts 1997b; Prados de la Escosura 2022a; Prados de la Escosura 2022b.

5. Taylor, Latham, and Woolhouse 2001, 985–6.

6. Quoted in Slack 1985, 22.

but they did so based on their assessment of private costs and benefits, not social ones. In the absence of appropriate signals, individual decisions did not take social costs and benefits into account.

Second, the market failed to reward people for producing and diffusing information about epidemic disease. Information is non-rival and non-excludable, so people trading in the market provide less of it than society would like them to. With less information available, individuals made decisions based on ignorance about what caused disease, whether it was currently in an epidemic phase, what its risks were, how they could protect themselves, and how they could improve immunity.

The market thus had both a good and a bad side when it came to controlling contagion. These two aspects of the market, as we have seen, were not separable. The market could generate the good things it did for epidemics only if it also generated bad things. In one epidemic after another over the past seven centuries, the market generated both the resources needed to control the epidemic and the contagion spillovers that needed to be controlled. Whether in Milan during the Black Death or in Asia during Covid-19, the cost of closing markets to prevent illness and death was high in terms of material consumption and human autonomy. But as in Florence during the Black Death or the USA during Covid-19, the cost of leaving markets open to maintain consumption and human autonomy was high in terms of illness and death.[7]

The dividing line between the good and the bad sides of the market was— and is—not clear-cut. It is blurred by the trade-off between different components of human welfare: income and health. Market exchange generated material resources needed for preserving lives in epidemics. But preserving lives generated the human resources—living and healthy producers and consumers—needed for market exchange to generate material resources. The market alone did not have the mechanisms to balance these two components of human well-being. This was because of contagion externalities and the public-good features of information, which markets struggle to deal with.

1.2. THE STATE

When markets fail, other institutions can provide remedies. One is state coercion. The state can compel us to pay attention to the costs our actions impose on others. It can extract resources from us to pay for public goods like information. As we have seen, in many epidemics down the centuries the state funded,

---

7. According to legend, when the Black Death came to Milan, the government walled up three infected houses and left their occupants to die, thereby saving the rest of the community; Florence supposedly failed to lock up the infected and close markets, causing it to suffer much higher mortality. For assessments, see Cohn 2010a, 48–9, 101; Johansen 2019.

enacted, and enforced measures to make people comply with rules governing sanitation, social and physical distancing, immunization, and diplomatic agreements to deal with cross-border spillovers. Increasingly, governments began to allocate at least some fiscal capacity to civilian public goods such as generating and diffusing information about epidemics.

But sheer state capacity was not enough. The state had to be motivated to collect knowledge about epidemics, negotiate politically with other institutions and groups, and prioritize public health over military, fiscal, and political purposes. Surprisingly few states did this. Governments with high fiscal capacity allocated it mostly to warfare and elite display, not to sanitation or supporting ordinary people through market closures. States with high legal capacity used it to intern people in pesthouses, which were so notoriously perilous that the infected avoided them—literally like the plague. States with high bureaucratic capacity devoted it to administering tax systems and armies, not to collecting epidemiological information or supporting medical science. States with high military capacity fuelled it with the lion's share of government expenditures, starving public health of resources.

The state also did things that made epidemics worse. States with capacity to organize colonial wars and imperial navies opposed travel inspections, quarantines, and isolation measures to serve military and political interests. Governments deliberately falsified information about epidemics to pursue their own fiscal and military ends. States extracted revenues by selling monopolies to waste management firms who provided such bad service that, as in Seoul in 1910, "shit piles up like mounds in and around people's houses".[8] States with high legal capacity used it to collaborate with religious and guild bans on smallpox variolation and limit access to vaccination. Authoritarian governments used public health measures as a pretext for surveillance and coercion. War, the most important single state activity, incubated epidemics from the Black Death to Covid-19.

As with the market, so too with the state: the good and the bad sides were hard to separate. The state could take effective action to control epidemics only by exercising coercion, whose use in other spheres exacerbated those very epidemics. Throughout history, the state generated both the coercion needed to control contagion and the misallocation of that coercion to activities that worsened contagion—waging war, granting privileges to special interests, banning innovations, and authoritarian overkill. Whether in north-west Europe during medieval plague epidemics or the USA during the Covid-19 pandemic, the cost of low state capacity was high in terms of morbidity and mortality. But as in nineteenth-century Russian cholera epidemics or China during Covid-19,

---

8. Quoted in T. Henry 2005, 656–7.

the cost of authoritarian overkill was high in terms of evasion, violence, economic stagnation, and constraints on human autonomy.

The blurred boundary between good and bad state capacity arose partly from trade-offs between different components of human welfare: individual autonomy and medical survival. State capacity generated the coercion needed for preserving lives in epidemics but stifled the autonomy needed for citizens to comply voluntarily, respond flexibly to new circumstances, or devise ways of ending the epidemic through material inputs or medical innovation. By itself, the state did not have the mechanisms to undertake trade-offs between these different components of human well-being—or at least not the "right" trade-offs from the perspective of society as a whole.

1.3. THE LOCAL COMMUNITY

The local community was another piece of the puzzle. It, too, had both good and bad effects on epidemics. The special strength of the community was its social capital of shared norms, information, sanctions, and collective action. Inevitably, the salience of local communities in epidemic control declined with the growth of market and state. But even in societies with well-functioning markets and high state capacity, the local community supported contagion control well into the modern period, and still plays an important role to this day. Sanitation, social distancing, and immunization were greatly enhanced when local communities directed their social capital to these ends. Peer pressure inside local communities deterred individuals from managing infectious waste in dangerous ways. Neighbourly monitoring detected violations of social distancing measures, especially home lockdown and curfew, more thoroughly and at lower cost than government inspections. Naming and shaming in their local face-to-face community motivated individuals to keep their neighbours safe by getting immunized.

But epidemics posed many challenges that communities could not address. Local communities are local, while epidemics spill beyond village walls or city limits to places where communal norms, information, and sanctions have no traction. Even inside the local community, peer pressure was often too informal to make people undertake costly sanitation, social distancing, or immunization choices. During epidemics, community leaders absconded, community councils collapsed, and communal levers easily fell into the hands of local oligarchies. Behind the harmonious façade of the community lurked conflicts fostered by multiplex relationships and worsened by epidemic stresses, reducing communal capacity to act collectively to contain disease.

Communities also had a dark side during epidemics. They deployed their social capital in ways that exacerbated contagion. Community trust helped organize collective opposition to public health measures. Communities whipped up vigilante action against groups they blamed for epidemics, ejecting scape-goats and pushing them into vulnerable living conditions where they lacked sanitation and could not observe social distancing. By acting in these ways, a local community brewed up a pool of contagion that spilled back inside the community and outward across the rest of society.

The boundary between the good and the bad sides of the community was not clearly marked. The community could generate the good things it did for epidemics only by virtue of its stock of social capital. But this social capital was precisely what enabled the community to do bad things during epidemics. Shared norms can be harmful, communal information can be false, communal sanctions can switch over to vigilantism, and communal action can be turned against unfamiliar information and disruptive practices even if those might help contain contagion. What decides whether communal social capital will be directed at good or bad ends is not just the structure of the community itself but how it interacts with the rest of the social framework.

1.4. RELIGION

Religion was part of that framework. Religion provided explanation, con-solation, and moral guidance that moved believers to cooperate in times of adversity. During historical epidemics religions exhorted the faithful to comply with public health measures organized by state or community. As the *Scientific American* blog rhapsodized in 2020, perhaps a trifle optimistically, "Religion and science can complement one another, as indeed they are already doing by reinforcing public health messages during the current pandemic."[9] Many religions established isolation hospitals and staffed them with their own per-sonnel and volunteers. Religions provided charitable relief, which indirectly supported social distancing by enabling poor people to isolate without starv-ing. Many religions provided theological and practical endorsement for immu-nization campaigns. Religions also helped project epidemiological and medical knowledge across international and cultural frontiers, most strikingly in the vaccination missions of the nineteenth century and to some extent during Covid-19 vaccine diplomacy after 2021.[10]

But religions did not always use their spiritual authority to control conta-gion. Tackling epidemics was often subordinated to more visceral religious objectives—pleasing sacred beings, benefiting religious elites, placating external sponsors, enhancing Church resources, increasing adherents. These purposes led many religions to coordinate activities that, however inadvertently, exac-erbated contagion. Some preached a fatalistic belief that epidemics were God's

---

9. Barmania and Reiss 2020.
10. Berkeley Center for Religion, Peace & World Affairs 2021.

will and should not be evaded. Others portrayed the human body as the temple of God, exhorting believers not to pollute it with immunization. Religious personnel even opposed epidemic sanitation, as in Russia in 1892 when rural priests warned parishioners against doctors who thought cholera could be better prevented by boiling water than by eradicating sin. Religions opposed scientific explanations, urging adherents to ignore sanitation, contagion, and immunization. Many religions continued to organize religious assemblies throughout epidemics, claiming they were needed to secure divine intercession. Many mandated pilgrimages, moving people across long distances, where they encountered new diseases in unsanitary conditions. Religions organized wars and crusades which triggered epidemics that afflicted not just soldiers and pilgrims but thousands of ordinary people along the march. No religion deliberately set out to cause contagion, but most went on organizing superspreader events regardless of the risks.

Like market, state, and community, the institution of religion illustrates the same blurred boundaries between good and bad effects on epidemics. Religion could do the good things it did for contagion only because it provided explanation, consolation, and moral guidance that moved the faithful to cooperate in ways that transcended their individual material advantage. But precisely those mechanisms also enabled religion to move believers to behave in ways that exacerbated contagion, even while they satisfied the epistemological, emotional, and ethical desires of the faithful—or at least of religious elites.

1.5. MEDICAL GUILDS AND ASSOCIATIONS

The guild or professional association is another part of the institutional package. During epidemics, medical associations had special strengths, particularly in processing knowledge for individuals, governments, and communities. A medical association can facilitate cooperation that is impossible if each practitioner acts independently, regulate training and quality to ensure good private and public health advice, monitor epidemiological knowledge, and validate innovations. Across the seven centuries of epidemics from the Black Death to Covid, medical associations provided individuals and governments with advice on how to diagnose diseases, identify their causes, and limit their spread. They certified members' skills and the quality of their services, monitored their probity, and penalized violations of professional standards, aiming to protect society against unqualified practitioners, false diagnoses, and fraud. Medical associations also deployed their specialist expertise to synthesize existing epidemiological knowledge and evaluate new ideas, issuing authoritative advice to practitioners, governments, and the public, and creating confidence in new knowledge about sanitation, social distancing, and immunization. As the Royal College of Physicians of Edinburgh declared during the Covid-19 pandemic, its role was to be "an advocate for our Fellows and Members and, ultimately, for the patients that we serve".[11] Medical associations often benefited society at large during epidemics by using their norms, information, sanctions, and collective action to solve problems that proved intractable for families, markets, states, communities, and religions.

But the medical association was another institution whose dark side loomed large during epidemics. It limited entry to medical practice on non-merit-based grounds, excluding wide swathes of skilled practitioners whose gender, skin colour, religion, or citizenship meant they could not surmount the entry barriers. This created a shortage of medical advice for patients and governments. The legal monopoly enjoyed by a medical association enabled its members to refuse to serve during epidemics and to mount successful opposition when patients, communities, or governments sought to employ substitutes from outside. Perhaps most seriously for the long-term management of epidemic contagion, many medical associations corrupted the flow of epidemiological information. To please governments, business elites, and communal public opinion, they issued authoritative declarations that emergent infections were not dangerous or that costly containment measures were not required. Some medical associations refrained from disciplining members who spread misinformation about epidemics, failed to challenge such information publicly, or even defended members who disseminated misinformation. Some abused their authority in order to obstruct innovative ideas and practices that threatened their monopoly of medical knowledge or their members' business practices. In epidemics throughout history, the claim to monopolize medical expertise led medical associations to oppose and reject measures such as quarantine, social distancing, variolation, and vaccination, with malignant effects on epidemic outcomes.

Again, there was a murky frontier between the good things medical associations did and the bad. They could not have done the good things they did had they not generated a social capital of norms, information, sanctions, and collective action inside the profession. But precisely the social capital they used to do these good things also enabled them to do bad ones, falsifying diagnoses, rationing training, creating scarcity, and blocking new knowledge and practices.

The Janus face of the medical association played a particularly important role during epidemics, which made medical knowledge and advice extraordinarily salient. When medical associations made authoritative pronouncements based on groupthink or authority, rejecting empirical observations or new ideas, they not only prevented medical knowledge from adjusting to the new epidemic reality. They also discredited science in general, because

11. A. Thomas et al. 2021, S10.

ordinary people and governments observed that medical authorities themselves were ignorant, prejudiced, or unresponsive to new circumstances. This made individuals and community mobs believe that the medical authorities were lying even when they were not, triggering attacks on health-care workers and resistance to public health measures. Worse still, it caused many ordinary people to reject all scientific recommendations, instead espousing supernatural explanations, state ideology, or communal prejudices. Because epidemics involve science taking place in real time, the groupthink and falsely authoritative pronouncements of medical associations can have far-reaching consequences for how individuals, institutions, and society process medical knowledge and respond to new ideas.

1.6. THE FAMILY

The institution of the family is a final piece of the puzzle. Throughout the many epidemics between the Black Death and Covid-19, the family played a positive role in limiting contagion. It regulated the secondary attack rate inside households, calibrated deathbed and funeral gatherings, and gave wives and mothers autonomy to make high-quality family health decisions. It shaped migration flows so as to provide migrants with safe domestic circumstances en route and at their destinations. Finally, the family created strong emotional incentives to protect vulnerable relatives by complying with anti-contagion measures itself and pressing others to do so. The family did many things that safeguarded its members from epidemics and thus, by reducing the number of people who contracted diseases, also reduced the number who transmitted contagion to the wider society.

But the family also had a dark side when it came to epidemics. In some contexts, its other interests led the family to form large, multigenerational households with high secondary attack rates that not only infected more family members but inevitably spilled over onto their contacts in the community. Family systems that relied heavily on reinforcing wide kinship links sometimes mandated large gatherings of relatives at deathbeds and funerals, which turned into superspreader events during epidemics. Patriarchal family systems limited women's autonomy, preventing mothers from getting children immunized or compelling them to evade male authority to do so. Where family systems exported solitary males to non-domestic living conditions, crowding and poor sanitation incubated epidemics. In societies lacking supportive nonfamilial institutions, the family prioritized its own interests at the expense of outsiders.

Again, the dividing line between the good and the bad sides of the family was not clear-cut. The family could do the good things it did to control contagion only because of its visceral role in coordinating residence, reproduction, nurturing, consumption, and production in such a way as to benefit its members. But that precise role in so many central aspects of private life gave the family the ability to act in ways that exacerbated contagion.

1.7. WHAT TIPS THE BALANCE?

Any institution, as this book has shown, could turn its dark side to epidemics. For one thing, it could fail to deploy its special strengths to control contagion for society at large. The market could fail to convey accurate prices, misleadingly signalling a low cost of contagious activities. The state could fail to deliver adequate compulsion to enforce sanitation, quarantine, or immunization. The local community could be too fissiparous to exercise effective peer pressure. Religion could be flaccid in exhorting believers to care about infecting others. A medical association could refuse to man a pesthouse or quarantine system. The family could pursue its own interests, heedless of how that might infect non-kin.

But the dark side of institutions went beyond this. Every institution could help coordinate activities that exacerbated contagion. Markets traded wares, animal vectors, or migrant labour that transmitted disease. States waged war, granted privileges, or taxed away the resources needed for public health measures. Communities threw out infected people or rioted against quarantine and vaccination. Religions organized superspreader gatherings or censored science. Medical associations limited supply, issued false announcements, or blocked innovations. Families escalated secondary attack rates, stifled female health choices, exported migrants to poor living conditions, or fostered amoral familism.

Each major institution of human society, therefore, contributed to controlling historical epidemics. But institutions arose for multiple reasons and people used them to coordinate multiple activities. Limiting contagion was seldom paramount, even during epidemics. It should not be surprising, therefore, that no institution was used solely for beneficial purposes, and that some had malignant effects. Offsetting forces impelled each institution to act in some ways that mitigated epidemics, in others that exacerbated contagion. One of the tasks of history is to investigate what tipped the balance to the bright rather than the dark side. A major component of the explanation is that the net effect of any institution depended on its interaction with the wider institutional framework within which it was embedded.

2. Greater than the Sum of Its Parts

What is the best institution for dealing with epidemic contagion? Once we start looking at epidemics and institutions, this question is hard to look away from. But history prescribes no magic pill. No single institution emerges from the past seven centuries as best for controlling epidemics.

Fortunately, no institution needed to be. Each institution we examined—market, state, community, religion, guild, and family—was just one component in a wider social framework. What worked best for contagion control was a combination of institutions, in which the surrounding framework supported the strengths of each component, compensated for its weaknesses, and curbed its excesses.

2.1. WHY INSTITUTIONS NEED HELP

One reason the surrounding social framework is important is that each institution needs help. Each institution has a special strength. But to deploy that strength effectively, it needs support from other institutions.

Why would this be? Why can each institution not operate on its own? First, each epidemic has specific characteristics—some living in infectious waste (cholera, typhus), others passing via social contacts (smallpox, influenza, Covid-19), others yielding to immunization (smallpox, Covid-19), many flourishing in multiple reservoirs (plague rodents in human rubbish, typhus lice on human skin, Covid-19 viruses on human food). Second, societies have devised multiple approaches to tackle any infectious disease—sanitation, immunization, social distancing in countless variants, cross-border coordination. Third, anti-contagion measures require multiple resources—money, labour, motivation, compulsion, expertise, information, innovation. Each institution has advantages in tackling particular epidemiological challenges, coordinating certain approaches to contagion, and mobilizing specific resources.

The market, in one form or another, exists in any society as a set of practices that coordinate exchange. A well-functioning market is the best institution that human beings have yet developed for achieving high incomes, economic growth, and the resources needed by individuals, states, and other institutions to control epidemic contagion. Simply by coordinating exchange, the market performs a key service for controlling contagion: helping generate material resources to allocate to social distancing, sanitation, immunization, and cross-border coordination.

But though the market is needed for economic growth to occur, non-market institutions are needed for the market to function.[12] At a bare minimum, the market cannot operate without other institutions to guarantee property rights, enforce contracts, and provide personal security to producers, consumers, and traders. As this book has shown, the wealth and incomes generated in the vibrant market societies of the medieval Middle East, late medieval Italy and Flanders, early modern Holland and England, and the developing economies

---

12. Ogilvie and Carus 2014, 404, 407–18.

of the nineteenth- and twentieth-century industrializing world were taxed by local governments, communities, and religions, which in turn allocated some of their fiscal take to public hygiene, isolation hospitals, inspections, quarantines, immunization campaigns, and information exchange. These revenues were also deployed by state, community, and Church to provide welfare payments and charitable relief to support poor households during lockdown, since, as the Jacobean statute of 1603 sapiently observed, the poor "must be by some charitable course provided for, lest they should wander abroad and thereby infect others".[13] Commercial variolators and vaccinators were employed by local governments, communities, religious organizations, and even some medical associations to improve the quality of immunization and expand its social diffusion. Commercial booksellers collaborated with state, clergy, and scientific associations to diffuse information such as the London Bills of Mortality and pamphlets based on them, which people purchased so that "the Rich might judge of the necessity of their removal, and Trades-men might conjecture what doings they were likely to have in their respective dealings".[14] The market was able to make these contributions to contagion control only when non-market institutions supported it to facilitate exchange, increase incomes, fund public health measures, and motivate knowledge diffusion. Indeed, the market was able to work as well as it did only because non-market institutions provided solutions to market failures arising from externalities and public goods.

Every society also has something like a state, which exercises legitimate coercion, extracts fiscal resources, provides public goods, and coordinates cross-border agreements. These activities are central to combatting epidemic contagion, as we have seen. But the state needs help, both to exercise coercion effectively and to direct it constructively. Fiscal capacity relied on markets to generate resources for the state to extract, communities and guilds to help with tax collection and government borrowing, religions to exhort obedience and taxpaying by the faithful. Communities, religions, and medical associations pressed for state expenditures to be allocated to public health, welfare provision, education, and medical research, instead of the military activities, princely display, vanity projects, and industrial subsidies favoured by rulers left to their own devices.[15] Governments could seldom implement public sanitation, quarantines, or immunization campaigns without the cooperation and support of civil society in the form of communal peer pressure, medical expertise, and religious endorsement, as in the 1603 English plague prayers declaring that non-compliance with social distancing was "a public and

13. Quoted in Champion 1993, 47 (spelling modernized).
14. Graunt 1662, preface, 1.
15. See the discussion in Ogilvie (2023).

manifest detriment to the state".[16] The key to effective state action was not centralization but subsidiarity—addressing problems at the most immediate level consistent with their solution. The state had to cooperate and coordinate with local communities, religious organizations, professional groups, and families.

The local community contributed its norms, information, and sanctions to contagion control in every society down the centuries, and still does so to this day. But it needs support if it is to use this social capital to help contain epidemics. Neighbourly monitoring could support sanitation and social distancing only in the shadow of formal regulation by local government and moral admonitions by religious institutions. Communal altruism helped feed the poor through lockdowns and market closures, but relied heavily on formal welfare provision by religious parish, local government, and central state. The Derbyshire village of Eyam accomplished its famous containment of plague in 1665 not just through communal social capital, but through resources and compulsion supplied by local governments, welfare institutions, philanthropic elites, and religious personnel. Community variolation and vaccination campaigns benefited from village peer pressure in China, England, and Sweden, but also relied on religion and local government to compile information and impose sanctions.[17] Hookworm eradication in the twentieth-century American South depended not just on communal shaming but also on medical professionals and philanthropic bodies posting maps showing which neighbours failed to upgrade latrines.[18] Even the most tightly knit communities deployed social capital most effectively to control contagion when they collaborated with other components of the institutional framework.

Religion supplies spiritual authority that helps to mediate the difficult trade-offs between individual and societal interests posed by epidemic disease. But it needs help from other institutions to do this effectively. State support gave religions the capacity and motivation to support public health measures, as in fourteenth-century Valencia and sixteenth-century London.[19] Integration into the local community increased the incentive and capacity of clergymen to endorse immunization, as in 1803 when the Botnang pastor advocated vaccination individually to each neighbour in his village.[20] The ability and motivation of religion to deploy spiritual authority to mitigate contagion was contingent on relations with secular institutions.

Occupational associations contributed to contagion control by regulating expertise, quality, information, and innovation. But they could do this only

16. Quoted in Slack 1985, 230.
17. Sköld 2000, 214; M. Bennett 2020, 372.
18. Shubinski and Iacobelli 2020.
19. Agresta 2020, 383 (Valencia); Grindal 1843, 8:271 (London).
20. Cless 1871, 105–8.

in collaboration with other institutions. Relations with the state were crucial in making medical associations supply advice and expertise for public purposes, as in early modern Italian and English cities when it required state health boards to extract advice and expertise from colleges of physicians "to preserve the whole, as well as to cure the infected".[21] Competitive pressures from the market pushed medical associations to liberalize their entry barriers and accept innovations, as in 1630 when the Florence doctors' guild tolerated the employment of 16 non-guild practitioners in the lazaretto,[22] or in the 1750s when the London College of Physicians publicly endorsed variolation partly because of the runaway success of commercial variolators who had ensured that it was "generally practised".[23] Relationships with state, market, religion, and community enabled, induced, and sometimes compelled medical associations to support social distancing, immunization, and other anti-contagion measures during epidemics.

The family coordinates many activities that feed into contagion but seldom acts independently of other institutions. The secondary attack rate of epidemics inside households depended not just on the family but also on the market for residential space, together with local government, community, and religion, which shaped the balance between home isolation and pesthouse internment. Kin gatherings at deathbeds and funerals took place in a framework of rules and pressure exerted by governments, religious bodies, communities, guilds, medical professionals, and feudal authorities. Women's decisions on family sanitation and immunization were influenced not just by marriage or patriarchy but also by opportunities and constraints emanating from other institutions, as in nineteenth-century Mexico where bishops exhorted women to vaccinate their children personally, while governments allowed medical associations to monopolize the procedure.[24] The magnitude, age structure, and gender balance of migration flows, and the degree to which they exacerbated or contained contagion, were shaped by labour markets, state compulsion, communal openness, and religious pressures. Familial conduct towards public health measures was shaped by availability of nonfamilial institutions—such as face-mask laws in Poland during Covid-19—to safeguard family members from epidemic contagion.[25] The very form the family took was influenced by the surrounding framework of nonfamilial institutions that could substitute for familial labour, insurance, and welfare services.[26]

21. Slack 1985, 218 (quotation); Cipolla 1976, 8, 23; Rose 2019, 162.
22. Henderson 2019, 113–14.
23. Quoted in G. Miller 1957, 170.
24. Poska 2022, 9–12, 14, 16–18; Few 2015, 187–8.
25. Burdyka 2020.
26. Dennison and Ogilvie 2014, 687.

2.2. WHEN INSTITUTIONS FAIL

Institutions not only supported one another. Sometimes they replaced each other. People used one institution as a substitute for others that malfunctioned, collapsed, or never existed. This partial substitutability among institutions was good because it increased social resilience. People could usually find some institution to help them coordinate responses to problems such as epidemics, improving their welfare compared to what they could achieve as isolated individuals. But substituting one institution that at least functioned for another that failed could also give rise to perverse effects for society at large.

As the history of epidemics has shown, successful social distancing depends on supporting the poor with money, food, and care so they can afford to withdraw from working, shopping, begging, and other activities required for material survival. This was already recognized in medieval plague epidemics and reactivated in furlough payments and other welfare transfers during Covid-19. Religious institutions have long played a major role in social transfers, substituting in many societies for a lack of capacity or motivation on the part of other institutions such as central states, local governments, communities, guilds, and kinship organizations. In the Mediterranean world in premodern plagues, in eastern Europe during nineteenth-century smallpox and cholera, and in the USA during Covid-19, religion played a central role in helping people survive the crisis. People participated in religious organizations not only because they genuinely held profound religious beliefs but also because religion provided a platform that combined spiritual with worldly services.[27] Religious organizations in early modern Mediterranean plagues and in the USA during Covid-19 provided welfare support, logistical help, and medical advice which in other societies, such as early modern north-west Europe or most twenty-first-century social market economies, were provided by local communities or local governments. There were undoubtedly spiritual as well as worldly reasons that by January 2021 people in many advanced societies said that the Covid-19 pandemic had increased their religious faith, but the percentage reporting this was much higher in the USA (28 per cent) than in most other advanced economies (13–16 per cent in Spain, Italy, and Canada; 9–10 per cent in France, Australia, the United Kingdom, South Korea, and Belgium; 5 per cent or less in Japan, Germany, Sweden, and Denmark).[28] Lower-income people in particular were far more likely to report that the Covid-19 pandemic had boosted their faith.[29] It seems probable that one reason for this intensification of religious faith among Americans and less well-off people was worldly

27. As argued by Seabright (2024).
28. Saghal and Schiller 2021, 6.
29. Saghal and Schiller 2021, 8.

support. In 2020, religiously inspired mutual aid organizations supported poor people through Covid-19 in many American cities, providing many forms of practical assistance, including paying bills, making medical appointments, and caring for family members—services either replacing or supplementing those of the state welfare and health system.[30] In many epidemics, therefore, religious organizations have provided support that was not supplied, for whatever reasons, by government, community, or other institutions.

But religion, community, and government, though they may provide overlapping services in the realm of welfare assistance and social transfers during epidemics, are not perfect substitutes. Religion, after all, is a platform. That is why it can supply both spiritual and practical services. But these services are interlinked. When religious organizations provided finance, logistical help, or medical advice during epidemics, these services were packaged with epistemological and ethical doctrines. This had the understandable result that individuals participating in religious platforms accepted not only worldly assistance but also religious explanations and admonitions. In some epidemics, both historical and modern, this involved rejection of social distancing or immunization. In medieval Mediterranean cities, early modern English ones, or twenty-first-century Indian ones, enjoying charitable or practical support from religious organizations also involved agreeing to participate in religious assemblies regardless of epidemic risks. In eighteenth-century France, nineteenth-century Europe, and twenty-first-century America, it involved signing up to the doctrine that immunization contradicted God's will. In nineteenth-century Europe, as we saw in chapter 5, anti-vaccination sentiment was strongest in the most pious sects, which provided a comprehensive platform of religious belief, financial support, and practical assistance to their adherents.[31] During the 2020–22 Covid-19 pandemic, American evangelical Protestant churches preached that Covid-19 was a divine message, that God's chosen people would be spared from infection, and that vaccination was the "mark of the beast"; as one Christian Nationalist Protestant church leader proclaimed in 2021, "We're anti-mask, anti-social distancing, and anti-vaccine." Covid-19 vaccination rates were significantly lower for White evangelicals than other Americans.[32] One quantitative study of American data during Covid-19 found that the epistemological and spiritual content of a religion was associated with a substantial reduction in its members' concern about disease, their support for public health regulations, and their willingness to protect others by voluntarily engaging in self-isolation or social distancing.[33] Religion provided essential services

30. *Economist* 2020d; J. Baker et al. 2020.
31. Baldwin 1999, 292.
32. Quoted in Barlow 2021.
33. Schnabel and Schieman 2022.

and helped people cope with pandemic hardship, substituting for the failures of state, community, market, and family. This increased individuals' well-being in many ways, but at a price: it fostered beliefs and behaviour that increased contagion both for them and for everyone else.

A second example is provided by the family. In many societies across the world, the family substitutes wholly or partially for other institutions in providing labour, credit, insurance, care, and household services. This takes place even in normal times.[34] But this pattern intensifies in emergencies. In many historical epidemics, the extended family provided a safety net for essential workers and substituted for government welfare support, which was minimal even in modern advanced economies until the 1930s.[35] The extended family also substituted for missing markets in the credit, insurance, care, and household services needed to help individuals survive lockdowns and quarantines.[36] Even in modern societies, people relied on extended family to help them deal with unexpected shocks to incomes, housing, and care services during Covid-19. The percentage of American young adults residing in parental households, for instance, increased from 47 to 52 per cent just in the six months from February to July 2020, levels not observed since the Great Depression.[37] By January 2021, over 40 per cent of people in some countries hard-hit by Covid-19, including Spain, Italy, the United Kingdom, and the USA, reported that the pandemic had strengthened their relationships with family members.[38]

In many epidemics, historical and modern, the extended family substituted for missing markets, states, and communities in providing essential services. That increased the welfare of family members, often proving essential in helping them survive the epidemic. But greater kin coresidence increased the secondary attack rate inside households. Even when it did not involve coresidence, more intense kin interaction exacerbated contagion, since it involved more informal social interaction alongside substitution of family services for those of market and state. When the extended family substituted for other institutions during epidemics, it benefited family members but increased contagion risks in the wider society.

---

34. Dennison and Ogilvie 2014, 686–7.

35. Lindert 1998, 113–14; Lindert 2004, 8, 12, 178; Lindert 2021, 80. Van Bavel and Rijpma (2016, 171) provide the most detailed long-term analysis, based on the Netherlands, United Kingdom, and Italy. They estimate that the entirety of formal social transfers (excluding informal, mainly familial, assistance), amounted to 1%–3% of GDP until the 1930s, 2%–5% by 1940, 7%–11% by 1950, and 10%–13% by 1960. Not until the 1970s and 1980s did it reach modern levels of 20% of GDP or more.

36. On the extended family during Covid-19 in the USA, see Gilligan et al. (2020, 435).

37. Fry, Passel, and Cohn 2020.

38. Saghal and Schiller 2021, 5.

Such examples can be multiplied. Epidemics pose existential challenges, in terms not just of infection but of unemployment, provisioning, care services, and everyday logistics. If market, local community, state, or any other institution is unable or unwilling to provide these services, people will use a different institution, even if it is not a perfect substitute and brings along additional baggage that has unintended epidemiological effects.

2.3. WHY ANY INSTITUTION NEEDS TO BE CURBED

A third way institutional frameworks influence contagion is when different institutions curb one another's excesses. We have seen again and again how each institution has malignancies during epidemics. People use the strengths of each institution for purposes that ignore contagion or even exacerbate it. The surrounding framework of other institutions can check these tendencies.

The market, as we saw, conveys inaccurate signals to people about the collateral damage—or unintended benefits—of their personal decisions. It also underprices and hence undersupplies information, leading market participants to make decisions in ignorance of epidemic risks and medical measures. This does not mean the market can be dispensed with. But the market operates better if it is embedded in a wider framework that curbs its failures. State compulsion, communal peer pressure, religious exhortation, medical admonitions, and familial affection can give people incentives to dispose of waste, withdraw from the market, get immunized, and consume or produce information, so they do not exacerbate contagion by infecting others.

States, too, exacerbate epidemics by using their coercive power to pursue military campaigns, overtax the poor, falsify information, and evoke evasion and resistance through authoritarian overreach. These state excesses can be monitored and checked by "civil society"—the aggregate of non-governmental institutions that advance the interests and desires of citizens. In different ways in different historical epidemics, market exchange, communal social capital, religious exhortations, professional expertise, and familial loyalty placed limits on the state. These non-governmental institutions constrained fiscal capacity, limited military action, tempered internal repression, and pushed for state spending to be allocated to civilian ends. They enforced subsidiarity, shifting power towards local governments, which were more responsive to local concerns and local information. Authoritarian activities that exacerbated epidemics were curbed when the institutional framework was more variegated, comprising different components that could compensate for state failures, control state excesses, and prevent state capture by other components.[39]

39. See Ogilvie and Carus 2014, 418–28.

The local community exacerbates coercion when it organizes resistance to public health measures or fails to consider societal interests beyond parochial boundaries. Other institutions can control these tendencies. During historical epidemics, states compelled communities to cooperate beyond their borders, since, as the grand duke of Florence admonished the community of Prato in 1630, "By eradicating the disease outside the walls, its eradication within is made easier."[40] Down the ages, the state obliged communities to pool risks and cooperate with one another in sanitation, market closures, lockdowns, quarantines, and vaccination mandates. The market gave communities access to non-local information and health inputs, supplied commercial immunization, and provided incentives for community members to increase their incomes by transacting with strangers. Religious institutions exhorted communities to practise charity and refrain from turning their poorest inhabitants into a disease reservoir that perpetually reinfected respectable citizens. Medical associations and their members sought to persuade unwilling communities to implement sanitary measures, comply with pesthouse isolation, participate in general inoculations, and acquiesce in vaccination campaigns.

Religion exacerbates epidemics by mandating superspreader assemblies, organizing pilgrimages and crusades, and preaching against contagion, science, and immunization. But secular institutions can overrule even divine mandates. States and local communities can limit superspreader events, as in 1630 when the grand duke of Tuscany and the Florence magistracy defended the Volterra health commissar against papal prosecution for closing churches.[41] The market can circumvent religious bodies by providing commercial variolation and vaccination, either openly as in eighteenth-century England or illicitly as in France and Spain. Families can use market, state, or community to secure immunization in the teeth of clerical prohibitions.

Medical associations exacerbate epidemics by limiting medical supply, spreading false information, and opposing immunological innovations. Other institutions can control these excesses. The state can grant exemptions from medical entry barriers and overrule pronouncements by medical associations that plague, cholera, or influenza is not contagious. The market can provide informal medical services, as in most medieval and early modern European societies where a vast penumbra of illicit practitioners—women, Jews, migrants—operated in the black market, harassed but never fully stamped out by the guilds, colleges, faculties, societies, and associations of licensed doctors and surgeons. Families can resort to market, community, religion, or state to obtain services rationed or denied by medical associations, as in eighteenth-century France where desperate customers evaded the legal ban on smallpox

---

40. Quoted in Cipolla 1973, 123.
41. Cipolla 1976, 37; Palmer 1982, 98; Mauelshagen 2005, 251.

immunization by paying black-market variolators to perform the operation on them in rented premises in out-of-the-way neighbourhoods.

The family can exacerbate epidemics by stifling female autonomy, mandating superspreader death gatherings, exporting unaccompanied male migrants to insanitary living conditions, and amorally evading public health measures. But these flaws can be checked by nonfamilial institutions. Market specialization offers alternative approaches to death rituals, as in fourteenth-century Florence or nineteenth-century Cairo when families substituted paid grave-diggers and mourners for large groups of relatives. Religions provide spiritual sanction for kin to distance themselves from deathbeds, as in seventeenth-century England where pastors exhorted family members to keep clear of plague victims. State, community, and medical professionals provide public health measures so families can safeguard their members—and incidentally the rest of society—through social distancing or vaccination.

Historical epidemics do not show that the institutions we observe in operation were the best of all possible solutions to contagion—quite the contrary. But nor do they show that institutions that neglected or exacerbated contagion were left unconstrained. No institution was either unalloyedly beneficent or irredeemably malignant. One reason was that most institutions do help people coordinate beneficial activities, whatever harmful ones they also help coordinate. But another reason was that every institution is embedded in a wider institutional framework. No institution operated in isolation, and thus no institution was by itself a patent remedy for limiting contagion or a toxic compound that exacerbated it.

2.4. WHAT MAKES A GOOD INSTITUTIONAL FRAMEWORK?

The finding that institutions affected historical epidemics by interacting in wider frameworks is important in itself. But do historical epidemics show what features of such frameworks favoured contagion control? The evidence in this book suggests three propositions.

First comes institutional diversity. Epidemic contagion was best contained by a framework comprising a diversity of institutions. Low institutional diversity meant that contagion control was subjugated to the capacity and interests of just one or two dominant institutions—the family and local community in a tribal or peasant society, the state in an authoritarian society, the occupational association in a corporative society, religion in a theocracy, the market in a capitalist society. Historical epidemics reveal serious flaws in each of these institutions, which exacerbated contagion when left unchecked. Without other institutions to curb their excesses, dominant institutions veered to extremes during epidemics, serving powerful interests regardless of the rest of society.

Does this mean that the most diverse possible institutional framework is best for contagion control? Here, there are offsetting forces. The benefit of institutional diversity is that multiple solutions for contagion are available, along with multiple mechanisms for curbing the excesses of dominant institutions. If each institution specializes in what it is good at, and is prevented from causing harm by a wide array of other institutions, who could object? One might imagine a sort of inter-institutional competition pushing each institution into providing only those services that benefit society. This is an evolutionary "efficiency" view, according to which institutions rise and survive because they are successful at solving social problems, being weeded out if they fail because no society that retained them could survive.[42]

But there is no reason things should work out this way, and history shows it seldom does. Institutional diversity has benefits, but also costs. The cost of diversity is that institutional friction can prevent effective contagion control. What if the sheer diversity of institutions in society imposes so many hindrances that no individual institution can exercise its special capacity to do good things any more than to do bad ones? Conversely, what if the elites that capture one institution share their booty with those controlling others, facilitating a malignant inter-institutional collaboration at the expense of society as a whole? This would be consistent with a "distributional" theory, according to which those institutional frameworks survive that serve the interests of powerful groups, redistributing ever-greater resources and power to those groups, which then use them to strengthen the frameworks that best serve their interests.[43] History shows that societies dominated by such malignant institutional equilibria—serfdom, slavery, corporatism, absolutism, colonialism—can survive for centuries. They do not flourish, but they take a long time to fail. Harmful institutional systems are not weeded out but rather provide a trough for elites to feed from, trapping society in an equilibrium of high epidemic contagion and poverty.

The answer is thus more complicated than a social evolution towards ever-more-diverse institutional frameworks whose components support only one another's beneficial tendencies and hinder only one another's malignant ones. The optimal degree of diversity in an institutional framework varies with the phenomenon to be tackled. When the matter at hand is contagion, which raises intricate problems of externalities, information asymmetries, public good problems, and innovation, the optimal diversity of institutions may be

---

42. See the argument advanced by Alchian (1950); for counter-arguments see Ogilvie (2007, 656, 665).

43. For a discussion of the "distributional" theory as applied to individual institutions rather than entire institutional frameworks, see Acemoglu, Johnson, and Robinson (2005); for the historical dimension, see Ogilvie (2007) and Ogilvie and Carus (2014).

unusually high. With economic growth, by comparison, it might be argued that a simpler institutional framework suffices, characterized by mechanisms to facilitate voluntary exchange, through property rights, contracts, and personal security. On the other hand, even economic growth may require a variegated institutional framework to deal with complex challenges such as market power, environmental degradation, or climate change.

In solving the problem of epidemic contagion, history suggests that high institutional diversity was a feature, not a bug. In the late medieval period, plague was controlled most effectively in the city-states of central and northern Italy, which rejoiced in a variegated institutional framework of lively markets, high state capacity, strong communities, active religious institutions, and vigorous medical associations. The less urbanized, more agrarian, more monolithic societies of central and northern Europe, and arguably also those of the theocratic and rural Ottoman Empire, managed plague contagion much less well. After around 1600, more effective contagion control emerged in the vibrant societies of the Dutch Republic, Flanders, and England, where markets became even more active than in Renaissance Italy, state capacity rose to the highest level in the world, multiple religions competed for adherents, rural and urban communities encroached on each other's hinterlands, and medical associations coalesced but never managed to dominate the medical marketplace. The rural, feudalized societies of early modern eastern Europe, the Balkans, and the Ottoman lands, dominated by overmighty rural magnates and imams, continued to suffer from high epidemic mortality. Institutional heterogeneity and flexibility emerged as even more of an advantage during the fight against smallpox in the eighteenth century and cholera in the nineteenth, when differences in tackling epidemic disease opened up even inside western Europe, with more highly urbanized and socially variegated societies along the North Atlantic seaboard creating a framework in which innovations such as variolation, vaccination, contagion theory, germ theory, chemical medicine, and other manifestations of medical and scientific inquiry found interstices where they could circumvent opposition by entrenched interests. A variegated institutional framework with a number of resilient and flexible institutions addressed the problem of contagion better than a monolithic framework with one or two dominant ones.

The market is a second key component. Any institutional framework that hoped to succeed in limiting contagion had a reasonably well-functioning market. Partly this was because limiting contagion was so resource-intensive. Only a high-performing market could achieve and sustain the economic growth needed to generate those resources. A large proportion of anti-contagion measures were undertaken privately by individuals and families, and the more resources they had at their disposal the better they could do this. Collective health measures, too, depended on the income level and growth rate of the underlying economy, funded through taxes and donations extracted from individuals by governments, communities, religions, and occupational associations. Finally, epidemic control required investments in knowledge, enabling experimentation with medical and institutional innovations. Without resources, these individual, collective, and experimental investments in contagion measures were likely to fail—or, more likely, never get off the ground. There may be better institutions than the market for generating high incomes and fast economic growth, but so far we have not discovered them.

The state is the third key feature. Any institutional framework hoping for success in tackling epidemic contagion needed to include something like a state. The state was central because the market was central. The market was needed to generate resources and spur innovation, but stumbled when facing the negative externalities of infectious waste and contagion, the positive externalities of immunization, the public good of information, and the cross-border externalities of epidemic disease. Epidemics created a situation in which market failures were particularly severe—so far-reaching, as we have seen, that they could not be remedied without at least some coercion. This required the institutional framework to include something like a state—an institution imposing rules over people in a territory, claiming priority over the rules of other organizations, and backed by legitimate coercion.

But not all states were created equal. In particular, the past seven centuries of epidemics showcase the difficulty states experienced in navigating between authoritarian and representative governance. Authoritarian states enjoyed greater capacity to enforce policies restricting individual decisions because they faced weaker constitutional constraints. They might also enjoy better incentives to do so because they did not need to secure electoral support from groups opposed to restrictions. Representative governments, by contrast, enjoyed greater capacity because they fostered information flow and consent from the governed. They enjoyed better incentives to implement policies benefiting the entire society because more social groups were represented in them. In non-epidemic periods, representative governments were unambiguously better at pursuing policies that benefited society, because individual citizens were the best judges of their interests when externalities were minor. In epidemic periods, authoritarian states gained ground, since they were able and willing to pursue policies that overruled individual choices and hence to contain contagion externalities. But the balance was unclear. Representative governments might impose too little coercion for society at large, but authoritarian ones might impose either too much or too little, since they sought benefits for the state rather than the wider society.

Historical epidemics show that successful anti-contagion measures were not associated with authoritarian government. Such measures did require a minimum fiscal, legal, and bureaucratic capacity, since the state had to exercise sufficient coercion to remedy market failures and make people take actions that they did not perceive to be in their individual interest. But beyond that threshold capacity, state motivation was what mattered, and that depended on five key features. First, the state had to be motivated to allocate resources to civilian purposes, a fundamental shift away from the typical military-dominated state expenditure pattern that prevailed well into the modern era. Second, the state had to allocate some of these resources to public goods with positive externalities for health, including (but not limited to) sanitary infrastructure, social distancing systems, epidemiological information, scientific research, and medical innovation. Third, the state had to aim not at maximum centralization or maximum devolution but rather at mastering the art of subsidiarity, addressing problems at the most immediate level consistent with their resolution. Often, but not invariably, this involved agreeing to devolve state capacity from the centre to provincial or local government; sometimes, by contrast, it involved delegating some control to supranational state institutions capable of tackling epidemics that spilled over beyond national frontiers. This required the fourth key feature: the state had to ensure cross-border cooperation both domestically and internationally. It had to bang municipal and provincial heads together within the polity, mediating and coordinating the interests of other domestic institutions and social groups. But it also had to devote attention to epidemic diplomacy beyond national borders, even when that consumed fiscal resources and political capital. The final feature was that the state had to interact productively with civil society. Governments had to be motivated to inform, consult, and respond to the governed, often through parliaments, but also through the aggregate of non-governmental institutions and organizations, even those unrepresented in parliament. The states that developed these features for coping with epidemics were not authoritarian but temperate—governments that fostered a two-way flow of information and consent with other components of the institutional framework.

That is why the central role of market and state in any successful institutional framework does not imply that other institutions were unimportant. Epidemic contagion involved many problems that neither market nor state could solve by itself. Communities provided peer pressure, religions provided ethical motivation, occupational associations provided professional expertise, and families provided emotional incentives. To tackle contagion, all were needed. Epidemic measures that ignored them were likely to fail.

3. Can We Compare Societies?

Over the past seven centuries, did some institutional systems deal with epidemic contagion better than others? Social scientists are always making comparisons, if only implicitly. But comparing societal solutions to epidemics is hard.

For one thing, controlling epidemic disease involves trade-offs. Contagion causes externalities, so limiting it involves restricting individuals' decisions in ways that can reduce their private happiness and deter them from engaging in activities—work, trade, investment, innovation—that are productive for society. Controlling contagion also directly swallows up resources, which are then unavailable for other purposes—individual consumption, social transfers, investment, research and development. During Covid-19, some societies achieved low pandemic mortality but at the expense of reducing important aspects of human well-being, such as individual autonomy and economic growth. Other societies achieved higher individual autonomy and economic growth but at the expense of higher Covid-19 morbidity and mortality. Can we say that one outcome is better than the other? For an individual, we cannot. Should Achilles have chosen glory over length of days? No one but Achilles could say. For a society, who chooses? How does a society decide whether it wants to be long-lived and poor or shorter-lived but rich? Even in normal times, different societies choose different combinations of outcomes, either deliberately or by default. Are we happy for the state to decide this, given the known imperfections in any political process, however democratic? Are we happy for individuals to choose in the market, given market failures and inequalities in resource endowments? But if not through these dominant institutions, then how is the trade-off to be decided?

A second reason comparisons are tricky is that societies differ in many ways, not just in their institutional systems, anti-contagion measures, and epidemic outcomes. Any observed difference may arise from underlying variables rather than from a particular institution or institutional framework. Even if a society's institutions do affect epidemic outcomes, they do so in multiple ways—by tackling contagion directly, but also by coordinating other outcomes such as economic growth or warfare, which affect contagion indirectly.

Third, the multiple variables that affect epidemic outcomes include many things that have not been observed. Some can in principle be observed— as this book has tried to do historically, both with individual institutions and with interactions among them. Other variables that affected epidemic contagion are not even observable in principle. Prime examples are cultural variables such as preferences, motivations, beliefs, and values, which take place inside human minds and can be observed only indirectly by trying to interpret what people say and do.

Despite these caveats, some historical epidemics over the past seven centuries display wide divergence across societies when it comes to mortality, other welfare measures (such as per capita GDP), and institutional regimes. We can at least draw attention to these differences, even if identifying definitive causal links is difficult, and evaluating whether one was preferable to another is impossible without spelling out people's preferences.

The first epidemic to consider is the Black Death, the earliest for which reasonably good records survive. The Black Death provides a good baseline, since it seems superficially to be a counter-example to almost any hypothesis about institutional influences on epidemic outcomes. Between 1346 and 1354, population mortality from this epidemic varied from place to place, but the current state of scholarship provides no definitive evidence that its mortality differed systematically between institutional regimes.[44] Almost the only difference among societies in the mid-fourteenth century was how long it took them to be visited by the Black Death, not how they coped once it arrived. Societies as various as the Netherlands, Bavaria, Bohemia, and Russia were originally thought to have escaped the pandemic. But more recent evidence has shown that the Black Death arrived there as well, and the initial impression was simply caused by gaps in the records rather than absence of plague. Even sub-Saharan Africa, one of the least well-documented continents in history, has revealed archaeological evidence of abandoned settlements in the later fourteenth century, suggesting the possibility of a great epidemic or another comparable disaster.[45] Certainly, we now know that the Black Death extended far beyond the places it was first recorded.[46]

Institutional systems differed across Europe, the Middle East, and Mediterranean Africa, but there is no systematic evidence of mortality differences during the Black Death.[47] Within Europe, the capacity of both market and state was higher in the Mediterranean world than in central, north-west or Nordic Europe. The same was true of large cities compared with small towns and villages. The south of Europe and large cities everywhere were also characterized by greater religious penetration of daily life and greater prevalence of medical associations. All these institutions organized responses to the Black Death, both individually and collaboratively. But there is no systematic evidence that these institutional initiatives systematically affected plague outcomes in the mid-fourteenth century.

What caused the Black Death to be so pervasive and its outcomes apparently so undifferentiated, despite institutional differences across fourteenth-century societies? The historical evidence may simply be too weak. Measuring morbidity and mortality accurately requires vital registration (baptism, marriage, and death registers), preferably in combination with census-type listings.[48] These become available only in the first half of the sixteenth century

44. Alfani 2023a, 16.

45. Kacki 2020, 9.

46. M. Green 2020, 1603–5.

47. As discussed in chapter 3, claims that mortality was systematically lower in "autonomous" cities are undermined by data problems.

48. Edwards and Ogilvie 2022b, 1231–2; Edwards and Ogilvie 2022a, 10–11, 35.

for most European societies, and much later for most non-European ones. At the time of the Black Death, the demographic evidence may simply be too fragile to measure epidemic outcomes at the level of detail needed to assess whether they varied between institutional systems.[49]

If Black Death outcomes did not vary systematically across institutional regimes, then several explanations are possible. One hypothesis is that the plague variant that raged around 1350 was epidemiologically distinctive because it was passed via rats and rat fleas rather than interpersonal contact. Intermediation by rodents and their insect parasites may have reduced the epidemiological gap between town and countryside, between urbanized south and rural north, diminishing any effect of human social arrangements.[50] Later plague variants may have been more easily transmitted between human beings, and other epidemic diseases certainly were. On the other hand, the insusceptibility of the Black Death to interpersonal contact may be an exaggeration. There is evidence even from the Black Death itself, let alone from later episodes of bubonic plague, that human bodies, clothing, and even wool and grain carried infection for lengthy periods.[51] Furthermore, as we saw in chapter 2, during the Black Death epidemic mortality did differ between rich and poor, suggesting that human arrangements—housing, sanitation, nutrition, nursing, flight, market withdrawal—could affect outcomes even for a disease transmitted primarily through an idiosyncratic rodent–insect vector chain.

A second possible explanation for undifferentiated Black Death mortality is compatible with the first. The Black Death was much more lethal than any other recorded pandemic, including later plague epidemics. In the face of such an extraordinary catastrophe, perhaps no existing institutional mechanism could have reduced contagion. Private decisions and expenditures by individuals clearly did have some effect, judging by the higher survival rates of richer and higher-status people. But collective decisions and expenditures by larger social groups or entire societies may never before have had to cope with an epidemic of this magnitude. So it is possible that no institutional arrangements had ever been developed to tackle the contagion externalities generated by such a severe pandemic.

A third and related explanation is that previous epidemics that might have been as lethal as the Black Death lay too far in the past. The last severe and

49. Datasets currently in use for analysing Black Death mortality rates and epidemic duration are comprehensively criticized by Roosen and Curtis (2018), though without dismissing the possibility of improving them.

50. Dimitrov 2020, 108–10.

51. Alfani 2023a, 5. On how plague-infected fleas could live for extended periods (up to 50 days) in grain, raw wool, and stockfish: Dols 1977, 71; Benedictow 2004, 200–1; Benedictow 2021, 54–5; H. Barker 2021, 106. On plague carried on human possessions in the early modern Netherlands: Rommes 2015, 52, 57.

comprehensive pandemic was the Justinianic plague, which started eight centuries before the Black Death (in 541 CE) and petered out six centuries before it (around 750 CE). Little is known about contagion-control measures during the Justinianic plague, and even its mortality rate is vigorously debated. But institutional memory of this plague withered away even in the Middle East, and disappeared altogether in Europe, across the intervening 600–800 years.[52]

The Black Death, however, was not typical. Historians might not be able to pin down any definitive relationship between epidemic outcomes and institutional regimes in the mid-fourteenth century. But every other epidemic in the seven centuries since the Black Death worked out differently in different societies and thus enables comparisons between one institutional framework and another.

The recurrent plague epidemics that struck Europe and the Middle East from 1350 to 1600 provide a first test case. In the centuries that followed the Black Death, plague mortality was much better controlled in central and northern Italy than elsewhere in Europe. Between 1550 and 1600, much of central and northern Italy virtually freed itself from plague, and suffered only sporadic outbreaks when the disease was reintroduced from outside.[53] In central, north-west, and Nordic Europe, by contrast, the sixteenth century still saw very serious plague epidemics. It was precisely this severity that motivated individuals and governments in Europe north of the Alps to investigate and imitate what they finally came to understand as the successful anti-contagion measures of the western Mediterranean, especially central and northern Italy. In the Middle East, the recurrent plague epidemics after the Black Death initially resembled those in Europe, but by around 1500 began to be characterized by greater frequency and severity than those in the western Mediterranean.[54] By 1731, the Venetian Governor General of Dalmatia took for granted that across the nearby border with the Ottoman Empire, plague was much more widespread, plague mortality was higher, and virtually no institutional measures existed to limit its spread.[55]

What caused this growing cross-country variation in plague outcomes between 1350 and 1600? One possible explanation is institutional. Contemporaries in northern Europe, as we have seen, certainly believed that plague was better controlled in Italy. English policymakers relied on translations of books in Italian and French, modelling English plague measures on those already used in Mediterranean Europe. Italian states such as Venice had higher fiscal capacity than England or any European state outside the Dutch Republic until well into

52. Alfani 2022, 19; Alfani 2023a, 7.
53. Alfani and Murphy 2017, 329; Alfani, Bonetti, and Fochesato 2023, 2.
54. Varlik 2015, 127, 159.
55. Andreozzi 2015, 117–18, 121, 133.

the eighteenth century.[56] Market performance was also extraordinarily good in central and northern Italy, with per capita GDP higher in this part of Italy than in England or most other European societies until around 1700.[57] With this combination of high state capacity and high market capacity, it is not so surprising that anti-contagion measures in central and northern Italy outperformed those in most other societies for the 250 years after the Black Death.

After 1600, there was a complete about-turn. The seventeenth century saw the most lethal European plague epidemics since the Black Death. This time around, mortality differed hugely across countries. Moreover, unlike the 1350–1600 period, after 1600 societies north of the Alps outperformed those of Mediterranean Europe. Plague intensity—the cumulative number of plague victims across the seventeenth century as a percentage of each society's population in 1600—was highest in Italy (at 30–37 per cent), exactly the part of Europe which had controlled plague most effectively in the preceding 250 years. Conversely, plague intensity was remarkably low in England (9 per cent) and France (13 per cent), which had suffered high plague intensity between the Black Death and the sixteenth century. Other European societies— southern Germany, the Dutch Republic, Spain—experienced plague intensity of 18–22 per cent, higher than England but much lower than Italy. Why was plague intensity highest in Italy, where anti-contagion measures had so long been better than anywhere else?

Multiple factors probably contributed. Urbanization might have become a bug rather than a feature if, as is sometimes argued, the plague microbe mutated after 1600 to become more infectious person to person than it had been during the Black Death.[58] Greater interpersonal transmission could have made plague more serious in highly urbanized societies such as Italy, southern Germany, the Dutch Republic, and Spain, while sparing less-urbanized England and France.

State capacity mattered, though not always in a good way. The main activity of the state was warfare, which, as we have seen, was a major cause of epidemics. So it is not surprising that Italy and Germany, both cockpits of the Thirty Years War, suffered greater plague intensity than France and England, whose states conducted most of their military activities after 1600 outside their own territories. The fiscal and bureaucratic phases of the "military revolution" that occurred in Europe between 1560 and 1660 made wars larger, longer,

---

56. Freire Costa, Henriques, and Palma 2022.

57. Broadberry, Guan, and Li 2018.

58. On the lack of definitive conclusions about mutations in the virulence of *Yersinia pestis* across the second plague pandemic, see Kacki (2020, 10). On the finding that plague can be transmitted through body lice, and thus in ways that do not involve the indirect rodent–flea pathway, see Ó Gráda (2020, 11).

and more expensive. This not only transmitted epidemics directly through troop movements, refugee flows, and prisoners of war. It also sapped private incomes, fiscal capacity, and collective institutional responses to epidemic contagion. It intensified the downside of state capacity in directly exacerbating contagion through warfare, while weakening the upside of state capacity in deploying fiscal, legal, and bureaucratic capacity to control epidemics.[59]

The market probably played a role. By 1600, the vibrant market institutions of late medieval Italy were beginning to petrify under the influence of extractive urban oligarchies, corporative merchant elites, privileged craft guilds, and exploitative agricultural institutions.[60] In the North Atlantic economies, by contrast, urban privileges were gradually loosening, corporate regulation of industry and commerce was withering away, proto-industries were booming, and entrepreneurial peasants were fostering an agricultural revolution.[61] Economic growth stalled in extractive Italy while it soared in commercialized Holland and England. This increased market incomes, state fiscal capacity, communal welfare, and religious philanthropy in north-west Europe, generating resources that became available for anti-contagion measures. Greater market orientation also increased incentives to control epidemics so as to sustain commercial exchange, whether between town and countryside or across international borders.

Finally, as we saw in chapter 3, the specific mechanisms used to control plague differed between north-west and Mediterranean Europe. After around 1600, England used an approach based mainly on home lockdown, supported by generous welfare support from local government, local community, and religious parish to enable compliance, with the central state mandating risk-pooling across local boundaries. This approach required high per capita GDP, strong state capacity, and a collaborative, generous. and locally informed welfare system. This north-west European approach to epidemic control, as it emerged, may have begun to outperform the traditional Italian plague measures, which relied more heavily on centralized internment in pesthouses and hospitals. Indeed, the success enjoyed by central and north Italian societies in using those measures in the centuries since the Black Death, culminating in their virtual eradication of epidemic plague by 1600, might have lulled them into a false sense of security, attenuating incentives to be vigilant or to upgrade contagion measures.[62]

Plague outcomes also differed between Europe and the Middle East as the early modern period progressed. Between around 1500 and around 1700,

59. Parker 1988; Ogilvie 1992; P. Wilson 2019.
60. Alfani 2020, 203, 206; Alfani 2022, 22–3; Alfani 2023a, 15–16.
61. De Vries 1976; Ogilvie 2000.
62. Alfani and Murphy (2017, 329) argue that it might also have reduced population immunity.

epidemics were much worse in the Middle East than in any European society, even seventeenth-century Italy.[63] After around 1700, plague continued to rage across the Middle East but died out in Europe.[64] The few European plague epidemics after 1700 came from the Middle East and northern Africa: the 1708–12 Baltic plague from Constantinople via Poland, the 1720 Marseille plague from Lebanon via Livorno, the 1743 Corsican plague from the Ottoman lands via Corfu, the 1770–72 Russian plague from Ottoman Moldova, the 1819 Silesian outbreak in a cotton shipment from Smyrna, the 1820 Mallorcan plague from a "Moorish" ship.[65]

Institutions probably contributed to this divergence in plague outcomes between Europe and the Middle East. State capacity, as measured by per capita tax revenues, was lower and slower growing in the Ottoman lands than in most parts of Europe from 1500 to 1800, hindering the development of government anti-contagion policies.[66] By the sixteenth century, the Ottoman state had begun to improve urban hygiene and disposal of plague corpses, but social distancing and quarantines were notable by their absence.[67] The cordon sanitaire that hindered transmission of epidemics between the Ottoman and Habsburg Empires was maintained primarily by Habsburg, not Ottoman, state capacity. Markets also worked less well in the Middle East than in Europe. Per capita GDP in the Ottoman lands was low and stagnant from 1500 onwards, compared with higher levels and faster growth in most parts of Europe except for Poland and Russia.[68] Poorer market performance in the Ottoman lands limited the resources available for individual, state, community, and religious anti-contagion measures, and muted commercial incentives to control contagion to keep trade flowing. Other institutions such as religious organizations, local communities, and medical associations differed significantly between Europe and the Middle East, but much more research is needed to identify differences in their behaviour during epidemics.

Smallpox, which supplanted plague as the major epidemic disease in many places from the late seventeenth century onwards, also offers instructive comparisons across societies. Here, institutions governing immunization come into play. China practised smallpox variolation at latest by the mid-sixteenth century, and parts of India, the Ottoman lands, and Africa recorded the procedure by the late seventeenth. In all these societies, variolation was permitted and sometimes promoted by central and local governments, diffused via

63. Varlik 2015, 127, 159.
64. Alfani 2022, 33–4.
65. M. Harrison 2012, 63; Moll, Salas Vives, and Pujadas-Mora 2017, 140; Alfani 2023a, 19.
66. Freire Costa, Henriques, and Palma 2022, table 1; Ogilvie 2023, 29, fig. 1.
67. M. Harrison 2012, 11.
68. Ogilvie 2023, 30, fig. 2.

market commerce, practised by medical groups, blessed by religion, and adopted by the family. In Europe, by contrast, variolation remained an obscure and scattered folk practice until it was introduced to European elites from other continents in the decades between 1700 and 1720. Smallpox outcomes were almost certainly worse in Europe than in non-European societies whose institutional frameworks fostered immunization.

Even within what is now China, smallpox outcomes show sharp contrasts across institutional regimes. In the seventeenth century, the Manchus lived beyond the north-east frontier of China, had comparatively low smallpox infection rates, lacked knowledge of variolation, and sought to control the disease by strict social distancing. In China south of the Manchu border, by contrast, smallpox was widespread, social distancing lax, and variolation widespread. In 1644, the Manchus conquered China, and introduced strict social distancing to avoid smallpox infection. The new Manchu rulers had so little contact with their new subjects that they did not learn of variolation until the 1660s, and adopted the practice only gradually. Further analysis is needed to explain the contrast between Chinese and Manchu smallpox regimes. Urbanization and population density were higher in pre-1644 Han China, a proximate cause of smallpox prevalence.[69] But were urbanization and population density outgrowths of Han Chinese institutions, with greater market commercialization, higher state capacity, and worldlier religious organizations, while the Manchu world retained an institutional system which was less variegated or just quite different in ways that have yet to be analysed? The sharpness of the frontier between the two epidemiological regimes is easier to explain: state institutions, with their military activities and dynastic segregation, prevented cross-border knowledge transfer that could have improved contagion control.

Europe also displayed sharp contrasts between different societal approaches to smallpox control during the eighteenth century. The introduction of variolation to Europe between 1700 and 1720 was facilitated by market trade with China and Africa, diplomatic links with the Ottoman world, and scientific correspondence between China and Anatolia on the one hand and Britain, France, and Italy on the other. Once introduced to Europe, however, variolation was adopted readily in England, Scotland, and Ireland in the 1720–50 period, but in Sweden not until the mid-1750s, in France and Spain not until the late 1760s or the 1770s, and in most parts of Germany not until the 1780s or 1790s. Much of the European continent thus continued to suffer higher smallpox mortality than England for many decades after knowledge of variolation became available. In England, market, local government, community, religion, and family spread variolation, and medical associations initially tolerated and later endorsed the practice. Sweden and some German states legalized variolation in the second

69. Hanson 2011, 107–8.

half of the eighteenth century, but then allowed privileged medical associations to monopolize the procedure, rendering it costly and inaccessible for ordinary citizens. In France and Spain until the late 1760s or early 1770s, variolation was banned by medical associations, damned by religion, and prohibited by governments, preventing commercial variolators from operating and families from consuming their services (though they sometimes did so illegally). Even once variolation was legalized in these societies, medical and religious disapproval hindered its adoption, sustaining a reservoir of infection that kept smallpox rates high compared with places with more flexible institutional systems.

Even inside particular societies, variolation regimes and smallpox outcomes varied with institutional regimes. In the English south and Midlands, local governments, communities, and parish vestries allocated resources to limiting smallpox contagion through pesthouse construction, welfare-supported home isolation, and collective variolation. In English north, by contrast, local institutions did not invest in pesthouses, social distancing, or variolation, tolerating much higher smallpox rates. The difference might have arisen partly from preferences, with southern parishes valuing the benefits of low smallpox rates more than northern ones. But institutions played a role: southern parishes had richer local governments, stronger welfare systems, and livelier market relationships, increasing their capacity and motivation to limit epidemics.

Vaccination regimes differed across societies, too. In almost every society across the world, governments permitted vaccination, and some made it compulsory. But whether this resulted in widespread implementation depended on the wider institutional framework. Medical associations accepted the procedure in Europe and Spanish America, but rejected it in parts of India and Africa where it competed with local medical practitioners' variolation business. But even where medical associations accepted the practice, they often monopolized the operation, giving rise to lower vaccination rates than where vaccination was open to religious, philanthropic, commercial, and familial practitioners. Religious institutions promoted vaccination in Catholic Baden but opposed it in Lutheran Württemberg, where smallpox morbidity and mortality remained significantly higher. Societies with greater autonomy for local communities such as Russia or Württemberg saw greater communal resistance to vaccination mandates, while those with greater cooperation between community and state such as England or Baden achieved higher vaccination rates and lower smallpox mortality because of greater community information and consent.

Cholera took epidemiological centre stage in the nineteenth century, and here too institutional differences affected outcomes. Cross-border diplomacy played a role, with the British government opposing quarantines and inspections to placate Indian commercial and religious interest groups, Middle Eastern states lukewarm about anti-contagion measures so as to sustain the lucrative pilgrimage industry and retain theological legitimacy, while France, Spain, and other southern European states pushed for stronger international regulation. Local governments differed greatly, with German cities building sewerage and water infrastructure to satisfy wealthy industrial residents, while English and American cities delayed such measures to placate tax-averse middle-class voters. Authoritarian states in eastern Europe failed to communicate or negotiate with local communities, provoking popular resistance against contagion controls and higher cholera mortality than societies where governments conveyed information to the governed and secured their consent. Religious leaders resisted limits on superspreader pilgrimages in many parts of Asia and the Middle East, even when such controls were advocated by central states, local governments, or communities. Where medical associations were more powerful, they declared cholera non-contagious and even dismantled quarantine measures, increasing mortality and opening the gates to recurrent epidemics.

Influenza mortality in 1918–19 also differed across institutional regimes. In a cross-country perspective, influenza mortality was increased by state military activities, as shown by higher mortality in countries involved in the First World War or in their own civil wars. Influenza outcomes were also affected by the institution of the family, with high-fertility demographic regimes involving early and universal marriage giving rise to a younger age structure and hence higher influenza mortality, though cross-country variation was greater than can be explained by differences in population age structure alone.[70] Influenza mortality was much higher in India than in Europe, which can be ascribed to family institutions involving high fertility, state institutions with lower public health capacity, and poorly performing markets giving rise to lower availability of food and other health inputs.[71]

Influenza outcomes also varied with institutional arrangements inside countries. Within the United States, cities where multiple non-pharmaceutical interventions were implemented early in the epidemic had significantly lower peak death rates, shallower epidemic curves, and lower cumulative excess mortality.[72] Comparisons across the 10 largest US cities in 1918–19 show that the timing, number, and type of non-pharmaceutical interventions adopted were influenced by a wide range of institutions, including state governments, municipal governments, medical professionals, religious authorities, business leaders, community organizations, and even bowling clubs.[73] Inside India, too, there were huge regional differences in influenza mortality in 1918, with the eastern provinces resembling Europe while the western provinces had mortality

70. Spreeuwenberg, Kroneman, and Paget 2018, 2565–6.
71. Spreeuwenberg, Kroneman, and Paget 2018, 2563.
72. Hatchett, Mecher, and Lipsitch 2007, 7584–5.
73. Ott et al. 2007; Tomes 2010.

10 times higher.[74] Lower mortality in the east was affected by state military activity (troops returning from the First World War introduced influenza first to the western city of Mumbai), market exchange (eastern India was less urbanized and commercialized), and institutional learning (eastern India had time to develop anti-contagion measures before the new virus steamed in by train).[75]

Comparing epidemic outcomes is complicated. History shows that every major epidemic in the seven centuries since the Black Death displayed different outcomes in different societies. Mortality differences were often *associated* with differences in social institutions—both those affecting society in general and those specifically targeting epidemics. But it is seldom possible to establish a definitive causal relationship. Societies differ not only in epidemic outcomes and institutional regimes, but also on many other dimensions.

The patterns that emerge from the past seven centuries of epidemics are thus descriptive, occasionally suggestive, but seldom definitively causal. They do, however, reveal certain institutional clusters that were historically better at controlling epidemic contagion: commercialized and responsive markets; democratic and non-militaristic states; outward-looking and welfare-oriented local communities; moderate and philanthropic religions; liberal and open-minded medical associations; families that cooperated with the rest of the institutional framework rather than carrying out all operations inside the household; and variegated rather than monolithic institutional frameworks. Such institutional clusters were not a magic pill in themselves. But on average they helped to protect against epidemic contagion.

4. Do Societies Learn?

"Destroyer and teacher" was how one American doctor described the influenza pandemic in 1918.[76] But how effective was this teacher? Did suffering a terrible epidemic that killed and maimed millions of victims at least spur societies to devise better ways to mitigate contagion when it returned? Did societies learn from epidemiological successes abroad? Is societal learning possible?

Societies sometimes learned. Central and northern Italy got much better at social distancing during the recurrent plague epidemics in the 250 years following the Black Death. So consequential was this institutional learning that, as we have seen, by around 1600 much of northern and central Italy had virtually freed itself from epidemic plague. Central and north-west Europe did not learn from the Black Death until later, despite equal or greater epidemic severity. It was not until the 1450–1550 period that France started adopting

74. Spreeuwenberg, Kroneman, and Paget 2018, 2563.
75. Chandra and Kassens-Noor 2014, 9.
76. Quoted in Tomes 2010, 49.

plague measures, and during this process different regions learned from different foreign neighbours, with southern French cities imitating nearby Italy while northern French towns copied the Burgundian Netherlands.[77] England started borrowing plague measures from Italy and France, though only in the 1550–1600 period, in response to travellers' astonished reports about how the Italians "are carefull to avoyde infection of the plague and to that purpose in every citty have Magistrates for Health".[78] Southern Italy began in the seventeenth century to adopt sanitary and social distancing measures long used in the centre and north of the peninsula. In the eighteenth century, Russia and Romania learned about plague control from central and western Europe via diplomatic contacts, state visits, and individual migrants, often from German-speaking central Europe. Openness to trade, breaks in warfare, peaceful diplomacy, and merit-based professional exchange made a difference to whether societies learned from one another.

Smallpox control also shows societal learning. As we have seen, in China after 1644 the new Manchu elite initially failed to learn about variolation but within a generation was experimenting with the practices of its new subjects. Variolation was all but unknown in the West before around 1720, but after that date societal learning led to gradual European and American adoption of this key innovation from the Ottoman lands, China, and Africa. Like Manchu China, England and America did not adopt the new anti-contagion technique immediately. But after a generation or so their central states tolerated it, their markets spawned commercial variolators, their families allowed mothers to immunize children, their local governments and communities organized general inoculations, their medical associations scrutinized the practice, and their religions grappled with the epistemological conflict between immunization as Christian love and epidemic disease as God's will. Soon variolation began to spread from the English-speaking world to the European continent, sometimes with government approval, as when the Swedish Crown sent the physician David Schultz to investigate variolation in England,[79] sometimes informally or even illicitly, when entrepreneurial migrants from Ireland and Scotland set up as commercial variolators in Germany and Spain, where variolation was frowned on.[80] After vaccination was invented in England in 1796, the new immunization procedure was adopted and indigenized in Europe, North America, China, Africa, and Latin America, although societal learning was slower in parts of Europe, India, and Africa because of opposition by entrenched religious and medical groups.

77. N. Murphy 2013, 153–4.
78. Quoted in Cipolla 1973, 16.
79. Sköld 1996a, 249–50; Sköld 1996b, 231, 236, 260–2.
80. Penschow 2022, 42–6, 56–8, 64.

Cholera, too, displays some instances of societal learning. American cities such as New York and Philadelphia, which started to construct municipal water systems as early as 1798, reduced cholera morbidity and mortality during the 1832 cholera epidemic, creating a demonstration effect that greatly influenced other American cities, further reducing urban cholera mortality by 1873, sometimes below that prevailing in adjacent rural areas.[81] In the second half of the nineteenth century, German cities learned of sanitary measures that had been pioneered in England and America, implemented them locally, and rapidly improved on them.[82] With the invention of germ theory in France and the discovery of the cholera bacterium in Germany, the policy implications were communicated to scientists and medical practitioners, and sometimes implemented by governments, throughout the rich world. The Russian state learned what needed to be done, especially via migrant German doctors and officials, but authoritarian overreach prevented cholera control measures from being accepted in Russian society beyond the urban elites.

Even in the brief span of the influenza epidemic between 1918 and 1920, societal learning took place. As we have seen, influenza mortality in India was 10 times lower in the east of the country than in the west, partly because of societal learning. Western India had no time to develop anti-contagion measures, since returning troops brought the infection back to Mumbai in 1918, where it immediately unleashed huge mortality in a society where state, community, medicine, and religion were unprepared. The pandemic diffused eastwards across the subcontinent, but gradually enough for eastern provinces to obtain information about the disease and develop measures such as simple social distancing.[83] In the United States, likewise, cities that the Spanish flu reached later in time had lower mortality peaks because they adopted non-pharmaceutical interventions at an earlier stage in their epidemics, as local governments and medical professionals learned from cities that had been afflicted earlier.[84] Because the 1918–19 influenza epidemic moved along railway networks, the spread of the disease was sufficiently gradual to permit societal learning. With Covid-19, by contrast, air travel spread the infection in 2020 faster than most societies could learn, and it took until 2021 for the internet to spread information (e.g. about face masks, ventilation, and vaccines) that helped societal learning catch up—at least in those societies able and willing to absorb it.

But every epidemic over the past seven centuries also shows notable failures of societal learning. During the century and a half after the Black Death,

81. L. Anderson 1984, 215–16.
82. John Brown 1988, 310, 316–18.
83. Chandra and Kassens-Noor 2014, 9.
84. Hatchett, Mecher, and Lipsitch 2007, 7584–5.

best practice on sanitation and social distancing diffused widely from one society to the next in central and northern Italy. But for many generations this information failed to diffuse even into the rural areas surrounding those cities, let alone to the Italian south, the adjacent eastern Mediterranean, or Europe north of the Alps. The absence of well-functioning markets to generate resources and muscular local governments to use them for plague control helps account for some of these failures. But we also find concerted opposition to adopting unfamiliar anti-contagion measures by entrenched groups. Societal learning was blocked by religious fissures between Christianity and Islam, as well as between different Christian confessions after the 1520s. Cross-border learning was also blocked when medical associations hindered immigration of knowledgeable south European professionals into more backward towns and territories north of the Alps.

Central and northern Italy itself lost societal memory in the sixteenth century, perhaps because its very success in largely eradicating epidemic plague interrupted institutional continuity, so that Italy was under-protected when plague returned with a vengeance after 1600. Italy also failed to learn from the advances in social distancing developed after around 1600 in England and other parts of north-west Europe. These societies developed approaches to segregating the infected through home lockdown supported by local welfare payments, which may have produced better mortality outcomes and certainly did not produce worse ones. Home isolation could more easily be scaled down for small rural settlements than the lumpy investments in centralized internment common in huge Italian cities. Entrenched investments by political, medical, and religious elites in the system of hospitals and lazarettos in Mediterranean Europe may even have blocked greater use of welfare-supported, decentralized home lockdowns on the north-west European model, which achieved greater social acceptance among the poor but offered fewer rents for powerful elites to extract.[85]

Smallpox control also displayed spectacular failures of societal learning. Variolation was ignored by the new Manchu dynasty for a generation after 1644, as we have seen, and was still hardly practised beyond royal and military circles well into the eighteenth century. In many parts of eighteenth-century Europe, religious elites and medical associations blocked their societies from adopting the new immunization procedure, explicitly objecting to learning new practices from other cultures, as in 1764 when an eminent French doctor excoriated variolation as emanating from "infidel calculations".[86] Even inside

85. On the lucrative business of operating quarantine lazarettos in Mediterranean ports, see Harrison (2012, 14–15). On profiteering in urban pesthouses in various European societies from the seventeenth to the nineteenth century, see chapter 3 above.

86. Quoted in Rusnock 2002, 87.

Britain, variolation benefited from little societal learning between southern and northern regions of England during most of the eighteenth century because of differences in markets, local governments, and parish communities. After the invention of vaccination, religious institutions, medical associations, and strong village communities managed to block societal learning between such culturally adjacent societies as the south-west German states of Baden and Württemberg, in the teeth of state vaccination mandates issued at almost identical dates.[87]

Cholera control measures also ran into obstacles to societal learning. Despite knowing that public water and sewerage infrastructure reduced cholera contagion, English and American local governments made slow progress in building it, hindered by blocking coalitions in municipal governments. Medical associations impeded societal learning by fostering a resurgence of anticontagionism between 1820 and 1870, which was taken seriously enough to oppose, weaken, or dismantle quarantine measures. Even when Robert Koch identified the cholera microbe in 1883, he lamented how epidemic policies remained uninformed by "thoroughly established and scientifically elaborated bases".[88] Failure to learn and adopt cholera isolation measures from successful societies in western Europe was exacerbated by authoritarian states in Russia, India, and the Ottoman lands, where state overreach and poor relations with local communities gave rise to lethal popular resistance and widespread rejection of societal learning.

During the 1918–19 influenza epidemic, societal learning was also limited. In most large and medium-sized American cities, local governments, medical associations, and the general public were highly informed about sanitation and social distancing, yet different cities followed different policies and their flu mortality diverged.[89] This failure of societal learning arose partly from the differing institutional composition of different American cities. But it also alerts us to a further source of disparate epidemic outcomes: divergent preferences. One issue that repeatedly arose among and within American cities in 1918 concerned "what constituted essential vs. unessential activities"—that is, differences in preferences about the trade-off between epidemic outcomes and other forms of human well-being.[90]

In the Covid-19 pandemic, too, differences in preferences about such trade-offs shaped public health measures and societal learning. Despite widespread concern about cultural homogenization across the globe, different societies still display different preference orderings among health, wealth, religious

---

87. Mühlhoff 2022.
88. Quoted in Lacey 1995, 1412.
89. Tomes 2010, 52–8.
90. Tomes 2010, 54.

observance, individual autonomy, and other forms of human utility. Some studies have argued that these preferences, alongside institutions, contributed to differences in willingness to accept market closures, mask wearing, social distancing, and vaccination during Covid-19.[91]

Despite all these imperfections of societal learning during historical epidemics, we must recognize one big fact. The risks of epidemic disease declined hugely over the past seven centuries. Acute epidemics weakened, they occurred less frequently, and they infected and killed fewer people when they did take place.[92] By the end of the nineteenth century, epidemic infection and mortality were much lower than they were in the fourteenth century. In the early twenty-first century they have fallen even more spectacularly. Why is that?

Earlier, this chapter offered three propositions about institutional frameworks that were better at limiting epidemics. First, institutional diversity fostered resilience in tackling epidemic contagion. Second, a relatively strong and well-functioning market was a key component of any institutional framework that hoped to succeed in limiting contagion. And third, any successful institutional framework included a state with sufficient capacity to compel individuals to take account of externalities but sufficiently curbed by other institutions to be motivated to devote that capacity to contagion control. What did human societies learn about these three things between the Black Death and Covid-19?

The answer that emerges from this book is the following. Over these 700 years, societies learned both to innovate and to coordinate. A well-functioning market, a temperate state, and institutional diversity worked together to create an openness to innovation. These features also helped societies coordinate among individuals and organizations that had diverse capacities and interests.

By the market we refer not to specific market locations such as trade fairs or shopping arcades. Rather, we mean something much broader and deeper: a set of practices, customs, and procedures that facilitates exchange by means of prices that convey information to producers and consumers about the scarcity and value of goods and services. When the market functioned well, it created a framework within which individual innovators could offer new solutions (to shortages, to individual needs, to new epidemic threats) which could be adopted by new users through a process of voluntary exchange, unhindered by the power of established authorities or entrenched interests. Of course, as this book has shown, these market solutions sometimes created negative externalities.

But that is where a temperate state intervened. To make the market work well, society needed an institution that could exercise moderate coercion—strong

---

91. Geloso, Hyde, and Murtazashvili 2022, 57–9.
92. Omran 1971; Santosa et al. 2014; Alfani 2022, 33–4.

enough to remedy market failures but sufficiently curbed by other institutions to allocate its capacity to containing contagion rather than exacerbating it.

It is also where institutional diversity stepped in. A social framework comprising a diversity of institutions was more successful at providing solutions to epidemic contagion, because it was open not just to medical innovation but to institutional innovation. Sometimes the innovation required for successful epidemic control was not one that could be implemented by individual market participants. In many cases, as we have seen, the innovation had to be undertaken by the state, community, religion, medical association, or family.

Increasing contact among different parts of the globe accelerated the transmission of pathogens and created new challenges for contagion control. But it also gave societies an incentive to innovate in socially useful directions. First, it facilitated competitive emulation between societies, both inside continents such as Europe and increasingly between continents, so that societies that were productively different learned from each other. Second, it encouraged trade, which transmitted not just goods but information, both embodied in migrants and written down in letters, pamphlets, and books, giving societies knowledge of what other societies were doing, what human societies had done in the past, and how well it worked, providing the basis for innovating in socially useful directions.

Coordination played a key role in this. The spectacular fall in epidemic mortality starting in the late nineteenth century was due not just to the spread of immunization (a result of innovation), but to improvements in non-pharmaceutical interventions: sanitation infrastructure, sophisticated forms of social distancing, and cross-border agreements such as quarantines, environmental agreements, and vaccination diplomacy. This required governments, communities, religions, medical associations, and families to coordinate practices that individuals lacked the capacity and motivation to undertake. However, those collective institutions knew which interventions to undertake only because of prior innovation, in which the market played a key role. And they had the incentive to make these interventions only because of competitive emulation, itself a product of a highly diverse institutional framework, both nationally and globally.

5. Us versus Them

What comes out of the past seven centuries of interaction between populations of microbes and populations of humans? Historical epidemics encourage neither biological catastrophism nor utopian complacency. Human societies were never entirely helpless in the face of even the most calamitous epidemics. Each of the core social institutions explored in this book helped people cooperate to deal with epidemic contagion. Markets enabled people to produce and trade in ways that generated growth in the available resources, which individuals, states, religions, communities, guilds, and families could allocate to controlling contagion. Markets also provided a framework within which innovators could experiment with new solutions to epidemic threats without being held back by established authorities and entrenched interests. To make individuals take account of the infection costs their choices imposed on others, states provided compulsion, communities fostered social capital, and religion supplied moral suasion. Medical associations cultivated professional expertise and ethics to direct health advice and services. Families supported anti-contagion measures to safeguard vulnerable members.

Yet each of the institutions discussed in this book also had flaws. Markets failed to deal with negative externalities, conveying price signals that motivated people to work, trade, or socialize for their own benefit regardless of the infections they inflicted on others. States pursued military conflicts that spread contagion and drained resources from public health measures. Local communities took health decisions based on parochial interests and organized collective action to resist anti-contagion measures. Religions mandated superspreader events and preached against social distancing, immunization, and science. Medical associations limited entry, created supply shortages, censored knowledge, and blocked innovations. Families sought the interests of their own members at the expense of the rest of society.

What decided whether the good or the bad side came out on top was seldom the characteristics of any individual institution in isolation. Rather, historical epidemics show clearly that what mattered most was the surrounding institutional framework. Each institution needed help to deploy its special strengths, and that help could be provided or withheld by other components of the institutional framework. Each institution also had weaknesses, and other institutions substituted for those weaknesses, sometimes in effective ways and sometimes in perverse ones. Finally, every institution had malignancies, and the surrounding framework of other institutions could curb those excesses.

The development of three key features over the past seven centuries created institutional frameworks in some societies that were better at controlling epidemic contagion. The first was institutional heterogeneity: epidemics were more successfully controlled in societies characterized by a variegated ecosystem of institutions with diverse strengths and weaknesses. Second, any institutional framework that hoped to limit contagion needed a relatively strong and well-functioning market to provide resources for individual health expenditures, collective contagion control, and investments in new biological and social knowledge. A third feature of a successful institutional framework was a temperate state, with sufficient coercive power to remedy problems of externalities and public goods while not careening off into authoritarian excess. This did not mean that community social capital, religious ethical motivation, guild professional expertise, and familial emotional incentives were unimportant, and indeed they contributed to the institutional diversity that helped keep market and state honest. But they were less salient than the top three.

These institutional features enabled societal learning. Between the Black Death and Covid-19, the risks of epidemic disease hugely declined because societies learned two things: how to coordinate and how to innovate. They learned how to coordinate among individuals and organizations that had diverse capacities and interests, and they learned how to innovate—not just scientifically but also socially.

How to limit lethal epidemic diseases and how to constrain malignant institutional regimes are vital components of societal learning. The process has been imperfect. It has taken at least seven centuries. And we are still dealing with its imperfections to this day. Nonetheless, epidemic risks are much lower now than seven centuries ago, and that is partly because of three big steps in societal learning: institutional diversity, a well-functioning market, and a temperate state. Institutional clusters with these three features make it possible for people to innovate and coordinate, gradually and unevenly improving our modus vivendi with humans' inseparable microbial companions.

BIBLIOGRAPHY

Published Sources

Aassve, Arnstein, Guido Alfani, Francesco Gandolfi, and Marco Le Moglie. 2021. "Epidemics and Trust: The Case of the Spanish Flu", *Health Economics*, 30: 840–57.

Abbara, Aula, et al. 2020. "Coronavirus 2019 and Health Systems Affected by Protracted Conflict: The Case of Syria", *International Journal of Infectious Diseases*, 96: 192–5.

Abbasi, Kamran. 2020. "COVID-19: State Failure Is Our Misery and Their Jackpot", *Journal of the Royal Society of Medicine*, 113: 419–20.

Aberth, John. 1995. "The Black Death in the Diocese of Ely: The Evidence of the Bishop's Register", *Journal of Medieval History*, 21: 275–87.

———. 2005. *The Black Death: The Great Mortality of 1348–1350. A Brief History with Documents* (New York: Palgrave Macmillan).

Acemoglu, Daron. 2003. "Why Not a Political Coase Theorem? Social Conflict, Commitment and Politics", *Journal of Comparative Economics*, 31: 620–52.

Acemoglu, Daron, Simon Johnson, and James A. Robinson. 2005. "Institutions as a Fundamental Cause of Long-Run Growth", in Philippe Aghion and Steven N. Durlauf (eds), *Handbook of Economic Growth* (Amsterdam: Elsevier), 385–472.

Ackerknecht, Erwin H. 1948. "Anticontagionism between 1821 and 1867", *Bulletin of the History of Medicine*, 22: 562–93.

———. 2009. "Anticontagionism between 1821 and 1867: The Fielding H. Garrison Lecture", *International Journal of Epidemiology*, 38: 7–21.

Adair-Toteff, Christopher. 2016. *Max Weber's Sociology of Religion* (Tübingen, Germany: Mohr Siebeck).

Adams, Christopher P., and Van V. Brantner. 2006. "Estimating the Cost of New Drug Development: Is It Really $802 Million?", *Health Affairs*, 25: 420–8.

Agresta, Abigail. 2020. "From Purification to Protection: Plague Response in Late Medieval Valencia", *Speculum*, 95: 371–95.

Aidt, Toke S., Romola J. Davenport, and Felix Gray. 2023. "New Perspectives on the Contribution of Sanitary Investments to Mortality Decline in English Cities, 1845–1909", *Economic History Review*, 76: 624–60.

Akasoy, Anna. 2007. "Islamic Attitudes to Disasters in the Middle Ages", *Medieval History Journal*, 10: 387–410.

Akerlof, George A. 1970. "The Market for 'Lemons': Quality Uncertainty and the Market Mechanism", *Quarterly Journal of Economics*, 84: 488–500.

Albrecht, Peter. 2005. "Von den vergeblichen Mühen, die Bevölkerung der Stadt Braunschweig von der Nützlichkeit des Impfens gegen Blattern zu überzeugen (1754–1787)", in Petra Feuerstein-Herz (ed.), *Gotts Verhengnis und seine Straffe. Zur Geschichte der Seuchen in der frühen Neuzeit* (Wiesbaden, Germany: Harrassowitz Verlag), 127–37.

Alchian, Armen A. 1950. "Uncertainty, Evolution, and Economic Theory", *Journal of Political Economy*, 58: 211–21.

Alebić, Tamara, and Helena Marković. 2017. "Development of Health Care in Dubrovnik from 14th to 16th Century: Specific Features of Ragusan Medicine", *Collegium anthropologicum*, 41. https://www.collantropol.hr/antropo/article/view/1578.

Alexander, James Edward. 1830. *Travels to the Seat of War in the East, through Russia and the Crimea, in 1829: With Sketches of the Imperial Fleet and Army, Personal Adventures, and Characteristic Anecdotes* (London: H. Colburn and R. Bentley).

Alexander, John T. 1980. *Bubonic Plague in Early Modern Russia: Public Health and Urban Disaster* (Baltimore, MD: Johns Hopkins University Press).

Alfani, Guido. 2013a. *Calamities and the Economy in Renaissance Italy: The Grand Tour of the Horsemen of the Apocalypse* (New York: Palgrave MacMillan).

———. 2013b. "Plague in Seventeenth-Century Europe and the Decline of Italy: An Epidemiological Hypothesis", *European Review of Economic History*, 17: 408–430.

———. 2020. "Pandemics and Asymmetric Shocks: Evidence from the History of Plague in Europe and the Mediterranean", *Journal for the History of Environment and Society*, 5: 197–209.

———. 2022. "Epidemics, Inequality, and Poverty in Preindustrial and Early Industrial Times", *Journal of Economic Literature*, 60: 3–40.

———. 2023a. "Epidemics and Pandemics: From the Justinianic Plague to the Spanish Flu", in Claude Diebolt and Michael Haupert (eds), *Handbook of Cliometrics* (Berlin: Springer), 1–35.

———. 2023b. "Epidemics, Inequality and Poverty: from the Black Death to the Spanish Flu", paper presented at the Oxford Research Seminar in Economic and Social History, 6 June 2023.

Alfani, Guido, and Marco Bonetti. 2019. "A Survival Analysis of the Last Great European Plagues: The Case of Nonantola (Northern Italy) in 1630", *Population Studies*, 73: 101–18.

Alfani, Guido, Marco Bonetti, and Mattia Fochesato. 2023. "Pandemics and Socio-economic Status: Evidence from the Plague of 1630 in Northern Italy", *Population Studies*, 78: 21–42.

Alfani, Guido, and Matteo Di Tullio. 2019. *The Lion's Share: Inequality and the Rise of the Fiscal State in Preindustrial Europe* (Cambridge: Cambridge University Press).

Alfani, Guido, Victoria Gierok, and Felix S. F. Schaff. 2022. "Economic Inequality in Preindustrial Germany, ca. 1300–1850", *Journal of Economic History*, 82: 87–125.

Alfani, Guido, and Alessia Melegaro. 2010. *Pandemie d'Italia. Dalla peste nera all'influenza suina: L'impatto sulla società* (Milan: Egea).

Alfani, Guido, and Tommy E. Murphy. 2017. "Plague and Lethal Epidemics in the Pre-industrial World", *Journal of Economic History*, 77: 314–43.

Alfani, Guido, and Cormac Ó Gráda. 2018. "Famine and Disease", in Matthias Blum and Christopher L. Colvin (eds), *An Economist's Guide to Economic History* (New York: Palgrave), 133–42.

Alfani, Guido, and Wouter Ryckbosch. 2016. "Growing apart in Early Modern Europe? A Comparison of Inequality Trends in Italy and the Low Countries, 1500–1800", *Explorations in Economic History*, 62: 143–53.

Allen, Bob. n. d. "Wage and Price Datasets, European Cities", Nuffield College, University of Oxford, accessed 24 May 2024. https://www.nuffield.ox.ac.uk/people/sites/allen-research-pages/.

Alsan, Marcella, and Claudia Goldin. 2018. "Watersheds in Child Mortality: The Role of Effective Water and Sewerage Infrastructure, 1880–1920", *Journal of Political Economy*, 127: 586–638.

Alston, Richard. 1998. "Trade and the City in Roman Egypt", in Helen Parkins and Christopher Smith (eds), *Trade, Traders, and the Ancient City* (London: Routledge), 168–202.

Aminjonov, Ulugbek, Olivier Bargain, and Tanguy Bernard. 2021a. "Gimme Shelter. Social Distancing and Income Support in Times of Pandemic", *Bordeaux Economics Working Papers*, 2021–12.

———. 2021b. "Poverty and Exposure to COVID-19: The Role of Income Support", *VoxEU*, 9 October 2021.

Ammannati, Francesco. 2020. Review of *Florence under Siege: Surviving Plague in an Early Modern City* by John Henderson, *Journal of Interdisciplinary History of Ideas*, 18. https://journals .openedition.org/jihi/2123.

Amster, Ellen J., and Rajae El Aoued. 2021. *Medicine and the Saints: Science, Islam, and the Colonial Encounter in Morocco, 1877–1956* (Austin: University of Texas Press).

Amundsen, Darrel W. 1977. "Medical Deontology and Pestilential Disease in the Late Middle Ages", *Journal of the History of Medicine and Allied Sciences*, 32: 403–21.

Andersen, Asger Lau, Emil Toft Hansen, Niels Johannesen, and Adam Sheridan. 2020. "Pandemic, Shutdown and Consumer Spending: Lessons from Scandinavian Policy Responses to COVID-19", arXiv preprint, arXiv:2005.04630.

Anderson, D. Mark, Kerwin Kofi Charles, and Daniel I. Rees. 2022. "Reexamining the Contribution of Public Health Efforts to the Decline in Urban Mortality", *American Economic Journal: Applied Economics*, 14: 126–57.

Anderson, Letty. 1984. "Hard Choices: Supplying Water to New England Towns", *Journal of Interdisciplinary History*, 15: 211–34.

Andrea, Alfred J. 1997. *The Capture of Constantinople: The "Hystoria Constantinopolitana" of Gunther of Pairis* (Philadelphia: University of Pennsylvania Press).

Andreozzi, Daniele. 2015. "The 'Barbican of Europe': The Plague of Split and the Strategy of Defence in the Adriatic Area between the Venetian Territories and the Ottoman Empire (Eighteenth Century)", *Popolazione e storia*, 16: 115–37.

Anon. 1767. *The Tryal of Mr. Daniel Sutton: For the High Crime of Preserving the Lives of His Majesty's Liege Subjects, by Means of Inoculation* (London: S. Bladon).

———. 1862. "Small-Pox", *Lancet*, 80: 290–1.

———. 1918. "The Etiology of Influenza", *Journal of the American Medical Association*, 71: 2097–100.

Apthorp, Kirrily. 2011. "As Good as an Army: Mapping Smallpox during the Seven Years' War in North America", BA thesis, University of Sydney.

Arcini, Caroline, et al. 2016. "Living Conditions in Times of Plague", in Per Lagerås (ed.), *Environment, Society and the Black Death: An Interdisciplinary Approach to the Late-Medieval Crisis in Sweden* (Oxford: Oxbow Books), 104–40.

Ardeleanu, Constantin. 2020. *The European Commission of the Danube, 1856–1948: An Experiment in International Administration* (Leiden, Netherlands: Brill).

———. 2023. "From 'the Dirtiest to the Best Water' in Romania: Public Health, Sanitary Diplomacy and Water in Sulina (1890s–1914)", *Water History*, 15: 247–62.

Arenas, Alberto. 2021. "Pandemics, Capitalism, and an Ecosocialist Pedagogy", *Journal of Environmental Education*, 52: 371–83.

Armstrong-Partida, Michelle, and Susan McDonough. 2023. "Singlewomen in the Late Medieval Mediterranean", *Past & Present*, 259: 3–42.

Arnold, David. 1986. "Cholera and Colonialism in British India", *Past & Present* 113: 118–51.

———. 1993. *Colonizing the Body: State Medicine and Epidemic Disease in Nineteenth-Century India* (Berkeley: University of California Press).

———. 2015. "Disease, Rumor, and Panic in India's Plague and Influenza Epidemics, 1896–1919", in Robert Peckham (ed.), *Empires of Panic: Epidemics and Colonial Anxieties* (Hong Kong: Hong Kong University Press), 111–30.

———. 2019. "Death and the Modern Empire: The 1918–19 Influenza Epidemic in India", *Transactions of the Royal Historical Society*, 29: 181–200.

———. 2020. "Pandemic India: Coronavirus and the Uses of History", *Journal of Asian Studies*, 79: 569–77.

Arnt, Nilton, and Leo Morris. 1972. "Smallpox Outbreaks in Two Brazilian Villages: Epidemiologic Characteristics", *American Journal of Epidemiology*, 95: 363–70.

Arroyo Abad, Leticia, Elwyn Davies, and Jan Luiten van Zanden. 2012. "Between Conquest and Independence: Real Wages and Demographic Change in Spanish America, 1530–1820", *Explorations in Economic History*, 49: 149–66.

Atmar, Robert L., Janet A. Englund, and Hunter Hammill. 1992. "Complications of Measles during Pregnancy", *Clinical Infectious Diseases*, 14: 217–26.

Aum, Sangmin, Sang Yoon Tim Lee, and Yongseok Shin. 2020. "COVID-19 Doesn't Need Lockdowns to Destroy Jobs: The Effect of Local Outbreaks in Korea", NBER Working Paper no. 27264.

Babcock, Emily Atwater, and August C. Krey (eds). 1943. *A History of Deeds Done beyond the Sea: By William, Archbishop of Tyre* (New York: Columbia University Press).

Bader, Richard-Ernst. 1985. "Sopono, Pocken und Pockengottkult der Yoruba: Erster Teil", *Medizinhistorisches Journal*, 20: 363–90.

———. 1986. "Sopono, Pocken und Pockengottkult der Yoruba: Zweiter Teil", *Medizinhistorisches Journal*, 21: 31–91.

Baek, ChaeWon, Peter B. McCrory, Todd Messer, and Preston Mui. 2020. "Unemployment Effects of Stay-at-Home Orders: Evidence from High Frequency Claims Data", Institute for Research on Labor and Employment Working Paper no. 101-20.

Baer, Gabriel. 1964. *Egyptian Guilds in Modern Times* (Jerusalem: Israel Oriental Society).

———. 1970. "The Administrative, Economic and Social Functions of Turkish Guilds", *International Journal of Middle East Studies*, 1: 28–50.

Bairoch, Paul, Jean Batou, and Pierre Chèvre. 1988. *La population des villes européennes: Banque de données et analyse sommaire des résultats, 800–1850* (Geneva: Droz).

Baker, Joseph O., et al. 2020. "Religion in the Age of Social Distancing: How COVID-19 Presents New Directions for Research", *Sociology of Religion*, 81: 357–70.

Baker, Robert B. 2018. "The American Medical Association and Race", *American Medical Association Journal of Ethics*, 16: 479–88.

Balaguer i Perigüell, Emili. 1997. "Arnau de Vilanova: La medicina, la ciencia y la técnica en tiempos de Jaime II", in Juan Antonio Barrio Barrio, José Vicente Cabezuelo Pliego, and Juan Francisco Jiménez Alcázar (eds), *Congreso internacional Jaime II 700 años después: Actas (1996–1997)* (Alicante, Spain: Universidad de Alicante), 13–27.

Baldwin, Peter. 1999. *Contagion and the State in Europe, 1830–1930* (Cambridge: Cambridge University Press).

Baljet, B. 2000. "The Painted Amsterdam Anatomy Lessons: Anatomy Performances in Dissecting Rooms", *Annals of Anatomy—Anatomischer Anzeiger*, 182: 3–11.

Balmford, James. 1603. *A Short Dialogue concerning the Plagues Infection: Published to Preserue Bloud, through the Blessing of God* (London: Richard Boyle).

Bamji, Alexandra. 2017. "Health Passes, Print and Public Health in Early Modern Europe", *Social History of Medicine*, 32: 441–64.

Banfield, E. C. 1958. *The Moral Basis of a Backward Society* (Glencoe, IL: Free Press).

Barberia, L. G., and E. J. Gómez. 2020. "Political and Institutional Perils of Brazil's COVID-19 Crisis", *Lancet*, 396: 367–8.

Barker, Hannah. 2021. "Laying the Corpses to Rest: Grain, Embargoes, and *Yersinia pestis* in the Black Sea, 1346–48", *Speculum*, 96: 97–126.

Barker, Sheila. 2006. "Art, Architecture, and the Roman Plague of 1656", *Roma moderna e contemporanea*, 14: 243–62.

———. 2017. "Miraculous Images and the Plagues of Italy, c. 590–1656", in Sandra Cardarelli and Laura Fenelli (eds), *Saints, Miracles and the Image: Healing Saints and Miraculous Images in the Renaissance* (Turnhout, Belgium: Brepols), 29–52.

Barlow, Monique Dean. 2021. "Christian Nationalism Is a Barrier to Mass Vaccination against COVID-19", *Conversation*, 1 April 2021. https://theconversation.com/christian-nationalism -is-a-barrier-to-mass-vaccination-against-covid-19-158023.

Barmania, Sima, and Michael J. Reiss. 2020. "Religion and Science in a Time of COVID-19: Allies or Adversaries?", *Scientific American Blog Network*, 11 June 2020. https://www.scientificamerican .com/blog/observations/religion-and-science-in-a-time-of-covid-19-allies-or-adversaries/.

Barnes, Kent B. 2014. "Social Vulnerability and Pneumonic Plague: Revisiting the 1994 Outbreak in Surat, India", *Environmental Hazards*, 13: 161–80.

Barry, John M. 2005. "1918 Revisited: Lessons and Suggestions for Further Inquiry", in Stacey Knobler, Alison Mack, Adel Mahmoud, and Stanley M. Lemon (eds), *The Threat of Pandemic Influenza: Are We Ready? Workshop Summary* (Washington, DC: National Academies), 58–68.

———. 2018. *The Great Influenza: The Story of the Deadliest Pandemic in History* (New York: Penguin Books).

Bartik, Alexander W., et al. 2020. "Measuring the Labor Market at the Onset of the COVID-19 Crisis", NBER Working Paper no. 27613.

Basco, Sergi, Jordi Domènech, and Joan R. Rosés. 2021. "Unequal Mortality during the Spanish Flu", CEPR Discussion Papers no. 15783.

Bastos, Cristiana. 2009. "Borrowing, Adapting, and Learning the Practices of Smallpox: Notes from Colonial Goa", *Bulletin of the History of Medicine*, 83: 141–63.

Batniji, Rajaie. 2021. "Historical Evidence to Inform COVID-19 Vaccine Mandates", *Lancet*, 397: 791.

Bauch, Martin. 2020. "'Just the Flu' in 1323? The Case Study of a Highly Contagious Epidemic with Low Mortality and Its Possible Origins in Late Medieval Europe", *Journal for the History of Environment and Society*, 5: 53–63.

Bautista, M. C., and B. G. Lopez-Valcarcel. 2019. "Review of Medical Professional Organizations in Developed Countries: Problems of Decentralized Membership Registers", *AIMS Public Health*, 6: 437–46.

Beach, Brian, Joseph Ferrie, Martin Saavedra, and Werner Troesken. 2016. "Typhoid Fever, Water Quality, and Human Capital Formation", *Journal of Economic History*, 76: 41–75.

Beale, Norman, and Elaine Beale. 2005. "Evidence-Based Medicine in the Eighteenth Century: The Ingen Housz-Jenner Correspondence Revisited", *Medical History*, 49: 79–98.

Beech, Peter. 2020. "What We've Got Wrong about China's 'Wet Markets' and Their Link to COVID-19", *World Economic Forum*, 18 April 2020. https://www.weforum.org/agenda/2020 /04/china-wet-markets-covid19-coronavirus-explained/.

Beland, Louis-Philippe, Abel Brodeur, and Taylor Wright. 2020. "COVID-19, Stay-at-Home Orders and Employment: Evidence from CPS Data", IZA Discussion Paper no. 13282.

Bell, Dean Phillip. 2020. "Learning from Disasters Past: The Case of an Early Seventeenth-Century Plague in Northern Italy and Beyond", *Jewish Social Studies*, 26: 55–66.

Bellavitis, Anna, and Beatrice Zucca Micheletto (eds). 2018. *Gender, Law and Economic Well-Being in Europe from the Fifteenth to the Nineteenth Century: North versus South?* (London: Routledge).

Belton, L. 1882. *Les anciennes communautés d'arts et métiers à Blois* (Blois, France: Marchand).

Bencard, Adam. 2021. "Epidemics before Microbiology: Stories from the Plague in 1711 and Cholera in 1853 in Copenhagen", *APMIS*, 129: 372–80.

Benedict, Carol. 1988. "Bubonic Plague in Nineteenth-Century China", *Modern China*, 14: 107–55.

———. 1993. "Policing the Sick: Plague and the Origins of State Medicine in Late Imperial China", *Late Imperial China*, 14: 60–77.

Benedictow, Ole Jørgen. 1987. "Morbidity in Historical Plague Epidemics", *Population Studies*, 41: 401–31.

————. 2004. *The Black Death, 1346–1353: The Complete History* (Woodbridge, UK: Boydell).

————. 2021. *The Complete History of the Black Death* (Martlesham, UK: Boydell).

Bennett, Judith M. 2019a. "Married and Not: Weston's Grown Children in 1268–1269", *Continuity and Change*, 34: 151–82.

————. 2019b. "Wretched Girls, Wretched Boys and the European Marriage Pattern in England (c. 1250–1350)", *Continuity and Change*, 34: 315–47.

Bennett, Michael J. 2008. "Jenner's Ladies: Women and Vaccination against Smallpox in Early Nineteenth-Century Britain", *History*, 93: 497–513.

————. 2009. "Smallpox and Cowpox under the Southern Cross: The Smallpox Epidemic of 1789 and the Advent of Vaccination in Colonial Australia", *Bulletin of the History of Medicine*, 83: 37–62.

————. 2020. *War against Smallpox: Edward Jenner and the Global Spread of Vaccination* (Cambridge: Cambridge University Press).

Bercé, Yves-Marie. 1984. *Le chaudron et la lancette: Croyances populaires et médecine préventive, 1798–1830* (Paris: Presses de la Renaissance).

Berche, P. 2022. "The Enigma of the 1889 Russian Flu Pandemic: A Coronavirus?", *La presse médicale*, 51: 104111.

Berkeley Center for Religion, Peace & World Affairs. 2021. "2021 Strategic Note on Religion & Diplomacy", Berkeley Center for Religion, Peace & World Affairs, 17 May 2021. https:// berkleycenter.georgetown.edu/publications/2021-strategic-note-on-religion-diplomacy.

Bernard, J. Y., E. Cohen, and M. S. Kramer. 2016. "Breast Feeding Initiation Rate across Western Countries: Does Religion Matter? An Ecological Study", *British Medical Journal Global Health*, 1: e000151.

Berridge, Virginia, and Griffith Edwards. 1981. *Opium and the People: Opiate Use in Nineteenth-Century England* (London: Allen Lane).

Berti, Lucia. 2021. "Early Reception of Smallpox Inoculation in Italy: Insights from the Correspondence of the Fellows of the Royal Society", *Diciottesimo secolo: Rivista della Società Italiana di Studi sul Secolo XVIII*, 6: 5–18.

Besl, Friedrich R. 1998. "Febris flava ad portas: Massnahmen in Liechtenstein und Graubünden gegen eine Epidemie 1804/05", *Bündner Monatsblatt: Zeitschrift für Bündner Geschichte, Landeskunde und Baukultur*, 1998 (4): 264–73.

Besley, Timothy, and Chris Dann. 2022. "When We Talk about State Capacity to Deal with COVID, We Shouldn't Ignore Interpersonal Trust", *LSE Thinks Blog*, 5 January 2022. https://blogs .lse.ac.uk/covid19/2022/01/05/when-we-talk-about-state-capacity-to-deal-with-covid-we -shouldnt-ignore-interpersonal-trust/.

Besley, Timothy, and Torsten Persson. 2009. "The Origins of State Capacity: Property Rights, Taxation, and Politics", *American Economic Review*, 99: 1218–44.

————. 2011. *Pillars of Prosperity: The Political Economics of Development Clusters* (Princeton, NJ: Princeton University Press).

————. 2013. "Taxation and Development", in Alan J. Auerbach, Raj Chetty, Martin Feldstein, and Emmanuel Saez (eds), *Handbook of Public Economics* (Amsterdam: Elsevier), 51–110.

Beveridge, W.I.B. 1991. "The Chronicle of Influenza Epidemics", *History and Philosophy of the Life Sciences*, 13: 223–34.

Bhatnagar, O. P. 1952. "Smallpox Vaccine: Its Introduction under Wellesley", *Indian Historical Quarterly*, 28: 186–9.

Bhattacharya, Sanjoy, Mark Harrison, and Michael Worboys. 2005. *Fractured States: Smallpox, Public Health and Vaccination Policy in British India, 1800–1947* (Hyderabad, India: Orient Longman).

Bhimraj, A., et al. 2022. "Therapeutic Emergency Use Authorizations (EUAS) during Pandemics: Double-Edged Swords", *Clinical Infectious Diseases*, 74: 1686–90.

Biller, Peter. 2001. *The Measure of Multitude: Population in Medieval Thought* (Oxford: Oxford University Press).

Biraben, Jean-Noël. 1968. "Certain Demographic Characteristics of the Plague Epidemic in France, 1720–22", *Daedalus*, 97: 536–45.

———. 1975. *Les hommes et la peste en France et dans les pays européens et méditerranéens*, vol. 1, *La peste dans l'histoire* (Paris: Mouton/École des hautes études en sciences sociales).

———. 1976. *Les hommes et la peste en France et dans les pays européens et méditerranéens*, vol. 2, *Les hommes face à la peste* (Paris: Mouton/École des hautes études en sciences sociales).

Blackburn, Peter. 2020. "Government Makes Wearing Face Masks Mandatory", British Medical Association, News and Opinion, 14 July 2020. https://www.bma.org.uk/news-and-opinion /government-makes-wearing-face-masks-mandatory.

Blaser, Martin J. 1998. "Passover and Plague", *Perspectives in Biology and Medicine*, 41: 243–56.

Blümcke, Otto. 1884. *Die Handwerkszünfte im mittelalterlichen Stettin* (Stettin, [Poland]: Herreke und Lebeling).

Blume, Stuart. 2006. "Anti-Vaccination Movements and Their Interpretations", *Social Science & Medicine*, 62: 628–42.

Bodemann, Eduard. 1883. *Die älteren Zunfturkunden der Stadt Lüneburg* (Hannover: Hahn).

Bodenhorn, Howard. 2020. "Business in a Time of Spanish Influenza", NBER Working Paper no. 27495.

Boerner, Lars, and Battista Severgnini. 2021. "Measuring and Comparing Economic Interaction Based on the Paths and Speed of Infections: The Case Study of the Spread of the Justinianic Plague and the Black Death", in Koenraad Verboven (ed.), *Complexity Economics: Building a New Approach to Ancient Economic History* (Cham, Switzerland: Palgrave Macmillan), 327–56.

Böhr, Dr. 1833. Review of *Relation historique et médicale de l'épidémie de choléra qui a régné à Berlin en 1831* par H. Scoutetten, *Cholera-Archiv mit Benutzung amtlicher Quellen*, 3: 169–81.

Boissonnade, P. 1900. *Essai sur l'organisation du travail en Poitou* (Paris: H. Champion).

Bolaños, Isacar A. 2019. "The Ottomans during the Global Crises of Cholera and Plague: The View from Iraq and the Gulf", *International Journal of Middle East Studies*, 51: 603–20.

Bolt, Nanno. 2021. "Monopoly, Competition and Regulation: Medieval Apothecaries in the State of Burgundy, 1300–1600", *Pharmaceutical Historian*, 51: 1–5.

Boomgaard, Peter. 2003. "Smallpox, Vaccination, and the Pax Neerlandica: Indonesia, 1550–1930", *Bijdragen tot de Taal-, Land- en Volkenkunde*, 159: 590–617.

Bootsma, Martin C. J., and Neil M. Ferguson. 2007. "The Effect of Public Health Measures on the 1918 Influenza Pandemic in U.S. Cities", *Proceedings of the National Academy of Sciences of the USA*, 104: 7588–93.

Born, Benjamin, Alexander Dietrich, and Gernot J. Müller. 2020. "Do Lockdowns Work? A Counterfactual for Sweden", CEPR Working Paper no. DP14744.

Borsch, Stuart J., and Tarek Sabraa. 2017. "Refugees of the Black Death: Quantifying Rural Migration for Plague and Other Environmental Disasters", *Annales de démographie historique*, 134: 63–93.

Bos, Gerrit (ed). 1992. *Qusṭā ibn Lūqā's Medical Regime for the Pilgrims to Mecca: The Risāla fī tadbīr safar al-ḥajj* (Leiden, Netherlands: Brill).

Bosma, Ulbe. 2019. *The Making of a Periphery: How Island Southeast Asia Became a Mass Exporter of Labor* (New York: Columbia University Press).

Botticini, Maristella, Zvi Eckstein, and Anat Vaturi. 2019. "Child Care and Human Development: Insights from Jewish History in Central and Eastern Europe, 1500–1930", *Economic Journal*, 129: 2637–90.

Bourdieu, Pierre. 1980. "Le capital social", *Actes de la recherche en sciences sociales*, 31: 2–3.

Boyar, Ebru. 2018. "Medicine in Practice: European Influences on the Ottoman Medical Habitat", *Turkish Historical Review*, 9: 213–41.

Boylston, Arthur. 2012. "The Origins of Inoculation", *Journal of the Royal Society of Medicine*, 105: 309–13.

Bradley, Leslie. 1977. "The Most Famous of All English Plagues: A Detailed Analysis of the Plague at Eyam, 1665–6", in Paul Slack (ed.), *The Plague Reconsidered* (Matlock, UK: Local Population Studies), 63–94.

Brent, John. 1860. *Canterbury in the Olden Time* (Canterbury, UK: A. Ginder).

Brévart, Francis B. 2008. "Between Medicine, Magic, and Religion: Wonder Drugs in German Medico-pharmaceutical Treatises of the Thirteenth to the Sixteenth Centuries", *Speculum*, 83: 1–57.

Brewer, Noel T., et al. 2022. "Incentives for COVID-19 Vaccination", *Lancet Regional Health—Americas*, 8: 100205.

Briggs, Chris. 2009. *Credit and Village Society in Fourteenth-Century England* (Oxford: Oxford University Press).

Brimnes, Niels. 2004. "Variolation, Vaccination and Popular Resistance in Early Colonial South India", *Medical History*, 48: 199–228.

———. 2013. "Coming to Terms with the Native Practitioner: Indigenous Doctors in Colonial Service in South India, 1800–25", *Indian Economic & Social History Review*, 50: 77–109.

Brivio, Alessandra. 2017. "Plague Spreaders: Political Conspirators and Agents of the Devil. A Study of Popular Belief in 17th-Century Milan", PhD dissertation, University of California, San Diego.

Broadberry, Stephen N. 2021. "Accounting for the Great Divergence: Recent Findings from Historical National Accounting", CEPR Discussion Papers no. DP15936.

Broadberry, Stephen, and Roger Fouquet. 2015. "Seven Centuries of European Economic Growth and Decline", *Journal of Economic Perspectives*, 29: 227–44.

Broadberry, Stephen, Hanhui Guan, and David Daokui Li. 2018. "China, Europe, and the Great Divergence: A Study in Historical National Accounting, 980–1850", *Journal of Economic History*, 78: 955–1000.

Broadberry, Stephen, and John Joseph Wallis. 2017. "Growing, Shrinking, and Long Run Economic Performance: Historical Perspectives on Economic Development", NBER Working Paper no. w23343.

Broadhurst, R.J.C., and Robert Irwin. 2019. *The Travels of Ibn Jubayr* (London: Bloomsbury).

Brockliss, L.W.B. 2010. "Medicine, Religion and Social Mobility in 18th- and Early 19th-Century Ireland", in Fiona Clark and James Kelly (eds), *Ireland and Medicine in the Seventeenth and Eighteenth Centuries* (Farnham, UK: Ashgate), 73–108.

Brockliss, L.W.B., and Colin Jones. 1997. *The Medical World of Early Modern France* (Oxford: Clarendon).

Brohm, Ulrich. 1999. *Die Handwerkspolitik Herzog Augusts des Jüngeren von Braunschweig-Wolfenbüttel: (1635–1666). Zur Rolle von Fürstenstaat und Zünften im Wiederaufbau nach dem Dreißigjährigen Krieg* (Stuttgart: Steiner).

Brook, Timothy. 2020. "Comparative Pandemics: The Tudor–Stuart and Wanli–Chongzhen Years of Pestilence, 1567–1666", *Journal of Global History*, 15: 363–79.

Broomhall, Susan. 2004. *Women's Medical Work in Early Modern France* (Manchester: Manchester University Press).

Brown, Jeremy. 2022. *The Eleventh Plague: Jews and Pandemics from the Bible to COVID-19* (Oxford: Oxford University Press).

Brown, John C. 1988. "Coping with Crisis? The Diffusion of Waterworks in Late Nineteenth-Century German Towns", *Journal of Economic History*, 48: 307–18.

———. 1989a. "Public Reform for Private Gain? The Case of Investments in Sanitary Infrastructure: Germany, 1880–1887", *Urban Studies*, 26: 2–12.

————. 1989b. "Reforming the Urban Environment: Sanitation, Housing, and Government Intervention in Germany, 1870–1910 [Dissertation Summary]", *Journal of Economic History*, 49: 450–2.

Browne, Joseph. 1720. *A Practical Treatise of the Plague, and All Pestilential Infections That Have Happen'd in This Island for the Last Century* (London: J. Wilcox).

Bruijn, Iris Diane Rosemary. 2009. *Ship's Surgeons of the Dutch East India Company: Commerce and the Progress of Medicine in the Eighteenth Century* (Leiden, Netherlands: Leiden University Press).

Brunton, Deborah C. 1990. "Pox Britannica: Smallpox Inoculation in Britain, 1721–1830", PhD dissertation, University of Pennsylvania.

Buell, Paul D. 2012. "Qubilai and the Rats", *Sudhoffs Archiv*, 96: 127–44.

Bullough, Vern L. 1958. "The Development of the Medical Guilds at Paris", *Medievalia et humanistica*, 12: 33–40.

————. 1959. "Training of the Nonuniversity-Educated Medical Practitioners in the Later Middle Ages", *Journal of the History of Medicine and Allied Sciences*, 14: 446–58.

————. 1970. "Education and Professionalization: An Historical Example", *History of Education Quarterly*, 10: 160–9.

Buonanno, G., L. Morawska, and L. Stabile. 2020. "Quantitative Assessment of the Risk of Airborne Transmission of SARS-CoV-2 Infection: Prospective and Retrospective Applications", *Environment International*, 145: 106112.

Burdyka, Konrad. 2020. "Amoralny familizm? O samopomocy rodzinno-sąsiedzkiej w społeczności wiejskiej czasu pandemii" [Amoral familism? Family and neighbourhood self-help in a rural community during a pandemic], *Wieś i rolnictwo*, 3: 141–59.

Burgess, Kaya. 2021. "Pastor 'Sold Divine Plague Kits to Protect from COVID'", *The Times*, 17 August 2021.

Burt, Ronald S. 2001. "Bandwidth and Echo: Trust, Information and Gossip in Social Networks", in Alessandra Casella and James E. Rauch (eds), *Networks and Markets: Contributions from Economics and Sociology* (New York: Russel Sage Foundation), 30–74.

Byrne, Joseph P. (ed.). 2012. *Encyclopedia of the Black Death* (Santa Barbara, CA: ABC-CLIO).

Caldwell, John C. 1976. "Toward a Restatement of Demographic Transition Theory", *Population and Development Review*, 2: 321–66.

Campbell, Anna Montgomery. 1931. *The Black Death and Men of Learning* (New York: Columbia University Press).

Campbell, Gwyn. 1991. "The State and Pre-colonial Demographic History: The Case of Nineteenth-Century Madagascar", *Journal of African History*, 32: 415–45.

Campos-Mercade, Pol, et al. 2021. "Monetary Incentives Increase COVID-19 Vaccinations", *Science*, 374: 879–82.

Cantisano, Pedro Jimenez. 2022. "A Refuge from Science: The Practice and Politics of Rights in Brazil's Vaccine Revolt", *Hispanic American Historical Review*, 102: 611–42.

Caracausi, Andrea. 2014. "Textiles Manufacturing, Product Innovations and Transfers of Technology in Padua and Venice between the Sixteenth and Eighteenth Centuries", in Karel Davids and Bert De Munck (eds), *Innovation and Creativity in Late Medieval and Early Modern European Cities* (Aldershot, UK: Ashgate), 131–60.

Carmichael, Ann G. 1983. "Plague Legislation in the Italian Renaissance", *Bulletin of the History of Medicine*, 57: 508–25.

————. 1986. *Plague and the Poor in Renaissance Florence* (Cambridge: Cambridge University Press).

————. 1998. "The Last Past Plague: The Uses of Memory in Renaissance Epidemics", *Journal of the History of Medicine and Allied Sciences*, 53: 132–60.

————. 2008. "Universal and Particular: The Language of Plague, 1348–1500", *Medical History*, 52: 17–52.

Caron, Vicki. 1998. "The Antisemitic Revival in France in the 1930s: The Socioeconomic Dimension Reconsidered", *Journal of Modern History*, 70: 24–73.

Carpenter, Daniel P. 2010. *Reputation and Power: Organizational Image and Pharmaceutical Regulation at the FDA* (Princeton, NJ: Princeton University Press).

Carter, Francis W. 1972. *Dubrovnik (Ragusa): A Classic City-State* (London: Seminar).

Carter, Kerstine, et al. 2023. "Regulatory Guidance on Randomization and the Use of Randomization Tests in Clinical Trials: A Systematic Review", *Statistics in Biopharmaceutical Research*, 1–13. https://doi.org/10.1080/19466315.2023.2239521.

Carvalho, Vasco M., et al. 2020. "Tracking the COVID-19 Crisis with High-Resolution Transaction Data", CEPR discussion paper no. DP14642.

Caselli, Francesca, Francesco Grigoli, and Damiano Sandri. 2022. "Protecting Lives and Livelihoods with Early and Tight Lockdowns", *B.E. Journal of Macroeconomics*, 22: 241–68.

Chais, Charles. 1754. *Essai apologétique sur la méthode de communiquer la petite vérole par inoculation où l'on tâche de faire voir que la conscience ne sauroit en être blessée, ni la religion offensée* (The Hague: Pierre de Hondt).

Champion, J.A.I. 1993. "Epidemics and the Build Environment in 1665", in Champion (ed.), *Epidemic Disease in London* (London: Centre for Metropolitan History), 35–52.

Chandra, Siddharth, Julia Christensen, and Shimon Likhtman. 2020. "Connectivity and Seasonality: The 1918 Influenza and COVID-19 Pandemics in Global Perspective", *Journal of Global History*, 15: 408–20.

Chandra, Siddharth, and Eva Kassens-Noor. 2014. "The Evolution of Pandemic Influenza: Evidence from India, 1918–19", *BMC Infectious Diseases*, 14 (510): 1–10.

Chang, Chia-Feng. 1996. "Aspects of Smallpox and Its Significance in Chinese History", PhD dissertation, School of Oriental and African Studies, University of London.

————. 2002. "Disease and Its Impact on Politics, Diplomacy, and the Military: The Case of Smallpox and the Manchus (1613–1795)", *Journal of the History of Medicine and Allied Sciences*, 57: 177–97.

Chapman, Jonathan. 2019. "The Contribution of Infrastructure Investment to Britain's Urban Mortality Decline, 1861–1900", *Economic History Review*, 72: 233–59.

Chatterjee, P. 2010. "Trouble at the Medical Council of India", *Lancet*, 375: 1679.

Chaturvedi, Vinayak. 2006. "The Making of a Peasant King in Colonial Western India: The Case of Ranchod Vira", *Past & Present*, 192: 155–85.

Chen, Sophia, Deniz Igan, Nicola Pierri, and Andrea F. Presbitero. 2020. "Tracking the Economic Impact of COVID-19 and Mitigation Policies in Europe and the United States", IMF Working Paper no. 20/125.

Chetty, Raj, et al. 2020. "How Did COVID-19 and Stabilization Policies Affect Spending and Employment? A New Real-Time Economic Tracker Based on Private Sector Data", NBER Working Paper no. 27431.

Chorniy, Anna, James Bailey, Abdulkadir Civan, and Michael Maloney. 2021. "Regulatory Review Time and Pharmaceutical Research and Development", *Health Economics*, 30: 113–28.

Chouin, Gérard. 2018. "Reflections on Plague in African History (14th–19th C.)", *Afriques*, 09. https://doi.org/10.4000/afriques.2228.

Christakos, George, R. A. Olea, Marc L. Serre, Hwa-Lung Yu, and Linlin Wang. 2005. *Interdisciplinary Public Health Reasoning and Epidemic Modelling: The Case of Black Death* (Berlin: Springer).

Christensen, Daniel Eric. 2004. "Politics and the Plague: Efforts to Combat Health Epidemics in Seventeenth-Century Braunschweig-Wolfenbüttel, Germany", PhD dissertation, University of California, Riverside.

Christensen, Peter. 2003. "'In These Perilous Times': Plague and Plague Policies in Early Modern Denmark", *Medical History*, 47: 413–50.

Chronopoulos, Dimitris K., Marcel Lukas, and John O. S. Wilson. 2020. "Consumer Spending Responses to the COVID-19 Pandemic: An Assessment of Great Britain", SSRN Working Paper no. 3586723.

Ciappara, Frans. 2021. "Confraternal Devotions in Malta, 1670–1798", *Journal of Religious History*, 45: 68–90.

Cingolani, Luciana. 2013. "The State of State Capacity: A Review of Concepts, Evidence and Measures", MERIT Working Papers no. 2013-053.

Cipolla, Carlo M. 1973. *Cristofano and the Plague: A Study in the History of Public Health in the Age of Galileo* (Berkeley: University of California Press).

———. 1976. *Public Health and the Medical Profession in the Renaissance* (Cambridge: Cambridge University Press).

CitiesX. 2018. "Venetian Responses to Plague", Youtube, 26 January 2018. https://www.youtube.com/watch?v=TTM-WfSBNkQ&t=2s.

Clark, G. N. 1964. *A History of the Royal College of Physicians of London* (Oxford: Clarendon).

Clay, Karen, Joshua Lewis, and Edson Severnini. 2019. "What Explains Cross-City Variation in Mortality during the 1918 Influenza Pandemic? Evidence from 438 U.S. Cities", *Economics & Human Biology*, 35: 42–50.

Cless, Georg von. 1871. *Impfung und Pocken in Württemberg* (Stuttgart: Schweizerbart (E. Koch)).

Clouse, Michele L. 2013. *Medicine, Government and Public Health in Philip II's Spain: Shared Interests, Competing Authorities* (Aldershot, UK: Ashgate).

Cohen, Mark R. 2021. *The Autobiography of a Seventeenth-Century Venetian Rabbi: Leon Modena's Life of Judah* (Princeton, NJ: Princeton University Press).

Cohen, Robert. 1991. *Jews in Another Environment: Surinam in the Second Half of the Eighteenth Century* (Leiden, Netherlands: Brill).

Cohn, Samuel K. 1998. "Women and Work in Renaissance Italy", in Judith C. Brown and Robert C. Davis (eds), *Gender and Society in Renaissance Italy* (London: Longman), 107–26.

———. 2007. "After the Black Death: Labour Legislation and Attitudes towards Labour in Late-Medieval Western Europe", *Economic History Review*, 60: 457–85.

———. 2010a. *The Black Death Transformed: Disease and Culture in Early Renaissance Europe*, 2nd ed. (London: Arnold).

———. 2010b. "Changing Pathology of Plague", in Simonetta Cavaciocchi (ed.), *Le interazioni fra economia e ambiente biologico nell'Europe preindustriale. Sett. XIII–XVIII. Economic and Biological Interactions in Pre-Industrial Europe from the 13th to the 18th Centuries* (Florence: Firenze University Press), 35–56.

———. 2010c. *Cultures of Plague: Medical Thinking at the End of the Renaissance* (Oxford: Oxford University Press).

———. 2012. "Pandemics: Waves of Disease, Waves of Hate from the Plague of Athens to A.I.D.S.", *Historical Research*, 85: 535–55.

Cohn, Samuel K., and Guido Alfani. 2007. "Households and Plague in Early Modern Italy", *Journal of Interdisciplinary History*, 38: 177–205.

Coleman, James S. 1988. "Social Capital in the Creation of Human Capital", *American Journal of Sociology*, 94: S95–120.

Colet, Anna, et al. 2014. "The Black Death and Its Consequences for the Jewish Community in Tàrrega: Lessons from History and Archeology", *Medieval Globe*, 1: 63–96.

Columbus, Aaron. 2022. "'To Be Had for a Pesthouse for the Use of This Parish': Plague Pesthouses in Early Stuart London, c. 1600–1650", *Urban History*, 51: 1–21.

Condran, Gretchen A. 1987. "Declining Mortality in the United States in the Late Nineteenth and Early Twentieth Centuries", *Annales de démographie historique*, 1998: 119–41.

Connolly, Elizabeth Anne. 2017. "A Dynamic Equilibrium: Doctors and Patients in Seventeenth-Century England", PhD dissertation, University of Adelaide.

Cook, Sherburne Friend. 1943. *The Conflict between the California Indian and White Civilization* (Berkeley: University of California Press).

Coomans, Janna. 2018. "In Pursuit of a Healthy City: Sanitation and the Common Good in the Late Medieval Low Countries", PhD dissertation, University of Amsterdam.

——. 2019. "The King of Dirt: Public Health and Sanitation in Late Medieval Ghent", *Urban History*, 46: 82–105.

——. 2021. *Community, Urban Health and Environment in the Late Medieval Low Countries* (Cambridge: Cambridge University Press).

——. 2022. "Making Good and Breaking Bad: Materiality and Community in Netherlandish Cities, 1380–1520", *English Historical Review*, 137: 1053–81.

Coomans, Janna, and Claire Weeda. 2020. "Politics of Movement: Exploring Passage Points in Responses to COVID-19 and the Plague in the Fifteenth-Century Netherlands", *Journal for the History of Environment and Society*, 5: 79–89.

Correia, Sergio, Stephan Luck, and Emil Verner. 2020. "Pandemics Depress the Economy, Public Health Interventions Do Not: Evidence from the 1918 Flu", SSRN Working Paper no. 3561560.

Cortese, Delia, and Simonetta Calderini. 2022. *Women and the Fatimids in the World of Islam* (Edinburgh: Edinburgh University Press).

Corvi, Antonio. 1996. "L'apothicairerie de la 'Cà Granda', fondée en 1470", *Revue d'histoire de la pharmacie*, 312: 167–74.

Cotter, Wendy. 1996. "The *Collegia* and Roman Law: State Restrictions on Voluntary Associations, 64 BCE–200 CE", in John W. Kloppenborg and Stephan G. Wilson (eds), *Voluntary Associations in the Graeco-Roman World* (London: Routledge), 74–89.

Cox, Eugene L. 1967. *The Green Count of Savoy: Amadeus VI and Transalpine Savoy in the Fourteenth Century* (Princeton, NJ: Princeton University Press).

Crafts, Nicholas. 1997a. "The Human Development Index and Changes in Standards of Living: Some Historical Comparisons", *European Review of Economic History*, 1: 299–322.

——. 1997b. "Some Dimensions of the 'Quality of Life' during the British Industrial Revolution", *Economic History Review*, 50: 617–39.

Crisciani, Chiara, and Michela Pereira. 1998. "Black Death and Golden Remedies: Some Remarks on Alchemy and the Plague", in Agostino Paravicini Bagliani and Francesco Santi (eds), *The Regulation of Evil: Social and Cultural Attitudes to Epidemics in the Late Middle Ages* (Florence: Sismel), 7–39.

Crosby, Alfred W. 1972. *The Columbian Exchange: Biological and Cultural Consequences of 1492* (Westport, CT: Greenwood).

——. 2003. *America's Forgotten Pandemic: The Influenza of 1918* (Cambridge: Cambridge University Press).

Cuffe, Robert. 2021. "Coronavirus: Four Numbers That Reveal the Real Trends", *BBC News*, 14 October 2021. https://www.bbc.co.uk/news/health-57984170.

Cuffel, Alexandra. 2012. "Environmental Disasters and Political Dominance in Shared Festivals and Intercessions among Medieval Muslims, Christians and Jews", in Margaret Cormack (ed.), *Muslims and Others in Sacred Space* (Oxford: Oxford University Press), 108–46.

Cukierman, Henrique. 2021. "The Vaccine Revolt of 1904, Rio De Janeiro, Brazil", *Oxford Research Encyclopedia*, Latin American History, 31 August 2021. https://oxfordre.com/latinamericanhistory/display/10.1093/acrefore/9780199366439.001.0001/acrefore-9780199366439-e-851.

Cummins, Neil, Morgan Kelly, and Cormac Ó Gráda. 2016. "Living Standards and Plague in London, 1560–1665", *Economic History Review*, 69: 3–34.

Curta, Florin. 2019. *Eastern Europe in the Middle Ages (500–1300)* (Leiden, Netherlands: Brill).

Curtis, Daniel R. 2016. "Was Plague an Exclusively Urban Phenomenon? Plague Mortality in the Seventeenth-Century Low Countries", *Journal of Interdisciplinary History*, 47: 139–70.

———. 2020. "Preserving the Ordinary: Social Resistance during Second Pandemic Plagues in the Low Countries", in Chris Gerrard, Peter Brown, and Paolo Forlin (eds), *Waiting for the Ends of the World: Perceptions of Disaster and Risk in Medieval Europe* (London: Routledge), 280–97.

———. 2021a. "The Female Experience of Epidemics in the Early Modern Low Countries", *Dutch Crossing*, 45: 3–20.

———. 2021b. "From One Mortality Regime to Another? Mortality Crises in Late Medieval Haarlem, Holland, in Perspective", *Speculum*, 96: 127–55.

Curtis, Daniel R., and Qijun Han. 2021. "The Female Mortality Advantage in the Seventeenth-Century Rural Low Countries", *Gender & History*, 33: 50–74.

Cutler, David M., and Grant Miller. 2005. "The Role of Public Health Improvements in Health Advances: The Twentieth-Century United States", *Demography*, 42: 1–22.

Damon, Inger K. 2012. "Smallpox, Monkeypox, and Other Poxvirus Infections", in Lee Goldman and Andrew I. Schafer (eds), *Goldman's Cecil Medicine*, 24th ed. (Philadelphia, PA: W. B. Saunders), 2117–21.

Darrāǧ, Aḥmad. 1961. *L'Egypte sous le règne de Barsbay 825–841/1422–1438* (Damascus: Institut français de Damas).

Dasgupta, Partha. 2000. "Economic Progress and the Idea of Social Capital", in Dasgupta and Ismail Serageldin (eds), *Social Capital: A Multifaceted Perspective* (Washington, DC: World Bank), 325–424.

Dasgupta, Partha, and Martin Weale. 1992. "On Measuring the Quality of Life", *World Development*, 20: 119–31.

Davenport, Romola. 2020a. "Cultures of Contagion and Containment? The Geography of Smallpox in Britain in the Pre-vaccination Era", in Véronique Petit, Kaveri Qureshi, Yves Charbit, and Philip Kreager (eds), *The Anthropological Demography of Health* (Oxford: Oxford University Press), 61–84.

———. 2020b. "Urbanization and Mortality in Britain, c. 1800–50", *Economic History Review*, 73: 455–85.

Davenport, Romola, Max Satchell, and Leigh Matthew William Shaw-Taylor. 2018. "The Geography of Smallpox in England before Vaccination: A Conundrum Resolved", *Social Science & Medicine*, 206: 75–85.

Davidson, Helen. 2020. "First COVID-19 Case Happened in November, China Government Records Show Report", *Guardian*, 13 March 2020. https://www.theguardian.com/world/2020/mar/13/first-covid-19-case-happened-in-november-china-government-records-show-report.

Davies, Matthew, and Ann Saunders. 2004. *The History of the Merchant Taylors Company* (Leeds, UK: Maney).

Davis, Nicola. 2023. "COVID Vaccines Should Be Available to Buy Privately in UK, Scientists Say", *Guardian*, 17 August 2023. https://www.theguardian.com/world/2023/aug/17/covid-vaccines-should-be-available-privately-uk-scientists-say.

Defoe, Daniel. 1722. *A Journal of the Plague Year* (London: E. Nutt).

De Kadt, Daniel, et al. 2020. "The Causes and Consequences of the 1918 Influenza in South Africa", Stellenbosch University Department of Economics Working Papers no. 12/2020.

Dekker, Theo. 2023. "Coping with Epidemics in Early Modern Chronicles, the Low Countries, 1500–1850", in Asperen Hanneke and Jensen Lotte (eds), *Dealing with Disasters from Early Modern to Modern Times* (Amsterdam: Amsterdam University Press), 229–48.

DeLacy, Margaret. 1993a. "The Conceptualization of Influenza in Eighteenth-Century Britain: Specificity and Contagion", *Bulletin of the History of Medicine*, 67: 74–118.

———. 1993b. "Influenza Research and the Medical Profession in Eighteenth-Century Britain", *Albion: A Quarterly Journal Concerned with British Studies*, 25: 37–66.

Delumeau, Jean. 1978. *La peur en occident, XIVe–XVIIIe siècles: Une cité assiégée* (Paris: Fayard).

De Meyer, Isaac Joseph. 1842. *Origine des apothicaires de Bruges* (Bruges: De Pachtere).

De Moor, Tine, and Jan Luiten van Zanden. 2010. "Girlpower: The European Marriage Pattern and Labour Markets in the North Sea Region in the Late Medieval and Early Modern Period", *Economic History Review*, 63: 1–33.

Denecke, Dietrich. 1986. "Straße und Weg im Mittelalter als Lebensraum und Vermittler zwischen entfernten Orten", in Bernd Herrmann (ed.), *Mensch und Umwelt im Mittelalter* (Stuttgart: Deutsche Verlags-Anstalt), 203–19.

Deneweth, Heidi, and Patrick Wallis. 2016. "Households, Consumption and the Development of Medical Care in the Netherlands, 1650–1900", *Journal of Social History*, 49: 532–57.

Dennison, Tracy. 2011. *The Institutional Framework of Russian Serfdom* (Cambridge: Cambridge University Press).

———. 2023. "Weak State, Strong Commune: Authority in the Russian Countryside", *Revista storica italiana*, 135: 623–54.

Dennison, Tracy, and Sheilagh Ogilvie. 2007. "Serfdom and Social Capital in Bohemia and Russia", *Economic History Review*, 60: 513–44.

———. 2014. "Does the European Marriage Pattern Explain Economic Growth?", *Journal of Economic History*, 74: 651–93.

———. 2016. "Institutions, Demography, and Economic Growth", *Journal of Economic History*, 76: 205–17.

Depping, Georges-Bernard (ed.). 1837. *Réglemens sur les arts et métiers de Paris, rédigés au XIIIe siècle et connus sous le nom du "Livre des métiers" d'Étienne Boileau* (Paris: Imprimerie de Crapelet).

Derosas, Renzo. 2003. "Watch out for the Children! Differential Infant Mortality of Jews and Catholics in Nineteenth-Century Venice", *Historical Methods: A Journal of Quantitative and Interdisciplinary History*, 36: 109–30.

Devi, Sharmila. 2020. "COVID-19 Exacerbates Violence against Health Workers", *Lancet World Report*, 396: P658.

Devos, Isabelle. 2021. "Belgium: The Nineteenth-Century Anti-vaxxer?" (using HISSTER database), Ghent University, Quetelet Center, January 2021. https://www.queteletcenter.ugent.be/en/belgium-the-nineteenth-century-anti-vaxxer/.

Devos, Isabelle, et al. 2021. "The Spanish Flu in Belgium, 1918–1919: A State of the Art", *Historical Social Research*, supplement, 33: 251–83.

De Vries, Jan. 1976. *The Economy of Europe in an Age of Crisis, 1600–1750* (Cambridge: Cambridge University Press).

———. 1984. *European Urbanization 1500–1800* (Cambridge, MA: Harvard University Press).

De Vries, Jan, and Ad van der Woude. 1997. *The First Modern Economy: Success, Failure, and Perseverance of the Dutch Economy, 1500–1815* (Cambridge: Cambridge University Press).

Devroey, Jean-Pierre. 2000. "Men and Women in Early Medieval Serfdom: The Ninth-Century North Frankish Evidence", *Past & Present*, 166: 3–30.

DeWitte, Sharon N. 2014. "Mortality Risk and Survival in the Aftermath of the Medieval Black Death", *PLOS One*, 9: e96513.

DeWitte, S. N., and G. Hughes-Morey. 2012. "Stature and Frailty during the Black Death: The Effect of Stature on Risks of Epidemic Mortality in London, A.D. 1348–1350", *Journal of Archaeological Science*, 39. https://doi.org/10.1016/j.jas.2012.01.019.

DeWitte, Sharon N., and James W. Wood. 2008. "Selectivity of Black Death Mortality with Respect to Preexisting Health", *Proceedings of the National Academy of Sciences of the USA*, 105: 1436–41.

Dharampal. 1971. *Indian Science and Technology in the Eighteenth Century: Some Contemporary European Accounts* (Delhi: Impex India).

Diamond, Jared. 1997. *Guns, Germs and Steel* (New York: W. W. Norton).

Dias, Jill R. 1981. "Famine and Disease in the History of Angola c. 1830–1930", *Journal of African History*, 22: 349–78.

Di Gialleonardo, Luca, Mauro Marè, Antonello Motroni, and Francesco Porcelli. 2021. "Family Ties and the Pandemic: Some Evidence from SARS-CoV2", MPRA paper no. 106735.

DiMasi, J. A., R. W. Hansen, and H. G. Grabowski. 2003. "The Price of Innovation: New Estimates of Drug Development Costs", *Journal of Health Economics*, 22: 151–85.

DiMasi, J. A., R. W. Hansen, H. G. Grabowski, and L. Lasagna. 1991. "Cost of Innovation in the Pharmaceutical Industry", *Journal of Health Economics*, 10: 107–42.

Dimitrov, Theodor. 2020. "'And Everything Here Was Filled with Misery and Tears': A Few Notes on the Black Death Demographic Impact on Byzantium, 1347–1453", *Etudes balkaniques*, 56: 105–25.

Dimsdale, Robert. 2017. "Mixed Blessing: The Impact of Suttonian Smallpox Inoculation in the Later Eighteenth Century", Study Group on Eighteenth-Century Russia, SGECR Occasional Series, no. 1. https://www.sgecr.co.uk/dimsdale/article.html.

Dincecco, Mark. 2015. "The Rise of Effective States in Europe", *Journal of Economic History*, 75: 901–18.

———. 2017. *State Capacity and Economic Development: Present and Past* (Cambridge: Cambridge University Press).

Dincecco, Mark, and Gabriel Katz. 2016. "State Capacity and Long-Run Economic Performance", *Economic Journal*, 126: 189–218.

Dincecco, Mark, and Massimiliano Gaetano Onorato. 2018. *From Warfare to Wealth: The Military Origins of Urban Prosperity in Europe* (Cambridge: Cambridge University Press).

Dinges, Martin. 1994. "Nord-Süd Gefälle in der Pestbekämpfung: Italien, Deutschland und England im Vergleich", in Wolfgang Uwe Eckart (ed.), *Das europäische Gesundheitssystem: Gemeinsamkeiten und Unterschiede in historischer Perspektive* (Stuttgart: Franz Steiner), 19–51.

D'Irsay, Stephen. 1927. "Defense Reactions during the Black Death of 1348–1349", *Annals of Medical History*, 9: 169–79.

Ditrich, Hans. 2017. "The Transmission of the Black Death to Western Europe: A Critical Review of the Existing Evidence", *Mediterranean Historical Review*, 32: 25–39.

Dixon, C. W. 1962. *Smallpox* (London: J. and A. Churchill).

Dobson, Mary J. 1992. "Contours of Death: Disease, Mortality and the Environment in Early Modern England", *Health Transition Review*, 2: 77–95.

Dols, Michael Walters. 1977. *The Black Death in the Middle East* (Princeton, NJ: Princeton University Press).

Donahue, Charles. 2008. *Law, Marriage, and Society in the Later Middle Ages: Arguments about Marriage in Five Courts* (Cambridge: Cambridge University Press).

Dönges, Philipp, et al. 2023. "SIR-Model for Households", arXiv preprint, arXiv:2301.04355v1.

Dorin, Rowan. 2021. "The Bishop as Lawmaker in Late Medieval Europe", *Past & Present*, 253: 45–82.

Dorst, Eva. 2019. "Taming an Epidemic: The 'Praagse Brief' and Its Reflections in Late Medieval Municipal Legislation", MA thesis, University of Leiden.

Doyle, Shane. 2000. "Population Decline and Delayed Recovery in Bunyoro, 1860–1960", *Journal of African History*, 41: 429–58.

Dueñas, Alcira. 2010. *Indians and Mestizos in the "Lettered City": Reshaping Justice, Social Hierarchy, and Political Culture in Colonial Peru* (Boulder: University Press of Colorado).

Duffin, Jacalyn. 2010. *History of Medicine: A Scandalously Short Introduction*, 2nd ed. (Toronto: University of Toronto Press).

Duggan, A. T., et al. 2016. "17th Century Variola Virus Reveals the Recent History of Smallpox", *Current Biology*, 26: 3407–12.

Duncan-Jones, R. P. 1996. "The Impact of the Antonine Plague", *Journal of Roman Archaeology*, 9: 108–36.

———. 2018. "The Antonine Plague Revisited", *Arctos*, 52: 41–72.

Durey, Michael. 1979. *The Return of the Plague: British Society and the Cholera, 1831–2* (Dublin: Gill and Macmillan).

Earn, David J. D., et al. 2020. "Acceleration of Plague Outbreaks in the Second Pandemic", *Proceedings of the National Academy of Sciences of the USA*, 117: 27703–11.

Ebot, Jane O. 2015. "'Girl Power!': The Relationship between Women's Autonomy and Children's Immunization Coverage in Ethiopia", *Journal of Health, Population and Nutrition*, 33 (18): 1–9.

Echenberg, Myron. 2002. "Pestis Redux: The Initial Years of the Third Bubonic Plague Pandemic, 1894–1901", *Journal of World History*, 13: 429–49.

———. 2007. *Plague Ports: The Global Urban Impact of Bubonic Plague, 1894–1901* (New York: New York University Press).

———. 2008. "Cholera: Fourth through Sixth Pandemics, 1862–1947", in Joseph P. Byrne (ed.), *Encyclopedia of Pestilence, Pandemics, and Plagues* (Westport, CT: Greenwood), 105–14.

Economist. 2020a. "Sealed Off: Tough Quarantine Measures Have Spread across China", 1 February 2020, 51–52.

———. 2020b. "As COVID-19 Spreads, Indonesia's President Has an Unhappy Eid", 24 May 2020.

———. 2020c. "Restrictions and Rebellion Follow New York City's COVID-19 Surge", 17 October 2020.

———. 2020d. "Mutual-Aid Groups Spread in COVID-Stricken America", 19 December 2020.

———. 2021a. "Opposites Attract: The Anti-lockdown Movement Is Still Going Strong", 3 July 2021.

———. 2021b. "Fighting for Their Right to Party: Britain Tests the Limits of Mass Vaccination", 20 July 2021.

———. 2022a. "Graphic Detail: Global Normalcy Index. The World Is Almost Back to Pre-Covid Activity Levels", 10 September 2022.

———. 2022b. "China's Leaders Ponder an Economy without Lockdowns—or Crackdowns", 20 December 2022.

———. 2023. "Kim Jong Un Has No Desire to Let His Country Rejoin the World: Ongoing Pandemic-Era Seclusion Hurts North Koreans—but Suits Their Dictator", 24 July 2023.

Edgington, Susan. 2007. *Albert of Aachen: "Historia ierosolimitana", History of the Journey to Jerusalem* (Oxford: Oxford University School of Archaeology).

Edwards, Jeremy, and Sheilagh Ogilvie. 2022a. "The Black Death and the Origin of the European Marriage Pattern", Oxford Economic and Social History Working Papers no. 204.

———. 2022b. "Did the Black Death Cause Economic Development by 'Inventing' Fertility Restriction?", *Oxford Economic Papers*, 74: 1228–46.

Egan, Joseph R. 2010. "A Plague on Five of Your Houses: Statistical Re-assessment of Three Pneumonic Plague Outbreaks That Occurred in Suffolk, England, between 1906 and 1918", *Theoretical Biology and Medical Modelling*, 7: 39.

Ehlers, Maren Annika. 2011. "Poor Relief and the Negotiation of Local Order in Early Modern Japan", PhD dissertation, Princeton University.

Ehmer, Josef. 1997. "Worlds of Mobility: Migration Patterns of Viennese Artisans in the 18th Century", in Geoffrey Crossick (ed.), *The Artisan and the European Town, 1500–1900* (Aldershot, UK: Scolar), 172–99.

———. 2000. "Wien und seine Handwerker im 18. Jahrhundert", in Karl Heinrich Kaufhold and Wilfried Reininghaus (eds), *Stadt und Handwerk in Mittelalter und Früher Neuzeit* (Cologne: Böhlau), 195–210.

Eisenberg, Merle, and Lee Mordechai. 2022. "The Short- and Long-Term Effects of an Early Medieval Pandemic", in Adam Izdebski, John Haldon, and Piotr Filipkowski (eds), *Perspectives on Public Policy in Societal-Environmental Crises: What the Future Needs from History* (Cham, Switzerland: Springer International), 291–303.

Ellis-Petersen, Hannah, and Shaik Azizur Rahman. 2020. "Coronavirus Conspiracy Theories Targeting Muslims Spread in India", *Guardian*, 13 April 13 2020. https://www.theguardian .com/world/2020/apr/13/coronavirus-conspiracy-theories-targeting-muslims-spread -in-india.

Eriksen, Anne. 2013. "Cure or Protection? The Meaning of Smallpox Inoculation, ca. 1750–1775", *Medical History*, 57: 516–36.

Ermus, Cindy. 2020. "When Bubonic Plague Hit France in 1720, Officials Dithered. Sound Famil-iar?", *Stat News*, 25 May 2020. https://www.statnews.com/2020/05/25/bubonic-plague -outbreak-1720-france-officials-dithered-sound-familiar/.

Esfandiary, Helen. 2023. "'A Thankless Enterprise': Lady Mary Wortley Montagu's Campaign to Establish Medical Unorthodoxy amongst Her Female Network", *Notes and Records: the Royal Society Journal of the History of Science*, 77: 235–50.

Esteves i Perendreu, Francesc. 1996. "Ordinacions de la confraria i collegi de doctors en medicina i mestres en cirurgia de Lleida (26 d'abril de 1600)", *Gimbernat* 26: 73–93.

Evans, James P., and Michael S. Watson. 2015. "Genetic Testing and FDA Regulation: Over-regulation Threatens the Emergence of Genomic Medicine", *Journal of the American Medical Association*, 313: 669–70.

Evans, Richard J. 1992. "Epidemics and Revolutions: Cholera in Nineteenth-Century Europe", in Paul Slack and Terence Ranger (eds), *Epidemics and Ideas: Essays on the Historical Perception of Pestilence* (Cambridge: Cambridge University Press), 149–74.

Ewing, E. Thomas. 2021. "The Ispanka in Historical Context: The 1918 Influenza Epidemic in the Soviet Union", in Guy Beiner (ed.), *Pandemic Re-awakenings: The Forgotten and Unforgotten "Spanish" Flu of 1918–1919* (Oxford: Oxford University Press), 244–57.

Fabbri, Christiane Nockels. 2007. "Treating Medieval Plague: The Wonderful Virtues of Theriac", *Early Science and Medicine*, 12: 247–83.

Fabretti, A. 1850. "Brevi annali della città di Perugia dal 1194 al 1352", *Archivio storico Italiano*, 16: 53–68.

Falck, Ludwig. 1975. "Das Mainzer Zunftwesen im Mittelalter", in Alfons Schäfer (ed.), *Ober-rheinische Studien*, vol. 3, *Festschrift für Günther Haselier aus Anlaß seines 60. Geburtstages am 19. April 1974* (Karlsruhe, Germany: Braun-Verlag), 267–88.

Farzanegan, Mohammad Reza, and Hans Philipp Hofmann. 2021. "A Matter of Trust? Political Trust and the COVID-19 Pandemic", CESifo Working Paper no. 9121.

Favereau, Marie. 2021. *The Horde: How the Mongols Changed the World* (Cambridge, MA: Belknap Press of Harvard University Press).

Fenn, Elizabeth A. 2000. "Biological Warfare in Eighteenth-Century North America: Beyond Jeffery Amherst", *Journal of American History*, 86: 1552–80.

Fenner, Frank. 1988. *Smallpox and Its Eradication* (Geneva: World Health Organization).

Ferragud i Domingo, Carmel. 2002. "Els professionals de la medicina (fisics, cirurgians, apotecaris, barbers i menescals) a la Corona d'Aragó després de la Pesta Negra (1350–1410): Activitat econòmica, politica i social", PhD dissertation, University of Valencia.

Ferrari, Luisa. 2020. "Spanish Flu in Turin as Told by Historical Autopsy Reports", *Pathologica— Journal of the Italian Society of Anatomic Pathology and Diagnostic Cytopathology*, 112: 110–14.

Ferrie, Joseph P., and Werner Troesken. 2008. "Water and Chicago's Mortality Transition, 1850–1925", *Explorations in Economic History*, 45: 1–16.

Fetzer, Thiemo. 2022. "Subsidising the Spread of COVID-19: Evidence from the UK's Eat-Out-to-Help-Out Scheme", *Economic Journal*, 132: 1200–17.

Few, Martha. 2015. *For All of Humanity: Mesoamerican and Colonial Medicine in Enlightenment Guatemala* (Tuscon: University of Arizona Press).

Field, John. 2008. *Social Capital* (London: Routledge).

Fifield, Anna. 2020. "Africans in China Allege Racism as Fear of New Virus Cases Unleashes Xenophobia", *Washington Post*, 13 April 2020. https://www.washingtonpost.com/world/asia _pacific/africans-in-china-allege-racism-as-fear-of-new-virus-cases-unleashes-xenophobia /2020/04/13/7f606cd8-7d26-11ea-84c2-0792d8591911_story.html.

Fildes, Valerie A. 1986. *Breasts, Bottles and Babies: A History of Infant Feeding* (Edinburgh: Edinburgh University Press).

Finlay, Roger. 1981. *Population and Metropolis: The Demography of London 1580–1650* (Cambridge: Cambridge University Press).

Finley, Theresa, and Mark Koyama. 2018. "Plague, Politics, and Pogroms: The Black Death, the Rule of Law, and the Persecution of Jews in the Holy Roman Empire", *Journal of Law and Economics*, 61: 253–77.

Fleck-Derderian, Shannon, et al. 2020. "Plague during Pregnancy: A Systematic Review", *Clinical Infectious Diseases*, 70: S30–6.

Flecknoe, Daniel, Benjamin Charles Wakefield, and Aidan Simmons. 2018. "Plagues & Wars: The 'Spanish Flu' Pandemic as a Lesson from History", *Medicine, Conflict and Survival*, 34: 61–8.

Føllesdal, Andreas. 1998. "Survey Article: Subsidiarity", *Journal of Political Philosophy*, 6: 190–218.

Foreman-Peck, James, and Peng Zhou. 2018. "Late Marriage as a Contributor to the Industrial Revolution in England", *Economic History Review*, 71: 1073–99.

Forman, Rebecca, Soleil Shah, Patrick Jeurissen, Mark Jit, and Elias Mossialos. 2021. "COVID-19 Vaccine Challenges: What Have We Learned So Far and What Remains to Be Done?", *Health Policy*, 125: 553–67.

Fors, Hjalmar. 2016. "Medicine and the Making of a City: Spaces of Pharmacy and Scholarly Medicine in Seventeenth-Century Stockholm", *Isis*, 107: 473–94.

Forsythe, Eliza, Lisa B. Kahn, Fabian Lange, and David Wiczer. 2020. "Labor Demand in the Time of COVID-19: Evidence from Vacancy Postings and UI Claims", *Journal of Public Economics*, 189: 1–7.

France, Reginald Sharpe. 1938. "A History of Plague in Lancashire", *Transactions of the Historic Society of Lancashire*, 90: 1–175.

Francke, Marc, and Matthijs Korevaar. 2021. "Housing Markets in a Pandemic: Evidence from Historical Outbreaks", *Journal of Urban Economics*, 123: 103333.

Franco-Paredes, Carlos, Lorena Lammoglia, and José Ignacio Santos-Preciado. 2005. "The Spanish Royal Philanthropic Expedition to Bring Smallpox Vaccination to the New World and Asia in the 19th Century", *Clinical Infectious Diseases*, 41: 1285–9.

Frandsen, Karl-Erik. 2010. *The Last Plague in the Baltic Region, 1709–1713* (Copenhagen: Museum Tusculanum).

Frank, Johann Peter. 1779–1827. *System einer vollständigen medicinischen Polizey*, 9 vols (Mannheim, Germany: C. F. Schwan).

Fraser, Christophe, et al. 2011. "Influenza Transmission in Households during the 1918 Pandemic", *American Journal of Epidemiology*, 174: 505–14.

Freckelton, Ian. 2020. "COVID-19: Fear, Quackery, False Representations and the Law", *International Journal of Law and Psychiatry*, 72: 101611.

Fredriksen, Paula. 2006. "Christians in the Roman Empire in the First Three Centuries CE", in D. S. Potter (ed.), *A Companion to the Roman Empire* (Oxford: Blackwell), 587–606.

Freire Costa, Leonor, Antonio Henriques, and Nuno Palma. 2022. "Anatomy of a Premodern State", University of Manchester Economics Discussion Paper Series no. EDP-2208.

Frieden, Nancy M. 1977. "The Russian Cholera Epidemic, 1892–93, and Medical Professionalization", *Journal of Social History*, 10: 538–59.

Frost, Peter. 2017. "The Hajnal Line and Gene-Culture Coevolution in Northwest Europe", *Advances in Anthropology*, 7: 154–74.

Fry, Richard, Jeffrey S. Passel, and D'Vera Cohn. 2020. "A Majority of Young Adults in the U.S. Live with Their Parents for the First Time since the Great Depression", Pew Research Center, Short Reads, 4 September 2020. https://pewrsr.ch/351SVsl.

Fukuyama, Francis. 1999. *The Great Disruption: Human Nature and the Reconstitution of Social Order* (London: Profile Books).

———. 2020. "The Thing That Determines a Country's Resistance to the Coronavirus", *Atlantic*, 30 March 2020. https://www.theatlantic.com/ideas/archive/2020/03/thing-determines-how -well-countries-respond-coronavirus/609025/.

Fuleihan, Christina. 2022. "Shattering the Mirage: The FDA's Early COVID-19 Pandemic Response Demonstrates a Need for Reform to Restore Agency Credibility", *American Journal of Law and Medicine*, 48: 307–42.

Fusco, Idamaria. 2017. "The Importance of Prevention and Institutions: Governing the Emergency in the 1690–92 Plague Epidemic in the Kingdom of Naples", *Annales de démographie historique*, 134: 95–123.

Gajurel, K., and S. Deresinski. 2021. "A Review of Infectious Diseases Associated with Religious and Nonreligious Rituals", *Interdisciplinary Perspectives on Infectious Diseases*, 2021: 1823957.

Gallagher, Daphne E., and Stephen A. Dueppen. 2018. "Recognizing Plague Epidemics in the Archaeological Record of West Africa", *Afriques*, 09. https://doi.org/10.4000/afriques.2198.

Gallardo-Albarrán, Daniel. 2020. "Sanitary Infrastructures and the Decline of Mortality in Germany, 1877–1913", *Economic History Review*, 73: 730–57.

Galletta, Sergio, and Tommaso Giommoni. 2020. "The Effect of the 1918 Influenza Pandemic on Income Inequality: Evidence from Italy", SSRN Working Paper no. 3634793.

Galley, Chris. 1995. "A Model of Early Modern Urban Demography", *Economic History Review*, 48: 448–69.

Gambetta, Diego. 1988. "Can We Trust Trust?", in Diego Gambetta (ed.), *Trust: Making and Breaking Cooperative Relations* (Oxford: Blackwell), 213–37.

Gao, J., and P. Zhang. 2021. "China's Public Health Policies in Response to COVID-19: From an 'Authoritarian' Perspective", *Front Public Health*, 9: 756677.

García-Ballester, Luis, Michael R. Mcvaugh, and Agustia Rubio-Vela. 1989. "Medical Licensing and Learning in Fourteenth-Century Valencia", *Transactions of the American Philosophical Society*, 79 (6): i–vii, 1–128.

Garfias, Francisco, and Emily A. Sellars. 2020. "Epidemics, Rent Extraction, and the Value of Holding Office", *Journal of Political Institutions and Political Economy*, 1: 559–83.

Garnel, Rita. 2014. "Disease and Public Health (Portugal)", in Ute Daniel et al. (eds), *1914–1918 Online: International Encyclopedia of the First World War*, issued by Freie Universität Berlin, Berlin, 1 November 2014. https://doi.org/10.15463/ie1418.10494.

Gasquet, Francis Aidan Cardinal. 1908. *The Black Death of 1348 and 1349* (London: G. Bell).

Gelfand, Toby. 1993. "The History of the Medical Profession", in W. F. Bynum and Roy Porter (eds), *Companion Encyclopedia of the History of Medicine* (Abingdon, UK: Routledge), 1119–50.

Gelman, Andrew. 2020. "Positive Claims Get Publicity, Refutations Do Not: Evidence from the 2020 Flu", *Statistical Modeling, Causal Inference, and Social Science Blogroll*, 6 May 2020. https://statmodeling.stat.columbia.edu/2020/05/06/theyre-not-looking-for-a-needle-in-a -haystack-theyre-looking-for-a-needle-in-a-pile-of-needles/.

Geloso, Vincent, Kelly Hyde, and Ilia Murtazashvili. 2022. "Pandemics, Economic Freedom, and Institutional Trade-Offs", *European Journal of Law and Economics*, 54: 37–61.

Geloso, Vincent, and Michael Makovi. 2022. "State Capacity and the Post Office: Evidence from Nineteenth Century Quebec", *Journal of Government and Economics*, 5: 100035.

Geloso, Vincent J., and Alexander W. Salter. 2020. "State Capacity and Economic Development: Causal Mechanism or Correlative Filter?", *Journal of Economic Behavior & Organization*, 170: 372–85.

Geltner, Guy. 2020. "The Path to Pistoia: Urban Hygiene before the Black Death", *Past & Present*, 246: 3–33.

Gentilcore, David. 1995. "'Charlatans, Mountebanks and Other Similar People': The Regulation and Role of Itinerant Practitioners in Early Modern Italy", *Social History*, 20: 297–314.

———. 2012. "Purging Filth: Plague and Responses to It in Rome, 1656-7", in Mark Bradley (ed.), *Rome, Pollution and Propriety: Dirt, Disease and Hygiene in the Eternal City from Antiquity to Modernity* (Cambridge: Cambridge University Press), 153–68.

Gestoso Singer, Graciela. 2017. "Beyond Amarna: The 'Hand of Nergal' and the Plague in the Levant", *Ugarit Forschungen: Internationales Jahrbuch für die Altertumskunde Syrien-Palästinas*, 48: 223–47.

Gieringer, D. H. 1985. "The Safety and Efficacy of New Drug Approval", *Cato Journal*, 5: 177–201.

Gilligan, M., J. J. Suitor, M. Rurka, and M. Silverstein. 2020. "Multigenerational Social Support in the Face of the COVID-19 Pandemic", *Journal of Family Theory & Review*, 12: 431–47.

Glatter, Kathryn A., and Paul Finkelman. 2021. "History of the Plague: An Ancient Pandemic for the Age of COVID-19", *American Journal of Medicine*, 134: 176–81.

Glick, Thomas F. 1972. "Muhtasib and Mustasaf: A Case Study of Institutional Diffusion", *Viator*, 2: 59–82.

Goh, Robbie B. H. 2021. "Protestant Evangelical Pilgrimages: Hagiography, Supernatural Influence, and Spiritual Mapping", *Journal of Cultural Geography*, 38: 1–27.

Goldberg, P.J.P. 1991. "The Public and the Private: Women in the Pre-plague Economy", in P. R. Coss and S. D. Lloyd (eds), *Thirteenth Century England III: Proceedings of the Newcastle-Upon-Tyne Conference 1989* (Woodbridge, UK: Boydell), 75–89.

Gómez-Díaz, Donato. 2008. "Cholera before the Pandemics", in Joseph P. Byrne (ed.), *Encyclopedia of Pestilence, Pandemics, and Plagues* (Westport, CT: Greenwood), 95–96.

Gooday, A. F. 1853. "The Royal College of Physicians and the Cholera", *Lancet*, 62: 513–14.

Good Law Project. 2023. "We Need Your Help to Ensure the GMC Delivers on Its Main Obligation—to Protect the Public", Crowdfunder, accessed 30 July 2023. https://actions.goodlawproject.org/gmc.

Goolsbee, Austan, and Chad Syverson. 2020. "Fear, Lockdown, and Diversion: Comparing Drivers of Pandemic Economic Decline", NBER Working Paper no. 27432.

Gorsky, Martin, Bernard Harris, Patricia Marsh, and Ida Milne. 2021. "The 1918/19 Influenza Pandemic and COVID-19 in Ireland and the UK", *Historical Social Research*, supplement, 33: 193–226.

Gottfried, Robert Steven. 1983. *The Black Death: Natural and Human Disaster in Medieval Europe* (London: Robert Hale).

Göttmann, Frank. 1977. *Handwerk und Bündnispolitik: Die Handwerkerbünde am Mittelrhein vom 14. bis zum 17. Jahrhundert* (Wiesbaden, Germany: Steiner).

Gottschang, Thomas R., and Diana Lary. 2020. *Swallows and Settlers: The Great Migration from North China to Manchuria* (Ann Arbor: University of Michigan Press).

Gotuzzo, Eduardo, and Carlos Seas. 2012. "Cholera and Other Vibrio Infections", in Lee Goldman and Andrew I. Schafer (eds), *Goldman's Cecil Medicine*, 24th ed. (Philadelphia, PA: W. B. Saunders), 1865–8.

Grabowski, H., J. Vernon, and J. A. DiMasi. 2002. "Returns on Research and Development for 1990s New Drug Introductions", *Pharmacoeconomics*, 20 (suppl. 3): 11–29.

Grabowski, H. G., J. M. Vernon, and L. G. Thomas. 1978. "Estimating the Effects of Regulation on Innovation: An International Comparative Analysis of the Pharmaceutical Industry", *Journal of Law & Economics*, 21: 133–63.

Gramlich-Oka, Bettina. 2009. "The Body Economic: Japan's Cholera Epidemic of 1858 in Popular Discourse", *East Asian Science, Technology, and Medicine*, 30: 32–73.

Grant, Alicia. 2019. *Globalisation of Variolation: The Overlooked Origins of Immunity for Smallpox in the 18th Century* (Hackensack, NJ: World Scientific).

Graunt, John. 1662. *Natural and Political Observations Made upon the Bills of Mortality* (London: Thomas Roycroft).

Green, Andrew. 2020. "Li Wenliang", *Lancet*, 395: 682.

Green, Monica H. 2018. "Putting Africa on the Black Death Map: Narratives from Genetics and History", *Afriques*, 09. https://doi.org/10.4000/afriques.2125.

———. 2020. "The Four Black Deaths", *American Historical Review*, 125: 1601–31.

Greenough, Paul R. 1980. "Variolation and Vaccination in South Asia, c. 1700–1865: A Preliminary Note", *Social Science & Medicine, Part D: Medical Geography*, 14: 345–7.

Greer, Scott L., et al. (eds). 2022. *Everything You Always Wanted to Know about European Union Health Policies but Were Afraid to Ask*, 3rd, rev. ed. (Copenhagen: European Observatory on Health Systems and Policies).

Greif, Avner. 2006. "Family Structure, Institutions, and Growth: The Origins and Implications of Western Corporations", *American Economic Review: Papers and Proceedings*, 96: 308–12.

Greif, Avner, and Guido Tabellini. 2010. "Cultural and Institutional Bifurcation: China and Europe Compared", *American Economic Review: Papers and Proceedings*, 100: 135–40.

Grindal, E. 1843. *The Remains of Edmund Grindal: Successively Bishop of London and Archbishop of York and Canterbury*, edited by W. Nicholson (Cambridge: Cambridge University Press).

Gross, Dominik. 1999. *Die Aufhebung des Wundarztberufs: Ursachen, Begleitumstande und Auswirkungen am Beispiel des Konigreichs Württemberg (1806–1918)* (Stuttgart: Steiner).

Gründer, Johann W. Ludwig. 1859. *Geschichte der Chirurgie von den Urzeiten bis zu Anfang des achtzehnten Jahrhunderts* (Breslau, [Poland]: Trewendt et Granier).

Gubert, Vladislav. 1896. *Ospa i ospoprivivanīe* (Saint Petersburg: Tip. P. P. Soĭkina).

Guiteras, Raymond P., et al. 2016. "Disgust, Shame, and Soapy Water: Tests of Novel Interventions to Promote Safe Water and Hygiene", *Journal of the Association of Environmental and Resource Economists*, 3: 321–59.

Gupta, Sumedha, et al. 2020. "Effects of Social Distancing Policy on Labor Market Outcomes", NBER Working Paper no. 27280.

Guterres, António. 2021. "Secretary-General's Statement to the Global Health Summit [as delivered]". United Nations, 21 May 2021. https://www.un.org/sg/en/content/sg/statement/2021-05-21/secretary-generals-statement-the-global-health-summit-delivered.

Guy, John R. 1982. "The Episcopal Licensing of Physicians, Surgeons and Midwives", *Bulletin of the History of Medicine*, 56: 528–42.

Haider, Najmul, et al. 2022. "The Global Case-Fatality Rate of COVID-19 Has Been Declining Disproportionately between Top Vaccinated Countries and the Rest of the World", medRxiv: 2022.01.19.22269493.

Hajnal, John. 1965. "European Marriage Patterns in Perspective", in D. V. Glass and D.E.C. Eversley (eds), *Population in History: Essays in Historical Demography* (London: Arnold), 101–43.

———. 1982. "Two Kinds of Preindustrial Household Formation System", *Population and Development Review*, 8: 449–94.

———. 1983. "Two Kinds of Pre-industrial Household Formation System", in Richard Wall, Jean Robin, and Peter Laslett (eds), *Family Forms in Historic Europe* (Cambridge: Cambridge University Press), 65–104.

Hakes, Nicholas A., Jeff Choi, David A. Spain, and Joseph D. Forrester. 2020. "Lessons from Epidemics, Pandemics, and Surgery", *Journal of the American College of Surgeons*, 231: 770–6.

Haldon, John, et al. 2018. "Plagues, Climate Change, and the End of an Empire. A Response to Kyle Harper's *The Fate of Rome* (2): Plagues and a Crisis of Empire", *History Compass*, 16: e12506.

Hallam, H. E. 1985. "Age at First Marriage and Age at Death in the Lincolnshire Fenland, 1252–1478", *Population Studies*, 39: 55–69.

Hamadeh, Shirine. 2017. "Invisible City: Istanbul's Migrants and the Politics of Space", *Eighteenth-Century Studies*, 50: 173–93.

Hammer-Luza, Elke. 2021. "'Lässt nicht impfen': Widerstände gegen die Vakzination in der Steiermark in der ersten Hälfte des 19. Jahrhunderts", *Virus—Beiträge zur Sozialgeschichte der Medizin*, 20: 101–30.

Hampton, Kathryn, Michele Heisler, Cynthia Pompa, and Alana Slavin. 2021. *Neither Safety Nor Health: How Title 42 Expulsions Harm Health and Violate Rights*, Physicians for Human Rights Report, July 2021. https://phr.org/wp-content/uploads/2021/07/PHR-Report-United-States -Title-42-Asylum-Expulsions-July-2021.pdf.pdf.

Hanson, Marta E. 2011. *Speaking of Epidemics in Chinese Medicine: Disease and the Geographic Imagination in Late Imperial China* (Abingdon, UK: Routledge).

Hardy, Anne. 1984. "Water and the Search for Public Health in London in the Eighteenth and Nineteenth Centuries", *Medical History*, 28: 250–82.

———. 1993. *The Epidemic Streets: Infectious Diseases and the Rise of Preventive Medicine 1856–1900* (Oxford: Oxford University Press).

Harper, Kyle. 2017. *The Fate of Rome: Climate, Disease, and the End of an Empire* (Princeton, NJ: Princeton University Press).

———. 2021. *Plagues upon the Earth: Disease and the Course of Human History* (Princeton, NJ: Princeton University Press).

Harris, James J. 2018. "H1N1 in the 'A1 Empire': Pandemic Influenza, Military Medicine, and the British Transition from War to Peace, 1918–1920", *Social History of Medicine*, 33: 604–21.

Harrison, Henrietta. 2015. "The Experience of Illness in Early Twentieth-Century Rural Shanxi", *East Asian Science, Technology, and Medicine*, 42: 39–72.

Harrison, Mark. 1992. "Quarantine, Pilgrimage, and Colonial Trade: India 1866–1900", *Indian Economic & Social History Review*, 29: 117–44.

———. 2012. *Contagion: How Commerce Has Spread Disease* (New Haven, CT: Yale University Press).

———. 2020. "A Dreadful Scourge: Cholera in Early Nineteenth-Century India", *Modern Asian Studies*, 54: 502–53.

Harvey, Gideon. 1696. *A Treatise of the Small-Pox and Measles: Describing Their Nature, Causes, and Signs, Diagnostick and Prognostick, in a Different Way to What Hath Hitherto Been Known* (London: W. Freeman).

Hasselgren, P. O. 2020. "The Smallpox Epidemics in America in the 1700s and the Role of the Surgeons: Lessons to Be Learned during the Global Outbreak of COVID-19", *World Journal of Surgery*, 44: 2837–41.

Hassett, Daniel E. 2003. "Smallpox Infections during Pregnancy: Lessons on Pathogenesis from Nonpregnant Animal Models of Infection", *Journal of Reproductive Immunology*, 60: 13–24.

Hatchett, Richard J., Carter E. Mecher, and Marc Lipsitch. 2007. "Public Health Interventions and Epidemic Intensity during the 1918 Influenza Pandemic", *Proceedings of the National Academy of Sciences of the USA*, 104: 7582–7.

Hatekar, Neeraj. 2003. "Farmers and Markets in the Pre-colonial Deccan: The Plausibility of Economic Growth in Traditional Society", *Past & Present*, 178: 116–47.

Haugland, Håkon. 2015. "'To Help the Deceased Guild Brother to His Grave': Guilds, Death and Funeral Arrangements in Late Medieval and Early Modern Norway, ca. 1300–1900", in Mia

Korpiola and Anu Lahtinen (eds), *Cultures of Death and Dying in Medieval and Early Modern Europe* (Helsinki: Helsinki Collegium for Advanced Studies), 152–83.

Hayden, Frederick G. 2012. "Influenza", in Lee Goldman and Andrew I. Schafer (eds), *Goldman's Cecil Medicine*, 24th ed. (Philadelphia, PA: W. B. Saunders), 2095–100.

Heckscher, Eli F. (1931) 1994. *Mercantilism* (London: Allen and Unwin).

Heffner, L. 1864. *Über die Baderzunft im Mittelalter und später, besonders in Franken* (Würzburg, Germany: Thein).

Heinrich, Torsten. 2021. "Epidemics in Modern Economies", MPRA Munich Personal RePEc Archive, paper no. 107578. https://mpra.ub.uni-muenchen.de/107578/.

Henderson, John. 1989. "Charity in Late-Medieval Florence: The Role of the Religious Confraternities", in Gian Carlo Garfagnini and Craig Hugh Smyth (eds), *Florence and Milan: Comparisons and Relations. Acts of Two Conferences at Villa I Tatti in 1982–1984* (Florence: Nuova Italia), 147–63.

———. 1992. "The Black Death in Florence: Medical and Communal Reactions", in Steven Bassett (ed.), *Death in Towns: Urban Responses to the Dying and the Dead, 100–1600* (Leicester, UK: Leicester University Press), 136–50.

———. 2006. *The Renaissance Hospital: Healing the Body and Healing the Soul* (New Haven, CT: Yale University Press).

———. 2019. *Florence under Siege: Surviving Plague in an Early Modern City* (New Haven, CT: Yale University Press).

———. 2020. "The Invisible Enemy: Fighting the Plague in Early Modern Italy", *Centaurus*, 62: 263–74.

Henley, Jon. 2020. "Fauci Apologises after Implied Criticism of UK's 'Rushed' COVID Vaccine Approval", *Guardian*, 4 December 2020. https://www.theguardian.com/world/2020/dec/04/anthony-fauci-apologises-for-implied-criticism-of-speedy-uk-vaccine-approval.

Henrich, Joseph Patrick. 2020. *The WEIRDest People in the World: How the West Became Psychologically Peculiar and Particularly Prosperous* (London: Allen Lane).

Henry, John. 2010. "Religion and the Scientific Revolution", in Peter Harrison (ed.), *The Cambridge Companion to Science and Religion* (Cambridge: Cambridge University Press), 39–58.

Henry, Todd A. 2005. "Sanitizing Empire: Japanese Articulations of Korean Otherness and the Construction of Early Colonial Seoul, 1905–1919", *Journal of Asian Studies*, 64: 639–75.

Herbert, Eugenia W. 1975. "Smallpox Inoculation in Africa", *Journal of African History*, 16: 539–59.

Herlihy, D. 1974. *The Family in Renaissance Italy* (St Charles, MO: Forum).

Herlihy, David, and Christiane Klapisch-Zuber. 1985. *Tuscans and Their Families: A Study of the Florentine Catasto of 1427* (New Haven, CT: Yale University Press).

Hernández, Pedro. 1802. *Orígen y descumbrimiento de la vaccina / traducido del frances con arreglo a las ultimas observaciones hechas hasta el mes de mayo de 801, y enriquecido con varias notas*, 2nd ed. (Madrid: B. Garcia).

Hilts, P. J. 2004. *Protecting America's Health: The FDA, Business, and One Hundred Years of Regulation* (Chapel Hill: University of North Carolina Press).

Hoffman, Philip T. 2015. "What Do States Do? Politics and Economic History", *Journal of Economic History*, 75: 303–32.

Holasová, Martina. 2005. "Každodenní život městského obyvatelstva za časů morové epidemie v 16. a 17. století (České Budějovice 1680)", *Historicka demografie*, 29: 5–28.

Hong, Y. J., and S. H. Park. 2017. "Medical Care or Disciplinary Discourses? Preventive Measures against the Black Death in Late Medieval Paris: A Brief Review", *Iran Journal of Public Health*, 46: 286–92.

Honigsbaum, Mark. 2013. "Regulating the 1918–19 Pandemic: Flu, Stoicism and the Northcliffe Press", *Medical History*, 57: 165–85.

———. 2019. *The Pandemic Century: One Hundred Years of Panic, Hysteria and Hubris* (London: Hurst).

Horn, Maurycy. 1993. "The Chronology and Distribution of Jewish Craft Guilds in Old Poland, 1613–1795", in Antony Polonsky, Jakub Basista, and Andrzej Link-Lenczowski (eds), *The Jews in Old Poland, 1000–1795* (London: I. B. Tauris), 249–66.

Horrox, Rosemary. 1994. *The Black Death* (Manchester: Manchester University Press).

Hotez, P. J. 2001. "Vaccines as Instruments of Foreign Policy: The New Vaccines for Tropical Infectious Diseases May Have Unanticipated Uses beyond Fighting Diseases", *EMBO Reports*, 2: 862–8.

———. 2014. "'Vaccine Diplomacy': Historical Perspectives and Future Directions", *PLOS Neglected Tropical Diseases*, 8: e2808.

Hotez, Peter J., and K. M. Venkat Narayan. 2021. "Restoring Vaccine Diplomacy", *Journal of the American Medical Association*, 325: 2337–8.

Hu, Cheng. 2010. "Quarantine Sovereignty during the Pneumonic Plague in Northeast China (November 1910–April 1911)", *Frontiers of History in China*, 5: 294–339.

Huang, Yanzhong. 2004. "The SARS Epidemic and Its Aftermath in China: A Political Perspective", in Stacey Knobler et al. (eds), *Learning from SARS: Preparing for the Next Disease Outbreak. Workshop Summary* (Washington, DC: National Academies), 116–36.

Huber, B. Rose. 2021. "A Better Understanding of 'Wet Markets' Is Key to Safeguarding Human Health and Biodiversity", Princeton University, News, 11 June 2021. https://www.princeton.edu/news/2021/06/11/better-understanding-wet-markets-key-safeguarding-human-health-and-biodiversity.

Huerkamp, Claudia. 1985. "The History of Smallpox Vaccination in Germany: A First Step in the Medicalization of the General Public", *Journal of Contemporary History*, 20: 617–35.

Huisman, Frank. 1989. "Itinerant Medical Practitioners in the Dutch Republic: The Case of Groningen", *Tractrix: Yearbook for the History of Science*, 1: 63–83.

Hull, Charles Henry. 1899. Introduction to Hull (ed.), *The Economic Writings of Sir William Petty: Together with the Observations upon the Bills of Mortality* (Cambridge: Cambridge University Press), lxxx–xci.

Human Rights Watch. 2020. "Cuba: COVID-19 Rules Used to Intensify Repression", Human Rights Watch, 7 December 2020. https://www.hrw.org/news/2020/12/07/cuba-covid-19-rules-used-intensify-repression.

———. 2023. *Human Rights Watch World Report 2023: Events of 2022* (New York: Human Rights Watch).

Hybel, Nils. 2002. "The Grain Trade in Northern Europe before 1350", *Economic History Review*, 55: 219–47.

Hybel, Nils, and Bjorn Poulsen. 2007. *The Danish Resources c. 1000–1550: Growth and Recession* (Leiden, Netherlands: Brill).

IFRC (International Federation of the Red Cross). 2022. "Plague: Disease Tool", IFRC Epidemic Control Toolkit, 16 June 2022. https://epidemics.ifrc.org/manager/disease/plague.

Imperato, Pascal James, and Gavin H. Imperato. 2014. "Smallpox Inoculation (Variolation) in East Africa with Special Reference to the Practice among the Boran and Gabra of Northern Kenya", *Journal of Community Health*, 39: 1053–62.

Jacques, David. 1992. *Essential to the Pracktick Part of Phisick: The London Apothecaries 1540–1617* (London: Worshipful Society of Apothecaries of London; San Francisco: Academia.edu). https://www.academia.edu/42797865/ESSENTIAL_TO_THE_PRACKTICK_PART_OF_PHISICK_The_London_Apothecaries_1540_1617.

Jannetta, Ann Bowman. 1987. *Epidemics and Mortality in Early Modern Japan* (Princeton, NJ: Princeton University Press).

Jarral, Farrah. 2016. "No Scrubs: How Women Had to Fight to Become Doctors", *Guardian*, 26 September 2016.

Jecker, Nancy S., and Caesar A. Atuire. 2021. "What's Yours Is Ours: Waiving Intellectual Property Protections for COVID-19 Vaccines", *Journal of Medical Ethics*, 47: 595–98.

Jedwab, Remi, Noel D. Johnson, and Mark Koyama. 2019. "Negative Shocks and Mass Persecutions: Evidence from the Black Death", *Journal of Economic Growth*, 24: 345–95.

Jedwab, Remi, Amjad M. Khan, Jason Russ, and Esha D. Zaveri. 2021. "Epidemics, Pandemics, and Social Conflict: Lessons from the Past and Possible Scenarios for COVID-19", *World Development*, 147: 105629.

Jegede, A. S. 2007. "What Led to the Nigerian Boycott of the Polio Vaccination Campaign?", *PLOS Medicine*, 4: e73.

Jenner, Mark S. R., and Patrick Wallis. 2007. "The Medical Marketplace", in Jenner and Wallis (eds), *Medicine and the Market in England and Its Colonies, c. 1450–c. 1850* (London: Palgrave Macmillan), 1–23.

Jensen, Lotte. 2023. "Cultural Resilience during Nineteenth-Century Cholera Outbreaks in the Netherlands", in Asperen Hanneke and Jensen (eds), *Dealing with Disasters from Early Modern to Modern Times* (Amsterdam: Amsterdam University Press), 121–36.

Jetter, Dieter. 1970. "Das Isolierungsprinzip in der Pestbekämpfung des 17. Jahrhunderts", *Medizinhistorisches Journal*, 5: 115–24.

Jit, Mark, et al. 2021. "Multi-country Collaboration in Responding to Global Infectious Disease Threats: Lessons for Europe from the COVID-19 Pandemic", *Lancet Regional Health—Europe*, 9: 100221.

Johansen, Mads Ilebekk. 2019. "To What Extent Was Milan Affected by the Black Death from 1348–1350?", prize-winning extended essay in Research Council of Norway essay competition, Kristiansand Cathedral School. https://www.forskningsradet.no/siteassets/unge-forskere/oppgaver-2020/ilebekk-johansen-mads.pdf.

Johnson, Noel D., and Mark Koyama. 2017. "States and Economic Growth: Capacity and Constraints", *Explorations in Economic History*, 64: 1–20.

Johnson, N. P., and J. Mueller. 2002. "Updating the Accounts: Global Mortality of the 1918–1920 'Spanish' Influenza Pandemic", *Bulletin of the History of Medicine*, 76: 105–15.

Johnson, Terence James. 1972. *Professions and Power* (London: Macmillan).

Joinville, Jean, Natalis de Wailly, and René Hague. 1955. *The Life of St. Louis* (London: Sheed and Ward).

Jones, Eric L. 1981. *The European Miracle: Environments, Economies, and Geopolitics in the History of Europe and Asia* (Cambridge: Cambridge University Press).

Juncker, Johann Christian Wilhelm. 1792–96. *Gemeinnützige Vorschläge und Nachrichten über das beste Verhalten der Menschen in Rücksicht der Pockenkrankheit: Erster Versuch für die mittlern Stände nebst einem Anhange für Aerzte* (Halle, Germany: H. Hahn).

Kacki, Sacha. 2020. "Black Death: Cultures in Crisis", in C. Smith (ed.), *Encyclopedia of Global Archaeology* (Cham, Switzerland: Springer International), 1–12.

Kaiserlichen Gesundheitsamte. 1888. "Die Regelung des Impfwesens in den neun älteren Provinzen Preußens bis zum Jahre 1874", in Kaiserlichen Gesundheitsamte (ed.), *Beiträge zur Beurtheilung des Nutzens der Schutzpockenimpfung nebst Mittheilungen über Maßregeln zur Beschaffung untadeliger Thierlymphe* (Berlin: Springer Berlin Heidelberg), 100–19.

Kaitin, Kenneth I., and Jeffrey S. Brown. 1995. "A Drug Lag Update", *Drug Information Journal*, 29: 361–73.

Kaitin, Kenneth I., Nancy Mattison, Frances K. Northington, and Louis Lasagna. 1989. "The Drug Lag: An Update of New Drug Introductions in the United States and in the United Kingdom, 1977 through 1987", *Clinical Pharmacology & Therapeutics*, 46: 121–38.

Kampfner, John. 2021. "Vaccine Competition May Now Be the World's Best Bet", *Chatham House Newsletter*, 30 June 2021. https://www.chathamhouse.org/2021/06/vaccine-competition-may -now-be-worlds-best-bet.

Kanbur, Ravi. 2001. "Cross-Border Externalities, International Public Goods and Their Implications for Aid Agencies", Department of Applied Economics and Management Cornell University Working Paper no. WP 2001-03.

Kaniewski, David, and Nick Marriner. 2020. "Conflicts and the Spread of Plagues in Pre-industrial Europe", *Humanities and Social Sciences Communications*, 7: 1–10.

Karaman, K. Kivanç, and Şevket Pamuk. 2010. "Ottoman State Finances in European Perspective, 1500–1914", *Journal of Economic History*, 70: 593–629.

Kettering, Sharon. 2001. *French Society 1589–1715* (Harlow, UK: Longman).

Kibre, Pearl. 1953. "The Faculty of Medicine at Paris, Charlatanism, and Unlicensed Medical Practices in the Later Middle Ages", *Bulletin of the History of Medicine*, 27: 1–20.

Kim, Min Joo, and Simon Denyer. 2020. "South Korea Is Doing 10,000 Coronavirus Tests a Day. The US Is Struggling for Even a Small Fraction of That", *Washington Post*, 13 March 2020: https://www.washingtonpost.com/world/asia_pacific/coronavirus-test-kits-south-korea-us /2020/03/13/007f14fc-64a1-11ea-8a8e-5c5336b32760_story.html.

Kim, S. Y., D. M. Yoo, C. Min, and H. G. Choi. 2021. "The Effects of Income Level on Susceptibility to COVID-19 and COVID-19 Morbidity/Mortality: A Nationwide Cohort Study in South Korea", *Journal of Clinical Medicine*, 10: 4733.

King, W. G. 1902. "The Introduction of Vaccination into India", *Indian Medical Gazette*, 37: 413–14.

Kinglake, Alexander William. 1844. *Eōthen, or Traces of Travel Brought Home from the East* (London: J. Ollivier).

Kiser, Edgar, and Steven M. Karceski. 2017. "Political Economy of Taxation", *Annual Review of Political Science*, 20: 75–92.

Klapisch, Christiane. 1972. "Household and Family in Tuscany in 1427", in Peter Laslett and Richard Wall (eds), *Household and Family in Past Times* (Cambridge: Cambridge University Press), 267–82.

Klebs, Arnold C. 1914. *Die Variolation im achtzehnten Jahrhundert. Ein historischer Beitrag zur Immunitätsforschung* (Berlin: De Gruyter).

Kleiner, Morris M. 2000. "Occupational Licensing", *Journal of Economic Perspectives*, 14: 189–202.

Kluge, Arnd. 2007. *Die Zünfte* (Stuttgart: Franz Steiner).

Knodel, John E., and Etienne van de Walle. 1967. "Breast Feeding, Fertility and Infant Mortality: An Analysis of Some Early German Data", *Population Studies*, 21: 109–31.

Knox, Ellis Lee. 1984. "The Guilds of Early Modern Augsburg: A Study in Urban Institutions", PhD dissertation, University of Massachusetts Amherst.

Kohn, George C. 2007. *Encyclopedia of Plague and Pestilence: From Ancient Times to the Present* (New York: Infobase).

Kollmann, Nancy Shields. 2000. "The Principalities of Rus' in the Fourteenth Century", in Michael Jones (ed.), *The New Cambridge Medieval History*, vol. 6, *c. 1300–c. 1415* (Cambridge: Cambridge University Press), 764–94.

Koponen, Juhani. 1988. "War, Famine, and Pestilence in Late Precolonial Tanzania: A Case for a Heightened Mortality", *International Journal of African Historical Studies*, 21: 637–76.

Koren, Ore, and Anoop K. Sarbahi. 2018. "State Capacity, Insurgency, and Civil War: A Disaggregated Analysis", *International Studies Quarterly*, 62: 274–88.

Kosaka, Makoto, et al. 2021. "Delayed COVID-19 Vaccine Roll-out in Japan", *Lancet*, 397: 2334–5.

Kowalewski, Mark R. 1990. "Religious Constructions of the Aids Crisis", *Sociological Analysis*, 51: 91–6.

Kramer, Stephanie. 2020. "With Billions Confined to Their Homes Worldwide, Which Living Arrangements Are Most Common?", Pew Research Center, Short Reads, 31 March 2020. https://www.pewresearch.org/fact-tank/2020/03/31/with-billions-confined-to-their-homes -worldwide-which-living-arrangements-are-most-common/.

Kresch, Evan Plous, Molly Lipscomb, and Laura Schechter. 2020. "Externalities and Spillovers from Sanitation and Waste Management in Urban and Rural Neighborhoods", *Applied Economic Perspectives and Policy*, 42: 395–420.

Krünitz, Johann Georg. 1768. *Verzeichniß der vornehmsten Schriften von den Kinderpocken und deren Einpfropfung* (Leipzig: Christian Gottlob Hilschern).

Krylova, Olga, and David J. D. Earn. 2019. "Patterns of Smallpox Mortality in London, England, over Three Centuries", bioRxiv preprint, bioRxiv:771220.

Kübler, Paul. 1901. *Geschichte der Pocken und der Impfung* (Berlin: Hirschwald).

Kuhnke, LaVerne. 1990. *Lives at Risk: Public Health in Nineteenth-Century Egypt* (Berkeley: University of California Press).

Kuronen, Jarmo, and Jarmo Heikkinen. 2019. "Barber-Surgeons in Military Surgery and Occupational Health in Finland, 1324–1944", *Military Medicine*, 184: 14–21.

Lacey, Stephen W. 1995. "Cholera: Calamitous Past, Ominous Future", *Clinical Infectious Diseases*, 20: 1409–19.

Ladero Quesada, Miguel Ángel. 1967. *Castilla y la conquista del Reino de Granada* (Valladolid, Spain: Editorial Sever-Cuesta).

Lahariya, C. 2014. "A Brief History of Vaccines & Vaccination in India", *Indian Journal of Medical Research*, 139: 491–511.

Lambring, Christoffer Briggs, et al. 2019. "Impact of the Microbiome on the Immune System", *Critical Reviews in Immunology*, 39: 313–28.

Lammel, Hans-Uwe. 2021. "Westeuropäische Wahrnehmung von und Vorstellungen über Seuchen in Osteuropa, dem Osmanischen Reich und dem Nahen Osten, 1650 bis 1800", *Saeculum*, 71: 79–110.

La Mottraye, Aubry de. 1723. *A. De La Motraye's Travels through Europe, Asia, and into Part of Africa* (London: printed for the author).

Landolt, Oliver. 2012. "'Ein mercklicher unerhörter grusamer sterbend.' Die Pest und ihre Auswirkungen im Länderort Schwyz im Spätmittelalter und in der Frühen Neuzeit", *Mitteilungen des Historischen Vereins des Kantons Schwyz*, 104: 43–75.

Laslett, Peter. 1977. "Characteristics of the Western Family Considered over Time", *Journal of Family History*, 2: 89–116.

———. 1988a. "The European Family and Early Industrialization", in Jean Baechler, John A. Hall, and Michael Mann (eds), *Europe and the Rise of Capitalism* (Oxford: Blackwell), 234–42.

———. 1988b. "Family, Kinship and Collectivity as Systems of Support in Preindustrial Europe: A Consideration of the 'Nuclear-Hardship' Hypothesis", *Continuity and Change*, 3: 153–76.

Laslett, Peter, and Richard Wall (eds). 1972. *Household and Family in Past Times* (Cambridge: Cambridge University Press).

Leadbeater, Rosemary. 2020. "'I Think It Highly Necessary to Have It Done before They Go out into the World': Inoculation, Responsibility and Patterns of Familial Transmission of Smallpox", *Local Population Studies*, 105: 37–46.

Leavitt, Judith W. 1976. "Politics and Public Health: Smallpox in Milwaukee, 1894–1895", *Bulletin of the History of Medicine*, 50: 553–68.

Lebrun, François. 1971. *Les hommes et la mort en Anjou aux 17e et 18e siècle. Essai de démographie et de psychologie historiques* (Berlin: De Gruyter Mouton).

Lee, Bruce Y. 2023. "Lee County, Florida, Republican Party Passes Resolution to Ban COVID-19 Vaccines", *Forbes*, 24 February 2023.

Leeson, Peter T., M. Scott King, and Tate J. Fegley. 2020. "Regulating Quack Medicine", *Public Choice*, 182: 273–86.

Leguay, Jean-Pierre. 1981. *Un réseau urbain au moyen âge. Les villes du Duché de Bretagne aux XIVème & XVème siècles* (Paris: Maloine).

Leibniz, Gottfried Wilhelm. 1710. *Essais de Théodicée sur la bonté de Dieu, la liberté de l'homme et l'origine du mal* (Amsterdam: Isaac Troyel).

Lentin, Antony. 1974. *Voltaire and Catherine the Great: Selected Correspondence* (Cambridge: Oriental Research Partners).

Lespinasse, René de, and François Bonnardot (eds). 1879. *Le "Livre des métiers" d'Etienne Boileau* (Paris: Imprimerie Nationale).

Leung, Angela Ki Che. 1987. "Organized Medicine in Ming-Qing China: State and Private Medical Institutions in the Lower Yangzi Region", *Late Imperial China*, 8: 134–66.

———. 2008. "The Business of Vaccination in Nineteenth-Century Canton", *Late Imperial China*, 29: 7–39.

———. 2011. "'Variolation' and Vaccination in Late Imperial China, ca. 1570–1911", in Stanley A. Plotkin (ed.), *History of Vaccine Development* (New York: Springer), 5–12.

———. 2020a. "Chinese State and Society in Epidemic Governance: A Historical Perspective", *Centaurus*, 62: 257–62.

———. 2020b. "Glocalizing Medicine in the Canton–Hong Kong–Macau Region in Late Qing China", *Modern Asian Studies*, 54: 1345–66.

Liang, Qizi. 2009. *Leprosy in China: A History* (New York: Columbia University Press).

Liang, Shu Ting, Lin Ting Liang, and Joseph M. Rosen. 2021. "COVID-19: A Comparison to the 1918 Influenza and How We Can Defeat It", *Postgraduate Medical Journal*, 97: 273–4.

Lilley, Andrew, Matthew Lilley, and Gianluca Rinaldi. 2020. "Public Health Interventions and Economic Growth: Revisiting the 1918 Flu Evidence", SSRN Working Paper no. 3590008.

Lin, Bing, Madeleine L. Dietrich, Rebecca A. Senior, and David S. Wilcove. 2021. "A Better Classification of Wet Markets Is Key to Safeguarding Human Health and Biodiversity", *Lancet Planet Health*, 5: E386–94.

Lindemann, Mary. 1996. *Health and Healing in Eighteenth-Century Germany* (Baltimore, MD: Johns Hopkins University Press).

Lindert, Peter H. 1998. "Poor Relief before the Welfare State: Britain versus the Continent, 1780–1880", *European Review of Economic History*, 2: 101–40.

———. 2004. *Growing Public: Social Spending and Economic Growth since the Eighteenth Century* (Cambridge: Cambridge University Press).

———. 2021. "Social Spending and the Welfare State", in OECD (ed.), *How Was Life?*, vol. 2, *New Perspectives on Well-Being and Global Inequality since 1820* (Paris: OECD).

Lipson, Ephraim. 1915. *The Economic History of England*, vol. 1, *The Middle Ages* (London: A. and C. Black).

Litchfield, R. Burr. 2008. *Florence Ducal Capital, 1530–1630* (eBook) (New York: ACLS Humanities).

Liu, Chien-Ling. 2016. "Relocating Pastorian Medicine: Accommodation and Acclimatization of Medical Practices at the Pasteur Institutes in China, 1899–1951", PhD dissertation, University of California, Los Angeles.

Liu, Pengyu, Lisa McQuarrie, Yexuan Song, and Caroline Colijn. 2021. "Modelling the Impact of Household Size Distribution on the Transmission Dynamics of COVID-19", *Journal of the Royal Society Interface*, 18: 20210036.

Liu, Yuan, et al. 2020. "Aerodynamic Analysis of SARS-COV-2 in Two Wuhan Hospitals", *Nature*, 582: 557–60.

Livi-Bacci, Massimo. 2006. "The Depopulation of Hispanic America after the Conquest", *Population and Development Review*, 32: 199–232.

Logan, Gabriella Berti. 2003. "Women and the Practice and Teaching of Medicine in Bologna in the Eighteenth and Early Nineteenth Centuries", *Bulletin of the History of Medicine*, 77: 506–35.

Lomax, Elizabeth. 1973. "The Uses and Abuses of Opiates in Nineteenth-Century England", *Bulletin of the History of Medicine*, 47: 167–76.

Lourens, Piet, and Jan Lucassen. 2000. "'Zunftlandschaften' in den Niederlanden und im benachbarten Deutschland", in Wilfried Reininghaus (ed.), *Zunftlandschaften in Deutschland und den Niederlanden im Vergleich: Kolloquium der Historischen Kommission für Westfalen am 6. und 7. November 1997 auf Haus Welbergen* (Münster, Germany: Aschendorf), 11–43.

Low, Michael Christopher. 2008. "Empire and the Hajj: Pilgrims, Plagues, and Pan-Islam under British Surveillance, 1865–1908", *International Journal of Middle East Studies*, 40: 269–90.

Lucassen, Jan. 1987. *Migrant Labour in Europe 1600–1900: The Drift to the North Sea* (London: Croom Helm).

Lucenet, Monique. 1985. *Les grandes pestes en France* (Paris: Aubier).

Lundh, Christer. 2003. "Swedish Marriages: Customs, Legislation and Demography in the Eighteenth and Nineteenth Century", Lund Papers in Economic History no. 88.

Luscombe, Richard. 2023. "'That Decision Cost Lives': COVID Data Case Further Deflates Ron Desantis's Campaign", *Guardian*, 15 October 2023.

Lynteris, Christos. 2016. *Ethnographic Plague: Configuring Disease on the Chinese-Russian Frontier* (London: Palgrave Macmillan).

Lythgoe, Mark P., and Paul Middleton. 2021. "Comparison of COVID-19 Vaccine Approvals at the US Food and Drug Administration, European Medicines Agency, and Health Canada", *Journal of the American Medical Association Network Open*, 4: e2114531.

Ma, Jianxin, et al. 2020. "Exhaled Breath Is a Significant Source of SARS-CoV-2 Emission", medRxiv preprint, medRxiv:2020.05.31.20115154.

Macdonald, Fiona A. 1997. "Vaccination Policy of the Faculty of Physicians and Surgeons of Glasgow, 1801 to 1863", *Medical History*, 41: 291–321.

Machado, Silva Heslley. 2021. "100 Years Later, Little Has Changed in Brazil: Disinformation and Pandemic", *African Health Sciences*, 21: 1938–40.

Mackay, Ruth. 2006. *"Lazy, Improvident People": Myth and Reality in the Writing of Spanish History* (Ithaca, NY: Cornell University Press).

Mackenbach, Johan P. 2020. *A History of Population Health: Rise and Fall of Disease in Europe* (Leiden, Netherlands: Brill).

———. 2021. "The Rise and Fall of Diseases: Reflections on the History of Population Health in Europe since ca. 1700", *European Journal of Epidemiology*, 36: 1199–205.

Maehle, Andreas-Holger. 1995. "Conflicting Attitudes towards Inoculation in Enlightenment Germany", in Roy Porter (ed.), *Medicine in the Enlightenment* (Leiden, Netherlands: Brill), 198–222.

Malanima, Paolo. 1998. "Italian Cities 1300–1800: A Quantitative Approach", *Rivista di storia economica*, 2: 91–126.

Maloney, William, and Temel Taskin. 2020. "Determinants of Social Distancing and Economic Activity during COVID-19: A Global View", World Bank, Policy Research Working Paper no. 9242.

Mamelund, Svenn-Erik. 2006. "A Socially Neutral Disease? Individual Social Class, Household Wealth and Mortality from Spanish Influenza in Two Socially Contrasting Parishes in Kristiania 1918–19", *Social Science & Medicine*, 62: 923–40.

Mandić, Jelena Ilić. 2022. "The Military Frontier and Emigration Challenges in the 18th Century", in Zofia A. Brzozowska, P. Kernel, and I. Lis-Wielgosz (eds), *Migrations in the Slavic Cultural Space from the Middle Ages to the Present Day* (Lódź, Poland: Lódź University Press), 45–62.

Manguvo, Angellar, and Benford Mafuvadze. 2015. "The Impact of Traditional and Religious Practices on the Spread of Ebola in West Africa: Time for a Strategic Shift", *Pan African Medical Journal*, 22 (suppl. 1): 1–4.

March, R. J. 2021. "The FDA and the COVID-19: A Political Economy Perspective", *Southern Economic Journal*, 87: 1210–28.

Margerison, Beverley J., and Christopher J. Knüsel. 2002. "Paleodemographic Comparison of a Catastrophic and an Attritional Death Assemblage", *American Journal of Physical Anthropology*, 119: 134–143.

Marglin, Frederique Apffel. 1987. "Smallpox in Two Systems of Knowledge", WIDER Working Papers no. WP 17.

Martindale, Adam. 1845. *The Life of Adam Martindale: Written by Himself, and Now First Printed from the Original Manuscript in the British Museum*, edited by Richard Parkinson (Manchester: Chetham Society).

Marzocchi, Jérôme. 1967. "La corporation des barbiers-chirurgiens de Bastia et ses statuts de 1714", *Revue d'histoire de la pharmacie*, 192: 397–401.

Masterson, John M., et al. 2023. "Disparities in COVID-19 Disease Incidence by Income and Vaccination Coverage: 81 Communities, Los Angeles, California, July 2020–September 2021", *Morbidity and Mortality Weekly Report*, 62: 728–31.

Mather, Cotton, and Zabdiel Boylston. 1721. *Some Account of What Is Said of Inoculating or Transplanting the Small Pox. By the Learned Dr. Emanuel Timonius, and Jacobus Pylarinus. With Some Remarks Thereon. To Which Are Added, a Few Quaeries in Answer to the Scruples of Many About the Lawfulness of This Method* (Boston, [MA]: S. Gerrish).

Matsuo, Koji, et al. 2023. "Severe Maternal Morbidity and Mortality of Pregnant Patients with COVID-19 Infection during the Early Pandemic Period in the US", *Journal of the American Medical Association Network Open*, 6: e237149.

Mauelshagen, Franz. 2005. "Pestepidemien im Europa der Frühen Neuzeit", in Mischa Meier (ed.), *Pest: Geschichte eines Menschheitstraumas* (Stuttgart: Klett-Cotta), 237–65, 432.

———. 2020. "Leviathan in Crisis", *Journal for the History of Environment and Society*, 5: 125–33.

McCants, Anne E. C. 2021. "Who Is He Calling Weird?", *Journal of Interdisciplinary History*, 52: 251–61.

McCloskey, Deirdre N. 2010. *Bourgeois Dignity: Why Economics Can't Explain the Modern World* (Chicago: University of Chicago Press).

McCormick, Michael. 2003. "Rats, Communications, and Plague: Toward an Ancient and Medieval Ecological History", *Journal of Interdisciplinary History*, 34: 1–25.

McCullough, Laurence B., and Frank A. Chervenak. 2021. "The Profession of Medicine Is Secular: An Eighteenth-Century Idea with Implications for the Boundary between Medicine and Religion", *Science, Art & Religion*, 1: 57–63.

McGowan, Victoria J., and Clare Bambra. 2022. "COVID-19 Mortality and Deprivation: Pandemic, Syndemic, and Endemic Health Inequalities", *Lancet Public Health*, 7: e966–75.

McNeill, William Hardy. 1976. *Plagues and Peoples* (Garden City, NY: Anchor).

McVaugh, M. R. 1993. *Medicine before the Plague: Practitioners and Their Patients in the Crown of Aragon, 1285–1345* (Cambridge: Cambridge University Press).

Mehfooz, Musferah. 2021. "Understanding the Impact of Plague Epidemics on the Muslim Mind during the Early Medieval Period", *Religions*, 12: 1–11.

Melikishvili, Alexander. 2006. "Genesis of the Anti-plague System: The Tsarist Period", *Critical Reviews in Microbiology*, 32: 19–31.

Melling, Antoine Ignace. 1809. *Voyage pittoresque de Constantinople et des rives du Bosphore* (Paris: P. Didot, l'aine).

Mertens, Charles de. 1799. *An Account of the Plague Which Raged at Moscow, in 1771* (London: F. and C. Rivington).

Meyer, Victoria N. 2022. "Innovations from the Levant: Smallpox Inoculation and Perceptions of Scientific Medicine", *British Journal for the History of Science*, 55: 423–44.

Michaud, Francine. 2016. *Earning Dignity: Labour Conditions and Relations during the Century of the Black Death in Marseille* (Turnhout, Belgium: Brepols).

Mickwitz, Gunnar. 1936. *Die Kartellfunktionen der Zünfte und ihre Bedeutung bei der Entstehung des Zunftwesens: Eine Studie im spätantiker und mittelalterliche Wirtschaftsgeschichte* (Helsinki: Societas scientiarum Fennica).

Midura, Rachel. 2021. "Policing in Print: Social Control in Spanish and Borromean Milan (1535–1584)", in Nina Lamal, Jamie Cumby, and Helmer J. Helmers (eds), *Print and Power in Early Modern Europe (1500–1800)* (Helsingfors, Netherlands: Brill), 21–46.

Miller, Genevieve. 1957. *The Adoption of Inoculation for Smallpox in England and France* (Philadelphia: University of Pennsylvania Press).

Miller, H. I. 1988. "Failed FDA Reform", *Regulation*, 21: 24–30.

Miller, Richard J. 1978. *Japan's First Bureaucracy: A Study of Eighth-Century Government* (Ithaca, NY: Cornell University).

Mills, I. D. 1986. "The 1918–1919 Influenza Pandemic: The Indian Experience", *Indian Economic & Social History Review*, 23: 1–40.

Minsky, Lauren. 2009. "Pursuing Protection from Disease: The Making of Smallpox Prophylactic Practice in Colonial Punjab", *Bulletin of the History of Medicine*, 83: 164–90.

Mitchell, A. Wess, and Charles Ingrao. 2020. "Emperor Joseph's Solution to Coronavirus", *Wall Street Journal*, 6 April 2020. https://www.wsj.com/articles/emperor-josephs-solution-to-coronavirus-11586214561.

Mitsel'Makheris, V. G. 1960. "The Brotherhood of Vilensk Barber Surgeons (1509–1833)" [in Russian], *Vestn Khir Im I I Grek*, 85: 134–42.

Mokyr, Joel. 2002. *The Gifts of Athena: Historical Origins of the Knowledge Society* (Princeton, NJ: Princeton University Press).

———. 2005. "Useful Knowledge as an Evolving System: The View from Economic History", in Lawrence E. Blume and Steven N. Durlauf (eds), *The Economy as an Evolving Complex System*, Vol. 3, *Current Perspectives and Future Directions* (Oxford: Oxford University Press), 309–38.

Mokyr, Joel, and Guido Tabellini. 2023. "Social Organizations and Political Institutions: Why China and Europe Diverged", CEPR Discussion Papers no. DP18143.

Moll, Isabel, Pere Salas Vives, and Joana María Pujadas-Mora. 2017. "Vers une nouvelle modernité sanitaire: L'épidémie de peste de Majorque en 1820", *Annales de démographie historique*, 134: 125–49.

Montagu, Mary Wortley. 1837. *The Letters and Works of Lady Mary Wortley Montagu*, edited by James Archibald Stuart-Wortley Wharncliffe (London: R. Bentley).

Monter, E. William. 1971. "Witchcraft in Geneva, 1537–1662", *Journal of Modern History*, 43: 180–204.

Montoya-Galvez, Camilo. 2021. "Top CDC Official Told Congress Migrant Expulsion Policy Was Not Needed to Contain COVID", *CBS News*, 12 November 2021. https://www.cbsnews.com/news/cdc-official-told-congress-migrant-expulsion-policy-not-needed-to-contain-covid/.

Morabia, Alfredo. 2013. "Epidemiology's 350th Anniversary: 1662–2012", *Epidemiology*, 24: 179–83.

Mühlhoff, Katharina. 2021. "Why Covid19 Will Not Be Gone Soon: Lessons from the Institutional Economics of Smallpox Vaccination in 19th Century Germany", EHES Working Papers no. 208.

———. 2022. "Convincing the 'Herd' of Immunity: Lessons from Smallpox Vaccination in 19th Century Germany", *Economics & Human Biology*, 47: 101193.

Murdoch, Lydia. 2015. "Carrying the Pox: The Use of Children and Ideals of Childhood in Early British and Imperial Campaigns against Smallpox", *Journal of Social History*, 48: 511–35.

Murphy, Hannah. 2019. *A New Order of Medicine: The Rise of Physicians in Reformation Nuremberg* (Pittsburgh, PA: University of Pittsburgh Press).

Murphy, Neil. 2013. "Plague Ordinances and the Management of Infectious Diseases in Northern French Towns, c.1450–c.1560", in Carole Rawcliffe and Linda Clark (eds), *The Fifteenth Century*, 12, *Society in an Age of Plague* (Woodbridge, UK: Boydell and Brewer), 139–60.

Muurling, Sanne, Tim Riswick, and Katalin Buzasi. 2021. "The Last Dutch Smallpox Epidemic: Infectious Disease and Social Inequalities in Amsterdam, 1870–1872", SocArXiv Papers, last edited 25 June 2021. https://doi.org/10.31235/osf.io/szjp5.

Nair, Aparna. 2019. "Vaccinating against Vasoori: Eradicating Smallpox in the 'Model' Princely State of Travancore, 1804–1946", *Indian Economic & Social History Review*, 56: 361–86.

Nalapat, Suvarna. 2012. *Education in Ancient India: Valabhi and Nalanda Universities* (Kottayam, India: D. C. Books).

Naphy, William G., and Andrew Spicer. 2000. *The Black Death and the History of Plagues 1345–1730* (Stroud, UK: Tempus).

Nathan, Carl F. 1967. *Plague Prevention and Politics in Manchuria, 1910–1931* (Boston, MA: Harvard University Asia Center).

Naudé, Wim, and Paula Nagler. 2022. "COVID-19 and the City: Did Urbanized Countries Suffer More Fatalities?", *Cities*, 131: 103909.

Navarro, J. A. 2010. "Influenza in 1918: An Epidemic in Images", *Public Health Reports*, 125 (suppl. 3): 9–14.

Newman, Kira L. S. 2012. "Shutt Up: Bubonic Plague and Quarantine in Early Modern England", *Journal of Social History*, 45: 809–34.

Newson, Linda A. 1985. "Indian Population Patterns in Colonial Spanish America", *Latin American Research Review*, 20: 41–74.

Nicholas, David. 1995. "Child and Adolescent Labour in the Late Medieval City: A Flemish Model in Regional Perspective", *English Historical Review*, 110: 1103–31.

Nicholas, Ralph W. 1981. "The Goddess Śītalā and Epidemic Smallpox in Bengal", *Journal of Asian Studies*, 41: 21–44.

Noggler, Josef. 1936. "Die Wiener Apothekerordnungen 1564–1770", in Gesellschaft für Geschichte der Pharmazie (ed.), *Vorträge der Hauptversammlung in Stuttgart 1936* (Stuttgart), 27–46.

Noordegraaf, Leo, and Gerrit Valk. 1988. *De gave Gods: De pest in Holland vanaf de late Middeleeuwen* (Bergen, Netherlands: Octavo).

North, Douglass C. 1990. *Institutions, Institutional Change and Economic Performance* (Cambridge: Cambridge University Press).

———. 1991. "Institutions", *Journal of Economic Perspectives*, 5: 97–112.

Noy, Ilan, Toshihiro Okubo, and Eric Strobl. 2020. "The Japanese Textile Sector and the Influenza Pandemic of 1918–1920", CESifo Working Paper no. 8651.

Ober, William B., and Nabil Alloush. 1982. "The Plague at Granada, 1348–1349: Ibn Al-Khatib and Ideas of Contagion", *Bulletin of the New York Academy of Medicine*, 58: 418–24.

OECD (Organisation for Economic Co-operation and Development). 2021. *Government at a Glance 2021* (Paris: OECD).

Ogilvie, Sheilagh C. 1992. "Germany and the Seventeenth-Century Crisis", *Historical Journal*, 35: 417–41.

———. 2000. "The European Economy in the Eighteenth Century", in T.W.C. Blanning (ed.), *The Short Oxford History of Europe*, vol. 12, *The Eighteenth Century: Europe 1688–1815* (Oxford: Oxford University Press), 91–130.

———. 2001. "The Economic World of the Bohemian Serf: Economic Concepts, Preferences and Constraints on the Estate of Friedland, 1583–1692", *Economic History Review*, 54: 430–53.

———. 2003. *A Bitter Living: Women, Markets, and Social Capital in Early Modern Germany* (Oxford: Oxford University Press).

———. 2005. "The Use and Abuse of Trust: The Deployment of Social Capital by Early Modern Guilds", *Jahrbuch für Wirtschaftsgeschichte / Economic History Yearbook*, 2005: 15–52.

———. 2007. "'Whatever Is, Is Right'? Economic Institutions in Pre-industrial Europe", *Economic History Review*, 60: 649–84.

———. 2011. *Institutions and European Trade: Merchant Guilds, 1000–1800* (Cambridge: Cambridge University Press).

———. 2014a. "Choices and Constraints in the Pre-industrial Countryside", in Chris Briggs, Peter Kitson, and S. J. Thompson (eds), *Population, Welfare and Economic Change in Britain, 1290–1834* (Woodbridge, UK: Boydell and Brewer), 269–305.

———. 2014b. "The Economics of Guilds", *Journal of Economic Perspectives*, 28: 169–92.

———. 2019. *The European Guilds: An Economic Analysis* (Princeton, NJ: Princeton University Press).

———. 2021. "Thinking Carefully about Inclusiveness: Evidence from European Guilds", *Journal of Institutional Economics*, 17: 185–200.

———. 2023. "State Capacity and Economic Growth: Cautionary Tales from History", *National Institute Economic Review*, 262: 28–50.

Ogilvie, Sheilagh, and André W. Carus. 2014. "Institutions and Economic Growth in Historical Perspective", in Steven Durlauf and Philippe Aghion (eds), *Handbook of Economic Growth* (Amsterdam: Elsevier), 405–514.

Ogilvie, Sheilagh, and Jeremy Edwards. 2000. "Women and the 'Second Serfdom': Evidence from Early Modern Bohemia", *Journal of Economic History*, 60: 961–94.

Ó Gráda, Cormac. 2020. "On Plague and Ebola in a Time of COVID-19", *Investigaciones de historia economica*, 16: 10–22.

Ohadike, D. C. 1981. "The Influenza Pandemic of 1918–19 and the Spread of Cassava Cultivation on the Lower Niger: A Study in Historical Linkages", *Journal of African History*, 22: 379–91.

Ojala, Maija. 2014. "Protection, Continuity and Gender: Craft Trade Culture in the Baltic Sea Region (14th–16th Centuries)", PhD dissertation, University of Tampere.

Olberg, Franz. 1791. *Beiträge zur Litteratur der Blattern und deren Einimpfung, vom Jahre 1768 bis 1790* (Halle, Germany: J. G. Trampens Wittwe).

Olson, Kenneth R., and Edward Krug. 2020. "The Danube, an Empire Boundary River: Settlements, Invasions, Navigation, and Trade Pathway", *Journal of Water Resource and Protection*, 12: 884–97.

Omran, Abdel R. 1971. "The Epidemiologic Transition: A Theory of the Epidemiology of Population Change", *Milbank Memorial Fund Quarterly*, 49: 509–38.

Oram, Richard D. 2007. "'It Cannot He Decernit Quha Are Clean and Quha Are Foulle.' Responses to Epidemic Disease in Sixteenth- and Seventeenth-Century Scotland", *Renaissance and Reformation / Renaissance et Réforme*, 30: 13–39.

Osheim, Duane. 2012. "Plague Saints", in *Encyclopedia of Medieval Pilgrimage* (Leiden, Netherlands: Brill). https://doi.org/10.1163/2213-2139_emp_SIM_00251.

Ott, Miles, Shelly F. Shaw, Richard N. Danila, and Ruth Lynfield. 2007. "Lessons Learned from the 1918–1919 Influenza Pandemic in Minneapolis and St. Paul, Minnesota", *Public Health Reports*, 122: 803–10.

Ouin-Lacroix, C. 1850. *Histoire des anciennes corporations d'arts et métiers et des confréries religieuses de la capitale de la Normandie* (Rouen, France: Lecointe).

Outram, Quentin. 2001. "The Socio-economic Relations of Warfare and the Military Mortality Crises of the Thirty Years' War", *Medical History*, 45: 151–84.

Pagel, Christina. 2021. "There Is a Real Danger that COVID-19 Will Become Entrenched as a Disease of Poverty", *British Medical Journal*, 373: n986.

Palliser, David M. 1973. "Epidemics in Tudor York", *Northern History*, 8: 45–63.

Palmer, Richard John. 1978. "The Control of Plague in Venice and Northern Italy 1348–1600", PhD dissertation, University of Kent at Canterbury.

————. 1982. "The Church, Leprosy and Plague in Medieval and Early Modern Europe", *Studies in Church History*, 19: 79–99.

Pancier, F. 1936. "Quelques dates de l'histoire des apothicaires d'Amiens", *Revue d'histoire de la pharmacie*, 96: 410–14.

Pankhurst, Richard. 1965. "The History and Traditional Treatment of Smallpox in Ethiopia", *Medical History*, 9: 343–55.

Park, Katharine. 1985. *Doctors and Medicine in Early Renaissance Florence* (Princeton, NJ: Princeton University Press).

————. 1988. *The Military Revolution: Military Innovation and the Rise of the West 1500–1800* (Cambridge: Cambridge University Press).

Parkin, F. 1853. "The Cholera: Its Cause and Prevention", *Lancet*, 62: 422.

Parrish, Sean David. 2015. "Marketing Nature: Apothecaries, Medicinal Retailing, and Scientific Culture in Early Modern Venice, 1565–1730", PhD dissertation, Duke University.

Parry, Richard Lloyd. 2023. "North Koreans 'Sealed Off and Starved to Death in Pandemic'", *The Times*, 6 December 2023.

Pasichnyk, Kateryna. 2018. "Official Physicians within the Medical Landscape of the Russian Empire (1760s)", MA thesis, Central European University.

Patterson, K. David. 1983. "The Influenza Epidemic of 1918–19 in the Gold Coast", *Journal of African History*, 24: 485–502.

Pead, Patrick J. 2003. "Benjamin Jesty: New Light in the Dawn of Vaccination", *Lancet*, 362: 2104–9.

Pearce, Adrian J. 2001. "The Peruvian Population Census of 1725–1740", *Latin American Research Review*, 36: 69–104.

Pearce, Nathaniel. 1831. *The Life and Adventures of Nathaniel Pearce: Written by Himself, during a Residence in Abyssinia from the Years 1810 to 1819, together with Mr. Coffin's Account of His Visit to Gondar* (London: Henry Colburn and Richard Bentley).

Pellerin, J., and M. B. Edmond. 2013. "Infections Associated with Religious Rituals", *International Journal of Infectious Diseases*, 17: e945–8.

Pelling, Margaret. 2014. "Barber-Surgeons' Guilds and Ordinances in Early Modern British Towns—the Story So Far", Early Modern Practitioners, The Medical World of Early Modern England, Wales and Ireland, c.1500–1715 project, University of Exeter, Working Paper no. 1. http://practitioners.exeter.ac.uk/working-papers/.

————. 2020. "'Bosom Vipers': Endemic versus Epidemic Disease", *Centaurus*, 62: 294–301.

Peltzman, Sam. 1973. "An Evaluation of Consumer Protection Legislation: The 1962 Drug Amendments", *Journal of Political Economy*, 81: 1049–91.

Penschow, Jennifer D. 2022. *Battling Smallpox before Vaccination: Inoculation in Eighteenth-Century Germany* (Leiden, Netherlands: Brill).

Percoco, Marco. 2013. "Geography, Institutions and Urban Development: Italian Cities, 1300–1861", *Annals of Regional Science*, 50: 135–52.

Perrin, Faustine. 2022. "On the Origins of the Demographic Transition: Rethinking the European Marriage Pattern", *Cliometrica*, 16: 431–75.

Peterson, Jerome S. 1946. "Epidemiological Studies in Cholera: Secondary Attack Rate among Cholera Household Contacts, China, 1946", *Chinese Medical Journal*, 64: 285–8.

Petroff, Casey. 2023. "Essays in Political Economy", PhD dissertation, Harvard University.

Phillips, Derek L. 2008. *Well-Being in Amsterdam's Golden Age* (Amsterdam: Pallas).

Phillips, Howard. 2008. "Why Did It Happen? Religious Explanations of the 'Spanish' Flu Epidemic in South Africa", *Historically Speaking*, September/October 2008: 34–36.

Phillips, Joanna Elizabeth. 2017. "The Experience of Sickness and Health during Crusader Campaigns to the Eastern Mediterranean, 1095–1274", PhD dissertation, University of Leeds.

Phillips, Maile T., Katharine A. Owers, Bryan T. Grenfell, and Virginia E. Pitzer. 2020. "Changes in Historical Typhoid Transmission across 16 U.S. Cities, 1889–1931: Quantifying the Impact of Investments in Water and Sewer Infrastructures", *PLOS Neglected Tropical Diseases*, 14: e0008048.

Phipson, E. S. 1923. "The Pandemic of Influenza in India in the Year 1918", *Indian Medical Gazette*, 58: 509–24.

Popplow, Marcus. 2012. "Knowledge Management to Exploit Agrarian Resources as Part of Late-Eighteenth-Century Cultures of Innovation: Friedrich Casimir Medicus and Franz von Paula Schrank", *Annals of Science*, 69: 413–33.

Portas, L. 2003. "Dzieje chirirgii cyrulickiej w Rzeszowie", *Archiwum historii i filozofii medycyny*, 66: 119–33.

Porter, Elizabeth-Anne. 1998. "Medieval English Medical Practice and the Law: An Analysis of Cases", PhD dissertation, University of St Andrews.

Porter, Roy. 1985. "The Patient's View: Doing Medical History from Below", *Theory and Society*, 14: 175–98.

Poska, Allyson M. 2022. "'An Operation More Appropriate for Women': The Gendering of Small-pox Vaccination in the Spanish Empire", *Journal of Women's History*, 34: 5–25.

Prabhu, Maya. 2021. "A Deadly Alliance—War and the Pandemic Influenza of 1918", Vaccines-Work, 30 July 2021. https://www.gavi.org/vaccineswork/long-view-deadly-alliance-war-and-pandemic-influenza-1918.

Prados de la Escosura, Leandro. 2022a. "Health, Income, and the Preston Curve: A Long View", EHES Working Paper no. 224.

———. 2022b. *Human Development and the Path to Freedom: 1870 to the Present* (Cambridge: Cambridge University Press).

Preiser-Kapeller, Johannes. 2023. "Loyal Servants of the Realm or Swarms of Locusts? Mobilisa-tions of Military and Civil Labour for the Empires of Western Afroeurasia in the Aftermath of the First Plague Pandemic, Eighth–Ninth Centuries CE", Joseph C. Miller Memorial Lecture for the Bonn Center for Dependency & Slavery Studies, 6 March 2023. https://www.dependency.uni-bonn.de/en/outreach/events/joseph-c-miller-memorial-lecture-by-johannes-preiser-kapeller.

Price, George M. 1918. "Influenza—Destroyer and Teacher: A General Confession by the Public Health Authorities of a Continent", *Survey*, 41: 367–9.

Puaksom, Davisakd. 2007. "Of Germs, Public Hygiene, and the Healthy Body: The Making of the Medicalizing State in Thailand", *Journal of Asian Studies*, 66: 311–44.

Putnam, James Jackson. 1906. *A Memoir of Dr. James Jackson* (Boston, MA: Houghton Mifflin).

Putnam, Robert D. 2000. *Bowling Alone: The Collapse and Revival of American Community* (New York: Simon and Schuster).

Putnam, Robert D., Robert Leonardi, and Rafaella Y. Nanetti. 1993. *Making Democracy Work: Civic Traditions in Modern Italy* (Princeton, NJ: Princeton University Press).

Race, Philip. 1995. "Some Further Considerations of the Plague at Eyam", *Local Population Studies*, 54: 56–65.

Raithby, J. 1811. *The Statutes at Large, of England and of Great-Britain: From Magna Carta to the Union of the Kingdoms of Great Britain and Ireland* (London: G. Eyre and A. Strahan).

Rajan, Raghuram. 2019. *The Third Pillar: How Markets and the State Leave the Community Behind* (New York: Penguin Books).

———. 2021. "Communities, the State, and Markets: The Case for Inclusive Localism", *Oxford Review of Economic Policy*, 37: 811–23.

Ramírez, Paul F. 2018. *Enlightened Immunity: Mexico's Experiments with Disease Prevention in the Age of Reason* (Stanford, CA: Stanford University Press).

Ravallion, Martin. 1997. "Famines and Economics", *Journal of Economic Literature*, 35: 1205–42.

Rawcliffe, Carole. 2019. "The View from the Streets: The Records of Hundred and Leet Courts as a Source for Sanitary Policing in Late Medieval English Towns", in Rawcliffe and Claire Weeda (eds), *Policing the Urban Environment in Premodern Europe* (Amsterdam: Amsterdam University Press), 69–95.

Raynaud, Maurice. 1862. *Les médecins au temps de Molière: Moeurs, institutions, doctrines* (Paris: Didier).

Razzell, P. E. 1977. *The Conquest of Smallpox: The Impact of Inoculation on Smallpox Mortality in Eighteenth Century Britain* (London: Caliban Books).

Restifo, Giuseppe. 1992. "The Campaign against the Last European Epidemic of Plague (1743)", in *Transactions of the Eighth International Congress on the Enlightenment* (Oxford: Voltaire Foundation), 1115–18.

Reuters. 2022. "COVID Lockdown Protests Break Out in Western China after Deadly Fire", *Guardian*, 26 November 2022.

Ribeiro da Silva, Filipa, and Hélder Carvalhal. 2020. "Reconsidering the Southern European Model: Marital Status, Women's Work and Labour Relations in Mid-Eighteenth-Century Portugal", *Revista de historia económica / Journal of Iberian and Latin American Economic History*, 38: 45–77.

Riera Blanco, Manuel. 1994. "El Colegio de Medicos de Barcelona. Una extrana provision de la audiencia de Pedro IV, de 23 de Mayo de 1342", *Gimbernat*, 22: 193–222.

Risse, Guenter. 1999. *Mending Bodies, Saving Souls: A History of Hospitals* (Oxford: Oxford University Press).

Riswick, Tim, Sanne Muurling, and Katalin Buzasi. 2022. "Exploring the Mortality Advantage of Jewish Neighbourhoods in Mid-19th Century Amsterdam", *Demographic Research*, 46: 723–36.

Robarts, Andrew. 2010. "A Plague on Both Houses? Population Movements and the Spread of Disease across the Ottoman-Russian Black Sea Frontier, 1768–1830s", PhD dissertation, Georgetown University.

———. 2017. "Nowhere to Run to, Nowhere to Hide? Society, State, and Epidemic Diseases in the Early Nineteenth-Century Ottoman Balkans", in Nükhet Varlik (ed.), *Plague and Contagion in the Islamic Mediterranean: New Histories of Disease in Ottoman Society* (Leeds, UK: Arc Humanities), 221–42.

Robertson, Lesley A. 2022. "The Vanishing Link between Animalcules and Disease before the 19th Century", *FEMS Microbiology Letters*, 369: fnac022.

Robinson, Nathan. 2020. "Trump Says 'Don't Be Afraid of Covid': That's Easy for Him to Say". *Guardian*, October 6, 2020. https://www.theguardian.com/commentisfree/2020/oct/06 /trump-says-dont-be-afraid-of-covid-thats-easy-for-him-to-say.

Rodocanachi, Emmanuel. 1894. *Les corporations ouvrières à Rome depuis la chute de l'Empire romain* (Paris: A. Picard et fils).

Rodrik, Dani. 2021. "Globalisation after the Washington Consensus", in Luis Garicano (ed.), *Capitalism after COVID: Conversations with 21 Economists* (London: Center for Economic and Policy Research), 69–74.

Roehr, Bob. 2010. "Homophobia and Africa's HIV Epidemic", *British Medical Journal*, 340: 1165–8.

Rogers, Katie, Lara Jakes, and Ana Swanson. 2020. "Trump Defends Using 'Chinese Virus' Label, Ignoring Growing Criticism", *New York Times*, 18 March 2020.

Rojas, Felipe Lozano, et al. 2020. "Is the Cure Worse than the Problem Itself? Immediate Labor Market Effects of COVID-19 Case Rates and School Closures in the U.S.", NBER Working Paper no. 27127.

Rolleston, J. D. 1933. "The Smallpox Pandemic of 1870–1874: President's Address", *Journal of the Royal Society of Medicine*, 27: 177–92.

Rommes, Ronald. 2015. "Plague in Northwestern Europe: The Dutch Experience, 1350–1670", *Popolazione e storia*, 16: 47–71.

Roosen, Joris, and Daniel Curtis. 2018. "Dangers of Noncritical Use of Historical Plague Data", *Emerging Infectious Diseases*, 20: 103–10.

Rose, Colin. 2019. *A Renaissance of Violence: Homicide in Early Modern Italy* (Cambridge: Cambridge University Press).

Rosen, Mark. 2008. "The Republic at Work: S. Marco's Reliefs of the Venetian Trades", *Art Bulletin*, 90: 54–75.

Rosie, Alison. 2020. "'Stench, Corruption and Filth': The Leith Plague of 1645", *Open Book: National Records of Scotland Records and Archives* (blog), 18 June 2020. https://blog.nrscotland .gov.uk/2020/06/18/stench-corruption-and-filth-the-leith-plague-of-1645/.

Rosser, Gervase. 2015. *The Art of Solidarity in the Middle Ages: Guilds in England 1250–1550* (Oxford: Oxford University Press).

Rotermund, Hartmut O., and Royall Tyler. 2001. "Demonic Affliction or Contagious Disease? Changing Perceptions of Smallpox in the Late Edo Period", *Japanese Journal of Religious Studies*, 28: 373–98.

Roth, Cecil. 1953. "The Qualification of Jewish Physicians in the Middle Ages", *Speculum*, 28: 834–43.

Royal College of Surgeons in London. 1812. *A General List of the Members of the Royal College of Surgeons in London* (London: Royal College of Surgeons).

Rubin, Rita. 2022. "When Physicians Spread Unscientific Information about COVID-19", *Journal of the American Medical Association*, 327: 904–6.

Rue, George Michael la. 2016. "Treating Black Deaths in Egypt: Clot-Bey, African Slaves, and the Plague Epidemic of 1834–1835", in Anna Winterbottom and Facil Tesfaye (eds), *Histories of Medicine and Healing in the Indian Ocean World: The Modern Period* (New York: Palgrave Macmillan), 27–59.

Rupp, Johannes-Peter. 1975. "Die Entwicklung der Impfgesetzgebung in Hessen", *Medizinhistorisches Journal*, 10: 103–20.

Rupp, Johannes-Peter, Winfried Leist, and Jost Benedum (eds). 1974. *Hundert Jahre Impfgesetz: Ausstellung in der Universitäts-Bibliothek Gießen, 19.–26. April 1974* (Gießen, Germany: Universitätsbibliothek Gießen).

Rusnock, Andrea Alice. 2002. *Vital Accounts: Quantifying Health and Population in Eighteenth-Century England and France* (Cambridge: Cambridge University Press).

Sahgal, Neha, and Anna Schiller. 2021. "More Americans than People in Other Advanced Economies Say COVID-19 Has Strengthened Religious Faith", Pew Research Center, 27 January 2021. https://www.pewresearch.org/religion/2021/01/27/more-americans-than-people-in -other-advanced-economies-say-covid-19-has-strengthened-religious-faith/.

Saint-Exupéry, Antoine de. (1942) 1986. *Flight to Arras* (New York: Harcourt Brace).

Sample, Ian. 2020. "'Scaremongering' Ads for Face Masks Banned by UK Regulator: Advertising Authority Censures Companies That Appear to Stoke Coronavirus Fears", *Guardian*, 4 March 2020. https://www.theguardian.com/media/2020/mar/04/scaremongering-ads-for -face-masks-banned-uk-regulator-advertising-authority-coronavirus.

Sandvik, H., and J. Straand. 1996. "Fra bartskjaerlaug til legeforening. Et 400-årsjubileum", *Tidsskrift for den Norske Laegeforening*, 116: 3614–17.

Santosa, A., et al. 2014. "The Development and Experience of Epidemiological Transition Theory over Four Decades: A Systematic Review", *Global Health Action*, 7: 23574.

Sarasúa, Carmen. 2009. "Working Harder but Still Poor: The 'Industrious Revolution' in Eighteenth Century Spain", Paper presented at the 15th World Economic History Congress, Utrecht, 3–7 August 2009.

———. 2019. "Women's Work and Structural Change: Occupational Structure in Eighteenth-Century Spain", *Economic History Review*, 72: 481–509.

Sarett, Lewis H. 1974. "Impact of Regulations on Industrial R&D: FDA Regulations and Their Influence on Future R&D", *Research Management*, 17: 18–20.

Sarnowsky, Jürgen. 2015. "The 'Golden Age' of the Hanseatic League", in Donald J. Harreld (ed.), *A Companion to the Hanseatic League* (Leiden, Netherlands: Brill), 64–100.

Sarris, Peter. 2022. "New Approaches to the 'Plague of Justinian'", *Past & Present*, 254: 315–46.

Savinetsky, A. B., and O. A. Krylovich. 2011. "On the History of the Spread of the Black Rat (*Rattus rattus* L., 1758) in Northwestern Russia", *Biology Bulletin*, 38: 203–7.

Savoia, Paolo. 2019. "Skills, Knowledge, and Status: The Career of an Early Modern Italian Surgeon", *Bulletin of the History of Medicine*, 93: 27–54.

Schabel, Chris, and Fritz S. Pedersen. 2014. "Miraculous, Natural, or Jewish Conspiracy? Pierre Ceffons' Question on the Black Death, with Astrological Predictions by Gersonides and Jean de Murs / Firmin de Beauval", *Recherches de théologie et philosophie médiévales*, 81: 137–79.

Schama, Simon. 1987. *The Embarrassment of Riches: An Interpretation of Dutch Culture in the Golden Age* (London: Collins).

Scheidel, Walter. 2002. "A Model of Demographic and Economic Change in Roman Egypt after the Antonine Plague", *Journal of Roman Archaeology*, 15: 97–114.

Schepers, Rita. 1985. "The Legal and Institutional Development of the Belgian Medical Profession in the Nineteenth Century", *Sociology of Health & Illness*, 7: 314–41.

Scheutz, Martin. 2018. "Goldener Apfel, höfische Residenz und eine der Hauptstädte des Heiligen Römischen Reiches. Die Metropole Wien der Frühen Neuzeit", in Stephan Sander-Faes and Clemens Zimmermann (eds), *Weltstädte, Metropolen, Megastädte: Dynamiken von Stadt und Raum von der Antike bis zur Gegenwart* (Ostfildern, Germany: Jan Thorbecke), 111–44.

Schlenkrich, Elke. 2002. " Johann Gregor Gutturff: Vom Leben und von der Arbeit eines Pestbarbiers im 17. Jahrhundert", *Medizin, Gesellschaft und Geschichte*, 21: 23–62.

Schmelz, U. O. 1971. *Infant and Early Childhood Mortality among Jews of the Diaspora* (Jerusalem: Institute of Contemporary Jewry, Hebrew University).

Schmid, Boris V., et al. 2015. "Climate-Driven Introduction of the Black Death and Successive Plague Reintroductions into Europe", *Proceedings of the National Academy of Sciences of the USA*, 112: 3020–5.

Schnabel, Landon, and Scott Schieman. 2022. "Religion Protected Mental Health but Constrained Crisis Response during Crucial Early Days of the COVID-19 Pandemic", *Journal for the Scientific Study of Religion*, 61: 530–43.

Schneider, William H. 2009. "Smallpox in Africa during Colonial Rule", *Medical History*, 53: 193–227.

Schofield, Roger. 1977. "An Anatomy of an Epidemic: Colyton, November 1645 to November 1646", in Paul Slack (ed.), *The Plague Reconsidered: A New Look at Its Origins and Effects in 16th and 17th Century England* (Matlock, UK: Local Population Studies), 95–126.

Schulz, Jonathan F., Duman Bahrami-Rad, Jonathan P. Beauchamp, and Joseph Henrich. 2019. "The Church, Intensive Kinship, and Global Psychological Variation", *Science*, 366: eaau5141.

Schulz von Schulzenheim, David. 1767. *An Account of Inoculation for the Small-Pox* (London: J. Payne).

Schütte, Jana Madlen. 2017. *Medizin im Konflikt: Fakultäten, Märkte und Experten in deutschen Universitätsstädten des 14. bis 16. Jahrhunderts* (Leiden, Netherlands: Brill).

Schwartz, J. L. 2018. "The Spanish Flu, Epidemics, and the Turn to Biomedical Responses", *American Journal of Public Health*, 108: 1455–8.

Scott, David. 1965. *Epidemic Disease in Ghana, 1901–1960* (Oxford: Oxford University Press).

Seabright, Paul. 2024. *The Divine Economy: How Religions Compete for Wealth, Power, and People* (Princeton, NJ: Princeton University Press).

Seguino, S. 2011. "Help or Hindrance? Religion's Impact on Gender Inequality in Attitudes and Outcomes", *World Development*, 39: 1308–21.

Serikbayeva, Balzhan, Kanat Abdulla, and Yessengali Oskenbayev. 2021. "State Capacity in Responding to COVID-19", *International Journal of Public Administration*, 44: 920–30.

Shabana, Ayman. 2021. "From the Plague to the Coronavirus: Islamic Ethics and Responses to the COVID-19 Pandemic", *Journal of Islamic Ethics*, 7: 1–37.

Shah, Nayan. 2001. *Contagious Divides: Epidemics and Race in San Francisco's Chinatown* (Berkeley: University of California Press).

Shangguan, Z., M. Y. Wang, and W. Sun. 2020. "What Caused the Outbreak of COVID-19 in China: From the Perspective of Crisis Management", *International Journal of Environmental Research and Public Health*, 17: 1–16.

Sharp, Buchanan. 2016. *Famine and Scarcity in Late Medieval and Early Modern England: The Regulation of Grain Marketing, 1256–1631* (Cambridge: Cambridge University Press).

Shaw, Brent D., and Richard P. Saller. 1984. "Close-Kin Marriage in Roman Society?", *Man*, 19: 432–44.

Shefer-Mossensohn, Miri. 2011. "Communicable Disease in Ottoman Palestine: Local Thoughts and Actions", *Korot*, 21: 19–49.

Shen, Yubin. 2019. "Pneumonic Plagues, Environmental Changes, and the International Fur Trade: The Retreat of Tarbagan Marmots from Northwest Manchuria, 1900s–30s", *Frontiers of History in China*, 14: 291–322.

Shephard, Edward J. 1986. "Social and Geographic Mobility of the Eighteenth-Century Guild Artisan: An Analysis of Guild Receptions in Dijon, 1700–90", in Steven L. Kaplan and C. J. Koepp (eds), *Work in France: Representations, Meaning, Organization, and Practice* (Ithaca, NY: Cornell University Press), 97–130.

Sherstneva, E. V. 2011. "The Scientific Societies and Surgeons' Congresses in Russia: The Second-Half of XIXth–the Early XXth Centuries" [in Russian], *Problemy sotsial'noi gigieny, zdravookhraneniia i istorii meditsiny*, 4: 55–58.

Shih, Gerry. 2021. "China Turbocharges Bid to Discredit Western Vaccines, Spread Virus Conspiracy Theories", *Washington Post*, 20 January 2021. https://www.washingtonpost.com/world /asia_pacific/vaccines-coronavirus-china-conspiracy-theories/2021/01/20/89bd3d2a-5a2d -11eb-a849-6f9423a75ffd_story.html.

Shizume, Masato. 2022. "The Great Influenza Pandemic in Japan: Policy Responses and Socio-economic Consequences", *RIEB Discussion Paper Series*, Kobe University, no. DP2022–27.

Shojaei, Amirahmad, and Pooneh Salari. 2020. "COVID-19 and Off Label Use of Drugs: An Ethical Viewpoint", *DARU Journal of Pharmaceutical Sciences*, 28: 789–93.

Shoolbred, J. 1805. *Report on the Progress of Vaccine Inoculation in Bengal* (London: Blacks and Parry).

Shubinski, Barbara, and Teresa Iacobelli. 2020. "Public Health: How the Fight against Hookworm Helped Build a System", *Re:source*, 23 April 2020. https://resource.rockarch.org/story/public -health-how-the-fight-against-hookworm-helped-build-a-system/.

Sigdel, Rajesh, Gregory Carlton, and Bivek Gautam. 2023. "Resolving the Ganges Pollution Paradox: A Policy-Centric Systematic Review", *River*, 2: 126–41.

Silva, Cristobal. 2011. "Technologies of Inoculation", in Silva (ed.), *Miraculous Plagues: An Epidemiology of Early New England Narrative* (Oxford: Oxford University Press), 142–79.

Silverstein, Arthur M. 2009. *A History of Immunology* (San Diego: Elsevier Science and Technology).

Simonsen, Lone, Julia R. Gog, Don Olson, and Cécile Viboud. 2016. "Infectious Disease Surveillance in the Big Data Era: Towards Faster and Locally Relevant Systems", *Journal of Infectious Diseases*, 214: S380–5.

Sköld, Peter. 1996a. "From Inoculation to Vaccination: Smallpox in Sweden in the Eighteenth and Nineteenth Centuries", *Population Studies*, 50: 247–62.

———. 1996b. *The Two Faces of Smallpox: A Disease and Its Prevention in Eighteenth- and Nineteenth-Century Sweden*, Demographic Data Base, Umeå University, Report no. 12 (Umeå, Sweden: Umeå University).

———. 2000. "The Key to Success: The Role of Local Government in the Organization of Smallpox Vaccination in Sweden", *Medical History*, 44: 201–26.

Slack, Paul. 1985. *The Impact of Plague in Tudor and Stuart England* (London: Routledge and Kegan Paul).

———. 1986. "Metropolitan Government in Crisis: The Response to Plague", in A. L. Beier and Roger Finlay (eds), *London 1500–1700: The Making of the Metropolis* (London: Longman), 60–81.

———. 1988. "Responses to Plague in Early Modern Europe: The Implications of Public Health", *Social Research*, 55: 433–53.

Slater, Eric. 2006. "Caffa: Early Western Expansion in the Late Medieval World, 1261–1475", *Review (Fernand Braudel Center)*, 29: 271–83.

Smallman-Raynor, Matthew, and A. D. Cliff. 2004. *War Epidemics: An Historical Geography of Infectious Diseases in Military Conflict and Civil Strife, 1850–2000* (Oxford: Oxford University Press).

Smith, Adam. 1776. *An Inquiry into the Nature and Causes of the Wealth of Nations* (London: W. Strahan and T. Cadell).

Smith, B. 1998. "Camphor, Cabbage Leaves and Vaccination: The Career of Johnie 'Notions' Williamson, of Hamnavoe, Eshaness, Shetland", *Journal of the Royal College of Physicians of Edinburgh*, 28: 395–406.

Smith, Emily R., et al. 2023. "Adverse Maternal, Fetal, and Newborn Outcomes among Pregnant Women with SARS-CoV-2 Infection: An Individual Participant Data Meta-analysis", *British Medical Journal Global Health*, 8: e009495.

Smith, Pamela H. 2004. *The Body of the Artisan: Art and Experience in the Scientific Revolution* (Chicago: University of Chicago Press).

Smith, Richard M. 1979. "Some Reflections on the Evidence of the Origins of the 'European Marriage Pattern' in England", in Christopher C. Harris (ed.), *The Sociology of the Family: New Directions for Britain* (Keele, UK: University of Keele), 74–112.

———. 1983. "Hypothèses sur la nuptialité en Angleterre au XIIIe–XIVe siècles", *Annales: Economies, sociétés, civilisations*, 38: 107–36.

———. 1985. "Pre-industrial European Demographic Regimes", in Serge Ed Feld and Ron J. Lesthaeghe (eds), *Population and Societal Outlook: Agora Demography. Brussels, 26 October 1983–14 March 1984* (Brussels: Fondation Roi Baudouin), 31–49.

———. 1990a. "Monogamy, Landed Property and Demographic Regimes in Pre-industrial Europe: Regional Contrasts and Temporal Stabilities", in John Landers and Vernon Reynolds (eds), *Fertility and Resources* (Cambridge: Cambridge University Press), 164–88.

———. 1990b. "Women's Work and Marriage in Pre-industrial England: Some Speculations", in Simonetta Cavaciocchi (ed.), *La donna nell'economia secc. XIII–XVIII: Atti della "ventunesima Settimana di studi", 10–15 aprile 1989* (Prato, Italy: Istituto Francesco Datini di Prato), 31–55.

Smith, Robert S. 1936. "Barcelona 'Bills of Mortality' and Population, 1457–1590", *Journal of Political Economy*, 44: 84–93.

Smith, Thomas. 1825. *The History and Origin of the Missionary Societies*, vol. 2 (London: Thomas Kelly and Richard Evans).

Snowden, Frank M. 1995. *Naples in the Time of Cholera, 1884–1911* (Cambridge: Cambridge University Press).

———. 2019. *Epidemics and Society: From the Black Death to the Present* (New Haven, CT: Yale University Press).

Sobel, Joel. 2002. "Can We Trust Social Capital?", *Journal of Economic Literature*, 40: 139–54.

Söderberg, Johan, Ulf Jonsson, and Christer Persson. 1991. *A Stagnating Metropolis: The Economy and Demography of Stockholm, 1750–1850* (Cambridge: Cambridge University Press).

Solar, Peter M. 1995. "Poor Relief and English Economic Development before the Industrial Revolution", *Economic History Review*, 48: 1–22.

Song, Huai-Dong, et al. 2005. "Cross-Host Evolution of Severe Acute Respiratory Syndrome Coronavirus in Palm Civet and Human", *Proceedings of the National Academy of Sciences of the USA*, 102: 2430–5.

Spector, Benjamin. 1952. "The Growth of Medicine and the Letter of the Law", *Bulletin of the History of Medicine*, 26: 499–525.

Spreeuwenberg, Peter, Madelon Kroneman, and John Paget. 2018. "Reassessing the Global Mortality Burden of the 1918 Influenza Pandemic", *American Journal of Epidemiology*, 187: 2561–7.

Srivastava, Kalpana, Suprakash Chaudhry, A. V. Sowmya, and Jyoti Prakash. 2020. "Mental Health Aspects of Pandemics with Special Reference to COVID-19", *Industrial Psychiatry Journal*, 29: 1–8.

Stathakopoulos, Dionysios. 2007. "To Have and to Have Not: Supply and Shortage in the Centres of the Late Antique World", in Michael Grünbart, Ewald Kislinger, Anna Muthesius, and Dionysios C. Stathakopoulos (eds), *Material Culture and Well-Being in Byzantium (400–1453): Proceedings of the International Conference (Cambridge, 8–10 September 2001)* (Vienna: Verlag der Österreichischen Akademie der Wissenschaften), 211–17.

Statista. 2018. "Number of Smallpox Deaths per Million Inhabitants in Belgium, the Netherlands, Italy and Hungary from 1851 to 1900", Statista, accessed 18 May 2024. https://www.statista.com/statistics/1107421/smallpox-death-rate-european-historical/.

Stearns, Justin. 2009. "New Directions in the Study of Religious Responses to the Black Death", *History Compass*, 7: 1363–75.

Stevens Crawshaw, Jane L. 2012. *Plague Hospitals: Public Health for the City in Early Modern Venice* (Abingdon, UK: Routledge).

Stevenson, William Henry, et al. (eds). 1899. *Records of the Borough of Nottingham: Being a Series of Extracts from the Archives of the Corporation of Nottingham*, vol. 4 (London: Quaritch).

Strauss, George. 1963. "Professionalism and Occupational Associations", *Industrial Relations: A Journal of Economy and Society*, 2: 7–31.

Stuart, Kathy. 1999. *Defiled Trades and Social Outcasts: Honor and Ritual Pollution in Early Modern Germany* (Cambridge: Cambridge University Press).

Sung, H., et al. 2020. "Preparedness and Rapid Implementation of External Quality Assessment Helped Quickly Increase COVID-19 Testing Capacity in the Republic of Korea", *Clinical Chemistry*, 66: 979–81.

Suryanarayan, Pavithra. 2021. "State Capacity: A Useful Concept or Meaningless Pablum?", *Broadstreet Blog*, 12 April 2021. https://broadstreet.blog/2021/04/12/state-capacity-a-useful-concept-or-meaningless-pablum/.

Süßmilch, Johann Peter. 1761. *Die göttliche Ordnung in den Veränderungen des menschlichen Geschlechts, aus der Geburt, dem Tode und der Fortpflanzung desselben* (Berlin: Im Verlag des Buchladens der Realschule).

Sutherland, Ian. 1963. "John Graunt: A Tercentenary Tribute", *Journal of the Royal Statistical Society: Series A (General)*, 126: 537–56.

Sydenstricker, Edgar. 1931. "The Incidence of Influenza among Persons of Different Economic Status during the Epidemic of 1918", *Public Health Reports*, 121 (suppl 1): 191–204.

Szołtysek, Mikołaj, Sebastian Klüsener, Radosław Poniat, and Siegfried Gruber. 2017. "The Patriarchy Index: A New Measure of Gender and Generational Inequalities in the Past", *Cross-Cultural Research*, 51: 228–62.

Szreter, Simon. 1997. "Economic Growth, Disruption, Deprivation, Disease, and Death: On the Importance of the Politics of Public Health for Development", *Population and Development Review*, 23: 693–728.

Tabarrok, Alex. 2017. "Discussion: The FDA Is Unprepared for Personalized Medicine", *Biostatistics*, 18: 403–4.

Tahir, Darius. 2022. "Medical Boards Get Pushback as They Try to Punish Doctors for COVID Misinformation", *Politico Magazine*, 2 January 2022.

Taubenberger, Jeffery K., and David M. Morens. 2006. "1918 Influenza: The Mother of All Pandemics", *Emerging Infectious Diseases*, 12: 15–22.

Taylor, Louise H., Sophia M. Latham, and Mark E. J. Woolhouse. 2001. "Risk Factors for Human Disease Emergence", *Philosophical Transactions of the Royal Society of London, Series B: Biological Sciences*, 356: 983–9.

Temin, Peter. 2004a. "Financial Intermediation in the Early Roman Empire", *Journal of Economic History*, 64: 705–33.

———. 2004b. "The Labor Market of the Early Roman Empire", *Journal of Interdisciplinary History*, 34: 513–38.

Thacker, Stephen B, and Donna F. Stroup. 2013. "Origins and Progress in Surveillance Systems", in Ruth Lynfield, Chris A. van Beneden, Nkuchia M. M'ikanatha, and Henriette de Valk (eds), *Infectious Disease Surveillance* (Chichester, UK: John Wiley and Sons), 21–31.

Thomas, A., et al. 2021. "COVID-19: The Role of the Royal College of Physicians of Edinburgh", *Journal of the Royal College of Physicians of Edinburgh*, 51: S7–11.

Thomas, Mark Roland, et al. 2015. "The Economic Impact of Ebola on Sub-Saharan Africa: Updated Estimates for 2015", World Bank Working Paper no. 93721. https://documents .worldbank.org/en/publication/documents-reports/documentdetail/541991468001792719 /the-economic-impact-of-ebola-on-sub-saharan-africa-updated-estimates-for-2015.

Thorndike, Lynn. 1975. *University Records and Life in the Middle Ages* (New York: W. W. Norton).

Thorvaldsen, Gunnar. 2008. "Was There a European Breastfeeding Pattern?", *History of the Family*, 13: 283–95.

Tilly, Charles. 1990. *Coercion, Capital, and European States, A.D. 990–1990* (Oxford: Blackwell).

Tomes, Nancy. 2010. "'Destroyer and Teacher': Managing the Masses During the 1918–1919 Influenza Pandemic", *Public Health Reports*, 125: 48–62.

Torres Sánchez, Rafael. 2007. "Possibilities and Limits: Testing the Fiscal-Military State in the Anglo-Spanish War of 1779–1783", in Torres Sánchez (ed.), *War, State and Development: Fiscal-Military States in the Eighteenth Century* (Pamplona: Ediciones Universidad de Navarra), 437–60.

Toshkov, Dimiter. 2023. "Explaining the Gender Gap in COVID-19 Vaccination Attitudes", *European Journal of Public Health*, 33: 490–5.

Townsend, Joy, Katie Greenland, and Val Curtis. 2017. "Costs of Diarrhoea and Acute Respiratory Infection Attributable to Not Handwashing: The Cases of India and China", *Tropical Medicine & International Health*, 22: 74–81.

Trepavlov, Vadim V. 2018. "The Takht Eli Khanate: The State System at the Twilight of the Golden Horde", *Revue des mondes musulmans et de la Méditerranée*, 143. https://doi.org/10.4000 /remmm.11177.

Triggle, Nick, Aurelia Foster, and Jim Reed. 2023. "COVID Inquiry: First Lockdown Imposed a Bit Too Late—Whitty", *BBC News*, 21 November 2023. https://www.bbc.co.uk/news/health -67484656.

Troesken, Werner. 2015. *The Pox of Liberty: How the Constitution Left Americans Rich, Free, and Prone to Infection* (Chicago: University of Chicago Press).

Tronrud, Thorold John. 1985. "The Response to Poverty in Three English Towns, 1560–1640: A Comparative Approach", *Histoire sociale—Social History*, 18: 9–27.

Tulchinsky, Theodore H. 2018. "John Snow, Cholera, the Broad Street Pump: Waterborne Diseases Then and Now", *Case Studies in Public Health*, 2018: 77–99.

Tumbe, Chinmay. 2020. *The Age of Pandemics (1817–1920): How They Shaped India and the World* (Noida, India: HarperCollins India).

Tuszewicki, Marek. 2021. *A Frog under the Tongue: Jewish Folk Medicine in Eastern Europe* (London: Liverpool University Press).

Tymms, Samuel. 1853. "Notes towards a Medical History of Bury", *Proceedings of the Bury & West Suffolk Archaeological Institute*, 1: 33–49.

Udale, Charles. 2023. "Evaluating Early Modern Lockdowns: Household Quarantine in Bristol, 1565–1604", *Economic History Review*, 76: 118–44.

Underwood, E. A. 1948. "The History of Cholera in Great Britain", *Proceedings of the Royal Society of Medicine*, 41: 165–73.

Upenieks, Laura, Joanne Ford-Robertson, and James E. Robertson. 2022. "Trust in God and/or Science? Sociodemographic Differences in the Effects of Beliefs in an Engaged God and Mistrust of the COVID-19 Vaccine", *Journal of Religion and Health*, 61: 657–86.

US Attorney's Office, District of Utah. 2023. "Utah Doctor and Co-defendants Charged for Running a COVID-19 Vaccine Scheme to Defraud the Government and CDC", press release, 18 January 2023. https://www.justice.gov/usao-ut/pr/utah-doctor-and-co-defendants-charged-running-covid-19-vaccine-scheme-defraud-government.

Van Bavel, Bas J. P., and Oscar Gelderblom. 2009. "The Economic Origins of Cleanliness in the Dutch Golden Age", *Past & Present*, 205: 41–69.

Van Bavel, Bas J. P., and Auke Rijpma. 2016. "How Important Were Formalized Charity and Social Spending before the Rise of the Welfare State? A Long-Run Analysis of Selected Western European Cases, 1400–1850", *Economic History Review*, 69: 159–87.

Vanneste, Sarah Frances. 2010. "The Black Death and the Future of Medicine", MA thesis, Wayne State University.

Van Nijf, O. M. 1997. *The Civic World of Professional Associations in the Roman East* (Leiden, Netherlands: Brill).

Van Oosten, Roos. 2016. "The Dutch Great Stink: The End of the Cesspit Era in the Pre-industrial Towns of Leiden and Haarlem", *European Journal of Archaeology*, 19: 704–27.

Van Steenbergen, Jo. 2003. "The Alexandrian Crusade (1365) and the Mamluk Sources: Reassessment of the Kitab Al-Ilmam of an-Nuwayri Al-'Iskandarani (d. 1372 AD)", in K. Ciggaar and H.G.B. Teule (eds), *East and West in the Crusader States: Context—Contacts—Confrontations*, vol. 3 of *Acta of the Congress Held at Hernen Castle in September 2000* (Leuven, Belgium: Orientalia Lovaniensia Analecta), 123–37.

Van Steensel, Arie. 2016. "Guild Solidarity and Charity in Florence, Ghent and London, c. 1300–1550", ACUH Working Paper Series in Urban History no. 3.

Van Zanden, Jan Luiten, Sarah Carmichael, and Tine De Moor (eds). 2019. *Capital Women: The European Marriage Pattern, Female Empowerment and Economic Development in Western Europe 1300–1800* (Oxford: Oxford University Press).

Varlik, Nükhet. 2015. *Plague and Empire in the Early Modern Mediterranean World: The Ottoman Experience, 1347–1600* (Cambridge: Cambridge University Press).

Velimirovic, Boris, and Helga Velimirovic. 1989. "Plague in Vienna", *Reviews of Infectious Diseases*, 11: 808–26.

Vialls, Christine Mary. 1999. "The Laws of Settlement: Their Impact on the Poor Inhabitants of the Daventry Area of Northamptonshire, 1750–1834", PhD dissertation, University of Leicester.

Viazzo, Pier Paolo. 2003. "What's So Special about the Mediterranean? Thirty Years of Research on Household and Family in Italy", *Continuity and Change*, 18: 111–37.

Victoria County History. 2003. "Early Modern Chester 1550–1762: Demography", in C. P. Lewis and A. T. Thacker (eds), *A History of the County of Chester*, vol. 5, pt 1, *The City of Chester: General History and Topography* (London: Victoria County History), 90–7.

Vista Agenzia Televisiva Nazionale. 2020. "Zaia. I cinesi li abbiamo visti tutti mangiare topi vivi." YouTube, February 28, 2020. https://www.youtube.com/watch?v=YXEYddVR6kY.

Voigtländer, Nico, and Hans-Joachim Voth. 2013. "How the West 'Invented' Fertility Restriction", *American Economic Review*, 103: 2227–64.

Vollrath, Dietrich. 2019. "The Deep Roots of Development, Part 4", *Growth Economics Blog*, 17 March 2019. https://growthecon.com/feed/2019/03/17/Deep-Roots-4.html.

Wakley, T. 1853. Editorial, *Lancet*, 22: 393–4.

Walhout, Evelien C. 2010. "Is Breast Best? Evaluating Breastfeeding Patterns and Causes of Infant Death in a Dutch Province in the Period 1875–1900", *History of the Family*, 15: 76–90.

Walker, Brett L. 1999. "The Early Modern Japanese State and Ainu Vaccinations: Redefining the Body Politic 1799–1868", *Past & Present*, 163: 121–60.

Wallis, Patrick. 2002. "Controlling Commodities: Search and Reconciliation in Early Modern Livery Companies", in Ian A. Gadd and Wallis (eds), *Guilds, Society, and Economy in London, 1450–1800* (London: Centre for Metropolitan History), 85–100.

———. 2006. "A Dreadful Heritage: Interpreting Epidemic Disease at Eyam, 1666–2000", *History Workshop Journal*, no. 61: 31–56.

———. 2020. "Eyam Revisited: Lessons from a Plague Village", *1843 Magazine*, 16 April 2020.

Wang, Han, and Andrés Rodríguez-Pose. 2021. "Local Institutions and Pandemics: City Autonomy and the Black Death", *Applied Geography*, 136: 102582.

Ward, Thomas Joseph. 2003. *Black Physicians in the Jim Crow South* (Fayetteville: University of Arkansas Press).

Washington, Harriet A., et al. 2009. "Segregation, Civil Rights, and Health Disparities: The Legacy of African American Physicians and Organized Medicine, 1910–1968", *Journal of the National Medical Association*, 101: 513–27.

Weber, Max. 1920. *Gesammelte Aufsätze zur Religionssoziologie* (Tübingen, Germany: J.C.B. Mohr [Paul Siebeck]).

———. (1922) 1978. *Economy and Society: An Outline of Interpretive Sociology*, Edited by Guenther Roth, Claus Wittich, and Ephraim Fischoff. (Berkeley: University of California Press).

Weiner, Gordon M. 1970. "The Demographic Effects of the Venetian Plagues of 1575–77 and 1630–31", *Genus*, 26: 41–57.

Wesoly, Kurt. 1985. *Lehrlinge und Handwerksgesellen am Mittelrhein. Ihre soziale Lage und ihre Organisation vom 14. bis ins 17. Jahrhundert* (Frankfurt am Main: Kramer).

Wheelis, Mark. 2002. "Biological Warfare at the 1346 Siege of Caffa", *Emerging Infectious Diseases*, 8: 971–5.

Whelan, Edward. 2012. "The Guilds of Dublin and Immigrants in the Seventeenth Century: The Defence of Privilege in an Age of Change", *Irish Economic and Social History*, 39: 26–38.

White, Alexandre I. R. 2018. "Global Risks, Divergent Pandemics: Contrasting Responses to Bubonic Plague and Smallpox in 1901 Cape Town", *Social Science History*, 42: 135–58.

White, Michael. 2020. "Los testamentos de Timoteo O'Scanlan (1723–1795): Testimonio de un médico militar irlandés en la España del siglo XVIII", *Cuadernos de estudios del siglo XVIII*, 30: 773–97.

White, Sam. 2010. "Rethinking Disease in Ottoman History", *International Journal of Middle East Studies*, 42: 549–67.

Whitteridge, Gweneth. 1977. "Some Italian Precursors of the Royal College of Physicians", *Journal of the Royal College of Physicians*, 12: 67–80.

Whittles, Lilith K., and Xavier Didelot. 2016. "Epidemiological Analysis of the Eyam Plague Outbreak of 1665–1666", *Proceedings: Biological Sciences*, 283: 20160618.

Wickham, C. 2023. *The Donkey and the Boat: Reinterpreting the Mediterranean Economy, 950–1180* (Oxford: Oxford University Press).

Wieser, Florian. 2023. "The Ten Plagues of the New World: The Sensemaking of Epidemic Depopulation in Sixteenth-Century Mesoamerica", in Asperen Hanneke and Jensen Lotte (eds), *Dealing with Disasters from Early Modern to Modern Times* (Amsterdam: Amsterdam University Press), 157–76.

Wiggins, Steven N. 1981. "Product Quality Regulation and New Drug Introductions: Some New Evidence from the 1970s", *Review of Economics and Statistics*, 63: 615–19.

Williams, Gareth. 2010. *Angel of Death: The Story of Smallpox* (Basingstoke, UK: Palgrave Macmillan).

Williamson, Jeffrey G. 2010. "Five Centuries of Latin American Income Inequality", *Revista de historia económica / Journal of Iberian and Latin American Economic History*, 28: 227–52.

Williamson, Stanley. 2007. *The Vaccination Controversy: The Rise, Reign and Fall of Compulsory Vaccination for Smallpox* (Liverpool: Liverpool University Press).

Wilson, Edward. 1853. "Contagiousness of Cholera", *Lancet*, 62: 422.

Wilson, Nick, Stephen Corbett, and Euan Tovey. 2020. "Airborne Transmission of COVID-19", *British Medical Journal*, 370: m3206.

Wilson, Peter H. 2008. "Dynasty, Constitution, and Confession: The Role of Religion in the Thirty Years War", *International History Review*, 30: 473–514.

———. 2019. *The Thirty Years War: Europe's Tragedy* (Cambridge, MA: Harvard University Press).

Wing, Kevin, et al. 2022. "Association between Household Composition and Severe COVID-19 Outcomes in Older People by Ethnicity: An Observational Cohort Study Using the Opensafely Platform", *International Journal of Epidemiology*, 51: 1745–60.

Wischnitzer, Mark. 1928. "Die jüdische Zunftverfassung in Polen und Litauen im 17. und 18. Jahrhundert", *Vierteljahrschrift für Sozial- und Wirtschaftsgeschichte*, 20: 433–51.

Wolff, Eberhard. 1998. *Einschneidende Maßnahmen: Pockenschutzimpfung und traditionale Gesellschaft im Württemberg des frühen 19. Jahrhunderts* (Stuttgart: Franz Steiner).

Woods, Robert. 2007. "Ancient and Early Modern Mortality: Experience and Understanding", *Economic History Review*, 60: 373–99.

World Health Organization. 2008. *Interregional Meeting on Prevention and Control of Plague: Antananarivo, Madagascar, 1–11 April 2006* (Geneva: World Health Organization).

Wrightson, Keith. 2011. *Ralph Tailor's Summer: A Scrivener, His City, and the Plague* (New Haven, CT: Yale University Press).

Wyżga, Mateusz. 2022. "Women's Labour Migration and Serfdom in the Polish–Lithuanian Commonwealth (Sixteenth to Eighteenth Centuries)", in Beatrice Zucca Micheletto (ed.), *Gender and Migration in Historical Perspective: Institutions, Labour and Social Networks, 16th to 20th Centuries* (Basingstoke, UK: Palgrave Macmillan), 175–213.

Yolun, Murat, and Metin Kopar. 2015. "The Impact of the Spanish Influenza on the Ottoman Empire", *Belleten*, 79: 1099–120.

Yongdan, Lobsang. 2021. "Misdiagnosis or Political Assassination? Re-examining the Death of Panchen Lama Lobsang Palden Yeshe from Smallpox in 1780", *Revue d'études tibétaines*, 58: 60–80.

Young, Sera L. 2011. *Craving Earth: Understanding Pica—the Urge to Eat Clay, Starch, Ice, and Chalk* (New York: Columbia University Press).

Yue, Ricci P. H., Harry F. Lee, and Connor Y. H. Wu. 2016. "Navigable Rivers Facilitated the Spread and Recurrence of Plague in Pre-industrial Europe", *Scientific Reports*, 6: 34867.

Zaneri, Taylor, and Guy Geltner. 2022. "The Dynamics of Healthscaping: Mapping Communal Hygiene in Bologna, 1287–1383", *Urban History*, 49: 2–27.

Zhang, Shuxian, et al. 2020. "COVID-19 Containment: China Provides Important Lessons for Global Response", *Frontiers of Medicine*, 14: 215–19.

Zhang, Zhiming, and Dinah Gardner. 2023. *Families in Fear: Collective Punishment in 21st Century China* (Madrid: Safeguard Defenders).

Zintel, Stephanie, et al. 2023. "Gender Differences in the Intention to Get Vaccinated against COVID-19: A Systematic Review and Meta-analysis", *Journal of Public Health*, 31: 1303–27.

Zucca Micheletto, Beatrice. 2011. "Reconsidering the Southern Europe Model: Dowry, Women's Work and Marriage Patterns in Pre-industrial Urban Italy (Turin, Second Half of the 18th Century)", *History of the Family*, 16: 354–70.

———. 2013. "Reconsidering Female Labor Force Rates Using New Sources in Eighteenth-Century Turin", *Feminist Economics*, 19: 200–23.

Archival Sources

Brandenburgisches Landeshauptarchiv (BLHA), 78 IV Privilegien 108, "Privilegien für die Zunft der Bader, Barbiere und Chirurgen in Berlin", Deutsche Digitale Bibliothek, https://www.deutsche-digitale-bibliothek.de/item/SFI2PM7RZBDCJGAFZSGYXASDVUVK7CBJ?lang=de.

Landesarchiv Baden-Württemberg, Abt. Generallandesarchiv Karlsruhe, 171 Nr. 1826, "Die zu Pforzheim errichtete besondere Baderzunft", Deutsche Digitale Bibliothek, https://www.deutsche-digitale-bibliothek.de/item/DOAGCRSO7ULYBOND2NIO2UQSK26C7XUS?lang=de.

Landesarchiv Baden-Württemberg, Abt. Staatsarchiv Ludwigsburg, B 375 L Bü 631, "Künzelsauer Amtsbericht und Beschluss wegen Errichtung einer Färber- und Baderzunft", Deutsche Digitale Bibliothek, https://www.deutsche-digitale-bibliothek.de/item/GWWVQYIRALSS5ID MQLBBJU4KANQEY7K5?lang=de.

Landesarchiv Baden-Württemberg, Abt. Staatsarchiv Wertheim, F-Rep. 139 Nr. 10, "Errichtung einer eigenen Zunft von Seiten der Chirurgen in der Grafschaft Löwenstein", Deutsche Digitale Bibliothek, https://www.deutsche-digitale-bibliothek.de/item/H5O4KJA57EODOVC N7WIBCZIWR5VWAUSS?lang=de.

Landesarchiv Baden-Württemberg, Hohenlohe-Zentralarchiv Neuenstein, La 15 Bü 151, 3, "Geplante Errichtung einer Baderzunft in der Grafschaft Langenburg", Deutsche Digitale Bibliothek, https://www.deutsche-digitale-bibliothek.de/item/6NGVMKXYT5V6IK5NJ5 EHEHZTAFMV75AH?lang=de.

Landesarchiv Baden-Württemberg, Hohenlohe-Zentralarchiv Neuenstein, Oe 1 Bü 12772, "Bitte der Hohenloher Baderzunft um Bestätigung und Schutz", Deutsche Digitale Bibliothek, https://www.deutsche-digitale-bibliothek.de/item/UYJ26LT6EU4JCD67PKMY2PDHLO RCWM6D?lang=de.

Staatsarchiv Nürnberg, StAN Deutscher Orden, Meistertum Mergentheim, Regierung 7503, "Errichtung einer neuen Baderzunft zu Ellingen", Deutsche Digitale Bibliothek, https://www.deutsche-digitale-bibliothek.de/item/27LICWRND3JG6AKHM2RFMFVLLVEQLMUU?lang=de.

Stadt Wien, "Apothekerordnung", Wien Geschichte Wiki, last updated 17 October 2018, https://www.geschichtewiki.wien.gv.at/Apothekerordnung.

Note: Page numbers followed by a *t* or *f* indicate a table or figure on the designated page.

travel restrictions, 118, 157–163, 177, 186
Troesken, Werner, 128–129
Trump, Donald, 184
Turin plague epidemic, 147
Turkey: Adrianople (Edirne) plague, 62, 249; compulsory smallpox vaccination laws, 126*t*; Constantinople (Istanbul) plagues, 30*f*, 37, 39–40, 248, 321, 396

Ukraine, strong-kinship family systems, 396
United Kingdom (UK): approval of Pfizer/ BioNTech vaccine, 72; Covid-19 pandemic, 41, 146, 382, 432, 434; licensing of woman doctors, 350; promotion of inaccurate information, 146; religious opposition to vaccination, 262; role of British Medical Association, 298–299; spreading of false epidemic information, 347–348; vaccine diplomacy, 168; vaccine regulatory process, 72
United States (U.S.): American Public Health Association, 328; Covid-19 strengthening of family bonds, 434; creation of Marine Hospital Service (MHS), 328–329; development of polio vaccines with USSR, 168; early twentieth-century sanitation efforts, 95; efforts at controlling sanitation, 93, 98; Florida state governor's opposition to vaccination, 143; impact of Covid-19 on religious faith, 432–433; impact of high-density households, 384; infectious-disease notification systems, 135; investments in water provision, 95; issuing of false pandemic information, 328–329; New York Academy of Medicine, 328; 1918–1919 influenza pandemic, 39, 40, 57, 197, 319, 384, 452; plague-related ignorance, 138; resistance to national quarantine system, 328; San Francisco plague, 209, 215; social distancing implementation, 105; Trump's expulsion of refuge-seeking immigrants, 184; vaccination history, 81; vaccine diplomacy, 168; vaccine regulatory process, 72; variolation history, 76; vilification of variolation, 69
US National Agency of Allergy and Infectious Diseases, 72

vaccine diplomacy, 165–170; Cold War era successes, 168; continuing success of, 168; definition, 165; English Mediterranean Mission, 166; problems of, 167–168;

Russian Buttats Expedition, 166; by Spain, 167, 167*f*; spreading of smallpox vaccination, 166, 167*f*; successes of, 169–170
vaccines/vaccination: Africa, religious opposition to, 264–265; Afro-Brazilian religions' opposition to, 265; anti-vaccination riots, 20, 22; authoritarian governments' mandates for, 187; Catholicism's responses to, 266; China/ Chinese acceptance of, 265; Christian responses to, 263, 266; community campaigns for, 430; community opposition to, 213–214; comparison across societies, 450; comparison to variolation, 73–74, 77, 123–124, 154; Covid-19 vaccines, 168–169; cowpox vaccination, 81, 123; differences across societies, 450; Egypt's opposition to, 264; England, cowpox vaccination trial, 399–400; Europe, nineteenth-century anti-vaccination movements, 433; Europe's acceptance of, 268; fiscal capacity's impact on, 130; Florida state governor's opposition, 143; France, 344; free-of-charge for poor people, 63; governments and, 71–72, 123–131; India's opposition to, 214–215, 264, 282; influenza vaccine development, 326; Janssen vaccine, 72; Japan, rates of, 71–72; Japanese opposition to, 143; Jenner's invention of, 73–74, 75*t*, 77, 80–81; Latin America opposition to, 265; Madagascar, opposition to, 143; market diffusion of, 81; markets and, 80–84; mass vaccination in Java, 265; Moderna vaccine, 72; mRNA vaccines, 143, 169; Muslim/Hindus/animist responses to, 264; Nigeria, opposition to, 143; non-Christian responses to, 264, 265; non-European medical associations' restriction of access to, 346; Pfizer vaccine, 17–18, 72; polio vaccination, 163; Protestant opposition to, 266; role in controlling smallpox contagion, 154; Russian Orthodox Church opposition, 266; Scotland, acceptance of, 268; social benefits of, 125; Stockholm's vaccination rate, 370, 370*t*; Sweden, acceptance of, 268; Sweden, institutional features of, 371*t*; vaccination history, 11, 13, 73–74, 154, 166; virology development, 364; women, Covid-19 vaccination hesitancy, 403; women's role in, 400–401, 402*f*, 431

The Princeton Economic History of the Western World

Joel Mokyr, Series Editor

Recent titles

The Laissez-Faire Experiment: Why Britain Embraced and Then Abandoned Small Government, 1800–1914, W. Walker Hanlon

The Hidden Victims: Civilian Casualties of the Two World Wars, Cormac Ó Gráda

Pioneers of Capitalism: The Netherlands 1000–1800, Maarten Prak and Jan Luiten van Zanden

Pawned States: State Building in the Era of International Finance, Didac Queralt

Pliny's Roman Economy: Natural History, Innovation, and Growth, Richard Saller

Plague's upon the Earth: Disease and the Course of Human History, Kyle Harper

The Israeli Economy: A Story of Success and Costs, Joseph Zeira

Credit Nation: Property Laws and Institutions in Early America, Claire Priest

The Decline and Rise of Democracy: A Global History from Antiquity to Today, David Stasavage

Going the Distance: Eurasian Trade and the Rise of the Business Corporation 1400–1700, Ron Harris

Escape from Rome: The Failure of Empire and the Road to Prosperity, Walter Scheidel

Trade in the Ancient Mediterranean: Private Order and Public Institutions, Taco Terpstra

Dark Matter Credit: The Development of Peer-to-Peer Lending and Banking in France, Philip T. Hoffman, Gilles Postel-Vinay, and Jean-Laurent Rosenthal

The European Guilds: An Economic Analysis, Sheilagh Ogilvie

The Winding Road to the Welfare State: Economic Insecurity and Social Welfare Policy in Britain, George R. Boyer

The Mystery of the Kibbutz: Egalitarian Principles in a Capitalist World, Ran Abramitzky

GPSR Authorized Representative: Easy Access System Europe - Mustamäe tee 50, 10621 Tallinn, Estonia, gpsr requests@easproject.com

www.ingramcontent.com/pod-product-compliance
Ingram Content Group UK Ltd.
Pitfield, Milton Keynes, MK11 3LW, UK
UKHW030005200325
456435UK00003B/2/J